TALKING ABOUT PEOPLE

Readings in Contemporary Cultural Anthropology

FOURTH EDITION

William A. Haviland
University of Vermont, Emeritus

Robert J. Gordon
University of Vermont

Luis A. Vivanco
University of Vermont

Boston   Burr Ridge, IL   Dubuque, IA   Madison, WI   New York   San Francisco   St. Louis
Bangkok   Bogotá   Caracas   Kuala Lumpur   Lisbon   London   Madrid   Mexico City
Milan   Montreal   New Delhi   Santiago   Seoul   Singapore   Sydney   Taipei   Toronto

Published by McGraw-Hill, an imprint of The McGraw-Hill Companies, Inc., 1221 Avenue of the Americas, New York, NY 10020. Copyright © 2006 by The McGraw-Hill Companies. All rights reserved. No part of this publication may be reproduced or distributed in any form or by any means, or stored in a database or retrieval system, without the prior written consent of The McGraw-Hill Companies, Inc., including, but not limited to, in any network or other electronic storage or transmission, or broadcast for distance learning.

This book is printed on recycled, acid-free paper.

1 2 3 4 5 6 7 8 9 0 QPD/QPD 0 9 8 7 6 5

ISBN 0-07-299481-9

Editor in Chief: Emily Barrosse
Publisher: Phillip Butcher
Sponsoring Editor: Kevin Witt
Developmental Editor: Kate Scheinman
Permissions Coordinator: Karyn Morrison
Marketing Manager: Dan Loch
Production Editor: Leslie LaDow
Manuscript Editor: Judith Brown
Design Manager: Cassandra Chu
Cover Designer: Cassandra Chu
Interior Designer: Amy Evans McClure
Production Supervisor: Richard DeVitto
Photo Researcher: Brian J. Pecko
Composition: 10/12 Palatino by Thompson Type
Printing: 45# Scholarly Matte Recycled by Quebecor, Dubuque

Cover image: © Adina Tovy Amsel/Lonely Planet Images. Background: PhotoDisc Collection/Getty Images

LIBRARY OF CONGRESS CATALOGING-IN-PUBLICATION DATA

Talking about people : readings in contemporary cultural anthropology.—4th ed. / [edited by] William A. Haviland,
   Robert J. Gordon, Luis A. Vivanco.
      p. cm.
   Includes bibliographical references and index.
   ISBN 0-07-299481-9 (alk. paper)
   1. Ethnology. I. Haviland, William A. II. Gordon, Robert J., 1947– III. Vivanco, Luis Antonio, 1969–
GN316.T34 2006
305.8—dc22   2005041594

The Internet addresses listed in the text were accurate at the time of publication. The inclusion of a Web site does not indicate an endorsement by the authors or McGraw-Hill, and McGraw-Hill does not guarantee the accuracy of the information presented at these sites.

www.mhhe.com

To all the women in our lives

Preface

This anthology is designed as a supplement for introductory cultural anthropology courses. It consists of thirteen chapters with three to five articles each, and each chapter has a short introduction written by the editors that relates the articles to each other and to the topic of the chapter. The chapters themselves are arranged to complement the chapter topics and order found in most introductory texts and courses.

In the fourth edition, there are twenty-one new articles, and we've introduced an exciting new feature: "Anthropology and Public Debate." In this feature, we offer two opposing anthropological arguments on topics of current public relevance: gay and lesbian marriage, understanding what happened on September 11, 2001, and anthropology's participation in the "war on terror." This feature complements one that we introduced in the third edition, "Doing Fieldwork," that we believe gives a fuller picture than other anthologies of how anthropologists actually work.

FEATURES AND BENEFITS OF THIS BOOK

Freshness and Originality

Most anthologies reproduce with some regularity "old chestnuts." While we have nothing against the classics, we do feel that it creates the impression that nothing new has happened in anthropology. We want to introduce students to some of the more recent and provocative works of anthropologists (and a few nonanthropologists who have what we consider to be anthropological insights). We want students to read provocative articles, for one of the aims of the introductory course should be to shake up the students' comfortably ethnocentric beliefs about the world in which they live.

Focus on Contemporary Global Concerns

It is no secret that North Americans are surprisingly ignorant about the nature of the "global society" of which they are a part. In an era when North Americans constitute a small minority of the world's people and are increasingly dependent on the rest of the world for vital raw materials, manufactured goods, and markets for those products still made at home, reliable information about other peoples and the ways in which they live has become ever more important for the survival of North Americans themselves. These concerns about how Americans relate to the wider world have become especially urgent in the context of American pursuits of a globally unpopular "war on terrorism" during the past several years. Because anthropology has always been in the forefront of efforts to learn about other peoples, it has a special role to play in combating the insularity and provincialism that sometimes accompany students to college. Thus, the majority of articles in this anthology focus on common global interests. From William Klausner's examination of the question "Can one really go 'native'?" in Chapter 1 to Steven Rubenstein's analysis of Shuar migrants in Chapter 13, the volume highlights global concerns.

At the same time, this anthology seeks to show the exotic in the familiar by suggesting new and provocative ways of looking at the student's own society. We feel this closer examination is an essential way to combat racism and other invidious distinctions that North Americans like to draw between "us" and "them." From articles such as Emily Martin's "Flexible Survivors" in Chapter 4 and James Brain's "The Ugly American Revisited" in Chapter 12, readers will gain fascinating insights into their own culture.

International Authorship

In keeping with the global perspective of this anthology, we include a significant number of articles by authors from outside the United States. Anthropology is not, after all, an exclusive American preserve (and how arrogant we are to call ourselves Americans!). It is an exciting international discipline whose members are not all white middle-class males. We have tried to reflect the profession more closely by increasing the representation of not only foreign (British, Canadian, Australian, Irish, Congolese, Danish, French, Philippine, South African) but also female contributors, including a number of nonanthropologists. About 40 percent of the authors come from outside the United States, and 40 percent are women.

"Anthropology and Public Debate" and "Doing Fieldwork"

Because of the special insights gained through cross-cultural study and intensive fieldwork, anthropologists have a lot to contribute to contemporary social and political debates. In this edition we have introduced a new feature, "Anthropology and Public Debate," that aims to show students the relevance of anthropological perspectives on controversial public issues during the past several years. We take two opposing anthropological arguments on gay and lesbian marriage, understanding 9/11, and anthropological participation in the "war on terror." One advantage of this feature is that it demonstrates a more politically complex discipline than caricatures from outside academia often portray of disciplines like anthropology, based on images of liberal and progressive domination. In fact, as this feature demonstrates, the reality is more complex and the opinions diverse. Recognizing the centrality of fieldwork to anthropological knowledge, the fourth edition includes essays that deal specifically with the nature and dilemmas of fieldwork. These essays, several of which have already been published and several commissioned originally for this reader, consider the changing status of the field (is it a geographical space? a bounded social community? a process? an event?); the nature of anthropological learning in the field; and ethical issues and dilemmas. The advantage for teachers is that this feature provides vivid and focused readings on an aspect of fieldwork, which can then become the basis of classroom conversation or lectures about how we anthropologists actually create knowledge.

Incorporation of Gender Issues

Because anthropology is the study of women as well as men, we have deemed it important that gender issues be well represented by the articles here. Considerations of gender enter into virtually everything that people do, so we chose to spread the material on gender throughout the book. Notable examples of articles that deal with gender are Alma Gottlieb's "The Anthropologist as Mother" in Chapter 4; Roger Lancaster's "The Place of Anthropology in a Public Culture Reshaped by Bioreductivism" and David Bennett's "Hanky-Panky and Spanky-Wanky: Sex and the Single Boy" in Chapter 7; Brett Williams's "Why Migrant Women Feed Their Husbands Tamales" and Timothy Egan's "The Persistence of Polygamy" in Chapter 8; Sylvia Rodgers's "Feminine Power at Sea" in Chapter 11; and Faye Ginsburg's "The Anthropology of Abortion Activism" in Chapter 13.

Abundant Student Learning Aids

An annotated table of contents offers students previews of the various articles, and chapter introductions provide some contextual "glue" for the points made by the articles. Brief biographical sketches of the authors of each article enhance the international flavor of the volume and contribute further insights into what anthropology is all about. The references and notes for each article will appeal to the student who wants to know more, and the glossary and map showing the location of peoples and places discussed will be helpful to all students. Focus questions help the student make the most out of each selection by offering specific questions for reflection and class discussion. Finally, the index and list of articles by topic area contribute further to making this a user-friendly book.

A NOTE ON THE ARTICLES

While many of the articles are reprinted here in their entirety, some have been edited in order to keep the book to a reasonable length. For the most part, the cuts have involved details of methodology so as not to adversely affect either the substance or the spirit of the article.

We have compiled an anthology with authors from many countries to provide a global anthropological perspective. We retained the spellings from the original texts to give students the experience of reading other versions of the English language and learning to distinguish between British and U.S. spellings; we thought this would help students learn something about the frames of reference of the authors. That was our theory, but in practice the book is a bit more complicated than that.

We have included authors, North American and British-style (includes all non-U.S. anthropologists), who were educated all over the world. They wrote for U.S. publications with editors who liked "North American" spelling and for British-style publications with editors who liked "British" spellings. And finally, they moved from one country to another. As anthropologists, we are a global community who often spell in both styles, switching from one to another without realizing it. To the utter horror of all copyeditors, we leave with you this evidence of our international lives, a bit of linguistic anthropological research on the anthropologists themselves!

ACKNOWLEDGMENTS

Lots of people have contributed in one way or another to this volume. Those behind the scenes who have made vital contributions during early editions include Anita de

Laguna Haviland, who, besides riding herd on the editors to meet deadlines, put everything into the computer, caught numerous errors, tracked down a variety of information, and assisted in writing the Instructor's Manual. Rinda Gordon kept one of the editors in line and helped with the Instructor's Manual. Peggy O'Neill-Vivanco offered her own experiences as an undergraduate anthropology major, as well as key moral and technical support for the junior editor.

The changes in this new edition in part reflect the reactions in Gordon's and Vivanco's introductory anthropology courses at the University of Vermont. To the students we have taught through the years (Haviland has been teaching introductory students since 1965, Gordon in the United States since 1979 and before that in Papua New Guinea, and Vivanco at several U.S. universities and Costa Rica since the early 1990s), we are grateful for all we have learned about teaching and the kinds of material students find effective.

We'd like to thank the instructors who reviewed for the first and second editions, as well as the following instructors who reviewed for the third edition of *Talking About People:* Abigail E. Adams, Central Connecticut State University; Cindi Sturtz Sreetharan, California State University-Sacramento; Mark Moberg, University of South Alabama; Jean Rahier, Florida International University; and Kerriann Marden, Tulane University. Their advice and comments have been most helpful throughout the evolution of this anthology.

We would also like to thank our colleagues who have made helpful suggestions for revisions: Jennifer Dickinson, Corrine Glesne, Lourdes Gutierrez-Najera, Mike Sheridan, Geoff White, and Rob Welsch.

Many people, first at Mayfield Publishing Company and then at McGraw-Hill, have helped bring this project to fruition. First of all, we are grateful to Jan Beatty, who worked with us on the first two editions and provided numerous valuable suggestions. We are also grateful to Kevin Witt and Phil Butcher, who have supported our work on this new edition. We are no less grateful to the others at McGraw-Hill who have seen this volume through production, particularly Judith Brown, Karyn Morrison, Leslie LaDow, and Kate Scheinman.

Hats off to you all!

William A. Haviland
Robert J. Gordon
Luis A. Vivanco
Burlington, Vermont

Contents

CHAPTER V   ✦   Ecology: *How Do People Relate to Nature?*   87

CHAPTER VI   ✦   Economics: *How Do People Make a Living?*   109

CHAPTER VII   ✦   Gender and Sexuality: *How Do Women and Men Relate to Each Other?*   125

"Elm Valley," with it upwardly mobile new residents and less affluent residents living in close proximity, affords an excellent example of how symbolic indicators and patterns of association are indicative of social class. Also evident are the kinds of misunderstandings that result from class-related worldviews.

CHAPTER X   ✦   Politics: *How Do People Exercise Power Over Each Other?*   201

CHAPTER XI   ✦   Religion: *How Do We Make Sense of Peoples' Beliefs and Ritual Practices?*   223

List of Articles by Major Topic Area

Concordance with Major Textbooks

Since this reader is often used in conjunction with a cultural anthropology textbook, the table below indicates the correspondence between *Talking about People* and seven major textbooks. The following textbooks are included:

Bodley, John. 2005. *Cultural Anthropology: Tribes, States, and the Global System,* 4th edition. New York: McGraw-Hill.

Ember, Carol, and Melvin Ember. 2004. *Cultural Anthropology,* 11th edition. Upper Saddle River, N.J.: Prentice-Hall.

Haviland, William, et al. 2005. *Cultural Anthropology,* 11th edition. Belmont, Calif.: Thomson Wadsworth.

Kottak, Conrad Phillip. 2000. *Cultural Anthropology,* 10th edition. New York: McGraw-Hill.

Miller, Barbara. 1999. *Cultural Anthropology.* Boston: Allyn and Bacon.

Nanda, Serena, and Richard Warms. 2004. *Cultural Anthropology,* 8th edition. Belmont, Calif.: Thomson Wadsworth.

Robbins, Richard. 2001. *Cultural Anthropology: A Problem-Centered Approach,* 3rd edition. Itasca, Ill.: F.E. Peacock.

Talking about People	Bodley	Ember and Ember	Haviland	Kottak	Miller	Nanda and Warms	Robbins
Chapter 1 Introduction: What Is Distinctive about Anthropology?	1	1, 2	1	1, 2	1, 2	1, 3	1
Chapter 2 Basic Concepts: What Is the Meaning of Culture?	1, 5	2, 3	2, 3	3, 4	1, 2	4	1
Chapter 3 Communication: What Is the Relationship between Language and Culture?	5	4	4	7	12	5	4
Chapter 4 Socialization: How Do People Learn and Experience Their Culture?	5	13	5		5, 6, 7	6	6
Chapter 5 Ecology: How Do People Relate to Nature?	2, 3, 4	5	6	8	3	7	2
Chapter 6 Economics: How Do People Make a Living?	11	6	7	8	3, 4	8	2
Chapter 7 Gender and Sexuality: How Do Women and Men Relate to Each Other?	8, 9	8, 9	8	11, 12	8	11	4, 5
Chapter 8 Marriage and Kinship: What Does It Mean to Be in a Family?	2, 8	9, 10	9, 10	10, 11	8, 9	10	5

Chapter 9 Collective Identities: How Do People Express Status and Group Membership?	6, 10, 12	7, 11	11	5, 6	10, 11	13	7
Chapter 10 Politics: How Do People Exercise Power Over Each Other	6, 7, 10, 12	12	12	9	10, 11	12	3, 8
Chapter 11 Religion: How Do We Make Sense of Peoples' Beliefs and Ritual Practices?	5, 8, 9	14	13	13	13	15	4
Chapter 12 Change: What Does It Mean to Modernize?	1, 11, 12, 13	16, 17, 19	15	15, 16, 17	15, 16	17	2, 3, 9
Chapter 13 Old Issues, New Contexts: What Does the Future Hold for Anthropology?	14, 15	17, 19	16	17	15	17	9

INTRODUCTION

What Is Distinctive about Anthropology?

MOST ANTHROPOLOGISTS define **anthropology** as the study of man, claiming that it was derived from the Greek words *anthropos* and *logos,* meaning "man study." In fact, many introductory texts bear pretentious titles like "The Study of Mankind," or "Humanity." However, if one probes deeper into the Greek lexicon, *anthropos* and *logos* can also be glossed as "bearer of scandals or tales." This is why pioneering British social anthropologist Lucy Mair, to whom we pay tribute in titling this anthology, modestly defined her discipline in her lectures as simply "talking about people." Not only is talking about people, or gossiping, a pleasantly informal activity (and the fodder of the ubiquitous TV talk shows!), but, as this anthology shows, it can also be a disciplined, engrossing, and enriching experience leading to important personal and social insights. Indeed, "talking about people" is a basic social and cultural activity in which we humans engage in order to educate and place ourselves in the world and to make sense of our beings and universe.

We feel that this more modest stance has contributed substantially to the increasing popularity of anthropology in recent years. There are, of course, other reasons as well. Some attribute its popularity to the fact that, of the various social sciences, anthropology has the least amount of jargon—a situation derived in part from the fact that the people researchers have studied do not read their studies. This has changed, however, in a world that is increasingly becoming a global village—which may also account for anthropology's newfound status, as there are many more opportunities for cultural misunderstanding and thus more need for an understanding of other cultures. As a result of this process of **globalization,** many of us now realize the importance of the interrelationships between people in our part of the world and those from other parts of the planet. Graphic TV images of terrorism, drought, famine, and pestilence in the global

South have made us sense an impending crisis. A growing disillusionment with "development" and the fact that more and more people are asking penetrating questions about why development has failed have also propelled anthropology to prominence (see readings in Chapters 5 and 12). "Development experts" are starting to realize that possibly one reason for their failures of development is that they have not understood or talked to local people. It is the business of anthropology to shed light on these bigger questions by talking to such folks.

Indeed, it is precisely this emphasis on the "Other" that makes the study of anthropology attractive to many. In essence, anthropology is concerned with the study of alternative lifestyles and cultures. It looks at how other people solve common human problems. On a more personal level, people who are interested in alternative lifestyles and cultures tend to be dissatisfied with their own society. In short, they suffer from various degrees of alienation; this gives rise to the old saw about the definition of anthropologists: those who reject their own society before that society rejects them. There is merit in this joke in that anthropology has a distinguished record of attracting far more women and minorities than any other social science. Most first-year students can name some prominent female anthropologists, such as Americans Margaret Mead and Ruth Benedict or the British Lucy Mair, Audrey Richards, and Monica Wilson. This tradition still continues—over half of all presidents of the American Anthropological Association since World War II have been women. Other social sciences and humanities, such as sociology, political science, psychology, and history, are hard-pressed to even halfway replicate such a distinguished record.

There is nothing deviant or abnormal about being alienated from one's society. On the contrary, some would argue that it is inevitable given the present condition of modernity. Disciplining one's alienation and using it as a way of seeing can lead to important insights. Indeed, we would argue that this alienated perspective is crucial. When one of the authors first came to the United States, he asked a native what books he should read to understand his new country. He was surprised to be told to read de Tocqueville's *Democracy in America* and Gunnar Myrdal's *An American Dilemma.* In retrospect, what they have in common, apart from providing original and synthetic insights into the workings of the United States, is that both authors were clearly outsiders to the United States.

Perhaps the most important characteristic of anthropology is that it self-consciously takes an outsider perspective on society and culture. In Robert Burns's immortal words, "Aye wad the giftie gie us, tae see ourselves as others see us." As such, anthropology can be a wonderful antidote to **ethnocentrism** and its associated myths of **cultural arrogance.** This disciplined outsider perspective is typically acquired by travel, either geographical or imaginary. But, as we all know, travel does not necessarily broaden the mind; that only happens if one is predisposed to let it happen, and this is where the anthropological perspective comes in.

A concern with the Other, either real or imagined, leads directly and inevitably into a consideration of difference. What are the implications of difference? Is difference largely in the eye of the beholder? For example, a Papua New Guinean village would obey the district commissioner's instruction to "tidy up the village" by assiduously sweeping up all the dog and pig droppings but leaving all the papers and cans. To them, papers and cans are not dirty but a sign of affluence and status. Here is an example of the important role played by culture in defining difference. Culture is one of the key concerns of anthropology, and in Chapter 2 we concentrate exclusively on the concept. A concern with difference also raises a host of issues, such as how much difference should be tolerated. This issue manifests itself in many ways, ranging from a young New Yorker in Papua New Guinea rationalizing wearing a scanty bikini among bare-breasted women despite their disapproval because in New York she would not object to what *they* wore, to the explosiveness of **multiculturalism** that is gripping U.S. campuses.

The issue of the Other and cultural differences is the focus of the article by Marion Benedict. She relates her experiences as an ethnographer in the Seychelles, struggling to understand the islanders' lives as *they* live them, yet finding it impossible to be a mere "fly on the wall" herself. Her article demonstrates not only the difficulties of getting to know Others, but also the difficulties of accurately writing about a particular culture for an audience with a different background. How does one do this without the description becoming a caricature? At the same time, as William Klausner points out, it is exceedingly difficult to "go native."

For the novice, a quick look at any anthropology department would reveal a bewildering array of diverse individuals who appear to have nothing in common with one another, except perhaps a department secretary. This is illusionary, however, because what relates the **linguist,** the **social anthropologist,** the **ethnologist,** the **prehistorian,** and the **physical anthropologist** is precisely an appreciation for the role of culture in the construction of difference. Historically, this arose out of a shared concern for what were originally "tribal people," but the focus is now more and more on contemporary changes. Anthropologists are increasingly studying segments of their own society, using a distinctive **anthropological perspective.** Although anthropologists will debate the smaller details, most agree that the following constitute some of the defining characteristics:

1. **Fieldwork** is perhaps the characteristic of which anthropologists are proudest. According to Seligman (quoted in Lewis 1976:27), "What the blood of the martyrs was to the Early Church, Fieldwork was to anthropology." He was perhaps exaggerating, but only slightly. Indeed, many give this distinctive characteristic the status of a tribal initiation rite: One is not an anthropologist unless one has done fieldwork for an extended period of time.

2. Extended fieldwork leads almost naturally to a focus on local communities and a feel for grassroots issues. **Ethnographies,** studies of particular cultures based on firsthand knowledge, are one of fieldwork's key products.

3. Fieldwork immersion and the breadth of anthropological training emphasize **holistic** and **cross-cultural** perspectives, examining social relationships in the full context of their interrelationships, and through the lens of other cultures, respectively. While other social scientists might spend all their time examining the beauty of individual flowers, so to speak, anthropologists pause from this task to take in the beauty of entire fields from the mountaintop and thus see a broader pattern.

It is from these holistic and cross-cultural perspectives that anthropologists can engage in the increasingly important task of debunking myths about the Other and themselves. Furthermore, as Laura Nader argues in her essay here, these perspectives are more necessary now than ever before in the context of dramatic global changes and crises.

It goes without saying that doing anthropology is a complicated business. It requires a balance of humility and hubris, broad vision and intense focus, and a (sometimes excruciating) ability to get along with people who are radically different from oneself. And as Gregory Starrett shows in his article on the use of anthropological knowledge by the U.S. military in support of its operations in Iraq, doing anthropology is also deeply political. Anthropological studies, sometimes wittingly and sometimes unwittingly, serve agendas other than the pursuit of knowledge and intercultural encounter. Every anthropologist has to face the key questions: What is the purpose of cultural study, and whose interests might be served by it?

FOCUS QUESTIONS

As you read these selections, consider these questions:

✦ What preconceptions do you have about anthropologists and the subject of anthropology? Where do you think they come from? How does your image contrast with the representations of anthropology and anthropologists in these selections?

✦ How does anthropology compare with other social sciences you have encountered? How does it compare with natural sciences? How do anthropological research methods differ from those of other social science disciplines?

✦ What role do you think anthropology can play in the contemporary world? How might anthropological information help us understand the changing conditions of the world's peoples?

✦ What kinds of political dilemmas do you think anthropologists face in doing their work?

REFERENCE

Lewis, I. M. 1976. *Social Anthropology in Perspective.* Harmondsworth, England: Penguin.

– 1 –

Anthropology!
Distinguished Lecture—2000

Laura Nader

*Laura Nader is professor of anthropology at UC Berkeley. She received her PhD
from Radcliffe University in 1961. She is a prolific author and public intellectual
whose work crosses disciplinary boundaries between anthropology, law, politics,
and philosophy. She has published extensively on topics ranging from justice and
control in Zapotec societies of Oaxaca (Mexico) to legal anthropology, conflict
resolution, and anthropology of science and knowledge. In 1995 the Law and
Society Association awarded her the Kalven Prize for distinguished research on law
and society, and in 2000, the American Anthropological Association awarded her
the Distinguished Lecture Award. This selection is her Distinguished Lecture.*

Thank you for the opportunity to speak to you tonight about Anthropology! Though I am aware of the difficulties we face, I am moved to share my sense of hope that contemporary conditions of anthropology bring us again to an exciting turning point. This is a moment for new synthesis and renewed civic engagement, a troubled time when relations between universities and the public in the United States are being redefined, in a world that is both interconnected and disconnected, on a planet where long-term survival is at risk.

ANTHROPOLOGY'S IMPACT IN THE TWENTIETH CENTURY—VICTIM OF ITS OWN SUCCESS?

For most of the twentieth century, anthropology was marked by increased specialization. In the process, anthropology lost its confidence in a holistic discipline and lost the vision of the field as a whole. In the twenty-first century I can see a transformation, a reassembling, in new mixes that can take us from the periphery to centers of modernity and back, an anthropology that is inclusive of *all* humankind, reconnecting the particular with the universal, the local and the global, nature and culture.

As we know, our discipline is always changing, in one way or another responsive to the world around us. It has been called the uncomfortable discipline by Raymond Firth and others or, more graphically, "an institutionalized train wreck" by Matt Cartmill (1994:1–2), "caught between science and humanities." We were one academic discipline that at the start refused to specialize, a discipline that has made enormous contributions to human knowledge and to what it means to be human, a discipline that has striven to overcome prejudice, a discipline that is only in its fourth generation (Valentine and Darnell 1999).

American anthropology is also currently described as self-absorbed, trapped in a diminished reality, inaccessible to the general public, and one of the least integrated or "whitest" professions in the United States (Shanklin 2000). There is truth to these depictions, but the vision of our field as a whole and the present range of anthropological work are greater than these characterizations indicate, and looking back gives me reason for optimism (Darnell 1998).

In 1904 Franz Boas, who framed the discipline of holism, wrote "The History of Anthropology" for the International Congress of Arts and Sciences in St. Louis. In concluding, he lamented, "There are indications of [anthropology] breaking up. The biological, linguistic, and

"Anthropology!–Distinguished Lecture 2000" by Laura Nader from
American Anthropologist, September 2000, 103(3), pp. 609–620. Reprinted by permission of American Anthropological Association.

ethnologic-archaeological methods are so distinct" (1906:481). By 1929, however, the editorial staff of the *Encyclopedia of Social Sciences* noted:

> The anthropologist's way of thinking has reached beyond his formal contacts with the other social studies, and like psychoanalysis and relatively has entered into the main stream of twentieth-century thought. . . . Such an approach heightens the metabolism of our minds and breaks down our parochialisms. [Seligman 1930:203]

Jacques Barzun at 92 recalls: "Anthropologists put the final touch to it by defining culture among primitives as everything they did: the way they ate, their canoes, their marriage customs. When that idea was applied to history—you got cultural history" (Rothstein 2000: A15).

Now we also have cultural sociology, cultural psychology, cultural ecology, cultural studies, cultural geography, and cultural psychiatry. Success?

The two tendencies, fragmentation and holism, move us back and forth. With increasing specialization, we divide and subdivide and still call it anthropology. At the same time, the anthropological perspective, disrespectful as it is of boundaries and cherished truths, continues to permeate the social sciences and the humanities, other disciplines, intelligent lay people, people in high places. Although method is what defines our specialties, it is the anthropological perspective that those outside our field relish—a perspective that sees what others often do not see, that makes connections that are not made elsewhere, that questions assumptions and exoticizes behavior that is normalized, that asks plain questions like, "What's going on around here?

We are an outrageous science, along with ecology the first of the "new" sciences rather than the last of the "old," a science with a shapeless quality because it is both soft and hard, both humanities and science, between nature and culture, the past and the present, Us and Them—searching for new ways to understand the human condition writ large, one that includes the nonhuman world. What is standing in the way of further scientific discovery is not our ignorance but the illusion of knowledge.

Nineteenth-century archaeologists shook the bottom out of human history, replacing short chronologies of biblical origin with longer time depth. A bold physical and cultural anthropology questioned thinking of inequalities as innate. Observations on other cultures made us realize that our own culture is unusual in world context.

Twentieth-century anthropologists moved from the armchair to firsthand fieldwork. Their theories of cultural relativism challenged the predominant theories of their day developed by Marx, Freud, Malthus, and others. An-

thropology became a science in that it rested on disciplined observation and experimentation, but what kind of science was not clear. The four fields are now more than four, and there are many more subfields.

The fluctuations in what are considered urgent questions to explore have been impressive over 100 years and give the field that shapeless quality. Some say this has been the secret of our vitality: what other science is so adept at self-criticism? Others say that fragmentation is erasing anthropology, in the bookstores, in granting agencies, in the universities, in the public eye, in anthropology itself. Margaret Mead is referred to as a sociologist. The anthropology section in *Science* magazine (see Marler 2000) includes any scientist that uses the words *culture, sex,* or *evolution.*

Much of the controversy about whether anthropology is a science or not is a false problem set up by people who do not understand what science is, taking up energy better placed elsewhere. It might have been avoided had we recognized there are many science traditions, even within Europe itself. In a plea for "a new contract for science" (Lubchenco 1998), a past president of the American Association for the Advancement of Science, observed that the early twenty-first century is a fundamentally different era from the one in which the current scientific enterprise developed. Science evolves. Indeed, the battle over scientific instruments is not new, as historian of science Lynn White reminds us: "The laboratory method's power lies precisely in its isolation of the phenomenon being studied . . . ecological science is on principle antiscientific as science at present is usually conceived and practiced" (1980:76). The only science we have is *human* science: it has human limitations, human error, human ignorance. People who hew to method miss the evolution of science itself.

Emerging ethnographies of science are having a powerful effect on contemporary anthropology, as did earlier studies of political economy and colonialism. Such ethnographies recognize natural science practices as intermixed with reflexivity, interpretation, and politics, and this has made a difference in how we think about knowledge. After all, Nobel Prize–winning biologist Barbara McClintock had a feeling for the organism (Keller 1983). Comparisons of energy physicists in Japan and the United States, or comparisons of Japanese and American primatology, show that culture is at work in science practice, though that does not per se indicate there is no truth value in the work. Furthermore, principles of a physical model may not be true for all times and all places. Anthropologists working in African agriculture observe the devastating effects of a cultural preference for universal explanations that override ecological particularisms and site-specific knowledge. Biological scientists themselves are blurring boundaries as they cross paths with indigenous peoples or make boundaries as in *French DNA* (Rabinow 1999).

Throughout the twentieth century anthropologists observed the development of science and technology as measures of worth. By midcentury we recognized the ideological nature of such beliefs. By end of century what is at issue is whether Western ways of knowing provide us with the only source of truth. Think of recent discoveries in Peru of early climate prediction and the Pleiades (Orlove et al. 2000). Rapid globalization makes consideration of intermingling of knowledge systems inevitable.

The issues for our publics are about the function of dominant Western science, its cultural ascendancy, its ethnocentricity, and its universality as these pertain to the future of life on this planet (Nader 1996). The assumption that science functions autonomously is contradicted by findings in archaeology and ethnology and by the observation that science does not develop independent of its laity. Is the anthropology of science a scientific or a humanistic effort? And does it matter, since *humanistic* and *scientific* are adjectives of convenience that are not mutually exclusive?

ANTHROPOLOGY THROUGH THE EYES OF ONE PRACTITIONER

I came to anthropology before knowing such a discipline existed. My entrance followed a boundary crossing from literature—an existing enterprise, but my work on Mexican revolutionary novels was disallowed as writing about literature. Someone pointed me to Clyde Kluckhohn's prizewinning *Mirror for Man* (1949). I went to study at Harvard because Kluckhohn envisioned a big anthropology, a wide-angled inclusive discipline intolerant of boundaries in the pursuit of knowledge.

Graduate school at Harvard in the 1950s was a place of disciplinary optimism—some of it misplaced. There were two kinds of doctoral anthropology programs. Peabody anthropology gave classic four field training: archeology, physical anthropology, sociocultural anthropology, and linguistics; social relations trained anthropologists along with sociologists and psychologists in the behavioral sciences, reflecting a vocal anti-disciplinary move. Those of us at Peabody had to pass muster in general anthropology as well as cover social science theory. We were both disciplinary and interdisciplinary; we suffered bone lab and the old genetics, sweated the Paleolithic, and many attended the Summer Institute of Linguistics. We also read the sociologists Parsons, Homans, and Sorokin and the psychologists. Specialization beyond area courses was only beginning to be a strong call and anthropology had not yet turned inward. But there were glimmerings of what was to come (Golde 1970).

Bateson's second edition of *Naven* (1958) spurred many discussions about the construction of ethnography and the experimental moment. At the same time, scientific and linguistic models were in vogue. British structural-functionalism, Lévi-Straussian structuralism, cross-cultural comparison, cognitive models, and middle-range theory were center stage. Ethnographies of fieldworkers came later.

We read V. Gordon Childe, Le Gros Clark, W. W. Howells—anthropologists who wrote books like *Man Makes Himself* (Childe 1951) for publics interested in the larger questions. Childe and Clark took the first steps toward an energy theory of cultural evolution. Kroeber (1944) was writing about open societies and *Configurations of Cultural Growth,* Kluckhohn (Gottschalk et al. 1944) was exploring life histories, Barnes in 1951 was writing about the invention of tradition and history. Turner (1957) on social drama, disputes, and language rhetoric provided a frame for processual analysis; Leach (1954) brought in power; and in our free time we read Wittgenstein, Langer, Cassirer on the philosophies in a new key, as well as Collingswood's *The Idea of History* (1948). With specialization came a tendency for the units of study to shrink, and so, too, the larger questions (Fardon 1990).

Fieldwork, especially fine-grained, *thick* fieldwork, is good preparation for working with multisited publics, for when we speak to our publics it is the broad perspective that differentiates us from narrower specialist disciplines. Mel Konner put the problem well when he observed:

> The problem is not that we know more about less and less. The problem is that we know more and more about more and more. . . . The time will come when we know so much about so many things that no one person can hope to grasp all the essential facts . . . needed to make a single wise decision. Knowledge becomes collective in the weakest sense and science becomes like men and women in a crowd, looking for one another, each holding a single piece of a very expensive radio. [1982:xii]

My fieldwork helped me see how and why energy scientists wished to confine the energy problem to a technical box.

During a decade of work on nuclear and alternative energies, a wide-angled anthropology was a requirement—one that drew on holism, appreciation of history and time depth, thinking of consequences arising from how language frames thought (Nader 1979, 1980, 1981).

The discourse of energy specialists was often one of no option. They appeared to be caught in growth models. They were unilineal evolutionists with no time depth. They understood that civilizations rise but not that they collapse (Yoffee and Cowgill 1988). Many thought that technological progress equaled social progress. The idea that experts might be part of the problem was novel to them. The idea that the energy problem had human dimensions slowly sank in as did the notion that the workplace in national laboratories affected their frame of reference. Their science was framed by a cultural outlook that held some dangers of the sort of indifference that makes reckless experimentation with living beings possible. The capacity of humans to change the globe in irreversible ways was limited until recently. Physical scientists run the risk of tunnel vision.

As informants reported back to me, however, it emerged that there were varieties of energy scientists. Many worked with a crisis theory of change, change by punctuated events, paralleling a view in biology; crises were justifications for shifting gears. Linear models of change were attached to the "can't turn back" people. Incremental models allowed more flexibility and room for unexpected alliances and innovative new technologies. In the end, new practices appeared in what Lévi-Strauss elsewhere describes as "bricolage," enlightened tinkering done by people who can see with different eyes and utilize what exists. Isn't that what anthropologists do?

MIRRORED IMAGES: THE WEST SEEN FROM DIFFERENT PERSPECTIVES

The energy work led me to think about extant civilizations and what others regard as progress (Nader 1989b). Useful in this endeavor was a literature mostly ignored by anthropologists but appreciated by multicultural classrooms, the ethnographic filtering of the West by literate people from other "civilizations"—Chinese, Japanese, Indian, Islamic, for example—travelers, diplomats, and missionaries who over the centuries came west and encountered Euro-American society for the first time. Al-Jabarti, and Arab chronicler, recorded firsthand the history of Napoleon's French Expedition to Egypt in 1978 *as well as* the attitude of learned Egyptians toward the French occupation.

By 1826, the first delegation of Egyptians traveled to France under the supervision of Rafic al-Tahtawi, a 25-year-old imam and scholar. Al-Tahtawi lived in Paris five years and in 1834 published his study of early-nineteenth-century France—its manner, mores, habits of everyday life—a study of the psychodynamics of the East–West en-

counter in an era of European colonial expansion, comparable but superior to Edward Lane's *The Manners and Customs of the Modern Egyptians* ([1836] 1973). Al-Tahtawi was impressed by French science and technology yet regarded the East as positionally superior to the barbaric West. His balance of praise and censure breaks down when he comes across the body of an Egyptian resister of Napoleonic occupation turned into a museum artifact where "some parts" of the corpse are on display. Al-Tahtawi points to a people concerned with the welfare of animals, yet inattentive to the dignity of other human beings, and ponders the possibility of a compromise between East and West, of the possibility of forging a harmonious relation between equal, if different, parts (Nader 1989b).

It was the first time a document representing a coherent political system in operation in a Western country was made available to an Arab-speaking readership. Al-Tahtawi made the alien familiar by using Arab proverbs or mirrored (East–West) images. He knew the power of comparison and contributed context to a commonly repeated observation of early and even contemporary travelers to the West from Japan to Gibralter, "The West—they have technology, but they have no culture, no civilization."

The idea that technological development need not be equated with civilization is alive today in spite of the strangeness of humanity united by industrialisms and an ideology of economic plenty. The disjunctures of modernity may not easily erase cherished continuities. Moreover, the problems that foreign observers see as present in the globalizing market economy were historically here where industrialization happened earlier. This was the subject of Anthony F. C. Wallace's underappreciated book *Rockdale* (1978), which is summarized in his elaborate subtitle: *An Account of the Coming of the Machines. The Making of a New Way of Life in the Mill Hamlets, the Triumph of Evangelical Capitalists over Socialists and Infidels, and the Transformation of the Workers into Christian Soldiers in a Cotton-Manufacturing District in Pennsylvania in the Years before and during the Civil War.*

The concept of progress, as Kroeber noted in 1948, has a powerful hold on the unconscious as well as the conscious thought of our day: it is an idea that forbids looking backward as we advance. Progress, Kroeber notes, is an a priori assumption that is adhered to with considerable fervor of emotion, something to be analyzed rather than taken for granted. To what extent is it continuous and inevitable? These are old questions still interesting to our publics, students among them, who ponder the directionality of our world and wonder if they should buy into the "inevitability syndrome," the belief that the economy, like the universe will continue to expand.

CHANGING CONTEXTS: POST–WORLD WAR II, COLD WAR, AND MULTICULTURALISM

The "anthropological attitude" that values detachment and involvement as a mode of rethinking existing assumptions has not changed much in the past 100 years, nor have the social prejudices that it challenged: ethnocentrism, racism, sexism, the use of inadequate measures of human worth. What really has changed is the world around us as it affects who we are, what we study, and with what consequence, forcing us to probe the question why we take the stand we do.

Factors external to the profession that were critical to anthropology in this country during the Cold War are still with us and merit remembering. In his work on American anthropology and McCarthyism, David Price (2000) observes that social anthropologists were attacked more for their stance on racial and economic inequalities than for holding Marxist positions. Gene Weltfish used U.S. Army data indicating that southern whites had lower IQs than northern blacks and was called before the House Un-American Activities Committee. On the other hand, technologies of military origin such as remote sensing drew archeologists and physical anthropologists into national laboratories—institutions not usually frequented by sociocultural anthropologists (Nader 1997a, 1997b). There was benefit but also a double edge: Geographic Information Systems, so important to archaeologists and ecological anthropologists, are also used to locate sites for bombing the people sociocultural anthropologists study (and sites dear to archaeologists). And in physical anthropology, funding increased for projects addressing a human species faced with the possibility of extinction. There were unexpected consequences. Physical anthropologist Earle Reynolds, who worked on the Atomic Bomb Casualty Commission, became an anti-bomb activist and sailed into a U.S. H-bomb test zone, as well as into Vladivostok to protest testing by the former U.S.S.R. The different legacies are still with us.

Other external factors hit archaeology later. The Native American Grave Protection and Repatriation Act (NAGPRA, 1990) is reorienting the nature of Native American/archaeologist dialogue. Its impact on museums and American archaeology coincided with a more diverse composition among American archaeologists. The pasts created by the discipline now compete not only with biblical accounts but with others' versions of the past. The Hopi employ archaeologists who document a Hopi past sometimes at odds with the national American past and use them in negotiations with non-Hopi; they are diagnosing America, confronting dangerous truths and memory theory. At the same time, archaeologists are opened to new self-realizations about perspectives that blind (Kehoe 1998).

A frequently cited story of normative blindness is that of Cahokia—hidden in plain sight, as one archaeologists put it. Robert Silverberg's *Mound Builders of Ancient America* (1968) demonstrated how archaeologists' interpretation was influenced by their social milieu. A rediscovery of Cahokia, at the confluence of the Missouri and Mississippi Rivers, tells of monumental cities visited by George Washington, recorded by Thomas Jefferson's associates, and then forgotten (Pauketat and Emerson 1997). The Manifest Destiny ideology that required the downgrading of the inhabitants who competed for land with white settlers resulted in normative blindness.

In the center of Cahokia stands the third largest structure in preindustrial North America—Monk's Mound. Only the great Pyramid of Cholula and Teotihuacan's pyramid of the Sun are larger. It is an area of 83 hectares—a city of some twenty thousand people in a region of some fifty thousand people that some speculate was comparable in size to eleventh- or twelfth-century Venice—larger than London, Paris, and Cologne and smaller only than Constantinople and Seville. Notions of a vanishing race of savages implied that America's First Nations never reached a level of civilization comparable to that of the invading conquerors, but now a whole New World archaeology is being uncovered as a property of indigenous peoples, from the Andes, to Mesoamerica, to Mound Builders of the eastern woodlands—a vertical world system, south–north (Kehoe 1998).

Bruce Trigger (1998) points out that each epistemology adopted by archaeologists privileges a different aspect of reality—something that could be said as well of linguistics or sociocultural anthropology. Processual archaeologists privilege the study of human behavior over the study of beliefs; post-processualists portrayed them as ecological determinists denying agency to human beings and questioned the assumption that the ideological sphere was of secondary importance. Transformations in archaeology led to new awareness of biases by ethnic prejudice as in Cahokia, by gender as in man the hunter and woman the gatherer, by class as in favoring elites over peasants or slaves. But as Trigger also points out, multiple standpoints need not simply create multiple, incompatible archaeologies or anthropologies. They challenge us to use this multiplicity to create more holistic syntheses. Trigger also warns that the combination of moral earnestness and acute critical self-consciousness "encourages the accumulation of increasing amounts of unverified and often mutually reinforcing speculation" (1998:29).

Novel ideals must be subject to some form of rigorous selection if they are to do more than destabilize the discipline, but unfortunately uncovering biases serves both to shake up the discipline *and* to obliterate disciplinary memory. A hundred years ago Boas erased not only the evolutionists with whom he disagreed but also anthropologists like James Mooney (1896) with whom he should have had much in common. Malinowski and the fieldwork revolution erased the diffusionists along with attention to culture contact, movement, and the destructive changes that imperialisms were inflicting on indentured laborers (Rivers 1922). Mooney and Rivers would be at home in contemporary anthropology, having a drink with Orin Starn or having tea with Aihwa Ong. Likewise, the interpretivists of the 1970s erased, revised, or essentialized pre-1960s anthropology because they thought that a break was needed to make space for new influences—from philosophy, literary criticism, and other social sciences (Marcus and Fisher 1986). But anthropologists working during the colonial period were at least as unaware of the settings that enmeshed them as we are today of corporate domination and control.

While the auto-critique of the 1960s and 1970s helped us adapt to what some call the incoherent conditions of accelerated history, it was the changed relationship between those who study and those being studied that forced anthropologists to consider the conditions under which their knowledge has been acquired. This new self-awareness had consequences.

In 1973 Talal Asad was concerned with the political and administrative inequality between colonial anthropologists and colonized informants. By 1986 anthropologists were concerned with ethnographic texts. The exploration of the effects of colonial inequality on ethnographic perspectives became the investigation of the distorting effects of authoritative writing styles. One result was that questioning of political and military power was subsumed within literary representation. The so-called crisis of representation created anxiety in younger anthropologists and paralyzed some. There was a retreat from standard English.

The postanthropological literary project is rooted in the methods and interests of literary criticism. As one of my colleges argued at the time, the critique was *about* anthropological works, but it was not anthropological (Rabinow 1986). Thick fieldwork and the lives of others were replaced by thick representation. Ethnographies were taken out of the field in both a disciplinary and a methodological sense. Dissenting views were set aside rather than engaged or argued. The linguistic anthropologists missed an opportunity when they failed to analyze the linguistic stoppers such as "it's not interesting," "it's trivial," "old fashioned," "quibbling," "not important," or "anti-scientific" that impeded exchange. By the twenty-

first century the inevitable reaction is in swing, and critiques of the critiques now emerge by Reyna (1998, 1999), Trencher (2000), Thu (1999), and others. Anthropology is grounded in life, not text; the marked absence of civic engagement in any but abstract terms is now recognized for what it was: escapism. Unlike fictional characters, the Samoans and Tikopeans exist, and it matters to them how they are represented, as noted earlier in *Reinventing Anthropology* (Hymes [1969] 1999). Adam Kuper (1999) warned American anthropologists of the unintended consequences of celebrating identity politics as versus social solidarity; he was vindicated in the November 2000 presidential election.

INTEGRATING PERSPECTIVES

Anthropology is now in a position to fully integrate the critiques. We know that history is contingent, that culture is situational, that culture is political, that the writing of culture involves ethical and intellectual stand taking, and that in taking stands, questions of aesthetics and form must be considered. We also know that ethnographic context involves multiple and shifting perspectives and necessarily includes questions of positional superiority. These are, however, no longer new and exciting discoveries that we draw from current research. They are methodological starting points that help us formulate richer and more relevant questions about social transitions and cultural change, about globalization and the reorganization of nation-states, about the shifting boundaries of nature and culture, about time and space. We do have empirical projects, many of them.

As early as the 1930s anthropologists wondered how we studied colonized peoples without studying colonizers, missionaries, and the anthropologist; now we are doing it. We wondered how so many scientific anthropologists could have omitted so much in their holistic study; now we begin to understand the blinders at work and we move forward. Along with Weber, we know that what we accomplish in science in some degree will be dated in 10, 20, 50 years. The "discovery" of women's wealth among Malinowski's Trobrianders (Weiner 1987) was crucial to an understanding of the political system that governed both men and women. Analyses of caloric intake among the San hunters and gatherers valorized gathering females over occasional male hunters. The original picture changes, reworked in the framework of gender and sexuality, and new mixes begin to unfold. Histories and the role of language in the making of history enter anthropology again, not solely to investigate where people came from and why but to value how people themselves saw history, to investigate memory and the means invented for recording memory.

Collingwood (1948) argued that history is the present's view of the past. Linguistic anthropologists are turning diachronicity into an event. Language ideologies as in marketing the discourse of cholera are powerful in framing and reframing social reality (Briggs 1999). The dynamics of interlingual conversion is at the heart of mestizo and Indian identity. These are not crises that put in question anthropological existence; they are challenges to find ways to understand the relationship of language to power with the help of social theory. We need a division of labor in anthropology, not antagonistic competitions.

Anthropology is now a worldwide discipline, not just Euro-American. Social anthropologists in France, Brazil, Mexico, the Middle East, Japan, Korea, and India point to different consequential ethnological traditions. The Anglo-Saxon tradition, for instance, has difficulty in coming to terms with power, while the French fieldwork tradition sees research inherently fraught with power relations in which there is no such thing as an unobtrusive participant. In archaeological anthropology, interlinkage of the different fields has been closest in North America, though now somewhat estranged, while in Britain and Europe there is increasingly more convergence, as with the declaration "Archaeology is anthropology or it is nothing." The same applies to biological and sociocultural anthropology. Fences make good neighbors (Ellison 1999), but do they make good anthropologists? One archaeologist asked what would archaeology be like without exchange, kinship, gender, symbolism (Gosden 1999). What would social/cultural anthropology be like if we were still working with short chronologies? Four million years throw present ways of life into perspective.

NEW CONNECTIONS: NATURE OF NATURE, FINANCE AND WORLD SYSTEMS, ENVIRONMENT AND INTELLECTUAL PROPERTY

Biological anthropology at the turn of the nineteenth century was central to evolutionary biology and to social research addressing social Darwinism and eugenics. A century later, population biology and advances in brain science generated new questions and a new eugenics. Earlier findings, such as the idea that physical types, language, and culture evolve independently, the rejection of race as the dominant paradigm for human variation, and primate adaptations as indicators in the evolution of humans, are being considered in a new context. If the biological category of race is without meaning, the social

category of race is determining life chances. A theoretical attachment to natural selection and adaptation theory can limit understanding of biological plasticity that has been played upon and developed in response to an evolution riddled with chance, coincidence, and chaos (McKee 2000; see also Fix 1999).

The discovery of DNA and what followed revolutionized physical anthropology. Our findings became relevant to scientists writing for *our* publics. Geneticist Cavalli-Sforza (2000) uses materials from archaeology, linguistics, and physical and cultural anthropology, doing what physical anthropologist John Moore notes we should and would do better. Physiologist Jared Diamond's bestseller, *Guns, Germs, and Steel* (1997), suffers a misplaced and Eurocentric emphasis on technology over culture. Paul Ehrlich's new book, *Human Natures* (2000), uses anthropology to argue that how people act is not all in their genes, a position that, though not new to us, apparently needs restating. In another mode, *Ishmael* (1993) by Daniel Quinn is an anthropological conversation between a gorilla and a young man about human history from before the neolithic to the present in which acceleration of environmental destruction is keyed to "civilization." Anthropology has much to say about human destiny and the taken for granted. We should say it and replace the "pundits." *Civilization* magazine recently published two headlines: "Why Corporate Colonialism Is Good" and "When Dying Cultures Shouldn't Be Saved" (Blake 2000). A challenge for young anthropologists: The time is ripe.

Today chemical and technological revolutions are unmatched in their power to remake living beings on the planet (Stone 1994). Wildlife stories corroborate the global drop in sperm count among healthy males over a period of 50 years. At the same time, biotechnologies are reshaping agriculture, animal husbandry, medicine, and pharmaceuticals and creating new inequalities, as are hormone-modulating pollutants. There is a wholesale reseeding of the Earth's biosphere with a bioindustrial nature, an alteration of the human species, and some say, a "backdoor to eugenics" (Duster 1990), justified by revised theories of evolution. A new narrative about evolution suggests that the ways in which we are reorganizing our economy are merely amplifications of nature's own principles. Multinationals scout the globe in search of microbes, plants, and animals with rare genetic traits that may have economic return for which they seek patent protection.

In this context, look at the controversy stirred up by Cavalli-Sforza's Human Genome Diversity Project organized to take blood samples from the world's linguistically distinct populations. Concern about its use came alive when the U.S. government sought patents on a virus derived from the cell line of a 26-year-old Guaymi Indian woman from Panama thought to be useful in AIDS and leukemia research. A few months later the U.S. government filed for patent claims on cell lines from Solomon Islanders and New Guinea Papuans, and then in California came the precedent-setting case over John Moore's cell line.

New technologies affect the way we marry and have babies, raise of children, work, eat, make kinship (Luoma 1999; Strathern 1992). The nineteenth-century debate over the issue of human slavery reemerges in the new context: can a human being be made the commercial property of another human being or, stranger yet, legal person? Exoticism may be passé in describing The Other, but as a vehicle of self-examination its potential is ripe. Anthropologists who study the invention of tradition also now study the invention of life and the rapidly changing nature of nature. Different interests in anthropology are interesting. Is aggression connected to a gene, or is it, as Frans de Waal (2000) says, a tool of competition and negotiation? Should it be medicalized? Violence is considered uncivilized except when exercised in the name of civilization. Part of the need to re-emphasize the anthropological perspective comes from the fact that new technologies have been created that link behavior to biological factors. How the link is viewed may be among the biggest questions of our time, and we need to be prepared.

These are extremely important issues that delve into "traditional" anthropology questions in a new context. Culture is part of nature, and the changing nature of nature is a subject for all of us. A study of mythologies of menopause in Japan and North America (Lock 1993) asks, can menopause really be a disease? Biological anthropologists look for connections among early menarche, late child-bearing, length of breast-feeding and long periods of menstruation and the incidence of breast cancer (Gladwell 2000; Straussman 1990). Can menstruation be a disease? Can ADD be a disease? Medical anthropologists are studying the buying and selling of human body parts as well as their theft, the significance of emerging concepts of "brain dead," and the more general problem of who owns the body (Scheper-Hughes 2000). Emerging economies use biopower for commercial and regulatory purposes, and though power need not be the theme for all anthropology, it is critical in examining central dogmas as they affect the body and the body politic.

The relationship between past and present is of great popular and philosophical concern (Milton 1999) yet not so easy to configure, as demonstrated by attempts to study changing English kinship with the advent of new biotechnologies. Economic assumptions underlying much of American policy are also challenged by globalization. Anthropologists interpret the ideology of the digital revolution and put it in a time frame as whole economies shift to digital. Islam forbids interest, yet Islamic financial concerns operate in 70 countries and have assets in the $200 billion range (Warde 2000). Dar Al-Maal Al Islami (DMI), the largest Islamic group, is headquartered in the Bahamas and operates primarily out of Geneva, yet it uses the language of the Islamic *unema.* New mixes link legal and economic anthropology, environmental anthropology with science practices and new technologies.

Interesting in this regard is the collaborative work of Agnar Helgason and Gísli Pálsson of Iceland—a biological anthropologist and a sociocultural anthropologist doing economic anthropology in a new key—on the commoditization of resource lights in Iceland (1997). Their work is a challenge to neoclassical claims as an all-embracing account of economic life in the West and elsewhere. They speak about "armchair fisherman or fish lords" and question Polanyi's influential but erroneous distinction between embedded economies elsewhere and disembedded economies in the West, unfettered by social relations of "externalities."

Debates in Iceland have to do with the transformation of common use rights into private property. With commoditization, boundaries are rearranged, social relations are transformed, and the allocation of commoditized fishing rights to boat owners has resulted in a privileging of capital over labor, shifting power from sea to land and widening the economic rift between boat owners and their employees. They know where they stand:

> The notion of scholarly practice that can be disassociated from moral debates "on the ground" is fallacious . . . the idea of standing objectively outside the flow of social life is overoptimistic . . . it is precisely by immersing themselves in the social and moral context of economic life that anthropologists can examine what the rather loose reference to "the market" entails. . . . The proximity of the ethnographic gaze is better suited to the data at hand than the detached neo-classical view from afar. [Helgason and Pálsson 1997:467]

As I said in "Up the Anthropologist" (Nader 1969), there is intellectual value in indignation.

And so it is with the nature of nature. *The Convention on Biological Diversity,* a United Nations product of 1992 and the Trade-Related Intellectual Property Rights conferred in 1994, part of the Uruguay Round negotiations leading to the creation of the WTO, reveals what counts as "nature" today (Jerome 1998). The products of traditional farmers are categorized as "raw nature" and therefore unpatentable, whereas nature found in laboratories, seed banks, and multinationals is "manufactured nature," deserving of intellectual property protection. Microorganisms and microbiological processes for the production of those plants are viewed as "nonnatural" and therefore deserving of intellectual property protection. Nature thus becomes a profoundly human construction, and as anthropologist Jessica Jerome points out, law is conscious in its construction of nature.

One of the hidden ideological premises necessary for the spread of the "free market" is the concept of nature as a resource or raw material. Indeed, conceptual categories are at the core of political struggles over biological diversity. The areas of high biodiversity are also those with high linguistic diversity. The loss of native languages means loss of knowledge and replacement by a new language as well as a new ecological frame, new resource economies, new discourses of "ecological modernization" that delegitimize conflict-based response—in favor of coercive harmony. The Kayapo of Brazil think that knowledge is a product of nature, not of human nature, and not always translated into useful products, not requiring invention, thereby colliding with legal issues of nature/human.

Thus anthropologists of law concern themselves with globalization studies; economic anthropologists, with financial institutions and kinship specialists; biological anthropologists, with feminist and medical anthropology, linguistics, and environmental anthropology. New mixes are taking form—as well as connections among nations, movements, international bureaucracies, and individuals with competing ideas about the meaning of nature.

From Germany, Stefan Beck (2000) examines the impact of genetic knowledge on marriage strategies and changing notions of blood and relatedness in Cyprus. He asks, How does nature enter into culture when genetic testing makes available new options that effect a transformation of the body and the body politic? A mandatory genetic test for thalassemia creates a "risk profile" for an individual. Endogamy, once thought to be predictably secure, is now considered risky. The complex interplay of genetic knowledge practices and ethnic nationalisms accelerates the ideologizing of biology and the unmaking of populations formerly bound by common narratives. There is now an international tourism in search of choices offered by genetics. Overlapping connections sustain a rich discipline.

DISCIPLINARY ISSUES

Where does professional practice fit in all this? (Baba 1994; Basch et al. 1999). There are those who would erase the distinction between theory and practice or academics and practice. We all practice anthropology. Teaching is practice and our primary engagement with the public, and all practice hinges on competence and professional autonomy. Without professional autonomy the anthropologist becomes an employee doing the bidding of his or her employer. There is precedent worth examining with increasing numbers of anthropologists employed outside academia. Look at what happened to the chemists or the engineers who, in spite of their revolt (Layton 1971), became indentured servants as industrial employees, without professional autonomy. Anthropologists should solve problems with people, not for them. We have to give thought to this issue and to the issue of regulation. People claim to be anthropologists who are not trained professionals. No anthropologist would for convenience call him- or herself a molecular biologist, or a lawyer, or even a literary critic; that the reverse is true indicates that there is still something sexy about being an anthropologist. Trained or not, people who call themselves anthropologists are working in questionable fields without consideration of ethics. We are properly attentive to possible infractions of anthropological ethics by those who work among the Yanomamo, but we close our eyes to practices on nuclear natives in the United States (Kuletz 1998), marketing to vulnerable populations such as children, the poor, the elderly, the infirm, or the unsuspecting, or in the Middle East where we actively participate in keeping the silence over Iraq, where since the Gulf War more people have died than at Nagasaki and Hiroshima put together.

We relegate to the margins our public intellectuals—anthropologists who practice anthropology by engaging wider issues. Louis Freedburg reports on the realities of immigration and education for the *San Francisco Chronicle*; Mary Ann Castle works imaginatively on abortion clinics and reproductive rights. Janine Wedel's recent work (1998) on Western aid to Eastern Europe in 1989–98 was ignored in anthropology but caught the attention of outside publics, in the *New York Times*, the *Wall Street Journal*, the *Los Angeles Times, Newsweek, Foreign Affairs,* and scholarly publications, or consultants, reformers, financiers, World Bank, IMF, and USAID. Wedel's prizewinning work is about how aid happens in Russia, involving Russian entrepreneurs, Harvard economists, and Vice President Al Gore. Pretty meaty stuff. Such anthropology resonates in many fora but interestingly not in anthropology itself.

Anthropologists who speak to a public wider than members of the discipline often have a greater immediate impact outside the discipline than in it. When I started to work on coercive harmony (Nader 1989a 1990, 1997c), the idea was slow to interest anthropologists (for reasons I examine elsewhere), while those who *felt* coercively harmonized—our publics—were quick to recognize its power, in the workplace with quality circles and "facilitators" (Nader 2000), in environmental movements at loggerheads with Clinton-style negotiation, on Native American reservations dealing with negotiations over nuclear waste (Ou 1996), in grade schools where harmony ideology is regularly taught in dispute resolution classes, in global arenas where lawyers are up against new international negotiators selling psychology instead of the rule of law (Nader 1995), or in national elections where debaters cannot disagree. If we are ignorant of debates outside academia, we increasingly find ourselves talking mainly to each other, trapped in a diminished space, working in cramped quarters (Auge 1998).

Recently a group of distinguished theoretical and mathematical ecologists, along with others, drafted a declaration of independence as a first step toward articulating a framework that allows their science to move beyond traditional paradigms (Gieryn 2000). It begins, "We hereby declare our independence from those current practices within the scientific community that restrict research."[1] "To be or not be specific is not the question" (Latour 1996); rather, they ask what kind of science can deal with dynamic, unstable heterogeneous reality that is knowable with difficulty as versus a stable, homogeneous, and readily knowable reality for which the old sciences had tools.

The case for a more generalist anthropology is not difficult to imagine. Anthropology, more than any other discipline, has the capacity to generate the kind of introspection that can influence the future role of human beings on earth, to impart the lessons of history, the experience of *Home sapiens* on the planet. More than any discipline we should not shrink from the big questions; every other discipline was designed to shrink. Though we may be a small part of the global transformation, we have a large part to play. The promise of science and technology to solve problems is initiated by the same old hubris that ignores other knowledges, long-term commonsense observations, and our own scientific culture and biases. We know even less of industrial subjects than we do of colonized ones. We need to abandon the practice of science as usual. Anthropology cannot be carved off into permanent parts—legal, political, gender, historical, biological, cognitive. We have the ability to judge "whether those with might have it right." We know how to do what needs to be done. Let's do it.

NOTES

Acknowledgments. Acknowledgments are never inclusive enough, but I would like to thank E. Colson and E. Hertz who read and commented on earlier drafts of this talk. In addition, many colleagues helped with focus and references, for which I feel a great gratitude. In particular I thank A. Dundes, A. Duranti, A. Ghani, R. Gonzalez, W. Hanks, J. Habu, M. Hiesinger, K. Lightfoot, J. Mahiri, J. Marks, K. Milton, J. Ou, P. Rabinow, and L. Wilkie. Holly Halligan miraculously kept the different versions straight, and Liza Grandia pitched in when necessary.

This essay was delivered as the Distinguished Lecture, 99th Annual Meeting of the American Anthropological Association, November 2000, in San Francisco, California.

1. The full text reads as follows:

> We hereby declare our independence from those current practices within the scientific community that restrict research, ways of knowing, citizen inclusion, and respect for non-humans.
>
> We affirm that science is social knowledge, that solving the environmental problems known to all of us is the mission of ecology, and that ecology is a co-operation among sciences, humanities, and human cultures.
>
> We will work to establish an American Science Foundation which emphasizes research that is accountable to people, nature, and quality of life; addresses questions of local, regional, and democratic significance; includes citizens in formulating and doing research; bridges the boundaries between the practical and the abstract; and uses knowledge in the service of life rather than in the service of power. [Gieryn 2000:2]

REFERENCES CITED

Al-Jabarti, Abdal-Rahman. 1975. Al-Jabarti's Chronicle of the First Seven Months of the French Occupation of Egypt under the French, 1798. Shmuel Moreh, ed. and trans. Leiden: E. J. Brill.

Al-Tahtawi, Rafic. [1834]1993. Takhlis al-ibriz fi talkhis Baris (An extraction of cold in the summary of Paris). Cairo: al Hay'ah al-Misriyyah al-Ammah lil-Kitab.

Asad, Talal, ed. 1973. Anthropology and the Colonial Encounter. London: Ithaca Press.

Auge, Marc. 1998. A Sense for the Other: The Timeliness and Relevance of Anthropology. A. Jacob, trans. Stanford: Stanford University Press.

Baba, Marietta L. 1994. The Fifth Subdiscipline: Anthropological Practice and the Future of Anthropology. Human Organization 53(2):174–186.

Barnes, J. A. 1951. History in a Changing Society. Rhodes-Livingstone Journal 11:1–9.

Basch, Linda G., Lucie Wood Saunders, Jagna W. Sharff, and James Peacock, eds. 1999. Transforming Academia: Challenges and

Opportunities for an Engaged Anthropology. Mary Moran, ed. American Ethnological Society Monograph Series, 8. Arlington, VA: American Anthropological Association.

Bateson, Gregory. 1958. Naven—The Culture of the Iatmul People of New Guinea as Revealed through a Study of the "Naven" Ceremonial. 2nd edition. Stanford: Stanford University Press.

Beck, Stefan. 2000. Human Genetics and the Making and Unmaking of Populations. Paper presented at the German–American Frontiers of Social and Behavioral Sciences Symposium for Young German and American Scholars, March 23–26. Stone Mountain, GA.

Blake, Michael. 2000. Rights for People, Not for Cultures. Civilization, August–September: 51–53.

Boas, Franz. 1906. The History of Anthropology. *In* Congress of Arts and Science Universal Exposition, vol. 5. Howard J. Rogers, ed. Pp. 468–482. St. Louis: Houghton Mifflin.

Briggs, Charles L. 1999. Sequentiality and Temporalization in the Narrative Construction of a South American Cholera Epidemic. *In* Theorizing the Americanist Tradition. Lisa P. Valentine and Regna Darnell, eds. Pp. 330–337. Toronto: University of Toronto Press.

Cartmill, Matt. 1994. Reinventing Anthropology. Yearbook of Physical Anthropology 37:1–9.

Castle, Mary Ann. 1999. The Invisible Anthropologist. *In* Transforming Academia: Challenges and Opportunities for an Engaged Anthropology. Linda G. Basch, Lucie Wood Saunders, Jagna W. Scharff, and James Peacock, eds. Pp. 253–267. American Ethnological Society Monograph Series, 8. Mary Moran, ed. Arlington, VA: American Anthropological Association.

Cavalli-Sforza, Luiga Luca. 2000. Genes, Peoples, and Languages. New York: North Point Press.

Childe, V. Gordon. 1951. Man Makes Himself. New York: New American Library.

Collingwood, Robin George. 1948. The Idea of History. Oxford: Clarendon Press.

Darnell, Regna. 1998. And Along Came Boas: Continuity and Revolution in Americanist Anthropology. Philadelphia: John Benjamin.

deWaal, Frans B. M. 2000. Primates—A Natural History of Conflict Resolution. Science 289:256–590.

Diamond, Jared. 1997. Guns, Germs, and Steel and the Fate of Human Societies. New York: W. W. Norton.

Duster, Troy. 1990. Backdoor to Eugenics. New York: Routledge.

Ehrlich, Paul R. 2000. Human Natures: Genes, Cultures, and the Human Prospect. Washington, DC: Island Press.

Ellison, Peter T. 1999. Good Fences Make Good Neighbors: Keeping Anthropology's Subfields Alive and Growing in the 21st Century. *In* Transforming Academia: Challenges and Opportunities for an Engaged Anthropology. Linda G. Basch, Lucie Wood Saunders, Jagna W. Scharff, and James Peacock, eds. Pp. 130–133. American Ethnological Society Monograph Series, 8. Mary Moran, ed. Arlington, VA: American Anthropological Association.

Fardon, Richard, ed. 1990. Localizing Strategies: Regional Traditions of Ethnographic Writing. Edinburgh: Scottish Academic Press; and Washington, DC: Smithsonian Institution Press.

Fix, Alan. 1999. Migration and Colonization in Human Microevolution. New York: Cambridge University Press.

Gieryn, Thomas. 2000. Applied Science Studies? Newsletter of the Section on Science, Knowledge and Technology (SKAT) of the American Sociological Association 76(3):2.

Gladwell, Malcolm. 2000. John Rock's Error; What the Co-Inventor of the Bill Didn't Know: Menstruation Can Endanger Women's Health. New Yorker, March 13:52–63.

Golde, Peggy, ed. 1970. Women in the Field. Chicago: Aldine Press.

Gosden, Christopher. 1999. Anthropology and Archaeology: A Changing Relationship. London: Routledge

Gottschalk, Louis R., Clyde Kluckhohn, and Robert Angell. 1944. The Use of Personal Documents in History, Anthropology, and Sociology. New York: Social Science Research Council Bulletin 53.

Helgason, Agnai, and Gísli Pálsson. 1997. Contested Commodities: The Moral Landscape of Modernist Regimes. Journal of the Royal Anthropological Institute 3(3):451–471.

Hymes, Dell, ed. [1969] 1999. Reinventing Anthropology. 2nd edition. Ann Arbor: University of Michigan Press.

Jerome, Jessica. 1998. How International Legal Agreements Speak about Biodiversity. Anthropology Today 14(6):7–9.

Kehoe, Alice B. 1998. The Land of Prehistory: A Critical History of American Archaeology. New York: Routledge.

Keller, Evelyn Fox. 1983. A Feeling for the Organism: The Life and Work of Barbara McClintock. New York: W. H. Freeman and Co.

Kluckhohn, Clyde. 1949. Mirror for Man: the Relation of Anthropology to Modern Life. New York: McGraw-Hill.

Konner, Mel. 1982. The Tangled Wing—Biological Constraints on the Human Spirit. New York: Henry Holt and Co.

Kroeber, Alfred. 1944. Configurations of Culture Growth. Berkeley: University of California Press.

———. 1948. Anthropology: Race, Language, Culture, Psychology, Prehistory. New York: Harcourt Brace.

Kuletz, Valerie L. 1998. The Tainted Desert: Environmental and Social Ruin in the American West. New York: Routledge.

Kuper, Adam. 1999. Culture: The Anthropologist's Account. Cambridge, MA: Harvard University Press.

Lane, Edward William. [1836] 1973. The Manners and Customs of the Modern Egyptians, New York: Dover.

Latour, Bruno. 1996. Not the Question. Anthropology Newsletter 37(3):4–5.

Layton, Edwin T., Jr. 1971. The Revolt of the Engineers: Social Responsibility in the American Engineering Profession. Cleveland: Case Western Reserve University Press.

Leach, E. R. 1954. Political Systems of Highland Burma—A Study of Kachin Social Structure. Cambridge, MA: Harvard University Press.

Lock, Margaret. 1993. Encounters with Aging—Mythologies of Menopause in Japan and North America. Berkeley: University of California Press.

Lubchenco, Jane. 1998. Entering the Century of the Environment: A New Social Contract for Science. Science 279:491–497.

Luoma, Jon R. 1999. System Failure. Mother Jones, July–August: 62.

Marcus, George E., and Michael M. J. Fisher. 1986. Anthropology as Cultural Critique: An Experimental Moment in the Human Sciences. Chicago: University of Chicago Press.

Marler, Catherine. 2000. Sex on the Brain. Science 289:1478–1479.

McKee, Jeffrey K. 2000. The Riddled Chain: Chance, Coincidence, and Chaos in Human Evolution. New Brunswick, NJ: Rutgers University Press.

Milton, Katherine. 1999. A Hypothesis to Explain the Role of Meat-Eating in Human Evolution. Evolutionary Anthropology 8(1):11–21.

Mooney, James. 1896. The Ghost Dance Religion and the Sioux Outbreak of 1890. *In* Fourteenth Annual Report of the Bureau of Ethnology, pt. 2. Washington, DC: Government Printing Office.

Nader, Laura. 1969. Up the Anthropologist—Perspectives Gained from Studying Up. *In* Reinventing Anthropology. Dell Hymes, ed. Pp. 285–311. New York: Pantheon Books.

———. 1980. Energy Choices in a Democratic Society. A Resource Group Study for the Synthesis Panel of the Committee on Nuclear and Alternative Energy Systems for the National Academy of Sciences.

———. 1981. Barriers to Thinking New about Energy. Physics Today 34(3):9, 99–102.

———. 1989a. The ADR Explosion: The Implications of Rhetoric in Legal Reform. Windsor Yearbook of Access to Justice. Pp. 269–291. Ontario: University of Windsor.

———. 1989b. Orientalism, Occidentalism, and the Control of Women. Cultural Dynamics, 2(3):323–355.

———. 1990. Harmony Ideology: Justice and Control in a Mountain Zapotec Village. Stanford: Stanford University Press.

———. 1995. Civilization and Its Negotiators. *In* Understanding Disputes: The Politics of Law. Pat Kaplan, ed. Pp. 39–63. Oxford: Berg Publishers.

———. 1996. Naked Science—Anthropological Inquiry into Boundaries, Power and Knowledge. New York: Routledge.

———. 1997a. The Phantom Factor—Impact of the Cold War on Anthropology. *In* The Cold War and the University: Toward an Intellectual History of the Postwar Years. Noam Chomsky et al., eds. Pp. 107–148. New York: New Press.

———. 1997b. Postscript on the Phantom Factor. General Anthropology Newsletter, November.

———. 1997c. Controlling Processes—Tracing the Dynamic Components of Power. Mintz Lecture. Current Anthropology 38(5):711–737.

Nader, Laura, with Roberto Gonzalez. 2000. The Framing of Teenage Health Care: Organizations, Cultures and Control. Culture, Medicine, and Psychiatry, June.

Nader, Laura, with N. Milleron. 1979. Dimensions of the "People Problem" in Energy Research and the Factual Basis of Dispersed Energy Futures. Energy 4(5):953–967.

Orlove, Benjamin S., John Chlang, and Mark A. Cane. 2000. Forecasting Andean Rainfall and Crop Yield from the Influence of El Niño on Pleiades Visibility, Nature 403:68–71.

Ou, Jay. 1996. Native Americans and the Monitored Retrievable Storage Plans for Nuclear Wastes: Late Capitalism, Negotia-tion, and Controlling Processes. Kroeber Anthropological Society Papers 80:32–89.

Pauketat, Tim R., and Thomas E. Emerson. 1997. Cahokia: Domination and Ideology in the Mississippian World. Lincoln: University of Nebraska Press.

Price, David. 2000. Anthropologists as Spies. The Nation, November 20:24.

Quinn, Daniel. 1993. Ishmael. New York: Bantam/Turner.

Rabinow, Paul. 1986. The Poetics and Politics of Enthnography. *In* Writing Culture. J. Clifford and G. Marcus, eds. Berkeley: University of California Press.

———. 1999. French DNA: Trouble in Purgatory. Chicago: University of Chicago Press.

Reyna, Stephen P. 1998. Right and Might: Of Approximate Truths and Moral Judgments. Identities 4(3–4):431–465.

———. 1999. The Owl in the Twilight: Cultural Anthropologies of Clifford Geertz and Marshall Sahlins. Reviews in Anthropology 26(3):173–187.

Rivers, William H. 1922. Essays in the Depopulation of Melanesia. Cambridge: Cambridge University Press.

Rothstein, Edward. 2000. A Sojourner in the Past Retraces His Steps. New York Times, April 15: A15–A17.

Scheper-Hughes, Nancy. 2000. The Global Traffic in Human Organs. Current Anthropology 41(2):191–224.

Seligman, E. R. A., ed. 1933. Anthropology. *In* Encyclopedia of Social Sciences, vol. 1. Pp. 199–203. New York: Macmillan.

Shanklin, Eugenia. 2000. Representations of Race and Racism in American Anthropology. Current Anthropology 41(1):99–103.

Silverberg, Robert. 1968. Mound Builders of Ancient America: The Archaeology of a Myth. Greenwich, CT: New York Graphic Society.

Stone, Richard. 1994. Environmental Estrogens Stir Debate. Science 265:308–310.

Strathern, Marilyn. 1992. After Nature: English Kinship in the Late Twentieth Century. Lewis Henry Morgan Lectures. Cambridge: Cambridge University Press.

Straussmann, Beverly T. 1990. Menstrual Cycling and Breast Cancer: An Evolutionary Perspective. Journal of Women's Health 8(2):193–202.

Thu, Kendall M. 1999. Anthropologists Should Return to the Roots of Their Discipline. Chronicle of Higher Education, April 30:A56.

Trencher, Susan R. 2000. Mirrored Images: American Anthropology and American Culture, 1960–1980. Westport, CT: Bergin and Gervey.

Trigger, Bruce. 1998. Archaeology and Epistemology: Dialoging across the Darwinian Chasm. American School of Archaeology 102:1–34.

Turner, V. W. 1957. Schism and Continuity in an African Society—A Study of Ndembu Village Life. Manchester: Manchester University Press.

Valentine, Lisa P., and Regna Darnell, eds. 1999. Theorizing the Americanist Tradition. Toronto: University of Toronto Press.

Wallace, Anthony F. C. 1978. Rockdale—An Account of the Coming of the Machines. The Making of a New Way of Life in the Mill Hamlets, the Triumph of Evangelical Capitalists over Socialists and Infidels, and the Transformation of the Workers into Christian Soldiers in a Cotton-Manufacturing District in Pennsylvania in the Years before and during the Civil War. New York: Alfred A. Knopf.

Warde, Ibrahim. 2000. Islamic Finance in the Global Economy, Edinburgh: Edinburgh University Press.

Wedel, Janine R. 1998. Collision and Collusion: The Strange Case of Western Aid to Eastern Europe, 1989–1998. New York: St. Martin's Press.

Weiner, Annette B. 1987. Women of Value, Men of Renown—New Perspectives in Trobriand Exchange. Austin: University of Texas Press.

White, Lynn, Jr. 1967. The Historical Roots of Our Ecologic Crisis. Science 155(3767):1203–1207.

———. 1980. The Ecology of Our Science. Science 80:72–78.

Yoffee, Norman, and George L. Cowgill, eds. 1988. The Collapse of Ancient States and Civilizations. Tucson: University of Arizona Press.

– 2 –

Fact versus Fiction
An Ethnographic Paradox Set in the Seychelles

Marion Benedict

Marion Benedict and her husband went to the Seychelles with their young children to do ethnographic fieldwork. She is at present a freelance author living with her anthropologist husband and her family in Berkeley, California.

The Seychelles are islands in the middle of the Indian Ocean, where my husband and I went for six months in 1960 and five months in 1975 to do anthropological fieldwork. Once we had decided to go there, I asked about the islands among my friends in London where we then lived. Everyone who had ever heard of the Seychelles had three things to say about them, and these were recited with remarkable agreement of thought and phrasing. First, the islands were breathtakingly beautiful, glittering like a necklace in a sun-splashed sea. Second, it was a land of free love where dark beauties, happy and carefree, all longed for white babies; and third, it was riddled with superstition and black magic.

Right away I wanted to look into that black magic, but my friends warned me not to. It was illegal, they said, and dangerous. Furthermore any investigations into such a subject would be construed as spying for the government, which would queer our fieldwork for good.

So I decided to take a sociological census. I had a notebook, a list of questions to ask, and an informant who could translate the local Creole for me and help me find my way around—and who might drop a few secrets along the way. My aim was to contribute to the world bank of ethnography and ultimately, to get to know people unlike myself—the "not me," the "Other."

Once in the field, in the confusion of new sights, sounds, smells and ways of thinking, I clung to that notebook and those questions as to a lifebelt. It represented the objective truth I was recording. It represented order and system; counting and measurement; collation and comparison; and objective observation. The notebook de-

fined my progress; it promised completion; it rationalized and legitimized my presence in that strange place among those strange people. It connected me to other collectors of ethnography and was a reassuring reminder of my own values, my own logical categories, the way I and my kind think—and, indeed, who I was.

But the facts I was trying to collect by asking questions tended to slide away. It had seemed an easy matter of question and answer, but the answer never came simply and directly, and sometimes never came at all, even after a long discussion of the topic. Lengthy digressions were the rule, and after my frustration wore off, I began to see that the important information lay in those very digressions, and not in the answers I was seeking. Important, I mean, in that my overall purpose was to comprehend these people in their own terms and not in terms of how they answered my questions, or of how they fitted into any readymade logical categories.

Furthermore, I suspected that many answers to my questions were inventions, and that the more directly the people answered me the more thoroughly they were lying. The vexed problem of what and whom to believe loomed larger and larger until I was forced to consider my own part in the dialogue. Upon what grounds did I decide what was true and what false? Sheerly on intuition, my own gut response based on some private mental/emotional grid far beyond the reach of any available logic.

And on what grounds had I chosen to record some things and not others? How did I sort out the significant from the insignificant? Again, it was on the seemingly illogical basis of intuition. And so the process of altering the text, or tampering with reality—that is, fictionalizing—had begun.

My intuition was at work in other ways, too. For instance, I had begun to think that one informant was paranoid in her fantastic suspicions that people were out to

"Fact versus Fiction: An Ethnographic Paradox Set in the Seychelles" by Marion Benedict from *Anthropology Today*, Vol. 1, No. 5, October 1985. Reprinted by permission of Blackwell Publishers.

"get" her. But how could I know for sure? And when I began to suspect that people were lying to me and laughing at me, how could I know that I was not catching her paranoia? Although I was able to check up on some facts and some of the answers given me, mostly I had to rely on guesswork.

I felt that the people were laughing at me and my concern with the tedious exercise of filling my notebook with their lies. I recall, during those first few weeks, bending my head constantly over the pages of my notebook, fingers smudged with ink, shooing away flies, writing up endless little facts that died as I pinned them down while the people around me nudged and winked and whispered and giggled, carrying on their real lives over my head . . . I was confronting head-on the difficulty of knowing the "Other." There was also the difficulty of how to write up the material and make it readable. How to begin, and what form to use? It seemed evident that the first step was to determine exactly what I wanted to say and then find the appropriate form in which to say it. In practice, however, there was a constant interchange between those two steps. Considering the form threw me back to reappraising the content, and considering the content threw me back to reappraising the form.

At first I tried the form of the anthropological monograph with its third person narration. That has the benefit of concentrating the reader's attention on the people by eliminating the "I" (except, of course, insofar as the author is always implied). But then I encountered the same difficulty as when collecting the material—without the personal, perceiving "I" the material was dull. In pursuing objectivity I had pushed out the felt life. So the "I" was moved in. But I still wanted to keep out the self: I wanted to write about them, not about me. So I thought of shaping the diary that I had kept in the field into readable form and presenting the material in that way.

The diary form had many advantages. In the first place, it was easy. Keeping my eye on the relations between the people and myself, I had only to shuffle around some times and places, cut irrelevancies, invent some transitions and the job was done. I could thus get rid of distracting disclaimers like "it seemed to me" and "or so I thought" because the personal point of view inhered in the diary form itself. The "I" was squeezed into the form, and so the reader's attention could fix itself upon the people.

The diary form also had the merit of accuracy, in that it was as exact an account of my activities in collecting the material as I could give in a readable form. It gave the sense of the present tense in all its immediacy, and transmitted my response to daily events as I saw them, and left it to the reader to do the work of fitting them into his own mental grid—that is, the work of interpretation.

But the diary had one big disadvantage; it did not have an organizing theme. It was anecdotal, episodic, and didn't go anywhere. There was nothing to carry the reader along; no build up, no suspense. Ultimately there was not enough meaning to make it interesting. It did not lead to any generalizations or argue any theory. So I shoved it into a drawer and did not look at it for several years.

When I did take it out again, I saw clearly that I had not sufficiently digested the material at the time I had written it. It was entertaining—amusing, even— but it didn't explain anything. I had not sufficiently engaged with what, all along, had been my underlying preoccupation.

But now I had digested the material. Now I saw a pattern emerging in my fieldnotes and a theme for my writing up. I saw that, in recording household compositions, behaviour, jokes told by fishermen and priests, schoolteachers and washerwomen, in noting down rituals and even the cost of raising pigs—I had been gathering an understanding about the nature of witchcraft. I had been recording evidence of how it works, and how that working radiates out to illuminate the most intimate and sensitive—and trivial—relations among the people of the Seychelles.

This new theme required a new form. I now saw that the ordering principle of my writing up must be the process of my understanding of witchcraft. In this way the search for content recapitulated the search for form. And the form required that the "I" be moved to centre stage.

This "I" had to be fictionalized. For the sake of coherence and emphasis on the important issues, I pretended to be a more naive observer than I really was. I took the reader by the hand and demonstrated, piece by piece, the evidence I had collected that led to my theory of witchcraft. I didn't actually *say* so, however, because I wanted the reader to go through the process of discovery for himself or herself. Sometimes I even planted clues so that the reader could see what was happening before I did.

Further fictionalizing was done in order to protect my informants. For that, I falsified names and put one person's words into another's mouth. For the sake of clarity and simplification I compressed several people into one. For instance, I really went to four fortunetellers, but I telescoped them into two. My main character herself is a composite of several women whom I had interviewed at length.

In order to clarify the narration I discarded material about whole families who, although they provided complexities and insights that my diary had included, nevertheless would distract the reader from the theme of witchcraft. The insights, however, helped to inform my final conclusions as I rearranged the actual process of discovery.

In order to show rather than to tell, I invented scenes of transition and thus imposed an order upon my narration that was never present in the field.

All this was done in the name of telling the truth and it resulted in a fiction. I had written a continuous narrative with suspense, a plot, fictional characters, a climax and a point—that is, a *novella*.

Fictionalizing continued as I invented another language to convey the rhythm and structure of my informants' diction. Their logic was roundabout; they told the middle first, then left me scrabbling for the subject and the message, so that it seemed a long and meaningless ramble until sometime later when I might have the good fortune to seize the point. But when my favourite informant spoke to her people she did not sound long-winded and tedious. The lilt of her Creole carried the knotty and treacherous structure along in an easy and natural flow that died when literally reproduced in my English on the printed page. Also, there was a freshness in her choice of words and a slyness in her digressions which alerted me to the calculated art that lay behind her kind of organization. But in order to convey the sense of this to my reader, I had to impose my own kind of organization as well as employ a free translation.

Witchcraft was a subject shrouded in secrecy and fraught with hysteria. Asking about it was like asking somebody to take hold of a live wire. The only way to approach it was indirectly. I had to go around in circles, pretending not to be interested in it to get close to it at all.

So my notebook is full of everything from very specific observations related to witchcraft—like accounts of my visits to witches—to the most conjectural. I recorded bits of gossip heavy with innuendo; half-guesses about oblique hints gleaned from informants; conversations with people describing their experiences with witches (or *bonhommes* or *bonnefemmes de bois,* as they called them). I noted behaviour that might be related to witchcraft and kept my eyes and ears open for signs of this hidden but ubiquitous phenomenon.

I was lucky to have, among my informants, an apprentice witch—not that she admitted it until the very end of my stay, by which time I already knew it. But the fieldnotes about my experiences with her became very valuable. They helped me to see, later on, how witchcraft works. I came to see that a witch can do harm simply because people believe that she can. People create the reality of spirits and magic simply by believing in them. They also believe that gossip can hurt them and so give it the power to do so. Gossip then takes on a life of its own, apart from being thoughts in people's minds and words on their tongues, and becomes what I have called gossip power. Gossip, when applied, becomes black magic. And conversely, black magic becomes applied gossip. I go to great pains to demonstrate that in my narration.

It was only through mulling over the material later that these generalizations sprang to mind. I also saw that the phenomenon of witchcraft is a prime example of how one's mental set shapes the world one sees. If somebody expects to see a spirit he will very likely do so. If he believes that his neighbour hates him and is practising black magic against him, he will then act in such a way that the neighbour will do just that. If he believes a fortuneteller's prediction that he will fall ill, he probably will. Thus subjective beliefs become objective reality.

This brings us back to the difficulties of objective truth, in this case of knowing what I now thought of simply as "others." I had wanted to keep myself out of the picture, to watch people interacting while I stood aside, just looking. But that simply did not work. If I stood aside I was ignored; nobody told me anything. It was like being erased. That nearly happened at first, when one of my informants pushed me aside and pursued her own ends at the beginning of my fieldwork. I accepted that for a while and watched from the sidelines, catching what attitudes and words I could as they flew by. But I was missing more than I was catching. Had I been part of their lives—able to help with their illnesses, or with getting jobs, I might have achieved a greater understanding. But as it was, their real lives eluded me because I was not sharing them. I could only achieve a deeper level of understanding through participating in the details and complexities of their everyday lives.

But how could I participate in their lives? The practical difficulties were too many: insufficient time; inadequate grasp of the language; not knowing enough about the people's pasts; not having been there when the important things had happened to them. All these played a part. But most important was the fact that I was an outsider. I was not one of them. I was richer and whiter and I could get out. They were there for life.

Even getting to know one person, as I tried to get to know my favourite informant, turned out to be difficult in a way I had not anticipated. She was watching me as closely as I was watching her. To be her friend required tact, respect, and reciprocity. She was very sensitive to anything I might do that could be construed as a slight. If she caught me in an insincerity she retaliated instantly with some egregious affectation of her own. Any suggestion of patronization maddened her and she would punish me by long absences. I don't think she ever resorted to witchcraft to take revenge upon me, as she did upon others, because she thought white people were not susceptible to black magic. But she could always get her own back by making me, foreigner that I was, a laughing-stock among her people.

She was suspicious of circumspection on my part—perhaps because she herself was so expert at it and knew what it concealed. She despised a doormat and ethnography was, to her, just another name for self-interest. She knew all about trade-offs and was determined to exact her quids-pro-quo.

She would walk all over anyone who let her. She tried it with me, and I called her bluff. It was only then, when I cared enough to show my spite and to pit my wits against hers, only then that I touched the quick of her life as she touched the quick of mine. I had to stand up to her, to talk back in order to win her respect. I could not beg it, or buy it—I had to earn it by becoming vulnerable myself, which involved, among other things, telling her my secrets as she had told me hers. It took my heart as well as my head, my intuition as well as my logic, my whole personality—that watchful, self-concealing ethnographer would never have uncovered her inner life.

There were also epistemological difficulties in knowing others. I had wanted an understanding distinct from self—but what could I know about others except what I could perceive through my own eyes and interpret through my own mental grid? The very cognitive process itself involved an "I" to observe and to know. How could I know anything that was "not me" when my very method of knowing was all me?

It was a paradox. Even though I came back to self when reaching out for the other, nevertheless something of the other did emerge in the process. That is, even though knowing may reside only in the knower, nevertheless some objective knowledge resides in my fictional *novella.*

– 3 –

Going Native?

William J. Klausner

William J. Klausner teaches law and anthropology, in both Thai and English, at Chulalongkorn University, Bangkok, and other Thai universities. Born in New York City, he graduated from Yale and has worked in Thailand since 1955. He has written extensively on law, culture, and popular Buddhism.

In a recent personal letter, the Editor of *Anthropology Today* referred obliquely to the ambivalence of my persona. He wondered aloud as to the pros and cons of becoming closely identified with the country of one's study and the possible loss of detachment in the process.

For the past forty years, I have been on a continuous pilgrimage seeking to fathom the intricate patterns of Thai culture. During this decades-long hegira, I didn't have to—and couldn't—forsake my Western heritage, but I could and did conveniently subject it to a traditional Thai massage. New intellectual and emotional pressure points were discovered. New dimensions to my nature emerged and hitherto familiar ways of thinking, acting and speaking were altered.

I remember being cautioned in Yale Graduate School not to forget that the anthropologist's very presence in the field can itself change the atmospherics and alter the very reality one seeks to capture. Actually, my experience, living for a year in a fairly remote northeastern Thai village, did not validate such an admonition. Very quickly, I found myself swept up into the rhythms of daily village life. Any impressions my footprints may have made on the village paths were quickly erased. If there was any meaningful alteration, it was in my own perceptions and perspectives. However, there was no wholesale change. In taking off my Ray-Ban glasses and trying on Thai shades, did I lose my detachment? I would hope not. Since I finished fieldwork almost four decades ago and began my teaching and foundation careers, I have been interpreting Thai culture and trying to bridge cultural chasms through lectures to and essays written for audiences of Western diplomats, businessmen and foreign aid workers and volunteers. Despite my close identification with and commitment to Thailand, I do not feel I have lost the detachment necessary for objective scholarship. Identification has led to empathy and sympathetic understanding; but, hopefully, intellectual distance has largely been preserved. The challenge has been to maintain my psychological equilibrium as a new identity, merging the newly acquired Eastern and the more familiar Western elements of my persona, has been shaped and formed.

Buddhism has had a profound influence in the development of my new identity. Despite my academic background, it was not its philosophical tenets that first drew me to the Buddhist faith. Rather, it was my introduction to village Buddhism in practice. Living within the confines of the temple for the first few months of my year's stay in the village, I soon found myself under the spell of the charismatic resident monks. They exuded an aura of serenity, equanimity and compassion as they fulfilled their daily religious and secular community service responsibilities. They, as well as their village parishioners, taught me to avoid confrontation and maintain a "cool heart." It was only in later years that I studied the Buddhist texts and found myself, as a humanist, attracted to what I felt was the quite compatible intellectual content of Buddhism.

On reflection, I believe the often stated contradiction between a close identification with a culture and the preservation of one's detachment is a false one. Of course, some may argue that subjectivity is not totally negative and that total objectivity is unattainable. I would agree that subjectivity can have a certain value at times, especially in instilling some passion into a foreign scholar's analysis and commentary. I would also accept that objectivity should be measured in terms of degree rather than in absolute terms. However, given the limitation of space, I hope I may be forgiven for treating the issues involved

"Going Native?" by William J. Klausner from *Anthropology Today*, June 1994, pp. 18–19. Reprinted by permission of Blackwell Publishers.

in this essay in more general and absolute terms. I am convinced that one can, for the most part, be both identified and detached. Those foreign scholars who deny completely their own heritage, their cultural roots, in their attempts to take on the coloration and hues of another culture, are fated to live in a fool's paradise. Such an expatriate does not—and I believe cannot—fully change his or her persona and become Thai, Japanese or Indonesian. Those that believe they have fully assumed the cultural identity of the country they have studied and identified with are, I would contend, deluding themselves. They have denied and lost one identity and yet not truly found a new one. They remain in limbo. For these cultural alchemists who have convinced themselves that such a total conversion has been achieved, objectivity and detachment are inevitably lost.

There are limitations to culture conversion, no matter how close one's identification, engagement, attachment and empathy. As in religious conversion, one often becomes more Papal than the Pope and loses one's perspective and objectivity. However, loss of detachment and objectivity does not mean one has actually assumed the essence, as well as the form, of a new cultural identity. One can study and grasp the intellectual meaning of a country's literature and history; of its language; its proverbs; its fairy tales; its religion and world view. However, unlike a child's enculturation process wherein literature, language, history, morality and appropriate behaviour are learned, largely uncritically, and impressed on a veritable cultural *tabula rasa*, the alien anthropologist, at a later stage in life, inevitably studies and learns through the lens of his or her own cultural and intellectual background; often rather heavy baggage.

For example, reading Thai literature and poetry of the past with its unmistakable hierarchical, patriarchal and male chauvinist bias can give one an appreciation of Thai social structure and gender bias. However, can such study for the scholar in his or her twenties, thirties, forties and beyond have the same emotional impact and intellectual meaning as for the native child whose received knowledge at a most impressionable age is constantly reinforced by his or her peers? One can record the prevalent practice of urban Thai schoolboys visiting prostitutes in one time-honoured *rite de passage* to manhood and note the double sexual standard involved. However, how can the adult foreign scholar ever internalize the emotional charge of participating in the above ritual passage encouraged, sustained and fortified by one's peers? The scholar can read of the extra-territorial courts in Thailand in the latter half of the 19th and early 20th centuries during the period of colonial influence, if not total control. One can intellectually appreciate the fixation of the Thai

judiciary on preserving its integrity and independence and the extreme sensitivity to any outside interference. However, can the foreign scholar ever truly expect to comprehend the emotional intensity of the older generation of Thai judges concerning the above without having experienced such judicial domination and intimation or been regaled about such interference on one's father's knee? How can the mature Western scholar, reading the skewed and biased historical accounts of relationships with the neighbouring countries of Laos, Burma and Cambodia, appreciate the building blocks of prejudice and stereotypes set and reinforced in primary and secondary Thai schools? Likewise, the rational and scientific mind and tools of the foreign scholar can be brought to bear in analysing the function of spirit worship in maintaining social harmony and communal solidarity and order in rural Thailand. However, can one ever expect to experience the fear and dread of and, at the same time, sense of reliance on spirits inculcated in the earliest years of childhood?

The above examples indicate the difficulty of truly "going native" in substance, rather than just form. In almost all cases, the end result is a shadow play, not reality. If in that process, one loses a sense of objectivity and detachment, the individual scholar must be faulted. One becomes, at that stage, a translator producing often beautifully crafted literal translations, but ones devoid of inner meaning. On the other hand, it is not impossible to achieve a sense of empathy and understanding after years of intimate and close identification with an alien culture and, in so doing, to interpret judiciously and objectively the essence of the culture with a close, if not absolute, approximation to emotional and intellectual certitude.

In the diminishing eyesight of this expatriate, I, thus, only see the positive side of close identification with an alien culture over a long period of time. Detachment and objectivity do not have to be sacrificed. If they are, then one loses the ability to interpret, to be a bridge between cultures. One retires, often in silence. One recalls the perhaps apocryphal anthropologist whose empathy and attachment to the Native American society he was studying were so compelling that he was accorded the rare honour of being initiated into the tribe's secret society. Alas, bound by oath, he never revealed its secrets and, thereafter, was forever reticent about writing about the tribe which had adopted him.

I believe governments, foundations and businesses have largely accepted the conventional wisdom of the contradiction between close identification and detachment. Thus, they continue to arbitrarily limit the duration of one's employment abroad in any one country to three, four or five years. Headquarters pride themselves on their success in avoiding their employees' close identification with the society in which they are working. Alas, a high price has been paid—unnecessarily so—for what is mistakenly assumed would be the commitment and concomitant loss of objectivity and detached judgment. What these institutions have actually lost is the insight and the unrivalled, informed analysis that can only come with many years of language study and the intimate identification with and engagement in the society and its culture.

Someday, perhaps, anthropologists, from whatever continent, about to venture into the field for the first time will be adequately advised by their university mentors to be prepared for their own ordeal by fire as their familiar ways of thinking and acting are tested. In the challenge and response of their first field experience, their intellectual and emotional horizons will expand. Whether one returns or remains, one may look forward to enhanced and enriched personas being forged. In these altered states, new identities emerge.

As for my own personal quest, my reflections on my sixtieth birthday are apposite: ". . . my fifth cycle is the continuation of a struggle to ensure the tensions of the Eastern and Western elements of my persona remain creative and that parallel paths ultimately merge into a single road of productive contemplation, which, supported by virtue, will lead to wisdom."

Culture Never Dies
Anthropology at Abu Ghraib

Gregory Starrett

Gregory Starrett is associate professor of anthropology at University of North Carolina Charlotte. He received his PhD from Stanford University. He specializes in anthropology of religion, history of anthropology, and anthropological theory, with a focus on the Middle East. He is author of Putting Islam to Work: Education, Politics, and the Transformation of Faith, *which examines how the development of mass education has transformed the Islamic tradition of contemporary Egypt.*

[For many of the Iraqi inmates at Abu Ghraib] living conditions now are better in prison than at home. At one point we were concerned that they wouldn't want to leave . . .

—General Janis Karpinski, Dec 2003

[T]he reorganization of the prisons has rendered them so comfortable that the [peasant] has no longer any fear of imprisonment, and makes no secret of saying that he is better treated in prison than at home, and the only privation he has to put up with is the temporary separation from his harem.

—Spencer Carr, British Consul in the Nile Delta, 1884

Official confidence that Western institutions of social control are more humane than Middle Eastern institutions of social support is an element of the long-standing use of the region as a mirror in which the West seeks its own inverted image.

PRISON/HOME

If prison and home are analogues, the home looks worse in comparison because of a gendered division of misery in which men suffer material want, while women and children suffer from patriarchy. Nineteenth century re-

formers lamented that "A great difficulty meets the legislator [in the Middle East] . . . namely, the complete exclusion of more than half the community from the action of the laws. . . . There is no power to penetrate into the harem, and whatever misdeeds are practiced there, neither police, nor laws, nor public opinion can reach. . . . No doubt fearful crimes and horrible abuses are perpetrated in those recesses which exclude all inspection, all interference, all control. The very organization of society thus stands in the way of justice" (John Bowring, 1840).

Family tradition is a prison, the world of policy is freedom. But since last spring the fearful crimes and horrible abuses from the recesses of Abu Ghraib reflect the analogy of prison and harem in a way none too flattering to policy. The homoerotic posing and piles of naked bodies are twisted contemporary versions of Victorian-era harem art. But the female slaves bathing the odalisque and the eunuchs guarding her virtue are now grinning American soldiers in blue latex gloves. The new odalisque is a feminized and humiliated male, the adult version of the boy in Gerome's familiar 1880 painting *The Snake Charmer*, facing the leers of soldiers participating in a complex system of war and expropriation. (See www.humboldt.edu/~rmj5/e465oart.html and www.orientalist-art.org.uk/harem.html for these images.)

POLITICS OF REPRESENTATION

In mid-May journalist Seymour Hersch identified anthropologist Raphael Patai's 1973 book *The Arab Mind* as one source of our government's understanding of the psychological vulnerabilities of Arabs, including the notion that Arab men are particularly subject to sexual shame. The book's posthumous 2002 edition bears a forward by retired Army Colonel Norvell B. DeAtkine, who assigns Patai to the officers he trains at the John F. Kennedy Special Warfare Center at Fort Bragg, NC. "It has been about 30 years," he writes, "since the majority of *The Arab Mind* was written . . . [but] it has not aged at all. The analysis is just as prescient and on-the-mark now as on the day it was written," particularly insofar as it illuminates "the social and cultural environment . . . and the modal personality traits that made [the 9/11 highjackers] susceptible to engaging in terrorist actions."

Denunciation of Patai's book by scholars and journalists was swift and fierce. It was also largely pointless, a writer's game of *cherchez le livre.* Manning Marable (Harvard) called on the Bush administration to publicly repudiate the book and stop using it as a source of information. Others belittled its methodology. Brian Whitaker of *The Guardian* scoffed at Patai's claim that there is homosexual behavior in Egypt. Ann Marlow of *Salon.com* dismissed his report of normative infant genital massage by mothers in some areas, which she interpreted as an accusation of maternal pathology. Evidence of both cultural commonality and difference were pegged as hateful smear rather than observations.

But many of the "Arab stereotypes" Patai outlines differ little from the characterizations Arab leaders and intellectuals articulate about their own cultures. What is at issue is the practical contexts in which they are deployed as strategies. Anthropology lies at a tense juncture of two public discursive fields, one entreating, "Are they exactly like us?" and the other demanding, "Or are they completely different?" Culture becomes the stuff of travel-guide advice on gift-giving or corporate seminars on managing multicultural workforces. And the stuff of the applied field of war. The military's interest in "cultural intelligence" began with heavy anthropological lobbying during WWII, extended through the Cold War and Vietnam, and currently enters the "global war on terror." Even before 9/11, the Marine Corps Warfighting Laboratory at Quantico, VA solicited input from anthropologists: "Cultural nuances that are of greatest significance in military operations—questions of loyalty, honor, and obligation, for example—are areas in which there is no substitute for very specific knowledge. . . . Due appreciation of . . . cultural intelligence will enable forces to 'operate smarter' and avoid the costly mistakes that can result from cultural ignorance."

Abu Ghraib reminds us of the costly mistakes made in trying to be too clever with cultural knowledge. Are Arabs ashamed by nudity? Maybe. But as Laurie King-Irani points out, anyone might be shamed when their rec-tum is being torn by a lightstick or they're being threatened by a snarling German shepherd. Could one seriously suggest that the ritual impurity of dogs is the key to understanding why naked Muslim prisoners are frightened by their snarling?

Scholars have distanced themselves from Patai's book by noting to journalists that "Its methodology . . . not to mention much of its content, was considerably behind the times even when it first appeared." This is either poor memory or face-saving in a field where the psychodynamics of sex and family are staples. In 1973 Robert Levy published the now-classic psychological ethnography *Tahitians,* and the *American Anthropologist* treated us to Evans-Pitchard's 40-year-old description of Zande copulation technique. Psychological anthropology was revitalizing itself in its new journal *Ethos,* whose second issue contained Robert Levine's survey of "Patterns of Personality in Africa." Levine argued that traditional black Africans tend to blame and fear others when under stress, and display a relative "concreteness of thought." Whatever its quality, Patai's approach did not stand out as abnormal. The few area specialists who reviewed *The Arab Mind*—from conservative historian Nadav Safran to radical sociologist Elaine Hagopian—dismissed it as a failure. The reviewer for *American Anthropologist,* on the other hand, called it outstanding, sympathetic and objective. Given the venue it's no comfort that the reviewer, Carroll Quigley, was not an anthropologist. (He was a wildly popular historian at Georgetown who inspired both Samuel Huntington and Bill Clinton.)

Significantly, Patai's early work showed little of the psychologizing of cultural difference so common among American anthropologists working for the U.S. government during the same period. In ethnographic work from the 1940s he showed how Palestinians' attitudes changed with the transformation of land tenure systems and political conditions. Economic self-interest rather than culture or mind drove interactions between Jews and Arabs. Tradition was a flexible inventory of symbols and practices to which ordinary people often had less attachment than their leaders, who manipulated them in response to internal and external conflicts. But Patai's approach changed as time went on, in ways that linked him first institutionally and then intellectually with the U.S. political, military and cultural establishments.

In 1956 the Human Relations Area Files, with Army funding, contracted him to prepare its country guides for Lebanon, Syria and Jordan. He was one of only two contract scholars without a university affiliation at the time. The other was Donald Wilber, an archaeologist charged with the volumes for Afghanistan and Pakistan. Two years previously Wilber had been the chief U.S. planner for the CIA-sponsored coup in Iran.

It is right to be troubled about how anthropological work can be harnessed in the service of violence and humiliation. But are hands on the genitalia worse than electrodes there? Far more interesting than anything Patai wrote is the issue of why military officers would use a book painting Arabs as fatalistic, unorganized and ineffectual to frame a devastating series of attacks that required years of careful planning and preparation. It should be clear to anthropologists that anything we say can and will be used in ways outside our control. To borrow the terms of Hermann Goering's famous quip, in contemporary conflicts any mention of culture may mask the sound of a revolver being drawn.

BASIC CONCEPTS

What Is the Meaning of Culture?

WHAT WOULD HAPPEN if a student went into a North American supermarket during rush hour and tried to haggle over the price of a 79-cent tube of toothpaste? Apart from causing considerable embarrassment and probable ejection from the store, the student would be illustrating the dangers of culturally inappropriate behavior. In many parts of the world, haggling is culturally appropriate.

As befits its centrality, the notion of **culture** is problematic and means many different things to different people, even to anthropologists—A. L. Kroeber and Clyde Kluckhohn's discussion of different anthropological definitions of culture, published in 1952, is a thick book! It is easier, however, to give examples of culture than to define it.

Culture, in brief, is what gives meaning to the world. It provides the lens through which people interpret and make sense of what they perceive the world to be. As such, it consists largely of knowledge and, like other resources, is not distributed equitably. By "making sense," it gives us a sense of patterning and thus of predictability, which allows us to anticipate events and actions. The importance of people being able to anticipate one another's social behavior is well illustrated in Luke Rinehart's novel *The Dice Man*. This book is about a psychotherapist who adopts a decision-making method of assigning odds and rolling dice. He literally "gets away with murder" because his decisions are all random and no "motive" can be assigned to his behavior.

Making sense of behavior becomes particularly problematic when one is in a foreign milieu, as are most anthropologists. Indeed, as Sir Raymond Firth recalled:

> Even with the pages of my diary before me it is difficult to reconstruct the impressions of that first day ashore—

to depersonalize the people I later came to know so well and view them as merely a part of the tawny surging crowd. . . . In his early experience in the field the anthropologist is constantly grappling with the intangible. The reality of native life is going on all around him, but he himself is not yet in focus to see it. He knows that what he at first records will be useless: it will be either definitely incorrect, or so inadequate that it must be later discarded. Yet he must make a beginning somewhere. He realizes that at this stage he is incapable of separating the patterns of custom from the accidentals of individual behavior, he wonders if each slight gesture does not hold some meaning which is hidden from him. . . . At the same time, he is experiencing the delights of discovery, he is gaining an inkling of what is in store; like a gourmet walking round a feast that is spread, he savors in anticipation the quality of what he will later appreciate in full.

> —Peacock and Kirsch 1980

Culture, in short, provides the patterns for behavior, whereas **society** is the product of patterns of behavior. Perhaps the safest way to define culture is to emphasize some of its most striking characteristics. Following Roger Keesing (1976), we can see it as a resource consisting of the sum total of learned, accumulated experience that is shared in varying degrees. As an abstraction it is a generalization—that is, no one has the exact same version. It is also a composite, insofar as no one knows all of it. Finally, it is dialectical—that is, it consists invariably of a number of **subcultures.**

Culture, then, is an interpretive dimension and knowledge; in making the world we experience more "predictable," it also creates categories. Implicit in such an exercise is the creation of boundaries of class, ethnicity, race, and gender. People create boundaries when they learn the appropriate **rituals** and habits of speech. For most people—except those with a probing anthropological perspective—these boundaries eventually become taken for granted and are unproblematic. Another way to think of this is the example of state borders, as Robert Thornton, an anthropologist from South Africa, explains:

> In crossing an "international boundary" we involve ourselves in a complex political ritual which includes elaborate signposts, people wearing austere uniforms with obscure insignia . . . gates and narrow corridors. There is always an element of risk, of interference with personal freedom, even death if the formalities of this particularly powerful political ritual are not acknowledged and complied with. The boundaries between countries in fact, exist only in the imagination. They are created through speech, text and gesture, and are enabled by the complex calculation of latitude and longitude which accurate clocks have made possible. We may see the power of culture in the political boundaries of states—a special kind of cultural category-making—for which most of us today are willing to risk all in modern warfare. (1988:27)

In a very real sense culture defines what we are, and the categories and activities all people take for granted are the object of important symbolic projections that vary from culture to culture. As the article by Lynn Morgan here explores, the very categories of "human" and "person" are culturally variable. The concept of **cultural relativism,** the proposition that one cannot understand another culture without suspending judgment to see how it works on its own terms, is a key component of cultural analysis. It is an antidote to ethnocentrism, or the assumption that one's own culture has the most appropriate ways of resolving common problems all humans face. As Sally Engle Merry argues in her essay in this chapter, human rights lawyers and journalists have mistakenly assumed that cultural relativism means that anthropologists uncritically accept the worth of any custom no matter how reprehensible—human sacrifices among the Aztecs, for example, or human rights abuses in other cultures. One can in fact take a critical stance toward any social practice or custom, but only *after* understanding it in its cultural and historical context. Even more important, Merry argues, it is naïve to indict a whole culture for the actions of certain individuals or groups, because all societies are internally heterogeneous.

Another key aspect of culture explored in this chapter is its dynamism. Cultures change and they are never static. People have always borrowed and shared things, ideas, and people from other societies, and the idea that so-called primitive peoples were isolated before European contact is a fantasy, although in some cases one that has been perpetuated by anthropology itself. The fact of cultural borrowing raises interesting questions about what happens when movements for cultural rights (such as indigenous rights movements) claim to "own" a culture and its material manifestations. Australian anthropologist Jane Mulcock did fieldwork on this politically charged issue, studying how white New Agers in Australia have adopted certain Aboriginal symbols. Mulcock suggests that this situation generated important dilemmas for her own fieldwork, forcing her to confront the fact that she did not agree with what New Agers were doing with Aboriginal cultural symbols, but her own disagreement was compromising her ability to understand how and why these groups borrowed cultural symbols. There are, as she says, no easy answers for these dilemmas.

FOCUS QUESTIONS

As you read these selections, consider these questions:

✦ What is culture, in an anthropological sense? How does it help people give meanings to their worlds?

✦ Have you ever been aware of profound cultural differences? What were the circumstances that led you to be aware of these differences? What did you learn about yourself in this situation? What did you learn about another culture?

✦ How does culture underlie our ideas about biological processes and human development?

✦ What are some reasons cultures change?

REFERENCES

Keesing, Roger. 1976. *Cultural Anthropology.* New York: Holt, Rinehart and Winston.

Kroeber, A. L., and C. Kluckhohn. 1952. *Culture: A Critical Review of Concepts and Definitions.* Cambridge, Mass.: Harvard University Press (Papers of the Peabody Museum of American Archaeology and Ethnology).

Peacock, James, and A. Thomas Kirsch. 1980. *The Human Direction: An Evolutionary Approach to Social and Cultural Anthropology.* 3rd ed. Englewood Cliffs, N.J.: Prentice-Hall.

Thornton, Robert. 1988. Culture: A contemporary definition. In *South African Keywords,* edited by Boonzaier Emiole and John Sharp. Cape Town: Philip.

– 5 –

When Does Life Begin?

A Cross-Cultural Perspective on the Personhood of Fetuses and Young Children

Lynn M. Morgan

Lynn M. Morgan has a PhD in medical anthropology, awarded jointly by the University of California, Berkeley, and the University of California, San Francisco. An associate professor at Mount Holyoke College, she has carried out fieldwork in Latin America; besides medical anthropology, her interests include development and political economy.

Participants in the U.S. abortion debate have argued about life and personhood from philosophical, religious, moral, biological, and political points of view, yet very few have examined the cultural dimensions of when life begins. Because they have overlooked the relevance of comparative cultural information, it has been difficult for participants in the debate to acknowledge the extent to which human life and personhood are culturally constructed. Perhaps a reflexive, cross-cultural perspective on personhood is an unaffordable luxury now, with the 1973 landmark *Roe v. Wade* Supreme Court decision legalizing abortion under fire from anti-abortion groups. Because the legality of abortion is seriously threatened, the subtleties and ambiguities about abortion are rarely acknowledged for fear of muddying the central policy issue.[1] In spite of the political stakes, however, I will argue that the discourse on personhood should be expanded to include perspectives from other cultures, thus encouraging Americans to confront and challenge the myriad culture-bound assumptions which permeate the U.S. debate over reproductive health policy.

The social recognition of fetuses, newborns, and young children is embedded within a wider social context. This observation is not new: a burgeoning literature illuminates the links between abortion, childrearing, women's status, social stratification, child welfare, ethnic and gender discrimination, and changing relations between the sexes. The process through which young human lives come to be valued is derived in part from these factors, but personhood is also a function of cultural divisions of the life cycle, attitudes toward death, the social organization of descent and inheritance, and social systems of authority and achievement. Anthropologists such as Mauss, Fortes, and La Fontaine[2] have documented a rich and remarkable range of variation showing the relationship among notions of self, body imagery, social organization, and ideational features such as consciousness and individuality. The cross-cultural evidence shows that the early thresholds of human life and personhood are just one issue in the larger question of whom society allows to become a person, under what circumstances, and why.

Every human being is potentially at risk of being aborted, miscarried, stillborn, or killed by natural cause or human agency before being accepted into a social community and labelled a person, yet there has been no recent systematic attempt to examine when other cultures come to value human life. . . .

Viewing the issue of personhood from a cross-cultural perspective helps to illustrate inconsistent and contradictory features of reproductive ethics debates in the United States. The ethnographic data show that the parameters of the U.S. abortion debate as presently constituted do not exhaust the realm of possibilities found among the earth's inhabitants. A close reading of the ethnographic evidence shows that killing neonates is often not regarded as murder, especially when the killing occurs before an infant is recognized as a human or person. Infanticide, then, with all the moral repugnance it evokes in the West, is a cultural construct rather than a universal moral edict. Apart from Tooley's influential "Abortion and Infanticide,"[3] few theorists have seriously considered the moral justifications for infanticide, yet the comparative cultural data indicate that this question deserves far more attention than it receives.

The cross-cultural evidence reveals two culturally constructed concepts used widely to divide the human life cycle continuum at its earliest stages: human-ness and personhood. In order to be granted status as a person, a fetus or neonate must first be recognized as a member of the human species. In some societies the decision to call a fetus "human" is not made until biological birth when the newborn's physical attributes can be assessed. Personhood, in contrast, is a socially recognized moral status. Neonates may not be labelled as persons until social birth rites are performed, often several days or months after biological birth. Social birth gives the neonate a moral status and binds it securely to a social community. Biological and social birth are not recognized as separate events in Western societies, even though they structure the onset of personhood in many non-Western societies. The U.S. abortion debate thus replicates Western divisions of the life cycle, overlooking the fact that even the human developmental cycle is socially patterned.

The attribution of personhood is a collective social decision, for the legal and ethical boundaries of personhood can only be negotiated within social settings. The limits of personhood are not decided by individuals, but by the entire society acting on shared cultural beliefs and values. For this reason, personhood—the value placed on human life—is not a concept which will be altered by religious mandate, nor by radical legislation by either the Right or the Left. Yet consensus is obviously eluding us, and seems destined to elude us as long as North Americans feel personal ambivalence and the compulsion to engage in increasingly polarized struggles over the issues surrounding abortion. Perhaps by reflecting on the social context of personhood and the value of fetuses and young children in other cultural contexts, we will be better able to understand how they are valued in our own.

"HUMAN" VERSUS "PERSON"

The furor over abortion in the United States has been waged in part through the manipulation of highly emotional symbols, resulting in a great deal of semantic confusion (a fetus may be called a "baby," an "unborn child," or "the product of conception").[4] I will make only one semantic distinction while examining the cross-cultural evidence: between the concepts of "human," and "person." . . .

Although "human" generally refers to a biological designation, the term is still subject to cultural influence and negotiation. In the United States, most people assume that the product of a human pregnancy will be human, yet the cross-cultural evidence shows greater variety. Among the Arunta of Central Australia, "[if] a child is born at a very premature stage, nothing will persuade the natives that it is an undeveloped human being, for it is nothing like a *Kuruna* [spirit] or a *retappa* [newborn]; 'they are perfectly convinced that it is the young of some other animal, such as a kangaroo, which has by mistake got inside the woman.'"[5] In Bang Chan, Thailand, women related episodes of "giving birth to 'gold,' 'jewels,' 'a monkey,' 'a fish's stomach,' and a mouse-like 'Golden Child.'"[6] In aboriginal Australia and Thailand, the products of conception are not assumed *a priori* to be human, for human status must be empirically verified.

In societies where humanity and personhood are defined separately, the determination of humanity always precedes the determination of personhood. On the island of Truk, for example, people waited until biological birth to see whether the newborn could be categorized as human. They did not take for granted the anthropomorphic character of the creature which would emerge from the womb. Abnormal or deformed infants were labelled as ghosts and burned or thrown into the sea: "Culturally this is not defined as infanticide and the suggestion of infanticide horrified the Trukese; a ghost is not a person and cannot be killed in any case."[7] This case, in which humanity itself was denied, is characteristic of the justification given for killing twins in some societies. Among the Tallensi in Africa, Fortes reports that twins were regarded suspiciously, because they may have been "malicious bush spirits" in human guise. After the first month of birth, a twin would be treated as any other child, but "only when it reaches the age of about four, and is placed under the spiritual guardianship of an ancestor spirit, is a twin definitely regarded as a complete social being."[8] A turn-of-the-century account of childhood in southern Africa noted that twins were regarded as more animal than human, and thus dangerously unpredictable: "No woman would care to marry a twin, for she would say that he was not a proper human being, and might turn wild like an animal, and kill her."[9] In these societies the neonate is not assumed to be born human, but is "anthropomorphized" after birth on the basis of physical characteristics which may or may not subsequently be endowed with moral significance. The criteria used to anthropomorphize newborns in different cultural contexts vary with caretakers' perceptions of the status of neonates.

DEFINING PERSONHOOD

Personhood is contingent on social recognition, and a person is recognized using established sociocultural conventions. Persons possess a special moral stature within their societies, yet in specific historical circumstances this status has been denied to certain groups, including women, children, slaves, prisoners of war, lepers, countless subordinate ethnic groups, and the insane. In all cultures, persons are living human entities whose killing is classed as murder; that is, the killing invokes some degree of moral condemnation and social retribution. The social construction of personhood varies according to the environmental, cosmological, and historical circumstances of different societies. What this means, in sum, is that "people are defined by people."[10] There can be no absolute definition of personhood isolated from a sociocultural context.

Burial customs may provide one source of data on cultural definitions of personhood, since only "persons" are buried. The data show a range of variation sufficient to highlight some of the contradictions in current U.S. policy. For example, on one extreme, a Chippewa Amerindian woman:

> knew her baby was two or three months along when she lost it . . . You could tell that it was just beginning to form. They cleaned it just like a child that is born and wrapped it. They gave a feast for it just like for a dead person and buried it in the same way. They believe that a child is human when it is conceived.[11]

Such behavior contrasts strikingly with burial practices in the United States, where fetuses weighing less than 500 grams are not buried, even in Roman Catholic hospitals where stated policy professes to respect human life from the time of conception.[12] On the other extreme, Ashanti children of Ghana who died before adolescence were reportedly thrown on the village midden heap,[13] indicating that burial rites and the full status of personhood were adult perquisites. In the United States, "fetuses ex utero over 500 grams are considered premature newborns, and therefore birth certificates must be issued for them and they must be buried,"[14] yet U.S. burial customs for children depend on more than the weight or size of the body. In New York City, a study revealed that many indigent children under one year of age were buried in unmarked graves in Potter's Field, where parents were not permitted to visit the gravesites.[15] Apparently child burial customs and the parents' right to graveside grieving are at least in part a function of social class in the United States, suggesting that the lives of poor children are valued less than those from wealthier families.

SOCIAL BIRTH

In Western industrialized societies, people generally believe that biological birth marks the entrance of a new being into the social community. The tenacity of this belief results from the cultural conviction that biological events have social significance. Unconsciously but relentlessly, Westerners have imbued that biological act of birth with profound importance, to the extent that legal and civil institutions confer personhood instantly when an infant is born alive. The social status of personhood is thus granted concurrently with a biological act: emerging from the womb. In several non-Western societies, however, members observe a period of transitional, liminal time between biological birth—when the infant can be seen, inspected, and evaluated—and social birth, when the infant is formally accepted into its social community. This is a stage of the life cycle which acknowledges and reinforces the cultural and cognitive divisions between the marginal, uncertain status of the fetus and the secure, protected status of a person. As a clearly bounded life cycle division, this period between biological and social birth so characteristic of many non-Western societies is unknown in 20th-century Western societies.

Until abortion became such a contentious issue, most people in the United States rarely stopped to question whether the social status of an infant could be separated from its biological status. It would be thought inappropriate to refer to the unborn fetus as a person complete with social identity (in part because the sex of the individual is essential to the construction of an individual's social identity). At birth the healthy child was automatically endowed with a social identity: as soon as the umbilical cord was cut, the neonate became a person. Biological birth was the major moral dividing line along the life cycle continuum: every individual who had passed the line was granted the rights and social status of persons,[16] while every individual shy of the line was not. Biological and social birth were inextricably intertwined in legal and medical institutions as well as in popular consciousness. This has changed only recently. In 1973, for example, *Roe v. Wade* established "viability" as the moral dividing line between fetuses which could be legally aborted and those which merited the protection of the State. Amniocentesis and other advances in medical technology have also altered the idea that persons could be distinguished from non-persons only at birth.

Many non-industrial societies, on the other hand, do not endow biological facts with the same degree of social importance. They separate the purely physiological act of birth from the social acceptance of the newborn. Social birth is marked by a ritual held sometime after biological birth, during which the newborn is granted a place in the social world. Social birth rituals often introduce the newborn formally for the first time to significant members of the community such as parents, siblings, godparents, other relatives, and community elders. The infant may also be presented to non-human entities considered important by the community, for example, sacred animals, natural entities, or supernatural beings. Social birth may be the occasion for some symbolically important event such as naming, hair cutting, depilation,[17] ear piercing,[18] removing incisor teeth,[19] or circumcision. Social birth may take place anywhere from a few days to several years after biological birth. It can be a one-time occurrence, or it may be a gradual process involving a number of socially significant events: crying, suckling, or weaning for the first time, or learning—as a small child—to perform certain chores.[20] Long, gradual transitions to personhood, sometimes lasting an entire lifetime, are common in non-Western societies,[21] yet a crucial induction into personhood often occurs early in life, with social birth. In a society where social birth rites are essential to personhood, an infant who dies before social birth has died before it was born.

DIVIDING THE LIFE CYCLE

Models of an individual life cycle, from the moment of conception to death and afterlife, are constructed differently from one society to the next. Societies divide the developmental cycle into segments, and mark transitions from one stage to the next by birthdays, marriage, parenthood, and religious rites of passage. Life cycle divisions are one way in which societies categorize their members. Life stages allow status to be monitored and evaluated by other members of society who look for age- and status-related cues to determine their attitudes and behavior toward those around them. Stages of life which North Americans take for granted, such as childhood, adolescence, and middle age, are in fact cultural constructions which have evolved in response to demographic, economic, and social factors. Anthropologists have been acutely aware of the social nature of the life cycle since Margaret Mead wrote about the nature of adolescence in Samoa. In the 20th-century United States, she said, adolescence had become known "as the period in which idealism flowered and rebellion against authority was

strong, a period during which difficulties and conflicts were absolutely inevitable."[22] In Samoa, however, teenagers did not pass through an analogous period of turmoil. Mead used the ethnographic evidence to show that adolescence was a phase of life unique to Western culture, specifically to the United States.

Childhood is another stage of life with a discernible social history, as Aries demonstrates for Western Europe. By analyzing European literature and iconography, Aries shows that children were not accorded the unique status they now occupy in the West until well after the advent of institutionalized schooling in the 16th and 17th centuries. Around that time, moralists began to argue that children needed to be trained, reformed, and subjected to "a kind of quarantine" before they would be fit company for adults.[23] The concept of infancy did not arise in western Europe until much later. British vital statistics did not distinguish among miscarried, stillborn, or infant deaths until late in the 19th century.[24] Until the mid-19th century, the French had no word for "baby."[25] During the first few months of life, when an infant could not interact with or respond to adult stimuli, it "simply 'did not count.'"[26] As the concept of childhood evolved in modern Europe, so did parents' ideals of the number and quality of children they desired, and society's expectations of the appropriate behaviors characterizing ideal adults and children.

Middle age, in addition to adolescence and childhood, is also a socially constructed life stage category. Brandes has shown that the American mid-life crisis (often associated with the fortieth birthday) is not a biological or developmental phenomenon, but cultural.[27] The turmoil and anxiety one feels on approaching the fortieth year is a reflection of our society's success in continuing the process of socialization through the adult years. Adults as well as children internalize society's popular wisdom and myths, one of which is that mid-life crisis is inevitable, natural, and almost genetically programmed. This relentlessly repeated message is deeply encoded in many realms of social life, including Western number symbolism. As a result, the American mid-life crisis has become a self-fulfilling prophecy: "the expectation of change at certain key times along the life course—especially if such expectation is elevated to the position of a shared, transmitted cultural norm—is likely actually to produce a change that might not otherwise occur."[28]

If the ethnographic evidence shows that the human developmental cycle is divided differently according to cultural and historical contingencies, then non-Western cultures can be expected to have divisions of the life cycle unfamiliar to Westerners. One well-known example is the clearly marked transition from childhood to adulthood celebrated by adolescent initiation rites in parts of Africa and Melanesia. Another such stage occurs early in life, during the period between biological birth and social birth.

PERSONHOOD, A CROSS-CULTURAL VIEW

When viewed in cross-cultural perspective, the criteria for personhood are widely divergent: in one society personhood may be an ascribed status, conferred automatically when an infant is born alive or given a name; in another society the status may be achieved only through a very long, gradual process of socialization. In Java "the people quite flatly say, 'To be human [i.e., "a person" in my terms] is to be Javanese.' Small children, boors, simpletons, the insane, the flagrantly immoral, are said to be *ndurung kjawa,* 'not yet Javanese'" and hence, not yet persons.[29] Evans-Pritchard reported that among the Nuer of the Nilotic Sudan, the death of a small child was not considered the death of a person:

> People do not mourn for a small child, for "a small child is not a person (*ran*). When he tethers the cattle and herds the goats he is a person. When he cleans the byres and spreads the dung out to dry and collects it and carries it to the fire he is a person." A man will not say he has a son till the child is about six years of age.[30]

A 1950s ethnographic account of Korea reported that the death of a newborn would receive "scarcely more deference than any other animal. If it lives only through a long course of learning and ceremonies will it obtain the position of a recognized personality."[31] Personhood is not a "natural" category or a universal right of human beings, but a culturally and historically constructed assemblage of behaviors, knowledge, and practices. For societies which observe social birth rites, biological birth and the recognition of humanity are only early indications of what an individual may become. Biological birth acknowledges potential, but carries no guarantee of eventual acceptance into the social community. . . .

LIMINALITY, DANGER, AND THE FATE OF THE NEONATE

In many societies, the period between biological and social birth is treated socially and symbolically as an extension of being in the womb. The newborn is kept in seclusion, sheltered indoors away from the view of all save its mother (and perhaps a midwife or other female caretaker). Danger is minimized by recreating and maintaining a womb-like environment in which the infant re-

sides until social birth. In the rural Philippines, for example, the newborn must be kept in strict seclusion for two weeks after biological birth, behind closed windows and above a well-sealed floor.[32] An ethnographer reporting on the Yavapai Amerindians of central Arizona wrote that mother and newborn stayed isolated and immobile for six days after parturition, resting on a bed of warm coals and earth and covered with grass.[33]

In society's terms none of these children have yet been born. They have emerged from their mother's uterus to a womb-like waiting room for pre-persons; their liminal status is perhaps analogous to a transitory phase at the other end of the life cycle known to Christians as purgatory.

Seclusion of infants is sometimes justified by citing the many perceived threats to their existence. Peoples of the Ghanaian Northern Territories told ethnographers that the infant may be reclaimed by spirits during the first seven days after biological birth:

> [A] newborn baby may in fact be a spirit-child, and not a human child at all. If it is a spirit, it will return to the world of spirits before a week is out, so for the first seven days after the birth the mother and child are confined to the room in which the birth took place, or at any rate to the house. If the child dies during that time, it is assumed that it was in fact a spirit-child. The body is mutilated and buried in a pot, to prevent its return in similar circumstances. The parents are not allowed to mourn its loss, but should show signs of joy at being rid of such an unwelcome guest.[34]

If the infant survives its first seven days outside the biological womb, it will be allowed to emerge from the symbolic social womb as well. At that point, "it is considered that the child is human, and it is 'out-doored,' or brought into the open for the first time."[35] Supernatural threats to the newborn also justify an eight-day hiatus between biological and social birth among the Ashanti of western Africa. Ashanti beliefs about conception and early infancy are known to anthropologists because of the *ntoro* concept, a spiritual bond passed from father to child in a society structured around matrilineal descent. At biological birth the Ashanti question whether the newborn is meant to stay in the human world or whether it is a wandering ghost who will soon return to the spirit world. For eight days the mother and child remain indoors, with no special efforts made to bind the child to the human world: "It is given any kind of old mat or old rag to lie upon; it is not addressed in any endearing terms; water or pap, if given to it, is administered out of an old banana skin or ground-nut husk. It is true it is permitted to feed at the mother's breast, but it is hardly encouraged."[36] If the child is still alive after eight days, a *Nteatea* rite is performed, "when the child is named for its senior *ntoro* relative, and it is then for the first time regarded as a member of the human family."[37]

Similar "out-dooring" ceremonies have been recorded in other parts of the world. In the Nilgiri hills in south India, the Toda keep the newborn indoors for three months after biological birth. The sun is not allowed to touch the child's face. One morning after three months have passed, a "face opening" ceremony is held at dawn. The infant is brought outdoors with its face covered, and unveiled when the first bird sings. During this social birth rite the infant is introduced to the temple, to nature, to buffaloes, and to its clansmen. The infant is not considered a person until the ceremony has been performed.[38] Greeting the sun was also a feature of social birth among the Hopi Amerindians a century ago. On the twentieth day after birth, a ceremony was held to purify the new mother, name the baby, and present the child to the sun. Great care was taken by the father to announce the precise moment the sun rose above the horizon. At that instant, the "godmother throws the blanket from the face of the baby" and presents a cornmeal offering to the sun.[39] All those present, including the newborn, then ate a ritual breakfast marking the entrance of a new person into the community.[40]

The above are quintessential examples of social birth rites: the newborn is kept indoors and out of sight for a specified period of time while the larger society remains symbolically unaware of its presence. This is a period of trial. The infant must "prove" it is worthy of personhood; first by managing to survive, then by exhibiting the vigor, health, and affect of one destined to become a functioning member of the community. If it survives and thrives, it is ready to pass through the social birth canal, to be ceremoniously welcomed as a person into the community. Completion of social birth rites ties the individual to the kin group and to the mortal world, granting it a moral status designed to protect it from harm by placing it under the protection of the group. If any of these criteria are not satisfied, the infant is classed as a non-person (and may in fact be labelled as non-human and hence not eligible for personhood, as with witches, ghosts and spirit-children). If it does not die of its own accord, it may be neglected until it does die, or it may be killed.

Infanticide is murder by definition, but most societies punish only the killing of human persons. It is problematic, then, to apply the label of infanticide to killing neonates before they are recognized as human or granted personhood. We might rather think of this as post-partum abortion, an image more applicable to the American experience. Induced abortion in the United States is rationalized (in part) by regarding the fetus as a pre-person,

not yet accorded the same sanctity of life applied to "babies." Societies without safe and effective means of inducing abortion at early gestational stages may delay valuing the infant until well after biological birth. During this interim between biological and social birth the unwanted fetus (and it *is* still regarded as a fetus by that society) can be killed while its caretakers remain immune from punishment. Infanticide is condemned in most societies, but only after the newborn has been accorded human status or recognized as a person:

> [I]nfanticide is most readily condoned if it occurs before the infant is named and has been accepted as a bona fide member of its society. It seems that the primary and fundamental restriction in most societies is the taboo on murder, i.e., killing a member of the ingroup. The less eligible a child is for membership in the group, the less seriously the act of killing the child is viewed.[41]

Thus the Bariba of Benin believe that some babies will be born witches, who may endanger their mothers' health and bring misfortune to the entire community. Witch babies can be identified at biological birth and should ideally be killed at that time to prevent future havoc.[42] In many societies the decision to expose or kill a neonate is made immediately at biological birth or within a few hours afterward. Among the Mohave Amerindians, if a newborn "was permitted to live long enough to be put to the breast, it was no longer subject to being killed."[43]

Post-partum abortion becomes infanticide if it is practiced after social birth rites are performed: "Thus in Athens the child could be exposed before the Amphidromia, a family ceremony at which the child was carried by its nurse around the hearth and thus received the religious consecration and its name."[44] In England during the 17th and 18th centuries, infanticide was practiced even though newborns were socially recognized as persons.[45] In those cases, however, personhood was granted incrementally, and infants were considered to be less significant persons than older children and adults. Under civil and religious law, killing a baby was a sin and a crime, but as practiced by the populace infanticide was less heinous than murdering an adult.

Becoming a person sometimes involves a long period of nurturing and socialization by the mother. This makes the infant's right to personhood in some societies contingent on the mother's survival and well-being. For example, an ethnographer reported that among the Toba Amerindians of the Bolivian Gran Chaco, if a woman died in childbirth the newborn would be buried alive with her body. If both lived, personhood was granted only when the infant gained physical autonomy from the mother after weaning. Before that time, neither abortion nor infanticide was considered immoral: "A new-born child is no personality and has not an independent existence; its parents, and particularly the mother, have full right to decide over its life."[46] Yanomamo infants, also living in lowland South America, were considered appendages of their mothers until weaned at the end of their third year. When nursing ended, "the child, which hitherto belonged to the flesh and blood of the mother, has become an independent human being."[47] The personhood of the newborn in these two societies was predicated, at least in part, on attaining physical independence from the mother.

Ethnographic accounts cite a wide range of socially significant events which mark the end of liminality and the beginning of personhood. Weaning is one example, but naming is by far the most common. A nameless infant, in many cases, is not considered a person. The social function of naming is discussed in Ford's cross-cultural study of reproductive behavior:

> Naming probably has derived its extremely widespread acceptance from the manifest advantages which result from the practice. A name facilitates social intercourse. . . . Naming a child helps to pull him into the framework of his society as an accepted member of the group. By virtue of being named the infant becomes a person like everyone else in the society; he is no longer a nameless outsider.[48]

Killing a child prior to naming was acceptable among certain societies, while killing a child after it was named would be tantamount to murder.[49] This was apparently the case among the Atayal aborigines of Formosa, where an early ethnographer reported "there is no punishment for the killing of an as yet nameless—i.e., less than two-or-three-year-old—child."[50] Among Arctic coast peoples, an ethnographer noted that infants were named after the deceased, thereupon reincarnating their ghosts: "naming may have restrained infanticide . . . because killing a named child could offend the reincarnated ghost."[51] Countless similar cases are found in the literature, where the name is a symbol of having become a person, and where a child who died prior to receiving a name was not regarded as a person.[52] Cherokee Amerindian babies were generally named a few days after birth. If the birth were prolonged or difficult, however, the child would be named during birth "so as to have something 'material' by which to exercise an influence upon it."[53] In the contemporary United States, where biological and social birth occur simultaneously, most newborns have names already chosen for them, which allows them to move directly from the womb into a permanent social identity.

Not everywhere, however, is a name the dominant symbol of the value placed on a newborn's life. Naming is delayed in many societies, but this behavior can have completely different meanings according to the social and environmental context. In northeast Brazil, where infant mortality is high, delayed naming is one of the emotional defenses which poor mothers use to shield themselves from the devastating psychological impact of frequent infant death. These Brazilian women view their children "as human, but [as] significantly less human than the grown child or adult."[54] Extreme poverty, widespread hunger, and high infant mortality rates affect the mother's emotional investment in her children: emotional deprivation is, in this context, a product of material scarcity.[55] Conversely in the Himalayas, where infant mortality is also high, children are not called their names precisely because their vulnerable young lives are highly valued. There Hindu children are named by a Brahmin priest on the tenth day after birth, but no one calls a child by this name for fear of making the child susceptible to the perils of "evil eye." Although not calling a child by its name may correspond with a denial of personhood in some societies, among the Hindus it is a "strong expression of the value and vulnerability placed on early lives, already begun but somehow requiring more protection."[56]

DISCUSSION

The ethnographic literature offers no universal consensus about who or what constitutes a person, for personhood is evaluated and bestowed on the basis of moral criteria which vary tremendously among and within different sociocultural contexts. The value placed on the lives of fetuses, neonates, and young children is determined according to a complex constellation of cultural factors, and cannot be determined simply by asking, "When does life begin?" Without a more general understanding of what it means to be a person in a given society, the beginnings of personhood can never be fully understood. An awareness of beginnings affords us only rudimentary insights into the social construction of personhood, which depends on the social relevance of gender, age, and material conditions and is in many contexts a gradual process. An example from West Africa will illustrate the point.

The Ashanti were mentioned earlier in connection with social birth rites which occur eight days after birth, but apparently these rites did not complete the transition to personhood. According to Rattray personhood was sometimes not solidified until adolescence: "In times not so very remote, persons dying before they reached adolescence were in no case accorded the ordinary funeral rites, and were often merely buried on the village midden heap. They were classed with the 'ghost children' who had not even survived eight days."[57] Not until passing through adolescent initiation rites did an Ashanti youngster become a complete person. As reflected in burial rites, children were not as highly valued as adults. This can be understood by examining the context and significance of personhood within Ashanti society. Among the Ashanti, differentiation between the sexes was an essential feature of adulthood, but sexual differentiation was insignificant until a child reached puberty and acquired the capacity to reproduce. Because reproduction was crucial to the perpetuation of the socio-political order, adolescent initiation rites symbolized the growth not only of the individual physical body but of the collective social body as well. Adolescents embodied society's hopes for its future. This point is made in Comaroff's discussion of healing among the Tshidi; there adolescent initiation rites "linked the natural maturation of the physical body to the reproduction of the socio-political system."[58] The importance of continuing the social formation is underscored by rites which grant personhood to adolescents: in La Fontaine's terms, "The concept [of person] serves to fuse the finite span of a human life with the unlimited continuity of social forms, by identifying personhood with self reproduction."[59] For the Ashanti child, to be a person meant to enjoy bodily autonomy with few corresponding social obligations, but to be an adult person meant that one's social responsibilities were multiplied, intensified, and enmeshed more tightly within the body politic.

So far we have been concerned with the valuation of fetuses and children cross-culturally, yet societal norms affect the personhood of the mother as well as the fetus, newborn, and young child. The mother's status as a person depends in most societies on her reproductive condition, the reproductive choices she makes, and her society's attitudes toward childbearing and child rearing. Feminist scholars writing in the United States argue that the abortion debate has focused too exclusively on fetal rights, virtually ignoring the role of women in society.[60] Recent attempts to reverse this trend include books by Luker, who demonstrates that U.S. women's opinions about abortion are conditioned by their life circumstances and perceived career options,[61] and Petchesky, who argues that the reproductive choices available to women must be understood within the broad socio-economic and political framework affecting the role of women.[62] Certainly these insights are applicable cross-culturally as well. Throughout the world women are primarily responsible for decisions affecting the lives and well-being of fetuses, neonates, and young children, and the choices women make in this regard are contingent on their own assessments of available options. The options change with the social tides, alternately restricting and expanding women's responsibilities for their born and unborn offspring. Such changes can be seen in a California lawsuit where a woman was charged with the wrongful death of her newborn child because she took illicit drugs and had sexual relations late in pregnancy, disregarding her doctor's orders. If this trend continues, American women will be increasingly held responsible for prenatal child abuse and neglect, even though fetuses have not been granted the rights of persons under the U.S. Constitution.

The ethnographic and historical literature is filled with accounts illustrating that a woman's status—even her claim to personhood and life itself—is contingent on her reproductive choices. In 15th-century England, for example, mothers known to have destroyed their newborn children were punished by death while wet nurses guilty of the same crime were not punished.[63] Piers argues that the reason for differential treatment was class bias, since wealthy women could afford to hire wet nurses for their children while poor women could not. Wet nurses were not executed for infanticide because breast milk was a rare and valuable commodity and wet nurses were scarce: "society simply could not have afforded to kill her."[64] Indigent natural mothers, in contrast, were relatively expendable, and these were the women most often found guilty of murdering their babies. The 15th-century criminal sentence for murdering an infant depended not on the value of the infant's life, but on the social class of the accused. The hierarchy of values ranked the lives of wet nurses above the lives of "natural" mothers, obscuring the fact that wet nurses were themselves natural mothers. While Christian moralists railed against child murder, society's response reflected how certain classes of women were so devalued and oppressed that their execution was condoned. Their crime was in reality the inability to afford a wet nurse.

A woman's status within society can be heightened, undermined, or made ambiguous by pregnancy. Generally if the pregnancy results in a healthy newborn (in some patrilineal societies only a healthy newborn boy is satisfactory) her status will be enhanced, but, if the pregnancy outcome is viewed as negative, she may suffer irreparable damage or even death. Devereux cites at least two societies where women could reportedly be killed with impunity for inducing an abortion.[65] The mother's status in such cases was rendered ambiguous by the liminal status of the fetus. Whereas before the pregnancy her murder would have been a punishable crime, in pregnancy her life was valued less than that of the fetus she carried.

Most often the woman making reproductive decisions is held directly responsible for her own actions, as interpreted through societal mores and prejudices. In some cases, though, the lives of several people may be affected by a woman's decision. The Azande of central Africa have a polygamous, patrilocal social structure which allowed a woman's reproductive decisions to have far-reaching repercussions:

> If the husband learns that his wife has used an abortifacient plant, he considers this tantamount to the assassination of his child. He therefore asks his father-in-law for a second wife, or else, in vengeance, he kills the wife of his father-in-law or one of his father-in-law's children.[66]

In this case, the woman's relatives paid the consequences of her actions, demonstrating the links between fetal status, female status, and the status of other members of society. A similar issue can be seen in the U.S. abortion debates: should the decision to induce abortion be made in private between a woman and her physician, or should the permission of the father also be required? To what extent is the personhood of the woman contingent on her relationship to others in her sphere of social relations? Anthropologists have shown that in some societies one's social identity and personhood [are] completely, inextricably embedded in the social structure, to the point where individuals cannot envision having relationships not dictated by social structural roles and statuses.[67] The very essence of personhood is negotiated, manipulated, bestowed, and denied in accordance with the tacit or considered approval of society's members.

In the United States, the abortion debate has been foreshortened by a culture-bound discourse on personhood. The discussion of fetal personhood and abortion legislation has been limited almost exclusively to the period between conception and biological birth, largely as a result of a shared, cultural belief that biological birth is the event which distinguishes persons from non-persons. Consequently, the only space left to negotiate the boundaries of personhood is prior to biological birth. We have framed the debate over abortion in such a way that we argue whether it would be defensible to push the dividing line earlier, toward conception, but not later, toward early childhood. In the process of limiting debate to this realm, we have largely ignored the expansive, multiple meanings of personhood in American society, including the implications for adult women and men of the social context which determines our life decisions.

How can the range of cultural variability discussed here affect the U.S. abortion policy debates? In spite of the relativist stance presented here, I will not argue that Americans should weigh the merits of post-partum abortion—that would be ignoring a fundamental U.S. cultural reality which gave us the term "infanticide." Nonetheless Americans have felt forced to construct convoluted philosophical justifications for their positions on these issues, even when contorted logic theoretically could be avoided by admitting the existence and relevance of cultural variation. Debates over fetal personhood would be more honest, although undoubtedly more agonizing, if it were easier to admit that the moral dividing of life between persons and non-persons at biological birth or "viability" is a cultural construction. The question is whether we can tolerate knowing that our beliefs and values are remarkably malleable, arbitrary products of our cultural milieu.

NOTES

1. Daniel Callahan, "How Technology Is Reframing the Abortion Debate," *Hastings Center Report* (February 1986): 33–42, esp. 41.

2. Marcel Mauss, "A Category of the Human Mind: The Notion of Person, The Notion of Self," in *The Category of the Person,* ed. M. Carrithers, S. Collins, and S. Luke (Cambridge: Cambridge University Press, 1985), 1–25; Meyer Fortes, "On the Concept of the Person Among the Tallensi," in *La Notion de la Personne en Afrique Noire,* ed. G. Dieterlen (Paris: Editions du Centre National de la Recherche Scientifique, 1973); J. S. La Fontaine, "Person and Individual: Some Anthropological Reflections," in *The Category of the Person,* ed. M. Carrithers, S. Collins, and S. Luke (Cambridge: Cambridge University Press, 1985), 123–140.

3. Michael Tooley, "Abortion and Infanticide," *Philosophy and Public Affairs 2* (1972): 37–65.

4. Leonard Kovit, "Babies as Social Products: The Social Determinants of Classification," *Social Science & Medicine 12* (1978): 347–351.

5. Ashley Montagu, *Coming Into Being Among the Australian Aborigines* (London: Routledge & Kegan Paul, 1974), p. 31.

6. Jane Richardson Hanks, *Maternity and Its Rituals in Bang Chan* (Ithaca: Cornell Thailand Project, 1963), esp. 34–35.

7. Thomas Gladwin and Seymour B. Sarason, *Truk: A Man in Paradise* (New York: Wenner-Gren Foundation, 1953), p. 133; quoted in George Devereux, *A Study of Abortion in Primitive Societies* (New York: International University Press, 1955), p. 344.

8. Meyer Fortes, *The Web of Kinship Among the Tallensi: The Second Part of an Analysis of the Social Structure of a Trans-Volta Tribe* (London: Oxford University Press, 1949), p. 271.

9. Dudley Kidd, *Savage Childhood: A Study of Kaffir Children* (London: Adam and Charles Black, 1906), p. 45.

10. Andie L. Knutson, "The Definition and Value of a New Human Life," *Social Science & Medicine 1* (1967): 7–29.

11. Devereux 1955, pp. 207–208.

12. Caroline Whitbeck, "The Moral Implications of Regarding Women as People: New Perspectives on Pregnancy and Personhood," in *Abortion and the Status of the Fetus,* ed. William B. Bondeson et al. (Dordrecht, Holland: D. Reidel Publishing Company, 1983), 247–272, esp. 258.

13. Robert S. Rattray, *Religion and Art Among the Ashanti* (Oxford: Clarendon Press, 1927).

14. Whitbeck, p. 258.

15. Peter Kerr, "Groups Fault City Policy on Burial of Poor Infants," *New York Times* (May 25, 1986), p. 30.

16. H. Tristram Engelhardt, Jr., "Viability and the Use of the Fetus," in *Abortion and the Status of the Fetus*, ed. William B. Bondeson et al. (Dordrecht, Holland: D. Reidel Publishing Company, 1983), 183–208, esp. 191.

17. Among the Siriono of eastern Bolivia, see Allan R. Holmberg, *Nomads of the Long Bow* (New York: Natural History Press, 1969).

18. Among the Argentine Araucanians, see M. Inez Hilger, *Araucanian Child Life and Its Cultural Background* (Washington: Smithsonian Miscellaneous Collections, Volume 133, 1957).

19. Performed among the Nuer when a child reached seven or eight years of age; see E. E. Evans-Pritchard, *Nuer Religion* (Oxford: Clarendon Press, 1956).

20. See Mead and Newton, p. 154, for examples.

21. La Fontaine, p. 132.

22. Margaret Mead, *Coming of Age in Samoa* (New York: American Museum of Natural History, 1928).

23. Philippe Aries, *Centuries of Childhood* (New York: Vintage Books, 1962), p. 412.

24. David Armstrong, "The Invention of Infant Mortality," *Sociology of Health and Illness* 8 (1986): 211–232, p. 214.

25. Aries, p. 29.

26. Aries, p. 128.

27. Stanley H. Brandes, *Forty: The Age and the Symbol* (Knoxville: University of Tennessee Press, 1985).

28. Brandes, p. 126.

29. Clifford Geertz, *The Interpretation of Cultures* (New York: Basic, 1973), p. 52.

30. Evans-Pritchard, p. 146.

31. Cornelius Osgood, *The Koreans and Their Culture* (New York: Ronald Press, 1951).

32. J. Landa Jocando, *Growing Up in a Philippine Barrio* (New York: Holt, Rinehart and Winston, 1969).

33. E. W. Gifford, "Northeastern and Western Yavapai," *University of California Publications in American Archaeology and Ethnology* 34 (1937): 247–354, esp. 300.

34. Barrington Kaye, *Bringing Up Children in Ghana* (London: George Allen & Unwin Ltd., 1962), pp. 56–57.

35. Kaye, p. 57.

36. Rattray, p. 59.

37. Edith Clarke, "The Sociological Significance of Ancestor Worship in Ashanti," *Africa* 3 (1930): 431–470, esp. 431.

38. David G. Mandelbaum, Department of Anthropology, University of California, Berkeley, personal communication.

39. J. G. Owens, "Natal Ceremonies of the Hopi Indians," *Journal of American Ethnology and Archaeology* 2 (1892): 163–175, esp. 170–173.

40. See Tilly E. Stevenson, "The Religious Life of a Zuni Child," *Fifth Annual Report of the Bureau of Ethnology* (1883–84): 539–555, esp. 546, for an account of a similar social birth rite which took place among the Zuni of western New Mexico.

41. Clelland S. Ford, "Control of Contraception in Cross-Cultural Perspective," *Annals of the New York Academy of Sciences* 54 (1952): 763–768; cited in Mildred Dickeman, "Demographic Consequences of Infanticide in Man," *Annual Review of Ecology and Systematics* 6 (1975): 107–137, esp. 115.

42. Carolyn Fishel Sargent, *The Cultural Context of Therapeutic Choice* (Dordrecht, Holland: D. Reidel Publishing Company, 1982), esp. 89–91.

43. George Devereux, "Mohave Indian Infanticide," *The Psychoanalytic Review* 35 (2, 1948): 126–139, esp. 127.

44. Glanville Williams, *The Sanctity of Life and Criminal Law* (New York: Knopf, 1957), p. 14.

45. Peter C. Hoffer and N. E. H. Hull, *Murdering Mothers; Infanticide in England and New England 1558–1803* (New York: New York University Press, 1981).

46. Rafael Karsten, *The Toba Indians of the Bolivian Gran Chaco* (Oosterhout N. B., The Netherlands: Anthropological Publications, 1967 [1923]), pp. 24–25; thanks to Beth Ann Conklin for providing me with this reference.

47. Hans Becher, *Die Surara und Pakidai, zwei Yanonami Stämme in Nordwestbrasilien* (Hamburg: Museum für Völkerkunde, Mitteilungen 26, 1960).

48. Clelland S. Ford, *A Comparative Study of Human Reproduction* (New Haven: Human Relations Area Files Press, 1964), p. 77.

49. Clelland S. Ford, *Field Guide to the Study of Human Reproduction* (New Haven: Human Relations Area Files Press, 1964).

50. O. Wiedfeldt, "Wirtschaftliche, rechtliche, und soziale Grundtatsachen und Grundformen der Atayalen auf Formosa," *Deutsche Gesellschaft für Natur– und Völkerkunde Ostasiens*, Mitteilungen 15 (Teil C, 1914): 1–55, esp. 23.

51. Asen Balicki, "Female Infanticide on the Arctic Coast," *Man* 2 (1967): 615–625, esp. 619.

52. Devereux, 1955, p. 232; Mead and Newton, p. 154; and Gerald T. Perkoff, "Toward a Normative Definition of Personhood," in *Abortion and the Status of the Fetus*, ed. William B. Bondeson et al. (Dordrecht, Holland: D. Reidel Publishing Company, 1983), 159–166, esp. 162.

53. James Mooney and Frans M. Olbrechts, "The Swimmer Manuscript: Cherokee Sacred Formulas and Medicinal Prescriptions," *Smithsonian Institution Bureau of American Ethnology* 99 (1932): 127.

54. Nancy Scheper-Hughes, "Culture, Scarcity and Maternal Thinking: Maternal Detachment and Infant Survival in a Brazilian Shantytown," *Ethos* 13 (1985): 291–317, esp. 312.

55. Scheper-Hughes, p. 292.

56. Lois McCloskey, School of Public Health, University of California, Los Angeles, personal communication.

57. Rattray, p. 61.

58. Jean Comaroff, "Medicine: Symbol and Ideology," in *The Problem of Medical Knowledge*, eds. P. Wright and A. Treacher (Edinburgh: Edinburgh University Press, 1982), 49–68, esp. 52.

59. La Fontaine, p. 132.

60. See Whitbeck, 1983.

61. Kristin Luker, *Abortion and the Politics of Motherhood* (Berkeley: University of California Press, 1984).

62. Petchesky, Rosalind P., *Abortion and Women's Choice: The State, Sexuality and Reproductive Freedom* (Boston: Northeastern University Press, 1985).

63. Maria W. Piers, *Infanticide* (New York: W. W. Norton & Company, 1978).

64. Piers, p. 51.

65. Devereux, 1955, pp. 58, 248.

66. Devereux, 1955, p. 188.

67. La Fontaine, 1985, p. 129.

REFERENCES

Aries, Philippe. 1962. *Centuries of Childhood.* New York: Vintage Books.

Armstrong, David. 1986. "The Invention of Infant Mortality," *Sociology of Health and Illness* Vol. 8: 211–232.

Balicki, Asen. 1967. "Female Infanticide on the Arctic Coast," *Man* Vol. 2: 615–625.

Becher, Hans. 1960. *Die Surara und Pakidai, zwei Yanonami Stämme in Nordwestbrasilien.* Hamburg: Museum für Völkerkunde, Mitteilungen 26.

Brandes, Stanley H. 1985. *Forty: The Age and the Symbol.* Knoxville: University of Tennessee Press.

Callahan, Daniel. 1986. "How Technology Is Reframing the Abortion Debate," *Hastings Center Report* (February 1986): 33–42.

Clarke, Edith. 1930. "The Sociological Significance of Ancestor Worship in Ashanti," *Africa* Vol. 3: 431–470.

Comaroff, Jean. 1982. "Medicine: Symbol and Ideology," in *The Problem of Medical Knowledge,* ed. by P. Wright & A. Treacher. Edinburgh: Edinburgh University Press.

Devereux, George. 1948. "Mohave Indian Infanticide," *The Psychoanalytic Review* 35 (2): 126–139.

Engelhardt, H. Tristram, Jr. 1983. "Viability and the Use of the Fetus," in *Abortion and the Status of the Fetus,* ed. by William B. Bondeson et al. Dordrecht, Holland: D. Reidel.

Evans-Pritchard, E. E. 1956. *Nuer Religion.* Oxford: Clarendon Press.

Ford, Clelland S. 1952. "Control of Contraception in Cross-Cultural Perspective," *Annals of the New York Academy of Sciences* Vol. 54: 763–768; cited in Mildred Dickeman, "Demographic Consequences of Infanticide in Man," *Annual Review of Ecology and Systematics* Vol. 6 (1975): 107–137.

Ford, Clelland S. 1964. *A Comparative Study of Human Reproduction.* New Haven, CT: Human Relations Area Files Press.

Ford, Clelland S. 1964. *Field Guide to the Study of Human Reproduction.* New Haven, CT: Human Relations Area Files Press.

Fortes, Meyer. 1949. *The Web of Kinship among the Tallensi: The Second Part of an Analysis of the Social Structure of a Trans-Volta Tribe.* London: Oxford University Press.

Fortes, Meyer. 1973. "On the Concept of the Person among the Tallensi," in *La Notion de la Personne en Afrique Noire,* ed. by G. Dieterlen. Paris: Editions du Centre National de la Recherche Scientifique.

Geertz, Clifford. 1973. *The Interpretation of Cultures.* New York: Basic.

Gifford, E. W. 1937. "Northeastern and Western Yavapai," *University of California Publications in American Archaeology and Ethnology* Vol. 34: 247–354.

Gladwin, Thomas, & Seymour B. Sarason. 1953. *Truk: A Man in Paradise.* New York: Wenner-Gren Foundation; quoted in George Devereux, 1955. *A Study of Abortion in Primitive Societies.* New York: International University Press.

Hanks, Jane Richardson. 1963. *Maternity and Its Rituals in Bang Chan.* Ithaca, NY: Cornell Thailand Project.

Hilger, M. Inez. 1957. *Araucanian Child Life and Its Cultural Background.* Washington, DC: Smithsonian Miscellaneous Collections, Vol. 133.

Hoffer, Peter C., & N. E. H. Hull. 1981. *Murdering Mothers; Infanticide in England and New England 1558–1803.* New York: New York University Press.

Holmberg, Allan R. 1969. *Nomads of the Long Bow.* New York: Natural History Press.

Jocando, J. Landa. 1969. *Growing Up in a Philippine Barrio.* New York: Holt, Rinehart and Winston.

Karsten, Rafael. 1967 [1923]. *The Toba Indians of the Bolivian Gran Chaco.* Oosterhout N.B., The Netherlands: Anthropological Publications.

Kaye, Barrington. 1962. *Bringing Up Children in Ghana.* London: Allen & Unwin.

Kerr, Peter. 1986. "Group Faults City Policy on Burial of Poor Infants," *New York Times* (May 25), p. 30.

Kidd, Dudley. 1906. *Savage Childhood: A Study of Kaffir Children.* London: Black.

Knutson, Andie L. 1967. "The Definition and Value of a New Human Life," *Social Science & Medicine* Vol. 1: 7–29.

Kovit, Leonard. 1978. "Babies as Social Products: The Social Determinants of Classification," *Social Science & Medicine* Vol. 12: 347–351.

La Fontaine, Jean. 1985. "Person and Individual: Some Anthropological Reflections," in *The Category of the Person,* ed. by M. Carrithers, S. Collins, & S. Luke. Cambridge, England: Cambridge University Press.

Luker, Kristin. 1984. *Abortion and the Politics of Motherhood.* Berkeley: University of California Press.

Mandelbaum, David G. Department of Anthropology, University of California, Berkeley, personal communication.

Mauss, Marcel. 1985. "A Category of the Human Mind: The Notion of Person, The Notion of Self," in *The Category of the Person,* ed. by M. Carrithers, S. Collins, & S. Luke. Cambridge, England: Cambridge University Press.

McCloskey, Lois. School of Public Health, University of California, Los Angeles, personal communication.

Mead, Margaret. 1928. *Coming of Age in Samoa.* New York: American Museum of Natural History.

Mead, Margaret, & Niles Newton. 1967. "Cultural Patterning of Perinatal Behavior," in *Childbearing: Its Social and Psychological Aspects,* ed. by S. A. Richardson & A. F. Guttmacher. New York: Williams and Wilkins, p. 153.

Montague, Ashley. 1974. *Coming into Being among the Australian Aborigines*. London: Routledge & Kegan Paul.

Mooney, James, & Frans M. Olbrechts. 1932. "The Swimmer Manuscript: Cherokee Sacred Formulas and Medicinal Prescriptions," *Smithsonian Institution Bureau of American Ethnology* Vol. 99: 127.

Osgood, Cornelius. 1951. *The Koreans and Their Culture*. New York: Ronald Press.

Ovens, J. G. 1982. "Natal Ceremonies of the Hopi Indians," *Journal of American Ethnology and Archaeology* Vol. 2: 163–175.

Perkoff, Gerald T. 1983. "Toward a Normative Definition of Personhood," in *Abortion and the Status of the Fetus*, ed. by William B. Bondeson et al. Dordrecht, Holland: Reidel.

Petchesky, Rosalind P. 1985. *Abortion and Women's Choice: The State, Sexuality and Reproductive Freedom*. Boston: Northeastern University Press.

Piers, Maria W. 1978. *Infanticide*. New York: Norton.

Rattray, Robert S. 1927. *Religion and Art among the Ashanti*. Oxford: Clarendon Press.

Sargent, Carolyn Fishel. 1982. *The Cultural Context of Therapeutic Choice*. Dordrecht, Holland: Reidel.

Scheper-Hughes, Nancy. 1985. "Culture, Scarcity and Maternal Thinking: Maternal Detachment and Infant Survival in a Brazilian Shantytown," *Ethos* Vol. 13: 291–317.

Stevenson, Tilly E. 1883–84. "The Religious Life of a Zuni Child," *Fifth Annual Report of the Bureau of Ethnology:* 539–555.

Tooley, Michael. 1972. "Abortion and Infanticide," *Philosophy and Public Affairs* Vol. 2: 37–65.

Turner, Victor. 1964. "Betwixt and Between: The Liminal Period in Rites of Passage," in *Symposium on New Approaches to the Study of Religion*, ed. by J. Helm. Seattle: American Ethnological Society.

U.S. Senate Subcommittee on Separation of Powers. (1981). *Report to the Committee on the Judiciary*. The Human Life Bill—S. 158. 97th Congress. Washington, DC: U.S. Government Printing Office, p. 12.

Van Gennep, Arnold. 1960 [1908]. *The Rites of Passage*. Chicago: University of Chicago Press.

Whitbeck, Caroline. 1983. "The Moral Implications of Regarding Women as People: New Perspectives on Pregnancy and Personhood," in *Abortion and the Status of the Fetus*, ed. by William B. Bondeson et al. Dordrecht, Holland: Reidel.

Wiedfeldt, O. 1914. "Wirtschaftliche, rechtliche, und soziale Grundtatsachen und Grundformen der Atayalen auf Formosa," *Deutsche Gesellschaft für Natur– und Völkerkunde Ostasiens*, Mitteilungen 15 (Teil C., 1914): 1–55.

Williams, Glanville. 1957. *The Sanctity of Life and Criminal Law*. New York: Knopf.

Human-Rights Law and the Demonization of Culture

Sally Engle Merry

Sally Engle Merry is Marion Butler McLean Professor in the History of Ideas and professor of anthropology at Wellesley College. She has published extensively on the themes of colonialism, law, and justice. Her recent book, Colonizing Hawai'i: The Cultural Power of Law, *received the J. Willard Hurst Prize from the Law and Society Association. She is currently completing a book on international human rights and localization.*

Why is the idea of cultural relativism anathema to many human rights activists? Is it related to the way international human-rights lawyers and journalists think about culture? Does this affect how they think about anthropology? I think one explanation for the tension between anthropology and human-rights activists is the very different conceptions of culture that these two groups hold. An incident demonstrated this for me vividly a few months ago. I received a phone call from a prominent radio show asking if I would be willing to talk about the recent incident in Pakistan that resulted in the gang rape of a young woman, an assault apparently authorized by a local tribal council. Since I am working on human rights and violence against women, I was happy to explain my position that this was an inexcusable act, that many Pakistani feminists condemned the rape, but that it was probably connected to local political struggles and class differences. It should not be seen as an expression of Pakistani "culture." In fact, it was the local Islamic religious leader who first made the incident known to the world, according to news stories I had read.

The interviewer was distressed. She wanted me to defend the value of respecting Pakistani culture at all costs, despite the tribal council's imposition of a sentence of rape. When I told her that I could not do that, she wanted to know if I knew of any other anthropologists who would. I could think of none, but I began to wonder what she thought about anthropologists.

Anthropologists, apparently, made no moral judgments about "cultures" and failed to recognize the contestation and changes taking place within contemporary local communities around the world,. This also led me to wonder how she imagined anthropologists thought about culture. She seemed to assume that anthropologists viewed culture as a coherent, static and unchanging set of values. Apparently cultures have no contact with the expansion of capitalism, the arming of various groups by transnational superpowers using them for proxy wars, or the cultural possibilities of human rights as an emancipatory discourse. I found this interviewer's view of culture wrong-headed and her opinion of anthropology discouraging. But perhaps it was just one journalist, I thought.

However, the recent article "From Skepticism to Embrace: Human Rights and the American Anthropological Association" by Karen Engle in *Human Rights Quarterly* (23: 536–560) paints another odd portrait of anthropology and its understanding of culture. In this piece, a law professor talks about the continuing "embarrassment" of anthropologists about the 1947 statement of the AAA Executive Board, which raised concerns about the Universal Declaration of Human Rights. Engle claims that the statement has caused the AAA "great shame" over the last fifty years (p 542). Anthropologists are embarrassed, she argues, because the statement asserted tolerance without limits. While many anthropologists now embrace human rights, they do so primarily in terms of the protection of culture (citing 1999 AAA Statement on Human Rights at www.aaanet.org). Tensions over how to be a

1947 AAA STATEMENT ON HUMAN RIGHTS

"Because of the great numbers of societies that are in intimate contact in the modern world, and because of the diversity of their ways of life, the primary task confronting those who would draw up a Declaration on the Rights of Man is thus, in essence, to resolve the following problem: How can the proposed Declaration be applicable to all human beings, and not be a statement of rights conceived only in terms of the values prevalent in the countries of Western Europe and America? . . ."

cultural relativist and still make overt political judgments that the 1947 Board confronted remain. She does acknowledge that not all anthropologists think about culture this way. But relativism, as she describes it, is primarily about tolerance for difference and is incompatible with making moral judgments about other societies.

But this incompatibility depends on how one theorizes culture. If culture is homogenous, integrated and consensual, it must be accepted as a whole. But anthropology has developed a far more complex way of understanding culture over the last two decades, focusing on its historical production, its porosity to outside influences and pressures, and its incorporation of competing repertoires of meaning and action. Were this conception more widely recognized within popular culture as well as among journalists and human-rights activists, it could shift the terms of the intractable debate between universalism and relativism. Instead, culture is increasingly understood as a barrier to the realization of human rights by activists and a tool for legitimizing noncompliance with human rights by conservatives.

One manifestation of the understanding of culture prevalent in human-rights law is the concept of harmful traditional practices. Originally developed to describe female genital mutilation or cutting, this term describes practices that have some cultural legitimacy yet are designated harmful to women, particularly to their health. In 1990, the committee monitoring the Convention on the Elimination of All Forms of Discrimination Against Women (CEDAW), an international convention ratified by most of the nations of the world, said that they were gravely concerned "that there are continuing cultural, traditional and economic pressures which help to perpetuate harmful practices, such as female circumcision," and adopted General Recommendation 14, which suggested that state parties should take measures to eradicate the practice of female circumcision. Culture equals tradition and is juxtaposed to women's human rights to equality. It is not surprising, given this evolving understanding of culture within human-rights discourse, that cultural relativism is seen in such a negative light. The tendency for national elites to defend practices oppressive to women in the name of culture exacerbates this negative view of culture.

Human-rights activists and journalists have misinterpreted anthropology's position about relativism and difference because they misunderstand anthropology's position about culture. Claims to cultural relativism appear to be defenses of holistic and static entities. This conception of culture comes from older anthropological usages, such as the separation of values and social action advocated in the 1950s by Talcott Parsons. Since "culture" was defined only as values, it was considered inappropriate to judge one ethical system by another one. For Melville Herskovitz, the leader of the AAA's relativist criticism of the Universal Declaration of Human Rights in 1947, cultural relativism meant protecting the holistic cultures of small communities from colonial intrusion (AAA 1947 statement, *AA* 49: 539–543).

If culture is understood this way, it is not surprising that cultural relativism appears to be a retrograde position to human-rights lawyers. Nor is it puzzling that they find anthropology irrelevant. As human-rights law demonizes culture, it misunderstands anthropology as well. The holistic conception of culture provides no space for change, contestation or the analysis of the links between power, practices and values. Instead, it becomes a barrier to the reformist project of universal human rights. From the legal perspective on human rights, it is the texts, the documents and compliance that matter. Universalism is essential while relativism is bad. There is a sense of moral certainty which taking account of culture disrupts. This means, however, that the moral principle of tolerance for difference is lost.

When corporate executives in the United States steal millions of dollars through accounting fraud, we do not criticize American culture as a whole. We recognize that these actions come from the greed of a few along with sloppy institutional arrangements that allow them to get away with it. Similarly, the actions of a single tribal council in Pakistan should not indict the entire culture, as if it were a homogeneous entity. Although Pakistan and

---

1999 AAA STATEMENT ON HUMAN RIGHTS

"Anthropology as a profession is committed to the promotion and protection of the right of people and peoples everywhere to the full realization of their humanity, which is to say their capacity for culture. When any culture or society denies or permits the denial of such opportunity to any of its own members or others, the American Anthropological Association has an ethical responsibility to protest and oppose such deprivation. This implies starting from the base line of the Universal Declaration of Human Rights and associated implementing international legislation, but also expanding the definition of human rights to include areas not necessarily addressed by international law. These areas include collective as well as individual rights, cultural, social, and economic development, and a clean and safe environment. . . ."

---

many of its communities have practices and laws that subordinate women, these are neither homogeneous nor ancient. Pakistan as a "culture" can be indicted by this particular council's encouragement to rape only if culture is understood as a homogenous entity whose rules evoke universal compliance. Adopting a more sophisticated and dynamic understanding of culture not only promotes human-rights activism, but also relocates anthropological theorizing to the center of these issues rather than to the margins, where it has been banished.

– 7 –

Ethnography in Awkward Spaces
An Anthropology of Cultural Borrowing

Jane Mulcock

Jane Mulcock is currently a postdoctoral fellow in anthropology at the University of Western Australia, which is also where she received her PhD. Her research interests focus on environmental values, beliefs, and practices, and she is currently involved in an ethnographic research project that is investigating people-nature relations in the urban setting of Perth, Australia.

What does it mean to "own" culture? What happens when one group of people borrow or appropriate the cultural property of another group? Why are some kinds of cultural property more rigorously defended than others? These are a few of the core questions that have informed my research over the past four years. My doctoral project focuses on cultural borrowing in the alternative health and spirituality movement (alias "New Age"[1]) in Australia. More specifically, I have been exploring the incorporation of indigenous imagery into contemporary, non-institutional forms of spiritual expression. Most of my fieldwork has been conducted "at home" in Perth, Western Australia and has involved a combination of participant observation,[2] one-on-one interviewing and textual analysis. My intention in this paper, however, is not to provide an account of the project's outcomes, but rather to highlight some of the methodological challenges that I faced during the course of the fieldwork. These experiences have led me to think about the kinds of roles required of anthropologists who choose to explore research questions that involve working with two or more deeply divided communities. Such "fieldsites" may constitute extremely uncomfortable, but potentially rich, settings for the ethnographer. These are the awkward spaces to which I refer.

Reproduced by permission of the Society for Applied Anthropology from Jane Mulcock, "Ethnography in Awkward Spaces: An Anthropology of Cultural Borrowing," SFAA 2001, *Practicing Anthropology*, Vol. 23, No. 1, pp. 38–42.

Before I embarked on this study I had no personal experience of the alternative health and spirituality movement. My only exposure to this range of cultural phenomena had been through occasional forays into "New Age" shops to gaze at the displays of crystals, talismans and faery figurines and to test out the infinite varieties of incense and essential oil. Even then I really didn't know what I was looking at. After a few visits I began to notice that a selection of indigenous imagery was constantly present among the range of merchandise that these shops carried. Collections of posters, greeting cards, books, jewellery and ritual tools, featuring strong references to "traditional" indigenous cultures, most often from North or South America, Australia and Africa, took their places alongside books on Celtic mythology, Feng Shui, Tibetan Buddhism, Astrology, Spiritualism and UFOs. In almost every instance, the indigenous cultures represented were heavily spiritualised, highly romanticised and almost completely de-politicised.

Having recently completed an honours dissertation on Indigenous Knowledge Systems and Sustainable Development, I began to wonder if the interest in indigenous ecological knowledge expressed by members of the international environmental conservation movement had any parallels with "New Age" interests in the spiritual traditions of indigenous people. What particular attraction did indigenous cultures hold for a group of mostly urban, mostly white, mostly middle-class consumers? And how did indigenous people themselves feel about being the objects of such an attraction?

Around the same time that I was asking myself these questions, Dumbartung Aboriginal Corporation, a Perth-based indigenous arts advisory body, headed by local Noongar[3] man, Robert Eggington, stepped up its international campaign against the American New Age author Marlo Morgan and her best-selling book, *Mutant Message Down Under*. Eggington and his supporters published a declaration "against the continued spiritual colonisation" of Indigenous West Australians and their cultures and made statements to the media expressing their concern and anger at Morgan's exploitation of Aboriginal culture for personal profit.

The declaration, entitled *Janagga Meenya Bomunggur* (translated as "The Smell of the White Man is Killing Us"), denounces all non-indigenous uses of Aboriginal imagery. It accuses non-Aboriginal people, including anthropologists and other academics, of "Grossly Distorting *Noongar* Spirituality and Culture," reinforcing "the Publics' negative Stereotyping of *Noongar* People" and gravely impairing *Noongar* self-esteem. One of the groups that this document specifically targets is the alternative health and spirituality movement. It states that ". . . Individuals and Groups involved in the New Age Movement, Women's Movements, Neo Pagan Cults and Shamanism Workshops have all exploited the Spiritual and Cultural Traditions of *Noongar* people by imitation of Ceremonial Understanding and molten Meshing this with Non-Aboriginal Occult Practice." In the wake of Eggington's campaign, local newspapers carried articles with headings such as "It's War on Culture Theft" and "Indigenous Push for Intellectual Property Rights." This passionate, political response to the offences of misrepresentation was much more in keeping with my own expectations of indigenous Australians than the glossy photos and idealised drawings of mystics and warriors that I had seen in various New Age shops. My anthropological training had primed me to interpret indigenous political resistance to mainstream stereotyping as appropriate and heroic. My bias on this issue was clear.

Before I competed my undergraduate training I was already of the opinion that if I ever undertook postgraduate research of my own it would have to be with non-indigenous Australians. I was highly sensitive to Indigenous characterisations of anthropology as a particularly insidious form of colonialism and felt, rightly or wrongly, that it would be inappropriate for me, as a young, white student to initiate an independent research project that focussed on indigenous issues. This feeling was very much intensified by Eggington's attack on white academics and students in the Declaration mentioned earlier. However, I did want my research on cultural appropriation to benefit Aboriginal Australians. I

knew I wanted to support the cause, a particular kind of positioning that I think well reflects what Marcus (1998:85) refers to as the tendency of anthropologists to favour the "subaltern point of view." I naively made up my mind to put my project and myself at the disposal of Robert Eggington and his campaign for indigenous intellectual and cultural property rights. In retrospect I am grateful to my supervisors who strongly advised me against this plan of action. I did try to pass on information that I thought might be of use to Eggington, but had I aligned myself more closely with his campaign I doubt that I would have encountered the awkward, confronting spaces that I was forced to occupy by merit of inhabiting the middle ground. In fact, my understanding of cultural borrowing, and perhaps even of the anthropological enterprise itself, may be richer as a result of this unanticipated and somewhat undesired positioning.

I had decided that I did not want to "study" indigenous responses to cultural appropriation for ideological reasons so I was left with the obvious strategy of focussing on the people doing the appropriating. I had some vague hesitations about researching a group whom I would inevitably end up critiquing, but beyond that I thought very little about the people I would be working with and the kind of situations and events I would be required to participate in over the course of the project I was proposing. It was not until I attended my first fieldwork event that the reality of this situation began to dawn on me. As it happened the first two events that I took part in were actually facilitated by Aboriginal people. The first, entitled "Belonging and Being in Australia: Aboriginal Spirituality for Australians," focused around a well-known male Elder from an Aboriginal community in the Kimberley region of Western Australia. The second, a day-long workshop for female participants only, entitled "The Ancient Wisdom of Aboriginal Women," was run by an Aboriginal woman from central Queensland. Both workshops were firmly linked into the alternative health and spirituality movement. It suddenly became starkly obvious that the line between the appropriated group and the appropriating group was not as clearly defined as I had imagined. However, this need for a conceptual shift was not what I found most challenging. The real indication that I had entered what I have come to think of as an awkward ethnographic space emerged from the particular ways that the expectations of the workshop facilitators and the other participants impacted upon my own expectations and understandings of sociality and self.

The second workshop, "The Ancient Wisdom of Aboriginal Women," organised and facilitated by Tjanara Goreng-Goreng, brought the issue of expectations sharply into focus for me. This event, and many others that I subsequently attended, emphasized the primary importance of experiential involvement. Full participation was required at all times. No one was permitted to sit on the sidelines and observe, especially not me, the "head-bound," over-intellectualising researcher (admittedly, it is difficult to be certain about how much of this message was communicated to me by the other women in the group and how much of it actually arose from my own feeling of being very out of place). The contradictory roles of participant and observer presented me with my first major dilemma. My job as a researcher seemed to require that I step back from the activity, at least in my mind, so that I could record and interpret what was happening. The imperative for many of the workshop participants, however, and perhaps for the facilitator, was to push aside so-called rational thought and to tap deeply into intuition, to focus on feeling and imagination. This was most evident when it came to learning about healing. Goreng-Goreng demonstrated what she described as a form of traditional Aboriginal healing using hands and breath to identify and manipulate energy blocks within the body. She then directed all the women in the room to select a partner and to take turns experimenting with the techniques she had showed us. For many of the participants who had prior interests in or previous experiences of alternative healing this was not a daunting exercise. For me, attempting to "heal" another person through a process I wasn't sure I believed in felt like an enormous compromise of my own integrity and my partner's dignity.[4]

As with many similar events that have emerged under the umbrella of the alternative health and spirituality movement, simply being present seemed to imply a willingness to experience some form of altered consciousness, an openness to attaining a shift in awareness, from material to non-material realms. Genuine participation in this setting required a kind of "letting go," a surrendering to the process, a turning inward that would immediately disable the observatory function necessary for the kind of research I wanted to do. Although I had a journal with me throughout the day-long workshop, I was constantly hesitant to take notes for fear of offending other participants by betraying my own lack of emotional engagement in the process. After all, this was a day for reflection and getting in touch with feelings. Intellectual analysis and careful description seemed to be barred from this environment by definition. This intuition was affirmed at some events that I attended later in my fieldwork. In these instances note-taking was actively discouraged because it was seen as a distraction from the actual experience that the workshop facilitator was attempting to provide for the participants.

At the beginning of the day, each person in the group was asked to explain briefly why they had chosen to attend the workshop. Most responses were deeply personal, indicating vulnerability, assuming trust, demanding mutual respect and disallowing critique. I felt the need to spiritualise my own discourse, to translate, or transform, my purpose for attending the workshop, from postgraduate research on cultural appropriation, into research on the importance of indigenous religious traditions for contemporary Euro-Australian spirituality. I struggled to pull some kind of spiritual reflection out of my interior space as an additional offering to convince the group that I was willing to make a personal investment in the day, that my interest and commitment to the process went beyond my academic agenda. Again, my sense of personal integrity in the presence of this group of seemingly vulnerable strangers felt painfully compromised. I felt like a fraud, a sceptic in a room full of people longing for transformation. I did not enter my "fieldsite" in search of spiritual transformation, instead I was searching for evidence of cultural appropriation in other people's transformative experiences. The particular voyeurism intrinsic to my position was deeply confronting.

Throughout the day I had to repeatedly force myself to submerge powerful, life-long inhibitions in order to take part in the dancing and the singing, the face painting and the ritual solemnity. I also had to silence the tape that was constantly replaying in my head, reminding me over and over that I was inadvertently supporting a movement that many indigenous people felt was exploitative. The fact that the day's activities, even though facilitated by an Aboriginal woman, seemed to exemplify the kind of "appropriation" that Eggington and others railed so angrily against increased my discomfort. I felt cornered by the need to conform, pinned down by the necessity of acceptance. My research agenda seemed to demand that I initiate and maintain a very unnatural set of relationships "in the field." I was suddenly stunned by an awareness of what doing this kind of ethnographic fieldwork was going to require of me. I needed these people to feel comfortable with me, I needed them to trust me, I needed them to allow me to access part of their lives. And they did not need me at all. For many, in fact, my analytical approach seemed to typify the very influence that they found obstructive in the context of their own lives.

Although I did talk briefly to other participants during the day I found it impossible to engage much beyond the sharing of pleasantries. By the end of the day I had only managed to make one rather wary contact, and then purely on the basis of getting copies of the audio-recordings she had made of the session. I was desperate for the workshop to come to an end, but as a researcher, my attendance funded by a departmental grant, I felt bound to stay until the very last. We finished almost an hour overtime and it was clear that the other participants were reluctant to leave. The euphoria in the air left me cold.

I returned home from this workshop with a throbbing headache, feeling completely drained, and terribly disoriented. The headaches ceased after several entries and exits from "the field," but the intense feelings of disorientation, alienation and emotional exhaustion never left me.

While one can argue that all ethnographic spaces are awkward by definition I want to suggest that some are more unyielding in their awkwardness than others. I think the awkward spaces that I experienced as part of my fieldwork resulted from a combination of factors. One of these was my prior political position on the evils of cultural borrowing. Another was my personal discomfort at being expected to participate fully in group ritual performances. The nature of the "fieldsite" itself further contributed to the difficulties that I experienced. For example, opportunities to conduct participant observation were usually limited to independently organised, once-only public workshops. These were often very structured and restricted to a fairly tight time frame. They tended to be expensive and intensely task oriented; as a result participants, understandably, had little inclination to spend valuable time talking to an anthropologist. Each workshop inevitably attracted a different group of participants, many of whom treated such events as "timeout" from their everyday lives, a space for personal reflection and retreat, a form of leisure. In retrospect it is easy to see why these people might have been hesitant to engage with a researcher who almost certainly wanted to question and analyse and explain their activities. Indigenous imagery, similar formats and philosophical themes, and my own presence were probably the only factors common to all of the events that I attended during my fieldwork. The potential for building ongoing relationships, characterised by trust and intimate rapport, was very limited in such settings.[5]

I have a sense that talking or writing publicly about negative fieldwork experiences, whilst not outlawed, is somewhat taboo in anthropological discourse. Perhaps this reflects concerns that to do so could undermine the credibility of the ethnographer, or of ethnographers in general. Perhaps it suggests a betrayal of the people with whom the ethnographer has worked, depicting them as unfriendly, unhelpful or otherwise unpleasant. I certainly do not intend anything of this kind in my own discussion of fieldwork realities. On the contrary, while some of the people I encountered "in the field" were, predictably, a little wary of me, the majority were tolerant and friendly. What's more, a number of these people generously invited me into their homes and willingly gave up their time, outside of the workshop setting, to answer my questions. Rather, I want to make a methodological point. I want to suggest that intensely uncomfortable experiences, experiences that often feel like downright failures, can often be just as informative as any other ethnographic data. When analysed reflectively such unsatisfying ethnographic experiences can not only contribute to our understanding of anthropological methodology, but they can also offer valuable and contstructive insights into the cultural spaces in which they occurred.

Throughout my postgraduate fieldwork I struggled constantly with the inevitable and intense feelings of confusion that surrounded my dual role of researcher and participant, the incompatibility of which seemed to be heightened by the particular cultural setting in which I was immersed. For example, one thing that became clear to me in the very early stages of my fieldwork was that if I wanted to avoid putting the people I hoped to interview on a defensive footing, or alienating them altogether, I would have to stop talking about "cultural appropriation." I started referring to "cultural borrowing" instead. This seemed to be less confronting to the individuals involved, perhaps because it allowed for a greater openness and curiosity on my part and perhaps because it lacks the political overtones of "appropriation." In retrospect, this shift in terminology was crucial for the way in which my understanding developed. Training myself to think about cultural borrowing, rather than cultural appropriation, allowed me to see far enough beyond my own postcolonial preconceptions to hear something more of what the people I was interviewing had to say. I was better able to acknowledge the role of cultural exchange as an ordinary part of everyday life, and to recognise some of the many ways in which cross-cultural imagery pervades contemporary Australian culture. Uncomfortable as it was at the time, the necessary act of de-politicising my key concept, and thus resisting my own ideological bias, helped me to arrive at a greater appreciation of the complexity inherent in processes of cross-cultural exchange. I came to see that a balanced analysis of the issue first required that I problematise the simple dichotomy I had imagined existed between colonial thieves and indigenous victims.

For a long time I attributed the painful sense of increasing rather that decreasing awkwardness that I experienced in my "fieldsite" to a series of failures and inadequacies of my own. I never developed the sense of "belonging" that I expected would come from doing extended ethnographic research, and I was unable to build the kind of rapport that I imagined was necessary to write a successful ethnographic account. Of course, perceptions of failure are intimately connected to the set of expectations that define success. I entered "the field" with a number of preconceptions about what makes a good anthropologist. Most of the anthropological fieldwork accounts I have read tell stories of anthropological heroes who struggle and struggle for social acceptance, and who finally, after many months of perseverance, generosity, flexibility and angst, manage to overcome the uncomfortable awkwardness of being outsiders on the outside. The protagonist happily graduates to the position of outsider on the inside and goes on to develop those much sought after feelings of belonging and rapport. Eventually the anthropologist reluctantly leaves the field carrying the warm responsibilities of connectedness, indebtedness and friendship, all of which signal a job well done. However, some ethnographic research, such as is evident in my own postgraduate work, does take place in spaces that never cease to be painfully awkward for the anthropologist.

An anthropology of cultural borrowing requires a strong degree of sensitivity to the arguments of both the borrowers and the "borrowees." In the case of indigenous spiritual traditions there are two intensely divided positions to take into account along with the innumerable positions that fall somewhere in between them. An anthropological approach potentially offers a very constructive analysis of such a conflict by merit of its ability to take a relativist stance on both perspectives and the assumptions and values underlying them. However, to do so, the anthropologist needs to be prepared to find herself locked into uncomfortable, interstitial spaces, the sort of awkward spaces that ensure that her conclusions meet with the approval of neither of the conflicting factions. In such instances perhaps it is this very lack of approval that signifies a job well done.

While I certainly do not deny the considerable value of developing the kind of intimate rapport with one's research participants that the discipline of anthropology has upheld as a mark of successful participant observation for a many decades, I do want to challenge the perception that this is the only way to do good ethnography. My point is that sometimes the research topic or setting itself, combined with the personal characteristics of the individual ethnographer, and perhaps the particular practical constraints of the project, such as time frames and available resources, can make the task of achieving this ethnographic ideal close to impossible. In such instances the reflective ethnographer may still be able to gain valid and valuable insights into the setting under investigation; in fact, in some specific cases, the researcher's non-aligned, interstitial position may even enhance his or her understanding of the social action at hand.

The lessons that my postgraduate experience has taught me about the potential benefits, or indeed the occasional imperative, of inhabiting the ethnographic middle-ground, promise to stand me in good stead for future anthropological work whether it be a long-term ethnographic study or short-term rapid appraisal projects. In fact, the latter may be well served by this call to the interstices given the inevitable restrictions imposed by most "contract anthropology" upon the discipline's idealisations of intimate rapport and ongoing relationship with those people "in-the-field" with whom we engage. As anthropology's circumstances continue to change, so too must its expectations along with its collection of alternative ethnographic strategies.

NOTES

1. The term "New Age" tends to carry a number of negative connotations, both for participants and for non-participants; I prefer to describe this cultural phenomenon more generally as the alternative health and spirituality movement.

2. My major methodological aim was to track the use of indigenous imagery through a variety of "New Age" settings. In this respect my project was multisited. Marcus (1998:90) explains that "[m]ulti-sited research is designed around chains, paths, threads, conjunctions or juxtapositions of locations in which the ethnographer has some form of literal, physical presence." The nature of the alternative health and spirituality movement, and the fact that I wanted to get a sense of how indigenous imagery was used across the movement, meant that opportunities for participant observation were largely limited to single, independently organised public events such as seminars, workshops and rituals.

3. Noongar is the name used by Aboriginal people from the southwest of Western Australia. The Noongar cultural area stretches roughly from Geraldton in the north to Esperance in the south.

4. Goreng-Goreng did incorporate a mini-lecture on Aboriginal history into her program, thus encouraging us to engage with our heads as well as our hearts. However, this constituted a small part of the introductory session. The bulk of the time was spent on other activities.

5. Marcus (1998) discusses the notion of anthropological rapport in some detail. He describes it as long-term "regulative ideal" (p. 127) of the discipline and suggests that it represents a very simplified account of the complex and variable interrelationships that constitute ethnographic fieldwork.

REFERENCE

Marcus, G. 1998. *Ethnography Through Thick and Thin*. Princeton, N.J.: Princeton Univerity Press.

COMMUNICATION

*What Is the Relationship between Language
and Culture?*

ONE OF THE THINGS THAT people spend a great deal of time doing is talking to one another. The reason we do so is simple—we have a great deal to communicate. For one thing, as social creatures, we need to let one another know how we are feeling and what we are up to at a given moment; doing this allows us to adjust our behavior in appropriate ways so that we don't antagonize one another or operate at cross-purposes. For another, because we rely so heavily for survival on the learned body of knowledge we call culture, there is an extraordinary amount of information that must be passed from one person to another and from one generation to the next. Of course, humans are not alone in our need to communicate, nor are we the only animals for whom learning plays an important role in our survival. In the past few decades, for example, studies of both captive and free-living monkeys and apes have shown the importance of learned behavior in their lives and revealed hitherto unsuspected communicative abilities among them. Indeed, so highly developed are these abilities that several captive apes have been taught to converse with humans using such systems as American Sign Language, and some have even taught this to others of their kind. Yet, the sheer complexity of what humans must learn in order to function adequately requires some means of **communication** surpassing those normally used by monkeys and apes. Although the latter can be taught to "talk" in a variety of nonverbal ways, their language skills (so far) do not progress beyond those of a two- to three-year-old human child (Miles 1994:46). Furthermore, they do not normally develop to this point on their own. Humans, by contrast, are "programmed" by our biology to talk, and it is virtually impossible to pre-

vent us from doing so. All normal individuals growing up in appropriate social environments will learn to talk at the proper time; precisely which language we learn to speak depends upon what is spoken by the people among whom we live.

As Raymond Williams has observed, "A definition of language is always, implicitly or explicitly, a definition of human beings in the world" (1977:21). Although spoken **language**—a system of sounds that, when put together according to certain rules, conveys meanings intelligible to all its speakers—is the primary means by which humans communicate, it is not our sole means of communication. Two others that accompany language are **paralanguage,** a system of extralinguistic noises that have meaning, and **kinesics,** a system of body motions used to convey messages. Both represent survivals of the gesture-call systems relied upon by other primates, such as monkeys and apes, to communicate their current states of being (contented, irritated, uncomfortable, sleepy, restless, and so forth) as well as their immediate intentions. Among humans, kinesics, or "body language," has received much attention and even popular interest. Paralanguage has received less attention in spite of our awareness of its importance, as signified by the phrase "It's not so much what she said as how she said it." As anthropologists William O'Barr and John Conley point out in their article, in courtroom proceedings *how* things are said is often more important than *what* is said.

Naturally enough, since humans rely primarily on language to communicate our hopes and aspirations, our upsets and concerns, and to transmit our accumulated wisdom from one generation to the next, specialists in the field of **linguistic anthropology** have devoted a great deal of time to its study. In addition to analyzing the structure of languages **(structural linguistics)** and their historical development **(historical linguistics),** they have investigated the important relationship between language and culture—for instance, how social variables such as class, gender, and status of the speaker will influence his or her use of a language **(sociolinguistics).** Such interests are represented in this chapter by the article by Salikoko S. Mufwene, a native of the Democratic Republic of the Congo, who describes his reaction to the different usage of forms of address in the United States, as compared with his central African homeland. As he puts it, "coming from my Third World background, there was more to be overwhelmed by than space-age technology."

The example of forms of address introduces another important point: Besides enabling us to communicate with one another, language serves other purposes as well. For one thing, it establishes boundaries between **social groups,** the members of which speak different languages or dialects of a particular language. Conversely, the imposition of one group's language or dialect upon another group has been a means by which one people has asserted its dominance over another. The interest in how language organizes peoples' lives, institutions, and their interrelations is the territory of **language ideology.**

Ideologies of language are not about language alone, but about "the construction and legitimation of power, the production of relations of sameness and difference, and the creation of cultural stereotypes about the types of speakers and social groups" (Spitulnik 1998:154). As Jane Hill describes in her essay in this chapter, language ideology is also about the link between social and racial inequality and forms of talk: When non-Latinos speak "Mock Spanish" (speak with a fake Spanish accent), the effect of their act not only contributes to the social marginalization of actual Latino speakers with accents in English, but assumes unaccented English as the implicit marker of what it means to be white. Other examples of language ideology explore how children are socialized to talk in certain ways that mark gender identity, or how the use of honorifics reflects and reinforces social status and inequality (Shieffelin, Woolard, and Kroskrity 1998). In her essay in this section, Jacqueline Urla explains that doing research on Basque language politics in Spain raises important ethical and political questions for the anthropologist about the nature of inequality, political rights, social justice, and freedom of speech. These questions are becoming ever more urgent in a period in which, as Urla notes, governments equate minority groups and their languages to "terrorists."

FOCUS QUESTIONS

As you read these selections, consider these questions:

✦ What role does language play in culture? How is it different from culture?

✦ How does the use of a language reflect a social identity or group membership?

✦ Why is it important to pay attention to *how* people say things, not simply *what* they say? What situations can you think of in which knowing *how* something is said (as opposed to *what* is said) could mean the difference between success and failure?

✦ What can a single word reveal about cultural processes?

✦ Do you speak another language besides your native language? What are the major differences between your native language and this other language? Do you express yourself differently in the other language than you would in your native language? Why or why not?

REFERENCES

Miles, H. Lyn White. 1994. Language and the orang-utan: The old person of the forest. In *The Great Ape Project*, edited by Paola Cavalieri and Peter Singer. New York: St. Martin's.

Shieffelin, Bambi, Kathryn Woolard, and Paul Kroskrity, eds. 1998. *Language Ideologies: Paractice and Theory.* Oxford: Oxford University Press.

Spitulnik, Debra. 1998. "Mediating Unity and Diversity. The Production of Language Ideologies in Zambian Broadcasting." In Shieffelin, Woolard, and Kroskrity, pp. 163–188.

Williams, Raymond. 1977. *Marxism and Literature.* Oxford: Oxford University Press.

8

When a Juror Watches a Lawyer

William M. O'Barr and John M. Conley

William M. O'Barr has a joint professorship in the departments of cultural anthropology and sociology at Duke University and is an adjunct professor of law at the University of North Carolina. He received his PhD from Northwestern University in 1969. His research has involved peoples of Africa as well as the United States, and his interests include legal anthropology, sociolinguistics, and discourse analysis. He also researches the anthropology of advertising.

John M. Conley is a professor of law at the University of North Carolina, where he currently holds the Ivey Research Chair. He is also an adjunct professor in anthropology at Duke and practiced trial law for a number of years. His recent book, Fortune and Folly, *is an anthropological look at institutional investors on Wall Street. Conley received his JD from Duke in 1977 and his PhD in anthropology from Duke in 1980.*

How things are said in court, as any successful trial lawyer knows, may be much more important than what is actually said.

Not only in the court, but in our everyday language, all of us have an intuitive notion that subtle differences in the language we use can communicate more than the obvious surface meaning. These additional communication cues, in turn, greatly influence the way our spoken thoughts are understood and interpreted. Some differences in courtroom language may be so subtle as to defy precise description by all but those trained in linguistic analysis. No linguistic training is necessary, however, to sense the difference between an effective and an ineffective presentation by a lawyer, a strong and a weak witness or a hostile versus a friendly exchange. New research on language used in trial courtrooms reveals that the subliminal messages communicated by seemingly minor differences in phraseology, tempo, length of answers and the like may be far more important than even the most perceptive lawyers have realized.

Two witnesses who are asked identical questions by the same lawyer are not likely to respond in the same way. Differences in manner of speaking, however, are usually overlooked by the court in its fact-finding quest.

Once an initial determination of admissibility has been made, witnesses may follow their own stylistic inclinations within the broad bounds of the law of evidence.

Scrutinize carefully the following pairs of excerpts from trial transcripts, and consider whether, as the law of evidence would hold, they are equivalent presentations of facts.

EXAMPLE 1

Q. What was the nature of your acquaintance with her?
A_1. We were, uh, very close friends. Uh, she was even sort of like a mother to me.
A_2. We were very close friends. She was like a mother to me.

EXAMPLE 2

Q. Now, calling your attention to the 21st day of November, a Saturday, what were your working hours?
A. Well, I was working from, uh, 7 a.m. to 3 p.m. I arrived at the store at 6:30 and opened the store at 7.

Compare this answer to the following exchange ensuing from the same question.

A. Well, I was working from 7 to 3.
Q. Was that 7 a.m.?
A. Yes.
Q. And what time that day did you arrive at the store?
A. 6:30.
Q. 6:30. And did, uh, you open the store at 7 o'clock?
A. Yes, it has to be opened.

EXAMPLE 3

Q. Now, what did she tell you that would indicate to you that she . . .
A. (interrupting) She told me a long time ago that if she called, and I knew there was trouble, to definitely call the police right away.

Compare the above with the slightly different version, where the lawyer completes his question before the witness begins answering.

Q. Now, what did she tell you that would indicate to you that she needed help?
A. She told me a long time ago that if she called, and I knew there was trouble, to definitely call the police right away.

Two years of study of language variation in a North Carolina trial courtroom, sponsored by the National Science Foundation, have led us to conclude that differences as subtle as these carry an impact which is probably as substantial as the factual variation with which lawyers have traditionally concerned themselves.

POWER LANGUAGE AND GETTING POINTS ACROSS

The three examples of differences in testimony shown here are drawn from separate experiments which the team has conducted. The study from which Example 1 is taken was inspired by the work of Robin Lakoff, a linguist from the University of California at Berkeley.

Lakoff maintains that certain distinctive attributes mark female speech as different and distinct from male styles. Among the characteristics she notes in "women's language" are:

- A high frequency of *hedges* ("I think . . . , It seems like . . . ," "Perhaps . . . ," "If I'm not mistaken . . .")

- *Rising intonation* in declarative statements (e.g., in answer to a question about the speed at which a car was going, "Thirty, thirty-five?" said with rising intonation as though seeking approval of the questioner)

- *Repetition* indicating insecurity

- *Intensifiers* ("very close friends" instead of "close friends" or just "friends")

- High frequency of *direct quotations* indicating deference to authority, and so on

We studied our trial tapes from the perspective of Lakoff's theory and found that the speech of many of the female witnesses was indeed characterized by a high frequency of the features she attributes to women's language. When we discovered that some male witnesses also made significant use of this style of speaking, we developed what we called a "power language" continuum. From powerless speech (having the characteristics listed above), this continuum ranged to relatively more powerful speech (lacking the characteristics described by Lakoff).

Our experiment is based on an actual ten-minute segment of a trial in which a prosecution witness under direct examination gave her testimony in a relatively "powerless" mode. We rewrote the script, removing most of the hedges, correcting intonation to a more standard declarative manner, minimizing repetition and intensifiers, and otherwise transforming the testimony to a more "powerful" mode.

From the point of view of the "facts" contained in the two versions, a court would probably consider the two modes equivalent. Despite this factual similarity, the experimental subjects found the two witnesses markedly different. The subjects rated the witness speaking in the powerless style significantly less favorably in terms of such evaluative characteristics as believability, intelligence, competence, likability and assertiveness.

To determine whether the same effects would carry over for a male witness speaking in "power" and "powerless" modes, we took the same script, made minor adjustments for sex of witness, and produced two more experimental tapes. As with females, subjects were less favorably disposed toward a male speaking in the powerless mode.

These results confirm the general proposition that how a witness gives testimony may indeed alter the reception it gets. Since most juries are assigned the task of deciding upon relative credibility of witnesses whose various pieces of testimony are not entirely consistent, speech factors which may affect a witness's credibility may be critical factors in the overall chemistry of the trial courtrooms.

These findings are not limited to a single study. Similar patterns have been discovered with other kinds of variation in presentational style.

Example 2 comes from a study of differences in the length of answers which a witness gives in the courtroom. Treatises on trial practice often advise allowing the witness to assume as much control over his testimony as possible during direct examination. Implicit in such advice is an hypothesis that relative control of the questioning and answering by lawyer versus witness may affect perception of the testimony itself.

To test this hypothesis we again selected a segment of testimony from an actual trial. The original testimony was rewritten so that, in one version, the witness gave short attenuated answers to the lawyer's probing questions. In the other version, the same facts were given by the witness in the form of longer, more complex answers to fewer questions by the lawyer.

BUT THEN, HOW LONG SHOULD A WITNESS SPEAK?

Contrary to our expectations, the form of answer did not affect the subjects' perception of the *witness,* but it did have a significant influence on the judgments about the *lawyer.* When the lawyer asked more questions to get the same information, subjects viewed him as more manipulative and allowing the witness less opportunity to present evidence.

The subjects' perceptions of the lawyer's opinion of his witness were also colored by the structure of the witness's answers; however, the differences were significant only when the witnesses were male. When more questions were asked by the lawyer, subjects believed the lawyer thought his witness was significantly less intelligent, less competent and less assertive.

On this point, then, standard trial practice theory is confirmed indirectly. The lawyer who finds it necessary to exert tight control over his witness will hurt his presentation by creating a less favorable impression of himself and suggesting that he has little confidence in the witness.

A LOT DEPENDS ON WHO INTERRUPTS WHOM

Example 3 is part of a study of interruptions and simultaneous talk in the courtroom. We wanted to know what effect a lawyer's interrupting a witness or a witness's interrupting a lawyer would have. Preparing a witness for a courtroom examination often includes an admonishment against arguing with the opposition lawyer during cross-examination, and a lawyer often advises his own witness to stop talking when he interrupts what the witness is saying.

To study some aspects of this complex phenomenon, we focused on the relative tendency of the lawyer and the witness to persist in speaking when the other party interrupts or begins to speak at the same time. This is one of the most subtle factors of language variation in the courtroom which we have studied, but, like the other differences, this too alters perception of testimony.

Working from the same original testimony, four experimental tapes were prepared: one in which there were no instances of simultaneous talk by lawyer and witness, one in which the witness primarily yielded to the lawyer

during simultaneous talk by breaking off before completion of his statement, one in which the lawyer deferred to the witness by allowing the witness to talk whenever both began to talk at once, and finally one in which the frequency of deference by lawyer and witness to one another were about equal.

All four tapes are clearly "hostile" and "unfriendly" in tone. The three containing simultaneous speech, or overlaps between lawyer and witness, would be difficult to distinguish by a person untrained in linguistic analysis of sequencing of questions and answers. Yet these subtle differences in patterns of deference in overlapping speech can be and are perceived differently by experimental subjects.

Findings from this study, like those from the second experiment, show significant effects on the perception of the lawyer. Subject-jurors rate the lawyer as maintaining most control when no overlapping speech occurs. The lawyer's control over the examination of the witness is perceived to diminish in all those situations where both lawyer and witness talk at once.

Comparing the situation in which the lawyer persists to the one in which the witness persists, interesting results also emerge. When the lawyer persists, he is viewed not only as less fair to the witness but also as less intelligent than in the situation when the witness continues. The lawyer who stops in order to allow the witness to speak is perceived as allowing the witness significantly more opportunity to present his testimony in full.

The second and third experiments thus show speech style affecting perceptions of lawyers in critical ways. Modes of speaking which create negative impressions of lawyers may have severe consequences in the trial courtroom. In all adversarial proceedings, lawyers assume the role of spokesmen for their clients. Impressions formed about lawyers are, to some degree, also impressions formed about those whom they represent.

The implications of these findings may be most severe in those criminal trials where the defendants elect not to testify, but they apply as well to all situations where lawyers act as representatives of their clients.

THE FACT IS: A FACT MAY BE MORE THAN A FACT

While the results of these particular experiments are undoubtedly important for the practicing lawyer, we feel that the true significance of the project lies in its broader implications. In a variety of settings, we have shown that lay audiences pay meticulous attention, whether consciously or unconsciously, to subtle details of the language used in the trial courtroom.

Our results suggest that a fact is not just a fact, regardless of presentations; rather, the facts are only one of many important considerations which are capable of influencing the jury.

As noted earlier, the law of evidence has traditionally concerned itself primarily with threshold questions of admissibility. The guiding principles have always been held to be ensuring the reliability of evidence admitted and preventing undue prejudice to the litigants. If it is true that questions of style have impact comparable to that of questions of fact, then lawyers will have to begin to read such considerations into the law of evidence if they are to be faithful to its principles.

As judges and lawyers become increasingly sensitized to the potentially prejudicial effects of speech style, one remedy might be to employ cautionary instructions in an effort to control jury reactions. For example, might it not be appropriate for a court confronted with a witness speaking in an extreme variant of the powerless mode to instruct the jury not to be swayed by style in considering the facts?

Additionally, lawyers themselves might begin to give greater recognition to stylistic factors while addressing the jury during voire dire, opening statement and closing argument.

Lawyers are already accustomed to calling jurors' attention to such presentational features as extreme emotion in urging on them particular interpretations of the evidence. What we suggest is merely an extension of a familiar technique into newly explored areas. . . .

REFERENCES

Lakoff, Robin T. 1976. *Language and Woman's Place.* New York: Octagon Books.

Lakoff, Robin T. 1990. *Talking Power: The Politics of Language in Our Lives.* New York: Basic Books.

9

Forms of Address

How Their Social Functions May Vary

Salikoko S. Mufwene

Salikoko S. Mufwene, a native of the Democratic Republic of the Congo, came to the United States in 1974 as a graduate student at the University of Chicago. He received his PhD in linguistics in 1979 and is now a professor of linguistics at his old alma mater. Previously he taught at the University of the West Indies in Jamaica and at the University of Georgia. Among his research interests is the relationship between language and culture, as well as pidgin and Creole speech.

The point of view presented in this essay is primarily Bantu, one of the several groups of sub-Saharan Africans typically characterized as black. Moreover, the outlook is that of a person who grew up in the central African colony of Belgian Congo during its transition to the independent nation of Zaire (called the Democratic Republic of the Congo since 1997) and was educated in a system that fosters an interesting coexistence of colonial European and local African cultures. From a sociolinguistic point of view, French, inherited from the colonial days as the official language and the medium of education from the fourth grade up to higher education, has been adapted to convey this marriage of African and colonial European cultures heavily anchored in the African tradition.

In this essay, I show how this background affected my reaction over fifteen years ago to English forms of address, as used at a major midwestern American university. With time, I have also learned that the customs described in this essay do not apply universally to the overall American society. However, I think that these first impressions reflect best my then unacculturated perception of a facet of American culture.

The term "form of address" is used in this essay as much for names, like *Peter, Mary,* and *Bob,* as for titles, like *Mr., Mrs., Dr.,* and *Professor,* which are normally used before last or full names, for example, *Mr. (Paul) Simon* or

"Forms of Address: How Their Social Functions May Vary" by Salikoko Mufwene, as appeared in *Distant Mirrors* edited by P. DeVita and J. Armstrong. Reprinted by permission of Salikoko Mufwene, University of Chicago.

Dr. (Alice) Rosenfeld. The term is also used for other titles such as *sir* and *ma'am,* normally used without a name; for kinship terms such as *Dad, Mom,* and *son* used to address relatives; for pet names such as *buttercup* and *cupcake;* or for any word used to address a person. Ethnographically, these forms of address specify the relation between the speaker and the addressee (for example, pals, professionals, parent-child, lovers) and the terms of their interaction (for example, distant, close, intimate), depending sometimes on the specific circumstances of the communication. To take an American example, a person named *Alice Rosenfeld* may be addressed in various ways, depending on context. She may be addressed as *Dr. Rosenfeld* in formal professional interaction, as *Mrs.* or *Ms. Rosenfeld* in situations where she is not well known, as *Mom* by her children, as *Alice* by her husband and colleagues in places where professional relations are not formal, and as *dear, darling,* or *honey* by her husband in intimate interaction.

I will restrict my observations on the American system to the usage of forms of address after the first time people have been introduced to each other. I will ignore those situations where preestablished relationships might allow usage of pet names and kinship titles, for instance, the title *uncle* extended to friends of the speaker's parents or blood uncles. However, it will help to provide more general background information about myself at this point, so that the reader may understand my original shock at how Americans address each other, at least at the university I attended.

In my Bantu background, addressees' names are often avoided in quite a variety of situations in order to express deference and/or intimacy. For instance, in the Bantu vernacular languages, people of the same age as one's parents are addressed by the same titles as the parents of the same sex, with the terms *papa* or *tata* (father) or *mama* (mother) prefixed to their names to express deference, for example, *Papa Kaniki* or *Mama Moseka*. These honorifics (that is, special forms of address for respect) are also used alone, without a name, to express both deference and intimacy when the speaker knows the addressee closely. For instance, in Kikongo-Kituba (my regional lingua franca), a close relation of the speaker's family who is of approximately the same age as, or older than, his or her father may be addressed as follows: *Papa, ebwe?* (Papa, how are you?)

When used alone to address strangers, the honorifics *papa* and *mama* are simple markers of politeness corresponding to the English honorifics *sir* and *ma'am,* used without a name, or to the honorifics *Mr., Mrs., Ms., Dr.,* and the like prefixed to the last names in formal interaction. These honorifics also are often used for addressees of the age group of the speaker's children as affective forms of address, corresponding to, for instance, the use of *son* by a nonkin. Thus, the sentence *Papa, ebwe?* used by an adult to a child is affective and may be translated idiomatically as "How are you, son/darling/dear?" All these Bantu forms of address fit in a system in which addressees' names are generally avoided, a practice to which I return below.

People of the age group of the speaker's older siblings are addressed in Kikongo-Kituba either by prefixing the kinship honorific *yaya* (older sibling) to their names for deference or by using the title alone for both deference and intimacy, for example, *Yaya Kalala.* Ethnographically, this corresponds in American English to addressing such a close relation by his or her first name or nickname.

A number of older male persons are assimilated to uncles and are addressed on the same pattern as above with the kinship honorific *noko* (uncle), for example, *Noko Mukoko.* However, note that many of the people addressed with this honorific would not be addressed with the honorific *uncle* in American English, since they may not be close friends of the speaker's parents or blood uncles.

Adult close friends often address one another by their professional titles, if these are considered as achievements (for example, *Munganga, ebwe?* [Dr. (MD), how are you?]), or by their nicknames or play names (for example, *Mbongo mpasi, ebwe?* [Hard Money, how are you?]). This custom is to express intimacy. In the case of professional titles, close associates bear the responsibility of setting up examples for others to follow; deference starts at home. Once more, usage of addressees' names is gener-

ally restricted to situations where it is absolutely necessary to make clear which person is being addressed, for instance, when more than one person in the same setting may be addressed by the same honorific.

Much of the same behavior is carried on in local French, except that the honorifics *monsieur* (sir), *madame* (ma'am), and *mademoiselle* (miss) are generally substituted for the traditional honorifics derived from kin terms. More recently, the honorifics *citoyen* (male citizen) and *citoyenne* (female citizen) were used by a political-ideological decree from the government in 1971 to distinguish the natives from foreigners.[1] Like the Bantu honorifics based on kin terms, they are generally used alone without the addressees' names. In all such cases, it is generally thought that only deference, not social distance, is expressed. Thus, translations with western European honorifics generally distort the ethnographic meaning somewhat, since they suggest social distance where none is suggested in either the Bantu forms of address with honorifics for deference or the local French adaptations to the system. For instance, the translation of the local French sentence *Suivez-moi, citoyen(ne)* (Follow me, citoyen(ne)) either becomes odd if *citoyen(ne)* is also translated as *citizen* or distorted if it is translated idiomatically as *sir* or *ma'am.* In the latter case, the idiomatic translation assigns higher status to the addressee, whereas the honorific *citoyen(ne)* does not.

Last, aside from the fact that names are generally avoided, it matters little in the Bantu system whether the first name or the surname is used. In any case, to make up for the tradition, speakers of local French often use the traditional Bantu honorifics, the kind of thing that is done less comfortably in a native French setting, unless all the interactants are from the same Bantu background. Note also that, as a rule, French requires that the polite pronoun *vous*, rather than the intimate pronoun *tu*, be used to address people concomitantly with the above titles. In fact, *vous* in the construction *Vous pouvez partir, monsieur/madame* (You may leave, sir/ma'am) assigns high status to the addressee. Using the traditional Bantu honorifics makes allowance for the intimate or status-free pronoun *tu*, which in a construction such as *Tu peux partir, papa* (You may leave, father) conveys both deference and intimacy or lack of status, depending on the case. Using *vous* together with *papa* makes explicit either the higher status of the addressee or the speaker's decision to establish social distance in the interaction.

In my American experience, I had to learn new norms of conduct. Honorifics based on age, and often even on rank, are commonly avoided.[2] My shock started in my first class, when the professor asked to be addressed as Jerry. Most of the other professors did likewise, regardless of age.[3] I found out that generally people do not give their titles when introducing themselves. More often than not, they either give only the first name or ask to be addressed by the first name. Further, the first names have usually been clipped to monosyllabics or disyllabics; for example, *Fred* is short for *Frederick* and *Ed* is short for *Edward*. Sometimes first names have been replaced by seemingly unrelated short nicknames; for example, *Bob* and *Bobby* are short for *Robert* and *Ted* is short for *Edward*. The native French transitional address system according to which persons are addressed by their honorifics and the pronoun *vous*, until there is a tacit or explicit agreement to convert to an intimate and informal mode of address, does not exist in America.

There is more to this American system of address. Foreigners are rebaptized, so to speak! The often long and "complicated" first names are replaced by nicknames. Ever since my first class, I have usually been addressed as *Sali*. The few Americans that say "Salikoko" either find the name "musical" or want to show off their familiarity with foreign names, in contrast with the regular reaction "I can't say that one."

However, addressing people by their first names does not necessarily mean a close relationship or intimacy. As suggested above, there are ways of expressing closeness or intimacy, but these will not be discussed here. The American system of address is basically a sign of informality, which is created from the onset of a social relationship, much sooner than I would have expected in the mixed cultural background I came from.

I also learned something else about names. As noted above, it makes little difference in the Bantu system whether one is addressed by one's first name or by one's surname, whenever names must or can be used. Names are typically avoided when addressing some relations, such as close friends, and names are taboo in addressing or referring to one's own parents. In the case of friends, professional titles or descriptive nicknames dealing with events in one's life are normally used. Name avoidance is a sign of closeness or intimacy. It is considered disrespectful to address ascending and descending in-laws by their names. Their kinship titles must be used not only to express deference but also to reassert the close social bond of the extended family by marriage. The expectation to use kinship honorifics in this case applies even to spouses' relatives when they interact among themselves, for instance, when the wife's cousin interacts with the husband's cousin.

The Bantu custom is in sharp contrast with the American custom of using first names or nicknames between close friends and with most in-laws.[4] In the beginning, I found it bizarre to see ascending and descending in-laws (fathers- and mothers-in-law and sons- and daughters-in-law, respectively) address each other by their first names and to see them interact casually with each other. (In my background, ascending and descending in-laws maintain avoidance relationships.) The new custom gave me the impression that Americans did not care much about these special, affined ties and that all social relations were of the same kind. I also assumed then that Americans did not distinguish between acquaintances and friends. In addition, I thought that Americans became personal with people they had just met rather quickly. (This impression was due essentially to the stereotypical French address system I had learned in school.) As noted above, acculturation to American ways has now taken the original shock away. However, coming from my Third World background, there was more to be overwhelmed by than space-age technology.

ACKNOWLEDGMENTS

I am grateful to James Armstrong, Kathleen MacQueen, and Jennifer Eason for feedback on drafts of this essay. I alone assume full responsibility for its shortcomings.

NOTES

1. This custom was patterned on the French system during Napoleon Bonaparte's regime in the nineteenth century to suggest an egalitarian revolution in the way Congolese interact with each other. The corruption and the socioeconomic discriminatory system it was meant to eradicate have grown stronger, starting from the political leadership, and a reactionary trend has now reverted to the current French forms of address with *monsieur* (sir), *madame* (ma'am), or *mademoiselle* (miss) when formality is required.

2. I will disregard here professional titles such as *Dr.* (for medical doctors) that act as part of the name in professional settings. Constraints are more complex here regarding when the title may be dropped.

3. There are apparently some exceptions to this observation. In my graduate school experience, I knew of some professors in their sixties that most students addressed as Mr. _____, though their much younger colleagues still addressed them by their first names.

4. I do not wish to ignore cases of assimilation where in-laws are addressed by the same kinship titles the spouse uses for them. However, coming from my background, another peculiarity here is that the assimilation applies almost only to the speaker relative to his or her spouse's relatives; his or her own relatives do not assimilate and show intimacy or closeness by using first names.

10

Language, Race, and White Public Space

Jane H. Hill

Jane Hill is Regents Professor and professor of anthropology with a joint appointment in linguistics, at the University of Arizona. She received her PhD from UCLA. She is a sociolinguist of Native American languages, and has worked with Tohono O'odham and Nahuatl speakers on issues of identity and self-construction. She has served as president of the American Anthropological Association.

THE STUDY OF RACISM IN ANTHROPOLOGY

Anthropologists share a contradictory heritage: Our intellectual ancestors include both founders of scientific racism and important pioneers of the antiracist movement. After many years in which anthropologists have given far less attention to racism as an object of cultural analysis than have many of our sister disciplines, we are now returning to work that honors and advances our antiracist heritage.

Racism should be as central a question for research in cultural anthropology as "race" has been in biological anthropology. We have always been interested in forms of widely shared apparent irrationality, from divination to the formation of unilineal kin groups to the hyperconsumption of (or abstention from) the flesh of cattle, and racism is precisely this kind of phenomenon. Why, if nearly all scientists concur that human "races" are imaginary, do so many highly educated, cosmopolitan, economically secure people continue to think and act as racists? We know that "apparent irrationalities" seldom turn out to be the result of ignorance or confusion. Instead, they appear locally as quite rational, being rooted in history and tradition, functioning as important organizing principles in relatively enduring political ecologies, and lending coherence and meaning to complex and ambiguous human experiences. Racism is no different: As Smedley (1993:25) has argued, "race . . . [is] a worldview . . . a cosmological ordering system structured out of the political, economic, and social realities of peoples who had emerged as expansionist, conquering, dominating nations on a worldwide quest for wealth and power." Racism challenges the most advanced anthropological thinking, because racial formation processes (Omi and Winant 1994) are contested and contradictory, yet global in their scope. At the local level racial practices (Winant 1994) can be very complex. Yet emerging global "racialscapes" (Harrison 1995:49, borrowing from Appadurai 1990) encompass even the most remote populations, as when the Taiap of the backwaters of the Lower Sepik River feel themselves to be "Black" as against "White" (Kulick 1993).

FROM "ALL LANGUAGES ARE EQUAL" TO THE STUDY OF RACIALIZING DISCOURSES

Like other anthropologists (and other linguists), linguistic anthropologists have made "education," with its implicit assumption of a confrontation with "ignorance," their central antiracist strategy. Attempts to inoculate students against beliefs in "primitive languages," "linguistic deprivation," or the idea that bilingualism (in certain languages) is inevitably seditious can be found in every introductory textbook in linguistics, and major scholars in the field have tried to spread the message not only as classroom educators, but as public intellectuals in a wide range of functions. And what have we to show for these efforts? "Official English" legislation on the books in many states, and, in the winter of 1996–97, a nationwide "moral panic" (Hall et al. 1978)[1] about whether "Ebonics" might be discussed in the classrooms of Oakland,

California. In the case of the Ebonics panic, the nearly universal reaction among linguists[2] and linguistic anthropologists was "We must redouble our efforts at education! How can we make classroom and textbook units on the equality of all languages, let alone all varieties of English, more effective? How can we place opinion pieces to fight this nonsense?" The problem here, of course, is that such interventions not only neglect the underlying cultural logic of the stigmatization of African American English, but also neglect the much deeper problem pointed out by James Baldwin: "It is not the Black child's language which is despised: It is his experience" (Baldwin 1979, cited in Lippi-Green 1997)—and Baldwin might have added, had he not been writing in the *New York Times*, "and his body."

Antiracist education in linguistics and linguistic anthropology has centered on demonstrations of the equality and adequacy of racialized forms of language, ranging from Boas's ([1889]1982) demolition of the concept of "alternating sound" and "primitive languages" to Labov's (1972) canonical essay on "The logic of non-standard English."[3] But until very recently, there has been little research on the "culture of language" of the dominant, "race-making" (Williams 1989) populations. New studies are beginning to appear, such as Fabian (1986), Silverstein (1987), Woolard (1989), and Lippi-Green (1997). Urciuoli's (1996) ethnography of speaking of Spanish and English among Puerto Ricans in New York City is perhaps the first monograph on the talk of a racialized population that foregrounds, and contributes to, contemporary theories of racial formation processes through her analysis of cultural phenomena such as "accent" and "good English."

A central theoretical commitment for many linguistic anthropologists, that "culture is localized in concrete, publicly accessible signs, the most important of which are actually occurring instances of discourse" (Urban 1991:1), prepares us to contribute in new ways to the untangling of the complexity of racism. Furthermore, such study is an obvious extension of an active line of research on linguistic ideologies (Woolard and Schieffelin 1994). We can explore questions like: What kinds of signs are made "concrete and publicly accessible" by racializing discourses? What kinds of discourses count, or do not count, as "racist," and by what (and whose) cultural logic? What are the different kinds of racializing discourses, and how are these distributed in speech communities? What discourse processes socialize children as racial subjects?[4] What are the discourses of resistance, and what do they reveal about the forms of racism? What discourse processes relate the racialization of bodies to the racialization of kinds of speech? And all of these questions must, of course, be qualified by the question, in what kinds of contexts?

"SPANISH ACCENTS" AND "MOCK SPANISH": LINGUISTIC ORDER AND DISORDER IN WHITE PUBLIC SPACE

To illustrate a linguistic-anthropological approach to these issues, I build on an analysis by Urciuoli (1996), recentering it from her research on bilingual Puerto Ricans in New York City to a national community of Whites.[5] I have been looking at uses of Spanish by Whites, both through on-the-spot observation of informal talk and through following as wide a range as possible of media and sites of mass reproduction such as advertising fliers, gift coffee cups, souvenir placemats, and greeting cards, for several years. First, I review Urciuoli's analysis of the racialization of Puerto Ricans through attention to their linguistic "disorder."

Puerto Rican Linguistic Marginalization: Disorderly Order

Urciuoli argues that her consultants experience language as differentiated into two spheres. In an "inner sphere" of talk among intimates in the household and neighborhood, the boundaries between "Spanish" and "English" are blurred and ambiguous both formally and functionally. Here, speakers exploit linguistic resources with diverse histories with great skill and fluency, achieving extremely subtle interactional effects. But in an "outer sphere" of talk (and engagement with text) with strangers and, especially, with gatekeepers like court officers, social workers, and schoolteachers, the difference between Spanish and English is "sharply objectified" (Urciuoli 1996:2). Boundaries and order are everything. The pressure from interlocutors to keep the two languages "in order" is so severe that people who function as fluent bilinguals in the inner sphere become so anxious about their competence that sometimes they cannot speak at all. Among the most poignant of the intricate ambiguities of this duality are that worries about being "disorderly" are never completely absent from the intimacies of the inner sphere, and people who successfully negotiate outer-sphere order are vulnerable to the accusation that they are "acting White," betraying their friends and relatives.

Urciuoli observes that a (carefully managed) Spanish is licensed in the outer sphere in such contexts as "folklife festivals," as part of processes of "ethnification" that work to make difference "cultural, neat, and safe" (Urciuoli 1996:9).[6] But Whites hear other public Spanish as impolite and even dangerous. Urciuoli (1996:35) reports that "nearly every Spanish-speaking bilingual I know . . . has experienced complaints about using Spanish in a public place." Even people who always speak English "in public" worry about their "accents." While "accent" is a cultural dimension of speech and therefore lives largely in the realm of the imaginary, this construct is to some degree anchored in a core of objective phonetic practices that are difficult to monitor, especially when people are nervous and frightened. Futhermore, it is well-known that Whites will hear "accent" even when, objectively, none is present, if they can detect any other signs of a racialized identity.[7] Speakers are anxious about far more than "accent," however: they worry about cursing, using vocabulary items that might seem uncultivated, and even about using too many tokens of "you know." Mediated by cultural notions of "correctness" and "good English," failures of linguistic order, real and imagined, become in the outer sphere signs of race: "difference as inherent, disorderly, and dangerous" (Urciuoli 1996:9).

The main point for my argument is that Puerto Ricans experience the "outer sphere" as an important site of their racialization, since they are always found wanting by this sphere's standards of linguistic orderliness. My research suggests that precisely the opposite is true for Whites. Whites permit themselves a considerable amount of disorder precisely at the language boundary that is a site of discipline for Puerto Ricans (and other members of historically Spanish-speaking populations in the United States)—that is, the boundary between Spanish and English in public discourse. I believe that this contrast, in which White uses of Spanish create a desirable "colloquial" presence for Whites, but uses of Spanish by Puerto Ricans (and members of other historically Spanish-speaking groups in the United States) are "disorderly and dangerous," is one of the ways in which this arena of usage is constituted as a part of what Page and Thomas (1994) have called "White public space": a morally significant set of contexts that are the most important sites of the practices of racializing hegemony, in which Whites are invisibly normal, and in which racialized populations are visibly marginal and the objects of monitoring ranging from individual judgement to Official English legislation.

White Linguistic Normalcy: Orderly Disorder

While Puerto Ricans are extremely self-conscious about their "Spanish" accents in English, heavy English "accents" in Spanish are perfectly acceptable for Whites, even when Spanish speakers experience them as "like a fingernail on the blackboard." Lippi-Green (1997) points out the recent emergence of an industry of accent therapists, who offer their services to clients ranging from White southerners to Japanese executives working at American plant sites. But the most absurd accents are tolerated in Spanish, even in Spanish classes at the graduate level. I have played to a number of audiences a tape of a

Saturday Night Live skit from several years ago, in which the actors, playing television news writers at a story conference, use absurdly exaggerated "Spanish" accents in names for Mexican food, places, sports teams, and the like. The Latino actor Jimmy Smits appears and urges them to use "normal anglicizations" (Hill 1993a). Academic audiences find the skit hilarious, and one of its points (it permits multiple interpretations) seems to be that it is somehow inappropriate for Whites to try to sound "Spanish."

While Puerto Ricans agonize over whether or not their English is cultivated enough, the public written use of Spanish by Whites is often grossly nonstandard and ungrammatical. Hill (1993a) includes examples ranging from street names, to advertising, to public-health messages. *Wash Your Hands/Lava sus manos*, originally reported by Peñalosa (1980) in San Bernardino County, California, can be found in restrooms all over the southwestern United States. Peñalosa observed that this example is especially remarkable since it has as many grammatical errors as it has words.[8] An excellent case was the reprinting by the *Arizona Daily Star* (august 10, 1997) of an essay by the Colombian Nobelist Gabriel García Márquez that originally appeared in the *New York Times* (Ausgust 3, 1997). All of the diacritics on the Spanish words—and the problem of accent marks had been one of García Márquez's main points—were missing in the *Star* version. Tucson is the home of a major university and has a large Spanish-speaking population, and the audience for the piece (which appeared on the op-ed page of the Sunday edition) no doubt included many people who are literate in Spanish. Clearly, however, the *Star* was not concerned about offering this audience a literate text.

While Puerto Rican code switching is condemned as disorderly, Whites "mix" their English with Spanish in contexts ranging from coffee-shop chat to faculty meetings to the evening network newscasts and the editorial pages of major newspapers. Their "Mock Spanish"[9] incorporates Spanish-language materials into English in order to create a jocular or pejorative "key." The practices of Mock Spanish include, first, semantic pejoration of Spanish loans: the use of positive or neutral Spanish words in humorous or negative senses. Perhaps the most famous example is *macho*, which in everyday Spanish merely means "male." Equally important are Spanish expressions of leave-taking, like *adiós* and *hasta la vista,* used in Mock Spanish as kidding (or as serious) "kiss-offs" (Mock-Spanish "adios" is attested in this sense from the mid-nineteenth century). A second strategy borrows obscene or scatological Spanish words for use as Mock-Spanish euphemisms, as on the handwritten sign "Casa de Pee-Pee" on the door of the women's restroom in the

X-ray department of a Tucson clinic, a coffee cup that I purchased in a gift shop near the University of Arizona Main Gate that bears the legend "Caca de Toro," and, of course, the case of *cojones*, exemplified below. In the third strategy, elements of "Spanish" morphology, mainly the suffix *-o*, often accompanied by "Spanish" modifiers like *mucho* or *el*, are borrowed to create jocular and pejorative forms like "el-cheap-o," "numero two-o," or "mucho trouble-o." In a recent example, heard on PBS's *Washington Week in Review*, moderator Ken Bode observed that, had the "palace coup" in the House of Representatives in July 1997 not been averted, the Speaker of the House Newt Gingrich would have been "Newt-o-Frito." The last major strategy of Mock Spanish is the use of "hyperanglicized" and parodic pronunciations and orthographic representations of Spanish loan words, as with "Grassy-ass," "Hasty lumbago," and "Fleas Navidad" (a picture of a scratching dog usually accompanies this one, which shows up every year on Christmas cards).

Mock Spanish is attested at least from the end of the eighteenth century, and in recent years it has become an important part of the "middling style" (Cmiel 1990), a form of public language that emerged in the nineteenth century as a way for elites to display democratic and egalitarian sensibilities by incorporating colloquial and even slangy speech. Recent relaxations of proscriptions against public vulgarity have made even quite offensive usages within Mock Spanish acceptable at the highest level of public discourse, as when the then-Ambassador to the United Nations Madeleine Albright addressed the Security Council after Cuban aircraft had shot down two spy planes manned by Cuban exiles: Cuban president Fidel Castro, she said, had shown "not *cojones*, but cowardice." Although many Spanish speakers find this particular usage exceptionally offensive,[10] Albright's sally was quoted again and again in admiring biographical pieces in the major English-language news media after she was nominated to be Secretary of State (e.g., Gibbs 1996:33).

THE SEMIOTICS OF MOCK SPANISH

In previous work (e.g., Hill 1995), I analyzed Mock Spanish as a "racist discourse." That is, I took its major functions to be the "elevation of whiteness" and the pejorative racialization of members of historically Spanish-speaking populations. Mock Spanish accomplishes the "elevation of whiteness" through what Ochs (1990) has called "direct indexicality": the production of nonreferential meanings or "indexes" that are understood and acknowledged by speakers. Speakers of Mock Spanish say that they use

it because they have been exposed to Spanish—that is, they are cosmopolitan.[11] Or, that they use it in order to express their loyalty to, and affiliation with, the Southwest (or California or Florida)—that is, they have regional "authenticity." Or that they use it because it is funny—that is, they have a sense of humor. In one particular elaborate example, in the film *Terminator 2: Judgement Day*, Mock Spanish is used to turn Arnold Schwarzenegger, playing a cyborg, into a "real person," a sympathetic hero instead of a ruthless and terrifying machine. When Schwarzenegger, who has just returned from the future, answers a request with a curt Germanic "Affirmative," the young hero of the film, a 12-year-old White boy supposedly raised on the streets of Los Angeles, tells him, "No no no no no. You gotta listen to the way people talk!" He then proceeds to teach Schwarzenegger the Mock Spanish tags "No problemo" and "Hasta la vista, baby" as part of a register that also includes insults like "Dickwad."[12]

Analysis reveals that Mock Spanish projects, in addition to the directly indexed message that the speaker possesses a "congenial persona," another set of messages: profoundly racist images of members of historically Spanish-speaking populations. These messages are the product of what Ochs (1990) calls "indirect indexicality" in that, unlike the positive direct indexes, they are never acknowledged by speakers. In my experience, Whites almost always deny that Mock Spanish could be in any way racist. Yet in order to "make sense of" Mock Spanish, interlocutors require access to very negative racializing representations of Chicanos or Latinos as stupid, politically corrupt, sexually loose, lazy, dirty, and disorderly. It is impossible to "get" Mock Spanish—to find these expressions funny or colloquial or even intelligible—unless one has access to these negative images. An exemplary case is a political cartoon in my collection, showing a picture of Ross Perot pointing to a chart that says, among other things, "Perot for El Presidente." This is funny only if the audience can juxtapose the pompous and absurd Perot with the negative image of a banana-republic dictator, dripping with undeserved medals. It is only possible to "get" "Hasta la vísta, baby" if one has access to a representation of Spanish speakers as treacherous. "Mañana" works as a humorous substitute for "later" only in conjunction with an image of Spanish speakers as lazy and procrastinating. My claim that Mock Spanish has a racializing function is supported by the fact that on humorous greeting cards (where it is fairly common) it is often accompanied by grossly racist pictorial representations of "Mexicans."

I have labeled Mock Spanish a "covert racist discourse" because it accomplishes racialization of its subordinate-group targets through indirect indexicality, messages that must be available for comprehension but are never acknowledged by speakers. In this it contrasts with "vulgar racist discourse," which uses the direct referential function in statements like, "Mexicans just don't know how to work," or hate speech ("Lazy greaser!"), which seems to operate through the performative function as a direct verbal "assault" (Matsuda et al. 1993). It is not exactly like the kind of kidding around that most Whites will admit can be interpreted as racist, as when David Letterman joked that the artificial fat olestra, which can cause abdominal pain and diarrhea, was "endorsed by the Mexican Health Department" (*New York Times,* August 24, 1997:F12). It also contrasts with the "elite racist discourse" identified by van Dijk (1993). Van Dijk pointed out that like Mock Spanish this type has as one function the presentation by the speaker of a desirable persona. Since "being rascist" is an undesirable quality, tokens often begin with qualifications like "I'm not a racist, but . . ." and then continue with a racializing argument like "I really resent it that all these Mexicans come up here to have babies so that American taxpayers will support them." Such qualifications do not make sense with Mock Spanish: One cannot say, "I'm not a racist, but no problemo," or "I'm not a racist, but comprende?," or "I'm not a racist, but adios, sucker." The reason this frame does not work is because Mock Spanish racializes its objects only covertly, through indirect indexicality.

Mock Spanish sometimes is used to constitute hate speech (as in posters saying "Adios, Jose" held by demonstrators supporting anti-immigration laws in California), and co-occurs with racist joking and with vulgar and elite racist discourses as well. It is sometimes used to address apparent Spanish speakers; many of my consultants report being addressed as "amigo," and Vélez-Ibáñez (1996:86) reports an offensive use of "comprende?" (pronounced [kəmprɛndiy]). However, it is found very widely in everyday talk and text on topics that have nothing to do with race at all. Because of its covert and indirect properties, Mock Spanish may be an exceptionally powerful site for the reproduction of White racist attitudes. In order to be "one of the group" among other Whites, collusion in the production of Mock Spanish is frequently unavoidable.

In my previous work, reviewed above, I have assumed that the "elevation of whiteness" and the constitution of a valued White persona was accomplished in Mock Spanish entirely through direct indexicality. However, in the light of Urciuoli's new work on the imposition of "order" on Puerto Ricans, I now believe that Mock Spanish accomplishes the "elevation of whiteness" in two ways: first, through directly indexing valuable and congenial personal qualities of speakers, but, importantly,

also by the same type of indirect indexicality that is the source of its negative and racializing messages. It is through indirect indexicality that using Mock Spanish constructs "White public space," an arena in which linguistic disorder on the part of Whites is rendered invisible and normative, while the linguistic behavior of members of historically Spanish-speaking populations is highly visible and the object of constant monitoring.

Research on "whiteness" (e.g., Frankenberg 1993) has shown that Whites practice not only the construction of the domain of "color" and the exclusion from resources of those racialized as "colored," but also the constitution of "whiteness" as an invisible and unmarked "norm."[13] Like all such norms, this one is built as bricolage, from the bits and pieces of history, but in a special way, as what Williams (1989), borrowing from Gramsci, calls a "transformist hegemony": "its construction results in a national process aimed at homogenizing heterogeneity fashioned around assimilating elements of heterogeneity through appropriations that devalue and deny their link to the marginalized others' contribution to the patrimony" (Williams 1989:435).[14]

Bits and pieces of language are important "elements of heterogeneity" in this work. Urciuoli (1996) has shown that precisely this kind of "heterogeneity" is not permitted to Puerto Ricans. What I have tried to show above is that linguistic heterogeneity and even explicit "disorder" is not only permitted to Whites, it is an essential element of a desirable White public persona. To be White is to collude in these practices, or to risk censure as "having no sense of humor" or being "politically correct." But White practice is invisible to the monitoring of linguistic disorder. It is not understood by Whites as disorder—after all, they are not, literally, "speaking Spanish" (and indeed the phenomena of public ungrammaticality, orthographical absurdity, and parodic mispronunciations of Spanish are evidence that they go to some lengths to distance themselves from such an interpretation of their behavior [Hill 1993a]). Instead, they are simply being "natural": funny, relaxed, colloquial, authentic.

I have collected some evidence that members of historically Spanish-speaking populations do not share Whites' understanding of Mock Spanish. For instance, the sociologist Clara Rodríguez (1997:78) reports that she was "puzzled. . . with regard to [the] relevance" of the Mock Spanish in *Terminator 2: Judgement Day.* Literate Spanish speakers in the United States are often committed linguistic purists, and Mock Spanish is offensive to them because it contains so many grammatical errors and because it sometimes uses rude words. They focus on this concern, but of course they have little power to change White usage.[15] It is clear that many Spanish speakers do hear the racist message of Mock Spanish. In an interview,[16] a Spanish-speaking Chicano high school counselor in Tucson said, "You know, I've noticed that most of the teachers never use any Spanish around here unless it's something negative." A Spanish-speaking Chicano businesswoman said, "When you first hear that stuff, you think, that's nice, they're trying, but then you hear more and more and you realize that there's something nasty underneath." In lecturing on Mock Spanish, I have found that Chicano and Latino people in my audiences strongly concur with the main outlines of my analysis, and often bring me additional examples. Chicano scholars, especially Fernando Peñalosa (cf. 1980), have long pointed out the racist implications of disorderly Spanish usage by Whites. Thus, for thoughtful Spanish speakers, the fact that disorderly Spanish and "Mock Spanish" constitute a "White public space" is not news. One of the dimensions of this space is that disorder on the part of Whites (including not only Mock Spanish, but also cursing and a variety of locutionary sins of the "you know" type) is largely invisible, while disorder on the part of racialized populations is hypervisable to the point of being the object of expensive political campaigns and nationwide "moral panics."

MORE SOURCES FOR HOMOGENEOUS HETEROGENEITY

The "incorporation"[7] of linguistic elements into the linguistic "homogeneous heterogeneity" of White public space draws on many sources. Perhaps the most important is what Smitherman (1994) calls the "crossover" of forms from African American English (AAE).[18] Gubar (1997) builds on the work of Morrison (1992) and others in a richly detailed study of very widespread and pervasive incorporative processes in the usage of White artists and writers. However, AAE and White English are so thoroughly entangled in the United States that crossover is extremely difficult to study. While obvious "wiggerisms" like "Word to your Mother"[19] or moth-eaten tokens of minstrelsy like "Sho' nuff, Mistah Bones" are easy to spot, many other usages are curiously indeterminate.[20] Even where an AAE source is recognizable to an etymologist, it is often impossible to know whether the usage indexes any "blackness" to its user or audience. One way of understanding this indeterminacy might be to see it as a triumph of White racial practice. New tokens of White "hipness," often retrievable as Black in origin only by the most dogged scholarship (although often visible to Blacks), are constantly created out of AAE materials.

An example of indeterminate crossover appeared in the "For Better or for Worse" comic strip published in the *Arizona Daily Star* (August 22, 1997). Two White Cana-

dian lads discuss how Lawrence should deal with his partner's departure to study music in Paris. Bobby, who is straight, tries to reassure Lawrence, who is gay,[21] that falling in love is always worth it, even knowing the risk of loss. Lawrence jokes, "Let it be known that this speech comes from a guy who's in a 'happening' relationship." "Happening" in this sense comes from AAE "happenin," but it seems unlikely that here it is intended to convey anything more than the strip creator's alertness to "the speech of today's young people" (although the quotation marks around the form do suggest that she regards this register as not part of her own repertoire). Yet similar usages can be highly salient for Blacks: Lippi-Green (1997:196) quotes an audience member on an episode of Oprah Winfrey: "This is a fact. White America use black dialect on commercials every day. Be observant, people. Don't let nobody tell you that you are ignorant and that you don't speak right. Be observant. They started off Channel 7 Eyewitness news a few years ago with one word: whashappenin. So what's happening, America?"

Now, contrast the episode of "For Better or for Worse" described above with another episode, published a couple of years ago. Here the young people are on a ski slope, and one boy, Gordon, "hits on" (I am sure Smitherman [1994] is correct that this is AAE, but in my own usage it feels merely slangy) a pretty girl with our now-familiar token, "What's happening?" She "puts him down" (probably also AAE, but not in Smitherman 1994)[22] with "With you? Nada." While probably few White readers of this strip sense "blackness" in "What's happening?", most will immediately detect "Nada" as "Spanish." That is, while the "Black" indexicality of "What's happening" is easily suppressed, it is virtually impossible to suppress the "Spanish" indexicality of "Náda," which has in "Mock Spanish" the semantically pejorated sense "absolutely nothing, less than zero." It seems likely that there are tokens that originate in Mock Spanish where the original indexicality is suppressable (the word *peon*, pronounced [piyan], which appeared in English by the seventeenth century, may be an example of this type), but in general tokens of this practice are relatively easy to spot and interpret.

Because of this relative transparency of Mock Spanish, it is a good choice for linguistic-anthropological research. However, precisely because it is narrower in its range of opacity and transparency than is AAE "crossover," it must function somewhat differently in White public space, an issue that needs investigation. Furthermore, African Americans themselves apparently use Mock Spanish; Terry McMillan's novel, *How Stella Got Her Groove Back,* is rich in attestations in the speech of Stella, a beautiful and successful African American professional woman from California. In contrast, as far as I know no members of historically Spanish-speaking populations use Mock Spanish, at least not in anything like the routine way that Whites do.[23]

The same question, of different functions of such linguistic incorporations into White "homogeneous heterogeneity," occurs with borrowings from other languages. For instance, tokens of "mock French" like "Mercy buckets" and "bow-koo" do occur, but they are relatively rare, especially in comparison with the very extensive use of French in advertising, especially in the fashion industry, to convey luxury and exclusivity. "Mock Italian" seems to have been relatively important in the 1940s and 1950s but is apparently on the way out; I have found very few examples of it. "Mock Yiddish" is common but is used by members of historically Yiddish-speaking groups as well as by outsiders. "Mock Japanese" "sayonara" is perfectly parallel to Mock Spanish "adios," but may be the only widely used token of this type.[24] In summary, "Mock" forms vary widely in relative productivity and in the kinds of contexts in which they appear. By far the richest examples of linguistic incorporations are Mock Spanish and AAE crossover.

CAN MOCK FORMS SUBVERT THE ORDER OF RACIAL PRACTICES?

A number of authors, including Hewitt (1986), Gubar (1997) and Butler (1997), have argued that usages that in some contexts are grossly racist seem to contain an important parodic potential that can be turned to the antiracist deconstruction of racist categorical essentializing. Hewitt studied Black-White friendships among young teenagers in south London and found a "productive dialogue of youth" (1986:99) in which he identifies antiracist potential. Especially notable were occasions where Black children would tease White friends as "nigger," and the White teens would reply with "honky" or "snowflake." Hewitt comments, "This practice . . . turns racism into a kind of effigy, to be burned up in an interactive ritual which seeks to acknowledge and deal with its undeniable presence whilst acting out the negation of its effects" (1986:238). Gubar (1997) suggests that posters by the artist Iké Udé (such as a famous image of Marilyn Monroe, but in "blackface," and a transformation of Robert Mapplethorpe's infamous "Man in a Polyester Suit" with white skin and a circumcised penis) may use the symbolic repertoire of racism as "crucial aesthetic means of comprehending racial distinction without entrenching or denying it" (Gubar 1997:256). An example in the case of Spanish might be the performance art of Guillermo Gómez Peña,[25] who creates frenzied mixtures of English and multiple registers and dialects of Spanish (and even

Nahuatl). Butler (1997), writing in opposition to the proscription of the racist vocabulary by anti-hate speech legislation, argues that gays and lesbians have been able to subvert the power of "queer," and that other "hate words" may have similar potential. The kinds of games reported by Hewitt, however, remain reserved to childhood, unable to break through the dominant voices of racism; Hewitt found the kind of interracial friendship that permitted teasing with racist epithets essentially vanished from the lives of his subjects by the time they reached the age of 16. In the light of the analysis that I have suggested above, the "subversions" noted by Gubar and Butler can also be seen simply as one more example of "orderly" disorder that is reserved to elites in White public space, rather than as carnivalesque inversions. Or, perhaps we should say that carnivalesque inversions can be a "weapon of the strong" as well as a "weapon of the weak."[26] The art of a Gómez Peña, to the degree that it is acceptable to White audiences, may precisely "whiten" this performer and others like him.

An important possible exception is the phenomenon of "crossing," discussed by British sociolinguist Ben Rampton (1995), who reports extensive use of out-group linguistic tokens among British adolescents of a variety of ethnic origins, including strongly racialized populations like West Indians and South Asians as well as Whites. "Crossings," while they retain some potential to give offense, often seem simply to acknowledge what is useful and desirable in the space of urban diversity. Thus, working-class White girls learn the Panjabi lyrics to "bhangra" songs, and Bengali kids speak Jamaican creole (which seems to have emerged in general as a prestigious language among British youth, parallel to the transracial "hip-hop" phenomenon in the United States). Early reports by Shirley Brice Heath of new work with American adolescents has identified similar "crossing" phenomena.[27] However, only slightly more than a decade ago Hewitt (1986) found that such crossings did not survive the adolescent years. We cannot be sure that these phenomena are genuinely outside the linguistic order of racism until we understand dimensions of that order—within which age-graded cohorts may have a relatively enduring place. I have tried above to show how linguistic-anthropological attention to the history, forms, and uses of White language mixing can help us toward such an understanding.

NOTES

Acknowledgments. I would especially like to thank María Rodríguez, Bambi Schieffelin, and Kathryn Woolard, who have provided me with valuable material on Mock Spanish.

1. Hall et al. (1978) borrow the notion of "moral panic" from Cohen (1972).

2. In a survey of 34 entries, encompassing about 100 messages, under the heading "Ebonics" on Linguist, the list that probably reaches the largest number of linguists, I found only one explicit mention of "racism" by an author who used the expression "institutional racism." It is, perhaps, appropriate for linguists to focus on their special areas of scholarly expertise, and it is certainly the case that there may be a linguistic dimension to the educational problems confronted by many African American children, but the neglect of racism on the list was quite striking. It was sometimes addressed obliquely and euphemistically, as with one author's proposal of the "special" situation of African Americans in the United States.

3. The "all languages are equal" argument continues in spite of a warning by Dell Hymes (1973) that this claim is technically incorrect in many subtle ways.

4. Hirschfeld (1996) documents the very early association between raced categories and an essentialized understanding of "human kinds" for young children in the United States.

5. I am mindful of Hartigan's (1997) argument that "Whites" are by no means a homogeneous population. Indeed, in other work (Hill 1995) I have suggested that working-class speakers are less likely to use "Mock Spanish" than are other Whites. Much of my material comes from mass media that are part of the homogenizing project of "whiteness," and there is no question that different "Whites" experience this project in different ways. I use "Whites" here (perhaps injudiciously) as a sort of shorthand required first by lack of space and second because the data required to precisely characterize the population I have in mind are not available. Certainly it includes White elites such as screenwriters and nationally syndicated columnists.

6. Urciuoli (1996:16) points out that it is essential to use Spanish in the folklife festival context because to translate songs, the names of foods, and the like into English would render them less "authentic," this property being essential to claims on "ethnicity" that are one way to resist racialization.

7. Here the canonical study is the matched-guise test conducted by Rubin (1992). Sixty-two undergraduate native speakers of English listened to a brief lecture (on either a science or humanities topic) recorded by a native speaker of English from central Ohio. While they listened, one group of students saw a slide of a White woman lecturer. The other half saw a slide of an Asian woman in the same setting and pose (and even of the same size, and with the same hair style, as the White woman). Students who heard the lecture under the "Asian slide" condition often reported that the lecturer had an Asian accent and, even more interestingly, scored lower on tests of comprehension of the lecture.

8. It should be *Lavarse las manos*, the usual directive for public places being the infinitive (e.g., *No fumar* 'No Smoking,' *No estacionarse* 'No Parking'), the verb being reflexive, and body parts are not labeled by the possessive pronoun *su* unless they are detached from the body of their owner.

9. In earlier publications (e.g., Hill 1993b), I referred to these practices as "Junk Spanish." I thank James Fernandez for the expression "Mock Spanish" and for convincing me that "Junk Spanish" was a bad nomenclatural idea, and the source of some of the problems I was having getting people to understand what I was working on (many people, including linguists and anthropologists, assumed that by "Junk Spanish" I meant something like the "Border Spanish" of native speakers of Spanish, rather than jocular and parodic uses of Spanish by English speakers). The most extensive discussion of Mock Spanish available is Hill (1995).

10. I am indebted to Professor Raúl Fernández of the University of California-Irvine for a copy of a letter he wrote to the *Los Angeles Times* protesting the appearance of *cojones* in a film review. Ernest Hemingway is probably to blame for the widespread knowledge of this word among monolingual speakers of English.

11. While some Whites who use Mock Spanish have a classroom competence in that language (I was a case in point), most of the speakers I have queried say that they do not "speak Spanish."

12. An anonymous referee for the *American Anthropologist* argues that this analysis, suggesting that the "elevation of whiteness" is accomplished through direct indexicality, it is not exactly correct. Instead, the direct indexicality of Mock Spanish elevates the individual, conveying "I am a nice/easy-going/funny/ locally-rooted/ cosmopolitan person." The elevation of "whiteness" is then accomplished indirectly when combined with the indirectly indexed message "I am White." This is an interesting suggestion, but I think the *Terminator 2: Judgment Day* sequence argues that the indexicality is direct: Mock Spanish is precisely "the way people talk"—and "people" can only be that group that is unmarked and thereby "White." Thus positive individual qualities and "whiteness" are simultaneously indexed. (A direct version of this, perhaps mercifully obsolete, is the expression that applauds some act of good fellowship with "That's mighty White of you.")

13. As Harrison (1995) points out, a more explicit construction of whiteness often appears among marginalized Whites, as in the current far-right "White pride" movement. She notes that this "undermines whatever incipient class consciousness exists among poor Whites" (Harrison 1995:63). Thus we can see such movements as part of the very large cultural formation wherein "race" may be the single most important organizer of relationships, determinant of identity, and mediator of meaning (Winant 1994).

14. Williams focuses her analysis on the "national process," the creation of what she calls the race/class/nation conflation, but the construction of whiteness is probably a project of global scope, and in fact Mock Spanish seems to be widespread in the English-speaking world. Bertie, a character in the Barrytown novels (*The Commitments, The Snapper, The Van,* which depict life in working-class Dublin) by the Irish author Roddy Doyle, often uses Mock Spanish. For another example from outside the United States, I am indebted to Dick Bauman for a headline from the gardening section of a Glasgow newspaper, inviting the reader to "Hosta la vista, baby!" (that is, to plant members of the genus *Hosta* for their decorative foliage).

15. I have discovered only one case of apparent concern about Spanish-speaking opinion in reference to the use of Spanish in mass media. Chon Noriega (1997:88) reports that when the film *Giant* was presented for review to the Production Code

Administration in 1955, Geoffrey Shurlock, the head of the PCA, requested that the ungrammatical Spanish in the film (in which Spanish appears without subtitles) be corrected, apparently for fear of offending the government of Mexico, then seen as a "good neighbor."

16. Dan Goldstein and I have begun a project of interviewing members of historically Spanish-speaking populations about Mock Spanish. We have compiled a scrapbook of examples, and subjects are audiotaped as they leaf through these and comment on them.

17. I borrow this term from Raymond Williams (1977).

18. I do not include "Vernacular" (many scholars refer to "African American Vernacular English" or AAVE), because AAE has a full range of register ranging from street argot through middle-class conversational usage to formal oratory and *belles lettres*. Scholars like Smitherman (1988) and Morgan (1994) have criticized sociolinguists for typifying AAE only through attestations of street registers.

19. Smitherman (1994:237) defines *wigger* as "literally, a white NIGGER, an emerging positive term for White youth who identify with HIP HOP, RAP, and other aspects of African American Culture." She gives the proper form of the affirmation as "Word to the Mother," but I first heard it (from a young White woman) in the form given.

20. In the lexicon of AAE provided by Smitherman (1994) I recognized many forms in my own usage that she does not mark as "crossovers" (to give only one example, "beauty shop" for a hair-and-nails salon was the only term I knew for such establishments as I was growing up, and it was universally used by my grandmothers, aunts, and mother, all White ladies who would never have dreamed of essaying any "Dis and Dat" [Gubar's (1996) term for the adoption of AAE forms by White writers]). My grandfather, an egregious racist who grew up in southeastern Missouri, was very fond of "copacetic," which Smitherman attributes to the speech of "older blacks" and does not recognize as ever having "crossed over."

21. A number of U.S. newspapers refused to publish the series of episodes in which Lawrence mourns his partner's departure.

22. The *American Heritage Dictionary of the English Language* (Third Edition) lists "put down" as "slang." Unsurprisingly, their sentence of attestation comes from the work of Dr. Alvin Poussaint, an African American.

23. Some Spanish speakers find some of the greeting cards in my sample funny. One woman said that she might send a "Moochos Smoochos" card (illustrating hyperanglicized parody and the use of Spanish morphology to be funny) to her husband; she said, "That one's kinda cute."

24. "Honcho," from Japanese *han* "Squad" and *chō* "chief" (*American Heritage Dictionary of the English Language,* Third Edition) seems to be etymologically inaccessible as Japanese except to specialists; many Whites probably think that it is Spanish.

25. See, for instance, his *Warrior for Gringostroika* (1991). However, Gómez Peña uses so much Spanish that one must be bilingual to understand him; his art seems to be addressed mainly to multilingual Spanish-speaking audiences. Woolard's (1988) study of a comic in 1970s Barcelona, who entertained audiences with jokes that code switched between Castilian and Catalan during a period of extreme linguistic conflict and purism, provides another example of this type of subversion.

26. "Weapon of the weak" comes, of course, from Scott (1985). Work on discourses of resistance by scholars like Scott (see also 1990) and Bhabha (1994) often seems to imply that parody and humor are primarily strategies of resistance. However, it is obvious that humor is an important part of racist discourse, and the accusation that antiracists "have no sense of humor" is an important weapon of racists.

27. In a colloquialism presented to the Department of Anthropology, University of Arizona, Tucson, January 27, 1997.

REFERENCES CITED

Appadurai, Arjun. 1990. Disjuncture and Difference in the Global Cultural Economy. Public Culture 2:1–24.

Bhabha, Homi K. 1994. The Location of Culture. New York: Routledge.

Boas, Franz. [1889]1982. On Alternating Sounds. In The Shaping of American Anthropology, 1883–1911: A Franz Boas Reader. George W. Stocking, ed. Pp. 72–76. Chicago: University of Chicago Press.

Butler, Judith. 1997. Excitable Speech. New York: Routledge.

Cmiel, Kenneth. 1990. Democratic Eloquence. New York: William Morrow.

Cohen, Stan. 1972. Folk Devils and Moral Panics: The Creation of the Mods and the Rockers. London: MacGibbon and Kee.

Fabian, Johannes. 1986. Language and Colonial Power: The Appropriation of Swahili in the Former Belgian Congo, 1880–1938. Cambridge: Cambridge University Press.

Frankenberg, Ruth. 1993. White Women, Race Matters: The Social Construction of Whiteness. Minneapolis: University of Minnesota Press.

Gibbs, Nancy. 1996. An American Voice. Time 149(1):32–33.

Gómez-Peña, Guillermo. 1993. Warrior for Gringostroika. St. Paul, MN: Graywolf Press.

Gubar, Susan. 1997. Racechanges: White Skins, Black Face in American Culture. Oxford University Press.

Hall, Stuart, Chas Critcher, Tony Jefferson, John Clarke, and Brian Roberts. 1978. Policing the Crisis. London: The Macmillan Press Ltd.

Harrison, Faye V. 1995. The Persistent Power of "Race" in the Cultural and Political Economy of Racism. Annual Review of Anthropology 24:47–74.

Hartigan, John, Jr. 1997. Establishing the Fact of Whiteness. American Anthropologist 99:495–505.

Hewitt, Roger. 1986. White Talk Black Talk, Inter-Racial Friendship and Communication among Adolescents. Cambridge: Cambridge University Press.

Hill, Jane H. 1993a. Hasta La Vista, Baby: Anglo Spanish in the American Southwest. Critique of Anthropology 13:145–176.

———. 1993b. Is it Really "No Problemo"? In SALSA I: Proceedings of the First Annual Symposium about Language and Society—Austin. Robin Queen and Rusty Barrett, eds. Texas Linguistic Forum 33:1–12.

———. 1995. Mock Spanish: A Site for the Indexical Reproduction of Racism in American English. Electronic document. University of Chicago Lang-cult Site. http://www.cs.uchicago.edu/discussions/l-c.

Hirschfeld, Lawrence A. 1996. Race in the Making. Cambridge, MA: MIT Press/Bradford Books.

Hymes, Dell H. 1973. Language and Speech: On the Origins and Foundations of Inequality among Speakers. *In* Language as a Human Problem. Einar Haugen and Morton Bloomfield, eds. Pp. 45–72. New York: W. W. Norton and Co.

Kulick, Don. 1993. Language Shift and Cultural Reproduction. Cambridge: Cambridge University Press.

Labov, William. 1972. Language in the Inner City. Philadelphia: University of Pennsylvania Press.

Lippi-Green, Rosina. 1997. English with an Accent: Language, Ideology, and Discrimination in the United States. London: Routledge.

Matsuda, Mari J., Charles R. Lawrence III, Richard Delgado, and Kimberlé Williams Crenshaw, eds. 1993. Words that Wound: Critical Race Theory, Assaultive Speech, and the First Amendment. Boulder, CO: Westview Press.

McMillan, Terry. 1996. How Stella Got Her Groove Back. New York: Viking.

Morgan, Marcyliena. 1994. The African-American Speech Community: Reality and Sociolinguists. *In* Language and the Social Construction of Identity in Creole Situations. Marcyliena Morgan, ed. Pp. 121–150. Los Angeles: UCLA Center for Afro-American Studies.

Morrison, Toni. 1992. Playing in the Dark: Witness and the Literary Imagination. Cambridge, MA: Harvard University Press.

Noriega, Chon. 1997. Citizen Chicano: The Trials and Titillations of Ethnicity in the American Cinema, 1935–1962. *In* Latin Looks. Clara E. Rodríguez, ed. Pp. 85–103. Boulder, CO: Westview.

Ochs, Elinor. 1990. Indexicality and Socialization. *In* Cultural Psychology. James Stigler, Richard A. Shweder, and Gilbert Herdt, eds. Pp. 287–308. Cambridge: Cambridge University Press.

Omi, Michael, and Howard Winant. 1994. Racial Formation in the United States. 2nd edition. New York: Routledge.

Page, Helán E., and Brooke Thomas. 1994. White Public Space and the Construction of White Privilege in U.S. Health Care: Fresh Concepts and a New Model of Analysis. Medical Anthropology Quarterly 8:109–116.

Peñalosa, Fernando. 1980. Chicano Sociolinguistics. Rowley, MA: Newbury House Press.

Rampton, Ben. 1995. Crossing: Language and Ethnicity among Adolescents. London: Longman.

Rodríguez, Clara E. 1997. The Silver Screen: Stories and Stereotypes. *In* Latin Looks. Clara E. Rodríguez, ed. Pp. 73–79. Boulder, CO: Westview Press.

Rubin, D. L. 1992. Nonlanguage Factors Affecting Undergraduates' Judgments of Nonnative English-Speaking Teaching Assistants. Research in Higher Education 33:511–531.

Scott, James C. 1985. Weapons of the Weak: Everyday Forms of Peasant Resistance. New Haven, CT: Yale University Press.

———. 1990. Domination and the Arts of Resistance: Hidden Transcripts. New Haven CT: Yale University Press.

Silverstein, Michael. 1987. Monoglot "Standard" in America. Working Papers of the Center for Psychosocial Studies, 13. Chicago: Center for Psychosocial Studies.

Smedley, Audrey. 1993. Race in North America: Origin and Evolution of a Worldview. Boulder, CO: Westview Press.

Smitherman, Geneva. 1994. Black Talk: Words and Phrases from the Hood to the Amen Corner. Boston: Houghton Mifflin Company.

Smitherman-Donaldson, Geneva. 1988. Discriminatory Discourse on Afro-American Speech. *In* Discourse and Discrimination. Geneva Smitherman-Donaldson and Teun van Dijk, eds. Pp. 144–175. Detroit: Wayne State University Press.

Urban, Greg. 1991. A Discourse-Centered Approach to Culture. Austin: University of Texas Press.

Urciuoli, Bonnie. 1996. Exposing Prejudice: Puerto Rican Experiences of Language, Race, and Class. Boulder, CO: Westview Press.

Van Dijk, Teun A. 1993. Elite Discourse and Racism. Newbury Park, CA: Sage Publications.

Vélex-Ibáñez, Carlos G. 1996. Border Visions: Mexican Cultures of the Southwest United States. Tucson: University of Arizona Press.

Williams, Brackette. 1989. A Class Act: Anthropology and the Race to Nation across Ethnic Terrain. Annual Review of Anthropology 18:401–444.

Williams, Raymond. 1977. Marxism and Literature. Oxford University Press.

Winant, Howard. 1994. Racial Conditions: Politics, Theory, Comparisons. Minneapolis: University of Minnesota Press.

Woolard, Kathryn A. 1988. Codeswitching and Comedy in Catalonia. *In* Codeswitching: Anthropological and Sociolinguistic Perspectives. Monica Heller, ed. Pp. 53–70. Berlin: Mouton de Gruyter.

———. 1989. Sentences in the Language Prison. American Ethnologist 16:268–278.

Woolard, Kathryn A., and Bambi Schieffelin. 1994. Language Ideology. Annual Review of Anthropology 23:55–82.

- 11 -

Euskara

The "Terror" of a European Minority Language

Jacqueline Urla

Jacqueline Urla is associate professor of anthropology and director of the Modern European Studies Program at the University of Massachusetts Amherst. Her research specializes in gender and sexuality, youth and popular culture, resistance, visual anthropology, and language politics. She has done long-term ethnographic research on the Basque language revival movement, examining such issues as language standardization, youth community media projects, music, and the political uses of language censuses.

I arrived in San Sebastián, known locally as Donostia, a beautiful port city in the Basque Country, on 13 February [2003] of this year, ready to begin a period of research leave and to finish a book on Basque language politics. As an anthropologist, I have been coming here for over 20 years, chronicling the impressive efforts Basques have made to preserve the autochthonous language, Euskara, reputedly the oldest living language in Europe. I thought my book was almost written, but the events I have witnessed in the last few months have indicated to me that the anthropology of political dissent in Europe is called on to enter a new and profoundly disturbing era.

When I arrived, I was stunned at how tense and polarized the political climate was. The armed militant organization, Euskadi ta Askatasuna (Basqueland and Freedom, commonly known as ETA) had just assassinated a municipal councillor belonging to the ruling right-wing political party, Partido Popular. The anti-ETA organization Basta Ya! (That's enough!) was holding a conference in San Sebastián; police and bodyguards were everywhere, and inflamed declarations by political leaders filled the media. Within a week, the Basque-language revival movement and Basque civil society as a whole would themselves become the victims of a devastating and unprecedented police action. On 20 February Judge Juan del Olmo, of the Audiencia Nacional, the Spanish supreme court, ordered the closing of the Basque-language newspaper *Egunkaria* and the arrest of 10 members of its administrative board for preseumed collaboration with ETA. Approximately 300 officers of the Guardia Civil, the Spanish military police, were deployed in this operation that began at 1:00 a.m. and involved dragging the suspects out of their beds—in several cases breaking down their doors—and dispatching them to Madrid to be held incommunicado for five days. Meanwhile, the paper's offices were boarded up, its website and online archive were shut down, and all computers were confiscated. Basque people woke up the next day to find no paper at their kiosks and a drama that eerily recalled the days of Franco.

It is difficult to convey to AT's international readership the significance of this event and the sense of outrage that it provoked. Tens of thousands of people—many of whom had not been to a demonstration in years—filled the streets in massive and indignant protest on the Saturday two days after the arrests. To understand the despair felt at the closing of *Egunkaria*, one has to have a sense of the independent voice it offered in a fractured political landscape. It published communiqués from ETA, but also interviews with some of Basque nationalism's most virulent critics, including Fernando Savater, founding member of Basta Ya!. But most importantly, it published in

Basque. It was coming to be a major influence on the development of the language. On its pages, readers could find the words and style that reflected the urban and cosmopolitan life Basques had been taught to see as accessible only through other languages—Spanish, French, English.

To the many protesters, the closing of the Basque newspaper signifies an entirely new level of intervention, namely an extension of the anti-ETA clampdown into the domain of media and culture, and effectively the criminalization of Euskara itself. In retrospect, this turn of events is not surprising. Eliminating ETA, rather than resolving the conflict, has been a primary goal of the government of Prime Minister Jose Maria Aznar since its election. At the end of 1990s, while the various parties to the Northern Ireland conflict, including the British and Irish governments, were talking dialogue and disarmament, the Spanish government chose an increasingly nonnegotiable tough-guy approach to political violence. There was a brief period of optimism in the summer of 1998 when ETA declared a truce. But when this broke down in 1999, events took a turn for the worse. ETA extended death threats to virtually all political parties (Partido Popular and Partido Socialista, PSOE) as well as some well-known professors and journalists. Demand for bodyguards skyrocketed, and with each new assassination and arrest the general atmosphere became more and more tense and fearful.

The summer of 1997, however, was an especially significant time. Taking advantage of the public outrage over ETA's cruel assassination of town councillor Miguel Angel Blanco that summer, Spain's anti-terrorist campaign began a new strategy of pursuing not only ETA members, but what has been called the social and financial "infrastructure" upon which the organization was seen to depend. Under the leadership of the Spanish judge Baltasar Garzón, the government initiated a series of raids and arrests against radical nationalist youth and civil disobedience associations, the Basque nationalist newspaper *Egin*, and a grassroots adult language and literacy organization popularly known as AEK (Alfabetatze Euskalduntze Koordinakundea). In most, if not all, of these cases, the charges of belonging to ETA have yet to be proven—a fact rarely reported outside the Basque Country. As long as those arrested were youths and radicals, public protest was subdued. But now that the roundup has extended to respected intellectuals and scholars, the abuses inherent in the anti-terrorist campaign can no longer be ignored. The definition of terrorism has become so expansive and slippery that it has come to include even those who worked non-violently for Basque national independence or simply a distinctively Basque historical perspective and cultural identity. The charges

made against those arrested are widely regarded as ludicrous by virtually everyone familiar with Basque culture. To futher the outrage, when *Egunkaria's* editor, Martxelo Otamendi, and some others were released on bail, they stated that the police had beaten and humiliated them, and subjected them to torture methods such as the *"bolsa,"* an asphyxiation technique. The Spanish government has refused to investigate the charges and has indicted the victims on yet another charge of making false accusations against the public security forces. Amnesty International has called on the Spanish government to investigate the accusations, but its plea appears to have fallen on deaf ears.

As Begoña Aretxaga (2000) noted, over the years the Spanish state has eerily adopted the tactics and even the look of terrorism, attacking, like ETA, those whose speech they find objectionable. It is highly unlikely that these repressive tactics will resolve the conflict. But what they do accomplish is the effective criminalization of what has up to now been considered a legitimate dissenting political ideology. Disturbingly, the Aznar government's view and actions have gone largely unquestioned in Spain and the rest of Europe. The Catalans have supported the Basque-language media organizations, but the powerful liberal European newspapers—publications like *Le Monde* and *Libération*, no friends of Aznar to be sure, and strong defenders of freedom of press—have not uttered a word. Shortly after the arrests, the war against Iraq began and Spain became the site of some of the largest anti-war demonstrations in all of Europe. Yet the ferocity with which Spaniards, like other Europeans, rejected warmongering rhetoric did not translate into a new sensibility towards the Basques. In a recent national music awards ceremony, for example, rock musician Fermín Muguruza, recipient of an award for the best Basque song, chose to speak out against the closing of *Egunkaria*, but was virtually booed and whistled off the stage by artists and celebrities who spent the rest of the ceremony denouncing the war. There is a chilling dissonance and irony here.

The closing of the Basque newspaper is a wound that strikes deep into the heart of many Basque people for many reasons. *Egunkaria* was a project in culture-building, in language-building, and yes, in nation-building, if by that we understand, following Benedict Anderson, that the creation of a public sphere is a central dimension of imagining community. By its very existence, it disrupted notions of Spanish nationhood by articulating a distinct voice and topography of identity. Has this now become a crime? It remains to be seen. Three of the arrested remain in jail as of this writing, without option of bail and with no evidence yet produced against them. In a somber editorial, the acclaimed novelist Bernardo Atxaga wrote of how the sight of his friend Joan Mari Torrealdai, distinguished writer on Basque culture and director of the *Egunkaria* editorial board, hunched over and surrounded by police signalled to him the end of one era and the beginning of another. When, as under Judge Garzón's leadership, the object of sanction is no longer terrorism *per se*, but its *infrastructure*, a crucial and worrying boundary has been crossed. Following the closure of the newspaper, the Spanish government achieved another of its goals: banning the radical, left-wing nationalist party Batasuna and getting it placed on the United States' official list of terrorist organizations. First the closing of a newspaper, now the banning of a political party—all this at a time when negotiations in Northern Ireland have been giving an example of another possible path to peace.

The question we anthropologists and public intellectuals need to ask ourselves is how we can guard against and challenge abuses of this kind in the post-9/11 world. Now that terrorism is perceived to be everywhere, we can expect to see an increase in this kind of repressive action in the years to come outside of the regions historically associated with "ethnic strife." The work of Joseba Zulaika and William Douglass (1996) provides one example of how academics can use their training to expose the rhetoric of reductionisms, conflations and spectral associations that characterize the discourse on "terrorism." In addition, anthropologists with grounded knowledge of political and social conflicts need to speak out and offer insight into the experiences and perspectives of those people who are all too easily demonized. As the case of *Egunkaria* illustrates, the taint of terrorism can lead to whole societies and linguistic communities losing basic civil liberties, including that of speaking and writing in their own language about the political communities they aspire to create.

I should point out that the determined citizens of the Basque Country have not been easily silenced. They have raised money and organized to set up a new Basque-language newspaper, *Berria*, which began publishing in June. But theirs is a lesson that extends well beyond the Basque Country, showing how the war on terror can become a convenient cover for the repression of internal dissidents. In the United States, the newly created Department of "Homeland Security" is invested with as yet unknown powers for the surveillance and pursuit of terrorism. Censorship is on the rise, as is the erosion of basic civil liberties: As we look ahead in this new, post-9/11 era, we will need to be vigilant and critical in our examination of the impact of the discourses and tactics of "security," and the pall of suspicion and insecurity this casts not only over minority languages and cultures and their promoters, but over potential dissidents everywhere.

REFERENCES

Aretxaga, Begoña. 2000. Playing terrorist: Ghastly plots and the ghostly state. *Journal of Spanish Cultural Studies* 1(1):43–58.

Zulaika, Joseba and Douglass, William. 1996. *Terror and taboo: The follies, fables and faces of terrorism.* London and New York: Routledge.

CHAPTER

IV

SOCIALIZATION

How Do People Learn and Experience Their Culture?

IN 1925, A YOUNG anthropology graduate student named Margaret Mead set out for Samoa to test a theory widely accepted at the time: that the biological changes of adolescence could not be accomplished without a great deal of psychological and social stress. Three years later, she published a book that was to become a classic, *Coming of Age in Samoa: A Study of Primitive Youth for Western Civilization.* Although the work later was subjected to some criticism, it is generally credited as establishing culture and personality as a specialty within **cultural anthropology.** Originally concerned with the effects of different child-rearing practices on the formation of adult personalities, the specialty has since developed into the broader one of **psychological anthropology.**

Since culture is learned, rather than biologically inherited, it is only natural that anthropologists should have become interested in *how* culture is learned. Initially, anthropologists thought that the different ways in which societies raised their children ought to result in adult personalities that differed distinctively from one culture to another. Perhaps the most famous (and extreme) statement of this point of view was Ruth Benedict's attempt to categorize whole cultures in terms of certain personality types. In her best-selling book *Patterns of Culture,* published in 1934 (and still in print), she characterized the Kwakiutl Indians of North America's northwest coast as "Dionysian," the Zuni Indians of the southwestern United States as "Apollonian," and the Dobuans of New Guinea as "Paranoid." Aside from the fact that her labels reflect the biases of Western culture, what she overlooked was the range of variation to be seen in any culture. For example, to characterize the Zuni as "Apollonian," she focused on their distrust of individualism and rejection of excess and disruptive psychological states while ignoring such seemingly "Dionysian" practices as sword swallowing and walking over hot coals.

What we now know is that no culture can be characterized in terms of a single personality structure exhibited by all or even a majority of adults. Because each individual is born with a particular genetic potential, and because no two individuals have *precisely* the same childhood experiences, as adults their personalities show considerable variability. Nevertheless, it is true that each culture does hold up a particular ideal toward which individuals should aspire. That these ideals may vary considerably from one culture to another is illustrated in the article by Amparo B. Ojeda. In her own Filipino culture, children are raised to be obedient to authority, to respect elders, to recognize the primacy of the family over the individual, and to strive for harmony and "togetherness." This **dependence training,** which promotes compliance and dependence on one's domestic group, contrasts with the **independence training** that is stressed in the United States, which promotes independent, assertive behavior on the part of children, as they are taught to be self-reliant and able to look out for their own self-interests. Needless to say, it is difficult for people raised in one way not to regard the other as somehow "bizarre."

Greatly though a society may value one set of ideals in the abstract, its practices do not always live up to the ideal. In the United States, for example, in spite of the great value set on personal independence, authority often takes precedence in particular situations, as illustrated by Alma Gottlieb's paper on childbirth. Although pregnancy and childbirth are not diseases, in the United States, people generally behave as if they were. In pregnancy an emphasis is often placed on suffering, and, just as sickness prevents one's full participation in ordinary daily activities, so are pregnancy and motherhood often considered incompatible with everyday work. In fact, expectant mothers are expected to submit to the authority of the medical establishment and do as they are told.

Moreover, the birth itself typically takes place in a hospital, an institution otherwise dedicated to treatment of people who have genuine illnesses. As Gottlieb shows, pregnancy and childbirth do not have to be seen as "sickness," nor does a mother-to-be necessarily have to assume the status of "passive victim," even in the United States. To assert her independence in the face of medical authority, however, is no easy thing.

Given their interest in the relationship between childhood experiences and personality, it was inevitable that anthropologists early on would develop an interest in **psychoanalytic theory,** with its emphasis on the importance of early childhood experiences and the social significance of "manias." One problem with psychoana-lytic theory, however, is that its concepts have often been based in assumptions of Western culture. Another is that, clinical studies to the contrary notwithstanding, psychoanalytic theorists have done little systematic testing through recourse to cross-cultural data. Many of the early culture and personality studies carried out by anthropologists were explicit tests of psychoanalytic theory. As Emily Martin argues in her essay "Flexible Survivors," what it means to be a person is always contingent on cultural and historical specificities. New "manias" are always emerging, related to changes in capitalism and science. The important question is which kind of "manias" are socially acceptable, even celebrated, and which are sanctioned and disciplined.

FOCUS QUESTIONS

As you read these selections, consider these questions:

✦ Can you think of any examples from your childhood that show how you learned basic cultural values or perspectives? What role did your parents play in this? Friends? Institutions?

✦ Do you think different cultures create different personality types? Why or why not?

✦ Can you think of any situations in which a personality type goes "against the grain" of the dominant culture? What happens to that individual?

✦ Can you think of any examples in which a society's conception of people as individuals ("how people work") relates to its social institutions ("how society works")?

REFERENCES

Benedict, Ruth. 1934. *Patterns of Culture.* Boston: Houghton Mifflin.

Mead, Margaret. 1928. *Coming of Age in Samoa: A Psychological Study of Primitive Youth for Western Civilization.* New York: Morrow.

Growing Up American
Doing the Right Thing

Amparo B. Ojeda

Amparo B. Ojeda is a native Filipina who is now an associate professor of anthropology and linguistics at Loyola University, Chicago. After completing an MA in English literature from the University of San Carlos in the Philippines, she came to the United States for an MS in linguistics from Georgetown University. Her PhD in anthropology was earned at San Carlos in 1975. She has carried out fieldwork in the Philippines and in Chicago, where she is studying the adjustment of Filipino immigrants in the metropolitan area.

The earliest and closest encounter that I had with Americans, and a most superficial brush with their culture, goes back to my childhood days when an American family moved into our neighborhood. I used to gaze at the children, a boy and a girl, who were always neatly dressed and who would romp around their fenced front yard. Not knowing their names, I, together with a cousin, used to call them, *"Hoy, Americano!"* (Hey, American!), and they themselves soon learned to greet us with "Hey Filipino!" That was as far as our "acquaintance" went because in no time at all they were gone, and we never again heard about them.

That brief encounter aroused my curiosity. I wanted to know something more about the "Americanos." What kind of people are they? What food do they eat? Where is America? As time passed, I learned about America—about the people and about some aspects of their lifestyle—but my knowledge was indirect. The opportunity to experience the world of the "Americano" directly was long in coming, and when it did I was gripped with a sense of ambivalence. How would I fare in a strange and foreign land with an unfamiliar culture? That was how I finally found myself on the plane that would bring me on the first leg of my cultural sojourn to Hawaii.

Excited as I was, I could hear my heart thumping, and apprehension came over me. Suddenly, the thought hit me: I have journeyed far from home, away from the comforts and familiarity of my culture. You see, in this trip, my first outside of my homeland, I did not come as an anthropologist to do fieldwork. I came as a graduate student to study linguistics. Seven years later I would be an anthropologist. But I am getting ahead of myself.

My host family during my brief two-week stay in Honolulu was waiting at the airport. The whole family was there! The children's beaming faces and the family's warm and gracious greetings gave me a sense of assurance that everything was going to be fine. "There's nothing to it," we Fulbright scholars were reassured during a briefing on aspects of adjustment to American life and culture. So there I was in Hawaii, the first leg of my cultural sojourn (I stayed in the Midwest for another four weeks of orientation, before proceeding east to do graduate work), equipped with a theoretical survival kit designed and guaranteed to work. I would later discover that there were discrepancies between the ideal procedures and techniques and day-to-day behavior.

The differences between my culture and American culture became evident in the first few hours after my arrival. On our way out of the air terminal, the children began to fuss: "I'm hungry," "I'm tired," "I'm thirsty," "I want to go to the bathroom!" Over the whining and fidgeting of the children, my hosts and I tried to carry on a conversation but to no avail. Amazingly, despite the constant interruptions, the adults displayed considerable tolerance and patience. No voice was raised, nor harsh words spoken. I vividly recall how, as children, we were reminded never to interrupt while adults were talking, and to avoid annoying behavior, especially when in the

"Growing Up American: Doing the Right Thing" by Amparo B. Ojeda from *Distant Mirrors: America as a Foreign Culture,* edited by Philip R. DeVita and James D. Armstrong. Belmont, CA: Wadsworth, 1993. Reprinted by permission of Amparo B. Ojeda.

company of adults, whether these people were kin, friends, or strangers.

We left the main highway, drove on a country road, and eventually parked by a Howard Johnson restaurant. The children did not need any bidding at all. They ran inside the restaurant in search of a table for us. I was fascinated by their quite independent and assertive behavior (more of this, later). I had originally been feeling dizzy and drowsy from the long plane ride, but I wasn't anymore. My "cultural" curiosity was aroused by the children's youthful showmanship, or so I thought. As soon as we were all seated, a young man came to hand us menus. The children made their own choices. Not feeling hungry at all, but wanting to show appreciation, I settled for a cup of soup. When the food finally came, I was completely shocked by the portions each child had. I wondered if they could eat it all. Just as I feared, they left their portions only partially eaten. What a waste, I thought. I remembered one of my father's gems of thought: "Take only what you can eat, and make sure to eat the last morsel on your plate." I must confess that I felt very bad looking at mounds of uneaten food. How can so much food be wasted? Why were children allowed to order their food themselves instead of Mom and Dad doing it for them? Was it a part of independence training? Or were Mom and Dad simply indulgent of their children's wants? I did not have any answers, but I surmised that it wasn't going to be easy understanding the American way. Neither would it be easy accepting or adjusting to American customs. I realized later that my difficulty was brought about by my cultural bias and naïveté. Given the situation, I expected my own familiar behavioral/cultural response. For instance, in the Philippines, as well as in many other Asian countries, children are rarely allowed, if at all, to "do their own thing" without the consent of their parents. Consultation with parents, older siblings, aunts and uncles, or grandparents is always sought. In America, I found out that from an early age, a person is encouraged to be independent, to make up his or her mind, and to stand up for his or her rights. Individualism is encouraged among the American youth, whereas among Asians, including Filipinos, group unity, togetherness, and harmony are valued.

Values such as obedience to authority (older people are vested with authority) and respect for elders are seriously observed and practiced. The young address their elders using terms of respect. Among the Tagalog, the particle *po* (sir, ma'am) or *opo* (yes sir, yes ma'am) is always used. Not to do so is considered rude. Children do not call anybody older by their first names. This deference to age contrasts sharply with the American notions of egalitarianism and informality.

American children, I observe, are allowed to call older people by their first names. I recall two interesting incidents, amusing now but definitely bothersome then. The first incident took place in the university cafeteria. To foster collegiality among the faculty and graduate students, professors and students usually ate lunch together. During one of these occasions, I heard a student greet a teacher, "Hey Bob! That was a tough exam! You really gave us a hard time, buddy!" I was stunned. I couldn't believe what I heard. All I could say to myself was, "My God! How bold and disrespectful!"

Not long afterward, I found myself in a similar scenario. This time, I was with some very young children of new acquaintances. They called to say hello and to ask if I could spend the weekend with the family. At their place, I met more people, young and not so young. Uninhibited, the children took the liberty of introducing me to everybody. Each child who played the role of "introducer" would address each person by his or her first name. No titles such as "Mr.," "Mrs." or "Miss" were used; we were simply introduced as "Steve, this is Amparo" and "Amparo, this is Paula." Because I was not acquainted with the sociolinguistics of American communicative style, this took me quite by surprise. I was not prepared for the reality of being addressed as the children's equal. In my own experience, it took me some time to muster courage before I could call my senior colleagues by their first names.

A somewhat similar occurrence happened many years later. I had impressed on my little girl the proper and polite way to address older people, that is, for her always to say "Mr." or "Mrs." before mentioning their first names and family names. I used to prod and remind her often that it was the right thing to do. Imagine my surprise and embarrassment when one day I heard her greet our next-door neighbor saying "Hi Martha!" I asked her why she greeted her that way. She readily answered, "Mommy, Martha told me not to call her Mrs. _____, just Martha!" What could I say? Since then, she was always called Martha, but I had qualms each time I heard my daughter greet her. In the Philippines, older people, regardless of their status in life, whether they are relatives or strangers, are always addressed using respectful terms such as *mang* (title for an elderly man), *iyo* (abbreviated variant for *tiyo*, or uncle, a title for a male relative but also used to address someone who is elderly), *aling* (respectful title for an older or elderly woman), and *manang* (a regional variant for *aling*). However, one gets used to doing things in a certain way after a while. So did I! After all, isn't that what adaptation is all about? But my cultural adventure or misadventure did not end here. This was only a prelude.

I was introduced into American culture from the periphery, which provided me with only a glimpse of the people's lifestyle, their passing moods and attitudes, and their values and ideas. I did not have the time, effort, or desire to take a long hard look at the cultural environment

In most regions of rural Africa, such questions would simply make no sense: it is inconceivable for adults—both men and women—*not* to work while surrounded by little people. For one thing, children in such settings represent the future—and to some extent, even the present—labor force that will ultimately be trained to take over an adult's job. Even though most work days in the industrial West are arranged quite differently, due to a host of factors—including the ascendancy of the nuclear family, the rise of the public school system, and the extreme division of labor brought on by industrialization—nevertheless, I was very much affected by what I saw in Bengland. Without romanticizing our Beng hosts and hostesses, without ignoring the extraordinary hardships attendant on their grinding poverty, I still felt I had much to learn from the integrated nature of their daily working lives.

Soon, another part of Africa asserted itself: the urge to relish rather than conceal my impending motherhood. After only a month, my waistline swelled with the slightest hint of a bulge. In celebration, I bought my first installment of maternity clothes. At a party, someone teased me: "It's only a month, and already you're wearing baggy shirts? Come on, you're just showing off!"

"No, I really *have* gained a couple of pounds!" I protested, laughing through my embarrassment—for of course my friend was right: my pride in my pregnancy, rarely spoken of in the U.S., was unmasked. Indeed I came to hear the phrase *You're showing,* repeated more frequently as my pregnancy advanced, as ambivalent, with more than a touch of implicit criticism. In American women's lives, other bodily items that "show" are not meant to: bra straps, slip hems should all be concealed with great effort. If my pregnancy were "showing," was I supposed to somehow tuck it in like underwear?

Luckily my pregnancy was easy—no morning sickness; no lower back pain; not even any weird, midnight food cravings; and if anything, I felt more energetic than usual. But anytime I revealed my fortunate situation—especially to my pregnant friends, and to fellow classmates in a pregnancy aerobics class (and, later, a pregnancy yoga class)—I instantly regretted it, for in their awkward and resentful silences, I found that the discourse of pregnancy in my home country is a discourse of suffering: Eve all over again. Having nothing to lament meant I lacked anything legitimate to discuss.

During this time, my husband and I tried to imagine how our lives—which we had shared as a couple for some thirteen years—would be transformed by becoming a trio. It was hard, for we simply didn't see children very often. While lacking the formal age grades for which, for example, many East African societies are known, American society nevertheless segregates people by age quite systematically. Not only do children inhabit different social spaces from those populated by adults, but children are separated from each other by increments of only a year once they join nursery school or day care settings. I did begin to notice little people in public places where I'd previously overlooked them: restaurants, malls, waiting rooms. But their new visibility only confirmed what I'd already noticed after our first return from Côte d'Ivoire: even when older people and children inhabit the same places, they rarely intermix. Instead, parents spend much public time disciplining their young sons and daughters to conform to adults' rules of politeness—"Don't shout!" "Don't run!" "Don't play!" were incantations I now heard regularly from exasperated mothers and fathers in public places clearly never intended for children. Why were there no indoor playgrounds in shopping centers, airports, office buildings, I wondered. Why were children almost never invited to the parties we attended, whether among academic colleagues, at artists' get-togethers, or fund-raising soirées for our favorite political candidates?

At the same time, I started observing how the things we use daily are manufactured with adults in mind, causing children no end of frustration as they endeavor, often unsuccessfully, to negotiate oversized spaces and giant objects. Parenting books warned that before our baby started to crawl, we must get down on hands and knees and look up to imagine our rooms from the infant's perspective, anticipating heavy chairs that might be toppled, hot stove burners that might scald a child's curious fingers, food processor blades that could prove lethal. I compared all this with the lives of Beng village children. Their days are hardly idyllic, but a high, unreachable world isn't one of their troubles. Hand-carved, low wooden stools allow even young toddlers to sit comfortably, feet touching the ground; women cook over campfires, allowing the youngest children to have a peek in the pot without fear of overturning it, or to help stir the sauce without having to balance precariously on a shaky stepladder; small mortars and pestles permit even two-year-old girls to begin to master the techniques of pounding that are essential to Beng cuisine. I was discouraged to think that already, my culture's architects had planned for our as-yet-unborn child's exclusion.

Pondering all this led me to push away my fears and consider my inevitable labor. Because I'd encountered in Africa a medical system that emphasized personal rather than technological connections, I was tempted to have the birth at home. Curious about such alternatives, I turned to Brigitte Jordan's path-breaking book on childbirth in several cultural settings (1983), midwife Ina Mae Gaskin's journeys into the spiritually uplifting aspects of birth (1978), Robbie Davis-Floyd's developing work offering devastating critiques of American hospital births (e.g., Davis-Floyd 1988), as well as my own field notes—for I had also seen and heard much of births while conducting fieldwork among the Beng.[3]

The more I considered the anthropological documentation of childbirth in other places, the more I thought that, in theory, there was much to recommend a home birth. I'd feel at home in our bedroom, could assume any delivery position I found comfortable—maybe lean back into the comforting arms of a birthing companion, as I'd seen my laboring Beng friend Amenan do; listen to soothing music; even moan and scream without embarrassment if the pain gripped me. And I could avoid all those machines that measure a laboring woman's bodily events while ignoring her state of mind (Davis-Floyd 1990, 1992; Jordan 1992). In short, I could relocate birth from an event defined by sickness and danger to one that sees it as an intensely emotional experience that might encompass anything from terror to joy.

While Western medical textbooks monotonously emphasized all that could go wrong during childbirth, other books and articles suggested that a normal birth could easily avoid the sophisticated technologies that modern medicine has compulsively developed. Moreover, some researchers were now documenting how, ironically, a reliance on the sophisticated Western technology of fetal monitors actually increases the likelihood of medical complications, including unnecessary Caesarean-section deliveries.[4] And the more I heard friends' and colleagues' hospital birth stories, so often marked by frustration and disappointment, the more convinced I was that, except in unusual circumstances, Western hospitals are a poor choice for the ritual moment of birth.

I thought back to Lévi-Strauss's marvellous article (1963) on Cuna Indian childbirth chants, which I'd long admired for its poetics. If a Cuna woman of Panama does not make sufficient progress during labor, he wrote, an attending shaman undertakes a dangerous, invisible journey to the underworld of the woman's uterus that is inhabited by Muu, the goddess that formed the fetus. Travelling "Muu's way," Lévi-Strauss wrote, the shaman recounts to the woman how he is embarking on "a complicated itinerary that is a true mythical anatomy, corresponding less to the real structure of the genital organs than to a kind of emotional geography" (p. 195). Along the way, the shaman battles the powerful uterine forces that stole the woman's soul, and he emerges to inform the woman that her soul has been regained; then, the delivery can proceed normally. If a Cuna woman could have her blocked labor eased by such a song, I thought, surely there should be some other, equally noninvasive means to help birthing Western women in trouble.

Still, I was bothered that Lévi-Strauss failed to mention one important detail: what proportion of difficult labors were indeed helped by this mythic treatment? Conversely, what was the rate of death during childbirth for Cuna women? Confronting this frightening question forced me to consider the tragedy of my Beng friend, Kouakou Nguessan. One day her husband had come to fetch me while I was working in another village, imploring me to return immediately to drive Nguessan to the dispensary in town, almost an hour away, because she was having difficulty in her labor. Of course I agreed, and soon Philip and I found ourselves racing down the gravelly road, Nguessan screaming her agony in the back seat. Perhaps the bumps in the road helped advance the baby down the birth canal, or perhaps the massaging that the midwife's assistant and I soon administered to Nguessan helped, but whatever it was, Nguessan delivered her baby soon after settling into the delivery bed. Still, the tiny infant was clearly in distress—she emerged green, and she wasn't breathing. Only extraordinary efforts by the midwife's assistant revived the child.

At the time, I felt blessed to have been able to help in this event. But a few years later, I learned that the little girl born from that fateful ride, frail ever since her traumatic birth, had died, and Nguessan herself, once again pregnant and having no access to medical screening or transportation to town, had died in labor.

Nguessan's tragedy warned me not to romanticize: childbirth could indeed be dangerous. I thought back to the slow, mournful dance I'd seen of pregnant Beng women commemorating the loss of one of their compatriots in childbirth (Gottlieb & Graham 1993:150–151), and I recalled that the Asante, among others, liken childbirth to war (Rattray 1927:58–59).

I decided I'd better do some preliminary research into home birth in my own part of the world. As long as women considered at medical risk for a safe delivery were excluded, a home birth with a trained midwife presiding seemed to be at least as safe as a hospital birth. Yet I was surprised to find that 99% of all childbirths in the U.S. take place in hospitals, and of these, over 97% have doctors presiding.[5] One of the major explanations for this situation, I discovered to my dismay, is that most states in the U.S., including Illinois, place midwifery and/or home birth on an extremely shaky legal footing, and have done so since 1920 (Whitby 1986:992–93; Wolfson 1985–86:958–67). In many situations involving a birth at home, if the newborn or birthing mother were to have a medical complication, the attending health specialist—whether midwife or doctor—could be held legally liable—up to and including imprisonment.[6] Thus in most states, including ours, there was no publicly available listing of midwives willing to attend home deliveries—one discovered their identities through hush-hush conversations conducted amidst oaths to keep the names secret. Through the pregnant women's rumor mill, I even heard of a recent home birth tragedy not far away, with the attending midwife having been sued by the state. It was a sobering story.

With not a little ambivalence—and anger that we lived in a country whose leaders could think to make giving birth at home a crime—Philip and I decided to have a hospital birth . . . but only if we could together recast the hospital's vision of birth to our own. After all, having seen a very different system in action, we no longer accepted our culture's constructed set of knowledge as having a *unique* claim to authority. We vowed to compel the medical system operating in our local hospital to accommodate our vision of birth. But would it be possible?

We took tours of our town's two maternity wards. The nurse in the first hospital showed off their new intensive care unit, new fetal monitors, ordinary beds that "broke down" to classic delivery beds complete with metal stirrups, and an array of miscellaneous items of shiny steel—in this post-industrial age, such items of raw industry are oddly enough still meant to convey authority. When I asked about the possibility of a less technological birth, the nurse remembered that they owned one birthing chair; she rummaged around until she found the key to a closet in which the molded plastic chair was stored. But when questioned further, our tour guide admitted that not many women use the chair because the semi-circle cut out of the seat was too narrow, causing larger-headed newborns to get stuck. It was depressing to see how industrial production only executes its high standards for efficiency when the goals of the product in question are in synch with those of the culture (Davis-Floyd 1990, 1992). And why hadn't anyone in the hospital—say, a maintenance crew member—remedied the deficiency with a low-tech solution such as a saw? Perhaps that wouldn't be deemed appropriate—too imprecise for such a precise subject as medical supplies.

In the second hospital, the head nurse also showed off their latest equipment, concluding her sales pitch by saying that it's a competitive environment, and her hospital wanted to do everything possible to accommodate the desires of the birthing couple. I wasn't enthralled with her capitalist's analogy of birthing-mother-as-consumer, but at least this nurse seemed a bit more flexible than the other. Still, my husband and I began to realize that we would have to make serious efforts to shape our birth experience—otherwise the normal routines of the technology-crazy hospital would certainly take over.

We needed someone at the delivery who could serve as an advocate, fend off the monitor-wielding nurses, challenge the authority of this medical system's medically unnecessary practices. I thought back to the Beng women's births I knew about. They'd always had one kinswoman to lean against, another to catch the baby, another to dispose of the placenta. How nice it would be if I had female relatives who could do this for me. But with my family aging, fragmented and dispersed even more than the usual American middle-class family, this wasn't possible. Who could I find in their place?

Happily, my identities as professor and as mother-to-be converged when I stumbled upon the idea of asking a then-graduate student named Laura O'Banion to serve as my birth attendant. Laura was completing both an M.D. degree and a brilliant master's thesis in anthropology on American midwives: she was perfect. Together, we devised a strategy: once my labor started, I'd stay home as long as possible. The less time spent in the hospital, we reasoned, the less I'd have to reject the nurses' inevitable offers of drugs or fetal monitors.

My waters broke late at night. I looked in the mirror: after tomorrow, that image would forever be that of a mother.

"I can't believe it, we're about to become parents!" Philip said. "Do you think we should pack the suitcase?"

"Not yet," I said. "I'm afraid if we pack now, I'll be tempted to leave for the hospital right away. But I wonder how far along I am. Maybe we should call Laura."

After sleepily grilling me on the timing of my contractions, Laura said I was still in early labor, but she graciously offered to spend the rest of the night in our guest room. Philip and Laura caught a few hours of sleep; massaging my cramping stomach, changing positions every few minutes to settle into the quickening contractions, I was too pained—and too excited—to do anything but lie, wide-eyed, in our dark bedroom, trying to recall the signs that Indian women use to predict the sex of the unborn baby, or the name of the herb that Beng women use to hasten the delivery.

At the first light of dawn, feeling the need for company and sympathy, I roused Philip. He obligingly massaged my back and shoulders, but those contractions had already surpassed the intensity of menstrual cramps and his kneading hands could do nothing to soften them. When Laura woke, Philip said he thought he'd take a short break to mail a note he'd dashed off to his literary agent early last night—in which he'd written that this would be his last letter before becoming a father.

"How far is the mailbox?" Laura asked.

"Oh, just two blocks," Philip said, "I'll be back in a few minutes."

Laura turned to me. "Why don't you go along? You know, walking helps move the baby down the birth canal."

"Hmmm—okay," I said, eager for anything to distract me from those relentless pangs.

It was 7 a.m.—the hour of joggers and dog-walkers. Those two blocks possessed me, a Turnerian time out of time. I stared at the few people we passed, at once proud and, unfairly, a little annoyed that they'd stumbled on my private ritual; they stared back, no doubt appalled at the strangely un-American spectacle of a woman obviously in labor walking the streets. All I need, I thought, is to reach that mailbox—if only we were there, if only I could drop that letter down the chute, if only this baby would be born. Under an especially glistening turquoise sky, those pains so gripped me that I stopped to rest against every tree; finally, an hour later, we were back home.

We found Laura cheerfully making breakfast. The medical books had advised me to fast; the midwifery books had advised me to eat. I didn't know what Beng women ate or didn't eat during the hours of their labors. In any case, I wasn't the remotest bit hungry, so I watched disinterestedly as Philip sipped our usual Pep-Up milkshake and Laura cooked herself some eggs.

I paced and moaned through our house as the contractions intensified and I thought of my laboring Beng friend Amenan, sitting on her dirt floor, leaning back slightly against her mother, legs outstretched, forehead sweating, saying to me in her fine French, *"Je souffre un peu"* ("I'm suffering a little"). Her stoicism shamed me.

The day dragged on, the space between contractions shortened, but still Laura charted only the barest progress. I began to despair. Maybe I needed a fast, bumpy ride on a dirt road, like the one we'd offered Nguessan. Or was there something seriously wrong?

"How much longer?" I pestered Laura. If only she could throw cowry shells as the Beng diviner Lamine might, to see the outcome of this day. I thought of Nguessan suffering in her bedroom, I thought of Amenan's mother getting stuck in her labor for several hours before her sorcerer cousin who was bewitching her was finally killed by a falling tree sent by an avenging Earth, I thought of Amenan herself almost dying during her delivery of her son Kouadio, I thought of Nguessan finally succumbing during her next delivery. Had my Beng friends ever lost hope, imagining they might never emerge from their ordeals, or were they always confident that their bodies would cooperate, that the witches could be kept at bay, that a healthy baby would eventually be born?

Finally it was time to assemble our baggage for the hospital. A Beng woman would have laughed at all the gear we toted. But if I wasn't having a baby at home, I wanted to bring large chunks of home with me: we carried reading pillows covered with our own patterned sheets; some tapes and a boom box to play them on; and a pair of birthing stools now covered with a pink and white tie-dyed *pagne* from Côte d'Ivoire—a piece of another home.

Once inside the hospital, my first act was to decline a wheelchair ride to the maternity ward; my second was to decline the offer of an ugly hospital gown—no need to play the invalid, or to occupy an anonymous predecessor's birthing garments. Indeed, the theme of my hospital stay became refusal: No, I didn't want to be hooked up to machines, or take painkillers, or lie down in bed. The head nurse was unnerved by my constant rebuffs—after all, she was offering the best of what both her training and her years of experience had assured her was the right way to have a baby; who was I, a first-time not-yet-mother, to turn down all these nuggets of wisdom? Hoping for female solidarity, I was disappointed to find myself at odds with the woman before me, each of us sure of what we believed, eager for the other to convert. At least the young nurse-in-training was solicitous, especially when her boss left the room. Still open-minded, she hadn't yet settled on a single version of authoritative knowledge. How many births would she attend before that would happen?

My most serious resistance occurred when it was time to prepare for the delivery. The head nurse was adamant about resituating me in bed; in too much pain to have an opinion about anything any longer, I was about to capitulate when Laura gently suggested I try the birthing stool. Lacking the will to disagree with anyone, I limped over to the stool, which Laura set up in front of a love seat, so that Philip could sit behind me and massage my shoulders. The head nurse panicked: it seemed the baby would be born onto the carpeted floor, and what about all the germs? The idea was intolerable. I was too distracted to mention that during the delivery of my Beng friend Amenan that I had partially witnessed, not only was the baby born onto the floor, but it was a dirt floor at that—no attempts at sterility anywhere—and the baby didn't seem to suffer any from the experience. But to accommodate the nurse, Laura suggested they spread one of the many available clean sheets on the carpet in front of me. The nurse gazed at us as if we were insane, but Laura—an M.D.-in-training, after all—prevailed.

Soon my obstetrician entered the room. He took one look at the odd scene in front of him and exchanged glances with the head nurse—who, according to Philip, gave him an imploring look that Philip interpreted to mean: "At last! Can you please take charge and get this crazy woman up on the bed?" But my doctor, showing himself to be even more aberrant than I'd dared hope, walked casually over to the rocking chair in the corner and proceeded to watch as Philip and Laura helped me through my contractions.

Like the nurse in a birth story documented by Brigitte Jordan (1992), Laura discouraged me from pushing when I had the urge to do so. But unlike that nurse, Laura explained the reason and offered me a choice: if I decided I could accept an episiotomy, she'd perform it and I could push now. Otherwise, I could try to resist the urge to push—she'd help me breathe in a way that accomplished this—and wait until I was effaced enough to avoid a tear or an episiotomy. Offered these two alternatives, I mustered my last bit of strength and chose to delay the delivery. And so Laura and my husband puffed and massaged, the young apprentice nurse cooled my sweaty forehead with ice, the doctor rocked and smiled, and the birth proceeded—very slowly.

Looking back on that day over seven years ago, when our son Nathaniel emerged triumphantly—from a dark wet world to a new, and very different one—I am struck by the concatenation of power relations that encased both me and my medical team. As a laboring woman, I should have been structurally placed in the position of disempowered and frustrated patient, as Robbie Davis-Floyd and Emily Martin, among others, have so painfully demonstrated is usually the case in American hospitals. Yet lucky enough to have had an advanced education, I was motivated to read widely on the subject of birth and so was able to offer Facts and Case Studies to my doctor ahead of time in order to present my own case for a birthing style that was certainly unusual by American hospital standards. In other words, I confronted my physician with a different system of authority, but one that was nonetheless premised on evidence to which he could relate. Impoverished women in inner-city hospitals do not partake of this conceptual system, and thus are not so graciously accorded the opportunities I was of recasting their birthing experiences (Martin 1987). Yet even most middle-class American women who yearn for a "natural" birth emerge from their hospital experiences disappointed at least to some degree, and often profoundly so (Davis-Floyd 1992).

But perhaps this should not be surprising, for as Brigitte Jordan has written, authoritative knowledge is just that. Like religion, it takes on an "aura of factuality," as Geertz would put it (1973:90), to make it seem "really real" (ibid.:112). My own modest and partial resistance to the locally dominant system of medicine was inspired by my exposure to a radically different system of authoritative knowledge in another part of the world—another system of "really real" that focuses on the laboring woman rather than machines as a reliable source of information; that accommodates the woman in a familiar setting surrounded by kinswomen and neighbors; and that looks to disturbances in social and spiritual relations as causes of obstructed deliveries.

In these days of widespread American discontent with the medical system in general and the practices of modern obstetrics in particular, one wonders what it will take to change our all-too-often unsatisfying system of hospital births in any significant and meaningful way. In recent years, feminists in a variety of disciplines have begun to contemplate the roles, responsibilities and choices open to them, and to speculate on the impact, both practical and theoretical, of feminism on their own disciplinary practices, and on the newfound sense of taking seriously the personal, the domestic and the emotional (e.g., Harding 1987). In accord with this move, it may be that feminist anthropologists can seize a unique opportunity to contribute to the growing debate on the particular subject of childbirth by sharing their invaluable comparative perspectives. After all, the past two decades or so have seen an upsurge of the "practice" approach to social life which, among other things, offers the possibility of *multiple layers* of knowledge forms even within so-called simple societies (Ortner 1984). Perhaps the next wave of anthropological analyses of childbirth experiences cross-culturally will provide us with the intellectual tools to consider a significant slice of the multiplicity of knowledge forms available in post-industrial, Western society (cf. Davis-Floyd & Sargent, [1997]). Anthropologists, I suggest, have something important to contribute to this growing international conversation.

ACKNOWLEDGMENTS

This article was first presented as a paper at the Annual Meeting of the American Anthropological Association (San Francisco, 2–6 December 1992). I am grateful to Robbie Davis-Floyd for the invitation to join the session, and to Rayna Rapp for her illuminating comments.

I acknowledge with gratitude the following agencies that have supported my research into Beng society over the years: the Social Science Research Council; the Wenner-Gren Foundation for Anthropological Research; the National Endowment for the Humanities; the Woodrow Wilson Foundation; the American Association of University Women; the United States Information Agency; and the Center for African Studies, the Research Board, International Programs and Studies, and the Department of Anthropology, all at the University of Illinois at Urbana-Champaign.

On a more personal note, I am grateful to those Beng women, some of whom are mentioned in this essay, who allowed me to participate in their lives as mothers, farmers, and everything else; and to Laura O'Banion, Larry Lane, my husband Philip Graham, and our son Nathaniel Gottlieb-Graham, who each in their own way contributed to my own birth experience.

I dedicate this essay to the memory of Kouakou Nguessan.

NOTES

1. I borrow the notion of "authoritative knowledge" from Brigitte Jordan, who developed it with reference to technical and business settings (e.g., Jordan 1992), but it has proven quite useful in the anthropological analysis of childbirth (Davis-Floyd & Sargent, [1997]).

2. For a depressing array of U.S. obstetricians who have either ignored or actively challenged the observations and insights of their female patients, see, for example, Martin (1987) and Davis-Floyd (1992).

3. For descriptions of some Beng childbirths, see Gottlieb and Graham (1993).

4. For references to critiques of hospital-based birth techniques, see Whitby (1986:987, N. 10; 988, N. 15; 995, N. 70; 1025).

5. These statistics are derived from: U.S. Dept. of Health and Human Services (1987): Sect. 2, Table 2-1, p. 1, and Sect. 2, Table 2-2, p. 87.

6. For a listing of such cases nationally, see Wolfson (1985–86: 929–33); on the problematic legal status of midwifery in Illinois as of 1986, see Whitby (1986:999, N. 89).

REFERENCES

Davis-Floyd, Robbie. 1988. "Birth as an American Rite of Passage." In *Childbirth in America: Anthropological Perspectives,* ed. by Karen Michaelson. South Hadley, MA: Bergin & Garvey.

Davis-Floyd, Robbie. 1990. "The Technological Model of Birth." In *Annual Editions 89/90,* ed. by Elvio Angeloni. Guilford, CT: Dushkin.

Davis-Floyd, Robbie. 1992. *Birth as an American Rite of Passage.* Berkeley: University of California Press.

Davis-Floyd, Robbie, & Carolyn Sargent (Eds.). [1997]. *Childbirth and Authoritative Knowledge: Cross-cultural Perspectives.* Berkeley: University of California Press.

Gaskin, Ina Mae. 1978. *Spiritual Midwifery* (rev. ed.). Summertown, TN: The Book Publishing Company.

Geertz, Clifford. 1973 [1966]. "Religion as a Cultural System." In *The Interpretation of Cultures.* New York: Basic Books.

Gottlieb, Alma, & Philip Graham. 1993. *Parallel Worlds: An Anthropologist and a Writer Encounter Africa.* New York: Crown/Random House.

Harding, Sandra (Ed.). 1987. *Feminism and Methodology: Social Science Issues.* Bloomington: Indiana University Press.

Jordan, Brigitte. 1983. *Childbirth in Four Cultures* (3d ed.). Montreal: Eden Press.

Jordan, Brigitte. 1992. *Technology and Social Interaction: Notes on the Achievement of Authoritative Knowledge in Complex Settings.* Palo Alto, CA: Institute for Research on Learning. Unpublished ms.

Lévi-Strauss, Claude. 1963 [1949]. "The Effectiveness of Symbols." In *Structural Anthropology,* trans. by Claire Jacobson & Brooke Grundfest Schoepf. New York: Basic Books. (Original: *L'anthropologie structurale,* Paris, 1958).

Martin, Emily. 1987. *The Woman in the Body.* Boston: Beacon Press.

Ortner, Sherry. 1984. "Theory in Anthropology since the Sixties." *Comparative Studies in Society and History* Vol. 26, No. 1:126–66.

Rattray, R. S. 1927. *Religion and Art in Ashanti.* Oxford: Clarendon Press.

U.S. Department of Health and Human Services. 1987. *Vital Statistics of the United States, 1986. I: Natality.* Washington, DC: U.S. Dept. of Health and Human Services.

Whitby, Kathleen M. 1986. "Choice in Childbirth: Parents, Lay Midwives, and Statutory Regulation." *St. Louis University Law Journal* Vol. 30, No. 3:985–1028.

Wolfson, Charles. 1985–86. "Midwives and Home Birth: Social, Medical, and Legal Perspectives." *Hastings Law Journal* Vol. 37:909–76.

Flexible Survivors

Emily Martin

Emily Martin received her PhD in 1971 from Cornell University. Her initial research focused on ritual and politics in China (The Cult of the Dead in a Chinese Village, Chinese Ritual and Politics). *In recent years, she has focused on the historical and ethnographic study of science, medicine, and work, resulting in the books* The Woman in the Body: A Cultural Analysis of Reproduction *and* Flexible Bodies: Tracking Immunity in American Culture from the Days of Polio to the Age of AIDS. *She is a professor of anthropology at Princeton University.*

There are signs that mental conditions involving constant shifting in time and space, emotionally or cognitively—namely manic-depression and Attention Deficit Hyperactivity Disorder (ADHD)—have been undergoing a dramatic revision in American middle-class culture, from being simply dreaded liabilities, to being especially valuable assets that can potentially enhance one's life in the particular social and cultural world now inhabited by many middle-class Americans. To understand this change, I turn to the social concept of the "person," long a mainstay of anthropological analysis, a concept that is central to the earth-shaking changes many middle-class Americans are now undergoing. As Marcel Mauss made clear, what it means to be a person is deeply embedded in its social context, and highly various over time and space. A particular kind of person, the "individual," seen as owner of himself and his capacities, rather than as part of a social whole, has been prominent in Euro-American culture since 17th century liberal democratic theory.

THE DISCIPLINED PERSON

What it means to be owner of oneself, however, has involved very different degrees of control over the boundaries around the self in different historical periods. In the first half of the 20th century, for example, a premium was placed on discipline and control because of the require-

ments of work in industrial settings. The moving assembly line with its dedicated machinery was oriented to efficient mass production and, eventually, to profitable mass marketing. Corporate organizations were hierarchically structured bureaucracies whose ideal employee was passive, stable, consistent and acquiescent. The stress was placed on stability and solidity: Sherry Turkle observes that, "earlier in this century we spoke of identity as 'forged.' The metaphor of iron-like solidity captured the central value of a core identity" (1995).

THE ADAPTING PERSON

Since the 1970s, rending political and economic changes have begun to make themselves felt in the US. These changes have important implications for understanding contemporary concepts of the person. The internationalization of labor and markets, growth of the service economy and abrupt decline of redistributive state services have meant that the fabric of the world has become substantially rewoven. In the US, concentration of wealth and income at the top of the social order is more extreme than at any time since the depression, while poverty has grown correspondingly deeper. Successive waves of downsizing have picked off, in addition to the disadvantaged, significant numbers of people from occupations and classes unaccustomed to a dramatic fall in their prospects and standard of living. The imperative to become the kind of worker who can succeed in extremely competitive circumstances has intensified, while the stakes at risk for failing have greatly increased. As one sign of the unforgiving nature of the way increased competition is experienced, references to the "survival of the fittest" have increased exponentially in the news media every year since 1970.

The factory, which has often served as both a laboratory and a conceptual guide for understandings of human behavior, is also changing. The hierarchical factory of the mass production era, with its worker drones, is being replaced (mostly in the elite sectors of the global economy) with new forms: machines that process information and communicate with self-managed workers, who are in turn invested with greater decision making powers. Corporations are flattening hierarchies, downsizing bureaucracies, enhancing their corporate "culture," becoming nimble and agile to survive in rapidly changing markets. They seek organization in the form of fluid networks of alliances, a highly decoupled and dynamic form with great organizational flexibility. Workers and managers are "evolving" with the aid of self-study, corporate training sessions and an insistence on self-management when they are lucky enough to be employed inside a corporation, and then aggressive entrepreneurialism during the frequent periods they are now expected to spend outside. The individual is still owner of himself, but the stakes have risen and they are ever changing.

Given this procession of dramatic changes on many social, cultural, economic and political fronts, what concepts of the ideal person will be enabled by and enable these conditions? As the mechanical regularity avidly sought from the assembly line worker gives way to the ideal of a flexible and constantly changing worker, what will happen to the value previously placed on stability and conformity? Some answers to these questions have been suggested by Jacques Donzelot. What Donzelot calls "changing people's attitudes toward change" has made its appearance in France through the *legal* right of every worker to "continued retraining": people are thought to *require* an active attitude toward change, from childhood to old age. The individual consists in potentials to be realized and capacities to be fulfilled. Since these potentials and capacities take their shape in relation to the requirements of a continuously changing environment, their content—and even the terms in which they are understood—are also in constant change. The person is made up of a flexible collection of assets; a person is proprietor of his or her self as a portfolio. In the 1990s, there has been an increase in "home based work," based on telecommuting or the "You, Inc" phenomenon. People with the resources to do so think of themselves as mini-corporations, collections of assets that one must continually invest in, nurture, manage and develop. There is a sense, as the nation-state yields its prominence in world affairs to the multi-national corporation, that the individual moves from being a citizen, oriented to the interests of the nation, to being a mini-corporation, oriented primarily to its interests in global flows of capital.

MANIC STYLE

It might seem a long reach from workers in constant change to pathological mental conditions involving constant change, such as manic-depression or ADHD. But an anthropological concept of culture encourages us to look across cultural domains as well as within for meaningful comparisons and contrasts. The liability associated with these mental conditions has often been linked with creativity and perhaps for this reason, they are becoming highly fascinating in business, educational and popular culture. For example, ADHD has begun to appear as an asset in books for business entrepreneurs; manic-depression, frequently loosely associated with tormented geniuses, has begun to occupy the best-seller list in the form of memoirs and novels. Personal confessions by the rich and famous, especially in Hollywood and on Wall Street, who reveal their ADHD or manic-depression, abound. Both conditions have recently been flooding the press, best-seller list and airwaves.

In popular culture, representations of these two conditions appear to be in the process of redefinition from being a disability to a strength. In each case, the qualities praised fit perfectly with the kind of emergent self Donzelot described: always changing, scanning the environment, dealing with all aspects of the interface with the outside in creative and innovative ways. For ADHD, praise for the continuously changing person can be seen in the books, newsletter and Internet organizing of Thomas Hartmann. One of Hartmann's books on ADHD, *Focus Your Energy: Hunting for Success in Business with Attention Deficit Disorder* (1993), is usually shelved with the business books. A hunter's "strong sense of individualism, high creativity, and the ability to be a self-starter" make such a person far more able to start his or her own company than non-ADHD people (p 56).

In manic-depression, redefinition from a liability to an asset can be seen in the writings of Kay Jamison, who with her recent memoir, *An Unquiet Mind* (1995), "came out" as manic-depressive herself. In her writing Jamison takes great pains to describe the positive aspects of manic-depression alongside the negative: echoing the good traits of ADHD, manic-depression entails a "finely wired, exquisitely alert nervous system." These thought processes are characteristic of the manic phase: "fluency, rapidity, and flexibility of thought on the one hand, and the ability to combine ideas or categories of thought to form new and original connections on the other . . . rapid, fluid, and divergent thought" (p 105). Beyond these examples, what might be called "manic (or hyper) style," a style that draws on the "mania" in manic-depression and the "hyper" in ADHD, is being attributed to exuberant and creative people in a wide range of fields, from Jim Carey and Ted Turner, to "Seinfeld's" Cosmo Kramer and Virgin Inc's Richard Branson. A Rockport ad features monologuist Spaulding Gray sprawled in a chair, hair standing out electrically, claiming "I'm comfortable with my madness." In the popular imagination, Ted Turner is particularly insistently associated with manic-depression, even though, according to The Turner Broadcasting System, Inc, he has never been diagnosed with such a condition. Nonetheless, Ted Turner appears in the *Saturday Evening Post* in a pair of photographs showing different sides of organic genius. In one he is a business man, lecturing soberly behind a podium with a corporate logo, and in the other he is a wild-eyed ship's captain, fiercely gripping the wheel at the helm of his yacht. The caption notes that Turner's competition should be warned: he has stopped taking his Lithium (and so might well be about to launch a manic—and profitable—new venture).

Perhaps one reason for the mistaken attribution of manic-depression to Ted Turner is that the qualities of the "manic style" fit well with the kind of person frequently described as highly desirable in corporate America: always adapting by scanning the environment for signs of change, flying from one thing to another, while pushing the limits of everything, and doing it all with an intense level of energy focused totally on the future. An ad campaign currently running for Unisys captures both the multiple tasking and the unremitting energy of the manic style in its images of a computer monitor–headed man who designs a system to report election results for the city of Rome while he golfs, another who fixes problems with Amadeus, the leading global travel reservation system, while ski jumping, and a woman who reduces the time needed to process welfare applications in California while lounging companionably on the couch with her husband. In each case, the Unisys employees have a computer monitor instead of a head, and on the screen flash changing scenes related to the work that preoccupies them while they are golfing, skiing or relaxing.

Are certain forms of irrationality, which are in fact an intrinsic part of daily life in late capitalism, emerging into visibility in popular culture? Perhaps the irrationality of the market (and what you have to do and be to succeed in it) is being more openly recognized and "rational choice" is being seen as dependent on "irrational" impulses and desires. In the popular imagination, Ted Turner has excess both as capitalist and yacht captain (depicted

and experienced as talent), which contains signs of apprehension: greater knowledge of what capitalism entails and greater fear of what it may require of people. The caption under the two photographs of Turner in the *Saturday Evening Post* ends on a fearful note: Turner's father, like Hemingway's, committed suicide—raising the implied question: will Turner end his life by suicide as did Hemingway? A new analysis of the workings of late capital is even called *One World Ready or Not: The Manic Logic of Global Capitalism* (William Greider, 1997). It is filled with references to "manic capital," oscillating with depression, and the calamitous consequences of both. The recent drop and rapid recovery of the stock exchange in October 1997 inspired a flurry of domain crossing remarks, in newspapers, such as: "If Wall Street were a person we'd think he was mentally ill."

It remains to be seen what kinds of distinctions will be made as the discursive space around the categories "mania and hyper-activity" open up. Will two kinds of mania and hyper-activity emerge: a "good" kind, harnessed by Robin Williams, Ted Turner and the successful workers at Unisys; and a "bad" kind to which most sufferers of manic-depression and ADHD are relegated? In this case, even if the value given to the "irrational" experience of mania and hyper-activity increases, validity would yet again be denied to the mentally ill, and in fact their stigmatization might increase. After all, if they have, by definition, the ability to be manic or hyper-active, and if that ability comes to be seen as an important key to success, then why are they so often social and economic failures? Or, will the presence of a "manic style" in popular culture reduce the stigmatization of manic-depression and ADHD? Now that he is an acknowledged manic-depressive, could Robin Williams' performances as a standup comic contribute to moving the categories mania and hyper-activity away from being wholly stigmatized, because his performances give pleasure, bring rewards and in their inventiveness, produce forms of value? Do his funny, madcap antics present mania and hyper-activity to us as valuable intellectual property?

An anthropological approach to understanding changes in the concept of the kind of person one must become to survive as we approach the millennium promises to shed light on changes in the valuation of mental conditions and even rationality itself. In turn, these insights may well have implications for our understanding of ideals being sought in many cultural domains, such as models of childhood development, education, work, personality and intelligence.

ECOLOGY

How Do People Relate to Nature?

WITH IMAGES OF famine and drought very much at the forefront of the media, the question of how people subsist takes on an added urgency. The United States has ritually affirmed the importance of this issue by proclaiming World Food Day on October 16 and Earth Day on April 22. **Subsistence** at its most elementary entails the production of food and other necessities, requiring the application of human labor, techniques, and technologies to natural resources. In sum, it is a process in which energy is expended to produce energy in different forms. The way in which a society produces energy—preeminently in the form of food, but including fire, animal power, and fossil fuels—obviously has a significant impact on the way people live, since neither features of the environment nor technology can be changed limitlessly. At the same time, the environment will obviously impose constraints upon the type of subsistence people will practice.

Most anthropology textbooks discuss the different types of subsistence practices globally; they will thus not be discussed in depth here. Typically they include:

1. Foraging
   a. Pedestrian
   b. Equestrian
   c. Aquatic
2. Swidden/slash-and-burn/extensive agriculture
3. Pastoralism
   a. Transhumance
   b. Nomadism
4. Intensive/large-scale agriculture

There is much debate about which of these systems are the most "energy-efficient," an issue dramatized during the regular "energy crises" the United States undergoes. It is important to emphasize that these are generally ideal types and that in reality most people, especially in the current world society, practice a mix of these strategies. Even the most isolated **hunter-gatherers** like the Bushmen have been part of the world system for a long time. Much of the ivory used in the manufacture of pianos that were prized possessions in many late-nineteenth-century households in the United States, for example, was supplied by the Bushmen of Southwest Africa (Gordon 1992). The important point is that in the current world situation more and more people are locked together in ties of interdependence. While the official reason for the 2003 U.S. invasion of Iraq has changed over and over again, most people realized that the need for Middle Eastern oil was a major unspoken factor. We have also begun to realize how one form of subsistence—for example, large-scale agriculture as practiced in the United States—can have an irreversible impact on people practicing, say, **foraging** in the Amazon, and vice versa. At the same time, these types of subsistence can interpenetrate or encapsulate each other. What, for example, is homelessness in the United States but a form of foraging? Or, for that matter, commercial fishing? These are in sharp contrast to some of the ideal types of subsistence where people had a larger degree of autonomy and were not so dependent upon other people. As people believe that they can produce energy and goods more cheaply by specialization, ties of interdependence increase. One can see this even in the case of a traditional people like the Gabbra, pastoral nomads of East Africa. Even in the absence of much specialization, the importance of redistribution of livestock for people's survival is indicative of their interdependence.

People like the Gabbra are often looked upon today with disapproval for their nomadic ways. In East Africa, postcolonial states see the Gabbra's disregard of political boundaries as a threat to their authority and so try to curtail their nomadism by encouraging more sedentary ways. **Development economists** regard their traditional ways as an inefficient method of raising livestock; to them, the rational approach is to drill wells to provide permanent water sources, permitting more livestock to be raised for sale, with less need to move around. The result of this combined impetus from politicians and economists to settle down is often massive environmental degradation, which leads to criticism from environmentalists, who all too often blame the nomads themselves for their plight. What they fail to recognize is that nomads supported themselves successfully for millennia without destroying their environment. The keys to their success were that they kept no more animals than were sufficient for their own needs and that they were able to move about as necessary so as not to overgraze any one place. Daniel Stiles's article on the Gabbra depicts a successful adaptation that is now threatened by outside interests.

Traditional economic development schemes are not the only pressures on indigenous peoples; large-scale nature conservation efforts are as well. As Marcus Colchester observes in his article, indigenous peoples have been facing the negative effects of nature conservation approaches based on the Western assumption that humans are separate from the natural world—leading to the displacement and marginalization of communities that live in, interact with, and rely on wilderness areas. But he also shows how the indigenous peoples are orga-

nizing to push for collective rights over their traditional homelands and forcing Western conservation organizations and activists to reorient their paradigms about how to save biological diversity.

A key element of any culture's subsistence activities and modes of adaptation is how people think about and symbolize their natural environment. In his article on how the Wola of the Papua New Guinea Highlands understand their natural world, Paul Sillitoe addresses a classic issue in sociocultural anthropology: classification systems. According to William Sturtevant, an anthropologist associated with the subfield of **ethnoscience** concerned with such things, the goal of studying classification systems (everything from color categories and kinship names to taxonomies of natural species) is to describe and understand "the 'conceptual models' with which a society operates" (Sturtevant 1964:100). In this article, Sillitoe argues that there are certain similarities between how Wola and the West categorize the elements of the natural world. But there is a crucial difference in that the Wola see categorization as a process of negotiation, which is related to the fact that in this oral society things are not written down and there are no authorities to adjudicate disputes over categorization. The Wola classification system therefore operates to facilitate discussion rather than provide certainty. Sillitoe raises an intriguing question: Is this at all similar to how we in the West understand the natural world?

FOCUS QUESTIONS

As you read these selections, consider these questions:

✦   Is cultural change always adaptive? In what circumstances might it not be adaptive?

✦   How do a culture's ideas about nature relate to how its members use it?

✦   Food production and eating are central to being human. Have you ever been in a situation in which the food you eat, and how you eat it, is profoundly different from eating practices in your own culture? How did you react? What did you learn regarding your own ideas about food?

✦   What impacts do you think increasing globalization and technology have on human–nature relations?

REFERENCES

Gordon, Robert J. 1992. *The Bushman Myth: The Making of a Namibian Underclass.* Boulder: Westview Press.

Sturtevant, William. 1964. "Studies in Ethnoscience." In *Transcultural Studies of Cognition,* edited by A. Romney and R. G. D'Andrade, 99–131. Washington, D.C.: American Anthropological Association.

– 15 –

Nomads on Notice

Daniel Stiles

Daniel Stiles received a PhD from the University of California at Berkeley for work on prehistoric cultures of eastern and southern Africa and is now a consultant to the United Nations Environmental Programme. He is also a research associate at the British Institute in East Africa. He first met the Gabbra in 1971 when working as a student archaeological assistant at Richard Leakey's research site on Lake Turkana. His current interest is in food foragers of Kenya, Madagascar, and India who are suppliers of forest products; his hope is to use this economic importance as a means for saving biological and cultural diversity.

Northern Kenya is a land of extremes, with wind-blasted volcanic wastes in the lowlands and lush tropical forests on isolated mountains. The territory is divided among several tribes that vigilantly defend their domains. The Gabbra pastoralists, who number about 35,000, cluster around the cracked, salt-encrusted mud flats of the Chalbi Desert and along the eastern shore of Lake Turkana. Because rainfall is sporadic and localized, water sources and vegetation are scattered and unpredictable. (Oases near the lake often provide fresh water, but the jade-colored lake itself is bitter with accumulated salts.) The Gabbra must move periodically, often splitting up their camps to take advantage of nature's meager offerings.

The keys to the Gabbra's survival are mobility, hard work, and cooperation. During their lives, married men go through various life stages, becoming at different times "political elders" and then "ritual elders." Along with those chosen for specific leadership roles, these elders control Gabbra life and also provide moral guidance.

The Gabbra separate their herds of camels, cattle, sheep, and goats by species, age, and whether or not they are giving milk. Milk is the traditional staple, followed by meat and then blood, but the Gabbra now commonly buy cornmeal through the sale of small livestock. They keep milk-giving animals at the main settlements (*ola*) and, to avoid overgrazing, send the dry ones and most males off to distant locations. Because of the danger of raiding by other tribes, young warriors usually run the satellite camps, called *fora*. The zones separating enemy tribes are sparsely inhabited.

One of the insecure zones is around Koobi Fora, paleontologist Richard Leakey's research site. In 1971, while I was there on my first trip to northern Kenya, a raiding party of a neighboring nomadic group, the Dassenech, came across the border from Ethiopia, sending the Gabbra running and scaring the wits out of the researchers and camp crew. The Dassenech had guns; the Gabbra didn't.

In a few hours, the Gabbra can pack a settlement, tents and all, on the backs of their camels and be on their way to an area where rain has fallen. The household effects are simple: aluminum cooking pots; wooden and woven fiber containers for storing milk, meat, and fat; bed poles and sleeping skins; and various ritual sticks that symbolize status (for a young man, a married man, a father, a married woman, an elder, and so on). Between 6:30 and 11:30 one morning, I observed four women in an area called Bubissa pack up their four families' skin tents, along with their pole frameworks and assorted contents, and load them onto the backs of groaning camels. The four households then set off on camels across the stony plains to go to Maikona, a two-day walk. A settlement may move up to ten times a year, depending on grazing conditions and security.

The Gabbra define four seasons, according to temperature and rainfall. Although conditions vary from year to year, generally the long, heavy rains come between late March and early June, followed by the cool dry season from June to September. Short rains arrive in October and last until early December, when the hot dry season sets in. During the dry periods, the Gabbra tend to live in small settlements grouped around permanent water sources, while in wetter times they occupy larger, more widely scattered settlements. When water becomes available in rain pools, for example, the otherwise dry Huri Hills become a favored pasture area. Three times a year, as many family members as possible, together with their livestock, gather at the *ola* for a *sorio*, a ceremony to bless the community and the livestock and to pray for rain and fertility.

Camels make up the bulk of the tribe's holdings, and without them the Gabbra could not live where they do. As beasts of burden, camels enable the Gabbra to move the *ola* rapidly to find fresh pasture after a cloudburst. Camels also transport water to the settlement, permitting an *ola* to be situated in good pasture as much as thirty miles from water. The Gabbra prefer to have female camels, with as many lactating ones as possible. In dry lands, camels provide much more milk than cattle do, lactating on average for at least a year after bearing a calf. A good camel can give more than two and a half gallons of milk a day during the rainy season and two to five quarts during the dry season. In contrast, a typical cow lactates only seven to nine months, giving two quarts of milk a day when pasture is lush and just a pint a day—and eventually none at all—during the dry times.

Camels also do less damage to the environment than other livestock. Their soft feet do not scuff up topsoil, causing it to blow or wash away, as hoofs do; and they feed on various types of vegetation, particularly leaves, so that the land does not lose the soil-conserving grass. Owing to the camel's relatively varied diet, its milk is higher in vitamin C and certain other nutrients than cattle milk.

Despite their sense of separate identity, the Gabbra are of mixed origins, in part derived from neighboring peoples. Arriving in the region in the late nineteenth century, mainly from Ethiopia and from farther east in Kenya, they took the land they now occupy from the Rendille and Samburu, who were squeezed to the south. They have since defended their territory successfully against invasions by the Turkana, who live west of Lake Turkana, and the Masai, who once occupied much of central and southern Kenya.

The Gabbra retain a reputation as fierce warriors. In greeting and prayer, however, they often use the word *nagaya*—"peace"—a cultural trait they share with Semitic peoples of western Asia, who are members of the same Afro-Asiatic language family. They particularly abhor strife within the tribe. I once witnessed two children, a boy and a girl, get into a fight. The boy hit the girl on the head with a rock and knocked her down. While I was treating her wound with antiseptic, several adults ran around seemingly in a panic. By the time I had finished and calmed the girl down, the parents had organized an expiation ceremony on the spot. They recited prayers and sacrificed a sheep offered by the boy's parents. I received a goatskin bracelet made from the sacrificed animal, signifying welcome and peace.

Water is critical for survival in the desert, but the Gabbra carefully avoid fighting among themselves over access to the few wells and water holes. At the height of the dry season, hundreds of thirsty camels, cattle, sheep, and goats may bellow for water and kick up clouds of dust around a well as their herders struggle to keep them at bay and await their allotted turn. The "father of dividing," selected by the political elders (and almost always one himself), schedules each herd by species and ownership. He must be a man of fairness and iron will.

A chain of six or eight men position themselves in the well on dug-out ledges, projecting rocks in the wall, or scaffolding and pass the traditional giraffeskin containers up and down. The wells are often called "singing wells" because the men keep up a rhythmic chant as they draw the water up by hand from a depth of as much as fifty feet. The animals drink from a trough of molded mud, which needs constant repair from the damage caused by their jostling.

One of the biggest problems the Gabbra face is fulfilling labor needs. Averaging the wet- and dry-season regimes, researchers have calculated that nine people must work nine hours a day, every day, to mind one family herd and take care of the various household chores. To find the necessary labor, the Gabbra draw on a network of kinship and other social ties to look after the subdivided herds at the *ola* and the outlying camel, cattle, and small livestock camps.

In doing censuses, I learned that many more people are attached to a household than mom, dad, and the kids. For example, Wario Guyo, his wife, Shanu, and their young daughter slept in their house, while Wario's two nephews and an unmarried brother-in-law slept behind a thorn-branch windbreak out by the camel corral. A man belonging to a lower-status subgroup, the Wata, not allowed by tradition to sleep in the *ola*, lived to the west in the shade of an acacia tree. These additional household members each had a different herd of Wario's to care for and were paid in kind by food and stock offspring. Away from the *ola*, which was located on the eastern margin of the Chalbi Desert, two of Wario's sons looked after a *fora* near Lake Turkana, and the third was in school at Mount Marsabit, about sixty miles away.

To discover how many animals people owned, I had to unravel various types of loans and ownership arrangements. One young married man, Dub Boru, explained that most of his animals still belonged to his father, and that he had received them as an advance on his inheritance. He also had three camels and several sheep and goats that his *abuya*, a special uncle, had given him on important occasions, such as his circumcision. Dub also managed several milk camels obtained on loan. In exchange for taking care of the animals, he was entitled to their milk and their offspring, but had to give all subsequent generations of animals to the owner. Counting all the animals at Dub's *ola* and out at the *fora*, I estimated that he controlled at least eight lactating camels, two lactating cows, ten other adult camels, seven camel calves, four other cattle, and about sixty sheep and goats (small livestock reproduce quickly and are often sold or slaughtered, so exact figures are hard to come by). These animals provided food for six adults and adolescents and eight children.

Dub also exchanged animals. When his second child was born, for example, he traded one of his transport camels for a lactating cow; and when he needed money for cloth for his wife and school fees for a sister's son, he traded a heifer camel for ten goats, which he then sold. (Gabbra do not sell camels directly for money, for they fear this would bring misfortune.) Even with these maneuverings, Dub's animals weren't always sufficient to feed his family, owing to fluctuations in milk supply. So he pooled his herd with that of his brother-in-law, who was in a similar situation. The combined herds provided a more reliable source of milk.

The right of personal ownership does not, in the Gabbra's view, permit a man to monopolize more animals than he and his dependents need for survival. Through loans and gifts, excess animals are redistributed to the needy, allowing the whole community to survive. The secular authority of political elders and the moral authority of ritual elders ensure that these mechanisms of social cooperation are respected. One old man, Guracha Galgallo, is famous for owning about one thousand camels and many cattle and small livestock. Yet he dresses as all other Gabbra do, lives in the same style house, and eats the same food as the poorest Gabbra (although probably more regularly). Most of his animals are out on loan to those who have need of milk or transport or a bull for mating. His reward is respect.

The redistribution of livestock maximizes their use for food, transport, and cash. When there is a real surplus of animals, more than needed to meet the food requirements for the community as a whole (a rare occurrence), they are sacrificed and consumed at special ceremonial occasions to thank Waqa, the supreme being. As a result, the burden placed on the fragile environment is kept to a minimum. In contrast, many cattle pastoralists with more restricted systems of redistribution accumulate great numbers of animals. While their herds serve as insurance against drought and other calamities, they can cause serious land degradation.

Because food is usually in short supply, the Gabbra store little, although they have the technology to do so. For example, milk is soured and made into a kind of yogurt that lasts for weeks. And pieces of meat, stored with fat in small woven or wooden containers, can keep for more than a year. With food resources fluctuating from season to season and year to year, a group must manage enough animals to survive the worst conditions. To get by, an average family of six needs about twenty-eight camels, including six to eight that are lactating, or the equivalent in other cattle. Unfortunately, in 1991 drought and an undiagnosed camel disease reduced the herds below this level.

When the Gabbra and other northern Kenya pastoralists experienced hard times in the past, they always managed to endure. But now they are receiving food relief, and foreign relief agencies and other Westerners are exerting great influence on them. Because of the scarcity of livestock—and deteriorating security due to the troubles in Somalia and Ethiopia—raiding has also become much more frequent. Some Gabbra have moved to refugee camps to escape armed bandits.

If the neighboring countries regain political stability, and if the rains return, the Gabbra's traditional life should improve. But the last time I visited Gabbra country, I was not encouraged. Outsiders—famine relief workers, development-aid workers, missionaries, teachers, and government officers—are telling the Gabbra that they are backward and primitive. They are urging some to move to settlements on nearby Mount Marsabit and learn how to grow crops. There they would join Ethiopian immigrants, mission-settled refugees, southern Kenyan traders and administrators, and others who are encroaching on a "protected" national park forest.

Most Gabbra I know are horrified at the thought of taking up cultivation. One man, a ritual elder named Elema Arbu, told me that becoming a farmer was equivalent to becoming an outcast. "Without livestock, how can I provide bride price for my sons? How can I pay my stock debts? How can I make *sorio* and other sacrifices? How can I give the stock gifts at my nephews' circumcisions? Without herds, how can I hold my head up?"

16

Contested Knowledge, Contingent Classification

Animals in the Highlands of Papua New Guinea

Paul Sillitoe

Paul Sillitoe is professor of anthropology at the University of Durham in England. He received his ScD from Cambridge and has qualifications in both agricultural science and anthropology. His research interests focus on tropical farming systems and indigenous natural resource management strategies. He specializes in development and social change, subsistence and technology, land use issues, human ecology, and ethnoscience. He has conducted extensive fieldwork in Papua New Guinea and is currently involved in projects in South Asia, researching local agricultural knowledge and development programs.

What sense can we make of disagreements among people in a society over how they identify or classify objects in their environment? The purpose of classification is to structure our understanding of the world, to codify and communicate intelligence. While we might assume some culturally authorized agreement about classification within any one system, the potential for disagreement also exists. The implications of such disagreement are not only intellectual, about the nature of human understanding, but also political, about whose knowledge counts. I argue here that the development, organization, and usage of classification systems may reflect structures and negotiations of social power. The way we each individually classify may express our social position and relations.

Taxonomic disagreements of considerable degree are found in New Guinea, a classic anthropological location for the study of stateless tribal polities. Here classification of things, such as animals, may be of a different order to that of Western science, being considerably more fluid. The taxonomic discrepancies that people countenance embarrass some cognitive schemes, questioning the extent that hierarchical notions of nested classes necessarily structure natural taxonomies, which some writers con-

sider a universal organizing principle (Atran 1990:47, 142; Berlin 1992:13, 19, 39; Brown 1984, 1986:1–2). I argue that we should not think disagreements unusual and aberrant, to be explained away. Some classification systems anticipate confusion and contention, with intriguing implications for our understanding of human cataloguing behavior.

Within ethnoscientific contexts, there is nothing new in pointing out that people may disagree when classifying natural phenomena (Ellen 1975; Ellen et al. 1976; Gal 1973; Gatewood 1983; Whitehead 1995a). We have sophisticated attempts to explain the source of disagreement—informant variability, different contexts, variation in cues, and imprecise methods (Berlin 1992: 199–231; Ellen 1993: 126–148). Writers comment on the methodological implications, such as the death of the omniscient informant (Boster 1986; Ellen 1979; Gardner 1976). To date, we have no accommodation of disagreements so prevalent in some stateless contexts that they question the very existence of taxonomies as culturally sanctioned arrangements of phenomena.

We see the dual issues of the nature of understanding and of whose knowledge counts in so-called indigenous knowledge research in development currently, in which ethnoscientific interests feature prominently as they inform peoples' management of their natural resources. One of the objectives of this work is to relate local knowledge and practices to scientific research,

"Contested Knowledge, Contingent Classification: Animals in the Highlands of Papua New Guinea" by Paul Sillitoe from *American Anthropologist*, December 2002, 104(4):1162–1171. Reprinted by permission of American Anthropological Association.

aiming to effect technological change and development (Sillitoe 1998). The apparent incompatibility of some of the premises that underpin these dissimilar knowledge systems, which may have quite different objectives, is thwarting the advance of any coherent methodology. The differences also acquire a sharp political edge: As the various stakeholders caught up in any development program struggle to make their voices heard, vociferous negotiation and conflicts becoming increasingly common in the context of contemporary participatory approaches to development.

The challenge from medical anthropology to the universality of biomedical diagnoses illustrates these dual intellectual and political dimensions, with some wishing to confront scientific medicine's assumption of authority. This "critical medical anthropology" (Singer and Baer 1995), a Marxist and postmodern mix, seeks to challenge the imposition of scientific medicine on populations around the world. It looks to combat the dismissing of local realities and practices, their denigration to the possible detriment of a person's well-being. It calls for resistance against biomedicine as an agent of capitalist hegemony. A parallel challenge has emerged in Europe and North America with disquiet over dehumanizing medical engineering and the failure of scientific medicine faced with conditions such as myalgic encephalomyelitis and multiple sclerosis. An upsurge of interest in alternative therapies marks this confrontation with "expert" knowledge. It is not only people living in tribal societies but also those living in nation states who confront scientific classifications and explanations; those living in nation states differ by struggling to institute alternative authorities instead of recognizing none. Furthermore, the evidence suggests that these challenges are far from dethroning establishment science, in part because of the entrenched power structures, which change relatively slowly short of disruptive revolution, and in part because of science's demonstrated intellectual power—heart transplant surgery like evolutionary theory is no mean achievement.

Tribally ordered societies give us a novel perspective on these issues. In promoting egalitarian social environments, they seek to contain the equation of knowledge with power. They consequently tolerate levels of taxonomic dissonance that scientific authorities find difficult to conceive. They take us back to basics in considering the purpose of classification.

TAXONOMIC FAMILIES

The montane rain forest of the Southern Highlands Province of Papua New Guinea, where Wola highlanders live, is home to an Australasian fauna. Common mammals include cuscuses and possums, together with tree kangaroos, several rodents (including giant rats), and the egg-laying echidna. Birds are numerous, varied, and colorful, some sensational, such as renowned birds of paradise and the flightless cassowary. The reptile and insect populations are also numerous and varied, and there are, according to local people, frightening forest-dwelling demon creatures, too.

The zoological taxonomy comprises six life-form categories or *sem* (families), which contain the majority of named animals: *sab* (large mammals), *honez* (small mammals), *sor* (birds), *jiya* (frogs), *wen* (fish), and *elelbiy* (insects and some reptiles). A few other animals stand on their own as unique "unaffiliated taxa," such as *burun* (pythons), *shaen* (dogs), *showmay* (pigs), and *tenol* (human beings).[1] The taxonomic level below these sem (family) life-forms is central to naming and classification (as in many folk systems, Berlin, 1992:60–64). It equates largely with the genus and species levels of scientific zoology and the *blackbird* or *dormouse* terms of common English. Some of these secondary taxa are further subdivided into tertiary categories.

The Wola use the word *sem*, or *family*, widely in classifying phenomena, including kin groups associated with local communities, and subdivisions of these, down to extended and nuclear families (Lederman 1986; Ryan 1961; Sillitoe 1979a). The use of the same terms for taxonomic classes intimates some possible correspondence. It suggests that people conceive of social groups and zoological taxa as analogous in some senses, animal classes organized hierarchically, one descending from another like local groups traced on genealogies. We might conclude, when they classify some animals, that the Wola think of them as comprising nesting series, in a manner similar to zoology. It has long been thought that these principles underpin folk taxonomy (Bulmer 1974b:94–95), and many ethnoscientific studies make use of them.

The idioms used both support and question the assumption, suggesting both hierarchical descentlike notions and horizontal network arrangements. When discussing sem kin groups, the Wola sometimes draw on the imagery of bananas and taro. They may liken the generations that comprise kin groups to *diyr kat* (hands of bananas), overlapping hierarchically down a mature bunch. They use the taro metaphor to distinguish agnates from others, referring to them as *mausha* (from *ma iysha*, "mother taro plant"), whereas others are *aysha* (like *ma pora*, "lateral cormels" that grow at random from a "parent plant") (Sillitoe 1983).

These people recognize that some animals are similar and on occasion group them together. There is perhaps a certain intellectual compulsion here, as there is to recognizing biological descent among humans. The natural world may to some extent oblige such arrangements; people cannot help but see similarities as they exist *out there* (Atran 1990:25–29; Berlin 1992: 53; Rosch 1975), but when viewed in an acephalous sociopolitical context, there is an impulse to compromise any incipient notion of hierarchy. Others have made the same point for New Guinea populations (see Glick 1964:275). The correlation between social arrangements and classificatory structures is inconsistent and equivocal. While the sem (family) concept signifies recognition of the biological inevitability of descent from one generation to another, symbolized in the banana-stem metaphor, the groups are not exclusive. Although highlanders talk in terms of patrifilial ideology, they accommodate extensive bilaterality in practice. In allowing for both, Wola behavior contributes to the vague definition of sem (family) groups, with a bilateral fudging of any descent structured genealogical hierarchy. Their contingent approach to classification declares inevitable opposition to hierarchy, an egalitarian order opposed to structures of domination. We have an attempt to render taxonomy more as a network of classes, variably constituted on occasion, akin to the social group as the taro cormel metaphor.

TAXONOMIC ANOMALIES

Several aspects of these highlanders' taxonomy are at odds with the notion of a hierarchy, as noted for some other folk natural histories (Bright and Bright 1965; Ellen 1993:216–234; Healey 1978–79; Hunn 1976; Hunn and French 1984; Randall 1976). Some animals have "one name only" and are assigned to neither higher- nor lower-level classes. Ethnographers have reported elsewhere such "unaffiliated taxa," as the ethnoscientific literature calls them (Atran 1990:37–40; Berlin 1992:171–181). The life-form status of such animals is open to debate among the Wola, who are unsure to which, if any, superordinate category they belong. If asked to ascribe bats to a sem (family) life-form class, some persons might opt for sab (large mammals), others for sor (birds), and yet others assert that they belong to no named sem, instead they are *imbiy na wiy* (lit., "name not have").[2] Similarly, pythons and other large reptiles, which, although similar in behavior and appearance, are not accommodated by the shallow taxonomic scheme.

Another contrast with scientific zoological taxonomy is the absence of any equivalent to the kingdom term *animal*, or in ethnoscientific parlance a *unique beginner*. There are many reports in the ethnoscientific literature of classification systems with no unique beginners (in New Guinea, see Bulmer 1970; Diamond 1966; Glick 1964:279). The nearest Wola equivalent to English *animals* is *acha*, which parallels the Pidgin term *abus*, glossed as *game*. It applies to edible fauna only, not all animals. The absence of an all-inclusive kingdomlike term signals a different approach to animal taxonomy, people not conceiving of all creatures collected together at the apex of the classification scheme. Its absence sits uncomfortably with assumptions about taxonomic hierarchies (Brown 1974) and is an anomaly regarding current ethnobiological paradigms (see Berlin 1992:190–195).

The Wola further contradict the tenets of scientific classification by giving the same name to two or more animals, which, although similar, they acknowledge are not identical. Others do likewise in New Guinea (e.g., the Seltaman [Whitehead 1995a:3, 14]). This is particularly noticeable with sor (birds), although some individuals may repeat names with any animal. Several secondary invertebrate taxa also include sundry genera and species, paralleling English folk classes like butterfly and spider. The Wola sometimes give two or more different creatures the same name because they commonly occur together in pairs, sometimes referring to them as "father" and "mother." They are sometimes a male and female of the same species, complying with standard zoological practice, which is intriguing with birds, as the Wola deny they can sex them. At other times they may refer to such animals, if there is a marked size difference between them, as "large" and "small."

Furthermore, there are some animals that have no genera-species-equivalent names at all. These creatures are the reverse of bats and pythons; they belong to a life-form but have no secondary or tertiary taxa names. The absence of names for some natural phenomena has long been noted in ethnobiology (Atran 1990:41–42). The Wola have no name for many invertebrates that occur in their region. When asked about them, they reply that they are *imbiy na wiy* (nameless) or *elelbiy sem* (round-and-round family). While the implications of such partial naming for the notion of taxonomy have not been fully faced, they have fueled a debate over the rationale for folk naming of animals and plants, with "utilitarianists" on one side and "intellectualists" on the other (Berlin 1991, 1992:181–190; Berlin and Berlin 1983:319–322; Brown 1986, 1995; Bulmer 1970; Descola 1994:82; Hays 1982; Hunn 1982; Morris 1984; Posey 1984; Whitehead 1995b:154). Briefly, the "utilitarian" position argues that people name and classify things that play an important part in their lives, notably as food, raw materials, and so on, while the "intellectual" camp points out that people pay attention to many things for which they have no use, to paraphrase Descartes, they are there, hence they think about them.

In addition to their zoologically informed classification, the Wola may sometimes categorize animals using other criteria, although not in schemes of comparable complexity. Reflecting utilitarian concerns, they may distinguish between animals according to their appropriateness for certain uses, such as supplying plumes and pelts for self-decoration or bones for manufacturing pointed implements (Sillitoe 1988). Reflecting intellectual concerns, they may on occasion mark creatures as taboo (Sillitoe 1983:249–251). Although this is less prevalent today with the demise of many rituals in which taboos featured, such as those to promote the well-being of bachelors (Sillitoe 1979b), it never comprised an extensive system comparable to some populations in New Guinea such as the Ok speakers, in which taboos on certain game marked elaborate initiation sequences (Whitehead 2000). While they recount origin myths that sometimes feature animals in the founding of today's local kin communities (Sillitoe 1979a:43–45), these are not part of a totemic system. The adoption of Christianity makes it difficult to conduct enquiries to interpret these animal associations because people are unlikely to want to talk about them or may deny any knowledge of them, as an embarrassing ancestral heritage that contradicts biblical stories.

TAXONOMIC DISAGREEMENTS

Disagreements over the naming of animals further compromise any parallels with scientific taxonomy.[3] Data collected on mammals indicate the extent of disagreements. These comprise animal identifications from skulls on display in houses (men regularly collect skulls as trophies), together with some newly caught animals. All of the animals were identified once only by the persons who caught them, who saw the full gamut of morphological, behavioral, and ecological information at capture.[4] If we take the largest number of identifications that correlate with one zoological species as "correct," we find that 36 percent of sab (large mammal) and 53 percent of honez (small mammal) identifications disagree with the correct one.[5] There is scant correlation between the frequency with which people catch creatures (which we might suppose relates to the size of animal populations) and agreement over identifications. They are as likely to dispute the names of commonly seen animals as others.

These data probably underrepresent the extent of disagreements related to captured animals that people could inspect closely before naming them. The scope for disagreement must increase considerably for animals only glimpsed briefly in the wild. These data might be criticized as disingenuous, privileging zoological cues. After all, there is no evidence that Wola classes should match those of zoological science, although such correspondence is widely found in ethnoscientific work (see Berlin 1973, 1992:201; Berlin and Berlin 1983:322–324; Berlin et al. 1966; Boster et al. 1986; Hunn 1975). Zoological correspondence is used to assess the consistency of Wola identifications, on the grounds that scientific identifications are relatively constant, use carefully defined categories, and consistently apply specified criteria to specimens when making identifications (Bulmer 1969:5–6).

Others have broached these issues in different fields, such as medical anthropology (Kleinman 1995; Lewis 2000:11). They have challenged for some time the assumption that biomedical diagnosis is objective and universal, and, therefore, "correct"—a biomedical diagnosis attempts, as Glick (1998:25) points out in his study of Gimi ethnomedicine, to classify an illness and to guide people to select an appropriate treatment. It is necessary to distinguish between biological explanations and any particular group's thoughts and responses to disease because members of different societies may vary in their interpretations and experiences (Lewis 1993:94). While the physical facts may be the same—fever, sweats, and shivers, for example—the culturally informed diagnosis may be as different as witchcraft versus malarial attacks. Some writers consequently seek to distinguish between biomedical identifications of *disease* and local representations of *illness* (Lewis 1975:149, 1993:94), arguing that while biological and social factors may interact, the implication is not that there are no differences between them. The biological continues to offer scope for universality, the view of medical nosologies being that nature controls the expression of disease in a regular way, each with its "natural history." Nonetheless, it is widely agreed that, whatever the status of biomedical disease diagnoses, we should not attempt to read these into others' classifications of ill health.

The taxonomic disagreements over mammals may result from some confusion over objective cues. It is possible that the identifications are consistent according to some other criteria. Two contenders are body size and sexual dimorphism. Individuals may disagree in their subjective judgments of when animals cross size thresholds. Sexual dimorphism, which can relate to body size in some animals, may explain confusion over birds, but not mammals with external genitalia. Differences also vary with the level of classification attempted, and the fineness of the distinctions made in naming a creature. It is at the lowest taxonomic levels that disputed identifications are most probable, differences being more likely where discriminations are keen. On another critical tack, it is arguable that the zoologists who generously assisted me with the scientific identifications made mistakes, for some of the taxonomic discriminations based on dentition are fine and specialists can disagree.

Divergences are pervasive and occur at all levels. Disagreements over the identification of animals (i.e., their assignment to taxa) and disputes about the structure of the taxonomy (i.e., the arrangement of classes), while different, are related issues. Individual Wola, depending on what they expect from the taxonomy, may equally dispute the assignment of particular animals to named taxa and the classificatory arrangement of these classes. On occasions they cannot even agree if certain named classes exist at all. The considerable number of synonyms for similar groups of creatures reflects people's inventiveness. Sometimes individuals may devise their own category to accommodate their perceptions based on their experiences and knowledge, acquired in some measure from personal encounters. Furthermore, people not only disagree with others but also with themselves over identifications on different occasions.

The disagreements may reflect some social differentiation and structuring of knowledge. The two principal dimensions that come to mind are age and gender. Adults certainly know more than children about wildlife and children are unlikely to seriously dispute identifications with senior relatives. Those who teach children influence their knowledge and there is probably some ordering of knowledge according to kin network, relatives passing on their views to one another. Gender may inform knowledge, too, although this is difficult to assess. The expectations of the sexual division of labor appear to structure knowledge in some measure. It is men who hunt for larger animals and women usually defer to them over sab (large mammal) identifications, whereas it is women who customarily collect amphibians and men usually heed their opinions about naming jiya (frogs) (as Whitehead [1995a:4] has discussed in her work with the Seltaman of the Western Province). It is not that more bellicose males are more likely to dispute identifications and conciliatory females to agree on them. Data on frog identifications from women show similar disagreement when compared with scientific identifications; again, taking the largest number of identifications that correlate with any one zoological species as "correct," 33 percent of the frog determinations disagree.

The evidence suggests that disagreements over the identification of creatures follow few predictable social dimensions. We might anticipate the absence of any defined social structuring to knowledge in an egalitarian society that lacks social classes *in the know* (experts) and others *in the dark* (lay persons). In hierarchical social orders, "there is some body of people in society who have the right to stipulate what words should designate, relative to some domain of expertise" (Lakoff 1987:123), and

such social arrangements are an integral aspect of power relations, control, and manipulation. In egalitarian tribal regimes, disputing what is known reflects the reverse, social arrangements that subvert the emergence of any dominant class over others.

TAXONOMIC BOUNDARIES

The anarchic status of highlander taxonomy intimates the fractious nature of political relations. The disagreements are in some regards an inevitable aspect of the nonhierarchical political order; they reflect it in action. In an acephalous polity, where power is diffused equally between all households, there is by definition no authority to arbitrate when persons disagree, whether their dispute is over some serious wrongdoing or merely a difference over the identification of some wild animal. They have to rely on self-help and sort out the issue between themselves, aided and abetted by their kinsmen. In the event of a relatively trivial disagreement over the naming of an animal, they may argue or they may agree to disagree. This challenges our assumptions about taxonomy invariably relating to hierarchical ordering of phenomena, which may be inimical to the Wola view of the world.

Some ethnobiologists have pioneered the use of Vennlike diagrams, in an attempt to overcome the distortions introduced into folk classifications by the use of descent structures (Berlin 1992:36–51; Ellen 1979, 1993:146; Gardner 1976; Hunn 1976). They argue that these break away from hierarchical representations, better depicting class overlap or the polysemous use of some terms, allowing the representation of basic and extended ranges. Such diagrams present a new problem, namely the depiction of boundaries. Disagreements over identifications challenge the existence of firm boundaries to mark off agreed exclusive categories. The definition of bounded classes is a necessary prelude to any formal classificatory arrangement (Atran 1990:138–142); Berlin 1992:64–78), yet a blurred and contested view of boundaries is a more accurate conceptualization of relations in nature, which comprise a continuum (Rosch 1975:180). In his discussion of classification, Lakoff, for example, refers to "fuzzy set theory" and "memberships gradience: The idea that at least some categories have degrees of membership and no clear boundaries" (1987:12, 21–22). If we take the discrimination between closely related sympatric species, they pass gradually one into the other with no clear boundary between them; the transition is subject to debate between taxonomists. The inadequacy of hierarchical notions of classification is not some arcane "folk" problem, it is increasingly evident in scientific taxonomy, particularly with the advance of molecular techniques such as DNA analysis, and taxonomists are increasingly experimenting with computer aided multivariate systems. The highlanders' contingent zoological heritage unexpectedly chimes in with contemporary problems in science.

The boundary-drawing conundrum occurs at all levels in Melanisian culture (Hays 1993), not only in the classification of natural phenomena but also the definition of kin groups with their taxonomic parallels. The negotiable aspects of Wola affiliative behavior produce alternately *bounded* and *unbounded* representations of social corporations. The blend of *bilaterality* with a detectable *agnatic bias* undermines the boundedness. The cultural impetus is to obfuscate and dissemble boundaries, although looked at behaviorally from the participants' perspective, they sometimes make boundaries and at other times unmake them, as contested over time and prompted by context. The challenge to boundaries pertains to issues of centrality and exclusion, which are inevitable with bounded entities, as structures of ascendancy, those on the periphery being, by definition, marginal to those occupying the centre (Fernandez 2000; Lamont and Fournier 1992). We see this in the ethnobiological concepts of the *basic* or *core* reference of terms compared with their *extended* or *peripheral* meanings (Berlin 1992:41–41; Hunn 1976). Some taxa are outliers, less central in taxonomic terms. Centrality intimates asymmetrical power relations of exclusion and subordination, which stateless orders dissipate, esteeming equality—diffusing, not concentrating, sociopolitical power. It is axiomatic that boundaries should be diminished and blurred, reducing the demarcation of dominant relations.

The argument is not that this fuzzy-set classification of animals exists because of some social compulsion. Rather, it is embedded in a political context that gravitates toward this taxonomic approach; an imperative Ellen calls "prehension" (1993:229). A direct causal connection is not sought between social structure and form of classification (e.g., after Durkeim and Mauss 1963). The aim is more modest. It follows Lakoff's "experimentalists" approach, which "attempt(s) to characterize meaning in terms of the nature and experience of the organisms doing the thinking," as

> many of our most important truths . . . come about as a result of human beings acting in accord with a conceptual system that cannot in any sense be said to fit a reality completely outside of human experience. Human experience is, after all, real too—every bit as real as rocks and trees. [Lakoff 1987:266, 296]

Also, drawing on Putnam's "internalist metaphysical realism," there exists "some sort of ideal coherence of our beliefs with each other and with our experiences, as those experiences are themselves represented in our belief system" (1981:50).

Referring again to medical anthropology, it has been apparent for some time that categories relating to illness and health, both the folk and scientific, are socially and historically constructed (Engel 1977). Anthropologists have demonstrated how people may understand and experience sickness differently, and historians have reminded us that biomedical definitions of diseases have erred and changed over time (e.g., Foucault 1964). We have the idea of the "social construction of illness," that cultural representations and social conditioning inform understanding and experience of illness. Perhaps we have more readily conceded the scope for cultural variation in the classification of illness because there is no entirely objective animal-equivalent reference point available out there. While we may think of diseases as distinct, named entities, they are not discrete natural things that exist independently of sick persons, but, rather, selections of symptoms characteristically shown by them, as Lewis explains in his most recent study of illness among the Gnau of the Torricelli mountains.

> "Swelling" or "jaundice" are not discrete natural entities in the same way as a person or an animal is. They do not have separate independent existences. We may be more easily tempted to think of "malaria" or "measles" like that because there are parasites involved (but the parasite or the virus itself is not the illness—the sweating, fever, or spots, etc.). [Lewis 2000:11]

When we identify an illness we select from the symptoms a sick person shows, it is a culturally informed construction. Cultures may differ in the symptoms they pay attention to and the categories of illness they recognize (Glick 1998:25). Furthermore, individuals differ in their presentation of symptoms, no illness is exactly the same, and this subjective variation between sick persons offers further scope for diagnostic variation (Lewis 2000:13).

We can only characterize the properties relevant to the definition of categories in terms of people's experiences with both their physical and cultural environment. Consequently, we are not trying to establish why highlander zoological classes are constituted as they are and whether their taxonomic arrangement reflects the social order or not. For example, pointing out that in discussing the constitution of their social groups or animal classes, the Wola may use either as metaphors for the other, does not imply a causal link. The taxonomic system both reflects, and is a response to, the fractious, uncentralized social environment. A nonhierarchical taxonomy does not imply contested classification in itself, although this is likely if it is associated with an acephalous political environment of the kind that may promote such an arrangement. This stance reflects that expressed by Lakoff that "experience does not determine conceptual systems, but only motivates them" (1987:310). Acephalous sociopolitical constraints may feasibly be accommodated to taxonomically in many possible ways. The Wola "solution" is only one. But whatever it is, in egalitarian contexts it will likely pose a challenge to scientific hierarchical arrangements. We can expect conundrums, for in some senses we have to think more flexibly, rather than tendentiously interpreting such cultures, drawing on our intellectual tradition that customarily draws lines around phenomena to further understanding of them.

NEGOTIATED TAXONOMY

Fuzzy boundaries, disputed classes, and subverted hierarchies, while integral to acephalous political relations, query the status of taxonomy. The extent of disagreements can be disconcerting on occasion, threatening to overwhelm our notion of a classification, in the sense of an agreed arrangement of phenomena. The suggestion is not that the taxonomic system itself is nihilist, for people can generally agree over its broad "family" structure. It is the composition of classes they question and individuals' pigeonholing of creatures within them. We assume that members of the same culture who speak the same language will largely agree over the content of the words they use or they will be unable to talk to one another intelligibly. The Wola zoological evidence suggests considerable tolerance of dissonance. The change in animal names with dialect from one place to another across Wolaland further exacerbates the differences (likewise in the Ok-speaking region [Whitehead 1995a:16]). These changes are quite extensive, and it would be a large, even, perhaps, futile, undertaking to match up all dialect variations with animal identifications.

Returning to medical parallels, we know diagnoses differ in nature and aim between cultures and disease classifications may vary considerably. The classification of illnesses by the Huli, neighbors of the Wola, strikes a familiar chord, as they

> possess no complex taxonomic hierarchy of disease names . . . to attempt to arrange all their illness descriptions into sets of contrasting categories distinguished according to the nature of the symptoms would not reflect their view. [Frankel 1986:8]

Likewise, among the Gnau "a collection of descriptions of symptoms is not the same as a set of disease names: it does not necessarily imply a classification—at least not in the systematic or conceptual sense" (Lewis 1975:141). Furthermore, the Gnau, anticipating taxonomic disagreements, "leave room for ambiguity and different interpretations when they explain illness; often they describe the facts and circumstances but draw no definite conclusion" (Lewis 1993:106). All reports of Melanesian medical practices emphasize negotiation and point out that diagnosis focuses less on examining bodily symptoms than finding out more about the sick person's social circumstances. Here, diagnosis derives "from syndromes of circumstance rather than syndromes of clinical symptoms" (Lewis 1993:109). This underscores with a vengeance the "social construction of illness" and scope for cultural relativity in the interpretation of illness. If causes are not discernible from clinical signs, discriminating between these is not going to be a priority. Instead, diagnosis focuses on social context and relations because, as Glick puts it, "causes may turn out to be invisible as viruses, but never as impersonal" (1998:26). Comparison with biomedical diagnoses becomes difficult, as illustrated by 13 cases diagnosed by the Gnau as attacks by a certain spirit, which the physician diagnosed as ranging from heart failure and perirectal abscess to common colds (Lewis 1993:108).

We are led to ask to what extent such people are doing something analogous to classifying in scientific thinking when they order animals, diseases, or any other phenomena, into classes. The rationale, strange as it may seem, could be to facilitate agreed and mutually intelligible discourse. Highlanders, like all human beings, observe nature's discontinuities, which feature in their experience of the world. They distinguish between them and name animals to structure their observations and communicate their ideas to one another. Some of the variation they see and categorize by is small, particularly at the lowest taxonomic level involving closely related species or subspecies, and they cannot always agree among themselves about its significance. They recognize no zoological authorities who can arbitrate definitively. While people may acknowledge that some persons are skillful hunters, and that their success may consequently demonstrate a keen appreciation of animal behavior, others do not necessarily defer to them as authorities over taxonomic issues and may robustly disagree with them if they think that their own identification is "correct." In the event of irresolvable differences between individuals at the secondary or tertiary taxonomic level, they can turn to an agreed on higher-level term.

The taxonomic classes facilitate communication, albeit sometimes less precise, and help avoid unnecessary disputes. People cannot settle disagreements in any other way where there is no authority to adjudicate, where no one necessarily acknowledges a more knowledgeable and powerful party to settle disputes. There are few disagreements at the life-form level about the class to which any animal belongs, unlike lower taxa; people largely agree when a creature is a sab (large mammal) etc., although the *no name* category intimates scope for disagreement. This strategy complies with the idea of "category cue validity" (Lackoff 1987:52–53; Rosch et al. 1976), which cognitive psychologists define as the probability that something will fall into a certain category by virtue of it possessing some feature or cue. For example, if you see a creature with a beak, you can identify it with certainty as a bird, beaks having a cue validity of 1.0 for birds and 0 for other creatures. The higher the cue score, the more certain class ascription, and the sum of cue validities for higher level taxonomic categories will always be greater than those for lower level ones (Murphy 1982). There are parallels also with the "analog prototype" model of category cognition (Rosch 1975).

The criteria that inform the constitution of some of the animal classes discussed here support cue validity. Size is important in the definition of several primary and secondary taxa. It is a fairly reliable cue when an animal is only glimpsed briefly. "Was it a large or small furry animal?" is a question people can answer with fair certainty. Sometimes people use common adjectives to qualify life-form names further. They may refer to a sab (large mammal) or sor (birds) as large or small, or many (i.e., in a flock) or one (i.e., solitary), or they may refer to color. On occasion they may use more than one qualifying term and talk, for example, about a "large black bird," which will suggest to the knowledgeable a black sicklebill or Princess Stephanie's bird of paradise, or any other of several large black birds. When people are unsure or disagree about secondary taxon identifications, the use of such adjectives makes for more precise communication. Although they demonstrate that people are quite capable of perceiving mid-groups between formal named ones, to call these "covert categories" (i.e., classes for which people have no names but that the analyst deduces to exist using his or her taxonomic logic) is, I think, to misinterpret their significance. The status of these hidden classes and the ability of researchers to elicit them have been debated for some years (see Atran 1990:43–46; Berlin 1974, 1992:176–181; Berlin et al. 1968; Brown 1974, 1984; Descola 1994:81; Ellen 1993:119–121; Hays 1976; Taylor 1984). They are ad hoc and variable descriptions that vary from individual to individual and occasion to occasion.

If we interpret taxonomy as facilitating agreed communication, this accounts for some other anomalies. It accounts, for example, for the absence of any kingdom-level terms equivalent to animals or plants. These would be redundant. There is no reason to seek to integrate the primary life-form taxa into a higher-level order, to complete some nonexistent hierarchy. Closure at a higher level assumes a hierarchical conception that only makes sense backed up by a cultural construct such as an evolutionary theory, prompting taxonomic completion. For the Wola, the classification of animals is inherently dynamic and subject to negotiation; there can be no closure or final bounded version, no authoritative comprehensive arrangement. The absence of any life-form classes for some animals, such as bats, pythons, pigs, and dogs ("unaffiliated generics" [Berlin 1992;171–181]) also complies with this interpretation. For a long time (to confess to an embarrassing ethnocentric exercise), I have worried my friends into inventing "family" classes for these, in which others have invented "covert classes." They are an unnecessary fiction. While the Wola regularly disagree over the naming of many creatures, these "unaffiliated" animals are unlikely candidates. No one is likely to confuse them, as an exasperated friend put it, "everyone knows that a dog is a dog!" These animals are quite distinctive and stand out from others. Furthermore, if they were grouped together, they would comprise relatively small life-form classes with relatively few animals eligible for each. In other words, not only are they distinctive but also there are not many of them to confuse one with another.

AGREEING TO DISAGREE

The Wola have a taxonomy less in the Greek sense of a *taxis* (arrangement) of natural phenomena for intellectual purposes than an *arrangement* in the political sense of an agreement for settling differences. They employ their taxonomy to communicate everyday with one another about animals, without untoward disputation, not to arrange closely defined classes in a hierarchical scheme for debate about evolutionary-ecological relations nor symbolic exegeses. The "solution" to Wola disagreements, taxonomic anomalies, and indifference to an integrated classification is so straightforward that I find it hard to believe that I have puzzled over them for so many years. Perhaps it was, I have to confess, that a scientific education had blinded me to their reality.

It is possible that some of the observations made here will apply to other tribal people beyond the New Guinea highlands, such as some South American Indian populations. This region's rain forest is home to many animals and its human inhabitants have detailed classifications reflecting their sophisticated knowledge of mammals (Berlin and Berlin 1983; Patton et al. 1982), birds (Berlin et al. 1981; Boster et al. 1986), amphibians (Lescure et al. 1980), and invertebrates (Posey 1984). The Achuar Jivaro of the Peruvian Amazon, for example, distinguish 30 classes of animals, grouping them together on morphological and ecological grounds (Descola 1994:88). The four major ones are *kuntin* (game), *chinki* (sparrows), *namak* (big fish), and *tsarur* (minnows). These could facilitate agreement over the naming of animals, seen fleetingly, for example, when precise identification is difficult. As the ethnographer points out, "Any small bird too far away to identify by its proper name will be designated as chinki" (Descola 1994:89).[6] This may help explain the constitution of some otherwise puzzling classes, such as the Achuar *yawa* category that comprises certain carnivorous quadrepeds, including jaguars and dogs, to the exclusion of certain others of distinctive appearance. The principles put forward here may not, however, be absolute. The Achuar, for example, have no generic class for armadillo; each of their five species, which could conceivably be confused with one another, is of "unaffiliated" status. Nonetheless, the person who, seeing a bird, commented, "This one is diurnal, lives in the canopy, eats such-and-such foods, is hunted by this or that animal, lives in bands of seven or eight, sings this way, but I've forgotten it's name" (Descola 1994:83), catches perfectly the context when higher level class names are useful. The interesting analysis of Aguaruna ethno-ornithological data by Berlin et al. that explores the extent that "people agree closely on the appropriate name of some species and disagree markedly on the name of other species" (1981:96), further confirms it.

The frustrations of compiling an ethnoscientific record made me aware of the problems people can have in agreeing to details, which I subsequently came to realize is an intrinsic aspect of their approach to taxonomy. We can appreciate the scope for disagreement with hundreds of named creatures and no reference list to help people remember and distinguish between them. The absence of a local checklist equivalent relates to the problems that attend writing such oral schemes down. In committing such traditions to the written record, we extend to them an artificial sense of order and consensus, robbing them of their ongoing negotiated status and contingency. Some of the problems regarding the extent of disagreements are an artifact of this transition. In some regards, learning with notebooks, checklists, and sessions to discuss animals is quite foreign to people such as the Wola, who normally pass on and retain knowledge in a casual and piecemeal manner. When asked how they identify particular animals, informants vary in their responses. They are not accustomed to specifying what cues they look for as naming criteria. It is arguable that "analog" constituted categories are "an even more prevalent mode of cognitive processing for preliterate cultures where technical criteria for category membership may not normally be a subject of conscious verbalized concern" (Rosch 1975:202). They see any creature as a distinctive whole, considering simultaneously a range of observable cues, not seeking a few characteristic ones.

The methodological implications of taxonomic disagreements are considerable for ethnoscientific enquiries.

The problem is defining and glossing the continuously negotiated classes employed by tribal people in ordering their ethnozoological knowledge. Currently we have no accurate and unambiguous way to represent relations, for we inevitably rob them of some of their negotiated spontaneity. If persons cannot agree over the features that they use to distinguish between different named creatures, what is the status of ethnographies that purport to do so? We report formal accounts of taxonomies without explaining on what grounds we assume the authority to construct these and arbitrate between contested classifications. A written taxonomy assumes and imposes order and agreement. It represents a consensual view, what we think the majority would recognize as descriptions of named creatures. In compiling such records we override many disagreements. It is partly a negotiated outcome and partly an imposed one. This standardizing method, following accepted ethnoscientific practice, is perhaps dubious in its distortion of the system, but the alternative for the ethnographic record would be a chaotic jumble of information.

Acephalous politics put the postmodern critique about "who can assume to know what" in an interesting context. Here we find people who expect to argue over objective cues relating to animals and their subjective understanding of them. Irreconcilable and unavoidable disagreements are an inevitable part of the system in which we find no authority to arbitrate and pronounce on the correct identification. This accords with current ideas about social life as process never finalized in structure, that all knowledge may be contested. Disagreements are not peculiar to natural history or to medicine. Social life in the highlands is fractious and disagreements are common. The endless negotiations during sociopolitical exchanges can sometimes erupt into acrimonious differences of opinion. Interminable discussions likewise characterize many ceremonial activities as people wrangle over the correct procedure to follow. We have yet to devise rigorous methodologies to document the extent of such variation and assess its significance, a necessary first step to contrasting such systems with the scientific ones of state orders, and assess the political implications of interaction in development or other contexts.

NOTES

1. Such ethnozoological arrangements are common throughout the Highlands: The Gimi of the Eastern Highlands (Glick 1964:275) and Kalam of the Schrader mountains (Blumer 1974a), to cite two examples, have similar categories.

2. The status of bats is similarly ambivalent elsewhere (e.g., the Seltamen [Whitehead 1995a:32]).

3. For comparative data on birds and an interesting discussion of identification disagreements between people, see Berlin et al

(1981), who used bird skins in a series of identification experiments with the Aguaruna Jivaro of Peruvian Amazonia.

4. Subsequently, I collected the animal skulls, and in a few cases pelts, too, and some entire pickled smaller animals, for scientific identification. Every identification pertains to a separate animal (the 54 *P. vestitus* identifications, for instance, were made by 54 persons on 54 animals; they do not represent 54 persons looking at the same specimen out of context either as an intact animal or a skull). The total numbers of animals in the samples were sab = 341, honez = 31, and jiya = 56.

5. The Wola distinguish between the two mammal life-forms according to size; sab are larger and honez are smaller. They name 17 sab and 13 honez secondary taxa. Both categories include marsupial and placental mammals, and the former a monotreme, too, in contrast to zoology that uses differences in reproductive physiology to structure taxa. These calculations omit these animals for which there is only one example identified, as not possible to assess "correctness" of identification against others. They also omit unspecified taxa.

6. Their Aguaruna Jivaro neighbours apparently differ, using their cognate *chigki* for large game birds (Berlin et al. 1981:99).

REFERENCES CITED

Atran, Scott. 1990. Cognitive Foundations of Natural History: Towards an Anthropology of Science. Cambridge: Cambridge University Press.

Berlin, Brent. 1973. The Relation of Folk Systematics to Biological Classifications and Nomenclature. Annual Review of Ecology and Systematics 4:259–271.

———. 1974. Further Notes on Covert Categories and Folk Taxonomies. American Anthropologist 76:327–331.

———. 1991. The Chicken and the Egg-Head Revisited: Further Evidence for the Intellectualist Bases of Ethnobiological Classification. *In* Man and a Half: Essays in Pacific Anthropology and Ethnobiology in Honour of Ralph Bulmer. Andrew Pawley, ed. Pp. 57–66. Auckland: Polynesian Society.

———. 1992. Ethnobiological Classification: Principles of Categorization of Plants and Animals in Traditional Societies. Princeton: Princeton University Press.

Berlin, Brent, and Elois A. Berlin. 1983. Adaptation and Ethnozoological Classification: Theoretical Implications of Animal Resources and Diet of the Aguaruna and Huambisa. *In* Adaptive Responses of Native Amazonians. R. B. Hames and W. T. Vickers, eds. Pp. 301–328. New York: Academic Press.

Berlin, Brent, James Boster, and John P. O'Neill. 1981. The Perceptual Bases of Ethnobiological Classification: Evidence from Aguaruna Folk Ornithology. Journal of Ethnobiology 1:95–108.

Berlin, Brent, Dennis Breedlove, and Peter Raven. 1966. Folk Taxonomies and Biological Classification. Science 154:273–275.

———. 1968. Covert Categories and Folk Taxonomies. American Anthropologist 70:290–299.

Boster, James. 1986. "Requiem for the Omniscient Informant": There's Life in the Old Girl Yet. *In* Directions in Cognitive Anthropology. J. W. D. Dougherty, ed. Pp. 177–198. Urbana: University of Illinois Press.

James Boster, Brent Berlin, and John O'Neill. 1986. The Correspondence of Jivaroan to Scientific Ornithology. American Anthropologist 88:569–583.

Bright, J. O., and W. Bright. 1965. Semantic Structures in Northwestern California and the Sapir-Whorf Hypothesis. American Anthropologist 67:249–258.

Brown, Cecil H. 1974. Unique Beginners and Covert Categories and Folk Biological Taxonomies. American Anthropologist 76:325–327.

———. 1984. Language and Living Things: Uniformities in Folk Classification and Naming. New Brunswick, NJ: Rutgers University Press.

———. 1986. The Growth of Ethnobiological Nomenclature. Current Anthropology 27:1–18.

———. 1995. Lexical Acculturation and Ethnobiology: Utilitarianism versus Intellectualism. Journal of Linguistic Anthropology 5(1):51–64.

Bulmer, Ralph N. H. 1969. Field Methods in Ethno-Zoology with Special Reference to the New Guinea Highlands. Port Moresby: University of Papua and New Guinea, Anthropology Department.

———. 1970. Which Came First, the Chicken or the Egg-Head? *In* Échanges et communications: mélanges offerts à Claude Lévi-Strauss à l'occasion de son 60 ème anniversaire. J. Pouillon and P. Maranda, eds. Pp. 1069–1091. Paris: Mouton.

———. 1974a. Folk Biology in the New Guinea Highlands. Social Science Information 13:9–28.

———. 1974b. Memoirs of a Small Game Hunter: On the Track of Unknown Animal Categories in New Guinea. Journal d'Agriculture tropicale et de Botanique appliquée 21:79–99.

Descola, Phillipe. 1994. In the Society of Nature: A Native Ecology in Amazonia. N. Scott, trans. Cambridge: Cambridge University Press.

Diamond, Jared. 1966. Zoological Classification of a Primitive People (Fore, New Guinea). Science 151:1102–1104.

Durkheim, Emile, and Marcel Mauss. 1963. Primitive Classification. Rodney Needham, trans. London: Cohen and West.

Ellen, Roy F. 1975. Variable Constructs in Nuaulu Zoological Classification. Social Science Information 14:201–228.

———. 1979. Omniscience and Ignorance: Variation in Nuaulu Knowledge, Identification and Classification of Animals. Language in Society 8:337–364.

———. 1993. The Cultural Relations of Classification: An Analysis of Nuaulu Animal Categories from Central Seram. Cambridge: Cambridge University Press.

Ellen, Roy F., A. F. Stimson, and James I. Menzies. 1976. Structure and Inconsistency in Nuaulu Categories for Amphibians. Journal d'Agriculture tropicale et de Botanique appliquée 23:125–138.

Engel, George. 1977. The Need for a New Medical Model: A Challenge for Biomedicine. Science 196(April 8):129–135.

Fernandez, James W. 2000. Peripheral Wisdom. *In* Signifying Identities: Anthropological Perspectives on Boundaries and Contested Values. Anthony P. Cohen, ed. Pp. 117–144. London: Routledge.

Foucault, Michel. 1964. Histoire do la folie à l'âge classique. Paris: Gallimard.

Frankel, Stephen. 1986. The Huli Response to Illness. Cambridge: Cambridge University Press.

Gal, S. 1973. Inter-Informant Cariability in an Ethno-Zoological Taxonomy. Anthropological Linguistics 15:203–219.

Gardner, P. 1976. Birds, Words and a Requiem for the Omniscient Informant. American Ethnologist 8:446–468.

Gatewood, J. B. 1983. Loose Talk: Linguistic Competence and Recognition Ability. American Anthropologist 85:378–387.

Glick, Leonard B. 1964. Categories and Relations in Gimi Natural Science, special issue, American Anthropologist 66(4):273–280.

———. 1998. Medicine as an Ethnographic Category. The Gimi of the New Guinea Highlands. In The Art of Medical Anthropology. S. van der Geest and A. Rienks, eds. Pp. 23–37. Amsterdam: Het Spinhuis.

Hays, Terence E. 1976. An Empirical Method for the Identification of Covert Categories in Ethnobiology. Amercian Ethnologist 3:489–507.

———. 1982. Utilitarian/Adaptionist Explanations of Folk Biological Classifications: Some Cautionary Notes. Journal of Ethnobiology 2:89–94.

———. 1993. "The New Guinea Highlands": Region, Culture Area or Fuzzy Set. Current Anthropology 34:141–164.

Healey, Christopher. 1978–79. Taxonomic Rigidity in Folk Biological Classification: Some Examples from the Maring of New Guinea. Ethnomedizin 5(3–4):361–384.

Hunn, Eugene. 1975. A Measure of the Degree of Correspondence of Folk to Scientific Biological Classification. American Ethnologist 2:309–327.

———. 1976. Toward a Perceptual Model of Folk Biological Classification. American Ethnologist 3:508–524.

———. 1982. The Utilitarian Factor in Folk to Biological Classification. American Anthropologist 84:830–847.

Hunn, Eugene, and David H. French. 1984. Alternatives to Taxonomic Hierarchy: The Sahaptin Case. Journal of Ethnobiology 3:73–92.

Kleinman, Arthur. 1995. Writing at the Margin: Discourse between Anthropology and Medicine. Berkeley: University of California Press.

Lakoff, George. 1987. Women, Fire, and Dangerous Things: What Categories Reveal about the Mind. Chicago: University of Chicago Press.

Lamont, M., and M. Fournier, eds. 1992. Cultivating Differences: Symbolic Boundaries and the Making of Inequality. Chicago: University of Chicago Press.

Lederman, Rena. 1986. What Gifts Engender: Social Relations and Politics in Mendi, Highland Papua New Guinea. Cambridge: Cambridge University Press.

Lescure, Jean, Francoise Grenand, and Pierre Grenand. 1980. Les amphibians dans l'univers Wayapi. Journal d'Agriculture Traditionnel et de Botanique Appliquée. Appliquée 28:247–261.

Lewis, Gilbert. 1975. Knowledge of Illness in a Sepik Society. London: Athlone.

———. 1993. Some Studies of Social Causes of and Cultural Response to Disease. In The Anthropology of Disease. C. G. N. Mascie-Taylor, ed. Pp. 73–124. Oxford: Oxford University Press.

———. 2000. A Failure of Treatment. Oxford Univerity Press.

Morris, Brian. 1984 The Pragmatics of Folk Classification. Journal of Ethnobiology 4:45–60.

Murphy, Gregory L. 1982. Cue Validity and Levels of Categorization. Psychological Bulletin 91(1):174–177.

Patton, James L., Brent Berlin, and Elois A. Berlin. 1982. Aboriginal Perspectives of a Mammal Community in Amazonian Peru: Knowledge and Utilization Patterns of the Aguaruna Jivaro. In Mammalian Biology in South America. M. Mares and H. H. Genoways, eds. Pp. 111–128. Pittsburgh: Pymatuning Laboratory of Ecology.

Posey, Darrell. 1984. Hierarchy and Utility in a Folk Biological Taxonomic System: Patterns in the Classification of Arthropods by the Kayapó Indians of Brazil. Journal of Ethnobiology 4:123–134.

Putnam, Hilary. 1981. Reason, Truth, and History. Cambridge: Cambridge University Press.

Randall, Robert. 1976. How Tall Is a Taxonomic Tree? Some Evidence for Dwarfism. American Ethnologist 3:541–357.

Rosch, Eleanor. 1975. Universals and Cultural Specifics in Human Categorization. In Cross-Cultural Perspectives on Learning. R. W. Brislin, R. W. Boehner, and W. J. Lonner, eds. Pp. 177–206. New York: Wiley.

Rosch, Eleanor, Carolyn Mervis, Wayne Gray, David Johnson, and Penny Boyes-Braem. 1976. Basic Objects in Natural Categories. Cognitive Psychology 8:382–439.

Ryan, D'Arcy. 1961. Gift Exchange in the Mendi Valley. Ph.D. dissertation, University of Sydney.

Sillitoe, Paul. 1979a. Give and Take: Exchange in Wola Society. Canberra: Australian National University Press.

———. 1979b. Man-Eating Women: Fears of Sexual Pollution in the Papua New Guinea Highlands. Journal of the Polynesian Society 88(1):77–97.

———. 1983. Roots of the Earth: The Cultivation and Classification of Crops in the Papua New Guinea highlands. Manchester: University of Manchester Press.

———. 1988. Made in Niugini: Technology in the Highlands of Papua New Guinea. London: British Museum Publications.

———. 1998. The Development of Indigenous Knowledge: A New Applied Anthropology. Current Anthropology 39(2):223–252.

Singer, M., and H. Baer. 1995. Critical Medical Anthropology. New York: Baywood.

Taylor, P. 1984. "Covert Categories" Reconsidered: Identifying Unlabeled Classes in Tobelo Folk Biological Classification. Journal of Ethnobiology 4:105–122.

Whitehead, Harriet. 1995a. Identifying Game Species with the Aid of Pictures in Papua New Guinea. Pacific Studies 18(4):1–38.

———. 1995b. The Gender of Birds in a Mountain Ok Culture. In Naturalizing Power: Essays in Feminist Cultural Analysis. Sylvia Yanagisako and Carol Delaney, eds. Pp. 145–173. London: Routledge.

———. 2000. Food Rules: Hunting, Sharing, and Tobooing Game in Papua New Guinea. Ann Arbor: University of Michigan Press.

17

Conservation Policy and Indigenous Peoples

Marcus Colchester

Marcus Colchester is director of the Forest Peoples Programme of the World Rainforest Movement. He received his PhD in social anthropology from Oxford University in 1982. His primary work has focused on helping secure indigenous peoples' rights to their lands and livelihoods through local, national, and international campaigns and information sharing. His initial work in Venezuela focused on indigenous land rights, health, bilingual education, nature protection, and development policy. He is associate editor of The Ecologist *magazine and has received various prestigious honors recognizing his activism and scholarship, including a Pew Fellowship in conservation and the environment.*

The creation of protected areas has been a central element in conservation policy since its beginnings in the 19th century. From their inception, protected areas were conceived as areas of land alienated to the state and managed for the benefit of future generations but to the exclusion of residents. National parks, pioneered in the United States, denied indigenous people's rights, evicted them from their homelands, and provoked long-term social conflict. This model of conservation became central to conservation policy worldwide. But the emergence of indigenous peoples as a social movement and as a category in international human rights law has contributed to conservation agencies re-thinking their approach to conservation. A new model of conservation can now be discerned based on a respect for the rights of indigenous peoples and other bearers of "traditional knowledge."

Conservation policies emerged at a time of fierce prejudice against indigenous peoples and led to the worldwide acceptance of a model of "colonial conservation" which has caused, and continues to cause, widespread human suffering and resentment. Advances in human rights and in the thinking of conservationists have led to an acceptance that conservation can and must be achieved in collaboration with indigenous peoples and based on respect for their internationally recognized rights. However, on the ground, protected areas continue to be imposed according to the colonial model, calling into question the extent to which there is a real commitment to giving conservation a human face.

THE FIRST NATIONAL PARKS

The idea that certain areas of land valued for the natural species that live there should be set aside for recreation and protected from other uses can be traced back to Mesopotamia in the first millennium B.C. From there it spread east and west, into India and Europe (Colchester 1994 [2003]). The first national parks were established at the same time as a tumultuous rush of land-grabbing during the American conquest of the Wild West, when covered wagons, the U.S. cavalry, gold miners, cowboys, and Indians struggled to impose their different visions of life and land use on the continent.

The first such park, established in Yosemite in California in 1864, followed a bloody war of extermination of the Miwok people, and involved the repeated, forced eviction of remnant Miwok settlements over the following 105 years (Keller and Turek 1998). The Yellowstone National Park, established 34 years later in what is now Wyoming, also involved the denial of indigenous peoples' rights. The Yellowstone National Park was created at a time when a devastating series of "Indian Wars" was being waged to subdue Indian autonomy and realize the United States' "manifest destiny." The indigenous peoples who lived in and made use of the extensive woods, plains, and waters of Yellowstone—the Shoshone, Lakota,

"Conservation Policy and Indigenous Peoples" by Marcus Colchester from *Cultural Survival Quarterly*, Spring 2004, pp. 17–22. Reprinted by permission of Cultural Survival.

Crow, Bannock, Nez Perce, Flathead, and Blackfeet peoples—were thus excluded, leading to resistance and the subsequent killing of hundreds of Indians (Keller and Turek 1998).

Underpinning this approach to conservation lay the idea that nature could only be preserved as "wilderness," areas conceived as "primitive and natural" and which must be kept uninhabited—set aside for recreation and science but otherwise left untouched. John Muir, one of the main forces in the national parks movement in the United States, argued vehemently and successfully that wilderness areas should be set aside for recreation to fulfill an emotional need for wild places (Colchester 1994). Most protected areas established in the United States followed this approach although the great majority of these areas overlap lands owned and claimed by indigenous peoples (Keller and Turek 1998). In the following century, the U.S. model of nature conservation was to be exported worldwide and strongly influenced conservation policy in many countries.

Summarizing the recent history of conservation, the former chairman of the World Commission on Protected Areas has noted, "The opinions and rights of indigenous peoples were of little concern to any government before about 1970; they were not organized as a political force as they are now in many countries" (Phillips 2003).

SOCIAL IMPACTS OF PROTECTED AREAS

It has been estimated that, as a result of these policies, some 1 million square kilometers of forests, pasture, and farmlands were expropriated in Africa to make way for conservation, but equivalent statistics are lacking of the number of people displaced as a consequence (Nelson and Hossack 2003). An all-too-common testimony of such forced relocation comes from a Twa who was expelled from the Kahuzi-Biega National Park in the Democratic Republic of Congo in the 1960s (Kwokwo Barume 2000):

> We did not know they were coming. It was early in the morning. I heard people around my house. I looked through the door and saw people in uniforms with guns. Then one of them forced the door of our house and started shouting that we had to leave immediately because the park is not our land. I first did not understand what he was talking about because all my ancestors have lived on these lands. They were so violent that I left with my children.

Denied their traditional lands and livelihoods, these Twa—traditional hunting and gathering "Pygmies"—now exist in a number of squatter camps on the fringes of their once extensive forest territory. They suffer extreme malnutrition, landlessness, demoralization, and despair. As another Twa explains:

> Since we were expelled from our lands, death is following us. The village is becoming empty. We are heading toward extinction. Now the old people have died. Our culture is dying too.

Accurate statistics about just how many people have been displaced to make way for protected areas in Asia are also lacking. One estimate suggest that as many as 600,000 tribal people have been displaced by protected areas in India alone (PRIA 1993). The statistics in Latin America are equally unavailable. Sources suggest that as many as 85 percent of the protected areas in Latin America are in fact inhabited (Amend and Amend 1992).

However, though we lack overall numbers, the local consequences of these impositions of protected areas on the lives of indigenous peoples have been better documented. Summarizing the extensive literature and field studies,[1] indigenous peoples commonly experience:

- Denial of rights to land
- Denial of use of and access to natural resources
- Denial of political rights and the validity of customary institutions
- Disrupted kinship systems
- Disorganized settlement patterns
- Loss of informal social networks, fundamental to the local economy
- Undermining the livelihoods, loss of property, no compensation
- Poverty
- Disruption of customary systems of environment management
- Enforced illegality. People become "poachers," "encroachers," and "squatters" on their own land and are subject to petty tyrannies by park guards.
- Forced resettlement
- Leadership systems destroyed, for if the community leaders accept the relocation they are accused of betraying their people, but if they resist they are proved powerless. Forced resettlement presents a no-win situation to community leaders.
- Symbolic ties to environment broken
- Cultural identity weakened
- Intensified pressure on natural resources outside the protected areas
- Popular unrest, resistance, incendiarism, social conflict, and ensuing repression

It is now widely recognized that the exclusion of indigenous peoples and other local communities from protected areas can also undermine their conservation objectives by creating conflict between local communities and parks managers. As a World Wide Fund for Nature-International (WWF) report notes (Carey, Dudley and Stolton 2000):

> Loss of traditional rights can reduce peoples' interest in long-term stewardship of the land and therefore the creation of a protected area can in some cases increase the rate of damage to the very values that the protected area was originally created to preserve . . . Putting a fence around a protected area seldom creates a long terms solution to problems of disaffected local communities, whether or not it is ethically justified.

NEW PRINCIPLE OF CONSERVATION

Since 1975, the World Conservation Union (IUCN) and World Parks Congress (WPC) have been making important statements implying recognition of the rights of indigenous peoples and the need to accommodate these rights in protected areas. The Kinshasa Resolution of 1975 recognized the importance of traditional ways of life and land ownership, and called on governments to maintain and encourage customary ways of living. It urged governments to devise means by which indigenous peoples could bring their lands into conservation areas without relinquishing their ownership, use, and tenure rights. It also noted that indigenous peoples should not normally be displaced from their traditional lands by protected areas, nor should protected areas be established without adequate consultation with the peoples to be directly affected. The same resolution was recalled in 1982 at the World National Parks Congress in Bali, Indonesia, which affirmed the rights of traditional societies to "social, economic, cultural and spiritual self-determination" and "to participate in decisions affecting the land and natural resources on which they depend." The resolution advocated "the implementation of joint management arrangements between societies which have traditionally managed resources and protected area authorities."[2]

At the World Congress on Protected Areas held in Caracas in 1992, a central issue addressed by the participants was the fact that the great majority of protected areas are in fact inhabited, notably by indigenous peoples. The congress recognized that the denial of the existence and rights of residents was not only unrealistic but counter-productive. At that time the IUCN defined a "national park" in terms of state ownership or control: "Where the highest competent authority of the country has taken steps to prevent or eliminate as soon as possible exploitation or occupation of the whole area."[3]

In 1996, following several years of intensive engagement with indigenous peoples' organizations, the WWF adopted a Statement of Principles on Indigenous Peoples and Conservation, which endorses the Draft U.N. Declaration of the Rights of Indigenous Peoples; accepts that constructive engagement with indigenous peoples must start with a recognition of their rights; and upholds the rights of indigenous peoples to own, manage, and control their lands and territories and benefit from the application of their knowledge. That same year the World Conservation Congress, the paramount body of the IUCN, adopted seven resolutions on indigenous peoples, including one that recognizes indigenous peoples' rights to their lands and territories—particularly in forests, marine and coastal ecosystems, and protected areas—and a resolution that recognizes indigenous peoples' rights to manage their natural resources in protected areas either on their own or jointly with others. A third resolution endorses the principles enshrined in International Labor Organization's Convention 169 and the U.N. Draft Declaration of the Rights of Indigenous Peoples.

In 1997, the IUCN published a two-volume resource guide, *Beyond Fences*, which makes suggestions about how conservation objectives can be achieved through greater collaboration with local communities. The guide notes that the collaborative approach is not only justifiable in terms of conservation effectiveness but is also required if conservation is to be morally and ethically responsible.

In 1999, the World Commission on Protected Areas adopted guidelines for putting the principles contained in one of these seven resolutions into practice. These guidelines emphasize the co-management of protected areas, agreements between indigenous peoples and conservation bodies, indigenous participation in protected areas, and recognition of indigenous peoples' rights to "sustainable, traditional use" of their lands and territories. The link between sustainability and secure tenure has also been clearly recognized. As the 1999 IUCN study *Global Tenure and Sustainable Use* concluded:

> Co-Management is often hailed as the appropriate middle ground, within which the needs of all stakeholders can be negotiated and acceptable compromises achieved [but] . . . this would seem to be only part of the solution. Co-management strategies can only be effective if they are accompanied by parallel efforts to address issues of tenure in the related territory. If tenure arrangements do not secure the interests of local users, there is no incentive to practice sustainable use.

OBSTACLES TO IMPLEMENTATION

Putting these new principles into practice is easier said than done. Conservation initiatives take place within the same constraints as other "development" activities. They must deal with the same competing enterprises and vested interests that confront local communities everywhere. In particular they have to confront the all-too-common ingrained prejudices against indigenous peoples, held by both the general public and personnel in government agencies.

A review carried out by the Forest Peoples Programme (FPP) over the past seven years, which has included an examination of the experiences of indigenous peoples with 36 protected areas in Latin America, Africa, and Asia, has found that the new principles of conservation are not yet being widely applied in developing countries. The three regional conferences at which these case studies were presented and discussed concurred that, in general, protected areas continue to be established and administered in violation of indigenous peoples' rights and in ignorance of the new standards. In Central Africa, protected areas continue to oblige the forced relocation of indigenous peoples, often without any plans for resettlement or compensation (Nelson and Hossack 2003). Serious impoverishment is widely reported and participation is at the most elementary level. Only in southern Africa have participatory wildlife management systems gained currency (Duffy 2000). The San peoples have experienced uneven treatment: being evicted from reserves in Botswana,[4] while enjoying the restitution of some of their lands in South Africa (Chennells 2003).

In Asia, while the overall pattern of denial of rights remains clear, reform efforts are underway in some areas. Overall national laws and policies continue to be framed by the colonial model of conservation, but benefit-sharing through integrated conservation and development projects have a wider currency and in some areas sincere efforts have been made to involve local communities in decision-making and to accommodate (if not legally recognize) indigenous peoples' land rights.

In Latin America, the picture is more mixed. Most national constitutions now recognize indigenous peoples and the legislatures have enacted laws that recognize indigenous peoples' rights. Although implementation of these laws still leaves a lot to be desired, significant progress has been made. But corresponding reforms of conservation laws and policies lag behind these changes and most examples of indigenous-owned and run protected areas have been achieved outside the official protected area systems (Gray, Newing & Padellada 1997). Parallel studies suggest that conservationists in Latin America are only in the first phases of incorporating local communi-

ties into protected area management. Typically these measures include employing local people in such jobs as park guards, rangers, cooks, and secretaries. Community development projects are then the next stage of participation, after which involving communities in natural resource management is attempted. Actual recognition of rights in protected areas is, often, not yet even on the national agenda (Dugelby and Libby 1998).

These findings echo studies made in the United States, where the gradual move toward an accommodation of indigenous peoples' rights in protected areas took over half a century. As Robert Keller and Michael Turek note in *American Indians and National Parks*:

> To begin, park/Indian relations seem to fall into four phases: (1) unilateral appropriation of recreation land by the government; (2) an end to land-taking but a continued federal neglect of tribal needs, cultures and treaties; (3) Indian resistance, leading to aggressive pursuit of tribal interests; (4) a new National Parks Service commitment to cross-cultural integrity and cooperation.

The Forest Peoples Programme review finds that, in all three of the regions examined, examples can be found of protected areas where sincere efforts to apply these new standards are being made. These examples demonstrate that it is possible to recognize the rights of indigenous peoples and achieve conservation goals in the same areas. The case studies also show that a number of serious obstacles stand in the way of an effective recognition of indigenous rights in conservation practice. These include:

- Entrenched discrimination in national societies' attitudes toward indigenous peoples such that indigenous peoples' ways of life are seen as backward, dirty, or subhuman. In the context of conservation initiatives, the result may be a denial of rights and a feeling among affected peoples that they are treated as worse than animals.

- Absence of reform of government policies and laws regarding indigenous peoples. Many governments, especially in Asia and Africa, pursue integrationist or assimilationist social policies toward indigenous peoples, designed to elevate them from backward ways into the national mainstream while ignoring or denying their cultural traditions, customary institutions, rights, and preferences.

- National laws and policies with respect to land which deny indigenous peoples' rights to own and manage their lands.

- National conservation policies and laws still based on the old exclusionary model of conservation. Few of the countries studied have adopted legislation that would encourage community-owned protected areas in line with the revised IUCN protected area category system, which would allow communities and indigenous peoples to own and control protected areas.

- Conservation agencies and NGOs lack appropriate training, staff, and capacity to work with communities. In many cases, national chapters of the large conservation organizations have not been informed about the new policies and principles which have been adopted at the international level.

A NEW PARADIGM

In September 2003, some 150 persons representing indigenous peoples and loosely coordinated through an Ad Hoc Indigenous Peoples Working Group for the WPC attended the Fifth WPC, held in Durban, South Africa. They called on the 3,000 conservationists present at the meeting to respect their rights and to develop a work program to give such declarations real effect. Support organizations such as the Forest Peoples Programme, which had helped raise funds for this mobilization, also issued a series of publications (MacKay 2002) that called on conservationists to:

- Reaffirm their commitment to respect and uphold indigenous peoples' internationally recognized rights in all their protected area programs

- Give priority to reforming national laws, policies, and conservation programs so that they respect indigenous peoples' rights and allow protected areas to be owned and managed by indigenous peoples

- Ensure that sufficient funds are allocated to national conservation programs, and to the regional and international programs that support them, to carry out these legal and policy reforms.

- Retrain conservation personnel in both national and international bureaus so that they understand and know how to apply these new principles

- Establish effective mechanisms for open dialogue, the redress of grievances, and the transparent exchange of information between conservationists and indigenous peoples

- Encourage other major international conservation agencies to adopt clear policies on indigenous peoples and protected areas in conformity with their internationally recognized rights and these new conservation principles

- Combat entrenched discrimination in national and international conservation programs and offices and, where necessary, adopt affirmative social policies that recognize and respect cultural diversity

- Support the consolidation of indigenous peoples' organizations as independent, representative institutions

- Support initiatives by indigenous peoples to secure their territorial rights

- Initiate transparent, participatory, and effective procedures for the restitution of indigenous peoples' lands, territories, and resources incorporated into protected areas and compensate them for all material and immaterial damages in accordance with international law.

The strong presence of indigenous peoples in Durban was successful in getting conservationists to accept a new approach to protected areas. The Durban Accord, the consensus document of the whole congress, announces that the WPC has accepted a new paradigm for protected areas, "integrating them equitably with the interests of all affected people." The accord celebrates the conservation successes of indigenous peoples. It expresses concern at the lack of recognition, protection, and respect given to these efforts. It notes that the costs of protected areas are often borne by local communities. It urges commitment to involve indigenous peoples in establishing and managing protected areas and to participate in decision-making on a fair and equitable basis in full respect of their human and social rights

To implement this new vision, the Durban Accord Action Plan notes that the costs of past successes in establishing a global protected area system have been inequitably borne by local communities. To rectify this disparity, the congress now seeks as a major outcome that the rights of indigenous peoples be recognized and guaranteed in relation to natural resources and biodiversity conservation.

There are currently some 100,000 officially recognized protected areas worldwide covering as much as 12 percent of the land surface of the planet. The great majority of these areas are owned or claimed by indigenous peoples. Reforming these in conformity with international law and in line with the new commitments made in Durban is now going to require a major effort from policy makers and development agencies.

FROM STAKEHOLDERS TO RIGHTS-HOLDERS

The history of indigenous peoples' relations to protected areas can be seen as one of social exclusion and marginalization. Having once been independent nations within their own territories, many indigenous peoples have been pushed off their lands, which have been expropriated by government agencies in the name of conservation. This has facilitated the entry of a number of interests into these areas, ranging from the private sector to academia. Current development discourse, insofar as it recognizes indigenous peoples at all, tends to characterize them now as stakeholders who must compete with other interest groups to get their voices heard. This recognition is not enough. International law recognizes that indigenous peoples have rights to own, manage, and control their lands, and conservationists have now accepted this as the basis for a new paradigm of conservation. The challenge is to allow indigenous peoples to move back into control of their lands.

NOTES

1. For detailed reviews see: West and Brechin 1991; Kemf 1992; Colchester 1994; Ghimire and Pimbert 1996; Gray, Newing and Parellada 1997; Colchester and Erni 1999; Chatty and Cochester 2002; Nelson and Hosack 2003; Cernea and Schmidt-Soltau 2003

2. See www.iucn.org

3. Cited in West 1991

4. See www.survival_international.org

REFERENCES AND FURTHER READING

Amend, S., & Amend, T., Eds. (1992). Espacios sin habitantes? Parques Nacionales de America del Sur. Gland: IUCN.

Borrini-Feyerabend, Grazia, Ed. (1997). Beyond Fences: Seeking Social Sustainability in Conservation, 2 Volumes, Gland: IUCN.

Carey, C., Dudley, N., & Stolton, S. (2000). Squandering Paradise? The Importance and Vulnerability of the World's Protected Areas. Gland, Switzerland: World Wide Fund for Nature-International.

Cernea, M., & Schmidt-Soltau, K. (2003, May 19–23). Biodiversity Conservation versus Population Resettlement: Risks to Nature and Risks to People. Paper presented to the International Conference on Rural Livelihoods, Forests and Biodiversity, Bonn.

Chatty, D., & Colchester, M., Eds. (2002). Conservation and Mobile Indigenous Peoples: Displacement, Forced Settlement and Sustainable Development. Oxford: Berghahn.

Chennells, R. (2003). The Khomani San of South Africa. *In* From Principles to Practice: Indigenous Peoples and Protected Areas in Africa. Nelson, J., & Hossack, L., Eds. Moreton-in-Marsh: Forest Peoples Programme. Pp. 269–289.

Colchester, M. (1994). Salvaging Nature: Indigenous Peoples, Protected Areas and Biodiversity Conservation. UNRISD Discussion Paper 55, Geneva [and 2003, Revised Second edition, World Rainforest Movement, Montevideo].

Colchester, M., & Erni, C., Eds. (1999). Indigenous Peoples and Protected Areas in South and Southeast Asia: From Principles to Practice. Forest Peoples Programme and the International Work Group for Indigenous Affairs, Copenhagen.

Duffy, R. (2000). Killing for Conservation: Wildlife Policy in Zimbabwe. Oxford: James Currie.

Dugelby, B., & Libby, M. (1998). Analyzing the Social Context at PiP Sites. *In* Parks in Peril: People, Politics and Protected Areas. Brandon, K., Redford, K., & Sanderson, S. Washington D.C.: Island Press. Pp. 63–75.

Forrest, S. (1999). Global Tenure and Sustainable Use. Washington D.C.: IUCN Sustainable Use Initiative.

Ghimire, K., & Pimbert, M., Eds. (1996). Social Change and Conservation: Environmental Politics and Impacts of National Parks and Protected Areas. London: Earthscan.

Gray, A., Newing, H., & Padellada, A., Eds. (1997). Indigenous Peoples and Biodiversity Conservation in Latin America: From Principles to Practice. Copenhagen: International Work Group for Indigenous Affairs & Forest Peoples Programme.

IUCN. (1996). World Conservation Congress: Resolutions and Recommendations. Gland: IUCN.

Keller, R., & Turek, M. (1998). American Indians and National Parks. Tucson: University of Arizona Press.

Kwokwo Barume, A. (2000). Heading Towards Extinction: Indigenous Rights in Africa—the case of the Twa of the Kahuzi-Biega National Park, Democratic Republic of Congo. Copenhagan: Forest Peoples Programme and International Work Group for Indigenous Affairs.

MacKay, F. (2002). Addressing Past Wrongs: Indigenous Peoples and Protected Areas: The right to Restitution of Lands and Resources. Moreton-in-Marsh, U.K.: Forest Peoples Programme.

Nelson, J., & Hossack, L., Eds. (2003). From Principles to Practice: Indigenous Peoples and Protected Areas in Africa. Moreton-in-Marsh: Forest Peoples Programme.

[PRIA] Society for Participatory Research in Asia (1993, October 28–30). Doon Declaration on People and Parks. Resolution of the National Workshop on Declining Access to and Control over Natural Resources in National Parks and Sanctuaries. Dehradun: Forest Research Institute

WCPA & IUCN. (2000). Indigenous and Traditional Peoples and Protected Areas: Principles, Guidelines and Case Studies. Gland, Switzerland: Beltran, J., Ed..

West, P., & Brechin, S., Eds. (1991). Resident Peoples and National Parks: Social Dilemmas in International Conservation. Tucson: University of Arizona Press.

World Wide Fund for Nature-International (1996). WWF Statement of Principles: Indigenous Peoples and Conservation. Gland, Switzerland: WWF.

VI

ECONOMICS

How Do People Make a Living?

Generally two meanings are attached to the word **economics.** On the one hand, it refers to maximizing behavior, as when we have to "economize"; on the other hand, it also refers to a system of how production is organized, exchanged, or distributed and consumed. While we like to think of economic behavior as rational, values, tastes, fads, and other idiosyncrasies play a role in our decision making in such a way as to bedevil any apparent rationality. How many parents would charge their children interest for a loan? Why do we grow our own vegetables when it would be much cheaper to purchase them at the local supermarket?

At the same time, we have an institution known as the national economy in which we feel as if we are subject to forces beyond our control. While these two economies seem to be disparate and distinct, they share a number of common characteristics; most importantly, since very few people directly consume what they produce, both of them have to do with **exchange.**

Marshall Sahlins (1972), who defined the various types of exchange, distinguishes between reciprocal, redistributive, and market exchanges. There are three types of reciprocity. First is **generalized reciprocity,** where there is no expectation of an immediate counterflow of equal value. Two typical examples are the following:

- Bushmen foragers share the spoils of a hunt with other camp followers in the expectation that their generosity will be reciprocated in some distant time.

- Parents will spoil children in the hope that when the parents are old, the children will feel obligated to help them. In these types of exchanges the participants will deny that they are economic and will couch them in terms of kinship or friendship obligations.

Second, there is **balanced reciprocity,** or trade, where one has a direct obligation to reciprocate in order to continue the social relationship. Again, it need not be a single commercial transaction. For example, it might be cheaper for me to buy groceries at the supermarket, but I often prefer to use my local corner store, even though it is more expensive, because on occasion they will provide me with credit and other favors. Similarly, as most members of a social drinking group know, when one buys a round, everyone reciprocates. If one member does not drink beer, however, but prefers whiskey, very soon that person gets left out or changes his or her taste because the reciprocity becomes unbalanced and this somehow "spoils the atmosphere." Finally, there is **negative reciprocity,** which is impersonal, barter-based, and centered on one's own ends. In terms of economic behavior, it is the "most economic" and ranges from theft to exploitation. It has very little morality in it and is typically practiced on people separated by great social distance.

All types of reciprocity can be found in one relationship, as in the case of a marital relationship in which one's spouse is unfaithful. Even socially frowned-upon practices like corruption can be analyzed in terms of exchange, as is made clear by Sean McNamara's case study of how to bribe a policeman.

The second type of exchange that Sahlins mentions is **redistributive,** which is more coercive and entails the produce of labor from several individuals being brought to a central place where it is sorted, counted, and reallocated. Such redistribution can take two forms: egalitarian or stratified. A good example of **egalitarian redistribution** would be among the Yanomami, where the headman/ redistributer simply has to work harder than anyone else and gets nothing in return immediately except perhaps admiration. In **stratified redistribution** the redistributer withholds his or her own labor, retains the largest share, and ends up with more material wealth. Typically these exchanges are clothed in a rhetoric of kinship obligations.

Market exchange, the final type, is by far the most dominant; its most important form of exchange is buying and selling. Closely related to the capitalist system, in which the idea of a market is central, market exchange is not, however, the sole mechanism for exchange in a capitalist system. Prices on the market are determined by supply and demand. In the market, loyalties and values are not supposed to enter in, but they often do.

One of the great contributions of anthropology has been in the discovery of the informal sector, or dual economy, of the market. This notion, first pioneered by the anthropologist Keith Hart in 1973, has had a major impact on our understanding of how people survive economically. It refers essentially to the innumerable economic activities that are not recorded in government statistics as tax returns or licenses. In many parts of the world this vibrant sector was usually ignored by economists, principally because it is so difficult to track. Philippe Bourgois's study, "Crack in Spanish Harlem," is representative of this type of economic activity. In many parts of the world the informal sector is more important than the formal sector.

Anthropologists have long been interested in urban life, exploring the social, economic, and political organization of cities. They are also increasingly interested in the dynamics and impacts of globalization. Richard Sennett treats both these themes, arguing that capitalism's economic globalization provokes a host of changes, not only in the structure of economic relationships, but also in the social and political life of cities. New dilemmas arise over citizenship, participation in the public realm, the nature of labor, and concepts of conviviality with strangers.

FOCUS QUESTIONS

As you read these selections, consider these questions:

✦ How do industrialized and market-based economies differ from non-industrial economies?

✦ Why and how do "informal economies" get established?

✦ Can you provide any examples of non-monetary-based exchange systems in your own life? How and why did you get involved in this exchange system? How is the value of goods and services established?

✦ What impacts do changes in capitalism and labor have on your own city or neighborhood?

REFERENCE

Sahlins, Marshall. 1972. *Stone Age Economics.* Chicago: Aldine.

18

Learning How to Bribe a Policeman

Sean Cush McNamara

Sean Cush McNamara is a British anthropologist who has carried out fieldwork in Bolivia.

There has been some discussion by social scientists interested in development studies on the use of public office for private gain. Although this question has had general interest for me, I never thought I would have any experience to contribute to the discussion. Indeed, as for many law-abiding people in Britain, such interests appear rather exotic. It was therefore rather a surprise, during a recent visit to Bolivia, to find myself inside a prison and bribing my way out again. What was immediately interesting was that I did not know how to bribe someone. This does not seem to have been part of my education in life skills and I had to learn about the process.

How did I find myself in this situation? Well, with a friend I had just arrived in Santa Cruz from La Paz. Santa Cruz is of interest as one of the last remaining "frontier" regions of the world. This frontier has been created first of all by discovery of oil and the subsequent immigration this has stimulated. The sleepy town surrounded by forest of the early 1970s is now a bustling centre from which the forest has receded. It has the feel of the Wild West to match its situation but with new pick-up trucks, not horses, in the streets. Two hours after arrival in Santa Cruz we were in the central plaza looking at an exhibition of handicrafts, and about a quarter of an hour later we were in the police station. Later, out again and back in our hotel, we overheard an American couple talking of their brush with the law and of their near-imprisonment. So this was not an isolated incident. In order to understand the system which gives rise to harassment of foreigners in Santa Cruz there is a need to describe the most salient features of the local economy.

"Learning How to Bribe a Policeman" by Sean Cush McNamara from *Anthropology Today*, Vol. 2, No. 2, 1986. Reprinted by permission of Blackwell Publishers.

THE CONTEXT

In Bolivia there is an inflation rate variously estimated between 500 and 2,000% per year. This means salaries erode rapidly and rises granted every quarter or even every month cannot keep pace. Daily paid workers obtain rises daily. There are two exchange rates in operation: in early June 1985 the official rate was 75,000 pesos to the dollar while the parallel rate was rising rapidly from about 300,000 to 400,000 pesos. This means that there is a great desire among salaried people, including the police, to obtain dollars in order to retain the value of "savings" (i.e., cash that has not been spent today but which will be needed tomorrow). The general importance of these factors in the bribery of policemen will be seen later. I should stress that these are not sufficient conditions: there are special features of Santa Cruz which make it different from the rest of the country. Whilst the national economy is struggling, the economy of Santa Cruz is buoyant. Santa Cruz is the area where oil, cocaine, and contraband play major roles in the economy. The resultant dollar wealth has two consequences which are relevant here. First, there is an extremely unequal distribution of dollars. Second, every foreigner is a potential supply, as are street money changers and small-time cocaine dealers.

THE PROTECTION OF THE LAW

The general objective for a salaried policeman is to ensure his subsistence for the whole month. In June 1985 it was reckoned that his salary of approximately $28 would last about a fortnight. Other cash must be obtained from other sources. The operational problem to be resolved by many policemen (without access to other funds) is how to ensure a reasonable flow of cash. Here the policeman's duty of upholding the law is very useful as it can be used to generate further funds.

Dealing in cocaine or contraband is illegal. There is mounting international pressure to reduce the flow of cocaine from Bolivia, and the Bolivian government is itself concerned about increasing domestic drug addiction. However it is common knowledge in Santa Cruz that some drug dealers are very wealthy and powerful and manage to evade the law. The same cannot be said of small-time dealers with few connections. Such small-timers populate the local prison.

Currency transactions in the street are also illegal but can be considered almost a necessity if the illegal dollar earnings are to be used within the Santa Cruz economy. Perhaps in recognition of this, money changers continue to operate in the street but have been moving away from the central plaza to the ring road.

Because of the intense interest in drugs there is a justification for taking an interest in foreigners: every one is a potential drug smuggler. However there must usually be some pretext for questioning a foreigner. Such pretexts are easy to find: talking to a known money changer; not carrying passports; driving a foreign vehicle. Once contact has been established, the game plan is as follows:

- Talking to someone *is* changing money illegally.
- Not carrying passport *is* being a suspected drug smuggler.
- Parking a vehicle *is* parking illegally.

All these pretexts enable the law to be used to gain a top-up of salary. In our case we were talking in the plaza when a policeman asked for proof of identity. Our passports were in the hotel—theft of passports is quite common—and a driving licence was not considered sufficient.

At this point there are three options for a foreigner:

1. Walk away immediately and with determination.
2. Pay bribe on the spot.
3. Accompany officer to the police station.

The problem of the second option is that foreigners do not know how to do it, and the first option does not come to mind. The third option has the consequence that a senior officer is involved and he wishes to receive the bribe. However, in front of many people in the outer offices of the police station it will probably appear even more difficult to bribe a policeman. The opportunity is offered by the senior officer requesting all pockets to be emptied. Having cash in pesos and dollars is further "evidence" of illegal money changing. We had the impression that confiscation of dollars was possible at this stage, except that since we were carrying travellers' cheques in the main this was less likely.

Not resolving the issue at this stage brings about an escalation in police pressure. The protest of innocence to the first policeman is now interpreted as "threatening behaviour," and the suspect is removed to the inner courtyard. This is inhabited by minor drug dealers and others serving a range of sentences or simply being held in custody. The economy of this part of the prison involving sale of clothing to buy food, negotiations between guards and women also held there—would be an interesting study in its own right.

Once in the courtyard the charge is rumoured to have increased again to assaulting a policeman, and an even more senior officer (who never appears in person) is involved. The immediate prospect seems to be a few hours or days in this courtyard; this is clearly designed as a softening up until the bribe is paid.

LEARNING HOW TO PAY A BRIBE

In the courtyard the minor drug dealers know the rules. One, who had been in the main prison elsewhere, had secured his own transfer to the relative comfort of the courtyard. A laid-back character who has now kicked his own habit but with 20 years still to serve officially (having completed 5), he makes himself useful talking to newcomers and passing on information received. We had the feeling our story was being checked informally and we heard how the charges were escalating. Through this intermediary it was made known that a bribe could be made and initial negotiations began over the amount. At the same time a CID man was sent to the hotel to collect the passports. Also the police heard that it was difficult for us to give a "bribe."

The final arrangements were made by the officer from the outer offices. The charges about hitting a policeman were forgotten but a "fine" was to be paid for keeping the passports safely in the hotel. We were asked how much we would like to pay. Working on the basis that $1 would have probably been acceptable to the very first policeman and that $50 obtains an internal transfer for a drug dealer according to our new friend, a sum of approximately $15 was offered in pesos to compensate for the inconvenience we had caused the police. This was agreed. Possibly a lower "fine" would have been acceptable in dollars.

As a sidelight on the affair, the CID man who had collected the passports had to accompany us back to the hotel where the staff had made him sign a receipt for the passports. He asked for $2 for his inconvenience.

CONCLUSIONS

The experience brings out a number of points:

1. If a bribe is a "fine," cross-cultural difficulties are resolved.

2. The amount increases as the centre of the prison is approached, and more senior officers are involved. A visitor should avoid accompanying the officer to the police station.

3. The police require their own justifications—for making the first contact and for raising the "fine" and these are found by reference to the law.

4. Police harassment is determined in this situation by economic factors; the incidence of harassment increases as the month progresses (and the salary diminishes in value).

5. The contempt with which local people treated the local police almost amounted to counter-harassment, except that locals were very aware of how and when to walk away from confrontation.

Ironically we had been trying to obtain cash dollars in order to pay the airport tax but were not able to find any legally so on the way to the airport the ring road money changers proved useful—though they were reluctant to buy pesos. This was an illustration of how a system of law not founded in economic reality—i.e., having to pay airport tax in dollars but there being none offered legally for purchase—creates a necessity for illegality.

Finally, although the experience is unique, I hope it adds some local colour to the recent debate on the use of public office for private gain.

19

Crack in Spanish Harlem
Culture and Economy in the Inner City

Philippe Bourgois

Philippe Bourgois, an associate professor at San Francisco State University, was awarded the PhD by Stanford University in 1985. Bourgois has carried out fieldwork in the Caribbean and Central America as well as in Spanish Harlem and has research interests in political economy, ethnicity, immigration, and the work process.

The heavy-set, white undercover policeman pushed me across the ice-cream counter, spreading my legs and poking me around the groin. As he came dangerously close to the bulge in my right pocket I hissed in his ear "It's a tape recorder." He snapped backwards, releasing his left hand's grip on my neck and whispering a barely audible "Sorry." Apparently, he thought he had clumsily intercepted an undercover from another department because before I could get a close look at his face he had left the *bodega* grocery-store cum numbers-joint. Meanwhile, the marijuana sellers stationed in front of the *bodega* that Gato and I had just entered to buy 16-ounce cans of Private Stock (beer), observing that the undercover had been rough with me when he searched through my pants, suddenly felt safe and relieved—finally confident that I was a white drug addict rather than an undercover.

As we hurried to leave this embarrassing scene we were blocked by Bennie, an emaciated teenager high on angel dust who was barging through the door along with two friends to mug us. I ran to the back of the *bodega* but Gato had to stand firmly because this was the corner he worked, and those were his former partners. They dragged him onto the sidewalk surrounding him on all sides, shouting about the money he still owed, and began kicking and hitting him with a baseball bat. I found out later that Gato owed them for his share of the supply of marijuana confiscated in a drug bust last week. . . . After we finished telling the story at the crack/*botanica*[1] house where I had been spending most of my evening hours this summer, Chino, who was on duty selling that night with Julio (pronounced Jew-Lee-oh), jumped up excitedly calling out, "What street was that on? Come on, let's go, we can still catch them—How many were they?" I quickly stopped this mobilization for a revenge posse, explaining that it was not worth my time, and that we should just forget about it. Chino looked at me disgustedly sitting back down on the milk crate in front of the *botanica*'s door and turned his face away from me, shrugging his shoulders. Julio, whom I knew better and had become quite close to for a number of weeks last year, jumped up in front of me raising his voice to berate me for being "pussy." He also sat back down shortly afterwards feigning exasperated incredulity with the comment "Man you still think like a *blanquito*." A half dozen spectators—some of them empty-pocketed ("thirsty!") crack addicts, but most of them sharply dressed teenage drug-free girls competing for Chino's and Julio's attentions—giggled and snickered at me.

CULTURE AND MATERIAL REALITY

The above extract from sanitized fieldwork notes is merely a personalized glimpse of the day-to-day struggle for survival *and for meaning* by the people who stand behind the extraordinary statistics on inner city violent crime in the United States. These are the same Puerto Rican residents of Spanish Harlem, New York City, that Oscar Lewis in *La Vida* declared to be victims of a "culture of poverty" enmired in a "self-perpetuating cycle of poverty" (Lewis 1966:5). The culture of poverty concept has been severely criticized for its internal inconsisten-

"Crack in Spanish Harlem: Culture and Economy in the Inner City" by Philippe Bourgois from *Anthropology Today,* Vol. 5, No. 4, 1989. Reprinted by permission of Blackwell Publishers.

cies, its inadequate understanding of "culture" and ethnicity, its ethnocentric/middle class bias, its blindness to structural forces, and its blame-the-victim implications (cf. Leacock 1971; Valentine 1968; Waxman 1977; Stack 1974). Despite the negative scholarly consensus on Lewis's theory, the alternative discussions either tend towards economic reductionism (Ryan 1971; Steinberg 1981; Wilson 1978) or else ultimately minimize the reality of profound marginalization and destruction—some of it internalized—that envelop a disproportionate share of the inner city poor (cf. Stack 1974; Valentine 1978; see critiques by Maxwell 1988; Wilson 1987). More importantly, the media, public policy-makers and a large proportion of inner city residents themselves continue to subscribe to a popularized blame-the-victim/culture of poverty concept that has not been adequately rebutted by scholars.

The inner city residents described in the ethnographic vignette above are the pariahs of urban industrial US society. They seek their income and subsequently their identity and the meaning in their life through what they perceive to be high-powered careers "on the street." They partake of ideologies and values and share symbols which form the basis of an "inner city street culture" completely excluded from the mainstream economy and society but ultimately derived from it. Most of them have few direct contacts with non–inner city residents, and when they do it is usually with people who are in a position of domination: teachers in school, bosses, police officers, and later parole or probation officers.

How can one understand the complicated ideological dynamic accompanying inner city poverty without falling into a hopelessly idealistic culture of poverty and blame-the-victim interpretation? Structural, political economy reinterpretations of the inner city dynamic emphasize historical processes of labour migration in the context of institutionalized ethnic discrimination. They dissect the structural transformations in the international economy which are destroying the manufacturing sector in the United States and are swelling the low wage, low prestige service sector (cf. Davis 1987; Sassen-Koob 1986; Steinberg 1981; Tabb & Sawers 1984; Wilson 1978, 1987). These analyses address the structural confines of the inner city dynamic but fall prey to a passive interpretation of human action and subscribe to a weakly dialectic interpretation of the relationship between ideological processes and material reality, or between culture and class.

Although ultimately traceable directly to being products of international labour migrations in a transnational world economy, street-level inner city residents are more than merely passive victims of historical economic transformations or of the institutionalized discrimination of a perverse political and economic system. They do not passively accept their fourth-class citizen fate. They are struggling determinedly—just as ruthlessly as the railroad and oil robber-barons of the previous century and the investment-banker "yuppies" of today—to earn money, demand dignity and lead meaningful lives. Tragically, it is that very process of struggle against—yet within—the system which exacerbates the trauma of their community and which destroys hundreds of thousands of lives on the individual level.

In the day-to-day experience of the street-bound inner city resident, unemployment and personal anxiety over the inability to provide one's family with a minimal standard of living translates itself into intra-community crime, intra-community drug abuse, intra-family violence. The objective, structural desperation of a population without a viable economy, and facing systematic barriers of ethnic discrimination and ideological marginalization, becomes charged at the community level into self-destructive channels.

Most importantly, the "personal failure" of those who survive on the street is articulated in the idiom of race. The racism imposed by the larger society becomes internalized on a personal level. Once again, although the individuals in the ethnographic fragment at the beginning of this paper are the victims of long-term historical and structural transformations, they do not analyse their difficult situation from a political economy perspective. In their struggle to survive and even to be successful, they enforce on a day-to-day level the details of the trauma and cruelty of their lives on the excluded margins of US urban society.

CULTURAL REPRODUCTION THEORY

Theorists of education have developed a literature on processes of social and cultural reproduction which focus on the ideological domination of the poor and the working class in the school setting (cf. Giroux 1983). Although some of the social reproduction approaches tend towards an economic reductionism or a simple, mechanical functionalism (cf. Bowles & Gintis 1977), the more recent variants emphasize the complexity and contradictory nature of the dynamic of ideological domination (Willis 1983). There are several ethnographies which document how the very process whereby students resist school channels them into marginal roles in the economy for the rest of their lives (cf. Willis 1977; Macleod 1987). Other ethnographically based interpretations emphasize how success for inner city African-American students requires a rejection of their ethnic identity and cultural dignity (Fordham 1988).

There is no reason why these theories of cultural resistance and ideological domination have to be limited to the institutional school setting. Cultural reproduction theory has great potential for shedding light on the interaction between structurally induced cultural resistance and self-reinforced marginalization at the street-level in the inner city experience. The violence, crime and substance abuse plaguing the inner city can be understood as the manifestations of a "culture of resistance" to mainstream, white racist, and economically exclusive society. This "culture of resistance," however, results in greater oppression and self-destruction. More concretely, refusing to accept the outside society's racist role playing and refusing to accept low wage, entry-level jobs, translates into high crime rates, high addiction rates and high intra-community violence.

Most of the individuals in the above ethnographic description are proud that they are not being exploited by "the White Man," but they feel "like fucking assholes" for being poor. All of them have previously held numerous jobs in the legal economy in their lives. Most of them hit the street in their early teens working odd jobs as delivery boys and baggers in supermarkets and *bodegas*. Most of them have held the jobs that are recognized as among the least desirable in US society. Virtually all of these street participants have had deeply negative personal experiences in the minimum-wage labour market, owing to abusive, exploitative and often racist bosses or supervisors. They see the illegal underground economy as not only offering superior wages, but also a more dignified work place. For example, Gato had formerly worked for the ASPCA cleaning out the gas chambers where stray dogs and cats are killed. Bennie had been fired six months earlier from a night shift job as security guard on the violent ward for the criminally insane on Wards Island; Chino had been fired a year ago from a job installing high altitude storm windows on skyscrapers following an accident which temporarily blinded him in the right eye. Upon being disabled he discovered that his contractor had hired him illegally through an arrangement with a corrupt union official who had paid him half the union wage, pocketing the rest, and who had not taken health insurance for him. Chino also claimed that his foreman from Pennsylvania was a "Ku Klux Klanner" and had been especially abusive to him as he was a black Puerto Rican. In the process of recovering from the accident, Chino had become addicted to crack and ended up in the hospital as a gunshot victim before landing a job at Papito's crack house. Julio's last legal job before selling crack was as an off-the-books messenger for a magazine catering to New York yuppies. He had become addicted to crack, began selling possessions from out of his home and finally was thrown out by his wife who had just given birth to his son, who carried his name as Junior the IIIrd, on public assistance. Julio had quit his messenger

job in favour of stealing car radios for a couple of hours at night in the very same neighbourhood where he had been delivering messages for ten-hour days at just above minimum wage. Nevertheless, after a close encounter with the police Julio begged his cousin for a job selling in his crack house. Significantly, the sense of responsibility, success and prestige that selling crack gave him enabled him to kick his crack habit and replace it by a less expensive and destructive powder cocaine and alcohol habit.

The underground economy, consequently, is the ultimate "equal opportunity employer" for inner city youth (cf. Kornblum & Williams 1985). As Davis (1987: 75) has noted for Los Angeles, the structural economic incentive to participate in the drug economy is overwhelming:

> With 78,000 unemployed youth in the Watts-Willowbrook area, it is not surprising that there are now 145 branches of the rival Crips and Bloods gangs in South L.A., or that the jobless resort to the opportunities of the burgeoning "Crack" economy.

The individuals "successfully" pursuing careers in the "crack economy" or any other facet of the underground economy are no longer "exploitable" by legal society. They speak with anger at their former low wages and bad treatment. They make fun of friends and acquaintances—many of whom come to buy drugs from them—who are still employed in factories, in service jobs, or in what they (and most other people) would call "shitwork." Of course, many others are less self-conscious about the reasons for their rejection of entry-level, mainstream employment. Instead, they think of themselves as lazy and irresponsible. They claim they quit their jobs in order to have a good time on the street. Many still pay lip service to the value of a steady, legal job. Still others cycle in and out of legal employment supplementing their bouts at entry-level jobs through part-time crack sales in an almost perverse parody of the economic subsidy of the wage labour sector by semi-subsistence peasants who cyclically engage in migratory wage labour in third world economies (cf. Meillassoux 1981; Wallerstein 1977).

THE CULTURE OF TERROR IN THE UNDERGROUND ECONOMY

The culture of resistance that has emerged in the underground street-level economy in opposition to demeaning, underpaid employment in the mainstream economy engenders violence. In the South America context of extreme political repression and racism against Amerindians and Jews, anthropologist Michael Taussig has argued that "cultures of terror" emerge to become ". . . a high powered tool for domination and a principal medium for political practice" (1984: 492). Unlike Taussig's examples of the 1910s Putumaya massacres and the 1970s Argentine torture chambers, domination in the case of the inner city's culture of terror is self-administered even if the root cause is generated or even imposed externally. With the exception of occasional brutality by policemen or the bureaucratized repression of the social welfare and criminal justice institutions (cf. Davis 1988), the physical violence and terror of the inner city are largely carried out by inner city residents themselves.

Regular displays of violence are necessary for success in the underground economy—especially at the street-level drug dealing world. Violence is essential for maintaining credibility and for preventing rip-off by colleagues, customers and hold-up artists. Indeed, upward mobility in the underground economy requires a systematic and effective use of violence against one's colleagues, one's neighbours and, to a certain extent, against oneself. Behaviour that appears irrationally violent and self-destructive to the middle class (or the working class) outside observer can be reinterpreted, according to the logic of the underground economy, as a judicious case of public relations, advertising, rapport building and long-term investment in one's "human capital development."

The importance of one's reputation is well illustrated in the fieldwork fragment at the beginning of this paper. Gato and I were mugged because Gato had a reputation for being "soft" or "pussy" and because I was publicly unmasked as *not being* an undercover cop: hence safe to attack. Gato tried to minimize the damage to his future ability to sell on that corner by not turning and running. He had pranced sideways down the street, though being beaten with a baseball bat and kicked to the ground twice. Significantly, I found out later that it was the second time this had happened to Gato this year. Gato was not going to be upwardly mobile in the underground economy because of his "pussy" reputation and he was further cementing his fate with an increasingly out of control addiction to crack.

Employers or new entrepreneurs in the underground economy are looking for people who can demonstrate their capacity for effective violence and terror. For example, in the eyes of Papito, the owner of the string of crack franchises I am currently researching, the ability of his employees to hold up under gunpoint is crucial as stick-ups of dealing dens are not infrequent. In fact, since my fieldwork began in 1986, the *botanica* has been held up twice. Julio happened to be on duty both times. He admitted to me that he had been very nervous when they held the gun to his temple and had asked for money and crack. Nevertheless, not only did he withhold some of the money and crack that was hidden behind the bogus *botanica* merchandise, but he also later exaggerated to Pa-

pito the amount that had been stolen in order to pocket the difference.

On several occasions in the midst of long conversations with active criminals (i.e., once with a dealing-den stick-up artist, several times with crack dealers, and once with a former bank robber) I asked them to explain how they were able to trust their partners in crime sufficiently to ensure the longevity and effectiveness of their enterprise. To my surprise I was not given any righteous diatribes about blood-brotherhood trustworthiness or any adulations of boyhood loyalty. Instead, in each case, in slightly different language I was told somewhat aggressively: "What do you mean how do I trust him? You should ask 'How does he trust me?'" Their ruthlessness is their security: "My support network is me, myself and I." They made these assertions with such vehemence as to appear threatened by the concept that their security and success might depend upon the trustworthiness of their partner or their employer. They were claiming—in one case angrily—that they were not dependent upon trust: because they were tough enough to command respect and enforce all contracts they entered into. The "How can they trust me?" was said with smug pride, perhaps not unlike the way a stockbroker might brag about his access to inside information on an upcoming hostile takeover deal.

At the end of the summer Chino demonstrated clearly the how-can-I-be-trusted dynamic. His cocaine snorting habit had been degenerating into a crack addiction by the end of the summer, and finally one night he was forced to flee out of state to a cousin's when he was unable to turn in the night's receipts to his boss Papito following a binge. Chino also owed Papito close to a thousand dollars for bail that Papito had posted when he was arrested for selling crack at the *botanica* a few months ago. Almost a year later when Papito heard that Chino had been arrested for jumping bail he arranged through another associate incarcerated in the same prison (Rikers Island) to have Chino beaten up before his trial date.

My failure to display a propensity for violence in several instances cost me the respect of the members of the crack scene that I frequented. This was very evident when I turned down Julio and Chino's offer to search for Bennie after he mugged Gato and me. Julio had despairingly exclaimed that I "still [thought] like a *blanquito*," genuinely disappointed that I was not someone with common sense and self-respect.

These concrete examples of the cultivation of violent public behaviour are the extreme cases of individuals relying on the underground economy for their income and dependent upon cultivating terror in order to survive. Individuals involved in street activity cultivate the culture of terror in order to intimidate competitors, maintain credibility, develop new contacts, cement partnerships, and ultimately to have a good time. For the most part they are not conscious of this process. The culture of terror becomes a myth and a role model with rules and satisfactions all its own which ultimately has a traumatic impact on the majority of Spanish Harlem residents—who are drug free and who work honestly at poorly remunerated legal jobs, 9 to 5 plus overtime.

PURSUING THE AMERICAN DREAM

It is important to understand that the underground economy and the violence emerging out of it are not propelled by an irrational cultural logic distinct from that of mainstream USA. On the contrary, street participants are frantically pursuing the "American dream." The assertions of the culture of poverty theorists that the poor have been badly socialized and do not share mainstream values is wrong. On the contrary, ambitious, energetic, inner city youths are attracted into the underground economy in order to try frantically to get their piece of the pie as fast as possible. They often even follow the traditional US model for upward mobility to the letter by becoming aggressive private entrepreneurs. They are the ultimate rugged individualists braving an unpredictable frontier where fortune, fame and destruction are all just around the corner. Hence Indio, a particularly enterprising and ambitious young crack dealer who was aggressively carving out a new sales point, shot his brother in the spine and paralyzed him for life while he was high on angel dust in a battle over sales rights. His brother now works for him selling on crutches. Meanwhile, the shooting has cemented Indio's reputation and his workers are awesomely disciplined: "If he shot his brother he'll shoot anyone." Indio reaffirms this symbolically by periodically walking his turf with an oversized gold chain and name plate worth several thousand dollars hanging around his neck.

The underground economy and the culture of terror are experienced as the most realistic routes to upward mobility. Entry-level jobs are not seen as viable channels to upward mobility by high school dropouts. Drug selling or other illegal activity appear as the most effective and realistic options for getting rich within one's lifetime. Many of the street dealers claim to be strictly utilitarian in their involvement with crack and they snub their clients despite the fact that they usually have considerable alcohol and powder cocaine habits themselves. Chino used to chant at his regular customers "Come on, keep on killing yourself; bring me that money; smoke yourself to death; make me rich."

Even though street sellers are employed by the owner of a sales point for whom they have to maintain regular hours, meet sales quotas and be subject to being fired, they have a great deal of autonomy and power in their daily (or nightly) routine. The boss only comes once or twice a shift to drop off drugs and pick up money. Frequently, it is a young messenger who is sent instead. Sellers are often surrounded by a bevy of "thirsty" friends and [hangers-on]—frequently young teenage women in the case of male sellers—willing to run errands, pay attention to conversations, lend support in arguments and fights and provide sexual favours for them on demand because of the relatively large amounts of money and drugs passing through their hands. In fact, even youths who do not use drugs will hang out and attempt to befriend respectfully the dealer just to be privy to the excitement of people coming and going, copping and hanging; money flowing, arguments, detectives, and stick-up artists—all around danger and excitement. Other non-users will hang out to be treated to an occasional round of beer, Bacardi or, on an off night, Thunderbird.

The channel into the underground economy is by no means strictly economic. Besides wanting to earn "crazy money," people choose "hoodlum" status in order to assert their dignity at refusing to "sling a mop for the white man" (cf. Anderson 1976: 68). Employment—or better yet self-employment—in the underground economy accords a sense of autonomy, self-dignity and an opportunity for extraordinary rapid short-term upward mobility that is only too obviously unavailable in entry-level jobs. Opulent survival without a "visible means of support" is the ultimate expression of success and it is a viable option. There is plenty of visible proof of this to everyone on the street as they watch teenage crack dealers drive by in convertible Suzuki Samurai jeeps with the stereo blaring, "beem" by in impeccable BMWs, or—in the case of the middle-aged dealers—speed around in well-waxed Lincoln Continentals. Anyone can aspire to be promoted to the level of a seller perched on a 20-speed mountain bike with a beeper by their side. In fact, many youths not particularly active in the drug trade run around with beepers on their belts just pretending to be big-time. The impact of the sense of dignity and worth that can accompany selling crack is illustrated by Julio's ability to overcome his destructive addiction to crack only after getting a job selling it: "I couldn't be messin' up the money. I couldn't be fucking up no more! Besides, I had to get respect."

In New York City the insult of working for entry-level wages amidst extraordinary opulence is especially painfully perceived by Spanish Harlem youths who have grown up in abject poverty only a few blocks from all-white neighbourhoods commanding some of the highest real estate values in the world. As messengers, security guards or Xerox machine operators in the corporate headquarters of the Fortune 500 companies, they are brusquely ordered about by young white executives who sometimes make monthly salaries superior to their yearly wages and who do not even have the time to notice that they are being rude.

It could be argued that Manhattan sports a *de facto* apartheid labour hierarchy whereby differences in job category and prestige correlate with ethnicity and are often justified—consciously or unconsciously—through a racist logic. This humiliating confrontation with New York's ethnic/occupational hierarchy drives the street-bound cohort of inner city youths deeper into the confines of their segregated neighbourhood and the underground economy. They prefer to seek out meaning and upward mobility in a context that does not constantly oblige them to come into contact with people of a different, hostile ethnicity wielding arbitrary power over them. In the underground economy, especially in the world of substance abuse, they never have to experience the silent subtle humiliations that the entry-level labour market—or even merely a daily subway ride downtown—invariably subjects them to.

In this context the crack high and the rituals and struggles around purchasing and using the drug are comparable to the millenarian religions that sweep colonized peoples attempting to resist oppression in the context of accelerated social trauma—whether it be the Ghost dance of the Great Plains Amerindians, the "cargo cults" of Melanesia, the Mamachi movement of the Guaymi Amerindians in Panama, or even religions such as Farrakhan's Nation of Islam and the Jehovah's Witnesses in the heart of the inner city (cf. Bourgois 1986, 1989). Substance abuse in general, and crack in particular, offer the equivalent of a millenarian metamorphosis. Instantaneously users are transformed from being unemployed, depressed high school dropouts, despised by the world—and secretly convinced that their failure is due to their own inherent stupidity, "racial laziness" and disorganization—into being a mass of heart-palpitating pleasure, followed only minutes later by a jaw-gnashing crash and wide-awake alertness that provides their life with concrete purpose: get more crack—fast!

One of the most dramatic illustrations within the dynamic of the crack economy of how a cultural dynamic of resistance to exploitation can lead contradictorily to greater oppression and ideological domination is the conspicuous presence of women in the growing cohort of crack addicts. In a series of ten random surveys undertaken at Papito's crack franchises, women and girls represented just under 50% of the customers. This contrasts dramatically to the estimates of female participation in heroin addiction in the late 1970s.

The painful spectacle of young, emaciated women milling in agitated angst around crack copping corners and selling their bodies for five dollars, or even merely for a puff on a crack stem, reflects the growing emancipation of women in all aspects of inner city life, culture and economy. Women—especially the emerging generation which is most at risk for crack addiction—are no longer as obliged to stay at home and maintain the family. They no longer so readily sacrifice public life or forgo independent opportunities to generate personally disposable income. This is documented by the frequent visits to the crack houses by pregnant women and by mothers accompanied by toddlers.

A more neutral illustration of the changed position of women in street culture outside the arena of substance abuse is the growing presence of young women on inner city basketball courts. Similarly, on the national level, there are conclusive statistics documenting increased female participation in the legal labour market—especially in the working-class Puerto Rican community. By the same token, more women are also resisting exploitation in the entry-level job market and are pursuing careers in the underground economy and seeking self-definition and meaning through intensive participation in street culture.

Although women are using the drug and participating intensively in street culture, traditional gender relations still largely govern income-generating strategies in the underground economy. Most notably, women are forced disproportionately to rely on prostitution to finance their habits. The relegation of women to the traditional street role of prostitution has led to a flooding of the market for sex, leading to a drop in the price of women's bodies and to an epidemic rise in venereal disease among women and newborn babies.

Contradictorily, therefore, the underlying process of emancipation which has enabled women to demand equal participation in street culture and to carve out an expanded niche for themselves in the underground economy has led to a greater depreciation of women as ridiculed sex objects. Addicted women will tolerate a tremendous amount of verbal and physical abuse in their pursuit of a vial of crack, allowing lecherous men to humiliate and ridicule them in public. Chino, who is married and is the father of nine children, refers to the women who regularly service him with oral sex as "my moufs" [mouths]. He enjoys calling out to these addicted women from across the street. "Yo, there goes my mouf! Come on over here." Such a public degradation of a cohort of women who are conspicuously present on the street cannot be neutral. It ultimately reinforces the ideological domination of women in general.

DE-LEGITIMIZING DOMINATION

How can one discuss and analyse the phenomenon of street-level inner city culture and violence without reproducing and confirming the very ideological relationships that are its basis? In his discussion of the culture of terror,

Taussig notes that it is precisely the narratives about the torture and violence of the repressive societies which ". . . are in themselves evidence of the process whereby a culture of terror was created and sustained" (1984: 279). The superhuman power that the media has accorded to crack serves a similar mythical function. The *New York Times* has run articles and interviews with scientists that portray crack as if it were a miraculous substance beyond the power of human beings to control (cf. 25 June, 1988: 1). They "prove" this by documenting how quickly rats will ecstatically kill themselves when provided with cocaine upon demand. Catheterized rats push the cocaine lever to the exclusion of the nutrient lever until they collapse exhausted to die of thirst.

The alleged omnipotence of crack coupled with even the driest recounting of the overpowering statistics on violence ultimately allows US society to absolve itself of any real responsibility for the inner city phenomena. The mythical dimensions of the culture of terror push economics and politics out of the picture and enable the US to maintain in some of its larger cities a level of ethnic segregation and economic marginalization that are unacceptable to any of the other wealthy, industrialized nations of the world, with the obvious exception of South Africa. Worse yet, on the level of theory, because of the continued domination—even in their negation—of the North America–centered culture of poverty theories, this discussion of the ideological implications of the underground economy may take readers full circle back to a blame-the-victim interpretation of inner city oppression.

NOTE

1. A *botanica* is a herbal pharmacy and *santeria* utility store.

REFERENCES

Anderson, Elijah. 1976. *A Place on the Corner*. Chicago: University of Chicago Press.

Bourgois, Philippe. 1986. "The Miskitu of Nicaragua: Politicized Ethnicity." *Anthropology Today* Vol. 2, No. 2: 4–9.

Bourgois, Philippe. 1989. *Ethnicity at Work: Divided Labour on a Central American Banana Plantation*. Baltimore, MD: Johns Hopkins University Press.

Bowles, Samuel, & Herbert Gintis. 1977. *Schooling in Capitalist America*. New York: Basic Books.

Davis, Mike. 1987. "*Chinatown, Part Two?* The 'Internationalization' of Downtown Los Angeles." *New Left Review* Vol. 164: 65–86.

Davis, Mike, with Sue Ruddick. 1988. "Los Angeles: Civil Liberties Between the Hammer and the Rock." *New Left Review* 1970: 37–60.

Fordham, Signithia. 1988. "Racelessness as a Factor in Black Students' School Success: Pragmatic Strategy or Pyrrhic Victory?" *Harvard Educational Review* Vol. 58, No. 1: 54–84.

Giroux, Henry. 1983. "Theories of Reproduction and Resistance in the New Sociology of Education: A Critical Analysis." *Harvard Educational Review* Vol. 53, No. 3: 257–293.

Kornblum, William, & Terry Williams. 1985. *Growing Up Poor*. Lexington, MA: Lexington Books.

Leacock, Eleanor Burke (Ed.). 1971. *The Culture of Poverty: A Critique*. New York: Simon & Schuster.

Lewis, Oscar. 1966. "The Culture of Poverty." In *Anthropological Essays*. New York: Random House.

Macleod, Jay. 1987. *Ain't No Makin' It*. Boulder, CO: Westview Press.

Maxwell, Andrew. 1988. "The Anthropology of Poverty in Black Communities: A Critique and Systems Alternative." *Urban Anthropology* Vol. 17, No. 2 & 3: 171–191.

Meillassoux, Claude. 1981. *Maidens, Meal and Money*. Cambridge, England: Cambridge University Press.

Ryan, William. 1986 [1971]. "Blaming the Victim." In *Taking Sides: Clashing Views on Controversial Social Issues*, ed. by Kurt Finsterbusch & George McKenna. Guilford, CT: Dushkin.

Sassen-Koob, Saskia. 1986. "New York City: Economic Restructuring and Immigration." *Development and Change* Vol. 17, No. 1: 87–119.

Stack, Carol. 1974. *All Our Kin: Strategies for Survival in a Black Community*. New York: Harper & Row.

Steinberg, Stephen. 1981. *The Ethnic Myth: Race, Ethnicity and Class in America*. New York: Atheneum.

Tabb, William, & Larry Sawers (Eds.). 1984. *Marxism and the Metropolis: New Perspectives in Urban Political Economy*. New York: Oxford University Press.

Taussig, Michael. 1984. "Culture of Terror—Space of Death, Roger Casement's Putumayo Report and the Explanation of Torture." *Comparative Studies in Society and History* Vol. 26, No. 3: 467–497.

Valentine, Bettylou. 1978. *Hustling and Other Hard Work*. New York: Free Press.

Valentine, Charles. 1968. *Culture and Poverty*. Chicago: University of Chicago Press.

Wallerstein, Emanuel. 1977. "Rural Economy in Modern World Society." *Studies in Comparative International Development* Vol. 12, No. 1: 29–40.

Waxman, Chaim. 1977. *The Stigma of Poverty: A Critique of Poverty Theories and Policies*. New York: Pergamon Press.

Willis, Paul. 1977. *Learning to Labor: How Working Class Kids Get Working Class Jobs*. Aldershot, England: Gower.

Willis, Paul. 1983. "Cultural Production and Theories of Reproduction." In *Race, Class and Education*, ed. by Len Barton & Stephen Walker. London: Croom-Helm.

Wilson, William Julius. 1978. *The Declining Significance of Race: Blacks and Changing American Institutions*. Chicago: University of Chicago Press.

Wilson, William Julius. 1987. *The Truly Disadvantaged: The Inner City, the Underclass and Public Policy*. Chicago: University of Chicago Press.

20

Cities without Care or Connection

Richard Sennett

Richard Sennett is an internationally renowned social and cultural critic. He has written numerous books on global capitalism and changing urban experiences, including The Hidden Injuries of Class, The Fall of Public Man, *and* The Corrosion of Character. *He is University Professor of the Humanities at New York University and Centennial Professor of Sociology at the London School of Economics.*

Cities can be badly run, crime-infested, dirty and decaying. Yet many people think it worth living even in the worst of them. Why? Because, I would suggest, they have the potential to make us more complex human beings.

A city is a place where people can learn to live with strangers, to enter into the experiences and interests of unfamiliar lives. Sameness stultifies the mind; diversity stimulates and expands it. The city can thus allow people to develop a richer, more complex sense of themselves. They are not just bankers or road-sweepers, Asians or Anglo-Saxons, speakers of English or of Spanish, bourgeois or proletarian: they can be some or all of these things, and more. They are not subject to a fixed, classificatory scheme of identity. People can develop multiple images of their identities, knowing that who they are shifts depending upon whom they are with.

This is the power of strangeness—the freedom from arbitrary definition and identification. When the writer Willa Cather finally arrived in New York's Greenwich Village in 1906, she, who had been haunted in small-town America by the fear that her lesbianism would be discovered, wrote to a friend: "At last, in this indecipherable place, I can breathe." In public, the urbanite may don an impassive mask, act cool and indifferent to others on the street; in private, however, he or she is aroused by these strange contacts, his or her certainties shaken by the presence of others.

These virtues are not inevitable in the city. One of the big issues in urban life is how to make the complexities that a city contains actually interact—so that people become cosmopolitans rather than simply city-dwellers—and how to turn the crowded streets into places of self-knowledge rather than places of fear. The French philosopher Emmanuel Levinas has referred to "the neighbourliness of strangers," and the phrase aptly captures the aspiration we ought to have in designing cities.

My argument is that a great change in capitalism has transformed the context of urban cultural values, that city designers and planners are faced with quite new challenges.

Capitalism has been changed not only by globalisation, but also by a transformation in production which allows people today to work more flexibly, less rigidly.

The 19th-century German sociologist Max Weber compared modern business organisations to military organisations. Both worked on the principle of a pyramid, with the general or boss at the apex and the soldiers or workers at the base. The division of labour minimised duplication and gave each group of workers at the base a distinct function. Thus, the corporation executive at the apex could determine how the assembly line or back office functioned, just as the general could strategically command platoons far from his command post. And, as the division of labour progressed, the need for different kinds of workers expanded far more rapidly than the need for more bosses.

In industrial production, Weber's pyramid became embodied in Fordism, a kind of military micro-management of a worker's time and effort which a few experts could dictate from the top. It was graphically illustrated by the General Motors' Willow Run auto plant in America, a mile-long, quarter-mile-wide edifice in which raw iron and glass entered at one end and a finished car exited at the other. Only a strict, controlling work regime could coordinate production on this giant scale. In the white-collar world, the strict controls of corporations such as IBM in the 1960s mirrored this industrial process.

A generation ago, businesses began to revolt against the Weberian triangle. They sought to "de-layer" organisations, to remove levels of bureaucracy (using new information technologies in place of bureaucrats) and to destroy the practice of fixed-function work, substituting instead teams that work short-term on specific tasks. In this new business strategy, teams compete against one another, trying to respond as effectively and as quickly as possible to goals set by the top. Instead of each person doing his or her own particular bit in a defined chain of command, you have duplication of function: many different teams compete to do the same task fastest, best. The corporation can thus respond more quickly to changing market demands.

The apologists for the new world of work claim it is also more democratic than the old military-style organisation. But that is not so. The Weberian triangle has been replaced by a circle with a dot in the centre. At the centre, a small number of managers makes decisions, sets tasks, judges results; the information revolution has given it more instantaneous control over the corporation's workings than in the old system, where orders often modulated and evolved as they passed down the chain of command. The teams working on the periphery of the circle are left free to respond to output targets set by the centre, free to devise means of executing tasks in competition with one another, but no more free than they ever were to decide what those tasks are.

In the Weberian pyramid of bureaucracy, rewards came for doing one's job as best one could. In the dotted circle, rewards come to teams winning over other teams. The economist Robert Frank calls it the winner-take-all organisation; sheer effort no longer produces reward. This bureaucratic reformulation, Frank argues, contributes to the great inequalities of pay and perks in flexible organisations.

The mantra of the flexible workplace is "no long term." Career paths have been replaced by jobs that consist of specific and limited tasks; when the task ends, often the job is over. In the hi-tech sector in Silicon Valley, the average length of employment is now about eight months. People constantly change their working associates—modern management theory argues that the "shelf life" of a team ought to be a year at most.

This pattern does not dominate the workplace at present. Rather, it represents a leading edge of change, an aspiration of what businesses ought to become: no one is going to start a new organisation based on the principle of permanent jobs.

The flexible organisation does not promote loyalty or fraternity any more than it promotes democracy. It is hard to feel committed to a corporation that has no defined character, hard to act loyally to an institution that shows no loyalties to you. Business leaders are now finding that lack of commitment translates into poor productivity and an unwillingness to keep a corporation's secrets.

The lack of fraternity bred by "no long term" is rather more subtle. Task-work puts people under enormous stress; on losing teams, recrimination tends to mark the final stages of working together. Again, trust of an informal sort takes time to develop; you have to get to know people. And the experience of being only temporarily in an organisation prompts people to keep loose, not to get involved, since you are going to exit soon. Practically, this lack of mutual engagement is one of the reasons why it is so hard for labour unions to organise workers in flexible businesses or industries such as Silicon Valley; the sense of fraternity as a shared fate, a durable set of common interests, has been weakened. Socially, the short-term regime produces a paradox: people work intensely, under great pressure, but their relations to others remain curiously superficial. This is not a world in which getting deeply involved with other people makes much sense in the long run.

My argument is that flexible capitalism has precisely the same effects on the city as it does on the workplace itself. Just as flexible production produces more superficial, short-term relations at work, this capitalism creates a regime of superficial and disengaged relations in the city.

It appears in three forms. The most self-evident is physical attachment to the city. Rates of geographic mobility are very high for flexible workers. Temps are the single fastest-growing sector of the labour market. Temporary nurses, for example, are eight times more likely to move house in a two-year period than are single-employer nurses.

In the higher reaches of the economy, executives in the past frequently moved as much as in the present, but the movements were different in kind; they remained within the groove of a company, and the company defined their "place," the turf of their lives, no matter where they were on the map. It is just that thread which the new workplace breaks. Some specialists in urban studies have argued that, for this elite, style of life in the city matters more than their jobs, with certain zones—gentrified, filled with sleek restaurants and specialised services—replacing the corporation as an anchor.

The second expression of the new capitalism is the standardisation of the environment. A few years ago, I took the head of a large, new-economy corporation on a tour of New York's Chanin Building, an art-deco palace with elaborate offices and splendid public spaces. "It would never suit us," the executive remarked. "People might become too attached to their offices, they might think they belong here."

The flexible office is not meant to be a place where you nestle in. The office architecture of flexible firms requires a physical environment that can be quickly reconfigured—at the extreme, the "office" becomes just a computer terminal. The neutrality of new buildings also results from their global currency as investment units; for someone in Manila easily to buy or sell a hundred thousand square feet of office space in London, the space itself needs the uniformity, the transparency, of money. This is why the style elements of new-economy buildings become what the critic Ada Louise Huxtable calls "skin architecture," the surface of the building dolled-up with design, its innards ever-more neutral, standard and capable of instant refiguration.

Alongside "skin architecture," we have the standardisation of public consumption—a global network of shops selling the same commodities in the same kinds of spaces whether they are located in Manila, Mexico City or London. It is hard to become attached to a particular Gap or Banana Republic; standardisation begets indifference. Put another way: the problem of institutional loyalties in the workplace, now beginning to sober up managers once blindly enthusiastic about endless corporate re-engineering, finds its parallel in the urban public realm of consumption; attachment and engagement with specific places is dispelled under the aegis of this new regime. Cities cease to offer the strange, the unexpected or the arousing. Equally, the accumulation of shared history, and so of collective memory, diminishes in these neutral public spaces. Standardised consumption attacks local meanings in the same way that the new workplace attacks ingrown, shared histories among workers.

The third expression of the new capitalism is less visible to the eye. High-pressure, flexible work profoundly disorients family life. The familiar press images—neglected children, adult stress, geographic uprooting—do not quite get at the heart of this disorientation. It is rather that the codes of conduct which rule the modern work world would shatter families if taken home from the office: don't commit, don't get involved, think short-term. The assertion of "family values" by the public and by politicians has a more than right-wing resonance; it is a reaction, often inchoate but strongly felt, to the threats to family solidarity in the new economy. Christopher Lasch's image of the family as a "haven in a heartless world" takes on a particular urgency when work becomes at once more unpredictable and more demanding of adult time.

One result of this conflict, by now well documented on middle-aged employees, is that adults withdraw from civic participation in the struggle to solidify and organise family life; the civic becomes yet another demand on time and energies in short supply at home.

And that brings me to one of the effects of globalisation on cities. The new global elite, operating in cities such as New York, London and Chicago, avoids the urban political realm. It wants to operate in the city, but not rule it; it composes a regime of power without responsibility.

In Chicago in 1925, for example, political and economic power were co-extensive. Presidents of the city's top 80 corporations sat on 142 hospital boards, and accounted for 70 per cent of the trustees of colleges and universities. Tax revenues from 18 national corporations in Chicago formed 23 per cent of the city's municipal budget. By contrast, in New York today, few chief executives of global firms are trustees of its educational institutions and none sits on the boards of its hospitals. Footloose multinational companies, such as Rupert Murdoch's News Corp, manage largely to avoid paying taxes, local or national.

The reason for this change is that the global economy is not rooted in the city in the sense of depending on control of the city as a whole. It is instead an island economy—literally so within the island of Manhattan in New York; architecturally so in places such as Canary Wharf in London, which resemble the imperial compounds of an earlier era. As John Mollenkopf and Manuel Castells have shown, this global wealth does not trickle down or leach out very far beyond the global enclave. Indeed, the politics of the global enclave cultivates a kind of indifference to the city, which Marcel Proust, in an entirely different context, calls the "passive beloved" phenomenon. Threatening to leave, go anywhere in the world, the global firm is given enormous tax breaks to stay, a profitable seduction made possible by the firm appearing indifferent to the places where it touches down.

In other words, globalisation poses a problem of citizenship in cities as well as nations. Cities can't tap into the wealth of these corporations, and the corporations take little responsibility for their own presence in the city. The threat of absence, of leaving, makes possible this avoidance of responsibility; we lack, correspondingly, the political mechanisms to make unstable, flexible institutions contribute fairly for the privileges they enjoy in the city.

For all these reasons, cities face three new dilemmas: a dilemma of citizenship; of arousal in the public realm, since impermanence and standardisation leave people indifferent to public places; and the dilemma of sheer, durable attachment to the city.

Production has been set free, reflected in cities of globally mobile corporations and flexible workers—a dynamic capitalism bent on erasing routine. Yet this restless economy produces political disengagements, a standardisation of the physical realm, new pressures to withdraw into the private sphere.

These dilemmas in turn mark the "civil society" of the city. Urban civil society is now in a condition of mutual accommodation, achieved through mutual dissociation. That means the truce of letting one another alone, the peace of mutual indifference. This is one reason why, on the positive side, the modern city is like an accordion, easily able to expand to accommodate new waves of migrants; the pockets of difference are sealed. On the negative side, mutual accommodation through dissociation spells the end of citizenship practices that require understanding of divergent interests, as well as marking a loss of simple human curiosity about other people.

At the same time, the flexibility of the modern workplace creates a sense of incompleteness. Flexible time is serial—you do one project, then another unrelated one—rather than cumulative. But there is no sense that, because something is missing in your life, you should turn outward to others, toward the "neighbourliness of strangers."

That suggests something about the art of making better cities today. We need to overlay different activities in the same space, as family activity once overlay working space. The incompleteness of capitalist time returns us to the issue that marked the very emergence of the industrial city, a city that broke apart the *domus*—that spatial relation which had, before the coming of industrial capitalism, combined family, work, ceremonial public spaces and more informal social spaces. Today, we need to repair the collectivity of space to combat the serial time of modern labour.

VII

GENDER AND SEXUALITY

How Do Women and Men Relate to Each Other?

Why is it that the worst swearwords in our society are utterances like "Motherfucker" or always seem to refer to reproduction or the sexual organs and incest? While there are no ready answers to this question, it does underline the importance we attach to sexual activity and the rules attached to it, in particular those regarding incest.

The literature on **incest** is voluminous and cannot be summarized here. Suffice it to say that there are at present two main camps, the Freudians and the evolutionary theorists. The psychoanalytically oriented Freudian interpreters try to explain how individual development blocks the possibility of incest. Freud argued that the child normally represses erotic feelings toward the opposite-sex parent or sibling out of fear of reprisal from the same-sex parent (the **Oedipus complex**). In short, familiarity breeds attempt, and thus the incest taboo came into being to prevent this rivalry.

The evolutionary theorists take as their founding father Edward Westermarck, the Finnish anthropologist who in 1891 suggested that **natural selection** had endowed humans with a tendency to avoid inbreeding and its harmful effects on offspring. It was, in effect, a question of familiarity breeds contempt, or "Marry out or die out."

Obviously the last word on incest has not been said, and anthropologists bedevil the discussion by pointing out the large degree of variation in cultural practices, even those as basic as incest and marriage.

Theories and explanations of procreation, incest, marriage, and sex are interrelated and closely related to people's wider worldviews. From such a broader perspective the power of women has been substantially underestimated in many societies. Consider, for example, this statement by Nisa, a Bushman woman:

Women are strong; women are important. Zhun/twa men say that women are the chiefs, the rich ones, the wise ones. Because women possess something very important, something which enables men to live: their genitals. A woman can bring a man life even if he is almost dead. She can give him sex even if he is almost dead. She can give him sex and make him alive again. If she were to refuse, he would die! If there were no women around, their semen would kill men. Did you know that? If there were only men, they would all die. Women make it possible for them to live. (Shostak 1981)

If there is one thing anthropologists have shown, it is how even the most basic behavior of those whom we define as "male" and "female" is very much a cultural production. When anthropologists us the terms **gender, sex,** and **sexuality,** we are generally identifying how the key categories of human experience around our sexual selves are socially constructed. In anthropological thought, *gender* typically refers to the culturally specific elaboration of biological differences and ideologies of how women and men relate to each other; *sex* refers to the anatomical and physiological characteristics of male or female bodies; and *sexuality* to erotic desires, sexual practices, and sexual orientations. But for every single one of these categories—even the most apparently immutable category of sex—humans have found ways to modify, bend, and blur them. In the first essay in this chapter, Roger Lancaster explores what he calls "bio-reductivism" in American culture, or the folk belief that gender norms, sexual orientations, and social institutions are genetically or hormonally "hardwired." This belief is especially powerful in the age of the Human Genome Project, when scientists are announcing discoveries—it seems almost weekly—about the genetic basis of our bodies and social selves. But as Lancaster argues, we anthropologists have a duty to point out that when they relate to issues of gender, sex, and sexuality, such arguments fly in the face of documented cultural variations.

Their more worrisome implication is that they "naturalize" (render natural) certain culturally constructed norms at the expense of social groups (women, gays, and lesbians) typically marginalized by conventional moralities.

The reality is that biology is not necessarily destiny, and sexual practices are culturally constructed and can change over time, even in an individual life. This is the point of David Bennett's essay on "Hanky-Panky, Spanky-Wanky" at a British all-boys boarding school. As in other societies (particularly some in the so-called Semen Belt of Papua New Guinea, where certain rituals involve sharing semen between men and boys), this article suggests that in the West, homosexual and bisexual practices may be considered a phase in one's "normal" life, depending on the circumstances in which one finds oneself. In the case of semen sharing during rituals, the goal is often to share the masculine power of adult men with the boys; while in the case of this British boarding school, it would appear to be an issue of sexual curiosity and recreation. This realization raises the interesting and important question: Are *homosexuality* and *heterosexuality* permanent and exclusive conditions to begin with?

This is, as Lancaster points out in his essay, a loaded issue for some activists involved in gay and lesbian rights, who have held that same-sex desires are inborn, congenital, and immutable. While this debate rages on, a new one over the right of gay and lesbian couples to get married is currently capturing headlines. Anthropologists have a lot to contribute to these debates, as evidenced in our "Anthropology and Public Debate" section, which offers two radically different perspectives on gay and lesbian marriage. Peter Wood argues that anthropology should be used to defend "traditional marriage" between a man and a woman. Ellen Lewin, on the other hand, argues that recognizing same-sex marriages is an issue not just of extending civil rights and responsibilities to a new group, but of symbolically moving marginalized people "to the front of the bus." We round out this chapter by exploring the issue of Vermont's recognition of civil unions as a means of considering the nature of fieldwork. David Houston writes that trying to do ethnographic research on the topic was not as easy as he thought it would be. Instead of being a simple question of studying how Vermonters related to the issue, Houston realized that the "geography of the social" was constituted by a broader set of networks and relationships that transcended Vermont itself.

FOCUS QUESTIONS

As you read these selections, consider these questions:

✦   How are gender differences constructed and perceived in different cultures? What contributions can anthropology make toward understanding gender differentiation?

✦   Are *homosexuality* and *heterosexuality* permanent and exclusive conditions? What are the political implications of your answer?

✦   What are some anthropological arguments for and against gay marriage?

✦   How does an anthropologist do an ethnographic study of a politically charged debate over "gay marriage"?

REFERENCE

Shostak, Marjory. 1991. *Nisa*. New York: McGraw-Hill.

21

The Place of Anthropology in a Public Culture Reshaped by Bioreductivism

Roger N. Lancaster

Roger Lancaster is associate professor of anthropology and director of cultural studies at George Mason University. He received his PhD in anthropology from UC Berkeley in 1987. His research specialties include gender and sexuality, lesbian and gay studies, critical theory, political economy, and social movements in Latin America and the United States. He has published several books on Nicaragua, including Life Is Hard: Machismo, Danger, and Power in Nicaragua, *which won the C. Wright Mills Award (Society for the Study of Social Problems) and the Ruth Benedict Prize (Society of Lesbian and Gay Anthropologists). He is most recently the author of* The Trouble with Nature: Sex in Science and Popular Culture.

In anthropology, it's a truism that science is constrained by ideology and sometimes takes the form of folklore outright. But perhaps because most researchers' attention has been trained elsewhere in recent years—on the social and institutional implications of ongoing developments in biomedicine—science studies in anthropology has largely neglected the elephant in the living room.

Here's a snapshot of the elephant: Over the course of the past decade, biomythology has permeated American culture as never before. The idea that gender norms, sexual orientations, and social institutions are genetically (or neuro-hormonally) "hardwired" flourishes in the long shadow of the Human Genome Project. And in close sync, the ubiquitous narratives of evolutionary psychology circulate, without qualification or caveat, in prominent newspapers and newsweeklies.

These new bioreductivisms, now prevalent in both academic and popular cultures, not only reverse decades of sophisticated cultural theory and empirical research on cultural variation; they have come to occupy the place once held by anthropology in a progressively dumbed-down serious public sphere. The stakes are high, not only for the discipline, but also for the social groups (notably women, gays, and lesbians) whose interests are marginalized in prevailing theories, which above all else "naturalize" conventional gender and sexual norms.

Naturalization is, perhaps, as old as the concept "nature," and pseudo-scientific naturalizations of social arrangements are old as, well, science. Turn-of-the-millennium biomythology thus bears some resemblance to earlier variants of the same. But it is also worth noting three key differences.

Big Science (Especially Biotechnology) is Big Business, thus Big News, Which Creates a Big Space for Bioreductive Narratives and Pseudo-Science: Over the past two and a half decades, major newspapers have developed extensive science supplements to capture breaking research news. These grew and developed alongside the Human Genome Project, which also stimulated the apparently boundless phenomenon that Ruth Hubbard and other critics have dubbed "genomania": the unsound idea that there exists "a" "gene" "for" virtually every biological, psychological and social trait; the equally erroneous notion that the genome provides, in micro, a blueprint for the organism; and thus, an unmodulated rage for evermore exacting genetic explanations of the human condition.

For example, a Lexis-Nexis search reveals that from 1970 until 1984, direct references to the phrases "genetic cause," "genetic source," or "genetic origin" in major Anglophone newspapers ranged from zero to four per year. Most of these refer to genetic maladies or traits with established genetic correlates. Beginning in 1985, references increase, first slowly, then dramatically, until peaking in 2000 at 165. A great many of these latter references are fanciful, attributing genetic causation to institutional arrangements or complex symbolic action.

These changes have drawn in their wake the unprecedented positive attention given to sociobiology, evolutionary psychology, and other forms of bioreductivism. This set-up has also predicated how research news of the past 15 years has been covered. Editors want positive stories about new developments, new breakthroughs and new knowledge. They don't want stories about the inapplicability of biological research to social questions or the limits of scientific knowledge. Thus, studies purporting to find evidence of "genes" "for" homosexuality, risk-taking, schizophrenia, and other traits were announced with great fanfare in science journals and on the front pages of major newspapers. The same claims were quietly retired on page 19—if retractions appeared at all—when subsequent studies failed to replicate the results of the original studies.

Today's Bioreductivism Wistfully Narrates the Social Preoccupations of Modern Subjects as an Evolutionary Pageant: Evolutionary psychology, which purports to derive the contours of a generic human nature as the outcome of biological adaptations over eons of evolutionary time, gave "legs," as they say in show biz, to the pervasive genomania. Whereas once upon a time 1970s sociobiology had explained and rationalized the "ugly" side of human nature (violence, war, racism, rape and sexual inequality), evolutionary psychology has developed a kinder, gentler variant of bioreductivism.

The gist of evolutionary-psychological reasoning has been widely disseminated, from the early 1990s on, in terms that will be familiar to most readers. Men seem restless? Hunters are hardwired to be on the prowl. Women like to shop? It's the biological legacy of gathering. Sweet tooth? Jealous? It's primal biology. . . . Everybody loves a good story, and it's no accident that the heterosexual fables of evolutionary psychology have provided source material for an ABC sit-com, "Home Improvement," for Rob Becker's Broadway hit, "Defending the Caveman," and for endless invocation in entertainment culture and self-help books.

Today's evolutionary fables describe how men and women got to be the way they (supposedly) are at a postfeminist moment when just *what* they are, and what it might mean to be a man or a woman, is hotly contested. Evolutionary psychology spins timeless tales about heterosexual courtship rituals, pair-bonding for life, and the inevitability of the nuclear family at a time when all of these are in the throes of change and are said, by many, to be "in crisis."

Modern Bioreductivism Puts the "I" in Identity Politics: Lastly, what defines modern bioreductivism and distinguishes it from early variants is its radical adaptability to different conditions and demands. It's easy enough to see why the new bioreductivisms appeal to secular social conservatives (evolutionary psychology naturalizes conventional heterosexual morality) and free-market libertarians (genomania's plucky little gene is a miniaturization of classical liberalism's entrepreneurial individual). But bioreductivism is selectively endorsed by a great many others, as well.

A segment of the gay rights movement, for example, has always argued that same-sex desires are inborn, congenital, fixed, immutable and invariant. "The gay gene" was thus embraced by some activists as the basis for legal arguments for gay civil rights. Fables about the evolution of sexual differences—especially fables that stress how women evolved to be nurturant, altruistic, pacific creatures—have also proved irresistible to some cultural feminists. Meanwhile, men's movement enthusiasts, even some progressive ones, were invested from the start in stories about men's "inborn needs," the evolutionary heritage of manhood.

"Identity politics," the quintessentially modern, American justification for social action and political redress by appeal to deep-seated, essential identities, provides fertile ground for bioreductivism, and everybody—the marginal or oppressed and dominant alike—wants to get in on the act.

In each of these cases, the biological reductions are selective and opportunistic. Gays who champion the idea of a "gay gene," for instance, seldom acknowledge the deeply heteronormative sociobiology from which the concept derives. Likewise, feminists and men's movement activists can be seen picking and choosing—always the more comforting images from the repertoire of evolutionary psychology, never the biological scary monsters and genetic supercreeps.

This sort of opportunism suggests the basis for bioreductivism's rapid spread in American culture from the early 1990s on. More than anything, today's reductivism offers to stabilize identity in the *points de capiton* of biology—that is, it purports to secure stability and certitude in an era when nothing much seems anchored about either identity or biology.

Furthermore, this approach to securing basic rights and recognition resonates with a longstanding Western understanding of "nature" as that which exceeds conscious control and volition. It also follows, logically, from a broad tradition of American civil rights law, which prohibits discrimination on the basis of "immutable" characteristics.

Yet, there are other, more viable, ways of staking just political claims than by recourse to a biologically reified identity politics vulgate. The Supreme Court's broad ruling in Lawrence v Texas, which struck down the nation's remaining sodomy laws, based its reasoning on civil libertarian arguments about human freedom; it cited not biological claims about innate desires but social constructivist histories treating law, institutions and identities.

WHAT'S AN ANTHROPOLOGIST TO DO?

Notwithstanding the positive uses to which flawed arguments are sometimes put, I think it would be professionally derelict not to point out that the broader implications of bioreductive models are overwhelmingly conservative; that the evidence for hardwired gender roles and sexual orientations is scant (to put it mildly); and that the cross-cultural data suggests that *variety* and *adaptability* are the better plot lines of our evolutionary heritage.

I don't take it for granted that all lesbians, gays, bisexuals, and transgendered people will agree with my arguments about the location of identity politics in American culture. Nor do I assume that all anthropologists will understand sociobiology, evolutionary psychology, and related forms of bioreductivism as "biomythology" or "scientific folklore." But I do think there's an interesting and productive confluence of questions in play here.

Contrary to Stephen Pinker's recent legerdemain in *The Blank Slate,* anthropologists over several generations have developed a variety of robust, synthetic models for thinking about the relationship between biology and culture, for treating the phenomenology of sex and desire, for theorizing the manner in which institutions like kinship are constructed and function, and for gauging the parameters of social variation on these (and other) questions. The best of feminist and queer studies deepens research into this central subject matter of the discipline. The problem is that these findings go against prevailing trends in public culture, which remains caught in the tow of magical thinking associated with genomania. And the problem is that theory-building in the recondite mode has not served anthropology well in recent years (and has likely done much to diminish its social relevance and its public visibility).

Would that I had a pithy list of recommendations which, if followed, would set things right. Alas, I have no easy solutions. What we need, in part, is more of what we're already doing: studies that take up the central questions of the field in changing political-economic and social contexts. There's a lot of intellectual excitement to be had there yet—and a lot of insight to be shed over some of the burning social and political questions of our day: What should a family look like? How might marriage and kinship be legislated? Should gays and lesbians be allowed to wed? How do routines of toil, deprivation, and violence shape the body and affect personhood? And how do we, in making the conditions of our lives, also make and remake ourselves? More to the point, what we need are more studies that join ongoing political struggles in an accessible language.

22

Hanky-Panky and Spanky-Wanky

Sex and the Single Boy

David Bennett

David Bennett is currently chief of health and occupational safety at the Canadian Labor Confederation in Ottawa.

To an outsider, the Brits are incomprehensible. The name of the country does not appear on their postage stamps, and the name of their navy is the Royal Navy, not the British Navy. This effortless British—or rather, English—air of superiority is not contrived but ingrained. The regions around London are known as the Home Counties as if everyone else were from away. So with their schools. It is baffling enough that their private schools are called public schools. Even worse that their best schools are called merely public schools, not by any name more grand. Lesser schools there are, the "minor public schools." I went to a public school.

The school which I was sent in the mid-fifties was, like most, a boys' school, with a strong academic reputation. It was in some ways atypical (a charity school), but in one respect it was average: It had a homosexual culture which was the norm, not the exception.

The outside observer would now find three parties to this common pursuit: the schoolmasters, the adolescents and the pre-pubescent boys—children. We make a big distinction, for instance, between the sexual intercourse of a man and a youth, strictly underage, and those who assault children. The latter we now call by the misnomer paedophile, rather than the traditional paederast. In the culture of the English boarding school, there were no such distinctions. No one remarked on the sexual preferences of the schoolmasters, whether they took as bedfellows older boys, adolescents or children. Nothing turned on whether an older boy "had" a boy of his own age, a younger one, or a "small boy."

Of the sum total of all sexual encounters, the most common were between adolescents, post-puberty. The most basic question: What did they do? The answer is simple: They engaged in mutual masturbation, they wanked. How they came to the act is at once complex (there were different routes to coition) and simple. Take the simple part first. The act required privacy in an institution where there was no privacy worth the name. But only a minute or two was needed—in a toilet stall, behind the trees, anywhere in the dark, inside or outside. There was no foreplay or ritual: immediate erection, a fumbling of the pants, grasping the organ, wank, come and gone.

In the bed, in the dormitory, things were a little less bleak. After lights out, the suitor would visit the bed of his best beloved, those narrow beds with wafer-thin mattresses, bed boards and cast iron frame. Here again, little finesse: immediate wank to climax, then an interlude in which nothing much happened, until second erection, orgasm and prompt retreat. These happenings took place in pyjamas, since the act did not require disrobing. Besides, the dormitory lights might suddenly go on, perhaps with malice aforethought. It would never do to have to slink off, naked and erect, to one's own bed.

Consider the circumstances. A single bed gave little occasion for bedsports, with neighbours a few feet away, pretending they were asleep. From the far end of the dormitory, a question might be poised to the suitor, eliciting a muffled, non-committal reply, so as not to betray the origin of the response. With luck, the question might come during the interval between the acts. And constantly, the fear of discovery, not the turpitude of hanky-panky, merely a threat of exposure enough to make the act tense and joyless.

This is, however, hardly pertinent. Two boys might take off to a field near the school, relax and stretch out for an hour or so of intimacy, perhaps with a drink before and a cigarette after. The constraints of the institution and the English weather made such encounters rare. But what stands in need of explanation is why episodes such as this

"Hanky-Panky and Spanky-Wanky: Sex and the Single Boy" by David Bennett. David Bennett PhD is National Director, Health, Safety and Environment, Canadian Labour Congress in Ottawa, Canada. Reprinted by permission of the author.

were not the model of carnal knowledge, why the acts ever came to be so barren, cursory and slight in the first place. None of the variations were much of an improvement. Two boys, unable to wait for lights out, would sit together on the benches at the common room table during "prep," the evening period for home assignments. They would place a heavy coat between them, hands burrowing underneath in a silent, hidden manoeuvre, pulling open the fly and going round or through the underpants. All the while, doodling intently, never a shudder of orgasm, jerking without jerking off. Perhaps this was a kind of foreplay after all, the constraints being an asset, not a limitation, an arousal culminating in the act that was to follow.

One boy claimed to creep up to a neighbour in the dormitory after dark, and masturbate him (the verb was not then used transitively) while he slept. He could engage in touching and fondling in a way not usually done; in fact, he had to, otherwise the favoured individual would wake up. This itinerant, nocturnal wanker said that he had done this to several boys and while none had awoken, none had come either. The story has a superficial plausibility because men often awake at the height of a wet dream.

Other invasions of privacy were good clean fun. On one occasion, two laughing heads popped up over the door of a stall. The boy inside was wanking furiously, "I can't stop now, you bastards." Well he did, suddenly.

Relations between "big boy and small boy" were essentially the same, though there may have been (for all I know) more variations and foreplay on the part of the big boy, prior to intercourse. Small boys, especially those pretty boys who seemed to respond to the approaches of the big boy, were called tarts or flirts. But such feminization was confined to small boys. No one referred to a partner, of whatever age, as "she" or "her" or "queen." Small boys who could achieve orgasm were prized, no doubt because the liaison could be legitimized as a reciprocal relationship. Not so, of course: Small boys existed simply for the gratification of the big boy.

The schoolmasters who were active paederasts were few. Again, the pattern of sexual activity was similar to that between boys. Sex of all sorts was a constant topic of conversation among the boys, but since oral sodomy was rarely discussed (the boys had no name for it), it is unlikely that any of the masters engaged in it. In a society now obsessed with cocksucking, this is hard to imagine. Sodomy was buggery, but when I asked an older boy, a notorious wanker, what buggery was, he gave me the wrong answer. Sodomy was rare. Some of the masters did occasionally sodomize older boys but these (again as far as I am aware) were casual acts of gratification, done very late at night in the dormitory or in the master's nearby bedroom, not a regular liaison. Throughout English boarding schools, sodomizing small boys must have been very rare. Otherwise, a few court cases of child rape would have erupted into a national scandal, as with assaults in the residential schools of Canada.

Once, some senior boys stole the homoerotic diaries of a master, in which the names of small boys were named. They threatened to expose him unless he resigned, which he did. The fact that the boys may have mistaken homoeroticism for paederasty hardly excuses this act of calculated viciousness. From his married exile in Wales, the master continued to write to his former pupils, congratulating them on their success, whenever the Oxbridge scholarships were written up in *The Times*.

Apart from big boy–small boy relationships, the boys tended to choose partners of about their own age. Some of the older boys with something in common such as literature or some other aesthetic interest would form a circle of casual wanking. But multiple partners were, I believe, quite rare. Liaisons could be quite short, a few weeks being the norm. There were some that lasted over a number of terms, such as discreet liaisons with small boys.

The penis was the sole object of sexuality. The boys would hold competitions over the length, erect. But this did not seem to play a part in the choice of a partner. Without penetration, the dimensions of the member were of no consequence. Shape and size are as important as people make them. In my later limited experience, they have little to do with sexual prowess or fulfillment, more to do with the individuality of the lover. Some of those who have the penis lengthened are engaging in a form of narcissism, self-gratification.

Neither was cut or uncut an issue. I was, I suppose, unusual, in that I found the idea of sex with a circumcised male repellant, seeing even then the ugly signs of mutilation. A powerful ejaculation was prized, with stories, mainly apocryphal, about the extent of the spurt, sometimes marked in ball-point on the bedsheet. But again, this played no part in the act. Besides, how could they tell, with only sticky fingers to show for it? Simultaneous orgasm was nice too, but since most of the encounters were so cursory, this was a norm rarely even noticed.

Why did they do it? Mutual masturbation is of course one of the *ars amatoria*, but it is hardly a feast of love, and even this thin diet was artless. Some boys claimed to have what we now, in our wooden way, call a relationship. For the most part the whole thing, in an institution with little warmth and no privacy, looks like a quest for intimacy through recreational sex. But the constraints of the institution and the lack of privacy are not enough to explain the bleakness of sexual encounters. Consider the circumstances. Sexual activity was neither legitimized in the institution, nor was it condemned. It existed neither in a twilight world nor was it driven underground. In this sense it was marginal activity in which there were no rules of propriety, no rituals of courtship, no obligations created as a result of sex, nothing that one boy did for his partner as a consequence of the liaison. The great works of homoerotic literature were never seen as having any bearing on the sex life of a single boy. Of course, they had no such bearing, but at least we would have expected such questions to be raised.

A proposition took the form of making a pass at the genitals of another boy, which was accepted, rejected or taken as a promise of future copulation. The deplorable thing was not the sex but the fact that this was taken as the paradigm of the sexual approach. As sex education, it was hopeless. We should hardly even call it a culture of homosexuality. There was really no such culture, no cultivation of the homosexual impulse, no ghost of eros in the wings, waiting to be made flesh.

At the school, the only admonitions against homosexuality were fleeting homilies from the housemasters, "Now come on boys, we have to stop this wanking." Then a reaction set in. The Headmaster was fired, reputedly because he had condoned homosexual behaviour among the masters and the boys. There were purges in the houses, in which the leading wankers were publicly exposed and humiliated, threatened with expulsion. A few were so expelled, I suspect because they had multiple partners. A psychiatrist was hired to lecture the boys, who were preached culpable nonsense about how wanking led to homosexuality in later life. Oh Goody! the gays must have thought. Married quarters were built for the masters on campus, a dubious move, since most of the paederasts were single men. For those that weren't, the house only gave them an additional venue for sex.

Boarding schools were not hotbeds of manual sex, with everyone busy wanking everyone else. What is true is that most boys left the school with some significant homosexual experience. How significant in later life is not obvious. For a few, the boarding school enabled them to realize the male side of their bisexual nature. A mixed blessing, since most bisexuals wanted a stable partnership yet one which would permit them to pursue their bisexuality, not an easy combination. For the rest, there were no outstanding consequences, except perhaps a knowing look in later years with those they had fumbled and wanked with.

Our inclination is to say that someone who had been repeatedly assaulted as a small boy must have been scarred in some way. Even this is not clear. By the time an assault took place, the boy would likely have been introduced to the smutty talk, the sight of mature male genitalia and what boys of all ages did with each other. Groping among small boys was common. In turn, the

child became a perpetrator, but without consciousness of the categories of player we now impose on such society. While we are rightly outraged by the assaults in religious schools in North America and the lives which were undoubtedly ruined, we have to recognize that assaults are a social phenomenon which derive their identity from a particular culture. Acts in one culture are ruinous; in another, they are harmless.

The pernicious effects of the boarding school culture—the non-culture—of homosexuality concern social relations with women. It is obvious that the boys did not grow up with girls, nor were they in any way taught how. The test comes when we have ignorance of women combined with an assumption about how the sexual approach is made, based on the experience with males in the school. At their height, the English public schools were the training grounds for soldiers and colonial administrators. They became an anachronism when there were scarcely any colonies left to administer and no troops to put them down when there were. Women were not important; they had their place and their function, to be called on when needed. In mid-century, most public schools played a part in a society that no longer existed and their values of socialization, including relations with women, were otiose.

So the products went out into the world, not knowing how to relate to women and having no ideas about courtship. This is easy to exaggerate; but at its worst, it was terrible. The route to bed was a few matter-of-fact conversations, followed by the abrupt question, "Will you sleep with me?" Some never learned. Even now, I have an academic acquaintance, in his sixties, whose idea of courtship is to ask a young woman to come to his apartment "to go over your essay." Having divorced his wife, he spends his middle years in a series of pathetic attempts to get laid. The old English joke, "Come up and see my etchings" is uncomfortably close to the truth. The wife of an old schoolfriend told me she was usually uncomfortable in the company of her husband's schoolfriends. They were shifty and uneasy, unable to recognize she was there. Which in an important sense she was not.

If this were all, it would be no great loss. But the echoes were more profound. Having the sexual intercourse of the school as a foundation, the boys were let loose with no grounding in the texture of the adult life to come. In a school without eros, they had cultivated no sexual sensibility, no intimation that significant encounters with women—routine or casual—were charged with the nuances of sexuality. Affability in a woman was seen as a sign of sexual interest—or as prickteasing. These damaged specimens of humanity were unable to appreciate that most flirtation is subtle, without political purpose, a dance of which the players are barely conscious, which invariably ends with a parting. If it ends in bed, this is evidence enough that the game had delightful and unseen consequences—or that a different game had been played.

That this sexual sensibility is the essence of social life is easy to misapprehend, because it is too easily confused with sexual motive or seduction, like saying that a novel by John Updike is all about sex. Or it is seen in terms of a crude Freudianism in which every social interaction is really about sex. Look what happens when an individual ceases to be a sexual being, due to chronic stress or hormonal imbalance, or whatever. This is commonly described as loss of sex drive. The loss is actually more subtle, because what is lost is sexual sensibility, a predicament in which no social relations are sexually charged. When the previous condition is restored, the response is relief and celebration, not merely because sexual relations can be resumed but that the world can be seen again in its true light, a world alive with sexuality. Without this, the ex-public schoolboy as something less than a person is sadly true. In a supreme irony he loses too his appreciation of men, allowing no situation to arise where men too are as much a focus of sexual sensibility as women. Deeply, they perhaps fear engagement, because they see such social phenomena as a manifestation of homosexuality, discourse reduced to intercourse.

In mid-century, the English public school was a nasty, mean, brutish place. Like most others, my own school had a monitorial system in which the senior boys ran the houses (residences), directed the lives of the boys and administered punishment (normally being strapped on the behind with a leather belt). Pyjamas gave little protection against bleeding and bruising. The story was that during the Second World War, the school was light on teaching staff who were away fighting the war, putting an even greater burden of care on the senior boys. But instead of tightening discipline, what they did was to engender a regime and a society in which vicious bullying was the norm. Those on the receiving end of bullying became in turn sadistic bullies, a true cycle of violence. The extremes of bullying need not concern us. It became normal for a senior boy to hit a small boy about the head, for some minor breach of discipline or convention. That this boy, slight, scared, lonely and homesick, had no clue about how to live in this strange new world, was never a consideration. There was no such concept as callousness. But callous it was. One boy hit a small boy in the face. This boy was a new boy, on his own in England, his parents missionaries in Africa. His glasses shattered and he lost an eye. Forced later to confront the parents who were on leave from Africa, the senior boy apologized. But what was lost in this is that no one protested hitting boys about the face, which should have been stopped immediately. No one even noticed that the boy who lost his eye was a particularly sensitive and cultured child. As one of the social deficits of the system, wanking was not in the same league.

In my own case, I recovered from such hateful experience by recreating, in defiance of orthodoxy, an earlier infantile world of love, laughter and security. This was a personal revolution, but it did not take very long, a matter of a couple of years. What was more difficult was the slow realization that I had never grown up, that the school had stunted emotional growth. The school taught you how to be successful (in fact it did so in some admirable ways) but it did not teach or cultivate those aspects of social life which are the essence of being in the world. Instead, I lived a solitary, lonely psychic existence, never realizing where this predicament had come from, why I was the way I was. One thing has survived, an abiding animosity towards the boys' boarding school.

– 23 –

GAY AND LESBIAN MARRIAGE

Should Gays and Lesbians Have the Right to Marry?

Peter Wood is an associate professor of anthropology at Boston University. He received his PhD from the University of Rochester and specializes in anthropology of religion, art, and aesthetics, with a focus on North America. He is the author of Diversity: The Invention of a Concept.

Ellen Lewin is professor of anthropology and women's studies at the University of Iowa. She received he PhD from Stanford University, and her major research interests center on motherhood, reproduction, and sexuality, particularly as these are played out in American cultures. She is author of Recognizing Ourselves: Lesbian and Gay Ceremonies of Commitment.

Sex & Consequences: *An Anthropologist Vindicates the Traditional Family*

Peter Wood

Anthropology—hometown to cultural relativists and all-night diner for disaffected intellectuals—may not be where you would most expect to find good reasons to defend traditional American family values. But anthropology, in fact, guards a treasure house of examples of what happens when a society institutionalizes *other* arrangements.

Want to know what it really means for a society to recognize "gay marriage"? Or for society to permit polygamy? Or when the stigma of out-of-wedlock birth disappears? Care to know what happens to a human community that tolerates sexual experimentation among pre-adolescents and teenagers? Are fathers and mothers really interchangeable? Anthropology actually has a large amount of empirical evidence on all these matters—and many others that are now on the table in the United States thanks to various advocacy movements.

The Leftist political convictions of many of my fellow anthropologists tend to keep them silent about some of the

scientific findings that have accumulated over 150 years or so of systematic ethnographic study. But these findings strongly suggest that the family is a bedrock institution and that the kinds of modifications to the family advocated by gays, feminists, and others who speak in favor of relaxing traditional restrictions on sexual self-expression will have huge consequences.

Let's take an anthropologically informed look at two of these proposed changes to the family: gay marriage and polygamy.

INSTITUTIONALIZING MALE HOMOSEXUALITY

It is not especially difficult to find examples of societies that are considerably more relaxed about male homosexual behavior than American society has been, at least until recently. Some societies such as pre-communist China and Vietnam officially disapproved of homosexuality while tolerating large numbers of male homosexual prostitutes. Today's boy prostitutes in Thailand carry on a trade that

"Sex and Consequence: An Anthropologist Vindicates the Traditional Family" by Peter Wood from *American Conservative*, July 28, 2003. Reprinted by permission of American Conservative.

was remarked on by Western travelers of centuries past. A fair number of North American Indian societies made room for a homosexual "man-woman" (a *berdache*, as the French fur traders called him) who dressed and acted the part of a woman. But the *berdache* was an exceptional creature and did not represent anything like normalized homosexuality.

For that, we have to look to Melanesia, where there are perhaps dozens of very small-scale societies in which male homosexuality is given ritual significance and fully incorporated into the life of the community. This happened for example in the New Hebrides, New Caledonia, and in many parts of New Guinea. Here is one example:

> Among the Etoro, a tribe of about 400 living by hunting and small-scale gardening in the Strickland-Bosavi district of Papua New Guinea, from around age 12, every boy is "inseminated" orally more or less daily by a young man who is assigned to him as a partner. Late in his teenage years, an Etoro boy is formally initiated in an event involving many male sex partners, after which he becomes an "inseminator" rather than an "inseminee." In due course, the former older male partner often marries the younger man's sister.

Somewhat similar customs are reported for many other tribes in the remote mountains of New Guinea, and these cases collectively serve as proof that it is not beyond human ingenuity to channel homosexual behavior into a social system. But what kind of social system? For the Etoro, it is one that radically discounts the value of women as mothers and wives. Etoro men defer marriage as long as possible and, when they do marry, are concerned mostly with the advantages to be gained from re-inforced links with their male in-laws. The Etoro, as it happens, put significant obstacles in the way of hetero-sexual behavior. Husband and wife, for example, are per-mitted to have sexual relations only outside the communal household and only under conditions that rule out about two-thirds of the calendar year. The birth rate, unsurpris-ingly, is very low.

Does the behavior of a small tribe in New Guinea have any bearing on the debates in contemporary America about "respect" for homosexual lifestyles? Perhaps not. After all, requiring homosexual behavior is far from merely permitting it. But the Etoro and similar societies do illus-trate something about the logic of homosexual male rela-tions in human societies. When such relations are subject to cultural elaboration they almost always fit into a pat-tern of initiation into secrets, male exclusivity, and a low status for women.

Why this should be so is a complex question, involv-ing both biology and the underlying nature of human soci-ety. A short answer is that heterosexual marriage is shaped by the complicated interplay of marital sex, pregnancy, child-care, and the sustained dependence and interdepen-dence of husband, wife, and children. Male homosexual relations, because they are sterile and because they chan-nel relations of male dominance, are built on a narrower base of sex, subordination, and control.

CAN IT WORK HERE?

Vermont already has approved "civil unions," and as I write it looks very much as though the Massachusetts courts are about to give the United States some form of officially sanctioned "gay marriage." Many of its propo-nents say gay marriage is just the extension of a civil right to an unfairly excluded minority, and that liberal-minded argument sounds convincing to large numbers of Ameri-cans. I, however, am skeptical. The anthropological record, as I read it, shows that if a society treats male homosexual behavior as a fully legitimate option, it will end up not with a more expansively defined system of marriage, but with a dual-track system in which "marriage" is reduced to a bare transactional relationship, while male homosex-uality will flourish according to its own dynamic.

As a social scientist, I am perfectly prepared to admit that American society *can* normalize male homosexuality and that "gay marriage" moves us in that direction. Other societies have run this experiment, and, in a fashion, it "works." If America normalizes male homosexuality through gay marriage, our culture is not suddenly going to become exactly like the Etoro, or the Big Nambas of the northern New Hebrides, or other such tribes. Rather, we will follow out the biological and cultural logic of homosexuality in our own fashion. The general results, however, are predictable on the basis of the ethnography: Heterosexual marriage will be weakened; the birth rate will decline; the status of women as mothers will further erode; and young boys will be a much greater target of erotic attention by older males.

To say these things, I understand, is to excite vigorous disagreement from those who advocate gay marriage as just a step in the proper expansion of civil rights. The link between homosexual desire and erotic interest in children is especially contentious. Gay activists and their support-ers frequently point out that most child molestation is per-petrated by heterosexual males. And they emphasize that homosexuality has no *necessary* link to pedophilia: A great many gay men are primarily interested in other adult gay men. I grant both points, but we are also left with the stubborn empirical fact that societies that have indeed institutionalized something akin to "gay marriage" have done so in the form of older men taking adolescent boys as their partners. To imagine that we could have gay marriage in the United States without also giving strong encouragement to this form of eroticism is, in light of the ethnographic evidence, wishful thinking.

In any case, the American experiment in "gay marriage" looks to me all but inevitable. We will see for ourselves in the next generation or two who is right.

PLURAL MARRIAGE

The advocates of making America safe for plural marriage or polygamy are less visible than the advocates of gay marriage, but they certainly exist. A substantial percentage of Americans now believe that the government "has no business" enacting or enforcing laws on what adults do "in the privacy of their bedrooms," and those who believe this have already ceded that, in principle, polygamy is a legitimate option. What concern is it of the government whether a man has more than one wife or a woman more than one husband, provided that all the partners enter into the relationship of their own free will?

In this sense, polygamy is a good stand-in for the larger attitude that sexual relations and marriage are a "private" matter in which the larger community should have no say. That libertarian ideal applied to sexual relations is based on profoundly false assumptions about human societies. The relations between men and women in the family and between parents and children always have far-reaching social consequences.

In the United States, polygamy is illegal and relatively uncommon but nonetheless practiced by a few. The best-known examples are those 50,000 or so breakaway Mormons who reject the 1890 Mormon-Church edict that ended the practice of polygamy begun by their prophet Joseph Smith. Smith had cited biblical precedent and divine revelation for adopting polygamy, but the institution provided an expedient solution for a movement that initially attracted many more female converts than male. As the Mormons became a self-reproducing community in their own right, polygamy made less functional sense and continued only on the remote fringes of the movement.

Even so, Mormon polygamy follows a pattern thoroughly familiar to anthropologists. In societies where a man is permitted to have more than one wife, typically a minority of men actually do so; the members of that minority marry not just twice but several times; some of the co-wives are often sisters or cousins; the age difference between the husbands and wives is substantial and typically greater with each additional wife; and new wives are often teenagers. Polygamy (technically "polygyny" when it is a man with several wives) in other words is a system by which powerful older men assemble a household of young desirable women. Polygynous marriages almost always are part of a system of arranged marriages in which the women have little or no say about the matter.

That does not mean that the wives in a polygynous household are necessarily unhappy. For every Lu Ann Kingston, the Mormon woman who recently testified about being pressured at age 15 to become the fourth wife of her 23-year-old cousin, there are many others who accept the situation and take pleasure in the fellowship of their co-wives. Polygyny, in fact, is a perfectly workable way of arranging human affairs. But it has highly predictable consequences that most Americans would find unacceptable.

We probably don't want to embrace a system that shunts young girls into motherhood before they have an opportunity to get an education or that leads to fathers arranging the marriages of their teenage daughters.

But surely we are in no danger of heterodox Mormons imposing their system of polygyny on Methodists in New Hampshire or Baptists in Florida? No, we aren't. But polygyny has a brand-new set of apologists who have emerged all over the country in a little-heralded movement called "polyamory." The polyamorists might be thought of as a fetid blossom of the Swinging Sixties' free-love movement. They favor a redefinition of marriage as a combination of any number of men and women who join together in a kind of group family. Polyamorists expect and encourage sexual relations within this tangle to be both homosexual and heterosexual. And they are very far from any thought that their licentious groupings would provide an avenue for the emergence of a patriarch with a retinue of teen-wives.

But that just shows that the polyamorists are too busy groping toward their particular form of sexual self-expressions to understand the consequences of abolishing monogamy. Eliminate the one-man-one-wife rule and, yes, the polyamorists could openly do their thing but so could a lot of other people. Should the polyamorists have their way, plural marriage would, almost of a certainty, emerge in its classic form of rich older males dominating much younger vulnerable females.

This is not a "slippery slope" forecast. It is more definite than that, since we know for a fact that everywhere and at every time human societies have made plural marriage an option, this is what happens. Given a free market and no rules against plural marriage, human beings will find themselves in a hierarchy dominated by older men with multiple younger wives.

But why? Why wouldn't the polyamorist utopia of coupling, tripling, and quadrupling emerge instead? Or at least some tame version where most people are monogamists, but a fringe avails itself of the new option? The answer lies in something anthropologists don't like to talk about: human nature. The human sexes accommodate fairly easily to a dominant male hierarchy; human males are biologically primed to seek sexual variety; and the systems of reciprocity on which all human societies are based lend themselves very easily to dominant males consolidating their status by taking young wives.

There is a lot of argument in anthropology over these matters, and, for the moment, I would prefer to avoid a more strenuous attempt to explain why polygamy tends to crystallize in one particular form. What matters is that we have studied many hundreds of human societies, large and small, and in doing so have a pretty clear picture of polygamy as an institution. One version of polygamy, polyandry—the marriage of a woman with more than one husband—is very rare. (Various Himalayan tribes and the extinct culture of the Marquesan Islands in the Pacific provide examples.) But polygyny is common. Ask an anthropologist why and you are bound to hear a lot about the numerous variations and particularities that distinguish one case from the next. But in the end you will still have this essential truth: Polygamy is inseparable from older men imposing themselves on young women.

Nor do the consequences stop there. A society in which older men collect younger women creates a series of follow-on problems for itself in matters such as dealing with a large number of youngish widows who missed getting an education and have few marketable skills; disputes over inheritance among the children of co-wives; and a large cohort of young men who find it much more difficult to find wives of their own. Young men competing for an artificially limited number of young women tend to be extra aggressive. Hence it is no surprise that polygynous societies are often violence-prone.

Would the United States be an exception? Possibly. Perhaps our emphasis on "companionship" in marriage and the ideal that spouses love one another would tame the spirit of male domination that polygamy typically unleashes. But I doubt it.

THE LIBERTARIAN ILLUSION

Recently, Sen. Rick Santorum (R-Pa.) provoked an outcry when he observed, "If the Supreme Court says you have the right to consensual [gay] sex within your home, then you have the right to bigamy, you have the right to polygamy, you have the right to incest, you have the right to adultery, you have the right to anything." Among the replies posted on the Internet, I noted these:

- "Bigamy, polygamy, incest, and adultery—could you please tell me what, in a practical sense, is wrong with these from a 'public policy' point of view?"

- "What principled case can be made that any private-between-consenting-adults sexual expression *should* be off-limits?"

- "If all laws against consensual sex in the privacy of one's home are unconstitutional or should be—which seems to be the position of Santorum's critics—I can't imagine why laws against adultery, incest, polygamy, and (possibly) bestiality should be spared from this sweeping claim."

As the editorial page of the *New York Times* saw it, Santorum "equate[d] homosexuality with bigamy, polygamy, incest, and adultery." Well, no, he didn't *equate* these practices, but Senator Santorum did enunciate a context for thinking about the broader implications of treating "sexual expression" as something that ought to be of no concern to society at large.

The anthropological evidence is overwhelmingly on the side of those who argue that large social consequences follow from a society's decisions about which sexual practices are legitimate. The rules that govern marriage and sexual relations are, directly and indirectly, the basis of family life and have enormous influence over the formation of good (or bad) character in children. Marriage channels the primary relations between the sexes and the generations, and it is the template for most other relations in society. This is true not just in the United States. It is true everywhere. Alter the rules of marriage, and society will reshape itself around the new situation. But it doesn't necessarily reshape itself in the ways that the reformers hoped.

The sexual privatizers imagine a society in which adults can seek their pleasures without interference and somehow children will get born and properly raised. It is a sheer illusion. A society that doesn't restrict human sexual relations in effective ways is a society that doesn't have much interest in reproducing itself. People left to their own sexual whims will sometimes form stable families, but that is the exception, not the rule. The more we treat sex as merely recreational, the less important we make procreation. Demystifying procreation—making it just another event that may or may not require heterosexual married parents in a long-term relationship—leads to both low procreation and badly raised children. A society that abandons the effort to restrict and channel human sexual urges into approved forms loses control of the strongest emotional/biological force known to our species and invites a progressive dissolution into unconnected or randomly connected individuals.

It is indeed possible to have a viable society that puts a very low value on women's reproductive capacity. All the society really needs is a reliable way to attract new members. It can do that by raising children, or it can encourage high rates of immigration. Increasingly, it looks like we are choosing the latter.

The dream of unfettered sexual expression is very powerful. The advent of effective birth control and abortion on demand, along with a revolution in attitudes towards pre-marital sex and cohabitation, and the de-stigmatizing of out-of-wedlock birth, divorce, pornography, and homosexuality have gone very far towards creating a popular view that we *can* create a society in which sexual behavior has no public consequences. But, in the end, this is merely a fantasy.

Forms of "sexual expression" are, at a deeper level, modalities of social relationships that do have very real public consequences. Whatever a society accepts as legitimate "in the bedroom" inevitably becomes a choice affecting the status of husbands, wives, children, and many others. In this sense, every society in effect chooses to have a strong version of marriage in which husbands and wives are bound by public expectations of good behavior or it chooses a weak version in which people work out their dissatisfactions and hurts in private and walk away from the marriage when they can't. Likewise, a society chooses to respect women as mothers or treats them primarily as income-earners. It chooses to create families that invest love and attention in their children or alternatively to treat children as a luxury good. Society chooses whether children will be the focus of adult sexual interest; and it chooses whether it will cultivate families that care deeply about education or delegate the whole task to strangers, and so on. If we indulge the fantasy that "sexual expression" is only an individual matter of no valid concern to society at large, we choose our high rate of divorce, our ambiguous regard for motherhood, our unhappy children, and our poor schools. It doesn't seem like an especially good choice.

Of course, you don't really need an anthropologist to see that a breakdown in social rules governing marriage and the family has disastrous consequences. Consider some statistics: 1.35 million children in the U.S. born outside of marriage in 2001—33.5 percent of the total; 947,384 divorces in 2000, excluding those in California, Colorado, Indiana, and Louisiana, states that don't count divorces; by age 14, 14–20 percent of American girls and 20–22 percent of American boys are "sexually experienced"; about five million Americans are addicted to drugs, and 52,000 die each year from their addictions; 15 million new cases of sexually transmitted diseases occur in the U.S. each year, a quarter of them among teenagers; about 100,000 American children engage in prostitution, and about 85 percent of street prostitutes report being incestuously molested by a male family-member as a child.

The breakdown in the family is also a sadly familiar part of everyday life for most of us. Who doesn't know a single mom struggling to do her best for her children but inevitably coming up short? Who doesn't know of couples sundered by the small difficulties that, in previous generations, would have been taken in stride? And you don't need an anthropologist to sense the transformation of America from a family-friendly culture to a culture of me-first.

But if you want to see where these social trends are leading, anthropology has some answers. Humanity has been experimenting with ways to organize itself into viable social groups for many millennia. Almost any combination of sexual partners has been institutionalized somewhere and often in multiple places. We can and should read that record as a realistic check against the dreams of consequence-free sexual liberation that have seized the imaginations of so many of our fellow citizens.

....

"Why Marriage?"

Ellen Lewin

That same-sex marriage has emerged as the most passionately debated civil rights issue of the early 21st century should come as no surprise to anthropologists, many of whom, after all, have devoted their lives to studying

"Why Marriage?" by Ellen Lewin. Reproduced by permission of the American Anthropological Association from *Anthropology News*, 45:5 May 2004, pp. 11–12. Not for sale or further reproduction.

kinship. American kinship, as David Schneider pointed out many years ago, depends on metaphors of blood and law, metaphors that work as effectively as they do in organizing our lives because they are so deeply held and emotionally compelling. And these are, of course, the metaphors that rule in the current debates, embedded in an even more compelling set of images of nature that make the eventual resolution of this issue matter so much to actors on both sides.

Why has marriage become so central to questions of gay/lesbian rights? How has this happened when lesbians and gay men are themselves so divided over the issue? I would like to outline a few ways that we might think about these questions. I base my comments on the research I carried out on same-sex commitment ceremonies (*Recognizing Ourselves: Ceremonies of Lesbian and Gay Commitment* 1998), on other anthropological work I've done with lesbian and gay families in the US, and on my own experience as a participant in the struggle to achieve the right to marry. My views on this issue, which had long rested on a radical antipathy to marriage as a patriarchal institution, shifted dramatically after my spouse and I were united in a Jewish ceremony in 1992 and after I studied some 60 same-sex couples who staged commitment ceremonies of various kinds—none at that time legally sanctioned.

CELEBRATING COMMITMENT

Commitment ceremonies, weddings, and other ritual occasions that seek to celebrate lesbian and gay relationships are in many ways very diverse: Some are religious, some are secular; some are modest affairs, others involve conspicuous expenditure and lavish display; some are crafted with the intent of invoking convention and upholding "tradition," while others are playful, subversive, and self-consciously "queer." But what they all attempt is to situate a relationship within a broader community context, to proclaim the authenticity of the relationship in a public manner, and to achieve recognition that extends beyond the boundaries of gay/lesbian communities. These ceremonies are often gripping events, occasions at which participants may experience unanticipated reactions: It is not uncommon for guests at ceremonies, even those (heterosexuals) who are attending under duress, to burst into tears, or to reveal the powerful impact the ritual has on them in other displays of emotion. "Now I understand," they may cry, "It's all about love."

When I first witnessed these events, and heard these formulaic exclamations, my reaction was embarrassment. Can relationships be reduced to sentiments commonly associated with popular romance novels? But I soon learned that I was missing the point, and that "love" is a code that makes otherwise alien behavior understandable within a shared cultural matrix—for both actors and audience. Non-gay people in our society may not understand or sympathize with homosexuality when they have no choice but to think of it as some set of sexual practices they probably cannot imagine, but they are very likely to "get it" when the issue is commitment, loyalty, domesticity—in short, "love."

EXPRESSION OF STATE APPROVAL

Given that these rituals are successful—that is, transformative—even in the absence of legal marriage, one might think that the issue could end there, to be easily resolved with some codification of "civil unions" or other non-marital conventions. But that conclusion ignores how both material and linguistic accoutrements of weddings shape their symbolic dimensions. As satisfying as religious ceremonies, rings, flowers, gifts, and the other markers of "weddings" are, there is nothing quite as powerful as the expression of state approval.

Last summer, my spouse and I went to Toronto to get legally married, 11 years after our extra-legal Jewish wedding. Our decision to do so was largely political. We wanted to be among those pioneering couples who would have a part in future legal challenges to marriage codes in the US. But nothing prepared us for the emotional impact of having government officials routinely process our paperwork or of having a functionary licensed by the province perform our brief City Hall ceremony. No family or close friends could attend, and virtually all routine wedding insignia were absent. But we were moved far more deeply than either of us expected; we came home feeling convinced that we really were "married," and that feeling has persisted even as we've had to confront our inability to officially claim any of the privileges that accompany marriage in our own country.

MOVE TO THE FRONT OF THE BUS

While only a few years ago lesbian and gay couples were thrilled to have even the most meager sort of recognition thrown in our direction, many of us are now adamant that we must have marriage and nothing less. In large part, this sense of entitlement to the full package of rights and responsibilities reflects wide discussion of the level of discrimination same-sex couples endure because we can't get married. More than 1000 specific rights are restricted to heterosexually married couples, including tax benefits, pension rights, child custody, and survivor benefits, in other words, most entitlements that have to do with being someone's next of kin. These benefits are not trivial. They can directly affect our ability to survive under particular conditions. But I would argue that as marks of legitimacy and authenticity these entitlements are even more vital. They mediate the ability to claim a particular identity in the context of one's community, and they intervene in situations where shame may preclude naming one's most important relationships. They have to do with the dignity with which we move through life.

Let me use an example from the drama of marriage-related civil disobedience that has been unfolding around the country. A few days after the mayor of the village of New Paltz, New York began to perform same-sex weddings without marriage licenses, the *New York Times* featured an article about the first couple to take advantage of the new policy. Jeffrey S McGowan and Billiam van Roestenberg had told very few people of their relationship. They had long been afraid to purchase a home together, feeling that it would be safer to rent in case they had to move quickly "if too many people found out about us." Even after buying a house, they avoided neighbors, had separate phone lines installed, and even removed photographs from the house when friends and family came to visit. Van Roestenberg described the anguish he felt as friends would try to make matches for his partner: "I can tell you it is utterly humiliating for me to be with the person I love and have people discuss whether he is suitable or not for a particular woman. You smile, but it really does hurt inside."

The wedding by a public official, however insecure the legal grounds on which it rested, changed everything for these two men, enabling them to make their relationship public. Van Roestenberg put it aptly, "Jeff and I sat down in the front of the bus for the first time and began a new phase of our lives together." By drawing on this image from the black civil rights movement of the 1950s and 1960s, he not only situated the struggle for same-sex marriage in an honorable protest tradition, but he alluded to the psychological damage done by discrimination that was at the heart of moral opposition to racial segregation.

STANDARD OF LEGITIMACY

Stories like this are not rare. They emerged over and over again in the research I conducted in the mid-1990s with same-sex couples whose weddings occurred outside the legal system. Even for lesbian and gay couples who have not felt it necessary to enter into such elaborate forms of concealment, the notion that one's union is not quite legitimate, not exactly "the real thing" casts a pervasive shadow over our lives. Marriage may seem like a small

step, but it is what other people—other citizens—have access to, and it is what many lesbians and gay people, as participants in the wider culture, use as a standard of legitimacy. For many of the couples I studied, the issue was having access to some form of authority that they saw as attesting to the authenticity of their relationship: In some cases, the endorsement came from God, in other cases from the presence of family and non-gay friends; in still other instances, receiving gifts, wearing clothes associated with weddings, having a certificate of some sort, like a Jewish *ketubah,* or drawing on ethnic traditions in constructing the ceremony authenticated the event. For many couples, even an ambiguous mark of legitimacy opened the door to making other claims to equal marital rights, even if such claims involved nothing more than declaring their existence for the first time. Marriage certificates issued by the state or religious institutions clearly offer another example as they constitute evidence that the relationship is just what the couple claims it to be—a marriage.

Diversion among lesbians and gay men over this issue continues to be sharp, although the tone of the debate has been muted in the face of recent actions to demand the right to marry. It's hard to be against such dramatic instances of civil disobedience, even if one doesn't find marriage a compelling goal, and even if one is reluctant to launch this struggle in the year of a critical national election. Of course, lesbians and gay men are not yet in a position to *refuse* to get married, since such protest can only be coherent when leveled against a right we possess. What's important as the discussion continues is to resist thinking of legal marriage as nothing more than a way to gain access to a package of formal entitlements and economic advantages. These concrete benefits are significant, but in the end pale beside the more symbolic rewards that come with moving to the front of the bus. This is a process that anthropologists can document with particular clarity. Our voices need to be heard in the current debate, not only to challenge unfounded claims by demogogues about the universality of any particular marital configuration, but to support the rights of lesbians and gay men to build their lives as full citizens.

– 24 –

Are We There Yet?

Getting to the Field

David Houston

David Houston received his BA in anthropology from the University of Vermont in 1998 and his MA from McGill University in 2001. He is currently working toward his PhD at McGill on the cultural aspects of technology and computer use in developing countries. He works at the University of Vermont as a system administrator in the university's computer support unit and as a lecturer in the anthropology department.

This essay examines some of the inherent beliefs about that central tenet of anthropology: the field. What is it? How does one "get" there? And perhaps more usefully, *where* is it and why does it sometimes take longer to arrive than indicated by the miles that one can count between where one is and where one wants to be?

For anthropology, the essence of the discipline is often considered to be the field studies, or *fieldwork,* that is the culmination of a graduate student's efforts to obtain his or her advanced degree. For very nearly the entire history of the discipline, "the field" has been at the center of the anthropologist's work. It has simultaneously offered the promise of understanding as well as the ability to plumb the great depths of "culture." It has also served as a kind of lightning rod, attracting a great deal of attention and controversy as anthropologists everywhere struggled to come to terms with ideas that called the whole idea of fieldwork into serious question. For a very long time, the whole idea of being "out in the field" connoted a common understanding that the geographical location under study was indeed far away, often inaccessible, and certainly not a place where the anthropologist regularly lived his or her life. Following the sequestering in the field, the generally accepted practice has been to return to collect and analyze notes, tapes, transcripts, and photographs.

But while much of what constitutes "the field" has changed in the past twenty to thirty years, a great deal of the process involved has not changed much at all. Recent ethnographic accounts are not infrequently situated in the same locale as the anthropologist's "home turf" and are as vibrant and powerful as studies conducted fifty years ago by someone like Edward Evans-Pritchard in remote and often inaccessible places. The entire question of *who* to study has been given a thorough look, and other ways of doing and seeing are now generally accepted. Ultimately, whether one goes to Botswana or the Bronx, there is the matter of clearly and unambiguously identifying just what "the field" is: The *where* and the *who* are both essential questions that must be addressed.

In the fall of 1999 and the spring of 2000, I was a resident in the state of Vermont and making some reasonable headway in pursuit of my advanced degree in anthropology at McGill University. At the time, a legal case based on who was eligible for a marriage license was brought before the Vermont Supreme Court, challenging the state constitution. A gay couple had been denied their request for a marriage license in a small town and had decided to take up the matter in order to address what they felt was a wrong. This led ultimately to the passage of the Civil Union bill, signed into law by the governor, which granted most of marriage's "bundle of rights" to gay and lesbian couples. As passed, it was not marriage, but the legal equivalent. This particular topic captured my attention when I was confronted with the choice of a thesis project. It seemed ideal: marriage and kinship are rich an-thropological veins, and the questions raised with the in-troduction of the bill were many (and I'm certain you all have ensconced in memory somewhere the Hawaiian kin form, don't you?). Best of all, the location was perfect—I lived in "the field"! I confidently embarked on my quest to understand and apprehend the changes in culture and society that seemed only a hop, skip, and jump away.

The entire process of the bill's development, passage, and signing into law had been contentious. The state was sharply and often bitterly divided over the issue. Both pro– and anti–civil union groups sprang into action to bol-ster their cause. Making things more interesting were the impending elections in the fall of 2000. On one side was the incumbent governor—in for the past nine years and reasonably well liked. On the other, a strong Republican challenger, defeated by the same incumbent two years earlier and not at all reserved about how this Civil Union bill had trampled on the will of the people. Add to this volatile mix a third-party candidate and a slim controlling margin in both the House and the Senate—and the mak-ings of a very interesting scenario began to unfold.

Now I had believed that the process of "going to the field" was very simple. Here I was, a bona fide resident of the state, surrounded by "the Natives," familiar with their culture and customs, fluent in their language and writing, and taking up a research project that seemed a perfect fit. "How simple," I thought, as I went first to one event and then another, carefully recording what I saw and heard, and keeping the idea of such things as community and so-ciety and location in my mind as I tried to elicit responses from potential informants. At first, all seemed as I had expected it to be: the cities, the towns, the country, the people, all there as I immersed myself in the work. Cele-bratory occasions to mark the passage of the bill and town meetings following the election to clarify, explain, and re-assure the voters as to its intent started to provide me with a rich collection of ethnographic material.

As I began to move deeper into the project, however, I gradually recognized that what I had originally envi-sioned as "the field" was not quite what I had thought it to be. This perception was very subtle at first. It took form

as I interviewed a few informants and began to recognize that many of my assumptions were not quite right. The "geography of the social," following Robert Castel, was different in subtle and hard-to-identify ways. Initially, what seemed to me to be a collection of individuals and couples living in various communities—all of which when considered together defined "the field"—was not quite that way. In fact, some of the informants resident in Vermont established quite quickly that *their* "communi-ties" did not even live in the state at all, but instead were loose, informal collections of people from *other* states! And it became apparent, based on data that the state of Vermont kept on the application of the civil unions them-selves, that there were far more people coming into the state as *out*siders than there were living in the state as *in*siders and that these were the people availing themselves of the process. All of a sudden, the geography of the field changed: No longer simply Vermont, it included the United States and parts of Canada! This was not the Bora-Bora I had expected.

To try to put things back into a context that made sense, I then began to try very hard to make contact with local informants through an interview process. I assumed that they would be ready and willing to pour out their stories and enrich both my work and its analytical pur-pose. The gathering storm of the elections, however, made even this a serious challenge. It became apparent that the "natives" were not particularly interested in talk-ing about something that had become a source of real hardship for many. The tenor of the elections had become so severe as to make direct contact a dicey prospect. So what was with these natives, anyway? Did they really live here? And were they even part of the "culture" I was living in?

"The field," as it turned out, was not a singular place. It was not a specific point in time or space. It wasn't even easy to get to, even though I lived there already. Instead, that time-honored tradition that was fieldwork became instead a conundrum of people, places, and ideas, emo-tions and feelings. It was everywhere and nowhere all at once.

CHAPTER

VIII

MARRIAGE AND KINSHIP

What Does It Mean to Be in a Family?

A KEY ISSUE THE PREVIOUS CHAPTER demonstrates is that human reproduction involves much more than sex, touching on issues of folk knowledge, politics, socialization, and social justice, to name but a few. Of course, it is also central to the issues of **marriage, family, and kinship.** Marriage provokes many questions. Why do different arrangements occur, and why and how are they socially recognized? Marriage does not have a single function. It ties a bundle of rights and obligations into one of several packages, creating economic units, relating the individual to other kin groups, defining social status. It is a political instrument, as royal marriages in Europe, and gay and lesbian marriages show. It also regulates sex and creates a social security network. Seen from such a broad perspective, sex might have nothing to do with marriage, as every teenager knows! It is for this reason that one can find woman-woman marriages and even ghost marriages. As Serena Nanda shows in her article on arranging a marriage in India, where marriages are conceived as relationships between families, it is much too important to leave to the whims of young people. Marriage is, in many societies, a family decision.

As with apple pie, everyone, especially politicians on the stump, is in favor of "the family," yet few people specify what they mean by it and why they believe it to be the bedrock of North American society. Many anthropologists have also exhibited this belief. For example, George Murdock (1965), after surveying some 250 societies that all had a form of **nuclear family** (a married couple with dependent offspring), claimed that the family served a number of functions, such as preventing disruptive sex, enabling enculturation and the sexual division of labor, and protecting females during their reproductive years. In short, the family is seen as providing the domestic sphere in which the focus is on such essentials as food preparation, discipline, sex, and grooming. Of course, all these activities can be and are undertaken in some societies by other institutions; for example, among the Mae Enga of Papua New Guinea, men and women sleep in separate men's and women's houses. Sex is frequently a matter of coupling in the fields. In some societies where the household is organized around a group of related women, men eat at their sister's house. Similarly, in British society, much **enculturation** of boys takes place away from home at "exclusive public schools" like Eton and Harrow.

The conventional approach is increasingly questioned, and some anthropologists now argue that the family is not a concrete institution designed by God or even people to satisfy human needs; rather, it is an ideological construct tied up with the development of the state. Ideologically we feel that what happens in the family is of no concern to the state. Yet, as a number of observers have pointed out, domestic violence is tolerated to a far greater extent than other forms of violence. Indeed, whereas most of us would not hesitate reporting a theft by a stranger to the police, we probably would have doubts about reporting the same theft if it were committed by a family member. When the chips are down, even though we might personally dislike family members, we feel a sense of obligation to help them.

Revisionist thinking is evident in Brett Williams's article on migrant farmworkers. In the United States we hear a great deal about the breakdown of families among the poor; yet among Hispanic migrants, marital relationships show a strength that is often lacking in middle- and upper-class families. Looking at the wives in migrant communities, who are quite submissive to their husbands, one might conclude that they are oppressed and without power; yet the same women are sisters, mothers, grandmothers, aunts, and godmothers, all of whom in fact have considerable authority over men. Hence, the glib stereotype of the "oppressed woman" in migrant families needs rethinking.

Williams's paper also challenges another stereotype held by many North Americans: that families constitute independent social units. As she shows, the women in migrant Hispanic communities work long and hard at gathering and binding relations so that their families are firmly embedded in a wider network of kinship—what anthropologists would call a **kindred.** These are the relatives on whom an individual can call in time of need, and in migrant communities they are crucial in helping people cope with the exigencies of life.

In most human societies, families (where they exist) are likewise embedded within larger networks of kin. In **agrarian societies** there often exists a whole hierarchy of groups based on descent, with some form of **extended family** at the base. In traditional China, for example, upon marriage a woman would leave the family into which she had been born to go live with her husband in the family into which he had been born. Thus, all men in the family shared a common male ancestor, and as older members died off, younger members were born into the family. Several families together whose men could trace their descent through men back to a more distant common male ancestor constituted a larger male descent group that anthropologists would call a **lineage.** Finally, lineages sharing a common ancestry—**clans** in anthropological parlance—were also recognized.

The Chinese case constitutes an example of **patrilineal descent,** a common device for specifying group membership in societies in which men perform the bulk of productive work and hold political authority. In societies without centralized political organization, in which much of the productive work is done by women, descent is apt to be reckoned matrilineally, exclusively through women. The Hopi people of the U.S. Southwest are one example. An important correlate of how descent is reckoned is the way the family relationships are structured. In patrilineal societies a woman is apt to be isolated from her kin and must defer to the dictates of the men in her husband's family, in which she is something of an outsider. Under such conditions, women must show great resourcefulness if they are to find ways to protect their own self-interests. By contrast, although patrilineal societies are generally patriarchal, societies with **matrilineal descent** are not matriarchal.

The Mosuo of China (in Lu Yuan and Sam Mitchell's article) offer an example of a matrilineal society in which descent is traced through women, but which is not a matriarchy because men still have important public authority. The Mosuo also practice a "walking marriage," in which men and women do not formally marry and reside together. Although the father and his kin do have relationships with the children that result from these relationships, they do not have formal economic or social obligations to them.

Timothy Egan explores the persistence and dilemmas of **polygamy** in the western United States among Mormon communities. Polygynous unions (one husband with more than one wife) create complex family units that some participants feel offer adaptive advantages (for example, the ability to share child support among wives, feelings of security, and a sense of sisterhood). Recently, however, critics have brought their concerns about this form of marriage and family life to the legal system, arguing that anti-polygamy statutes must be enforced and that such unions can involve incidents of sexual abuse and ostracism within Mormon clans. The question we should ask is not why such forms of marriage and family persist, as if they were survivals from some evolutionarily earlier state of human development (with the nuclear family as the modern end point), but what purposes and dilemmas they offer participants.

In the final article in this chapter, Thomas Maschio explores how the refrigerator serves as a "command center" where mothers balance a number of different activities in contemporary U.S. middle-class families. He compellingly shows how anthropological fieldwork around an everyday object that we take for granted can reveal broader insights about kin relations in our own society and how we symbolize complex notions like "home."

FOCUS QUESTIONS

As you read these selections, consider these questions:

✦ Why do you think the nuclear family is not a universal form of family organization?

✦ What are the advantages and dilemmas associated with polygamous forms of marriage and family life?

✦ How do kin groups maintain a common identity if all the members do not reside in the same household?

✦ How would you describe the kin group to which you belong? To which descent group do you belong? How does that contrast with some of the examples in these selections?

REFERENCE

Murdock, George P. 1965. *Culture and Society, Twenty-Four Essays.* Pittsburgh: University of Pittsburgh Press.

25

Arranging a Marriage in India

Serena Nanda

Serena Nanda, who earned her PhD at New York University in 1973, is now a professor at John Jay College of Criminal Justice of the City University of New York. Her field research includes the study of tribal development in India, and her book, Neither Man nor Woman: The Higras of India, *won the 1990 Ruth Benedict Prize. She has also published on ethnicity, gender, and law in the United States, and her interests include urban and visual anthropology.*

Sister and doctor brother-in-law invite correspondence from North Indian professionals only, for a beautiful, talented, sophisticated, intelligent sister, 5'3", slim, M.A. in textile design, father a senior civil officer. Would prefer immigrant doctors, between 26–29 years. Reply with full details and returnable photo.

A well-settled uncle invites matrimonial correspondence from slim, fair, educated South Indian girl, for his nephew, 25 years, smart, M.B.A., green card holder, 5'6". Full particulars with returnable photo appreciated.

—Matrimonial Advertisements, *India Abroad*

In India, almost all marriages are arranged. Even among the educated middle classes in modern, urban India, marriage is as much a concern of the families as it is of the individuals. So customary is the practice of arranged marriage that there is a special name for a marriage which is not arranged: It is called a "love match."

On my first field trip to India, I met many young men and women whose parents were in the process of "getting them married." In many cases, the bride and groom would not meet each other before the marriage. At most they might meet for a brief conversation, and this meeting would take place only after their parents had decided that the match was suitable. Parents do not compel their children to marry a person who either marriage partner finds objectionable. But only after one match is refused will another be sought.

As a young American woman in India for the first time, I found this custom of arranged marriage oppressive. How could any intelligent young person agree to such a marriage without great reluctance? It was contrary to everything I believed about the importance of romantic love as the only basis of a happy marriage. It also clashed with my strongly held notions that the choice of such an intimate and permanent relationship could be made only by the individuals involved. Had anyone tried to arrange my marriage, I would have been defiant and rebellious!

At the first opportunity, I began, with more curiosity than tact, to question the young people I met on how they felt about this practice. Sita, one of my young informants, was a college graduate with a degree in political science. She had been waiting for over a year while her parents were arranging a match for her. I found it difficult to accept the docile manner in which this well-educated young woman awaited the outcome of a process that would result in her spending the rest of her life with a man she hardly knew, a virtual stranger, picked out by her parents.

"How can you go along with this?" I asked her, in frustration and distress. "Don't you care who you marry?"

"Of course I care," she answered. "This is why I must let my parents choose a boy for me. My marriage is too important to be arranged by such an inexperienced person as myself. In such matters, it is better to have my parents' guidance."

I had learned that young men and women in India do not date and have very little social life involving members of the opposite sex. Although I could not disagree with Sita's reasoning, I continued to pursue the subject.

"But how can you marry the first man you have ever met? Not only have you missed the fun of meeting a lot

---

"Arranging a Marriage in India" by Serena Nanda from *Stumbling toward Truth: Anthropologists at Work*, pp. 96–104. Waveland Press, 2000. Reprinted by permission of the author.

of different people, but you have not given yourself the chance to know who is the right man for you."

"Meeting with a lot of different people doesn't sound like any fun at all," Sita answered. "One hears that in America the girls are spending all their time worrying about whether they will meet a man and get married. Here we have the chance to enjoy our life and let our parents do this work and worrying for us."

She had me there. The high anxiety of the competition to "be popular" with the opposite sex certainly was the most prominent feature of life as an American teenager in the late fifties. The endless worrying about the rules that governed our behavior and about our popularity ratings sapped both our self-esteem and our enjoyment of adolescence. I reflected that absence of this competition in India most certainly may have contributed to the self-confidence and natural charm of so many of the young women I met.

And yet, the idea of marrying a perfect stranger, whom one did not know and did not "love," so offended my American ideas of individualism and romanticism, that I persisted with my objections.

"I still can't imagine it," I said. "How can you agree to marry a man you hardly know?"

"But of course he will be known. My parents would never arrange a marriage for me without knowing all about the boy's family background. Naturally we will not rely only on what the family tells us. We will check the particulars out ourselves. No one will want their daughter to marry into a family that is not good. All these things we will know beforehand."

Impatiently, I responded, "Sita, I don't mean know the family, I mean, know the man. How can you marry someone you don't know personally and don't love? How can you think of spending your life with someone you may not even like?"

"If he is a good man, why should I not like him?" she said. "With you people, you know the boy so well before you marry, where will be the fun to get married? There will be no mystery and no romance. Here we have the whole of our married life to get to know and love our husband. This way is better, is it not?"

Her response made further sense, and I began to have second thoughts on the matter. Indeed, during months of meeting many intelligent young Indian people, both male and female, who had the same ideas as Sita, I saw arranged marriages in a different light. I also saw the importance of the family in Indian life and realized that a couple who took their marriage into their own hands was taking a big risk, particularly if their families were irreconcilably opposed to the match. In a country where every important resource in life—a job, a house, a social circle—is gained through family connections, it seemed foolhardy to cut oneself off from a supportive so-

cial network and depend solely on one person for happiness and success.

Six years later I returned to India to again do fieldwork, this time among the middle class in Bombay, a modern, sophisticated city. From the experience of my earlier visit, I decided to include a study of arranged marriages in my project. By this time I had met many Indian couples whose marriages had been arranged and who seemed very happy. Particularly in contrast to the fate of many of my married friends in the United States who were already in the process of divorce, the positive aspects of arranged marriages appeared to me to outweigh the negatives. In fact, I thought I might even participate in arranging a marriage myself. I had been fairly successful in the United States in "fixing up" many of my friends, and I was confident that my matchmaking skills could be easily applied to this new situation, once I learned the basic rules. "After all," I thought, "how complicated can it be? People want pretty much the same things in a marriage whether it is in India or America."

An opportunity presented itself almost immediately. A friend from my previous Indian trip was in the process of arranging for the marriage of her eldest son. In India there is a perceived shortage of "good boys," and since my friend's family was eminently respectable and the boy himself personable, well educated, and nice looking, I was sure that by the end of my year's fieldwork, we would have found a match.

The basic rule seems to be that a family's reputation is most important. It is understood that matches would be arranged only within the same caste and general social class, although some crossing of subcastes is permissible if the class positions of the bride's and groom's families are similar. Although dowry is now prohibited by law in India, extensive gift exchanges took place with every marriage. Even when the boy's family do not "make demands," every girl's family nevertheless feels the obligation to give the traditional gifts, to the girl, to the boy, and to the boy's family. Particularly when the couple would be living in the joint family—that is, with the boy's parents and his married brothers and their families, as well as with unmarried siblings—which is still very common even among the urban, upper-middle class in India, the girl's parents are anxious to establish smooth relations between their family and that of the boy. Offering the proper gifts, even when not called "dowry," is often an important factor in influencing the relationship between the bride's and groom's families and perhaps, also, the treatment of the bride in her new home.

In a society where divorce is still a scandal and where, in fact, the divorce rate is exceedingly low, an arranged marriage is the beginning of a lifetime relationship not just between the bride and groom but between their families as well. Thus, while a girl's looks are important, her character is even more so, for she is being judged as a prospective daughter-in-law as much as a prospective bride. Where she would be living in a joint family, as was the case with my friend, the girl's ability to get along harmoniously in a family is perhaps the single most important quality in assessing her suitability.

My friend is a highly esteemed wife, mother, and daughter-in-law. She is religious, soft-spoken, modest, and deferential. She rarely gossips and never quarrels, two qualities highly desirable in a woman. A family that has the reputation for gossip and conflict among its womenfolk will not find it easy to get good wives for their sons. Parents will not want to send their daughter to a house in which there is conflict.

My friend's family were originally from North India. They had lived in Bombay, where her husband owned a business, for forty years. The family had delayed in seeking a match for their eldest son because he had been an Air Force pilot for several years, stationed in such remote places that it had seemed fruitless to try to find a girl who would be willing to accompany him. In their social class, a military career, despite its economic security, has little prestige and is considered a drawback in finding a suitable bride. Many families would not allow their daughters to marry a man in an occupation so potentially dangerous and which requires so much moving around.

The son had recently left the military and joined his father's business. Since he was a college graduate, modern, and well traveled, from such a good family, and, I thought, quite handsome, it seemed to me that he, or rather his family, was in a position to pick and choose. I said as much to my friend.

While she agreed that there were many advantages on their side, she also said, "We must keep in mind that my son is both short and dark; these are drawbacks in finding the right match." While the boy's height had not escaped my notice, "dark" seemed to me inaccurate; I would have called him "wheat" colored perhaps, and in any case, I did not realize that color would be a consideration. I discovered, however, that while a boy's skin color is a less important consideration than a girl's, it is still a factor.

An important source of contacts in trying to arrange her son's marriage was my friend's social club in Bombay. Many of the women had daughters of the right age, and some had already expressed an interest in my friend's son. I was most enthusiastic about the possibilities of one particular family who had five daughters, all of whom were pretty, demure, and well educated. Their mother had told my friend, "You can have your pick for your son, whichever one of my daughters appeals to you most."

I saw a match in sight. "Surely," I said to my friend, "we will find one there. Let's go visit and make our choice." But my friend held back; she did not seem to share my enthusiasm, for reasons I could not then fathom.

When I kept pressing for an explanation of her reluctance, she admitted, "See, Serena, here is the problem. The family has so many daughters, how will they be able to provide nicely for any of them? We are not making any demands, but still, with so many daughters to marry off, one wonders whether she will even be able to make a proper wedding. Since this is our eldest son, it's best if we marry him to a girl who is the only daughter, then the wedding will truly be a gala affair." I argued that surely the quality of the girls themselves made up for any deficiency in the elaborateness of the wedding. My friend admitted this point but still seemed reluctant to proceed.

"Is there something else," I asked her, "some factor I have missed?" "Well," she finally said, "there is one other thing. They have one daughter already married and living in Bombay. The mother is always complaining to me that the girl's in-laws don't let her visit her own family often enough. So it makes me wonder, will she be that kind of mother who always wants her daughter at her own home? This will prevent the girl from adjusting to our house. It is not a good thing." And so, this family of five daughters was dropped as a possibility.

Somewhat disappointed, I nevertheless respected my friend's reasoning and geared up for the next prospect. This was also the daughter of a woman in my friend's social club. There was clear interest in this family and I could see why. The family's reputation was excellent; in fact, they came from a subcaste slightly higher than my friend's own. The girl, who was an only daughter, was pretty and well educated and had a brother studying in the United States. Yet, after expressing an interest to me in this family, all talk of them suddenly died down and the search began elsewhere.

"What happened to that girl as a prospect?" I asked one day. "You never mention her anymore. She is so pretty and so educated, what did you find wrong?"

"She is too educated. We've decided against it. My husband's father saw the girl on the bus the other day and thought her forward. A girl who 'roams about' the city by herself is not the girl for our family." My disappointment this time was even greater, as I thought the son would have liked the girl very much. But then I thought, my friend is right, a girl who is going to live in a joint family cannot be too independent or she will make life miserable for everyone. I also learned that if the family of the girl has even a slightly higher social status than the family of the boy, the bride may think herself too good for them, and this too will cause problems. Later my friend admitted to me that this had been an important factor in her decision not to pursue the match.

The next candidate was the daughter of a client of my friend's husband. When the client learned that the family was looking for a match for their son, he said, "Look no further, we have a daughter." This man then invited my friends to dinner to see the girl. He had already seen their son at the office and decided that "he liked the boy." We all went together for tea, rather than dinner—it was less of a commitment—and while we were there, the girl's mother showed us around the house. The girl was studying for her exams and was briefly introduced to us.

After we left, I was anxious to hear my friend's opinion. While her husband liked the family very much and was impressed with his client's business accomplishments and reputation, the wife didn't like the girl's looks. "She is short, no doubt, which is an important plus point, but she is also fat and wears glasses." My friend obviously thought she could do better for her son and asked her husband to make his excuses to his client by saying that they had decided to postpone the boy's marriage indefinitely.

By this time almost six months had passed and I was becoming impatient. What I had thought would be an easy matter to arrange was turning out to be quite complicated. I began to believe that between my friend's desire for a girl who was modest enough to fit into her joint family, yet attractive and educated enough to be an acceptable partner for her son, she would not find anyone suitable. My friend laughed at my impatience: "Don't be so much in a hurry," she said. "You Americans want everything done so quickly. You get married quickly and then just as quickly get divorced. Here we take marriage more seriously. We must take all the factors into account. It is not enough for us to learn by our mistakes. This is too serious a business. If a mistake is made we have not only ruined the life of our son or daughter, but we have spoiled the reputation of our family as well. And that will make it much harder for their brothers and sisters to get married. So we must be very careful."

What she said was true and I promised myself to be more patient, though it was not easy. I had really hoped and expected that the match would be made before my year in India was up. But it was not to be. When I left India my friend seemed no further along in finding a suitable match for her son than when I had arrived.

Two years later, I returned to India and still my friend had not found a girl for her son. By this time, he was close to thirty, and I think she was a little worried. Since she knew I had friends all over India, and I was going to be there for a year, she asked me to "help her in this work" and keep an eye out for someone suitable. I was flattered that my judgment was respected, but knowing now how complicated the process was, I had lost my earlier confidence as a matchmaker. Nevertheless, I promised that I would try.

It was almost at the end of my year's stay in India that I met a family with a marriageable daughter whom I felt might be a good possibility for my friend's son. The girl's father was related to a good friend of mine and by coincidence came from the same village as my friend's husband. This new family had a successful business in a medium-sized city in central India and were from the same subcaste as my friend. The daughter was pretty and chic; in fact, she had studied fashion design in college. Her parents would not allow her to go off by herself to any of the major cities in India where she could make a career, but they had compromised with her wish to work by allowing her to run a small dress-making boutique from their home. In spite of her desire to have a career, the daughter was both modest and home-loving and had had a traditional, sheltered upbringing. She had only one other sister, already married, and a brother who was in his father's business.

I mentioned the possibility of a match with my friend's son. The girl's parents were most interested. Although their daughter was not eager to marry just yet, the idea of living in Bombay—a sophisticated, extremely fashion-conscious city where she could continue her education in clothing design—was a great inducement. I gave the girl's father my friend's address and suggested that when they went to Bombay on some business or whatever, they look up the boy's family.

Returning to Bombay on my way to New York, I told my friend of this newly discovered possibility. She seemed to feel there was potential but, in spite of my urging, would not make any moves herself. She rather preferred to wait for the girl's family to call upon them. I hoped something would come of this introduction, though by now I had learned to rein in my optimism.

A year later I received a letter from my friend. The family had indeed come to visit Bombay, and their daughter and my friend's daughter, who were near in age, had become very good friends. During that year, the two girls had frequently visited each other. I thought things looked promising.

Last week I received an invitation to a wedding: My friend's son and the girl were getting married. Since I had found the match, my presence was particularly requested at the wedding. I was thrilled. Success at last! As I prepared to leave for India, I began thinking, "Now, my friend's younger son, who do I know who has a nice girl for him . . . ?"

FURTHER REFLECTIONS ON ARRANGED MARRIAGE

The previous essay was written from the point of view of a family seeking a daughter-in-law. Arranged marriage looks somewhat different from the point of view of the bride and her family. Arranged marriage continues to be preferred, even among the more educated, Westernized sections of the Indian population. Many young women from these families still go along, more or less willingly, with the practice, and also with the specific choices of their families. Young women do get excited about the prospects of their marriage, but there is also ambivalence and increasing uncertainty, as the bride contemplates leaving the comfort and familiarity of her own home, where as a "temporary guest" she has often been indulged, to live among strangers. Even in the best situation, she will now come under the close scrutiny of her husband's family. How she dresses, how she behaves, how she gets along with others, where she goes, how she spends her time, her domestic abilities—all of this and much more—will be observed and commented on by a whole new set of relations. Her interaction with her family of birth will be monitored and curtailed considerably. Not only will she leave their home, but with increasing geographic mobility, she may also live very far from them, perhaps even on another continent. Too much expression of her fondness for her own family, or her desire to visit them, may be interpreted as an inability to adjust to her new family, and may become a source of conflict. In an arranged marriage, the burden of adjustment is clearly heavier for a woman than for a man. And that is in the best of situations.

In less happy circumstances, the bride may be a target of resentment and hostility from her husband's family, particularly her mother-in-law or her husband's unmarried sisters, for whom she is now a source of competition for the affection, loyalty, and economic resources of a son or brother. If she is psychologically or even physically abused, her options are limited, as returning to her parents' home or getting a divorce is still very stigmatized. For most Indians, marriage and motherhood are still considered the only suitable roles for a woman, even for those who have careers, and few women can comfortably contemplate remaining unmarried. Most families still consider "marrying off" their daughters as a compelling religious duty and social necessity. This increases a bride's sense of obligation to make the marriage a success, at whatever cost to her own personal happiness.

The vulnerability of a new bride may also be intensified by the issue of dowry that, although illegal, has become a more pressing issue in the consumer conscious society of contemporary urban India. In many cases, where a groom's family is not satisfied with the amount of dowry a bride brings to her marriage, the young bride will be harassed constantly to get her parents to give more. In extreme cases, the bride may even be murdered, and the murder disguised as an accident or a suicide. This also offers the husband's family an opportunity to arrange another match for him, thus bringing in another dowry. This phenomenon, called dowry death, calls attention not just to the "evils of dowry" but also to larger issues of the powerlessness of women as well.

26

Why Migrant Women Feed Their Husbands Tamales

Foodways as a Basis for a Revisionist View of Tejano Family Life

Brett Williams

Brett Williams is a professor of anthropology and director of American studies at American University, Washington, D.C. She received her PhD from the University of Illinois in 1975. Her fieldwork has been done in the United States, among migrant workers of Mexican descent from Texas, in a mixed ethnic neighborhood of a northeastern city (see Chapter 9), and among waitresses. She has written on all of these topics, as well as on Southern folklife and on the African American hero John Henry. Her research interests include poverty, the media, folklore, and politics and culture.

In the array of artifacts by which Tejano migrant farm-workers identify themselves, the tamale has no serious rival.[1] It is a complicated culinary treat demanding days of preparation, marking festive—sometimes sacred—occasions, signalling the cook's extraordinary concern for the diners, and requiring a special set of cultural skills and tastes to appreciate and consume appropriately. Tamales are served wrapped in corn husks which hold a soft outer paste of *masa harina* (a flour) and a rich inner mash prepared from the meat of a pig's head.

Only women make tamales. They cooperate to do so with domestic fanfare which stretches through days of buying the pigs' heads, stripping the meat, cooking the mash, preparing the paste, and stuffing, wrapping, and baking or boiling the final tamale. Women shop together because the heads are very bulky; they gather around huge, steaming pots to cook together as well. Tamales are thus labor-intensive food items which symbolize and also exaggerate women's routine nurturance of men. The rit-

ual and cooperation of tamale cookery dramatically underscore women's shared monopoly of domestic tasks.

For middle-class women, such immersion in household affairs is generally taken as a measure of a woman's oppression. We often tend to equate power and influence in the family with freedom from routine family tasks and find such tamale vignettes as those below disconcerting:

- At home in Texas for the winter, an elderly migrant woman, with her daughters-in-law, nieces, and god-daughter, spends several weeks preparing *200 dozen* tamales to distribute to friends, relatives, and local taverns for Christmas. The effort and expense involved are enormous, but she regards this enterprise as a useful and rewarding way to commemorate the holiday, to obligate those she may need to call on later, and to befriend the tavern owners so that they will watch over her male kin who drink there.

- In Illinois for six months a year, migrant women take precious time out from field labor to prepare elaborate feasts, with many tamales, commemorating the conclusion of each harvest (in asparagus, peas, tomatoes, pumpkins, and corn) as well as dates of biographical significance to others in the camp. An especially important day is the *quinceañera* or fifteenth birthday, on which a young girl who will most likely spend her life in field labor is feted with tamales, cakes, and dancing all night, just as though she were a debutante.

- A young migrant, with the full support of his wife's kin as well as his own, sues his wife for divorce in a smalltown Illinois court. His grounds are that she refuses to cook him tamales and dances with other men at fiestas. A disconcerted Illinois judge refuses to grant a divorce on such grounds and the migrant community is outraged: women argue with special vehemence that to nurture and bind her husband a proper wife should cook him tamales.[2]

Incidents like the last, focused on women, their husbands, elaborate domestic nurturance, and the jealous circumscription of sexuality in marriage, again seem to reveal the most repressed and traditional of females. Because migrant women are so involved in family life and so seemingly submissive to their husbands, they have been described often as martyred purveyors of rural Mexican and Christian custom, tyrannized by excessively masculine, crudely domineering, rude and petty bullies in marriage, and blind to any world outside the family because they are suffocated by the concerns of kin.[3] Most disconcerting to outside observers is that migrant women seem to embrace such stereotypes: they argue that they *should* monopolize their foodways and that they should *not* question the authority of their husbands. If men want tamales, men should have them. But easy stereotypes can mislead; in exploring the lives of the poor, researchers must revise their own notions of family life, and this paper argues that foodways can provide crucial clues about how to do so.[4]

The paradox is this: among migrant workers both women and men are equally productive wage earners, and husbands readily acknowledge that without their wives' work their families cannot earn enough to survive. For migrants the division of labor between earning a living outside the home and managing household affairs is unknown; and the dilemma facing middle-class wives who may wish to work to supplement the family's income simply does not exist. Anthropologists exploring women's status cross-culturally argue that women are most influential when they share in the production of food and have some control over its distribution.[5] If such perspectives bear at all on migrant women, one might be led to question their seemingly unfathomable obsequiousness in marriage.

Anthropologists further argue that women's influence is even greater when they are not isolated from their kinswomen, when women can cooperate in production and join, for example, agricultural work with domestic duties and childcare.[6] Most migrant women spend their lives within large, closely knit circles of kin and their work days with their kinswomen. Marriage does not uproot or isolate a woman from her family, but rather doubles the relatives each partner can depend on and widens in turn the networks of everyone involved. The lasting power of marriage is reflected in statistics which show a divorce rate of 1 percent for migrant farmworkers from Texas, demonstrating the strength of a union bolstered by large numbers of relatives concerned that it go well.[7] Crucial to this concern is that neither partner is an economic drain on the family, and the Tejano pattern of early and lifelong marriages establishes some limit on the whimsy with which men can abuse and misuse their wives.

While anthropology traditionally rests on an appreciation of other cultures in their own contexts and on their own terms, it is very difficult to avoid class bias in viewing the lives of those who share partly in one's own culture, especially when the issue is something so close to home as food and who cooks it. Part of the problem may lie in appreciating what families are and what they do. For the poor, public and private domains are blurred in confusing ways, family affairs may be closely tied to economics, and women's work at gathering and obligating or *binding* relatives is neither trivial nor merely a matter of sentiment. Another problem may lie in focusing on the marital relationship as indicative of a woman's authority in the family. We too often forget that women are sisters, grandmothers, and aunts to men as well as wives. Foodways can help us rethink both of these problematic areas and understand how women elaborate domestic roles to knit families together, to obligate both male and female kin, and to nurture and bind their husbands as well.

THE SETTING FOR FAMILY LIFE

To understand migrant family foodways, it is important to explore first the economic circumstances within which they operate. The two thousand Tejano migrants who come to Prairie Junction, Illinois, to work in its harvest for six months a year are permanent residents of the Texas Rio Grande Valley, a lush and tropical agricultural paradise.[8] Dominating that landscape are great citrus and truck farms, highly mechanized operations which rely on commuters from across the Mexican border for whatever manual labor they need. Lacking jobs or substantial property at home, Tejanos in the valley exit for part of each year to earn a living in the north. Agricultural pay is low and employment is erratic, guaranteeing no income beyond a specific hourly wage and offering no fringe benefits in the event of unemployment or disability.[9] As a consequence, migrant workers must be very flexible in pursuing work and must at the same time forge some sort of security on their own to cushion frequent economic jolts. Migrants use kinship to construct both the security and the flexibility they need to manage a very marginal economic place.

In extended families, all members are productive workers (or at the very least share in childcare duties), and migrants find a great deal of security within families whose members are mutually committed to stretching scarce resources among them. Kin call on kin often for material aid, housing, and emotional support; they cooperate in field labor and domestic tasks and freely share food, money, time, and space. Because resources are only sporadically available to individuals, depending on kin eases hard times. In turn, most persons are sensitive to their relatives' needs not only because they care about them but also because they recognize the great value of reciprocity over time.

Migrant families are not easily placed in a convenient anthropological category for they implicate relatives in binding ways while allowing husbands and wives a great deal of freedom to move and settle when they need to, and to return whenever they like. This relative independence of nuclear families allows them to scatter and regroup when pursuing erratic opportunities to work, but always underlying their travels is a sense of a long-term place within a wider circle of kin. I call migrant families *convoys*, for they should be conceptualized as a process rather than a structure; they literally join persons in travel, in work, and through the life course, sharing food as well as the most intimate of concerns.

In the rural Texas settlements (*colonias*) where most migrants spend jobless winters, and in the stark barracks of Prairie Junction where they work each summer, convoys come together (1) to produce and share food for economic survival, (2) to surround food with ritual in order to save one another's dignity in degrading situations, (3) to reaffirm their cultural identity through marking and crossing boundaries with outsiders, and (4) to gather and bind kin, including spouses, to accompany them through life.

STRATEGIES FOR SURVIVAL: ROUTINE

Just as tamales ritually underscore women's domestic commitments, the everyday preparation and sharing of food routinely reaffirms family ties and allows families to work as efficiently and profitably as possible. Especially in emergencies, the sharing of food attests to migrants' visions of their lives as closely, mutually intertwined. The discussion which follows explores the foodways of the Texas *colonias* and the Prairie Junction migrant camps,

the routines which surround them, and the ways they mobilize in crisis.

A newcomer to the Texas *colonias* is struck first by the appalling poverty in which migrants live there. Most are too far from the valley's urban centers to share in such amenities as running water, sewage disposal, or garbage collection. Hand-constructed shacks usually surround a primitive central area where fruits and vegetables grow, goats and chickens roam, and children play. The homes have many hastily constructed additions and ill-defined rooms, attesting to the mobility of the individual family members and seemingly indicating an impermanence to domestic life. This feeling of impermanence is belied, however, by the ongoing family-scale agricultural and pastoral system through which kin produce and share their own food over the Texas winters. Individuals may come and go; but through the extended family migrants adapt as peasants to those times when there is no income. The *colonias* offer evidence of creative domestic cooperation in stretching and sharing food within families and in the continuing migration of family members north from Mexico and back and forth to Illinois to work. These kin know that they can always find food from the winter gardens in Texas.

It is in this context that one can appreciate Sra. Compartida's great Christmas feasts of 200 dozen tamales for relatives, friends, and people she considers resources or contacts. She has worked for most of her life to allow her relatives in Mexico to join her, and in her old age she finds herself surrounded by kin who help her and whom she can count on. She feeds them still and is known especially for the beans and flour tortillas which she always cooks for those she welcomes home. She is clearly at the center of a convoy of cooperating kin whom she has organized and continues to remind of their obligations to one another.[10]

Sra. Compartida has worked for wages throughout her life and continues to do part-time housework when it is available. But, like other migrant women, she is a wife who appears much too submissive to her husband: she offers him extraordinary care, cooks everything he eats, and quietly abides his beer-drinking although she disapproves of it. On the other hand, her efforts on behalf of her family have compelled Sra. Compartida to learn English and cultivate respectable skills at negotiating bureaucracies such as immigration service. Her husband clearly depends on her as his ambassador, not only among kin but also with the outside Anglo world. They cooperate in setting their particular relationship apart through constructing roles in which he pretends to be boss, proclaiming extreme jealousy and expecting that she nurture him in elaborate ways. Yet one cannot dismiss their interaction by stereotype, for Sra. Compartida's authority and influence as mother, aunt, god-mother, sister, and grand-mother are so definite that she simply will not fit a category. Tamales help her maintain that influence, and she uses them to express affection and obligate others, as well as gather a network of tavern owners who watch out for her husband when she cannot be there.

Domestic cooperation extends to the Illinois migrant camps, long barracks of small single rooms originally designed to accommodate prisoners of war. The camps offer domestic convoys highly inappropriate living situations, for they allot these single rooms to conjugal families, and through separating kin dramatically defy their routine commitment to shared domestic tasks. Because observers often prefer that each family convene in a tidy still-life world, migrant family life in the camps has been portrayed by some as very chaotic.[11] Kin realign in this inappropriate space to share domestic duties, care for children, cook cooperatively, allow husbands and wives conjugal privacy, and meet recurring emergency needs. While a conjugal family might remain basically committed to a particular room, kin move in and out of one another's rooms throughout the day, often carrying pots of food or other supplies. Children gather with elderly caretakers in a central outdoor spot (for the small rooms are stifling), and it is sometimes difficult to identify their mothers and fathers. Other kin who have settled temporarily in town visit the camp frequently, bringing food and children back and forth with them.

Women cook together routinely, sharing and stretching short supplies, combining scarce ingredients to preserve what they can of traditional Tejano tastes. They transport clay pots, tortilla presses, and chilies from their homes to the camps each year, and replenish short supplies throughout the summer as kin travel back and forth to Texas. Thus, surrounded by Illinois cornfields, women simmer beans in the barracks, save tomatoes from the fields for sauces when they can, and do their best to stretch the family's wages to support a large group of relatives.

STRATEGIES FOR SURVIVAL: CRISIS

If the tamale symbolizes elaborate celebration and nurturance, the tortilla is probably the most symbolic of the last bit of food a woman has to share. Simply, quickly, expertly made by migrant women, tortillas are treated very much like bread. Women roll a dough from *masa harina* or plain white flour, lard, salt, and water, flatten it with a press or by hand, and fry it on a dry griddle for just a few minutes. It is the least expensive and most basic of their food items, and when women worry (as they often do) that their sup-

plies have dwindled to the ingredients for tortillas, they are speaking of real want. Tortillas stand for emergencies and it is through such crises that one can see perhaps most clearly how migrant family foodways work.

One family which has weathered many crises typical of migrant life is the Gomas. Their domestic convoy stretches through four generations and across several marriages, and their members are dispersed in Texas and Illinois but remain closely involved in one another's lives. The woman most central to this family is middle-aged and lives with her husband and their teenaged children off-and-on in Prairie Junction. Joana Goma and her husband have never been able to last for long in Illinois, for it is difficult for them to find work there, and they move back and forth to Texas often, sometimes leaving one of their children there for a time or returning with other young relatives so, as she puts it, "I won't have to be lonesome for them all winter." Each summer some two dozen of the Gomas' relatives arrive to work through the migrant season, and during that time Sra. Goma mobilizes on their behalf the resources of her Illinois networks—legal aid, public assistance, transportation, and a less formal example, a service station owner who will cash paychecks. She has worked hard to stretch and secure this network, often initially obligating friends through food. By sharing her locally famous taco dinners, Illinois residents act as though they are kin, and through time she finds that she can call on them for help as if they really were.

Although Joana Goma's marriage also appears quite traditional, with food and sex recurring metaphors for conjugal loyalty, she is the center of a world on which her husband and his kin depend.[12] When her sister-in-law was disabled because her hands were poisoned by pesticides, Sra. Goma saw to it that her own sister assumed the woman's cooking and housekeeping tasks. When her sister's nephew was stricken with hepatitis, Sra. Goma untangled the complicated legal procedures whereby a local hospital was compelled to provide free medical care for indigents, secured his bus fare to Texas from Traveler's Aid, and organized an investigation of the camp's drinking water. But these smaller, frequent emergencies are less telling than a more dramatic tortilla crisis in which the Gomas powerfully affirmed the importance of family to migrant workers.

One summer, Joana Goma's husband's brother, his wife, and their five children could not find work. They were penniless and planned to stay for several months, hoping there might be employment in a later crop. Joana brought her husband's employer to their home in the middle of the night to see for himself all those little children sleeping on the floor, thinking that she might persuade him to offer her brother-in-law a job. The employer stalled, and she worked at securing public aid for the family. This process is a lengthy one, and she soon found her household with no money or food left but tortillas, which they lived on for several days while Joana visited local ministers to ask for loans. On the day the welfare check at last arrived, her father and mother were critically injured in an automobile accident in Texas; and Joana and her children traveled there immediately, financed by this check.

Migrant family life may appear chaotic as kin realign inside and outside the camps, travel when they need to give support, and share what they have down to the last tortilla. Joana and her husband will never be rich, for they are unwilling to cast off the demands of kin. They love them, and they also seem to know that they are happier and more secure in the long run if they embed their marriage in a larger family circle. Again, Joana appears the most submissive of wives, but as a sister, daughter, and in-law she is the most highly regarded member of the family.

RITUAL AND AFFIRMATION

Beyond the routine domestic order and beyond using food in emergencies as a metaphor for the ways in which people's lives are intertwined, migrants give food special significance in ritual. Some observers have noted that migrants' rituals seem both wasteful and tawdry, at best a mere release of tension for the poor.[13] From a certain perspective migrant ritual seems absurd: women waste valuable working time preparing a feast to commemorate a harvest which is not really theirs and which in fact signals a slack time between crops; or women cook extravagantly to celebrate a young girl's birthday in what appears to be a tragic display of false consciousness about the course of her future life. Further, migrant rituals are tainted by the unavailability in Illinois of their preferred foods and crops: sometimes women must substitute barbecued chicken and potato chips for the tamales, chili, and beans which have for centuries marked such occasions and are deeply rooted in an oral tradition shared by women through recipes. Even so, such feasting seems to testify to migrants' involvement with kin in ways that reach far beyond the ritual moment.

Susana Sangre is the youngest of five sisters dispersed throughout Texas and Illinois. She stays fairly permanently with her mother, father, and small nephews, whom she cares for when she is not working in the fields. As her fifteenth birthday approached, her sisters gathered in the camp bringing tamales from Texas. With the help of their mother and other women, the Sangre sisters spent almost a week digging great barbecue pits, soaking

pinto beans to cook, and purchasing items such as cakes and potato chips in local stores. On the evening of Susana's birthday, almost everyone in the camp gathered to kiss and congratulate her, present her with inexpensive storebought gifts (most often handkerchiefs or jewelry), and feast and dance all night. She wore a long pink bridesmaid's dress, while the guests remained in their work clothes. Although her outfit seemed incongruous, it clearly reflected her honored status at the event, as did the great whoops and cheers which surrounded her as she opened each gift, initiated the dancing with her father, and graciously endured the evening's jolly courting. The effort and expense incurred by Susana's family were enormous, and one might argue that they should not delude her through such feasts about the significance or possibilities of her life.

The *quinceañera* feast does signal the importance of her life to *them*, and the lavish ritual expressions which surround occasions such as this work to bind kin, recreate obligations, and promise reciprocity. Most persons know that they too will be commemorated at the appropriate times, and that their lives are significant to others as well. Further, through ritual, migrants dramatically defy the degrading "total institutions" in which they spend half their lives: the monotonous surroundings and crowded, unsanitary conditions which tacitly proclaim their worthlessness.[14] Celebrating the harvest proclaims their part in it and denies that they are its slaves. And to prepare their own foods when possible is to reaffirm the dignity of Tejano identity in an Anglo world which offers it little respect, as well as to root the celebrants in a long and great tradition mediated—made present—by the family.

STRANGERS AND FRIENDS

Tamales are distinct and unique by place: Texans prepare them differently from Californians; Salvadorian migrants to this country often disdain those made in Mexico. Tamales testify to rich oral tradition, for the most part women's tradition, about how to buy and cook them. Although many Anglos in the Southwest enjoy Mexican food and have in part transformed the tamale into a regional artifact, for Tejano migrants the real thing is deeply theirs, rooted in their homes, and kept alive by the women who prepare, distribute, and teach others about it.[15]

In Prairie Junction this distribution is critical not only in knitting together families, but in negotiating relations with outsiders as well. Such negotiations may be crucial to family life—as, for example, when migrants befriend Anglos who have the skills, power, or resources to help their kin in various ways. In these negotiations it is evident how misleading it is to proclaim family life an isolating, stultifying, belittling activity for women, as women use food to make friends and allies as well as to identify outsiders who will or will not commit themselves to the Tejano family's concerns. Women ply prospective friends with tamales and tacos, taking an acceptance of the hospitality they offer both as a show of respect for Tejano culture and as a tentative commitment to kin-like relations.

Ethnic boundaries, of course, remain important.[16] Migrant workers do not expect that prospective Anglo friends will relish these foods as Tejanos do. Migrants joke that "gringos' stomachs are too weak" and claim that they must smuggle chilies into Illinois restaurants so that they can season Anglo food properly. Many appreciated the respectful, self-deprecating remarks of a young poverty program lawyer who found that he could not eat the tacos women offered him without a healthy dose of ketchup. While potential friends should be open to traditional Tejano food, it is best appreciated by Tejanos themselves. Significantly, those Tejanos who ingratiate themselves to Anglos are labelled "Tio Tacos," the Spanish equivalent of Uncle Toms: thus, food becomes a metaphor for those who seem untrue to their ethnic identity.[17] Migrants use foodways to preserve a sense of who they are in an alien cultural setting just as they mobilize foodways to approach and appraise friends, and, again, it seems that women purposefully monopolize those skills necessary for plying and obligating others and for keeping ethnicity alive.

The most active cook in Prairie Junction is also married to the president of a self-help organization whose goal is to help those migrants who wish to "settle out," or leave the migrant stream and try to build a life in Illinois. Although Sra. Mezclado's husband wields the official community action power among Prairie Junction's Tejanos, she is the one who mobilizes several dozen women to cook the large benefit dinners on which the organization depends for funds. Sr. Mezclado's networking philosophy is consistent with the mutual assistance tenets of Tejano family life: he and his organization hold that no conjugal family can "settle out" without aid in procuring furniture, housing, and employment. Yet even in this context of outreach beyond the family, Sra. Mezclado continues to monopolize the foodways, and, with other women, to use food to identify and enlist the support of friends. Although she seems obsequious in the home, her husband acknowledges her authority and often speaks of women generally as living representations of the Lady of Guadalupe.[18] Sr. Mezclado is especially obedient to his own mother who, when she visits, rouses him early every day for church and insists that he keep a large statue of the Lady enshrined on his television set. Other men mock these traditional religious activities because they see Sr. Mezclado as an otherwise thoroughly modern man, but he argues that his mother is *"la jefa* [the boss]. I just can't say no to her." Again the marital paradox: while acknowledging the influence of women like Sr. Mezclado's mother, both spouses insist upon constructing a marital relationship which severely circumscribes sexual nuances, grants the husband seemingly whimsical authority, and offers the wife an unchallenged monopoly over domestic life.

GATHERING KIN: MEN, WOMEN AND MARRIAGE

Families and family foodways must be worked at, and among migrants it is women who most vigorously do so. Women are much more likely than men to be involved as liaisons among kin, in stretching networks to draw in kin-like persons who can be helpful, providing the props which allow persons to preserve their dignity in demeaning situations, and negotiating ethnic boundaries.

While young, women begin to build domestic convoys whose members will accompany and sustain them through life. Marriage is a crucial step in that process wherein women find both husbands and many more kin who will share their lives. Even very young and seemingly modern women uphold traditional roles when they marry. One such woman, Dolores Abierta, works in the migrant children's educational program as a teacher's aide. She feels flattered that her husband circles the school in his pick-up truck to watch over her when he can and that he forbids her to swim or wear shorts in public. He also "presses on my stomach when my period is late," "holds me in his lap and lets me cry like a baby," and "loves my cooking." Dolores takes great pride in the fact that "when we got married he was skinny and I was fat. Now it is the other way around." She also respects the limits he places on conjugal life and appreciates his concern that sexuality be confined by marriage: "Before we got married my brother-in-law's cousin used to come into my room and bother me. Now he leaves me alone."

Dolores makes it very clear that she will not allow any of her four brothers to marry women who will not obey them, cook their meals for them, and be ever ready for their sexual overtures. She polices her brothers accordingly, and she is especially wary of Anglo women, "who don't know how to be a good wife." At the same time, she gathers her kin around her, bringing her crippled mother from Texas to live in the migrant camp, giving her husband's cousin the car so "he'll have wheels," arranging for her husband's mother to change rooms so that they can be closer together and so that Dolores can learn from her how to cook tamales.

Within their convoys of kin, women's special nurturance of their husbands makes a good deal of sense. Not only do they bind men more and more closely, but also both women and men cooperate in setting marriage apart as something special within a wide circle of people sharing resources as well as the most intimate of concerns. Sexuality is no longer a larger issue. And while women cook often for many people, in marriage the obligation is immediate and forthright and binding: their husbands must have tamales.

NOTES

1. There is a great deal of ambivalence among scholars and the people themselves about the appropriate ethnic label for migrant workers from Texas and of Mexican descent. Many migrants refer to themselves as "Tejanos" (or Texans), others prefer the term "Mexicans," others "Mexican Americans," still others "Chicanos." "Tejano" is used here, because it seems to capture the migrants' sense of themselves, as bicultural with the caution that some migrants might prefer to be identified in other ways.

2. These incidents are reported from the author's personal participant-observation in Texas and Illinois.

3. Cf. Leo Grebler, Joan Moore, and Ralph Guzman, *The Mexican-American People* (New York: Free Press, 1970); William Madsen, *The Mexican-Americans of South Texas* (New York: Holt, Rinehart and Winston, 1973); Harlan Padfield and William Martin, *Farmers, Workers, and Machines* (Tucson: Univ. of Arizona Press, 1965).

4. Recently a number of scholars have begun to revise earlier views which held that the poor were virtually without culture, that the family life of the poor in particular was dysfunctional; cf. Carol Stack, *All Our Kin* (New York: Harper and Row, 1974), and Stanley West and June Macklin, eds., *The Chicano Experience* (Boulder, Col.: Westview Press, 1980). However, few scholars have used foodways to focus on the culture of the poor.

5. Cf. Judith K. Brown, "A Note on the Division of Labor by Sex," *American Anthropologist* 72 (1970): 1073–78; Louise Lamphere and Michelle Rosaldo, eds., *Woman, Culture, and Society* (Stanford, Calif.: Stanford Univ. Press, 1974); Peggy Sanday, "Toward a Theory of the Status of Women," *American Anthropologist* 75 (1973): 1682–1700.

6. See note 5 above.

7. Cf. W. Eberstein and W. P. Frisbee, "Differences in Marital Instability Among Mexican-Americans, Blacks, and Anglos: 1960 and 1970," *Social Problems* 23 (1976): 609–21; *Census of the US Population* 19 (Washington, D.C.: U.S. Department of Commerce, Bureau of the Census, 1970).

8. The name of the town and personal names are pseudonyms.

9. For more on this subject, see Ernesto Galarza, Herman Gallegos, and Julian Samora, *Mexican-Americans in the Southwest* (Santa Barbara, Calif.: McNally and Loftin, 1969); Lamar Jones, *Mexican-American Labor Problems in Texas* (San Francisco: R&E Research Associates, 1971); John Martinez, *Mexican Emigration to the U.S.: 1919–1930* (San Francisco: R&E Research Associates, 1971); Carey McWilliams, *North from Mexico* (New York: Greenwood Press, 1968); David North, *The Border Crossers* (Washington, D.C.: Department of Labor, 1970); Brett Williams, *The Trip Takes Us: Chicago Migrants on the Prairie* (PhD diss. Univ. of Illinois at Urbana, 1975); Brett Williams, "Chicano Farm Labor in Eastern Illinois," *Journal of the Steward Anthropological Society* 7 (1976); Dean Williams, *Political and Economic Aspects of Mexican Immigration into California and the U.S. Since 1941* (San Francisco: R&E Research Associates, 1973).

10. Sra. Compartida has fostered almost a dozen children, most of whom were separated from their parents as infants. Recently, she has taken both her six-year-old grandniece and her very old and dying mother to live with her. One example of her kin-gathering activities occurred when she saw a young man in an orchard with, as she put it, "my husband's face," convinced him that he was her husband's nephew who had been separated from the family as a small child, took him home and reincorporated him in the family with great celebration and a tamale dinner.

11. See especially William Friedland and Dorothy Nelkin, *Migrant* (New York: Holt, Rinehart and Winston, 1971), treating Black migrants on the east coast.

12. He frequently threatens to "run off with a little 'mojadita!' (the diminutive female term for 'wetback')," she, to "throw him out and let him cook for himself, just like he did my cat." She also likes to boast about the time her doctor "played my legs, right in front of Pedro."

13. Friedland and Nelkin.

14. "Total institution" is a term used by Erving Goffman in *Asylums* (Garden City, N.J.: Doubleday, 1961). It refers to those institutions which are qualitatively more encompassing than most, segregating and degrading their inmates in dramatic ways, often by denying them ordinary access to the props and routines by which they build their lives.

15. For example, Gerald Ford was ridiculed by the San Antonio, Texas, press when, during his presidential campaign there, he attempted to eat a tamale without first removing the corn husk.

16. Cf. Frederik Barth, *Ethnic Groups and Boundaries* (Boston: Little, Brown, 1969), who argues that ethnic identity is realized most dramatically in the negotiation of boundaries among groups.

17. One such "Tio Taco" is criticized by others for avoiding his Tejano friends and trying very hard to align himself with his fellow (Anglo) factory workers. That he does this by taking big plates of tacos to the factory every day is especially offensive, for this is women's work. And that the Anglo workers do not reciprocate by attending the migrant organization's benefit dinners seems to indicate that "they don't care enough about our food to pay for it."

18. The Lady of Guadalupe is Tejanos' most beloved folk saint. She emerged in Mexico at the time of the Spanish Conquest, appears faintly Indian, and has been carried all over the world by Mexican migrants who turn to her frequently for help with many varied matters. As a saint, she is much like an earthly woman: She has no direct power of her own, but she has a great deal of influence as a liaison with Christ and because of this is both loving and approachable.

REFERENCES

Barth, Frederik. 1969. *Ethnic Groups and Boundaries.* Boston: Little, Brown.

Brown, Judith K. "A Note on the Division of Labor by Sex," *American Anthropologist* Vol. 72 (1970): 1073–78.

Census of the US Population 19. 1970. Washington, DC: U.S. Department of Commerce, Bureau of the Census.

Eberstein, W., & W. P. Frisbee. 1976. "Differences in Marital Instability Among Mexican-Americans, Blacks, and Anglos: 1960 and 1970," *Social Problems* Vol. 23: 609–21.

Friedland, William, & Dorothy Nelkin. 1971. *Migrant.* New York: Holt, Rinehart and Winston.

Galarza, Ernesto, Herman Gallegos, & Julian Samora. 1969. *Mexican-Americans in the Southwest.* Santa Barbara, CA: McNally and Loftin.

Goffman, Erving. 1961. *Asylums.* Garden City, NJ: Doubleday.

Grebler, Leo, Joan Moore, & Ralph Guzman. 1970. *The Mexican-American People.* New York: Free Press.

Jones, Lamar. 1971. *Mexican-American Labor Problems in Texas.* San Francisco: R&E Research Associates.

Lamphere, Louise, & Michelle Rosaldo (Eds.). 1974. *Woman, Culture, and Society.* Stanford, CA: Stanford Univ. Press.

Madsen, William. 1973. *The Mexican-Americans of South Texas.* New York: Holt, Rinehart and Winston.

Martinez, John. 1971. *Mexican Emigration to the U.S.: 1919–1930.* San Francisco: R&E Research Associates.

McWilliams, Carey. 1968. *North from Mexico.* New York: Greenwood Press.

North, David. 1970. *The Border Crossers.* Washington, DC: Department of Labor.

Padfield, Harlan, & William Martin. 1965. *Farmers, Workers, and Machines.* Tucson: Univ. of Arizona Press.

Sanday, Peggy. 1973. "Toward a Theory of the Status of Women," *American Anthropologist* Vol. 75: 1682–1700.

Stack, Carol. 1974. *All Our Kin.* New York: Harper and Row.

West, Stanley, & June Macklin (Eds.). 1980. *The Chicano Experience.* Boulder, CO: Westview Press.

Williams, Brett. 1975. "The Trip Takes Us: Chicago Migrants on the Prairie." PhD diss. Univ. of Illinois at Urbana.

Williams, Brett. 1976. "Chicano Farm Labor in Eastern Illinois," *Journal of the Steward Anthropological Society* Vol. 7.

Williams, Dean. 1973. *Political and Economic Aspects of Mexican Immigration into California and the U.S. since 1941.* San Francisco: R&E Research Associates.

27

Land of the Walking Marriage

Lu Yuan and Sam Mitchell

Lu Yuan and Sam Mitchell co-direct the China-Yunnan Study Abroad program for the School of International Training and are honorary professors at Yunnan Normal University. Lu is a journalist and Mitchell recently received a PhD in Asian history from the University of Hawaii.

There are so many skillful people,
  but none can compare with my mother.
There are so many knowledgeable people,
  but none can equal my mother.
There are so many people skilled at song and dance,
  but none can compete with my mother.

We first heard this folk song around a blazing fire in southwestern China in the spring of 1995. It was sung enthusiastically by women of Luoshui village—members of the Nari, an ethnic group more commonly known to outsiders as the Mosuo. During the past few years, we have returned several times to visit these people, who celebrate women in more than song. Although the majority of China's ethnic groups follow a strong patrilineal tradition, the Mosuo emphasize matrilineal ties, with matrilineally related kin assisting one another to farm, fish, and raise children. Women also head most households and control most family property.

Marriage as other cultures know it is uncommon among the Mosuo; they prefer a visiting relationship between lovers—an arrangement they sometimes refer to in their language as *sisi* (walking back and forth). At about the age of twelve, a Mosuo girl is given a coming-of-age ceremony, and after puberty, she is free to receive male visitors. A lover may remain overnight in her room but will return in the morning to his own mother's home and his primary responsibilities. Children born from such a relationship live with their mother, and the male relatives responsible for helping to look after them are her brothers. Many children know who their fathers are, of course, but even if the relationship between father and child is quite close, it involves no social or economic

obligation. And lovers can end their relationship at any time; a woman may signal her change of heart by simply no longer opening the door. When speaking Chinese, the Mosuo will call the *sisi* arrangement *zou hun* (walking marriage) or *azhu hunyin* (friend marriage, *azhu* being the Mosuo word for friend); nevertheless, the relationship is not a formal union.

Chuan-kang Shih, an anthropologist at the University of Illinois at Urbana-Champaign and an authority on the Mosuo, points out that many aspects of their family system have parallels elsewhere in the world. For example, although in most societies a husband and wife live together (usually near his relatives or hers), in others they continue to live in separate households, and one spouse must make overnight nuptial visits. Matrilineal kinship systems, in which a man looks after the interests of his sisters' children, are also well known. And although men commonly wield the power, even in matrilineal societies, women may play important political and economic roles. But the absence of a formal marital union may quite possibly be unique to the Mosuo. In this respect, only the pre-colonial practices of the matrilineal Nayar of southern India come close. As Shih explains, among some Nayar groups, a woman would take lovers (with due regard for social class), who would establish and maintain their relationships to her through a pattern of gift giving. Despite being expected to acknowledge paternity, the lovers incurred no obligations to their offspring. Still, the Nayar had a vestigial form of marriage: shortly before puberty, a girl would be wed to a young man; although this marriage lasted only three days and was often purely ceremonial in nature, the union marked the girl's transition to adult life and legitimized the birth of her children.

In Luoshui we stayed with thirty-year-old A Long, who runs a small guesthouse. His family consisted of his mother, grandmother, younger brother and sister, and sister's two-year-old son. Each evening A Long departed

---

"Land of the Walking Marriage" by Lu Yuan and Sam Mitchell reprinted by permission from *Natural History*, November 2000, pp. 58–64; copyright © Natural History Magazine, Inc., 2000.

with his small overnight bag; each morning he returned to help his mother and sister. After several days of eating with the family and becoming friendly with them, we asked A Long what he thought about the *sisi* system. "'Friend marriage' is very good," he replied. "First, we are all our mother's children, making money for her; therefore there is no conflict between the brothers and sisters. Second, the relationship is based on love, and no money or dowry is involved in it. If a couple feels contented, they stay together. If they feel unhappy, they can go their separate ways. As a result, there is little fighting." A Long told us that he used to have several lovers but started to have a stable relationship with one when she had her first child.

"Are you taking care of your children?" we asked.

"I sometimes buy candy for them. My responsibility is to help raise my sister's children. In the future, they will take care of me when I get old."

A Long's twenty-six-year-old sister, Qima, told us that the Mosuo system "is good because my friend and I help our own families during the daytime and only come together at night, and therefore there are few quarrels between us. When we are about fifty years old, we will not have 'friend marriage' anymore."

Ge Ze A Che is the leader of Luoshui, which has a population of more than 200 people, the majority of them Mosuo, with a few Han (China's majority ethnic group) and Pumi as well. He spoke proudly of this small settlement: "I have been the leader of the village for five years. There has been little theft, rape, or even argument here. 'Friend marriage' is better than the husband-wife system, because in large extended families everyone helps each other, so we are not afraid of anything. It is too hard to do so much work in the field and at home just as a couple, the way the Han do."

The Mosuo live in villages around Lugu Lake, which straddles the border between Yunnan and Sichuan provinces, and in the nearby town of Yongning. They are believed to be descendants of the ancient Qiang, an early people of the Tibetan plateau from whom many neighboring minority groups, including the Tibetans themselves, claim descent. As a result of Han expansion during the Qin dynasty (221–206 B.C.), some Qiang from an area near the Huang (Yellow) River migrated south and west into Yunnan. The two earliest mentions of the Mosuo appear during the Han dynasty (A.D. 206–222), and the Tang dynasty (618–907), in records concerning what is now southwestern China.

The Mosuo do not surface again in historical accounts until after Mongol soldiers under Kublai Khan subjugated the area in 1253. During the Yuan dynasty (1279–1368), a period of minority rule by the Mongols, the province of Yunnan was incorporated into the Chinese empire, and many Mongol soldiers settled in the Mosuo region. In fact, during the 1950s, when the government set out to classify the country's minority nationalities, several Mosuo villages surrounding Lugu Lake identified themselves as Mongol, and some continue to do so today. When we walked around the lake, as the Mosuo do each year in the seventh lunar month—a ritual believed to ensure good fortune during the coming year—we passed through villages that identified themselves variously as Mosuo, Mongol, Naxi, Pumi, and Han. The "Mongol" people we encountered dressed the same as the Mosuo and spoke the same language. Their dances and songs, too, were the same, and they sometimes even referred to themselves as Mosuo.

Tibetan Buddhism first entered the region in the late thirteenth century and has greatly influenced the lives and customs of the Mosuo. Before the area came under the control of the Communist government, at least one male from almost every family joined the monastic community. The local practice of Buddhism even incorporated aspects of the *sisi* system, although the women did the "commuting." On the eighth day of the fifth lunar month, monks traveling to Tibet for religious study would camp in front of Kaiji village. That night, each monk would be joined by his accustomed lover—a ceremonial practice believed to enable the monks to reach Lhasa safely and to succeed in completing their studies. And the local Mosuo monks, each of whom lived with his own mother's family, could also receive lovers. Such arrangements seem to defy the injunctions of many schools of Tibetan Buddhism, but by allowing the monks to live and work at home, outside the strict confines of monastic life, they helped the Mosuo maintain a stable population and ensure an adequate labor force to sustain local agriculture.

The area around Lugu Lake did not come under the full control of China's central government until 1956, seven years after the founding of the People's Republic. In 1958 and 1959, during the Great Leap Forward, the nearby monasteries, notably the one at Yongning, were badly damaged. Now, however, with a combination of government funds and donations from local people, they are slowly being rebuilt. One element of recent religious revival is the Bon tradition, which is accepted by the Dalai Lama as a school of Tibetan Buddhism but believed by many scholars to be derived from an earlier, animist tradition. During our walk around Lugu Lake, we witnessed a Bon cremation ceremony and visited the Bon temple on the eastern shore of the lake. The Mosuo also retain a shamanic and animist tradition of their own, known as Daba.

In the twentieth century, the West became acquainted with the Mosuo through the work of French ethnographers Edouard Chavannes and Jacques Bacot and through the contributions of Joseph Rock, a Vienna-born American who first journeyed to Yunnan in 1922 while on a botanical expedition. A flamboyant character, Rock traveled through remote Tibetan borderlands accompanied by trains of servants and bodyguards and equipped with such dubious necessities as a collapsible bathtub and a silver English tea set. He made the Naxi town of Lijiang his home for more than twenty years, until the victory of the Chinese Communist Party in 1949 spelled an end to foreign-funded research and missionary activity in the area.

Besides conducting botanical surveys and collecting plant and animal specimens, Rock took many photographs and became the West's foremost expert on the region's peoples and their shamanic practices. He identified the Mosuo as a subgroup of the Naxi, who, although their kinship system is patrilineal, speak a language closely related to that of the Mosuo. The Mosuo strongly contest this classification, but it has been retained by the present government, which has been reluctant to assign the Mosuo the status of a distinct minority. The Communists claim that the Mosuo do not fit the criteria for nationality status as defined for the Soviet Union by Joseph Stalin. According to Stalin, as he phrased it in a 1929 letter, "A nation is a historically constituted, stable community of people, formed on the basis of the common possession of four principal characteristics, namely: a common language, a common territory, a common economic life, and a common psychological make-up manifested in common specific features of national culture."

In keeping with Marxist interpretations of historical development, Chinese ethnologists have also regarded Mosuo society as a "living fossil," characterized by ancient marriage and family structures. This view draws on theories of social evolution formerly embraced by Western anthropologists, notably the American ethnologist Lewis Henry Morgan (1818–81). Morgan proposed that societies pass through successive natural stages of "savagery" and "barbarism" before attaining "civilization." He also proposed a sequence of marriage forms, from a hypothetical "group marriage" of brothers and sisters to monogamy. Chinese scholars have argued that a minority such as the Mosuo, with its unusual kinship system, fits into this scheme and thus validates Marxist views. Of course, the application of Morgan's theories to minority

cultures in China has also enabled the Han majority to see itself as more advanced in the chain of human societal evolution. This kind of thinking, long discredited in the West, is only now beginning to be reexamined in China.

With the coming of the Cultural Revolution (1966–76), the Mosuo were pressured to change their way of life. According to Lama Luo Sang Yi Shi (a Mosuo who holds a county-government title but is primarily a spiritual leader), "during the Cultural Revolution, the governnor of Yunnan came to Yongning. He went into Mosuo homes and cursed us, saying that we were like animals, born in a mess without fathers. At that time, all of the Mosuo were forced to marry and to adopt the Han practice of monogamy; otherwise, they would be punished by being deprived of food." During this period Mosuo couples lived with the woman's family, and divorce was not permitted. But even though they held marriage certificates and lived with their wives, the men kept returning to their maternal homes each morning to work.

Luo Sang Yi criticized this attempt to change the Mosuo and explained that "at the end of the Cultural Revolution, the Mosuo soon returned to their former system of 'friend marriage.' A small family is not good for work. Also, mothers and their daughters-in-law cannot get along well."

Today the Mosuo maintain their matrilineal system and pursue *sisi* relationships. Yet how long will this remain the case? The government of Yunnan recently opened Lugu Lake to tourism, and vans full of visitors, both Chinese and foreign, are beginning to arrive. To some degree, this added exposure threatens to envelop the Mosuo in a society that is becoming increasingly homogeneous. Yet the tourists are drawn not only by the beauty of the lake but by the exotic qualities of the Mosuo people. Ironically, their unique qualities may well enable the Mosuo to endure and prosper.

We asked Ge Ze A Che, the Luoshui village leader, if tourism would change the lives of the Mosuo. "It has already changed their lives to some extent," he observed. "Our young people now like to wear Han clothes, speak Chinese, and sing Chinese songs. In the future they will lose our people's traditions and customs."

And what would happen to "friend marriage"? we wondered.

"It will also change—but very, very slowly!"

28

The Persistence of Polygamy

Timothy Egan

Timothy Egan is a journalist for the New York Times.

Driving south on Utah's Highway 59, you slip out of the subdivisions sprouting in the desert, ascend to a lonely stretch of ink-colored juniper trees, then suddenly find yourself at the edge of the last century. There on the Arizona border, tucked behind towering flanks of red rock, is a town of about 5,000 people. Most are Mormon fundamentalists, and most are outlaws; it is the largest polygamous community in the United States.

Though polygamy is a felony, nobody has to hide from the law in this town, called Hildale on the Utah side of the state line, Colorado City on the other. More than a century after it was outlawed, polygamy is flourishing in Utah and small pockets of the American West, nurtured by religious directives and the hands-off stance of legal authorities.

Laura Chapman, 36, is the 25th child from a family with four mothers and 31 children, and she knows most of the people in Hildale and Colorado City, even the few she is not related to by blood. Chapman left the town years ago—she calls it "the land that time forgot." Today she is one of a new group of women who have fled plural families and want to draw attention to the reality of modern polygamy.

Forget the sepia-toned notion of kindly Mormon patriarchs frolicking with a bushel of happy wives, these women say. Forget about the polygamy of Abraham or the Mormon pioneer Brigham Young. Late-20th-century polygamy, practiced by people who seem unconcerned about the law or public opinion, is a Dark Ages hybrid, say women who have left the big families. They raise allegations of sexual abuse, pedophilia and incest. "This is organized crime, operating under the cover of religion," Chapman maintains.

If the charges of women like Chapman have been shrugged off before, that may be about to change. Last year a teen-age girl emerged with a story of incest, child abuse and forced marriage at the hands of one of Utah's biggest polygamous clans, the Kingstons—who are based right in Salt Lake City, within a few miles of the domed capital building. Whatever the outcome, Chapman and other ex-wives of polygamy hope the resulting trials, scheduled to begin in April, will force a reckoning with Utah's oldest ghost.

There are two worlds in the Beehive State. One is the Utah of first impressions, from the powder snow in the mountains to the brisk, overtly friendly business climate. The other Utah is harder to know. Mark Twain called it "a land of enchantment and awful mystery." Even now one side of the state's personality remains hidden.

After the Mormon Church denounced polygamy and Utah outlawed it in 1896—Washington had made this a condition of statehood—it was thought that the practice of taking multiple wives would ultimately disappear. But a century later the opposite has happened, with anywhere from 20,000 to 60,000 people living in families where one man is married to 2, 3, 5, as many as 30 women. No one has been prosecuted for polygamy in Utah for nearly 50 years, and the state's power structure has not made enforcement an issue. Last year Gov. Michael O. Leavitt, a Republican who is himself a descendant of polygamists, even said the practice is not often prosecuted in part because "these people have religious freedoms" (a statement he later amended in the wake of a public outcry).

The practice is still a minority one in this state of two million people, of course, and the mainstream Mormon leadership in Salt Late City strongly condemns it. But it survives in "clans"—massive patriarchal cabals linked by bloodlines and business ties, whose members generally tithe 10 percent of all wages and earnings to their church. Those leaders insist that their only crime is following the true word of God—they see the church's capitulation on polygamy as a blasphemous mistake. Sexual abuse is rare, they insist, and when it occurs it is not tolerated.

There are at least four major clans in Utah. One of these polygamous empires, based about 40 minutes south of Salt Lake, in Bluffdale, is run by Owen Allred, age 84. The state has long estimated its membership at about 5,000 people. But Janet Bennion, a Utah Valley State College anthropologist who spent five years studying the Allreds for a recent book, "Women of Principle" (Oxford University Press), says the number is closer to 10,000, with clusters all over the West.

At the Allred compound, the headquarters is a huge, windowless two-story building facing the Wasatch mountain range. Arrayed around it are massive houses, with two or three minivans in many of the driveways.

Lillian Bowles spent most of her life on this patch of arid land. She grew up in a trailer not far from Bluffdale's church, one of 40 children in a family in which her mother was one of eight wives. She is not even sure where she fits in the family chronology. "I think I'm No. 17," she says. She remembers a life of claustrophobia and fear of the outside world. "I knew early on that what we were doing was against the law," says Bowles, who is 26. "We were always taught to hide. We couldn't play in the front yard. When we drove somewhere, it was always 'Duck!' when you passed a police car."

At 16, she wanted to leave. But like other women who have fled polygamy, she says she had no idea how to. "We were taught early on that we were God's chosen people, and everyone else was condemned to hell. If you left, you were condemned." At age 17, she married a man who told her it was better to get married young, rather than wait to be a third or fourth bride. After six years of marriage, she says, Bowles left her husband when he decided to take on another wife.

Rowenna Erickson, 59, told me a similar tale when she described her life within another major clan, the Kingstons. She married her brother-in-law, Charles L. Kingston, and produced eight children. "The other wives kept telling me how this was all so wonderful because we were going to heaven," she says between baby-sitting chores for grandchildren in Salt Lake City. "But if it was so wonderful, how come I felt so horrible?"

I asked her if she was ever in love with her husband. "It was business," she says. "Produce the babies. Don't question your husband. But still, you get jealous. I remember when my husband had his eyes on a very young girl. My sister and I were so hurt." She went on to explain a marital routine I heard from members of polygamous families all over Utah, a sexual-rotation schedule with all the romance of being a hen at a poultry ranch. "When you're ovulating, the patriarch is called," she says.

Polygamous leaders tend to shrug off stories like those told by Bowles, Erickson and Chapman, dismissing them as bitterness with a political agenda. But they may have a more difficult time explaining away an episode that rocked Utah last spring, when a sobbing, badly bruised 16-year-old girl placed a 911 call from a truck stop in northern Utah. She told the police a story of indentured barbarism, alleging her father had forced her into becoming the 15th wife of her uncle. When she tried to flee, she maintained, she was whisked to a family ostrich ranch, taken into a barn and whipped by her father.

The leaders of the Kingston clan run one of the biggest and wealthiest family business empires in Utah. With 1,500 members and interests in everything from restaurants to casinos, the clan is worth $150 million or more, state officials estimate. The clan operates much of its business out of an old brick office on State Street just outside downtown Salt Lake City. The building has no identification on the outside, save an address.

In a December pretrial hearing, the girl gave a hint of what her life was like inside the clan. Her marriage was arranged by her father and uncle; the latter had sex with her the first time at her mother's home. "I guess it was my night, so he came over," the girl testified. Then she was moved into a small apartment, with another wife, one door away from a third wife. All the while, the girl said, she was terrified. "I felt trapped."

The girl's uncle David O. Kingston has been charged with three counts of incest and one count of unlawful sexual conduct. Her father, John D. Kingston, has been charged with child abuse. The two brothers will be tried separately in April, and both have pleaded not guilty. (The father's lawyer—and cousin—Carl E. Kingston refused to talk to me.)

But even in the face of the girl's court testimony that she had been forced to marry her uncle and join 14 other wives, the state has chosen not to bring polygamy charges.

To women like Laura Chapman, that decision by prosecutors not to enforce the anti-polygamy statute is just one more example of Utah's refusal to go after the practice that is at the core of the clans' existence. State officials insist the law is unenforceable because most polygamists have a marriage certificate only for the first bride; the others are sealed in church ceremonies, without a paper trail necessary for proof of crime. The last major attempt at prosecuting anyone on polygamy charges was in 1953, in Hildale/Colorado City—then called Short Creek. A big raid on the compound was written about and photographed by *Life* magazine, and what resulted was a furor over families being torn apart by the state.

Last year, six women from plural marriages—including Bowles, Erickson and Chapman—founded one of the most unusual private outreach groups in the country, an advocacy organization called Tapestry of Polygamy. When such women hear Senator Orrin Hatch of Utah intone about the sanctity of law and President Clinton's sexual misdeeds, they want to shout from the top of the Mormon Temple: "What about polygamy?"

Prompted in part by Tapestry, the state Attorney General's office recently sent emissaries to the Allred compound to discuss things like statutory rape, child abuse, the minimum wage and other basic legal facts of modern American life. They gave out phone numbers. According to the Attorney General's office, dozens of calls have come in—women and children asking basic questions about the outside world.

When Chief Deputy Attorney General Reed Richards said last year that polygamy was not only nearly impossible to prosecute but, technically, not a crime at all, it took the largely poor and unschooled ex-wives of polygamous men to point out the law to him. Polygamy is in fact covered by the statute that makes bigamy a felony, the women noted, and the law says nothing about a marriage certificate being needed for proof of crime, only that a husband or wife "purports to marry another person."

I read that statute to Richards and mentioned that prominent polygamists in Utah had their own Web sites and seemed to be bragging about breaking the law. One man, Graydon Henderson, whom I spoke to, lives openly with his five wives and 21 children in a suburb just south of Salt Lake. "I'm not a bit afraid of the law," he told me. "It's not even worth worrying about."

Richards finally said that he has no idea why polygamy was not prosecuted in his state. But he added, "If we cracked down on it, I think it would all go underground."

Carmen Thompson, another Tapestry co-founder, figures that what most of the people with power in Utah really want is for the ex-wives to go underground. Thompson, who is 41 and spent more than a decade as one of eight wives, points to the polygamous roots of many members of the state's power structure. "They all have this romantic view of how their grandfathers practiced it," she says. "But this is not grandpa's polygamy. As near as I can tell, Brigham Young was not a pedophile."

Mormons, from the very founding of their church by Joseph Smith Jr. in 1830, have been persecuted. Their fear of outsiders—or gentiles, as non-Mormons are called in Utah, where 70 percent of the population identify themselves as Mormon—is integral to their religious identity.

Smith told of how an angel appeared to him in upstate New York, directing him to gold plates bearing the story of ancient inhabitants of what is now Israel who had settled in the Western Hemisphere. That story forms the basis of the Book of Mormon, which with the Bible and Doctrine and Covenants are the sacred texts of the church.

It is in the latter book, Section 132, where God tells the prophet Joseph Smith that he can marry as many women as he wants. "And if he has 10 virgins given unto him by this law, he cannot commit adultery, for they belong to him and they are given unto him; therefore he is justified," Smith, with God speaking through him, explains.

Smith's successor, Brigham Young, took his followers West, establishing the territory of Deseret in what is now called Utah. The Mormons prospered in the Great Basin, but their plural marriages were an affront to the rest of the country. In 1857 the United States nearly went to war with the religious state that had formed on the Wasatch Mountain front. President Buchanan sent troops to the Great Salt Lake. Eventually, under threat of having their assets seized, the Church of Jesus Christ of Latter-day Saints (as the Mormon Church is formally known) denounced polygamy in 1890, saying it was no longer necessary. Ever since, Mormons who practice polygamy do so under threat of excommunication.

But for a swath of people who consider themselves true believers, this change of heart was mere political expediency. In Hildale/Colorado City today and in the Allred and Kingston compounds, residents consider themselves the followers of the true Mormon Church. In their view, the heretics are the ones operating out of Temple Square in downtown Salt Lake.

This history does not lend itself to easy sanitizing. On a tour of Temple Square, the global headquarters of the Mormon religion, one of the fastest-growing in the world, I asked the guide about Brigham Young's wives. We were in a former home of Young's, the Beehive House, about a block from the Temple, and the guide was explaining how the patriarch's wife made bread.

"Which wife?" I asked. Young had 27.

"These other wives were mostly widows," the tour guide replied.

That sort of historical revisionism ends up infuriating both the women who have fled polygamy and the people who defend it. Chapman wants Utah's Mormons to acknowledge that some of their most revered founding fathers had child brides. Fundamentalists want the basic facts of the polygamists' past to remain a central part of the Mormon narrative.

What seems to interest outsiders the most about polygamy is the sex. The famed 19th-century eroticist Sir Richard Burton traveled to Utah to have a firsthand look at a practice he considered quite natural. Some people who defend modern polygamy take the same approach, saying men are, after all, promiscuous animals by nature. "You look at the nature of men, and most of them are polygamous," says Mary Potter, who was once one of three wives of a policeman in a Salt Lake City suburb. (The family later split up.) She has now formed a group in support of plural marriages, and openly frets about "having to wear a scarlet P," as she calls the cries for legal action. "In polygamy, men are properly channeled."

She and other supporters of polygamy point to recent studies that maintain that men are evolutionarily wired for multiple sexual partners. "There's a desire on the part of men to have a diversity of mates—it's their natural urge—so sex is definitely a motivating factor for many of the patriarchs," says Janet Bennion, the anthropologist who has written about the Allred clan.

Viagra has been a blessing for a few of the older patriarchs, Bennion notes. "Some members of the Allred group are using Viagra because they just can't keep up with their younger wives," she says. "There is a big age difference for many of these men. If you've got three or four sexually active wives, that's a lot of work."

Bennion is sympathetic to polygamous families and thinks it would be a terrible thing if the state started prosecuting them. While she concedes that there have been incidents of sexual abuse, marrying of relatives and ostracizing of older, less attractive wives within the clans, she believes polygamy can offer a sense of security and a kind of sisterhood to modern women, and that's what accounts for the continued growth.

With its reputation for divinely sanctioned promiscuity, the Hildale and Colorado City community attracts its share of misguided visitors, says Dan Barlow, who is the town's mayor and an elder in the church that owns nearly every house here. "They think what goes on here is all about sex," he says. "It's foolish to make such a claim because we live a hundred miles or so from Las Vegas. If people want sex, that's where they should go."

The mayor took me on a tour. The houses he showed me were huge, some with as many as 15 to 20 bedrooms and others that looked more like half-finished motels or dormitories. On a weekday afternoon, every female in town was wearing an ankle-length dress.

All around town I glimpsed new additions to houses, businesses and public buildings. Church prophecies about millennial catastrophes have stepped up the pace of preparation for bad times, Barlow told me. We drove the wide streets, passing huge, never finished houses. "These are happy, joyous homes," Barlow said. With its extraordinary rate of reproduction, the community is growing by better than 10 percent a year, he said.

In conversation, the mayor at times sounded defensive as he tried to explain his town's unique culture to a curious outsider. "The roads lead in and out," he said. "The telephone lines go both ways. Women are free to leave if they want."

The law seemed a distant concern, but the raid of 1953 stands as a defining moment. "I was 21 at the time," Barlow told me. "I had three children. They were made wards of the state. Is that what these women want?"

Laura Chapman sees things differently. What she remembers most about growing up was a sense of being a prisoner in a life with no escape route. At age 11, she was pulled out of public school and taught at home. At age 18, her father took her to see the clan's spiritual leader, LeRoy S. Johnson, now dead. The prophet, then in his 70's, had taken as one of his wives Chapman's 17-year-old sister, she says.

"He says, 'Let's take care of this right now,' and he calls in an 18-year-old boy," Chapman recalls. "I got sick to my stomach. I told him I couldn't marry him. So, to get out of that marriage, I agreed to marry another boy. I was married in a week."

She wanted to work outside the home; she says her husband told her no. She wanted to practice birth control; he said he would have nothing to do with her if she did, she says. "I was in my late 20's before I even knew there was a law against statutory rape," says Chapman. "When I finally got out, at age 28, I had the knowledge of the outside world of an 11-year-old."

When her husband said he was ready to take another wife—his 18-year-old cousin—Chapman gathered up her five children and left. Ultimately she made it to college, and after seven years got a degree in sociology and human development (and has recently left Tapestry and plans to pursue a master's degree in social work). Her older sister, Rena Mackert, confirmed every detail of Chapman's life story. "I'm proud of her," says Mackert. "She was the most beaten-down child—timid, afraid of her own shadow. My little sister has come a long way."

Barlow scoffs at such tales. "They're a bunch of soreheads, those women," he says. Yes, marriages are arranged on occasion, and almost always approved by a spiritual leader. But that is an ancient and respected practice, says Barlow. As for the allegations that boys paw at their sisters and old men prey on young girls, he shakes his head. "Whenever you have people living together, you're going to have people problems, the same here as anywhere else."

It seems improbable that these two conflicting views of reality can coexist indefinitely, and perhaps a clash is now inevitable. Prompted by the recent furor, two bills introduced in the current state legislative session directly target polygamy. One would raise the legal age of marriage from 14 to 16. The other would provide money and shelters for women who want to flee but may not meet the specific admittance rules of traditional halfway homes.

"What these women have brought into broad daylight is a civil rights issue that is second to none in the history of Utah," says State Senator Scott Howell, the leader of the Democratic legislative minority in Utah, who introduced one of the bills. "Here, we've got all the world coming to town for the Olympics. Do we really want to be known as the place where we let old men marry little girls?"

For the women who brought polygamy out of Utah's closet, the 2002 Olympics remain the trump card. More than 10,000 visiting journalists will be deluged with information about the world's greatest snow, the glowing city in the Wasatch, the spotless facilities. And then, when they grow tired of the luge and the Tabernacle Choir stories, the press will have no trouble finding the women of Tapestry, who will tell them about Utah's other heritage.

"We toyed with the idea of giving out maps to the homes of famous polygamists, like maps to the stars," says Thompson, feeling the power of mischief. "Wouldn't that be a tourist attraction?"

– 29 –

The Refrigerator and American Ideas of "Home"

Thomas Maschio

Thomas Maschio is vice president of Westport, Connecticut–based Cultural Dynamics, a market research firm that specializes in ethnographic research on consumer attitudes and behaviors. He received his PhD from McMaster University, based on research in Papua New Guinea. He is author of To Remember the Faces of the Dead: The Plenitude of Memory in Southwestern New Britain *and is working on a book on American consumer culture.*

The particular refrigerator I recall literally was plastered over with pictures of children and certificates and citations that marked their athletic and educational accomplishments. There were photos of family gatherings, cousins, aunts and uncles, grandmother and grandfather. One could see that pictures considered most emotionally important to parents—the youngest son being hugged by a grandparent, a daughter riding the family dog—were placed at eye level, on the front of the fridge. Photos of distant relatives and business cards of the family insurance agent, plumber, painter and house remodeler were placed either below eye level on the front of the fridge, or on its side in a more peripheral space. Also, as the mom of the household explained to me, pictures sometimes were replaced as new and important family gatherings took place, or if children did something that merited that special "Kodak moment." Thus a process of creating or recycling family history, of outlining degrees of familial affection, of intimacy or of distance was spatially diagrammed on the refrigerator.

Having sharpened my analytical eye observing the rituals and mores of a remote Papua New Guinean tribal group, I began to see the refrigerator as an object ritually marked by this middle-class, Midwestern family. Ritual space, like that in which an initiation or a mortuary ritual is performed, usually is marked off from the surrounding area by objects that have a special "alerting" quality. The object can be something ordinary, even mundane, but some modification is done to it so that its nature is altered in a symbolic sense and it comes to convey a host of special meanings.

CREATING DOMESTICITY

This refrigerator, and millions like it that are put to similar symbolic uses, occupied central stage in a ritual performance that had as its aim the creation of domesticity, and a feeling of home. The refrigerator increasingly has become a sort of billboard advertisement for many strongly held values about what a home should be, what sort of emotional and moral tone should distinguish it, and how it should run.

What is the American culture of domesticity? What values go in to making it up, and how can we see these values pictured on our refrigerators? Well, to begin let's consider the issue of American mothers being responsible for the flow of household tasks. That is, one of the ways that the middle-class mom judges her success as a mom and housewife is by successfully coordinating or balancing a host of household activities. Running kids to soccer practice or little league, shopping for and preparing family meals, picking up kids from band practice . . . all these activities must be balanced and organized if the household is to function smoothly; indeed, if it is to function at all. Keeping the family activities running smoothly is not only a mother's key responsibility, but often a significant source of feelings of satisfaction, competence and pride. The family master schedule enshrines the values of balance and organization—helping to put order into a potentially chaotic environment, and provide the home with its particular rhythm and tone; placed on the fridge, it revealed the kitchen and the refrigerator surface to be family command and control centers, on which certain notions of how a home should run were displayed.

"WARMING-UP OF THE HOME"

The ritual of continually creating a domestic world also involves the evocation of sentiment. Many domestic acts and routines are specifically understood to be acts of emotional nurturing and caring. These accomplish what can be called an emotional "warming-up of the home." By placing photos of the household's children on the front of the fridge, the mom of the household was performing one of these acts of housewarming. The photos were evidence of parental care, concern and affection. Other photos that I saw on the fridge, such as those of distant relatives, also had a certain teaching function. The mom told me that she would often point out pictures of these kin to her young children as she told them who they were and how they were related to the children. Bits of family history were woven into these descriptions. The refrigerator had become a sort of memory board that functioned to evoke a feeling of family.

The children's art taped at odd angles of the fridge, the certificates of their educational and athletic accomplishments—an A received on a spelling test, a certificate awarded for good sportsmanship on a little league team—were testament to the fact that domestic life for this family also was about the emotional nurturance and praise of children. Keeping up the flow of emotional nurturance, as well as domestic routine, is an emotionally trying endeavor for many mothers. And so the proliferation of homilies—pithy and uplifting sayings that express sympathy for the mother and homemaker's lot, or that have a straightforward religious message—all usually plastered on the fridge so that the household's mom can take a dose of daily comfort and counsel.

UPSCALE REFRIGERATORS

This is not of course the whole of the story. Other American refrigerators I have seen in the course of my work reflect another definition of domesticity. In a number of more upscale homes, the kitchen is not so much a place for celebrating family values and children's achievements as a stage where one displays a sense of mastery of domestic arts—such as cooking—and where one can exhibit an overall social ease. Here refrigerators most often have a clean surface. In this sort of household, the refrigerator also serves as a ritual marker. What it marks, above all else, is its owner's taste and aesthetic judgment. The gleaming stainless steel surface and sharpness and boldness of line of the Sub Zero, for instance, connote a kind of mastery of a developed aesthetic vocabulary, as well as a real assertion of self. Here sharp lines and gleaming surfaces are associated with the suppression of domesticity and sentiment.

IX

COLLECTIVE IDENTITIES

How Do People Express Status and Group Membership?

IN ALL HUMAN SOCIETIES, kinship and residence are important for the organization of people into various groups. These are not the only **organizational principles,** however; others that are frequently used (and imposed) include sex, age, common interest, race, ethnicity, and stratification. In all societies some division of labor by sex exists. In some societies this division is relatively flexible, in that tasks normally performed by one sex may be performed by the other, as circumstances dictate, without "loss of face." This is the case among the Bushmen, where many tasks are shared between men and women. In some other societies, though, the sexes are rigidly separated in what they do, as among the Iroquoian peoples of what now is New York State. Among them the tasks of men took them away from their villages for purposes of hunting, warfare, and diplomacy (in the twentieth century, for high-steel work in urban areas), while the work of women was carried out in and near the villages.

Grouping by age involves the concepts of **age-grades** and **age-sets,** categories to which one belongs by virtue of age, and cohorts of individuals who move through a series of age-grades together. The concepts are familiar to college students: A particular "class" (of '04, '05, or whatever) constitutes an age-set whose members pass through the first year, sophomore, junior, and senior age-grades together. Age-grades, with or without age-sets, are found in many human societies, with important ritual activity often marking the transition from one age-grade to the next.

Common-interest groups, formed for a specific purpose and to which one belongs by virtue of an act of joining (as opposed to automatic assignment by virtue of descent, age, sex, and so on), are particularly characteristic of urban industrial societies, although they may be found in traditional agrarian societies as well. In the United States they exist in profusion, ranging all the way from street gangs to civic groups like the Lions or Elks clubs. Common-interest associations are especially well suited to industrialized and developing societies, where new needs are constantly arising, around which new associations can form.

Grouping by sex, age, or common interest may or may not involve a degree of inequality; after all, groups may exist for different purposes without being ranked as inferior or superior to one another. Among the Iroquoians, for example, the rigid separation of sexes was *not* associated with subordination of one sex to the dominance of the other. Rather, the tasks assigned each sex were regarded as of equal value, and neither sex could impose its will on the other. By contrast, stratification *always* involves inequality, as whole categories of people (**social classes** and **races**) are ranked high versus low relative to one another.

Members of one social class find ways to distinguish themselves symbolically from members of other social classes. One obvious way is through ownership of material things, like luxury items. **Stratification,** one of the defining features of **civilization,** is backed by the power of the state, which may use force to maintain the privileges of those most favored by the system. Needless to say, those in the uppermost class, the **social elite,** have prior claim to basic resources, whereas those at the bottom of the scale must make do with whatever those of higher rank leave them.

The articles by Matthew Gutmann and Brett Williams neatly illustrate social stratification in action. Two of the ways in which social classes are manifest is through **symbolic indicators**—activities and possessions indicative of one's status—and patterns of interaction— who interacts with whom, and in what way. "Elm Valley" affords good illustrations of both and highlights the misunderstandings that stem from somewhat different worldviews held by members of different social classes.

In his article Gutmann argues that in Mexico City, such differentiation has expressed itself in working class discontent with free trade agreements like the North American Free Trade Agreement (NAFTA). He shows how the poor, who appear to benefit least from free trade, have begun to assert that they have a duty to defend the Mexican nation. This is because the rich, who are hoping to get a piece of the pie in a globalized economy, are ceding Mexican economic and juridical sovereignty to wealthier countries and corporations.

Beyond social class, a society's system of stratification can be cast in racial or ethnic terms. Anthropologists have shown again and again that race, generally defined as a repressive framework that divides people into groups ranked by arbitrary qualities of biological superiority or cultural worth, has no biological basis. Yet race has played a powerful symbolic and political role in recent world history. (Although the difference with the term *race* is not always clear, **ethnicity** generally refers to nonbiological expressions of group membership, an ethnic group being people who share foods, clothing, language, and so on.) **Racism,** the ideology that evaluates people according to

racial identity and provides a justification for discrimination, is not simply a problem of the Americas and Europe; it is a major problem in many societies around the world. In his article on the **genocide** in Rwanda, Alex de Waal discusses how differentiated occupation and political statuses laid the groundwork for the emergence of racial extremism in a supposedly unified nation, an extremism that fueled one of the major tragedies of the twentieth century. In this selection, we see how the expression (and imposition) of racial identity and status can go beyond simple expressions of superiority and provide the basis for physical domination and violence.

In this chapter, we also consider the dilemmas of group identification and status for anthropologists themselves. In her article, Elizabeth Garland discusses how a raid by Rwandan rebels in her Ugandan fieldsite affected her ideas about Western privilege and its relationship to doing fieldwork and anthropology. In the midst of this experience, Garland reflects on the hypocrisy of the anthropological endeavor: As a white Western woman, she was provided a protected escape from the situation, while the Africans she studied were left behind. Garland argues that her own privileged status as a Westerner and anthropologist, as well as the assumptions she previously made about safety and danger, have unexpectedly prevented her from understanding how her informants experience their dangerous world.

FOCUS QUESTIONS

As you read these selections, consider these questions:

✦ Why do people organize themselves in common interest groups, like socioeconomic classes? What needs do these associations serve?

✦ In your experience, what are some of the ways people demonstrate their social statuses?

✦ How can stratified ethnic and occupational differentiations lead to discrimination and even lay the groundwork for violence or genocide?

✦ Have you ever been in a situation in which you were aware of social stratification? What were the circumstances of that situation, and what role did you play? How did you know there was stratification?

30

For Whom the Taco Bells Toll
Popular Responses to NAFTA South of the Border

Matthew C. Gutmann

Matthew Gutmann is associate professor of anthropology at Brown University. He received his PhD from UC Berkeley in 1995. His research focuses on change in Mexico through the lenses of gender, sexuality, ethnicity, race, and nationalism. His first book, The Meanings of Macho: Being a Man in Mexico City, *examines changing male identities and practices with respect to fathering, sexuality, housework, alcohol, violence, and the cultural history of machismo. He has also studied popular politics, as seen through criticisms of free trade agreements, and most recently has been studying Mexican men's reproductive health and sexuality.*

News item, 1992
With CEO John Martin saying "value and quality know no borders," Taco Bell opened its first outlet south of the border in Mexico City. (USA Today, 4 June 1992: A-1)

News item, 1998
According to Rocío Conejo, a spokeswoman in Mexico City for Taco Bell's new holding company (Tricon Global Restaurants, Inc., which also owns Kentucky Fried Chicken and Pizza Hut), "because Mexican tacos are very different from Taco Bell tacos no franchises are presently in operation or planned for Mexico." (phone interview, 6 January 1998)

ANGELA'S BIG FEET

For my friend Angela, the North American Free Trade Agreement (NAFTA) always held the promise of greater access to goods from the United States. In her case what she most wanted were size 10½-wide shoes for her grandmother's badly swollen feet. As for Angela's neighbor Toño, like most men in Colonia Santo Domingo in Mexico City, he has had a hard time finding steady employment in the 1990s.[1] To Toño the treaty represented the potential for growth of US business investment in central Mexico. Even if it meant slaving in a low-wage *maquiladora* assembly plant, Toño had high hopes for better job prospects after NAFTA went into effect on 1 January 1994.

On that fateful day, as it happens, thousands of Tzotzil, Tzeltal, Chol and other indigenous peoples made clear their very different interpretation and expectation for NAFTA: they launched an armed uprising in the southern Mexican state of Chiapas to denounce the Agreement and demand democracy, liberty, and justice for *indígenas* and all people in Mexico. Although there has to date been no Chiapas-like response to NAFTA in the *colonias populares* in Mexico City or other urban areas, and despite the views of some like Toño, disdain and contempt for the accord among the poor throughout the country have been widespread.

No matter how ambiguous and ill-defined popular opposition to NAFTA might be in the Mexican capital and the countryside, as Chiapas has so well reminded anthropologists, we must not engage in the violence of ethnographic indifference by ignoring politically dissident moods and activities, whether they are clearly voiced or muted and confusing. By the same token, and for similar reasons, it is important regularly to assess processes such as the individualization of responses to efforts like NAFTA, as this relates to the periodic waxing and waning of popular political interest in "politics" altogether.

"For Whom the Taco Bells Toll: Popular Responses to NAFTA South of the Border" by Matthew C. Gutmann from *Critique of Anthropology*, 1998, Vol. 18, No. 3, pp. 297–315. Reprinted by permission of Sage Publications, Inc.

Amid mountains of important analyses regarding more strictly economic and environmental aspects of NAFTA it is easy to miss critical cultural dimensions that point to equally momentous changes in the lives of millions of dispossessed on both sides of the Rio Grande/Bravo. NAFTA has meant far more than the commercial reorganization of relations between the United States, Canada, and Mexico.

The announcement of Taco Bell's arrival in Mexico City in 1992, for example, was greeted as more than absurd by the capital's poor. In the *colonias populares* of Mexico City, the appearance of these franchises "south of the border" was a symbolic tolling which heralded good times ahead for the upper middle class and elites alone. After all, the only people who could regularly patronize such establishments were the youth from these strata. The vast majority of Mexicans simply could not afford gringo fast food. Nonetheless, apparently North American tacos were too much for even these youth to stomach, which resulted in Taco Bell's evident failure to establish a foothold in Mexico. It seems that even the more affluent sectors of society took umbrage at this attempted gringo-ization of Mexico's national cuisine.[2]

In this article I address certain implications of the Free Trade Agreement for national and class identities and relations in Mexico. I examine how discontent and frustration among Mexico's urban poor are representative of contradictory political dissidence and popular nationalism, and I explore how and why these manifestations of popular political culture are both ardently felt and yet nonetheless lie dormant in all but exceptional historical moments. The tension between individual and collective strategies to oppose US domination are evidence, I conclude, of broader chaos and confusion with respect to the meanings of democratic and popular will in Mexico today.

Colonia Santo Domingo is a community that was formed by land invasion in the early 1970s, and today is home to well over 150,000 men and women, most of whom live on one to three "minimum salaries" (the semi-official standard of poverty in Mexico). Residents of the *colonia* clean homes in wealthy neighborhoods and buildings in the nearby National Univerity; they drive taxis and buses; and they work in factories and small enterprises throughout the capital city. Most adults are able to find paid work if they want it, yet few are able to survive on the wages from one job alone. In Santo Domingo, if someone has the temerity to ask a neighbor "How much do you earn?" the reply would be invariably "Don't ask how much I earn, ask how much I lose!"

I am interested here in why so many men and women in working-class barrios in Mexico City today believe that defending Mexico's national sovereignty has become the duty principally of the poor because, they feel, the elites have relinquished their national loyalties, and why among the poor this is seen so often as an individual rather than a collective project. If many working-class people in Mexico City would agree that in practice the rich generally put their own interests before those of the nation, residents in neighborhoods like Colonia Santo Domingo might nonetheless point out that the language of the elites has shifted in recent years. Now even the pretense of independence—for example, opposition to US foreign policy—has all but disappeared. It has been replaced, they say, with slogans like that of Jaime Serra Puche, the government official who called in 1991 for Mexicans to accept *"el reto de la interdependencia* [the challenge of interdependence]" between Mexico, the United States and Canada, that is, NAFTA (cited in García Canclini, 1992:5).

In this article I will also offer evidence that the perception among the poor—at least, those who worry about such matters—that defense of the Mexican nation is now their burden is related to the spreading conclusion among activists in Colonia Santo Domingo that popular social movements in the last two decades have focused too restrictively on ameliorating practical problems among the poor and in this way may have inadvertently relinquished political ground around international and global issues.[3]

Although many commentators have addressed the relationship of NAFTA to national identity, national sovereignty and political debate in Mexico, discussion of popular perceptions and responses to the treaty have been largely speculative if they have been reported at all. Ethnographic material has been sorely lacking, and thus this article also seeks to provide initial indications of popular political discourse and activity in response to the first four years of the Agreement.

PREFAB CURTAINS AND JAPANESE MELONS

If during its initial phase Angela and especially Toño looked more benignly upon the TLC (as the accord is known in Spanish, for Tratado de Libre Comercio), Marcos, another neighbor on Huehuetzin Street in Colonia Santo Domingo in the Mexican capital, had a more typical response: "The TLC is one more blow against the already *jodidos* [screwed]," one more instance of "the Mexican and gringo rich fleecing *la gente humilde* [the common folks]." Marcos works in maintenance at the National University next to Santo Domingo, and he reported that other janitors and groundskeepers felt similarly.

Other accounts of NAFTA's impact are more personal. One afternoon in late September 1994, Doña Josefina described to me what occurred to her husband, Guillermo, following Mexico's entry into the pact:

"Guillermo worked for many years as a *cortinero* [curtain maker] in a curtain shop," Josefina began. "He would go to people's homes to measure their windows and then make them custom curtains. One day his *patrón* told him that because of Tratado de Libre Comercio he was going to shut down the curtain shop."

"But what did TLC [NAFTA] have to do with shutting down the curtain shop?" I asked.

"I think he talked about tariffs [*aranceles*]. I'm not sure if it was taxes or what. I don't know . . . But what it did mean was that he could no longer pay what they were charging him because [with the Agreement] other prefabricated curtains were going to start coming in [to Mexico]. Much cheaper ones. That's what it was. And he declared bankruptcy. He couldn't pay the workers any more, or continue in business. That's what has happened to a lot of other people, too."

"Like . . . ?"

"Like some furniture workers."

"Have your friends who are furniture workers had problems finding work afterwards?"

"Yes, yes. And near here, as well, there was a factory that made plastic bottles. They also shut that."

"And you're sure this had to do with NAFTA?" I pressed.

"Yes, a lot of places shut down. For example, there was an umbrella shop. They also shut that down because umbrellas from Taiwan began to arrive. So more people were out of work. Look, we know little about the Tratado de Libre Comercio. The truth is that we know little about what the Tratado was really, because they're not going to . . . The *patrón* tells us, 'We're going to shut because of the Free Trade Agreement.' But really we don't know about free trade. They don't let us in on that."

"Do you have any idea," I continued, "who *is* making money with the Agreement?"

"I think the ones who are importing goods here [into Mexico]. Because if you go shopping everything is from another country, radios, grills, dishes, pots, batteries, games, like that. If you go to the supermarket there's also a lot of meat from the United States."

"Are there any Mexicans making money off the Agreement?"

"Well, maybe Serra Puche[4] and his people have gotten something. He was very optimistic [about the Agreement], because they think it's going to make us better and do well for us. Well, no, not really! So we see how Serra Puche and all are doing very well. Yes, they have made something. We don't aspire to great things like those who have power, so much power, the owners of so much power, even over lives! We don't aspire to all that but only what's necessary. That's why there's

struggle. Even if we're few in number that's what we want: that there not be so much injustice."

In late 1996, I also spoke about NAFTA with my good friend Jorge who spends 12–14 hours daily operating a small *tienda* corner store on Huehuetzin Street in Colonia Santo Domingo. Unlike Josefina, who went through only first grade, as an adolescent Jorge studied to be a lawyer. Today, in addition to minding the store and helping to raise his five small children, Jorge works with the local center-left Partido de la Revolución Democrática (PRD), especially at election time when he monitors polling stations in the *colonia* for vote fraud. NAFTA, gringolandia and Mexican national sovereignty are all subjects dear to Jorge's heart.

"So, my old friend, What the hell do you make of this, NAFTA?" I began.

Jorge began his sermon on the impact of NAFTA among various social strata in Mexico.

"For us in the lower middle class, it's of no benefit whatsoever. It doesn't benefit us mainly because in reality, here, in the city, instead of raising employment it has lowered it. In the countryside, *campesinos* have little money to export. And let's say they try to get a loan, as I did when I went back [to Tierra Blanca, his natal *pueblo* in the western state of Guerrero]. I applied for a loan from BANRURAL.[5] I'm sure you've seen the brochures they give out, or seen their commercials on the TV where they say, 'Apply for rural assistance—go to the Bank and . . .'."

"This is connected to NAFTA?" I ounce again asked.

"Well, yeah. Because if the banks assist *campesinos*, well, then the *campesinos* will get ahead. You know, the poor *campesinos*. There's land for planting and there's the will, too, but there's no money. NAFTA only . . . how shall I put this, it helps the *grandes* [big shots]. Those who plant on a large scale. The rich, those who have money."

"Are Gringos buying up land in Guerrero?"

"Only on the coast."[6]

"Not to plant?"

"No, not to plant. Only on the coast. There are talks, there are rumors that the government is going to build a dam financed by the Japanese. So there are a lot of plans. If you remember, where you entered, at the crossroads, it's all very flat there."

Jorge was referring to an ill-fated attempt I had made several years earlier to drive to the village, Tierra Blanca, where at the time he was tending the family cows for a few months. Together with my wife, Michelle, and our infant daughter we spent the better part of a day driving over creeks, boulders and fallen logs looking for Jorge's godforsaken birthplace. To this day I tease him that Tierra Blanca probably doesn't even exist and that he invented it to make a gringo look like a fool.

In the same conversation I taunted Jorge by saying that I wanted to divulge "the secrets" of the people from the village to my students in the United States.

"Why?" he asked. "Because Christ never went there?"

"No, man. Because no one has ever been there," I replied.

"Well, there's no gringos who go there! And, if you want," Jorge paused before adding in a whisper, "you can become a guerrilla there."

"It's that easy?"

"Out there, only the goats could give you away."

Jorge returned to his tale about the Japanese-financed dams:

"So they say that the Japanese want to finance the dam and pay a little rent to grow melons (I think that's what they say) on the land. Because the Japanese really like melons and it's a lot cheaper to grow them here [Mexico] than there [Japan]."

"So things are better or worse for poor folks after the Agreement?"

"Worse. Because, based on what I understand, the small industries used to have more chance of offering work here in Mexico, but now they have to compete with transitional companies. Games, a lot of other things they used to make here. But no longer. Why? Because they shut [the plants] down. Now the big North American chains, like Home Mart and I don't know what can offer everything less expensively."

"But people from Santo Domingo can't afford to go to Home Mart."

"Yes they can. For example, when they have some money they'll go for the sales and buy more. But for us, for the tiny merchants [*pequeñísimo comercio*], well folks are just coming to buy sodas from us. And that's what you sell the most of but earn the least from. The other thing is that my business is hurt by the Agreement simply because a lot of people are without work. So they obviously don't have money to spend in the *tienda*."

In the wake of renewed hopes for improved economic fortunes, as part of broader democratic transformations in Mexico, Jorge and many of his friends in Santo Domingo have been frustrated in the last decade at every turn. It has become increasingly difficult to imagine fundamental changes occurring in the country's domestic economy, much less in its political sphere or in Mexican–US relations and the concomitant emigration of the *paisanos* to the United States. He still works as a poll-watcher on election days, but, as Jorge himself begrudgingly ad-

mits, his distrust of political parties signals a more fundamental disenchantment with participation in collective forms of struggle and "politics" in general.

ANTI-AMERICANISM AND NAFTA

Beginning even before the Treaty of Guadalupe-Hidalgo was signed some 150 years ago, the United States has been central to debates regarding Mexico's geopolitical borders, the cultural frontiers of *lo mexicano,* and internal "boundary" disputes involving opposing sectors of the populace. So it is no coincidence that today NAFTA is generally emblematic of contemporary US–Mexican relations.

When listening to the new transnational gospel as preached by Mexican government and business leaders— "The purpose of Free Trade today is to allow Mexico to become the first Third World country to vault quickly into the ranks of the First World"—most in the popular urban sector of the country are more than slightly skeptical that such a transformation will take place. A recurring and rhetorical question asked by those still actively grappling with these issues in Colonia Santo Domingo is: How can we suddenly forget about history, especially that between Mexico and *"el otro lado"* (literally, the other side, meaning the United States)? The idea that the Free Trade Agreement has instantly nullified the arrogantly unequal relations between Mexico and *el otro lado* strikes more than a few as ridiculous. Only the gringos are served by such historical myopia, they feel.[7]

Some periods in history witness greater changes and transformations in social relations than others. The present epoch and the foreseeable future have the potential to be tumultuous periods, in no small part because of significant changes associated with transnational commerce, communication and migration. But as to the possibility that profound change will impact the vast majority of the poor in Mexico, doubts persist, and they are doubts rooted in long experience with persistent poverty and marginalization.

Incredulity regarding the prospects of Mexico leaping to first-world status reflect not simply popular cynicism. The California Chamber of Commerce (1993: 14), for instance, questions "the basis for Mexico's claim that it will soon be ready to join the group of industrialized nations." Men and women in *colonias populares* throughout Mexico have decades of experience and opinions regarding import substitution, foreign direct investment, IMF austerity measures and *maquiladoras*. Their views on NAFTA also represent oppositional judgments about the merits of *openly* tying Mexico's economic future so thoroughly to that of the United States, as evidenced by the fact that shortly after the Agreement was ratified in

Mexico, jokes began circulating in Santo Domingo that the best job prospects in the future would be those offered by the Pentagon.

If today, as John Gledhill (1997: 104) writes, for "the majority of Mexico's growing army of deracinated urban poor, the general class opposition between 'ricos' and 'pobres' has greatest salience to their conditions of life," this is by no means an automatic product of historical class schisms any more than it is an inevitable consequence of class position. How people in Santo Domingo and other colonias populares today view los ricos and los pobres is more particularly linked to the three remarkable and turbulent decades in which popular urban movements in Mexico, as elsewhere in Latin America, have involved millions of women and men in struggles over housing, social services, ethnic rights, domestic violence, Christian base communities, and movements around feminism, lesbian and gay rights, and ecology.[8] Especially in the 1980s, political cultures independent of the government and official parties emerged on a large scale in the popular urban sector in Mexico.

That said, it is important not to exaggerate the novelty of the cultural processes taking place. Arguments about Mexican cultural nationalism have long involved treatments of how class relates to nation, whether different classes share opposing and/or similar interests, and indeed whether and in what contexts it might be possible to speak of a Mexican national culture.[9] Carlos Monsiváis (1992a: 200) writes with reference to NAFTA and "Americanization" in particular, "The process is global, irreversible, and it must be examined from a perspective that does not characterize everything as 'cultural penetration' or presume perennially virginal societies."

Mexico entered the GATT (General Agreement on Tariffs and Trade) in 1986, in a preliminary effort to become qualitatively more "integrated" into Washington's market schemes, while Mexican elites in the mid-1980s were still attempting to resolve the country's 1982 financial collapse and prepare the way for neoliberalism's triumph in the (widely fraudulent) elections of 1988. Especially after the fall of the Soviet system in the late 1980s, it became a matter of course for business and political leaders in Mexico to locate their country's strategy for achieving "fast-track" modernity ever more exclusively under the North American (and NAFTA) umbrella.

With real minimum salaries in the 1990s standing at roughly the same levels as they did 30 years earlier, and workers' real earnings in 1990 less than half what they were before the 1982 crisis (see Barkin, 1991), and less still after the crisis of 1994–5, there was little confusion, or optimism, that the Agreement boded well in the short term for the poor in Mexico.

In 1993, after helping Don Armando gather hay for his animals in a rural village outside Mexico City, and after fielding his pointed questions regarding the US bombing of Iraq in January that year (see Gutmann, 1996: 7–8), I asked Armando if I could photograph him with his straw hat, deeply tanned wrinkles, and a new and nasty cut on one of his fingers. Don Armando shrugged and stared at me with his finger held up for the camera. Two days later, when I was again back in Santo Domingo, Armando's daughter came looking for me. She told me that her father was very worried about the photo I had taken. It occurred to Armando that I might be with the CIA or DEA (Drug Enforcement Administration).[10] I had to promise never to use the picture in classes I taught and never to publish it. Why the CIA or DEA might be interested in a photograph of Don Armando and what they might do with it were not discussed.[11]

To be sure, three years later, while skimming through my ethnography of Santo Domingo, Don Armando's daughter and others noticed the photos of some family members that I had published. But I was chastised for not including Don Armando's picture, that is, for taking his accusations and admonitions seriously. My friends and acquaintances in Colonia Santo Domingo are deeply ambivalent as to how to cope with the menace and the real power of the United States.

Although the otro lado can be a blessing for individual Mexicans, in the view of many it remains a scourge for Mexico as a whole. Over the course of several years, while wandering familiar and unknown streets in colonias populares in Mexico City, I have been the target of the insult "¡Gringo!" on many occasions. Walking through alleys or even driving down major avenues, men, usually young men, have often yelled at me "¡Gringo!" or "¡Pinche gringo! [goddamned gringo]." One time the accusation was accompanied by a piece of flying fruit that hit me on the head. Another time, a would-be assailant was wielding a screwdriver as if he meant to stab me. My friends Luciano and Marcos reason that this kind of cat-calling stems from simple resentment of gringos on the part of poor youth and a few adults.

What seems clear is that this kind of insult is not representative of a facile xenophobia. "Gringos" continue to be the popular target of resentment and anger, not foreigners in general, and as often as not "gringos" is a charge leveled against Mexicans who are perceived as wealthy and are unexpectedly encountered in poor neighborhoods in the capital.

On the River Plate futbol team made up of young men from Santo Domingo and the neighborhood of Los Reyes, an adjacent pueblo, most of the players had nicknames. In addition to one called Keé-kair (as in "kicker"), Conejo (rabbit), Calaca (for a wrist cast) and Choco (as in "chocolate," for dark brown skin), there were also Japonés (Japanese), Argentino (Argentine) and Francés (French). The name of the squad itself comes from the famous River Plate football club in Argentina. As with their middle-class compatriots, far from feeling a distaste for things foreign these young men from the poor barrios of Mexico City are especially intrigued and attracted to the exoticism of foreignness. Exoticism, too has its limits, and no one on the River Plate team has ever been nicknamed El Gringo; such a title would cross the bounds of acceptable humor and verge on gratuitous insult.

NATION-BUILDING AND THE THIRD MILLENNIUM

How Mexico's urban poor perceive NAFTA, and whether and to whom such perceptions might ultimately matter, are questions that remain far from clear. Undoubtedly for the purposes of US commercial and foreign relations "local" popular sentiments must be taken into account. A 1996 article in the *New York Times,* for instance examines "dispirited public sentiments" in Mexico with respect to NAFTA, and characterizes the overall mood among the poor as one in which "grumpiness reigns" (see Dillon, 1996). Nonetheless, lack of enthusiasm for the Agreement on the part of the working poor is not by itself a cause for entrepreneurial worries as long as this discontent is confined to amorphous and individualized "grumpiness."

More disturbing to globalizing elites, perhaps, is an emerging popular judgment that although it is increasingly easy for the rich to jet off to Houston for weekend buying sprees at the upscale Galleria shopping mall, for the vast majority of Mexicans crossing international borders still amounts to carrying out, on an individual and small-group level, the actual invasion of foreign territory. Transnationalism has not led to the withering away of the US Army or Border Patrol. In addition, whereas the same wealthy visitors are able to keep their money in dollars in Houston banks—or even in Swiss accounts—the greatest accomplishment most migrants hope to achieve is regular remittances in dollars they send back to communities wracked by peso devaluations.

The correspondence of transnationalism with rich *vendidos* (sell-outs) on the one hand, and of the Mexican nation with its poor *jodidos* (screwed) on the other, is far from casual in the minds of my neighbors in Mexico City. Many remark that the Free Trade Agreement merely confirms what they already knew to be the case: Mexico has long since lost a national sense of self, and that hereafter Mexico will not even feign national autonomy. So, with

the thin façade of independence dropped, for many people in Santo Domingo, Mexico's self-reliance has become a political myth that can no longer be sustained.

Partially in response to the rupture of popular support for state institutions and the growing influence of independent urban social movements in the 1980s, the regime of Carlos Salinas de Gortari (1988–94) launched the Solidaridad/PRONASOL program early in his administration. As one government functionary put it in 1992, "The intention behind PRONASOL is to create, through public works and services, a new urban base for the Mexican state. By the end of the 1980s the social bases of the Mexican state were unraveling" (cited in Dresser, 1994: 148).

Solidaridad/PRONASOL was also designed with the Free Trade Agreement in mind. Specifically, it represented what some analysts have called "Mexico's principal entry in the global sweepstakes to create new institutional arrangements and structures to sustain the open, market-oriented economic development strategies" of NAFTA and neoliberalism in general (Cornelius et al., 1994: 4).

Solidaridad/PRONASOL was, thus, a major federal effort designed at legitimizing the Mexican state (and the ruling PRI party) within a context of transnationalism and popular discontent. So while some men and women in Colonia Santo Domingo believe that the *maquiladoras* will shortly ride the NAFTA wave south to the capital, far more fear that the Agreement will lead to elimination of better-skilled employment through the importation of less expensive prefabricated products. Solidaridad/PRONASOL's rush to develop infrastructure like roads and electricity, to say nothing of a nation of consensual consumers, itself has never offered more than a few solutions to long-term employment problems in the urban areas of Mexico where most of the country's population is today concentrated.[12]

As my friend Roberto contended while he re-soldered the dented radiator on my car:

> Solidaridad was meant to trick us. It's just like they come round before election time and hand things out. You know, like a bucket with the candidate's name, or a coupon for an extra [plastic] bag of milk. Well, the only difference is that the handouts are all the time. But they still don't really help if you're poor. They don't fool anyone.

Promises aside, few are still under the nationalist spell of José López Portillo's challenge during his presidency (1976–82), "¡*Preparémonos para administrar la abundancia!* [Get ready to cope with prosperity!]" The petroleum fumes that clouded the heads of so many in the 1970s have been blown away in the economic and political cataclysms that followed López Portillos's fateful words.

And as petroleum promises were scattered to the winds, many contemporary premises anchoring nationalist unity suffered irreparable damage as well. Because, as Carlos Monsiváis notes, "Nationalism depends on common and individual memories and on a minimum confidence in progress" (1992b: 71).

It is all the more remarkable therefore that despite a profound displacement of even minimal confidence in progress and even the nation-state, evidence of nationalism and nationalist consciousness persists among the poor in Mexico City. What Florencia Mallon (1995: 3) calls "the active participation and intellectual creativity of subaltern classes" in imagining and creating nationalisms cannot be underestimated today any more than in the period in which the Mexican republic was consolidated following independence in 1821.

In many respects, of course, the nationalisms of the 21st century will be dramatically different from those of the 19th century that Mallon's study highlights. One noteworthy feature of NAFTA-era popular nationalism in Mexico is the heightened conviction on the part of many that they are unable to influence national politics, for instance, by expressing their belief that Mexico is being undermined openly and covertly by the United States. They grow less and less optimistic about Mexico's political future and increasingly disillusioned about the nature and import of democracy in their country.

The reality, most feel, is that only rarely can they control their own daily lives, and even less frequently can they influence any political process that might conceivably be regarded as democratic self-determination in Mexico. It is no surprise, then, that when they can affect either international relations, their personal existence, or both, many relish the opportunity.

In 1996, I went with Bernardino and Esther—though only in their late 20s, already veteran community militants—to a meeting to plan pre-Christmas Posada celebrations sponsored by a local chapter of the PRD. We brought along a roasted chicken and some chilies to share with the others who were to gather in an apartment in a neighboring area.

As we came into the narrow entryway into the *vecindad* (a group of single-room apartments with communal baths and sinks) we spotted two youths still in their *futbol* uniforms. After asking about the score of a nationally televised game earlier in the day, Berna asked where the meeting room was. The youths pointed us further down the walk toward some women who were washing clothes in the sinks and children in large metal washtubs. The women pointed us still further inside the *vecindad.*

Three men were already sitting in the meeting room when we arrived. Another man and a woman arrived while I was being questioned as to my purpose at the meeting, my political affiliations in the United States and Mexico, my relationship with the US government, and how they could be expected to trust my intentions to "help the community." They returned quickly to the matter of my connection to the US government—evidently there was strong suspicion that I was a (US) federal agent of some kind.

I had seen the man who was leading the impromptu inquiry at collective work days in a nearby lagoon where some community activists met on Sundays to clean up the water and surrounding playing fields. He had seen me participating in these clean-up efforts as well. As it appeared I was soon to be ordered out of the meeting and the *vecindad*—two people opposed my presence from the beginning while all but Bernardino and Esther seemed to have serious reservations—I decided to argue politics and not protocol. After reiterating my ethnographic purpose in Mexico City, my involvement as a community and political organizer in Chicago and Houston for many years, and my desire to respect the wishes of all attending the meeting, I told everyone that personally I would be astonished if the United States government were interested enough in such meetings deep in the poorer homes of the poorer neighborhoods of Mexico City that they cared to assign a gringo agent to investigate. I said I was fairly sure that the United States was uninterested in such meetings.

My approach backfired immediately and I was unceremoniously asked to leave the premises. Bernardino escorted me to the street, apologizing as we walked and assuring me that he would not face untoward repercussions for having invited me.

In retrospect, may actions and words that day strike me later as at best naive and at worst presumptuous. In the remainder of the article I discuss certain issues that pertain to Mexican popular nationalism and sovereignty as these are developing in the late 1990s, and in the process address recalcitrant theories of nationalism and class, including within critical theory, that settle for comfortable naivety and metropolitan arrogance in lieu of creative new approaches to understanding contemporary nationalism.

NATIONAL SOVEREIGNTY

It turned out that for me not to consider the pre-Posada gathering a threat to US national security was more disrespectful of popular nationalist politics than if I had been sent to spy on the meeting by the CIA director himself. The responses of those in attendance that December day cannot be reduced to knee-jerk anti-Americanism. Instead, or in addition, I believe, they represent real frustration and bewilderment on the part of many in the popular movements in Mexico as they try to make contemporary sense of the Mexican nation and of the United States.

In a process analogous to what Mercedes González de la Rocha (1991, 1994) calls the individualization and privatization of solutions to Mexico's economic crises of the 1980s and 1990s (see also Benería, 1992), for many in the *colonias populares* the defense of Mexico's nationhood and sovereignty has become a personal rather than collective responsibility. For numerous others, of course, this goal has become illusory in the extreme; discouragement at the possibility of defending the Mexican nation has contributed mightily to more endemic political malaise.

The individualization and privatization of popular nationalism in Mexico represents in part the fruits of two decades of social movements among the poor that have focused rather exclusively on survival and securing rudimentary services. In the *colonias populares,* little debate has occurred in the last 20 years on other than individual, or perhaps family and household, levels regarding the Mexican nation and watershed developments like NAFTA. If grassroots leftist politics in the late 1960s in Mexico, as elsewhere, too often neglected daily needs and realities for the masses of working and underemployed poor, the pendulum in the intervening decades has not infrequently been swung to the opposite extreme, as recent popular social movements have customarily ignored current debate on questions of transnationalism and nationalism.

Events such as the Chiapas uprising in 1994 and the presidential elections of 1988 and 1994 have become topics of heated discussion, of course, including as to what these events have to do with Mexico and modernity (see Gutmann, forthcoming). This was especially true in the period around the 1988 elections. Yet fundamental pillars of Mexican nationhood—institutions like the *ejido* lands formerly held in communal trust as well as the state monopoly over basic natural resources and services like oil and telephones—have in this recent period been undermined at home and marketed abroad, all with little organized popular protest, much less rebellion. With the demise of the *ejido* and state ownership of Mexico's inheritance, says Jorge the *tienda* owner in Santo Domingo, "Before long, only tequila, tardiness, and tourist art will carry the 'Made in Mexico' stamp" of authenticity.[13]

There is still a certain desire among many ordinary Mexicans in the cities to defend what they used to regard as the collective project of Mexican sovereignty. Few of my friends and acquaintances are consistent in their feelings and actions in this respect, but most experience at least periodic bouts of anti-Americanism and patriotic fervor.

Guillermo Bonfil Batalla (1992: 175) wrote that past "nationalization of oil, railroads, electricity, and later the banks were historic milestones which reaffirmed our na-

tional sovereignty." Especially in the face of repeated economic crises, most recently the drastic devaluation of the peso in 1994–5, NAFTA is far more than an ideological issue alone. Now, among the other problems heightened by the Agreement, Bonfil Batalla (1992: 167–8) wrote, is that of "cultural penetration, which translates into the imposition of the *american way of life* as a model for Mexican society".[14]

As epitomized by the Free Trade Agreement, domestic elites are selling the country to the highest foreign bidders and making a fortune for themselves in the process.[15] Despite this popular sentiment, or perhaps in part because of it, Claudio Lomnitz (1996: 56) notes, in official venues in Mexico during this same period of crippling crisis and the auctioning off of the national patrimony, the topic of democracy has received "obsessive attention." As part of this discussion on democracy, Lomnitz (1996: 64–6) reports, there occurred "a rift between state and nation" as the state became increasingly identified with "a small and unpopular Americanizing elite who parasitically depends on the Mexican nation" while nationalism itself became differentiated between elite and popular versions.

Whereas the Mexican upper crust has a program for transnational "integration" into a global network headquartered in Washington, DC, Lomnitz (1996: 66) cautions, the majority of the population who seek protection of the state against the global market "has not yet devised a political formula that can simultaneously work in a contested democratic field and provide the kind of state protection that revolutionary nationalism provided."

The issues are complex, involving new and evolving nationalist images in Mexico and international relationships in the global arena, overnight financial catastrophes and fortunes in Mexico, and widespread opposition to Mexican immigration that continues to grow within the United States. Moreover, just as the ideas and cultural goods are reappropriated and reconfigured daily regardless of national origins or original meanings—"LP" in Mexico signifies not only long-playing record but also *"litro de pulque"*[16]—so too can state activities inadvertently and profoundly impact national identities and awareness of international inequalities.[17]

ANGELA'S OIL

In discussing free trade, big shoes, runaway factories, and transnationalism once again with my grandmother's friend Angela, I asked her at one point what her overall impression was of NAFTA.

"It's for the US to get more control of our *petroleo*," she replied.

"Well, I don't want your *petroleo*," I said, trying again to distance myself from the generic *Gringo*.

To this she responded calmly, "*Ni yo lo tengo, tampico* [Nor do I have it, either]."

This resentment is not even particularly novel on the part of those Manual Azuela (1939) called *los fracasados* (the failed). Over 30 years ago, Oscar Lewis (1966: 7) quotes Manuel Sánchez, one of the famous "children of Sanchez," as saying:

> And gasoline, even though it is "ours," eighty *centavos* a liter. *Chingao*, we were better off when the *gringos* and the English had our oil! And now that the government has nationalized electricity, too, wait and see what those bastards are going to pull on us. And there's no stealing it now . . . you're robbing the nation!

In the midst of calls in the 1990s for global trade and international interdependence there is potential for questions regarding transnational democracy and international solidarity. Weary cynicism mixes with periodic and exasperated outbursts on the streets of Colonia Santo Domingo. In the capital city a passionate desire to make sense of the madness of modernity in Mexico is as characteristic of the epoch as ennui. "Many Mexicans now believe the train of modernity has stopped," writes Roger Bartra (1995: 144–5). "Yet this disenchantment and delegitimation seems to be precisely what is opening the door to democracy.

In 1994, for example, in addition to widespread political frustration and confusion in Mexico there was an armed uprising in Chiapas, the assassinations of national politicians, and presidential elections. In Santo Domingo there was, for a few months, an exhilarating sense that popular politics mattered and might just have real consequences for the political fortunes of millions of other Mexicans.[18]

Shortly after New Year's Day 1997, I asked Doña Josefina, whose husband Guillermo had lost his job as a curtain maker "because of NAFTA," what she thought would happen in Mexico in the next few years. As a local leader of the Unión de Colonias Populares (UCP) she felt it necessary to express optimism about the future. But there was also an angry edge to her political forecasting that I had not noticed before during our six years of friendship.

> We're going to be better off. That's what we want and that's what we'll get! If it's peaceful, so much the better. But if it's not peaceful, and if there's an uprising, if nothing else, some things will change. The country will get out of this mess, it can't continue as it is. This is too much already.

"Is it much harder to live today than before?" I asked, thinking of Josefina's early participation in founding the

colonia, her experiences as a domestic servant beginning when she was 13 or 14, her love for reading despite her lack of formal schooling, and how she and Guillermo had eloped after Josefina's stepfather forbade them to marry.

> Yes, it's much harder today. Before, even though we were living in plastic [sheeting for housing], using oil stoves, and sometimes . . . well, actually, most of us had plastic shoes. We didn't have anything, did we? But we protected each other. If someone was sick, we helped them, or they helped us. The area was very nice then.
>
> Even if it was beans, there weren't the pressures as there are now. You can lose your job at any time now. Before, if they fired you they'd still give you some money. Now, no! Now, no contracts, no work, no nothing!
>
> So it's up to us, the *pueblo* [people], whether the change comes peacefully or in another way. But we've got to change. Having a country like Mexico and a legacy of those who struggled before us, how could we continue with the way things are? Things cannot continue as they are.

NOTES

1. Fieldwork was conducted in 1992–3, with grants from Fulbright-Hays DDRA, Wenner-Gren, National Science Foundation, Institute for Intercultural Studies, UC MEXUS, and the Center for Latin American Studies and Department of Anthropology at UC Berkeley, and 1993–5, under a grant from the National Institute for Mental Health. My gratitude to the Centro de Estudios Sociológicos and the Programa Interdisciplinario de Estudios de la Mujer, both at El Colegio de México, and to the Departmento de Antropología, Universidad Autónoma Metropolitana-Iztapalapa, for providing institutional support during fieldwork in Mexico City. Thanks also to Claudio Lomnitz, Lynn Stephen and Thomas Wilson for comments on earlier versions of this article, and to John Gledhill for graciously accepting my endless excuses for not expanding it sooner.

2. In correspondence from Taco Bell International on 14 January 1998, I was informed that although nothing was available in Mexico, franchises were for sale elsewhere in Latin America, including in Chile, Costa Rica, the Dominican Republic, Ecuador, Guatemala, Honduras, Peru and Puerto Rico.

3. This article is thus meant to contribute to the emerging study of national culture and modernity in Mexico, for example, Claudio Lomnitz's (1996) work on contemporary Mexican nationalism and Florencia Mallon's (1995) exploration of how popular political cultures at the level of villages in Mexico and Peru interacted with regional and national arenas to construct national politics in the 19th century.

4. Jaime Serra Puche was formerly Mexico's Secretario de Comercio y Fomento Industrial, roughly equivalent to the Commerce Secretary in the United States. As indicated by his quest to engage with "the challenge of interdependence," Serra

Puche was an outspoken proponent of NAFTA in Mexico in the early 1990s.

5. BANRURAL is the Banco Nacional de Crédito Rural, the National Rural Credit Bank.

6. Guerrero's coast includes the resort areas of Acapulco, Ixtapa and Zihuatenejo.

7. During a conference for US scholars at the Chapultepec Castle in 1992, I was asked by then-US Cultural Attaché, John Dwyer, "Do you know the history of this place?" I replied, "You mean the Niños Héroes?" I was referring to Mexican military cadets who, in 1847, died defending the Castle from an invading army led by US General Winfield Scott. Dwyer slapped me lightly on the shoulder and said, "No, not *that* history." It turned out he had been referring to the Peace Accords signed at the Castle by government and guerrilla forces from El Salvador on New Year's Eve 1991.

8. On recent social movements in the region, see especially Alvarez et al. (1998), Eckstein (1989), Escobar and Alvarez (1992), Foweraker and Craig (1990), Massolo (1992).

9. See Ramos (1962), Paz (1961), Aguilar Camiín (1989), Monsiváis (1981), Bartra (1989, 1992), Lomnitz (1992, 1994).

10. The fact that the DEA is known in Mexico popularly by its acronym alone is an indication of the extent of its disrepute in Mexico.

11. Suspicions like this concerning North Americans are widespread among people in Latin America. Several acquaintances in Mexico City who are political *militantes* have asked me, "Is there anything in your publications that the CIA can learn from?" Such concerns reflect an awareness of extensive covert activities by US agents throughout the continent as much as unwarranted paranoia. For another typical CIA allegation, this one in Nicaragua in the late 1980s, see Lancaster (1992: 75–7).

12. On Solidaridad/PRONASOL's short-term infrastructure-building without long-term jobs creation, see Cornelius et al. (1994), Lustig (1994) and Dresser (1994).

13. *"Muy pronto sólo lleverán el sello 'Hecho en México' el tequila, la tardanza y los Mexican curios."*

14. Emphasis and orthography in English in original.

15. Lest we be tempted to overestimate the novelty of globalization and transnationalism, a commentary from 150 years ago:

> The bourgeoisie has through its exploitation of the world-market given a cosmopolitan character to production and consumption in every country. To the great chagrin of Reactionists, it has drawn from under the feet of industry the national ground on which it stood. All old national industries have been destroyed or are daily being destroyed . . . In place of old wants, satisfied by the productions of the country, we find new wants, requiring for their satisfaction the products of distant lands and climes. In place of the old local and national seclusion and self-sufficiency, we have intercourse in every direction, universal inter-dependence of nations. (Marx and Engels, 1969: 112)

16. A liter of *pulque,* an alcoholic beverage made from the sap of the maguey.

17. Cook (1994) discusses these issues in relation to the globalization of social movements.

18. For more on popular political culture, elections, and democracy see Gutmann (2002). For more on politics and identity in daily life in *colonias populares* in Mexico City, see Massolo (1992) and Díaz-Barriga (1998).

REFERENCES

Aguilar Camín, Héctor, ed. (1989). *En torno a la cultura nacional.* Mexico City: Consejo Nacional para la Cultura y las Artes and Instituto Nacional Indigenista. (Orig. 1976.)

Alvarez, Sonia E., Evelina Dagnino and Arturo Escobar, eds. (1998). *Cultures of Politics/Politics of Cultures: Revisioning Latin American Social Movements.* Boulder, CO: Westview Press.

Azuela, Manuel (1939). *Los fracasados.* Mexico City: Ediciones Botas.

Barkin, David. (1991). *Un desarrollo distorsionado: La integración de México a la economía mundial.* Mexico City: Siglo Veintiuno.

Bartra, Roger. (1989). "Culture and Political Power in Mexico," *Latin American Perspectives* 16(2): 61–9.

Bartra, Roger. (1992). *The Cage of Melancholy: Identity and Metamorphosis in the Mexican Character,* trans. Christopher J. Hall. New Brunswick: Rutgers University Press. (Orig. 1987.)

Bartra, Roger. (1995). "South of the Border: Mexican Reflections on Distorted Images," *Telos* 103: 143–8.

Benería, Lourdes. (1992). "The Mexican Debt Crisis: Restructuring the Economy and the Household," in Lourdes Benería and Shelley Feldman (eds.) *Unequal Burden: Economic Crises, Persistent Poverty, and Women's Work,* pp. 83–104. Boulder, CO: Westview Press.

Bonfil Batalla, Guillermo. (1992). "Dimensions culturales del Tratado de Libre Comercio," in Gilberto Guevara Niebla and Nestór García Canclini (eds.) *La educacíon y la cultura ante el Tratado de Libre Comercio,* pp. 157–78. Mexico City: Nexos/Nueva Imagen.

California Chamber of Commerce and California Trade and Commerce Agency. (1993). *North American Free Trade Guide: The Emerging Mexican Market and Opportunities in Canada under NAFTA: Creating Jobs Through Trade.* La Jolla, CA: Center for US-Mexico Studies.

Cook, Maria Lorena. (1994). "Regional Integration and Transnational Politics: The North American Free Trade Agreement and Popular Sector Strategies in Mexico (DRAFT)," paper presented at Latin American Studies Association Congress, Atlanta, 10–12 March.

Cornelius, Wayne A., Ann L. Craig and Jonathan Fox. (1994). "Mexico's National Solidarity Program: An Overview," in Wayne A. Cornelius, Ann L. Craig and Jonathan Fox (eds.) *Transforming State-Society Relations in Mexico: The National Solidarity Strategy,* pp. 3–26. La Jolla, CA: Center for US-Mexico Studies.

Díaz-Barriga, Miguel. (1998). "Beyond the Domestic and the Public: *Colonas* Participation in Urban Movements in Mexico City," in Sonia E. Alverez, Evelina Dagnino and Arturo Escobar (eds.) *Cultures of Politics/Politics of Cultures: Revisioning Latin American Social Movements,* pp. 252–77. Boulder, CO: Westview Press.

Dillon, Sam. (1996). "Free Trade? Don't Sell Us That," *The New York Times,* 4 August: E-6.

Dresser, Denise. (1994). "Bringing the Poor Back In: National Solidarity as a Strategy of Regime Legitimation," in Wayne A. Cornelius, Ann L. Craig and Jonathan Fox (eds.) *Transforming State-Security Relations in Mexico: the National Solidarity Strategy,* pp. 143–65. La Jolla, CA: Center for US-Mexico Studies.

Eckstein, Susan, ed. (1989) *Power and Popular Protest: Latin American Social Movements.* Berkeley: University of California Press.

Escobar, Arturo and Sonia E. Alvarez, eds. (1992). *The Making of Social Movements in Latin America: Identity, Strategy, and Democracy,* Boulder, CO: Westview Press.

Foweraker, Joe and Ann Craig, eds. (1990). *Popular Movements and Political Change in Mexico,* Boulder, CO: Lynne Rienner.

García Canclini, Néstor. (1992). "Políticas culturales integración norteamericana: Una perspectiva desde México," mss, Universidad Autónoma Metropolitana-Iztapalapa.

Gledhill, John. (1997). "Liberalism, Socio-Economic Rights and the Politics of Identity: From Moral Economy to Indigenous Rights," in Richard A. Wilson (ed.) *Human Rights, Culture and Context: Anthropological Perspectives,* pp. 70–110. London: Pluto.

González de la Rocha, Mercedes. (1991). "Family Well-Being, Food Consumption, and Survival Strategies during Mexico's Economic Crisis," in *Social Responses to Mexico's Economic Crisis of the 1980s,* Mercedes González de la Rocha and Agustín Escobar Latapi (eds.), pp. 115–27. La Jolla, CA: Center for US-Mexican Studies.

González de la Rocha, Mercedes. (1994). *The Resources of Poverty: Women and Survival in a Mexican City.* Oxford: Blackwell.

Gutmann, Matthew C. (1996). *The Meanings of Macho: Being a Man in Mexico City.* Berkeley: University of California Press.

Gutmann, Matthew C. (2002). *The Romance of Democracy: Compliant Defiance in Contemporary Mexico.* Berkeley: University of California Press.

Lancaster, Roger N. (1992). *Life Is Hard: Machismo, Danger, and the Intimacy of Power in Nicaragua.* Berkeley: University of California Press.

Lewis, Oscar. (1966). "A Thursday with Manuel," *New Left Review* 38: 3–21.

Lomnitz, Claudio. (1992). *Exits from the Labyrinth: Culture and Ideology in Mexican National Space.* Berkeley: University of California Press.

Lomnitz, Claudio. (1994). "Decadence in Times of Globalization," *Cultural Anthropology* 9(2): 257–67.

Lomnitz, Claudio. (1996). "Fissures in Contemporary Mexican Nationalism," *Public Culture* 9: 55–68.

Lustig, Nora. (1994). "Solidarity as a Strategy of Poverty Alleviation," in Wayne A. Cornelius, Ann L. Craig, and Jonathan Fox (eds.) *Transforming State-Society Relations in Mexico: The National Solidarity Strategy,* pp. 79–96. La Jolla, CA: Center for US-Mexico Studies.

Mallon, Florencia. (1995). *Peasant and Nation: The Meaning of Postcolonial Mexico and Peru.* Berkeley: University of California Press.

Marx, Karl and Frederick Engels. (1969). "Manifesto of the Communist Party," *Selected Works, Vol. 1,* pp. 98–137. Moscow: Progress Publishers. (Orig. 1847.)

Massolo, Alejandra. (1992). *Por amor y coraje: Mujeres en movimientos urbanos de la ciudad de México.* Mexico City: El Colegio de México.

Monsiváis, Carlos. (1981). "Notas sobre el estado, la cultura nacional y las culturas populares en México," *Cuadernos Políticos* 30: 33–43.

Monsiváis, Carlos. (1992a). "De la cultura mexicana en vísperas del Tratado de Libre Comercio," in Gilberto Guevara Niebla and Néstor García Canclini (eds.) *La educación y la cultura ante el Tratado de Libre Comercio,* pp. 179–209. Mexico City: Nexos/Nueva Imagen.

Monsiváis, Carlos. (1992b). "La identidad nacional ante el espejo," in José Manuel Valenzuela Arce (ed.) *Decadencia y auge de las identidades: Cultura nacional, identidad cultural y modernización,* pp. 67–72. Tijuana: El Colegio de la Frontera Norte.

Paz, Octavio. (1961). *The Labyrinth of Solitude: Life and Thought in Mexico,* trans. Lysander Kemp. New York: Grove. (Orig. 1947.)

Ramos, Samuel. (1962). *Profile of Man and Culture in Mexico,* trans. Peter G. Earle. Austin: University of Texas Press. (Orig. 1934.)

31

Owning Places and Buying Time
Class, Culture, and Stalled Gentrification

Brett Williams

Brett Williams is a professor of anthropology and the director of American studies at American University, Washington, D.C. She received her PhD from the University of Illinois in 1975. Her fieldwork has been done in the United States, among migrant workers of Mexican descent from Texas (see Chapter 8), in a mixed ethnic neighborhood of a northeastern city, and among waitresses. She has also written about Southern folklife and on the African American hero John Henry. Her research interests include poverty, the media, folklore, and politics and culture.

Gentrification allows ethnographers a rare glimpse of the interplay of class and culture in everyday life. But because dramatic displacement generally follows, we seldom find the chance to observe this process in detail. In the last few years, however, economic hard times have stalled gentrification, so that people who may not have intended to be neighbors have come to share problematic communities. They bring to these communities different resources, visions of neighborhood, expectations for neighbors, and patterns of everyday interaction. The limits and opportunities of class shape varied neighborhood traditions at the same time that these traditions stretch and enliven the constraints of class. Stalled gentrification thus makes everyday life a rich arena for exploring the interaction of passions, economics, habits, and ways of carving out a life.

My research, six years of participant-observation and structured interviews, took place in a neighborhood that I will call Elm Valley, where class divisions tend to coincide with renting and owning. A streetcar suburb in a northeastern city, Elm Valley lost many of its white residents in the 1950s and 1960s. After a period when its population was mostly Black American, Elm Valley—like other areas undergoing gentrification—has been rediscovered by white middle-class settlers (Allen, 1980; Goldfield, 1980; Hennig, 1982; McCaffrey, 1982). Other new immi-

grants have come as well, able, because of the city's strict rent control laws, to crowd into small apartments. Today the population of this neighborhood of about 5000 people is approximately 50% Black American, 20% Latin American, 20% white, and 10% immigrants from other parts of the world, especially Southeast Asia, East Africa, and the Caribbean. If the gentrification that began in the mid-1970s had continued, most of the Black owners would have been displaced by higher taxes and pressure from speculators; the tenants, too, would have been forced out by renovations and condominium conversions. Instead, city legislation and high interest rates have, since 1980, stalled gentrification. Thus, Elm Valley is surprisingly diverse, and home ownership crosses lines of race. Black families make up the majority of both owners and renters. Almost all non-Anglo immigrant groups rent, however; and most of the young, newer, white residents own their homes.[1]

In spite of the disruption of gentrification and displacement, the neighborhood might be a model of class and cultural integration. Distinctly bounded by a park and two avenues, it has a lively main street and many small businesses that allow neighbors to build contacts (Jacobs, 1961). The architecture of Elm Valley stresses the front porch, and its wide, deep alleys encourage informal, disclosing interaction from kitchens, around gardens, and over clotheslines out back. Finally, the Black families who bought houses in the 1950s, together with the core of white families who chose to stay, have given Elm Valley an unusual cross-racial bridge that until recently stretched out a tradition of civic activism.[2]

"Owning Places and Buying Time: Class, Culture, and Stalled Gentrification" by Brett Williams from *Journal of Contemporary Ethnography* (formerly *Urban Life*), October 1985, Vol. 14, No. 3, pp. 251–273. Reprinted by permission of Sage Publications, Inc.

These neighborhood qualities have shaped passionate attachments to Elm Valley, but with gentrification these attachments have failed to cross the barriers of social class. Neighborhoodwide organization has folded after 100 years. New owners wage an escalating memo and bulletin war against the men on the street. In the large apartment buildings that preserve Elm Valley's class diversity, tenants discriminate among themselves as they negotiate with their landlords about renovation and control. Elm Valley is a crumbling community of lost possibilities, even though people there are trying to resist chaotic change and take control of their lives. Yet they bring to these efforts disparate, sometimes distracting visions of neighborhood and of neighbors. This article explores the conflicts that have erupted from those perceptions, as well as the clues those conflicts hold to the interaction of class and culture.

RENTERS FACING OWNERS

On one block in Elm Valley a large dilapidated apartment building that I call The Manor faces attractive rowhouses across the street. Renters and owners do not enter one another's homes, but looking across the street allows them glimpses of others' lives. Renters see owners engaged in optional, honorable tasks such as carpentry, painting, and gardening. This renovation and tinkering ironically mirrors the deterioration of The Manor. In addition, most of [the] tenants' domestic duties are defensive, fighting back filth in their overcrowded apartments. When families postpone washing dishes, let food sit out overnight, or fail to mop their floors after meals, they invite pests that are especially problematic if the families sleep where they eat. Many one-bedroom apartments shelter from four to a dozen people, who sleep in the living/dining room area and, for example, store their shoes under the coffee table. Such intensive use means recleaning the same small space each day to reap the largely negative rewards of relatively fewer roaches and mice. The puttering, *offensive* tasks renters observe across the street cast these circumstances into sharp relief.

These same tasks also signal to tenants owners' control over the physical facades of their houses. By contrast, tenants feel strongly their own lack of control over a facade. For example, they are not allowed to use the grass in front of their building to play games or mind children. If they do, the resident manager may emerge from the building with a shrill public reprimand. This lack of control is obvious in other ways as well. Tenants would like a say about such strategic decisions as installing a security system, controlling pests, permanently repairing the elevator and the boiler. Many feel at the mercy of machines that swallow money more reliably than they dispense goods and services. The erratic support system of The Manor makes everyday life a gamble: A person might return home loaded with groceries and a child in a stroller to discover a broken elevator and face a four-floor walkup, or put off washing his or her hair until morning only to find that there will be no hot water for three days. The laundryroom is a source of special indignities; residents have to stand in line for the few machines that work, jealously defend their places between loads, and negotiate the treacherous transition from washers to even scarcer, often cold driers.

Even when tenants are inside their apartments, conversations and quarrels, the smell of meals, and the sounds of music and television seep through the walls and out into the halls; embarrassing substances drip through the floors and ceilings. As one woman put it, "I know everybody hears our little family things." And they did: This woman's husband was a notorious drinker who enjoyed playing Dr. King's "I Have a Dream" speech at top volume when high. Other families' secrets erupted as well, as a bathtub might overflow, smoke filter out, or a woman chase her husband into the hall.

Finally, tenants find telling the places where they see owners—outdoors but in charge, on their porches, in their yards, shovelling the snow from a small patch of sidewalk. These transitional spaces highlight the easy movement outdoors and back inside that tenants lack, for they must negotiate buffer zones such as hallways, elevators, and stairwells. Although they enjoy meeting neighbors in these places, tenants feel vulnerable there as well (Jacobs, 1961; Reed, 1974). The annexes to a house also bear witness to greater space inside (which families can use to separate eating, sleeping, and recreational activities), and to a more negotiable domestic organization (as families can divide themselves up in ways that parents who must lug small children with them to the laundry room cannot). Thus, these glimpses of owners' lives reflect varied features of life in a house and the rights and privileges that accompany owning one: easy access, choices about tasks and companions, negotiable space, taking the domestic offensive, and orchestrating a flexible family.

When owners look across the street at the dwellings of tenants, they see an impersonal shared facade with no options for outdoor tasks beyond fixing and washing cars. Some complain that the building blocks the sun. Some comment on what they consider to be an astonishing parade of foot traffic and a great deal of hauling. Rather than cars, most tenants depend on the multipurpose pull-along cart that is a centerpiece of low-income urban life. Those tenants who prefer the public laundromat to The Manor's whimsical machines join others who tow groceries and small children. All of these sights seem embarrassing as they testify to a less-controlled presentation of self, a perception shared by some tenants who complain about having to display their dirty laundry and who line their carts with plastic garbage bags to preserve what privacy they can. Finally, from the vantage point of owners, renters seem to engage in widespread, inappropriate use of the outside, a matter at the center of conflict in Elm Valley. Because owners know little beyond what they see at places like The Manor, the people who use the street seem to have become emblematic of renters. Their activities outdoors testify to contrasting strategies for living in a neighborhood.

THE WORK OF THE STREET

Elm Valley's tenants choose tremendous financial sacrifice to stay in a neighborhood they prefer to those suburbs rapidly swelling with the displaced poor. Some do not see this as a choice, citing the "time and trouble it takes to move" or "the money we'd spend commuting back into town," and claiming "I'd be back over here every day anyway." Others, however, are explicit about opting for a neighborhood. What I will call "the work of the street" reflects, encourages, and rewards that decision to stay.

The work of the street reflects in part the small, hot apartments, in which people feel they cannot entertain, and the sparse financial resources that prevent renters from traveling freely. Although women use the street freely during the day, and although there are women on the street and linked to the street at night as well, they do not gather there in the clear and dramatic ways that men do. Their networking strategies seem more varied and more likely to be inside, whether at work, at church, or inside their buildings. The work of the street seems to be largely the preserve of men.

On the street men bolster family economies. They network and they pool. They swap services such as rides, repairs, and hauling; exchange goods such as clothing, small appliances, furniture, food stamps, and things from work such as crabs, tostados, pesticides, and cleaning fluids. Men often trade goods for favors—souse meat or "gas money" for a ride; pirated or home-grown vegetables for babysitting; playing a number in exchange for "a taste"; help with moving in exchange for a crib; homemade soup for a watch. Sometimes men organize small cooperatives for a trip to a suburban farmers' market to shop in bulk. The pooling and swapping that is so important to the poor and so often the concern of women is in this situation an activity that men also share.

Some men earn their living by streetwork. One man owns a truck, which he uses for harvesting the surplus vegetables of suburban gardeners, moving furniture, delivering appliances, and salvaging trees to sell for firewood. Another man sells dresses, coats, and jewelry on the street and is generally available there to sweep and run errands for shopkeepers, help mind children for passersby, or deliver them to nursery school. Men like these two are conscientious and self-conscious custodians of the street, keeping careful track of what goes on during the day and often sharing information and delivering messages and warnings.

Other men do not live from streetwork but look to it to solve routine problems: to find information about a city bureaucracy, to look for jobs, to have appliances repaired, to locate help with moving, to fill ordinary, everyday needs. The street as *work* looms large in family negotiations; men stress its financial benefits when they bargain for time away from their homes: "I have to try to run into Ben so that I can tell him Maria needs firewood"; "I have to deliver these greens to Harper so that I can tell Jimmy to come around and fix the stereo"; "How do you expect me to find a job if you won't let me go to the tavern?" But the men of Elm Valley, like their counterparts in other cities, love the street (Hannerz, 1969; Liebow, 1967; Suttles, 1968; Williams, 1981). It is fruitless to untangle the financial benefits of streetwork from the other attractions of streetlife, and the men of Elm Valley would not do that, for finances are interwoven with a great deal of trust and talk, lasting social relationships, and the detailed knowledge that works just as well to manage stigma as to cook up deals.

In the intricate world of the street men do all they can to understand the details of one another's biographies. Because they memorize others' reputations, they tolerate a great deal of deviance and diversity. I was first struck by this early one morning when a slightly tipsy man approached me with a big sharp chisel. I was grateful when another man chorused, "Just getting off work, Curly?" and proceeded to tell me that Curly worked all night cleaning and repairing office buildings. I particularly appreciated this exchange because the second man had tried to make me feel safe on the street, but there are many other examples. One man is well liked but known to be a pickpocket; those whose pockets he picks generally blame themselves because they know, and know that he knows they know he does that. Another man is known as a soft touch but a terror "when he's drinking," yet another as a soft touch when he's drinking. Others are known to be "not drinking," a personal career linked to problems of health, family conflict, alcoholism, or probation.

The street is also an arena for preserving the culture of the Carolinas, through foodways (souse meat, greens, and many parts of the pig, including tails, ears, and knuckles); remedies (junction weed boiled with a penny for chicken pox, wild onion roots boiled with butter and Calvert whiskey for a cold, ear wax for chapped lips); expressions (to be pleasantly tipsy on Calvert is to be "high as a Georgia pine"). Men also identify real friends as "from Carolina" or "from my home town." On the street they share urban lore as well, organizing complicated neighborhood lotteries around football games, sharing stories about the numbers, playing strategies, lucky wins, narrow losses ("That's how the numbers get you"). Many residents agree that the more dire their straits, the more obliged they are to play. Beyond financial possibilities, however, numbers strategies and lore are much more than work; one's regular number, evolving tactics for choosing one and deciding where to play it, biography of wins and narrow losses are important parts of personal identity. Each person is a complex weave of vivid everyday detail acted out on the street.

The world of the street draws in its shopkeepers and muddles divisions between shopper and seller. One man, for example, claims that in 18 years he has done no shopping outside Elm Valley. He has long-term relationships with some of the older shopkeepers, relations which may involve credit or part-time employment. As new stores open, he entrenches himself in each, coming to be known by name and to entangle and complicate relationships, crossing all the usual boundaries of urban consumption. He arranges layaway at the drugstore, barter at the thrift shop (whose owner watches for and saves clothes that fit him and his family), charitable contributions for his children's nursery school from the new grocery store. He defines his needs so that they can be satisfied in Elm Valley and then redefines and stretches what it offers.

It is on the street that we see most clearly the passion for texture that is central to the renters' neighborhood world, a passion that emerges from the interplay of financial constraints and cultural traditions. This passion for texture is much like the thick description valued by folklorists and ethnographers (see Geertz, 1973). It includes a decided preference for depth over breadth, an interest in rich, vivid, personal, concrete, entangled detail. It involves repetition, density, mining a situation from many faces and angles. A joke, a story, a teasing line can be retold and rephrased many times, as long as the emphasis varies just slightly. Inside apartments I saw a love of texture in a desire to fill empty spaces with artifacts and objects and to manage the density of domestic life by weaving through it the sounds and colors and rhythms of television. It emerged in renters' interest in programs such as *Dallas* and *Dynasty*, which offer vivid, concrete, detailed entanglements. It is clear in many residents' preference for local over national news, for stories that can be followed from beginning to end. It is clearest on the street in the intimate knowledge men build of one another, in the

ways that roles, institutions, and relationships are complicated and rewoven, the formal and informal sectors muddled, interaction intimate and multifaceted.

THE METROPOLITAN VISION

Owners have also chosen a community in the face of other options. New owners' reasons for choosing Elm Valley vary. Some like the convenient commute, but keep more cosmopolitan personal attachments; some are fond of the lovely streetscapes and fine, historic architecture; some are nostalgic, even utopian in their hope of rooting themselves in an old-fashioned urban neighborhood; some are activists tackling international problems there. Many value the personal growth that they feel accompanies confronting diversity. Their perceptions of neighborhood life generally differ from those of renters, and these perceptions again reflect some of the complex class cultures, including varied resources for travel and indoor activities as well as radically different visions of what a neighborhood offers and how it should be used.[3] Looking at some of [the] owners' strategies for handling family needs should make this difference clear.

As a result of stalled residential gentrification, the commercial gentrification of Elm Valley is also incomplete (see Hennig, 1982). Although the commercial strip boasts an art and an antique store, there is no PLANTS, Etc. or California Café. Thrift shops, dry cleaners, and liquor stores rely on large numbers of clients rather than wealthy ones. Most owners find them uninteresting and inadequate and therefore shop outside the neighborhood, often while driving to and from work.

For child enrichment, many owners look outside Elm Valley for pools, schools, playgrounds, violin and ballet lessons. Few owners avoid the neighborhood completely; most use mixed strategies.[4] One woman, for example, devoted many hours of volunteer time to a local nursery school, for she felt that it offered her daughter an important multicultural experience. Now, however, she sends her child to elementary school outside the neighborhood. A strong advocate of hiring local people for domestic work, repairs, and childcare, she shops in remote parts of the metropolitan area and does not walk through Elm Valley because she considers it unsafe. (To some extent gender crosscuts class in limiting women's movement at night; however, cars do provide shells of sorts for metropolitan travel for those who own them.)

Another woman, active in a bid to have Elm Valley named a historic district, has led a fight to stop the local Korean grocery store from placing advertising leaflets under windshield wipers. It developed during a meeting on the topic that she had no idea that this store underpriced local supermarket chains, or that the owner had hired all local workers ("winos" in some versions) to cement neighborhood relations. It had not occurred to her to shop there. Her assumptions would be incomprehensible to many tenants; they had learned as much as they could about the new store as soon as it had opened, in part through the new workers, who gave the owners an immediate pipeline to the street.

Other owners juggle buffering and involvement in a number of ways; but strategies that may be appropriate for families can create problems for the community. Elm Valley already houses institutions inherently segregated by class: buses, church basement daycare centers, laundromats. Other places that might jumble people across class lines and encourage small contacts are segregated by default (see Jacobs, 1961; Love, 1973; Merry, 1980, 1981; Molotch, 1969). These range from the local elementary school to shops, taverns, and parks. That owners leave the neighborhood to find more elaborate toddler parks is especially hard on female tenants with small children. Women work parks to build contacts with other parents so that they can organize play groups, carpools, babysitting coops, birthday parties and everyday friendships (see Swartley, 1983). Most women are wary of Elm Valley's one rather inadequate park, which therefore remains in the hands of men, many of whom do take their children there, but most of whom hardly need another arena for building contacts.

Thus, the greater financial resources, shopping, and child enrichment strategies as well as the more metropolitan vision of many new owners deprive them of access to the street. To just hint at the complex interplay of race, ethnicity, and residence here, the more extended and established Black households are nearly always tied through at least one male member to the street. The few longer-term white residents of Elm Valley either work the streets or the alleys. Those tenants in group houses or small apartments, even if they are white and new to Elm Valley, are less likely to own cars, more likely to walk and to know at least some of the shopkeepers who are tied into street talk. But few of the newer white owners pursue these arenas.[5]

"HOW CAN WE GET THE BUMS OFF THE STREET?"

The various groups involved perceive one another's strategies differently. One day several men prominent on the street explained their vision of the situation: The newer owners are different from the older, "racial whites," who are "stuck in (Elm Valley) with its cheap beers and cheap (Black people) because they're too old or too poor to move." The newer residents "move in but don't associate." In part they may be afraid: "They hear a lot of garbage when they go outside the neighborhood to associate." This "garbage" is not challenged because those who hear it do not get to know the details of their neighbors' personalities. But mostly they do not associate because "they just don't know how—they weren't raised up that way." Although these men feel strongly that the newer residents should "learn how to speak on the street," their assessment is fairly benign in its stress on cultural background.

Their attention to detail also contributes to these men's feelings about the new owners. Some of the men on the street cite neighborhood history as a reason to feel benign: Whites have always lived in Elm Valley; integration was fairly painless; prejudiced individuals stand out and can be known. Some of these individuals, however, are regarded with affection simply because they are known. For example, one of the tavern owners is an 82-year-old native Kentuckian who freely uses racial epithets, organized hard for John Connally's presidential campaign, and tries to persuade Blacks that they should support the party of Lincoln. She is widely considered a cheap and temperamental employer and a vindictive, erratic hostess. Nonetheless, many details of her life are known: her concern for alcoholics; her personal rescue of a popular retarded man; the joy she takes in children. (Her case demonstrates, I believe, the extent to which a passion for detail and texture is ultimately a forgiving world view.)

Other men cite the fallout effects of class privilege as grounds for their relatively benign feelings toward the new owners. Property owners demand and receive decent city services, so that Elm Valley's streets, traffic lights, and curbs are better repaired and its trash more reliably hauled away than in the past. New owners also bring volunteer time, money, and knowledge to neighborhood activities; they organize block parties, renovate the local library, and heal the elm trees.[6]

Owners for the most part do not reciprocate this good will; their feelings seem to vary from indifference to tolerance or compassion to vague unease or active dislike. They lack many of the tenants' inclinations to build detailed cross-class portraits: Tenants (and certainly not the men on the street) do not bring tangible class resources into Elm Valley life; new owners do not call on neighborhood memories in evaluating biographies; many have a broader, more metropolitan vision rather than an eye for local detail. In any event, new owners are not often motivated to explore the texture of Elm Valley life. Their feelings toward tenants in general are not at issue here; my concern, like theirs, is the way in which some owners' more extreme feelings about the men on the street (as standing for tenants) are splitting Elm Valley apart.

Late in 1983 a cluster of angry residents organized a committee they called "Elm Valley's Corridor Committee." During their early months they distributed memos and handbills attacking the men on the street and citing particular abuses such as loitering, littering, drinking and using profanity. "What can we do about public urination?" queried one flier. Eventually this group circulated a letter to Elm Valley households with a list of demands, including one for foot patrols with guard dogs.

The city's charter establishes for each neighborhood an elected neighborhood council, composed of five members representing small districts within the neighborhood. Hearing murmurs of support for the Corridor Committee, this council invited city officials to a public meeting to air the complaints. The Corridor Committee's chair set the tone, asking in her introductory remarks, "How can we get the bums off the street?"

The committee's paper war had gone unnoticed by tenants, for it occurred outside the social system of personal exposure and talk which they see as structuring neighborhood life. The meeting was another matter. Few tenants attended, for they feel that the neighborhood council is a property owners' preserve. What most considered to be the vicious contents of the letter, however, had leaked out. Several of the more central and flamboyant men from the street therefore attended the meeting out of anger and curiosity. Also, the more politically active but usually distracted residents came to argue against what they saw as racist rabble-rousing, as did some of the men from established Black households with ties to the street. For the first time Elm Valley had a forum where people could talk and interpret acts across class.

At the meeting the owners made momentary alliance with feminists who did not want to be harassed on the street. Trying to reconcile these two interests, a white renter who also works as a nursery school social worker suggested that when walking the street a person "salute each man." She argued that the men on the street feel that they make it safer, because they watch out for their friends and they also know what goes on. They know who is likely to mug, and after the mugging they will hear about it. Some of the Black householders commented that outdoor toilets might address the public urination problem and that large trash cans might help with litter. A Latino leader argued that the men on the street "don't have homes." The only man to talk from the street complained that "the police always come down on us but not the Spanish people." The outcome of this long, angry and complicated meeting was the triumph of a liberal solution: Elected officials repeated their reluctance to "enforce manners"; the police chief cited "people's right to use the street"; beat officers explained the difficult logis-

tics of arresting someone urinating outdoors; and the council was charged to explore available social services.

The wide appeal of the Corridor Committee is puzzling, however, especially since it grew among people who had chosen to live in a varied urban community. To some extent class cultures can help to explain this appeal: We have seen that the interplay between traditions and resources that expresses class cultures encourages owners to choose breadth over depth in everyday life. The virtues of this choice are obvious, as these families preserve access to those facilities that they feel enrich and broaden their lives, and that offer them continuing advantages in school and at work. Yet probing for depth, texture, and intricacy seems to be a more successful strategy than buffering and juggling density if one wants to carve out a comfortable life in Elm Valley. Grasping the neighborhood's texture depends on a rich public life of inspection and exposure for at least the male members of renting families. Yet this occasion for building and exploring texture stigmatizes those who have figured out how well it works to build a community.

"YOUR BUILDING IS GOING DOWN, DOWN . . ."

The second arena of conflict is between landlords and renters irritated by the deterioration of their buildings. The Manor provides one example: A network of women tenants began to organize in winter, a time of intense sociability within the building and a time when tenants felt the building's problems more harshly. The women were angry about the malfunctioning machines, the erratic heat and hot water, and especially concerned about the stairs and hallways, which were emerging as popular places to socialize, smoke, and drink. They initiated a campaign of petition signing and letter writing. The most telling feature of the women's written complaints was the way they were framed. These frames reveal a sense of having paid with rent money and time for a home, a place where one belongs and feels secure. These women added a moral dimension as they called up a relationship between building a home and the kinds of people they are. They cited personal qualities to legitimize their requests. For example, each woman noted in her letter how long she had lived in The Manor: "I have lived here for 18 years," or "This is the first time in 13 years I have had to complain," or "We have been here 8½ years and have cooperated with the Agency in every way." This matter of ethos seems crucial in legitimizing their demands. The women asked for more say about transitional places and the mechanical support system. Their demands did not appeal to universal human rights or even to local law. They demanded particular privileges because they were particular sorts of people: moral, concerned, and settled. Ironically, the glimpses they have managed of owners' lives seem to have encouraged them to identify with owners as a kind of people.[7]

These personal letters offered details of the women's everyday lives ("I am often home alone in the afternoons and it is very cold") and tried out names rumored to attach to officers of the management corporation. The corporation response, however, was a less personal, masterful mass memo. Beginning "Dear Tenant," it mentioned the tenants' complaints as well as the grievances of owners across the street about litter on the lawn. It grouped hallways, stairwells, the laundry room, and the lawn as "public areas," and used them as evidence that tenants of the Manor were *not* like homeowners after all: They dumped trash on the floor, they left graffiti in the laundry room, they used the stairwell as a bathroom. Tenants should improve themselves, for "It's your home." Lumping all tenants denies the exceptional homeowning qualities the women attributed to themselves. The message is that these kinds of discriminations are inappropriate; while the women had invoked the cultural attributes surrounding connections and commitments to a place, management responded by lumping them by class.

Tenants offered varied explanations for the rapid and distressing decline of the building. One theory held that management was allowing it to deteriorate on purpose so that long-term tenants would leave. Turnovers allowed the landlords to raise rents; and if the building deteriorated enough to be condemned, the owners could gut it and convert into condominiums. Few of the renters believed that management would collaborate in the building's decline; many felt that owners would want to keep homeowning-like people in the building and would certainly want to keep the property up.

Another view suggested that a recent change in resident managers was responsible. Like many other mediators, resident managers give owners a face; they personalize landlords to tenants at the same time that they are known as tenants themselves. In theory they are neutral and fairly powerless mediators, there as go-betweens for owners and tenants to everyone's mutual benefit. In practice they are rarely neutral enough to jeopardize their jobs. As one manager put it (in response to a tenant's complaint that his negligence had meant that her friend's ceiling had collapsed and almost killed a baby), "I only got one friend and that's the man who gave me my job."

This manager, Mr. Ironsides, was a problem drinker who rarely responded to tenant requests for repairs. Coincident with stalled gentrification and the movement of Latino tenants into the building, he had died. He was replaced by a woman who proved to be competent and prompt at managing repairs. Mysteriously, tenants began to mutter within a few weeks that she was "too nice," "too weak," and "too soft." Mr. Ironsides reemerged in the public memory as a hero, a man who "roamed the halls with a blackjack" keeping order. Ms. Johnson's unpopularity was partly a matter of timing and partly a matter of gender. Some of the hostility reflected ethnicity—a Jamaican labeled "African" by the custodial staff, she was seen as too lenient toward other "foreigners." This hostility that Black renters felt toward her illuminates the third divisive arena in Elm Valley.

"THE DO DROP IN" OR HOME AS SANCTUARY

Many Black renters placed the bulk of the blame for the building's problems on the "Spanish people," a half-dozen extended families recently arrived from El Salvador. The complaints of women and men tenants against these families varied in revealing ways. Women tenants complained many times that "Spanish people use the hall like a porch." The young men liked to congregate in the halls, and they often failed to manage the stigma of public life in time-honored local ways, for example, by moving discreetly away from a woman approaching or by offering a wholesome-sounding greeting to signal benevolent intent. In addition, they cheerfully broke bothersome rules: One group, for example, simply commandeered the service elevator whenever the one designated for tenants was stuck somewhere else.

Most striking about Black women's antagonisms toward these young Latino men, however, was their use of labels emphasizing ethnicity rather than gender and age. Most of us are leery of groups of young men hovering in an ambiguous place, but what tenants stressed in encoding these groups was that they were "Spanish." Perhaps the stress on ethnicity reflected Latino families' general transformations of domestic life space. As large, extended families in desperate straits, they crowded many people into their small apartments. Other tenants claimed that "one might sign the lease and then they sneak all kinds of others in." Not knowing exactly who or how many occupied a unit disoriented other tenants, and their confusion was compounded by irritation at the efficient dispersal of Latino family members to manage tasks such as laundry. Those tenants who had developed ways to beat the laundry room rush soon found that there was never a time when several elderly Latinas were not in the laundry room minding infants and washing many loads of clothes. Even more annoying was the houselike use to which Latino families transformed their apartments. On two floors domestic networks spread out over several apartments, but because they shared many tasks and responsibilities, the families flowed between these units, left their doors open, and encouraged their children to play in the halls. They did, in fact, use the hall as a porch.

A hall is the closest thing to a porch that tenants have. It is an important transitional area for storing trash on the way to the trash room, packing urban carts, and chatting. Informal dress and even night clothes seem to be acceptable in the hall (see Reed, 1974). Latino families were drawing a fairly appropriate analogy between hall and porch that was consistent with the living arrangements most had known at home. But to other tenants this use of the hall as porch highlighted all its contradictions: This great, shared, indoor porch in which there was neither privacy nor say so demanded some sort of cooperation in limiting interaction. Families who used it detracted from others' right to have it not used.

Women saw these behaviors as proof that the Latino tenants were not like homeowners. Some were concerned about the preponderance of men in these families, and argued, "Women make an apartment more like a home." Others stressed transiency: "They think this is the 'Do Drop In,' they're like college students; they don't care about keeping it up because they don't want to make it a home."

Men phrased the problem a little differently. Many male tenants felt that Latinos "use the hall like the street," and that they did not make the appropriate overtures for sharing public space. In turn, they attributed all anonymous troubles to Latinos, including the trash room fires that grew common during the winter of 1983 and one episode in which 50 tires were slashed. As one man put it, "Spanish people only come out at night, because they think they're white then. Black people do what they want during the day."

There is an irony in this process that seems to parallel what is happening outdoors. Black renters' passion for texture and detail is thwarted by a language and set of customs they do not understand. Most of the refugees define home differently than Elm Valley's long-term tenants because they have radically different priorities for it. Many want to offer shelter to fellow refugees and, in fact, to use the promise of shelter to encourage kin and friends to migrate. They are not so interested in keeping up the property or necessarily in building ties. They want to use home as a sanctuary. Even those who may want more privacy soon face a choice between cutting off fellow refugees and doubling up. Their desperation has created scenes in several apartments featuring rows of cots and numbers of depressed and displaced people.

None of these things is particularly clear to other tenants, who know little of the circumstances in Central America that have propelled these refugees north. The theory they have built to explain The Manor's decline relies heavily on the immediate and concrete details of building life that they can observe every day. Whenever one family moves out, it is replaced by another of lesser quality. This gradual substitution of good tenants by worse ones means that the building inevitably deteriorates. Management is complicit "because they don't screen new tenants," but the problem is essentially one of tenant mobility. If tenants move out, there is likely to be something wrong with the building anyway; those who come in are by definition not settled or committed, and if they are willing to move into a declining building, they are doubly suspect. Speaking a different language and bringing culturally distinct and inappropriate traditions for inhabiting space further complicate the problem. In The Manor women argue that by settling in and taking an active, moral interest in a building one can act like a homeowner. This ethos then frames the rhetoric through which they demanded particular privileges and services. The frame turns out to be a divisive one that leads to blaming other tenants for problems with the landlord and for the decline of the building.

CONCLUSION

Stalled gentrification brings together residents who ordinarily would not be neighbors and who have disparate options, constraints, perceptions, and traditions that are expressed in varied, easily misunderstood strategies for urban life. New owners buy a piece of a place and feel that through property they have put down roots in the community. Acquiring the responsibility and concerns attached to property values makes them less sympathetic to the men on the street, who seem to endanger those things. Their more cosmopolitan attachments and broader visions place them to some extent outside Elm Valley's cultural system.

Unable to buy houses, Elm Valley's renters have bought time and used that time to dig in and build ties. Entangled in a rich weave of local ethnographic detail, renters have expressed their anger over the threat of displacement in part through efforts to align themselves with the qualities that seem to characterize owners: settledness, commitment, connections, control. They have thus built difficult divisions among themselves. Owners distance themselves from the characteristics that seem to stick to renters: inappropriate display, misuse of public space and time, immersion in immediate time and place.

Ironically, a rich, diverse community with many possibilities for truly intricate integration is torn apart by conflicts rooted in the constraints of class, the traditions through which people link themselves to ethnic and racial groups, and the playing out of those constraints and traditions in everyday life strategies.

NOTES

1. For many reasons that will become apparent, the name of this neighborhood is a pseudonym: the location disguised, the statistics rounded out, and the description of my research abbreviated. The research has involved a complicated constellation of residential patterns and community organizing activities as well as formal research strategies such as taped interviews and participant observation. Because I was the mother of two infants during the research, I have been worried about distorted findings, particularly regarding male-female relations and in describing such arenas as the laundry room. I have found Rosaldo's (1984) discussion of "the positioned observer" reassuring.

2. Some of these friendships continue on the integrated residential blocks. Because they are cross-racial and longstanding, they are an important kind of neighborhood glue.

3. To stress the circumstances of renting and owning is not to deny the importance of race and ethnicity. There is some evidence that the passion for texture has deep roots in Black culture, seen, for example, in urban street epics, children's clapping, rhyming and jumprope games, and blues music. The circumstances of renting thus encourage and bolster the emergence of a cultural form that has been expressed in other times, places, and media as well. It is significant in Elm Valley that many Black householders seem to entexture their alley communities or residential blocks and to link themselves to the street through at least one male family member. However, renting as a class constraint is still important in encouraging people to probe for depth. White renters are generally much more tied to the shops, schools, and sidewalks of Elm Valley than their counterparts who own. It is too soon to tell exactly what the strategies of the new, renting refugees from Southeast Asia and Central America will be: Early observations indicate that Latin men have begun to embrace the life of the street; Southeast Asian families may be building a public life around one apartment building.

4. In one unusual but representative situation, two men with two toddlers apiece grew to know each other when one was assigned to be the other's doctor and noted from his patient's file that they were neighbors. The children began to play together, but their paths soon split. The doctor had bought a house in Elm Valley before it was fashionable and he enjoys its international variety. He was, however, determined that his children not suffer culturally because of his decision. When the doctor was in charge of the children, they went to a park in a wealthy neighborhood, to swimming lessons in the suburbs, or to a museum. The patient minded his own children frequently, but he saw their early developmental tasks differently. Although he took them regularly to Elm Valley's seedy park, he also let them play right on the sidewalk while he talked to his friends, and he took them shopping and into taverns with him. He patiently herded them to the store, allowing them to inspect every plant and animal specimen, vehicle, pothole, stairwell, and construction site that caught their attention along the way. He taught them to greet and joke with all the shopkeepers, bus drivers, and people on the street. He wanted them to learn details, nicknames, reputations, stories and histories, what to expect and predict, how to capture texture for themselves.

5. Many of the owning families do seem to seek texture in particular places, revisiting, for example, a special park, a small museum, or the downtown dinosaurs. They bring to these places the same ethnographic affection that for many renters is an encompassing, definitive strategy for living in a neighborhood.

6. Hennig (1982) writes of gentrification that although planners expected it to boost cities' financial resources by increasing tax revenues and decreasing demand for social services, this has not been the case. New owners demand more, back up those demands, and dislike contributing to the public sector in exchange for services they are more likely to find elsewhere. This appreciation of class privilege in a multicultural situation is similar to what Rosen (1977, 1980) found in his research at a preschool: Middle-class parents stressed a desire to expose their children to cultural differences; poorer parents stressed the status of a school that middle-class children attended and a desire to reap the benefits in skills and resources that would help their children excel in schools later on.

7. The house is a well-worn centerpiece of the American Dream, in which it usually stands for happiness and success. Constance Perrin's (1978) interviews with people in the housing and banking industries revealed that they read a great deal into houses and in particular into owning one. Her informants easily painted owners as more independent, responsible, and rooted than tenants, whom they believed to be poor providers and decision makers, socially marginal, and uncommitted to a community. The mortgages that banks grant owners certify that they are properly climbing the ladder of life; and owning a house further encourages good character and valued behaviors, in part by liberating residents from the problematic relations that stem from tenants' shared use of common facilities. Realtors seem to have carried these associations even further, as their promotional materials refer to houses as "homes." "Home" to stand for even an empty house has crept into popular usage almost metaphorically, with all the nuances of connections, commitments, and roots that "home" used to pose in contrast to "house."

REFERENCES

Allen, I. 1980. "The Ideology of Dense Neighborhood Development." *Urban Affairs Q.* Vol. 15, No. 4: 409–428.

Geertz, C. 1973. *The Interpretation of Cultures.* New York: Basic Books.

Goldfield, D. 1980. "Private Neighborhood Redevelopment and Displacement." *Urban Affairs Q.* Vol. 15, No. 4: 453–468.

Hannerz, U. 1969. *Soulside.* New York: Columbia University Press.

Hennig, J. 1982. *Gentrification in Adams Morgan.* Washington, DC: George Washington University Press.

Jacobs, J. 1961. *The Life and Death of Great American Cities.* New York: Random House.

Liebow, E. 1967. *Tally's Corner.* Boston: Little, Brown.

Love, R. 1973. "The Fountains of Urban Life." *Urban Life and Culture* Vol. 2, No. 2: 161–209.

McCaffrey, P. 1982. "The Gentry Are Coming." *Perspectives* (Winter): 22–27.

Merry, S. 1980. "Racial Integration in an Urban Neighborhood." *Human Organization* Vol. 39, No. 1: 59–69.

Merry, S. 1981. *Urban Danger: Life in a Neighborhood of Strangers.* Philadelphia: Temple University Press.

Molotch, H. 1969. "Racial Integration in a Transition Community." *Amer. Soc. Rev.* Vol. 34: 878–893.

Perrin, C. 1978. *Everything in Its Place.* Princeton, NJ: Princeton University Press.

Reed, P. 1974. "Situated Interaction: Normative and Nonnormative Bases of Social Behavior in Two Urban Residential Settings." *Urban Life and Culture* Vol. 2, No. 4: 460–487.

Rosaldo, R. 1984. "Grief and a Headhunter's Rage," in *Text, Play, and Story,* ed. by E. Bruner. Washington, DC: AES.

Rosen, D. 1977. "Multicultural Education: An Anthropological Perspective." *Anthropology and Education Q.* Vol. 8: 221–226.

Rosen, D. 1980. "Class and Ideology in an Innercity Preschool." *Anthro. Q.* Vol. 53: 219–228.

Suttles, G. D. 1968. *The Social Order of the Slum.* Chicago: University of Chicago Press.

Swartley, A. 1983. "If This Were Any Other Job, I'd Shove It." *Mother Jones* Vol. 8 (May): 33–55.

Williams, M. 1981. *On the Street Where I Live.* New York: Holt, Rinehart & Winston.

32

The Genocidal State

Hutu Extremism and the Origins of the "Final Solution" in Rwanda

Alex de Waal

Since taking his doctorate at Oxford, Alex de Waal has been involved with numerous NGOs (nongovernmental organizations) concerned with human rights, disaster relief, and development in Africa. He is the author of a definitive study on the Sudanese famine and co-director of the organization African Rights.

It is hard for simple reportage . . . to do justice to the bloodshed in Rwanda. What we need to do now—and what may, paradoxically, be easier—is to begin to explain it.

Elements of the story can be sought in desperate land pressure in Rwanda, in rural poverty intensified by the collapse of the international coffee price, and in the determination of a privileged coterie to retain their commanding positions in the Government and the army in the face of political and economic "readjustment" of the state. These have been fuel for the fire. But what ignited the genocide is an extremist racial ideology, an ideology that would be laughable were it not so demonically powerful.

Rwanda is more than another collapsing African state. The interim government of Rwanda is fighting for the right—as it sees it—to free itself from the moral claims of the rest of the world. This requires not just the eradication of the Tutsi minority but the annihilation of the human-rights and democracy movement in Rwanda, and all the values it stands for. In this furnace, extremist politicians are re-forging the identity of the Hutu people. It is frightening to watch.

To understand Hutu extremism one needs to delve into the origins of Hutu identity. Anthropologists and historians unite in deriding the description of Hutu and Tutsi as "tribes," and even as distinct "ethnic groups." The two speak the same language, share the same territory and traditional political institutions, and—despite caricatures to the contrary—it is often impossible to tell which group an individual belongs to on the basis of physical appearance. Rwanda is—or was—one of the true nations in Africa. A century ago, the colonists found a powerful and relatively centralized kingdom, consisting of three groups, determined largely by occupational status, and a large number of clans, determined by landholding. They were not even distinct "ethnic groups."

The European conquerors, first German and then Belgian, seized upon the occupational categorization, imbuing it with a hierarchical racial classification. The Tutsi minority were identified as a Hamitic aristocracy, who ruled a state of such sophistication that they could only have originated from a place, geographically, culturally and above all racially nearer Europe, that is, Ethiopia. Mgr Leon Classe, the first Roman Catholic Archbishop of Rwanda and the individual most responsible for shaping colonial policies there, considered the Tutsi to have an Aryan strain, while his acolytes claimed to have retrieved their origin as a lost tribe of Christendom. The "Hamitic hypothesis"—which holds that all precolonial civilization in Africa was brought by outsiders, specifically the Hamitic branch of the Caucasian race—is no longer academically respectable. But when the Tutsi courtiers converted to Roman Catholicism, abandoning the traditional sacral kingship that underpinned their authority, they seized upon it as legitimation for their continued rule.

Meanwhile, the Hutu majority were designated Bantu peasants, consigned to a life of toil and denied the possibility of education or a political role. This persisted until 1959, when, with independence approaching, the Belgians assisted in a "social revolution" that swept away the Tutsi monarchy and installed a Hutu republic. Both

"The Genocidal State: Hutu Extremism and the Origins of the 'Final Solution' in Rwanda" by Alex de Waal from *Times Literary Supplement* (London), 1 July 1994, pp. 3–4. Reprinted by permission of Times Literary Supplement.

extremist politicians and many European missionaries still insist on talking of the "Hutu race." Hutu politicians have turned the Hamitic hypothesis back in the face of their former masters: the Hutu now elevated to the original inhabitants, the Tutsi condemned as foreigners in their own country. (One reason why so many corpses have been washed into Lake Victoria is that a prominent ideologue, Dr Leon Mugesera, exhorted the population to return their erstwhile masters to Ethiopia, via the short-cut of the Nyaborongo river.) The tiny group of Twa hunter-gatherers and potters were given the lowest status of all: aboriginal pygmies, a remnant of an earlier stage of human evolution. They remain one of the most despised and maltreated minorities in Africa.

It was common for European colonists to administer their territories through local intermediaries, creating or solidifying local oligarchies as they did so. Only in Rwanda and Burundi, however, was this overlaid with such an ex-plicitly racial ideology. These two countries were also un-usual in the extremes resorted to by the colonists. In the 1930s, the Belgians conducted a census and issued an iden-tity card for each individual, which specified whether they were Tutsi, Hutu or Twa. Such was the slender basis for the racial typology that the census-takers were obliged to use ownership of cows as a criterion: those with ten or more were Tutsi, those with less were Hutu, in perpetuity. On the basis of a cow or two hinged the status of overlord or serf, and with it access to education and every other privi-lege bestowed by the administration. The cards still exist today—they are the means whereby the road-block militi-amen know whom to kill and whom to spare.

As elsewhere in Africa, clan identity cuts across eth-nicity. Each of Rwanda's fourteen major and numerous minor clans contains Tutsi, Hutu and Twa lineages. Be-fore the late nineteenth century, social mobility across the categories was not uncommon. But Tutsi supremacy was cemented and extended, and "Tutsi" and "Hutu" became the most important political categories for Rwandese. This was most resented in northwest Rwanda, where the independent Hutu princedoms, known as Abahinza, were dismantled and Tutsi rulers imposed. Dr Ferdinand Nahimana, a leading Hutu extremist ideologue and Di-rector of Radio-Télévision des Libres Mille Collines, whose radio broadcasts have been instrumental in incit-ing the killings, built his academic career at the National University of Rwanda on chronicling the Abahinza. His papers (for example, "Les Principautés Hutu du Rwanda Septentrional," in *La Civilization ancienne des peuples des Grands Lacs,* Paris 1979) appear in scholarly publications. President Juvenal Habyarimana, who died in the plane crash of April 6 [1994], and his lieutenants, who have since presided over the genocide, hail from this area and see themselves as the heirs of the Hutu princes.

Specialists on Rwanda protest in vain that Hutu and Tutsi are not separate ethnic groups. But sixty years of colonial and Tutsi rule, and thirty-five years of Hutu su-premacy following the 1959 Revolution, which consigned half the Tutsi population to exile, have fundamentally changed the nature of the relationships between them. Political conflict, punctuated by intercommunal violence, has created distinct and mutually opposed Hutu and Tutsi identities, which, for all the hesitations of social sci-entists, are identifiably "ethnic."

Some insight into such processes of creating identity can be gleaned from the study of rather different, small-scale societies in southwest Ethiopia by David Turton, whose essay is the outstanding contribution to *Ethnicity and Conflict in the Horn of Africa:*

> If groups such as the Mursi are treated . . . as "given in nature," then the conflict which is seen to define their boundaries is also given in nature; it is simply the way in which independent political groups must relate to each other in the absence of overarching political structure. But, if a network of relations based on clanship and other identities is treated as primary, conflict begins to look like the means whereby independent and mutu-ally opposing political units are temporarily "carved out" from this "underlying" sociality in the first place.

This stands Hobbesian theory on its head; political orga-nization, and ultimately states, are not what constrains the individual's propensity to violence, but what shapes it. Turton continues:

> I suggest that for the Mursi and their neighbours, war-fare is not a means by which an already constituted political group seeks to defend or extend its territory, but a means by which the very idea of it as an indepen-dent political unit, free from the normative claims of outsiders, is created and kept alive.

In terms of human lives, this can be very costly. (Turton's analysis, developed over decades of familiarity with the Mursi, should be required reading for all who are in-volved in conflict resolution.)

Another paper in this collection, Tim Allen's account of the creation of ethnicity on the Sudan-Uganda border, charts a similar process whereby colonial administration, armed conflict and the popular currency of the notion of "tribe" have created the Acholi and Madi tribes, partly supplanting the more diffuse and complex relationships that existed beforehand. To argue that these tribes thus manufactured are artificial is to miss the point. As Allen points out, it is impossible to interpret recent events with-out recourse to tribal labels, and they are the labels used by the people themselves. Above all, people kill each other because of them.

Although derived from societies remote from centres of state power, the academic debate has insights for all concerned with the conundrum of the reinvigoration of nationalism and ethnic exclusivism. These are the currents tapped by politicians with a chauvinist agenda, and the resonances in Rwanda are compelling. On one side of the conflict are the leaders of the Tutsi-dominated Rwandese Patriotic Front (RPF). These are mostly children of refugees who fled to Uganda in 1959–63; their identities have been shaped by a generation of exile. Many fought as members of the Ugandan National Resistance Army (NRA) led by Yoweri Museveni, which captured Kampala and formed a government in 1986. Never fully accepted in Uganda, several thousand Rwandese members of the NRA deserted, formed the RPF, and invaded Rwanda on October 1, 1990.

Echoing their schooling at Makerere University, the RPF leaders complain that the ethnic labels Hutu and Tutsi are some sort of "mistake." They popularize this by harking back to the mythical origins of a unified Rwandese people unsullied by colonialism—conveniently skating over the Tutsi oppression of the Hutu in historical times. Their ideology has another intellectual lineage, traceable through the NRA to Frelimo in Mozambique, where Museveni first underwent training, and thence to Mao Tsetung. Maoist theories of guerrilla war stress social transformation through participation in a liberation struggle, and focus on socioeconomic tensions rather than ethnic solidarity. The RPF ideology is self-serving, designed for Western ears. Playing down ethnicity promotes the interests of a relatively wealthy and well-educated minority, and hides the enduring contempt many Tutsi commanders feel for the Hutu. Moreover, a display of military discipline strengthens the RPF's claim to dominate the future Rwandese army. But this politically cynical yet sociologically naive ideology has helped—so far—to prevent RPF soldiers wreaking a massive revenge on the Hutu populace.

On the other side, the Hutu racists regard the Hutu–Tutsi conflict as "given in nature," and repeatedly invoke the Hamitic-Bantu distinction. A Rwandan government pamphlet from 1990, entitled "The whole truth of the October 1990 war imposed upon Rwanda by the aggressors from Uganda armed forces," referring to President Museveni's origins in the "Hamitic" Hima people, enumerates "The true motives of the aggressors":

[To] set up an extended Hima-Tutsi kingdom in the Bantu area of the Great-Lakes region. It should be recalled that in identification with the Aryan race, both ethnic groups consider themselves as being superior to other ethnic groups and use the swastika of Hitler as their symbol.

The last claim is wholly untrue, but this is mild in comparison with the propaganda put out in the Kinyarwanda language. Evidence that the extremists believed their own propaganda is contained in an internal Ministry of Defence memorandum from 1992, "Definition and identification of the enemy." Passing through "Tutsi refugees" and "Hutu who are hostile to the regime" the list concludes with "The Nilo-Hamitic people of the region." Ironically, this racial fantasy is underwritten by Tutsi supremacists in Burundi, the mirror-image neighbouring country where government and army remain dominated by the Tutsi minority. There, too, mutually antagonistic identities have been created and reinforced by colonial rule and politically instigated communal violence.

As well as a bid for power, the mass killing in Rwanda is a struggle to define the identity of the Rwandese Hutu. In *The Cohesion of Oppression,* Catherine Newbury argues that Hutu identity itself was a creation of the common experience of Rwandese peasants excluded from power and privilege during the colonial era. Before that, "hutu" merely referred to the status of vassal. Divided by clan, region and their relationship to the precolonial states and substates within Rwanda's colonial borders, Rwandese farmers became "Hutu" by default, as access to state power came to define the Tutsi.

Earlier scholars have charted the central role of the Christian missions in giving shape to this consciousness. Ian Linden's *Church and Revolution in Rwanda* (1977) is the classic of this literature. The Roman Catholic White Fathers, under Mgr Classe, formed a Tutsi state Church in the heyday of colonial rule. Later—partly because the Anglicans and Baptists began evangelizing the Hutu—the Catholic Church switched, in time to underwrite the creation of the Republic. The late Catholic Archbishop, Mgr Vincent Nsengiyumva, who was captured and killed by RPF forces last month [June 1994], served on the Central Committee of Habyarimana's ruling party for fifteen years.

Newbury, deriving her account from a study of the southwest periphery of the kingdom, reveals how uneven the local experience of Tutsi rule was, challenging the previous orthodoxy that patron-client ties imbued the whole of Rwandese society. *The Cohesion of Oppression* is a valuable addition to the literature, running parallel to Linden's book in that its main aim is to explain the "social revolution" of 1959, a revolution that did indeed precisely reverse the political order.

Since then, Hutu politicians have ruled Rwanda. While still portraying the Hutu as downtrodden, they have used the same methods of ethnic discrimination to award the privileges of state power to themselves. A *coup* in 1973, announced by its leader, Major-General Habyarimana, as a "moral revolution," called a halt to anti-Tutsi pogroms and promised development without politics. But since 1990, with simultaneous economic crisis, populist mobilization for multiparty elections and the threat of the RPF, Hutu extremism has returned in a far more virulent form. The scholarly literature has yet to grapple with this.

Perhaps it is the very fact that Hutu ethnicity has such insubstantial foundations that compels the extremists to sharpen it, using methods that would be absurd were they not so inflammatory. The last few years have witnessed an outpouring of propaganda calling for no repetition of the "mistakes" of 1959, when the Tutsi were "allowed to escape" abroad. The message mixes traditional, religious and racial themes, often subverting them. For example, the third of the Hutu extremists' "Ten Commandments," published in 1990 in *Kangura,* a leading Rwandese newspaper, reads: "Are not [Hutu women] beautiful, good secretaries and more honest?" The sophisticated may laugh, but the list continues to number eight, "The Hutu should stop having mercy on the Tutsi" and number ten, "We shall consider a traitor any Hutu who will persecute his Hutu brother for having read, spread and taught this ideology."

The propagandists' principle of the bigger the lie, the greater the credulity, has been well observed. Peasants in areas overrun by the RPF are reportedly astonished that the Tutsi soldiers do not have horns, tails and eyes that glow in the dark—such is the content of the radio broadcasts they listen to. The terrorist principles perfected by Renamo are also in evidence: the symbolic inversion of moral values (churches and hospitals are favoured places for massacres) and forcing ordinary people to kill, so that they feel dehumanized and worthy only of the company of other killers.

The character of ethnicity in Rwanda presents the architect of genocide with another problem: how to distinguish his victims. It cannot be done by language or location, and—despite the best efforts of German and Belgian physical anthropologists—height and length of nose are uncertain guides. Checking identity cards is a time-consuming business, and the killers relied on speed for the success of their operation. The extremists solved this by mobilizing at least one militiaman from every ten households across the country, so that every Tutsi family could be pointed out by someone who knew them personally. Hence schoolchildren have been killed by their teachers, shopkeepers by their customers, neighbours by their neighbours.

Taking their name from the communal work groups that in the 1970s received the acclaim of aid agencies as the vanguard of equitable development, the militia are known as *interahamwe,* "those with a common goal."

Mass murder masquerades as civic duty. Catechists wield machetes, and archbishops have defended the Government as "peace-loving." By these means, the interim government of Rwanda has succeeded in perfecting an intermediate technology of genocide. Using fragmentation grenades, machetes and big clubs with nails sticking out, they have matched the industrialized methods of extermination developed by the Nazis.

But the killing in Rwanda is more extreme still than genocide, and in this lies a second, complementary strand of an explanation. There is a third ideology at work in Rwanda—one that again has both local and international roots. This is "democratization" in its various forms: "conflict resolution," "human rights," "civil society" and "good governance."

In accordance with the extremists' tenth commandment, the first and most prominent victims of the killing were Hutu: opposition politicians, academics, journalists, human-rights activists, lawyers, priests, businessmen. The cream of the country's civil society was slaughtered in a few days by the Presidential Guard, who had earlier compiled their wanted lists. A curfew, imposed under the pretence that uncontrollable ethnic strife had broken out, enabled the soldiers to hunt down their victims in their homes. It was the ultimate *putsch:* physical liquidation of all advocates of democratization. Observers were confused because some of the victims were themselves members of the Government. Agatha Uwilingiyimana, killed on the first day along with ten Belgian soldiers from the United Nations who were her guards, was both Prime Minister and an opposition politician. Her position reflects a deep irony, for, until April 6, Rwanda was a model for a transition to democracy and the peaceful resolution of armed conflict.

In 1990, President Habyarimana bowed to the "democracy wave" sweeping Africa and agreed to move from a single-party to a multiparty system. In the same year he also faced the RPF invasion. International pressure brought both sides to the negotiating table, and a series of accords were hammered out. Under close monitoring by the United Nations, cabinet posts were to be shared with the opposition, the police retrained, the national army and the rebel front merged and scaled down, and free elections held. Regional powers such as Tanzania and Zaire played a role, the Belgians backed the agreements, and a United Nations force was dispatched to demonstrate the commitment of the world.

Whenever Habyarimana prevaricated or stalled on the timetable to democracy, the international peace-brokers stepped in and forced him to keep his word. A desperate attempt by Hutu extremists to derail the process by assassinating a leading opposition politician on February 21 unleashed several days of violence by the *intera-hamwe* militia. But the UN, the Organization of African Unity and Rwanda's main Western donors did not flinch: Habyarimana was dragged back to the negotiating table, and forced to agree. Under countervailing pressure from his hardline coterie, he tried to wriggle again; the regional leaders called him for a conference in Dar es Salaam. The President was forced to agree once more: the transitional institutions would be set up. He left for home in his personal plane, but word of his latest capitulation had reached the Presidential Guard stationed near Kigali airport, and they shot him down.

Habyarimana was a victim of the international peace industry as well as of the hardliners he had hand-picked for the Presidential Guard. The peace process had failed to bring an important (albeit nasty) section of Rwandese society along with it. At times, those guiding the international diplomacy seemed to be closing their eyes and wishing the extremists away.

Before April 6, Rwanda had one of the most vigorous human-rights movements in Africa. Six independent human-rights organizations cooperated in exposing abuses by government and rebel forces. They also invited an International Commission of Inquiry, consisting of ten human-rights experts from around the world. The Commission visited Rwanda in 1993 and compiled a comprehensive and courageous report, documenting violations and naming those responsible—including senior members of the Government and army and extremist ideologues. Habyarimana was reported to have personally acquiesced to a massacre, with a nod of his head, in 1992.

Democracy implied justice. The individuals named were promised an amnesty, but knew that their actions were under scrutiny. Their strategy to escape justice was to kill all those who had collaborated in human-rights investigations. They killed most of them. It is a shocking reminder of just how high the stakes are in the human-rights business. There was plentiful evidence for preparations for mass killing. The UN Special Envoy publicly objected to the arming of militias on several occasions, and the names of the leaders of the "Zero Network" death squads were circulated by the civil opposition. But no contingency plans were made. This was particularly shortsighted because of the example of Burundi the previous year.

The democratization process in Burundi reached fruition in June 1993, with the election of Melchior Ndadaye as the first Hutu President. Entirely carried through by Burundis themselves, it was a shining example of peaceful transition—as one observer put it, "too good to be true." But, with their position under threat, on October 21 the Tutsi-controlled army mounted a *coup d'état*, assassinated

Ndadaye, and unleashed communal violence that killed up to 50,000 people. The international community reacted immediately to condemn the *putsch:* there was to be no foreign aid or diplomatic recognition unless the extremists backed down. The extremists duly returned to barracks (where they have been left undisturbed); and since then Burundi has been in a fragile state of power-sharing interrupted by sporadic assassinations.

When the storm erupted in Rwanda, the reaction of the Western world was merely to decry the anarchic savagery, evacuate its citizens, and pull out all but a handful of UN troops. Under this smokescreen the killers proceeded undisturbed; and the local human-rights activists were left to their fate. Since then, the pace of the diplomatic ball-game has been much slower than the momentum of the genocide. The UN Commission for Human Rights has met in extraordinary session and appointed a Special Rapporteur, but criminal indictments for genocide are still in the distant future. The foreign minister of the interim government was allowed to deliver a racist diatribe to the UN Security Council—no one even considered changing the diplomatic rules to prevent the advocacy of genocide at the UN's inner sanctum. In Kigali, the UN Special Envoy is still grasping at the standard formulas: ceasefire and political settlement. Maintaining "neutrality" by blaming both sides equally, he is apparently oblivious to the impossibility of an agreement between a government whose *raison d'être* is genocide, and a rebel force that will not stop its advance until it has saved every remaining Tutsi from the threat of the militias. It seems probable that the genocide will be resolved in time-honoured fashion—either the killers will run out of victims, or the rebel army will win the war. International troops sent with the wrong mandate—for example, to impose a ceasefire—will be a practical and moral irrelevance.

This should be giving sleepless nights to the advocates of peace and democracy in the United Nations, Western embassies and humanitarian foundations. Their own ideologues are spectacularly unable to deal with political philosophies such as Hutu extremism. For example, Ronald Cohen's keynote chapter in *Human Rights and Governance in Africa* persists in seeing the weakness of the state as the reason for ethnic conflict, even citing earlier rounds of killings in Rwanda and Burundi as an example of this. This is unreconstructed Hobbes: the "great beast" of popular violence must be constrained by a contract between the individual and the state.

Articulating an evolutionary view with similar credentials to the Hamitic hypothesis, Cohen argues in passing that ascribed rights based on race or ethnicity "can be predicted to atrophy over time." It is perhaps unfair to characterize the whole of a solid collection on the basis of a few remarks in one paper, but the student who reads the publisher's claims for "timeliness" and "originality" will be disappointed. Though the publication date is 1993, the papers for this volume were written in 1988. The Rwandese method of genocide was perfected in less time than it took for the proceedings of an academic conference on human rights to reach the publisher's catalogue.

Generals and genocidal ideologues continue to sharpen their tools faster than the proponents of peace and democracy. While human-rights advocates and relief agencies still shudder in shock from Rwanda, dictators are observing closely how the crime unfolds. Some, no doubt, have more than a little admiration for the sheer audacity of the Hutu extremists' attempted "final solution" to the threat of political opposition. If interim President Theodor Sindikubabwo, Major-General Augustine Bizimana, Dr Casimir Bizimungu and their coterie succeed—if they retain a stake in power, and remain legitimate interlocutors in the eyes of the international diplomatic corps—that will be an advertisement for mass political killing, and an open invitation for others to replicate it.

More is at stake in Rwanda even than the survival of the Tutsi people. The killers' aim is a "final solution" to the threat to their power and beliefs posed by human rights and democracy itself. Should they succeed, the armoury of political extremism worldwide will be enriched with a host of new techniques for propagandizing and swiftly executing mass murder, as well as methods of confusing, neutralizing and even co-opting the international peace industry. Should the killers fail, it will almost certainly be due to the few thousand guerrillas of the RPF, not to the troops of the UN or any other international pressure: an accidental defeat for genocide, not a victory for human rights.

Scholars, lawyers and diplomats expend huge energies refining the instruments and expanding the institutions of international human rights. But this community, too, is ultimately defined by the battles it fights. Should it refuse to enter the fray in Rwanda, it will be diminished. For a movement that ultimately depends on collective moral authority, this would be profoundly discouraging.

– 33 –

An Anthropologist Learns the Value of Fear

Elizabeth Garland

Elizabeth Garland is pursuing her PhD in sociocultural anthropology at the University of Chicago.

In the early morning of March 1, 1999, more than a hundred heavily armed Rwandan rebels attacked the headquarters of Bwindi National Park in southwestern Uganda, a park famous for being one of the few remaining mountain gorilla habitats in the world. A Ugandan park warden was killed in the raid, and fifteen people, fourteen of them Western tourists, were captured and marched at gunpoint into the rain forest in the direction of the nearby Congo border. Over the course of the day, the rebels killed eight of the hostages. The remaining seven they released with warnings that they wouldn't be as merciful the next time.

I was at Bwindi when the attack occurred, awakened in my tent by the gunfire, and although the rebels did search and loot the campground where I was—abducting another person staying there—they somehow didn't find my campsite, which was located at the periphery of the main camp and partially concealed from view by bushes. Within a couple of hours of hearing the first gunshots, I realized that there was a good chance that I would survive the attack. Sometime later a friend came to see if I was okay, signaling that it was safe to come out of my tent; and by the afternoon, I was on a chartered plane to Kampala, evacuated by the U.S. embassy with a number of other Westerners who had also hidden or been left behind by the rebels. Within a week, I was back at my home in western Massachusetts.

I had arrived in Uganda in December of 1998 to conduct the fieldwork for my doctoral dissertation in socio-

cultural anthropology on the symbolic and political aspects of mountain gorilla conservation in the Great Lakes region. I hoped to explore the ethical implications of Western concern for the endangered apes, given that mountain gorillas live in one of the most war-torn places in the world—a region where *human* life has historically been appallingly undervalued by the West. My actual research was to focus on the mountain gorilla tourism industry: I would live for a year or more in a rural village near a national park where tourists come to see gorillas in the wild. There, through a combination of interviews with tourists, "participant-observation" in the life of the village, and observations of the interactions between tourists and local African people, I would gain a sense of the ways in which the West's romantic image of Africa as a place of pristine nature intersects with indigenous African social, cultural, and political processes. From this local vantage point, then, I proposed to extrapolate about the ethical and political implications of such a nexus at a more global level.

By the beginning of March, things were going remarkably well. I had begun intensively studying Rukiga, the language spoken by the Bakiga people who live around Bwindi National Park, and had met with all the government officials, local leaders, and community groups necessary to gain permission to conduct my research there. I was having a house built for me in a village outside the Bwindi headquarters—my very own mud hut, as I happily described it—and while it was being completed, I had set up a temporary base in one of the park campgrounds, spending my evenings interviewing the tourists who stayed there. During the days, with the help of a research assistant and translator, I had slowly begun to gain my footing in the local community, learning things like who belonged to which clan, why people wore

"An Anthropologist Learns the Value of Fear" by Elizabeth Garland as appeared in *The Chronicle of Higher Education*, May 7, 1999, p. B4. Reprinted by permission of the author.

certain kinds of clothing and not others, what everybody really thought of the new local government official, and all sorts of other classically anthropological information. I had started to make some friends, and—not unrelated—people were increasingly calling on me for favors. I was just beginning to get invited to events like baptisms and weddings.

It is in this context that I experienced the rebel attack on Bwindi. Although at first I didn't realize just how purposefully the rebels had set out to destroy the park's tourism industry, I knew immediately that it was the presence of tourists that had made the park a target. With word of the abductions, I had to face the fact that from the rebels' perspective I was indistinguishable from a tourist myself—not only that I could easily have been captured along with the others, but also that, as a Western person in the park, I was implicated in the industry that had drawn the rebels in. As I walked around and looked at the dead body of the park warden, the burning buildings and vehicles, the looted homes and shops, and the many stricken faces of people I was just getting to know, this knowledge felt almost unbearable. I was very glad to be flown out of there by the U.S. embassy later that day, but I have never had to face the hypocrisy of the anthropological endeavor more directly than I did riding out of town on the back of a pickup full of white tourists, headed for the airstrip while "my people" watched from the doorways of their burned-out houses.

Back in the States, reading through what seems to me an obscenely large pile of newspaper clippings about the incident, I'm struck by how many of the articles are concerned with the question of travel safety. "The Dicey Game of Assessing Travel Risk," from the *New York Times,* is a typical example, describing the horror of the attack at Bwindi and locating it on a timeline with a number of other incidents in areas where political violence or natural disasters have resulted in the deaths of tourists.

I find myself enraged by these articles. Not only do they cast the rest of the world's terrible problems as potential hindrances to some rich American's vacation but they also implicitly assume that all newspaper readers potentially *are* rich American vacationers, as if we should all relate to places like Uganda foremost as destinations for our touristic consumption. In light of how guilty and worried I feel about all the people I left behind at Bwindi—people who have very recently been harmed by the existence of the international tourism industry—this sort of depoliticized self-absorption seems more like a part of the problem than simple, innocent advice.

It's not lost on me that I should probably be more angry at the rebels for nearly killing me than at a bunch of American journalists for developing an ethnocentric story angle. But these articles have struck a nerve for me, for I can't help but share many of the safety concerns they voice myself, and I don't enjoy the thought—the same one I had the morning of the attack on Bwindi—that my own status as a professional anthropologist is indistinguishable from that of the average tourist in many fundamental respects.

The truth is, like a tourist, I did worry quite a bit about safety in the course of planning my fieldwork trip to Uganda. Knowing that there were rebel groups active in the eastern part of the Democratic Republic of Congo, and appreciating the overall political volatility of the region, I designed my project carefully to try to mitigate the dangers I thought I might encounter while in the field. I researched the security situations at all four gorilla parks in the Great Lakes region, and, like most gorilla tourists, chose Bwindi because it was located entirely within Uganda, which is more stable than neighboring Rwanda and Congo, where gorillas are also found. I consulted with the U.S. State Department, the U.S. embassy in Kampala, the Uganda Wildlife Authority, and many researchers, tour operators, conservationists, and development workers who work in and around the park. On their advice, I decided to live close to the Bwindi park headquarters rather than in a more remote part of the park, reasoning that, should things heat up, I would be protected by the presence of the park rangers and tourists. In the end I had concluded that these measures would keep me safe and had convinced my partner, advisors, and family to let me go on that basis.

Underlying my planning to minimize risk in my fieldwork, as well as articles about the risks of travel, is a sense of entitlement about safety—an expectation of it—that seems to me now to be part of a singularly privileged, perhaps even a uniquely American worldview. Who else in the world feels so invulnerable that they expect to be able to travel wherever they like and return home again unscathed? How many people can afford to speak of such serious matters as safety and danger in the self-assured, agency-filled language of games and risks? Certainly few Ugandans—not to mention Yugoslavs or Iraqis—are likely to feel invulnerable in the face of danger these days. And yet this conceit that safety is somehow the default position has become so naturalized in the United States that we've come to think of danger as a thing that we can avoid if we so choose, forgetting (or repressing) that it is precisely the fact that danger is out of our control that makes it dangerous.

It's not that we—even we privileged Americans—actually *are* safe, of course. Cancer routinely strikes our lives, and so do car accidents, heart attacks, AIDS, and scores of other tragedies. And we also die violently all the time, as often at the hands of our spouses, children, and police officers as at the hands of those we hold at a distance with labels like "psychopath" and "terrorist." But the fantasy that we are safe is a key component of our national self-image: danger is something *over there*, in Africa, not something here at home.

The practice of international tourism plays a central role in this fantasy of domestic safety. Through imagining ourselves as tourists in foreign lands, we displace our everyday fears and vulnerabilities onto more exotic dangers (like being abducted by Hutu rebels) that we might conceivably encounter someplace else. Displacing our fears in this way undoubtedly helps to justify our systematic failure to attend to many of the dangerous problems that exist within our own society. In addition, it provides us with a tantalizing vision of danger to which we are not ourselves subject. We act as tourists *by choice*, after all; no one forces us to vacation in dangerous places. By traveling to them anyway, we unconsciously assert ourselves as the sort of people who are intrinsically invulnerable to the dangers they have to offer. One might even say that it is the prospect of encountering and surviving danger—or at least a bit of "excitement"—that energizes our desire to leave home in the first place. When wealthy Americans travel to the war zones of western Uganda in order to trek through dense jungle in search of wild gorillas, they do so in full expectation of being challenged by the experience. But they equally expect to return home safely at the end of their trip, shored up in their confidence that they are brave and strong enough to handle the more mundane challenges of life at home.

Anthropologists notoriously conceptualize dissertation fieldwork as a transformative rite of passage in much the same way. By custom, graduate students in anthropology are designated either "pre-field" or "post-field," the experience of fieldwork acting as a crucial credentialing process, *the* way that we become experienced enough to count as real scholars. Although, in this present era of ethnographic reflexivity, anthropologists have come to pay far greater critical attention to their own role in the fieldwork process than they did in the more positivist days of yore, an awareness of the "dialogic" nature of anthropological research has done little to alter disciplinary assumptions about the transformative effect that fieldwork has on the novice anthropologist. When I went into the field in Uganda, I fully expected to be shaken up by my research—to be pulled on, and pushed around, and entangled in webs of obligation, attraction, repulsion, and maybe even hostility. But in the end I also assumed that I would emerge from it all constituted as an anthropologist, which is to say I expected that fieldwork would form me into a person more qualified to succeed in my chosen world here in the United States. I certainly didn't expect that it might kill me in the process.

Like many things about the discipline of anthropology, my assumption that I would not only survive but also profit from my fieldwork in Africa rests squarely on a set of colonial and post-colonial power relations between the West and the non-Western world. Like the tourists who feel safe even in the middle of war zones, Western anthropologists have often carried out research in places where others were being brutally repressed or otherwise endangered, first with the backing and protection of colonial administrators and soldiers and, more recently, with the sense of security that comes from a position of privilege within the post-colonial world order.

By designing my dissertation project to focus on the practice of tourism and the ways in which Western assumptions and values affect the position of African people within the world system, I have tried to incorporate a self-consciousness about the legacy of colonialism into my work in a central way. And yet, when it came down to designing my actual fieldwork, the things I imagined myself doing bore a striking resemblance to a classically colonial model of anthropological research: I would live for a long, uninterrupted time in a rural African village, learning the local language and immersing myself in the sociocultural dynamics of the local community. I took for granted that something called "the local community" existed, and I also assumed that, provided I took the appropriate measures, this community would eventually welcome me in and look after me (indeed, integrating oneself into a community is a classic piece of advice on staying safe in the field). Even with my awareness of the regional political context, and in spite of the explicitly transnational focus of my research, I failed to consider the possibility that a local village outside the park headquarters simply wasn't the relevant social unit, that I had neglected to factor in the rebels—known to be living only miles away on the other side of the Congo border. As a white American, I approached the prospect of my fieldwork in much the same way as a tourist planning to travel to a potentially dangerous place. Because I wanted it to be so, I decided that my research at Bwindi was viable—that, for someone like me, it would be safe enough.

By attacking the tourism industry at Bwindi, the rebels made clear that they reject the worldview that has enabled me to be so sure of myself in this regard and that they mean to challenge the power relations that underpin it in their part of the world. From the perspective of my proposed topic, surely this is a fascinating turn of events, for now I've had a glimpse of what it would look like if the symbolic structure I'm analyzing were itself to be destabilized. That is, rather than just setting out to document the harms and benefits caused by the West's imagination of Africa as a natural and wild place, defined in subordinate relation to our own "civilized" society, I now have the opportunity to study a forceful African critique of this very imagined relationship.

The difficulty I face at the moment is how to proceed with my research. Because the practice of anthropology has for so long depended on Western privilege to keep us safe in the field, we have very few models for doing research under conditions in which we feel ourselves inherently to be unsafe. It's not that anthropologists have failed to think about how to minimize danger while in the field—on the contrary, a number of people have written quite thoughtfully about the strategies they've used to manage the risks of fieldwork in dangerous conditions. My problem is that I used many of these strategies in setting up my research in Bwindi, and yet it was only arbitrary, inexplicable luck (fate, divine intervention, witchcraft—pick your idiom), not my own efforts at all, that kept me alive. Rather than techniques for risk management, what I'm looking for now is a way to carry on while relinquishing the idea that danger and safety are things over which I have very much control. I'm scheduled to head back to Uganda, and the only thing I'm certain of is that I can't be sure that I'll be safe. My hope is that my fear will make me a better anthropologist, more open to the ways in which the people I'm studying experience their dangerous world.

CHAPTER

POLITICS

How Do People Exercise Power Over Each Other?

THE CONCEPTS OF **political organization** and **social control** are about the ways power is distributed and embedded in society. Power is found in all social relationships. In this chapter, Clifford Shearing and Philip Stenning show that even in seemingly innocuous places like Disney World, people are controlled in subtle and not so subtle ways. Power is not about physical force alone, but involves the use of space, voluntary submission, and ideology, all of which make the study of power so fascinating. An insightful perspective on these events can be gained from the world traditionally studied by anthropologists.

The events of the Colonial Era, the short but intense period from about 1884 to 1960 when the industrialized European powers acquired large amounts of colonial real estate in Africa and Asia, set the parameters for the political structures under which the majority of the world's population live. **Colonialism** reorganized or undermined traditional social, political, and economic autonomy, and colonial authorities were largely oblivious to what they were doing because the way in which they saw the world and asked questions was shaped by their Victorian outlook. To consolidate their position, the British and the other colonizers used remarkably similar strategies. They created a class of **subalterns,** local indigenes who were propelled into positions of petty power and who ruled on the colonizers' behalf.

In this they were aided by missionaries who provided the subalterns with the minimal educational skills and who played a further important role in legitimating colonial rule. At the same time, missionaries also provided the seedbed for the later anticolonial movements. Legitimacy, with its rich invocation of symbols, is a key concern in the politics about power.

Pierre van den Berghe's study provides a graphic illustration and polemical account of the relationship between **nations** and **states.** Most of the states in the contemporary world are the product of colonialism, and rather than simply accept them as necessary, we need to ask some probing questions about their nature. Why is it that states are so often controlled by people of one nation, who use their power to suppress the rights of other nationalities living within the same state?

As Archie Mafeje, a leading African anthropologist, put it: Those who control state bureaucracies "think that the way to fish is by emptying the pond." There are a number of reasons for such a predatory worldview, which is intimately tied to how the people in control view the state. Certainly they do not see the state the way Western political theorists see it, as some sort of neutral umpire protecting and caring for its citizens in exchange for taxes. As a Papua New Guinean said to one of this book's editors, "The State is a money box in a tent which is controlled by the senior officials." This intellectual legacy is still very much with us and indeed will probably grow as Africa and the other southern hemisphere countries become increasingly marginalized and hence less subject to public scrutiny.

As Whitney Azoy, an anthropologist and former diplomat, shows in his article in this chapter, apparently politically "advanced" democracies like the United States operate in similar ways, even as we distinguish "our" political processes as transparent and fair and "theirs" as corrupt and unfair. He explores how the Iranian term *waaseta* (personal connections) aptly describes how our politicians work in favor of corporate campaign donors and even "win" dubious elections.

Many anthropologists see autonomy and how **cultural pluralism** is tolerated within the state as the major issues at the beginning of a new century. This view is perhaps overstated to make the point. Consider Papua New Guinea as an example: It is a country of some 3 million people with over 700 different nations, of which the largest language group has fewer than 200,000 speakers. Ask any Papua New Guineans what they regard as the major achievement of their Australian colonizers (Papua New Guinea rather reluctantly became an independent state in 1975), and they will say the creation of **law** and order. They will say that prior to colonization everyone fought, but the Australians brought peace to the country. Papua New Guineans are renowned for their **egalitarian ethos.** Politically they have no strongly developed **hierarchies** with chiefs or kings. This meant that if they had a dispute, they had to settle it between themselves, largely through warfare and related compensation payments. The Australians brought peace by creating overarching third-party dispute management forums for hearing disputes. In short, they said, if you have a problem, do not make a war but bring it to the district commissioner. This principle of **dispute management** was not new. Indeed, it forms one of the rationales for the creation of the World Court of International Justice. What is important, though, is why these triadic structures were successful during the colonial heyday but not in the post-independence era. Many commentators have interpreted the new "lawlessness" confronting many parts of the globe as a resurrection of "primitive" or "tribal" warfare. That the matter is not so simple is well argued in the essay by Neil Whitehead and Brian Ferguson. In the final article, we go to the field with Andrew Cornish, who illustrates how he came to understand dispute settlement processes in Thailand after he had a motorcycle accident—a serendipitous situation that sheds light on the nature of fieldwork.

FOCUS QUESTIONS

As you read these selections, consider these questions:

✦   How does the use of physical space reflect social control?

✦   What evidence have you seen in our political system that "personal connections" play a role in achieving political ends?

✦   Why do people organize themselves in large, formal systems like states, and what do they gain and lose when they do?

✦   Why are images of "tribal warfare" problematic?

✦   Think of the different kinds of disputes in which you have found yourself. How were they resolved? Why did you arrive at a particular resolution? How does that differ from the examples in these selections on conflict management in other cultures?

Say "Cheese!"

The Disney Order That Is Not So Mickey Mouse

Clifford D. Shearing and Philip C. Stenning

Clifford Shearing is a criminologist at the University of Toronto currently attached to the Community Law Center at the University of the Western Cape, South Africa.

Philip Stenning is a criminologist at Victoria University of Wellington, New Zealand.

One of the most distinctive features of that quintessentially American playground known as Disney World is the way it seeks to combine a sense of comfortable—even nostalgic—familiarity with an air of innovative technological advance. Mingled with the fantasies of one's childhood are the dreams of a better future. Next to the Magic Kingdom is the Epcot Center. As well as providing for a great escape, Disney World claims also to be a design for better living. And what impresses most about this place is that it seems to run like clockwork.

Yet the Disney order is no accidental by-product. Rather, it is a designed-in feature that provides—to the eye that is looking for it, but not to the casual visitor—an exemplar of modern private corporate policing. Along with the rest of the scenery of which it forms a discreet part, it too is recognizable as a design for the future.

We invite you to come with us on a guided tour of this modern police facility in which discipline and control are, like many of the characters one sees about, in costume.

The fun begins the moment the visitor enters Disney World. As one arrives by car one is greeted by a series of smiling young people who, with the aid of clearly visible road markings, direct one to one's parking spot, remind one to lock one's car and to remember its location and then direct one to await the rubber-wheeled train that will convey visitors away from the parking lot. At the boarding location one is directed to stand safely behind guard rails and to board the train in an orderly fashion. While climbing on board one is reminded to remember the name of the parking area and the row number in which one is parked (for instance, "Donald Duck, 1"). Once on the train one is encouraged to protect oneself from injury by keeping one's body within the bounds of the carriage and to do the same for children in one's care. Before disembarking one is told how to get from the train back to the monorail platform and where to wait for the train to the parking lot on one's return. At each transition from one stage of one's journey to the next one is wished a happy day and a "good time" at Disney World (this begins as one drives in and is directed by road signs to tune one's car radio to the Disney radio network).

As one moves towards the monorail platform the directions one has just received are reinforced by physical barriers (that make it difficult to take a wrong turn), pavement markings, signs and more cheerful Disney employees who, like their counterparts in other locations, convey the message that Disney World is a "fun place" designed for one's comfort and pleasure. On approaching the monorail platform one is met by enthusiastic attendants who quickly and efficiently organize the mass of people moving onto it into corrals designed to accommodate enough people to fill one compartment on the monorail. In assigning people to these corrals the attendants ensure that groups visiting Disney World together remain together. Access to the edge of the platform is prevented by a gate which is opened once the monorail has arrived and disembarked the arriving passengers on the other side of the platform. If there is a delay of more than a minute or two in waiting for the next monorail one is kept informed of the reason for the delay and the progress the expected train is making towards the station.

Once aboard and the automatic doors of the monorail have closed, one is welcomed aboard, told to remain seated and "for one's own safety" to stay away from open windows. The monorail takes a circuitous route to one of the two Disney locations (the Epcot Center or the Magic Kingdom) during which time a friendly disembodied voice introduces one briefly to the pleasures of the world one is about to enter and the methods of transport available between its various locations. As the monorail slows towards its destination one is told how to disembark once the automatic doors open and how to move from the station to the entrance gates, and reminded to take one's possessions with one and to take care of oneself, and children in one's care, on disembarking. Once again these instructions are reinforced, in a variety of ways, as one moves towards the gates.

It will be apparent from the above that Disney Productions is able to handle large crowds of visitors in a most orderly fashion. Potential trouble is anticipated and prevented. Opportunities for disorder are minimized by constant instruction, by physical barriers which severely limit the choice of action available and by the surveillance of omnipresent employees who detect and rectify the slightest deviation.

The vehicles that carry people between locations are an important component of the system of physical barriers. Throughout Disney World vehicles are used as barriers. This is particularly apparent in the Epcot Center, . . . where many exhibits are accessible only via special vehicles which automatically secure one once they begin moving.

Control strategies are embedded in both environmental features and structural relations. In both cases control structures and activities have other functions which are highlighted so that the control function is overshadowed. Nonetheless, control is pervasive. For example, virtually every pool, fountain, and flower garden serves both as an aesthetic object and to direct visitors away from, or towards, particular locations. Similarly, every Disney Productions employee, while visibly and primarily engaged in other functions, is also engaged in the maintenance of order. This integration of functions is real and not simply an appearance: beauty *is* created, safety *is* protected, employees *are* helpful. The effect is, however, to embed the control function into the "woodwork" where its presence is unnoticed but its effects are ever present.

A critical consequence of this process of embedding control in other structures is that control becomes consensual. It is effected with the willing cooperation of those being controlled so that the controlled become, as Foucault has observed, the source of their own control. Thus, for example, the batching that keeps families together provides for family unity while at the same time ensuring that parents will be available to control their children. By seeking a definition of order within Disney

World that can convincingly be presented as being in the interest of visitors, order maintenance is established as a voluntary activity which allows coercion to be reduced to a minimum. Thus, adult visitors willingly submit to a variety of devices that increase the flow of consumers through Disney World, such as being corralled on the monorail platform, so as to ensure the safety of their children. Furthermore, while doing so they gratefully acknowledge the concern Disney Productions has for their family, thereby legitimating its authority, not only in the particular situation in question, but in others as well. Thus, while profit ultimately underlies the order Disney Productions seeks to maintain, it is pursued in conjunction with other objectives that will encourage the willing compliance of visitors in maintaining Disney profits. This approach to profit making, which seeks a coincidence of corporate and individual interests (employee and consumer alike), extends beyond the control function and reflects a business philosophy to be applied to all corporate operations (Peters and Waterman, 1982).

The coercive edge of Disney's control system is seldom far from the surface, however, and becomes visible the moment the Disney-visitor consensus breaks down, that is, when a visitor attempts to exercise a choice that is incompatible with the Disney order. It is apparent in the physical barriers that forcefully prevent certain activities as well as in the action of employees who detect breaches of order. This can be illustrated by an incident that occurred during a visit to Disney World by Shearing and his daughter, during the course of which she developed a blister on her heel. To avoid further irritation she removed her shoes and proceeded to walk barefooted. They had not progressed ten yards before they were approached by a very personable security guard dressed as a Bahamian police officer, with white pith helmet and white gloves that perfectly suited the theme of the area they were moving through (so that he, at first, appeared more like a scenic prop than a security person), who informed them that walking barefoot was, "for the safety of visitors," not permitted. When informed that, given the blister, the safety of this visitor was likely to be better secured by remaining barefooted, at least on the walkways, they were informed that their safety and how best to protect it was a matter for Disney Productions to determine while they were on Disney property and that unless they complied he would be compelled to escort them out of Disney World. Shearing's daughter, on learning that failure to comply with the security guard's instruction would deprive her of the pleasures of Disney World, quickly decided that she would prefer to further injure her heel and remain on Disney property. As this example illustrates, the source of Disney Productions' power rests both in the physical coercion it can bring to bear and in its capacity to induce cooperation by depriving visitors of a resource that they value.

The effectiveness of the power that control of a "fun place" has is vividly illustrated by the incredible queues of visitors who patiently wait, sometimes for hours, for admission to exhibits. These queues not only call into question the common knowledge that queuing is a quintessentially English pastime (if Disney World is any indication Americans are at least as good, if not better, at it), but provide evidence of the considerable inconvenience that people can be persuaded to tolerate so long as they believe that their best interests require it. While the source of this perception is the image of Disney World that the visitor brings to it, it is, interestingly, reinforced through the queuing process itself. In many exhibits queues are structured so that one is brought close to the entrance at several points, thus periodically giving one a glimpse of the fun to come while at the same time encouraging one that the wait will soon be over.

Visitor participation in the production of order within Disney World goes beyond the more obvious control examples we have noted so far. An important aspect of the order Disney Productions attempts to maintain is a particular image of Disney World and the American industrialists who sponsor its exhibits (General Electric, Kodak, Kraft Foods, etc.). Considerable care is taken to ensure that every feature of Disney World reflects a positive view of the American Way, especially its use of, and reliance on, technology. Visitors are, for example, exposed to an almost constant stream of directions by employees, robots in human form and disembodied recorded voices (the use of recorded messages and robots permits precise control over the content and tone of the directions given) that convey the desired message. Disney World acts as a giant magnet attracting millions of Americans and visitors from other lands who pay to learn of the wonders of American capitalism.

Visitors are encouraged to participate in the production of the Disney image while they are in Disney World and to take it home with them so that they can reproduce it for their families and friends. One way this is done is through the "Picture Spots," marked with signposts, to be found throughout Disney World, that provide direction with respect to the images to capture on film (with cameras that one can borrow free of charge) for the slide shows and photo albums to be prepared "back home." Each spot provides views which exclude anything unsightly (such as garbage containers) so as to ensure that the visual images visitors take away of Disney World will properly capture Disney's order. A related technique is the Disney characters who wander through the complex to provide "photo opportunities" for young children. These characters apparently never talk to visitors, and the reason for this is presumably so that their media-based images will not be spoiled.

As we have hinted throughout this discussion, training is a pervasive feature of the control system of Disney Productions. It is not, however, the redemptive soul-training of the carceral project but an ever-present flow of directions for, and definitions of, order directed at every visitor. Unlike carceral training, these messages do not require detailed knowledge of the individual. They are, on the contrary, for anyone and everyone. Messages are, nonetheless, often conveyed to single individuals or small groups of friends and relatives. For example, in some of the newer exhibits, the vehicles that take one through swivel and turn so that one's gaze can be precisely directed. Similarly, each seat is fitted with individual sets of speakers that talk directly to one, thus permitting a seductive sense of intimacy while simultaneously imparting a uniform message.

In summary, within Disney World control is embedded, preventative, subtle, cooperative and apparently noncoercive and consensual. It focuses on categories, requires no knowledge of the individual and employs pervasive surveillance. Thus, although disciplinary, it is distinctively noncarceral. Its order is instrumental and determined by the interests of Disney Productions rather than moral and absolute. As anyone who has visited Disney World knows, it is extraordinarily effective.

While this new instrumental discipline is rapidly becoming a dominant force in social control . . . it is as different from the Orwellian totalitarian nightmare as it is from the carceral regime. Surveillance is pervasive, but it is the antithesis of the blatant control of the Orwellian State: its source is not government and its vehicle is not Big Brother. The order of instrumental discipline is not the unitary order of a central State but diffuse and separate orders defined by private authorities responsible for the feudal-like domains of Disney World, condominium estates, commercial complexes and the like. Within contemporary discipline, control is as fine-grained as Orwell imagined but its features are very different. . . . It is thus, paradoxically, not to Orwell's socialist-inspired Utopia that we must look for a picture of contemporary control but to the capitalist-inspired disciplinary model conceived of by Huxley who, in his *Brave New World*, painted a picture of consensually based control that bears a striking resemblance to the disciplinary control of Disney World and other corporate control systems. Within Huxley's imaginary world people are seduced into conformity by the pleasures offered by the drug "soma" rather than coerced into compliance by threat of Big Brother, just as people today are seduced to conform by the pleasures of consuming the goods that corporate power has to offer.

The contrasts between morally based justice and instrumental control, carceral punishment and corporate control, the Panopticon and Disney World and Orwell's and Huxley's visions are succinctly captured by the novelist Beryl Bainbridge's observations about a recent journey she made retracing J. B. Priestley's celebrated trip around Britain. She notes how during his travels in 1933 the centre of the cities and towns he visited were defined by either a church or a centre of government (depicting the coalition between Church and State in the production of order that characterizes morally based regimes).

During her more recent trip one of the changes that struck her most forcibly was the transformation that had taken place in the centre of cities and towns. These were now identified not by churches or town halls, but by shopping centres; often vaulted glass-roofed structures that she found reminiscent of the cathedrals they had replaced both in their awe-inspiring architecture and in the hush that she found they sometimes created. What

was worshipped in these contemporary cathedrals, she noted, was not an absolute moral order but something much more mundane: people were "worshipping shopping" and through it, we would add, the private authorities, the order and the corporate power their worship makes possible.

REFERENCES

Bainbridge, B. 1984. Television interview with Robert Fulford on "*Realities*" Global Television, Toronto, October.

Foucault, M. 1977. *Discipline and Punish: The Birth of Prison.* New York: Vintage.

Peters, T., & R. H. Waterman, Jr. 1982. *In Search of Excellence: Lessons from America's Best-Run Companies.* New York: Warner.

Priestley, J. B. 1934. *English Journey: Being a Rambling but Truthful Account of What One Man Saw and Heard and Felt and Thought during a Journey through England the Autumn of the Year 1933.* London: Heinemann and Gollancz.

35

Waaseta (Personal Connections)

Whitney Azoy

Whitney Azoy, who received his PhD in anthropology from the University of Virginia, has worked as a columnist for the Bangor Daily News *(Maine) and as a diplomat in Muslim countries, including Afghanistan and Iran. In recent years he has been an advisor to Afghani Interim President Hamid Karzai. He is author of the book* Buzkashi: Game and Power in Afghanistan, *which examines the game that entails an aggressive struggle between horsemen over a calf carcass.*

This is a tale of two conversations separated by nearly three decades and about 3,000 miles. Its theme is the power of personal connections, known in Persian as *waaseta*. It deals, as the best stories do nowadays, with Them (traditional Muslims) and Us (modern Westerners). It asks three questions: (1) Does the concept of personal connections mark a difference between Them and Us? (2) Is this difference growing or shrinking? (3) Is that movement (the growing or the shrinking) for the good?

The first conversation took place in 1973 Iran, during the Watergate investigation back home. I was a diplomat serving under Ambassador Richard Helms, the former CIA director (1967–1973) who knew too much about the break-in cover-up and thus had to be gotten out of Washington. A young man then, I felt at first blush much ashamed of President Nixon and, by extension the political culture of my country. I knew a dean at Tehran University. We came to be "friends," a concept that in the Persian sense can mean almost anything but which, for us, entailed a semblance of trust.

One day we got to talking about Watergate. I am—as all readers should be—suspicious of so-called remembered conversations, especially when they're rendered in quotation marks, but this writer asks for your trust as he tries to recall word-for-word.

U.S. diplomat: "Off the record, I have to admit it. Watergate's awful. Nixon's lying. I feel ashamed. If I weren't on the embassy staff, I'd say so out loud."

Iranian dean: "Whatever you do, don't say so out loud. You're a grown man. Don't act like a child. But tell me: Why on earth do you feel so ashamed? What's there to feel ashamed about?"

U.S. Diplomat: "My president's lying. Everyone knows it. I feel so embarrassed."

Iranian dean: "Are you lying for him?"

U.S. diplomat: "No, not yet. But I'm supposed to represent the United States. I'm an American, and now Americans look like fools."

Iranian dean: "On the contrary, you look like citizens. Americans have never looked better to Iranians, certainly not since 1953 when your government with people like Helms wrecked our government. [In that year CIA agent Kermit Roosevelt, son of W's hero T. R., staged a coup which ousted nationalist prime minister Mohammed Mossadegh and reinstalled the exiled Shah Mohammed Reza Pahlevi. The issue, of course, was oil—Iran's oil. Iranians haven't forgotten.] But for now the ordinary American people look pretty good."

U.S. Diplomat: ???

Iranian dean: "You Americans—the people, I mean—are speaking up and taking action. You're going to get Nixon. You're going to do it despite his being president, despite his power, despite his personal connections. No one—no matter how powerful and well-connected—is above your laws. You've got checks and balances. We wish to God it were the same in Iran. We'd get rid of this shah that you forced on us. You're doing it yourselves at home. Why can't you let us do it here in our home?"

It was shortly thereafter that the U.S. diplomat switched to anthropology . . . and soon returned, less well paid and pampered, to the Persian-speaking world. I kept my (now lifelong) embassy friends, developed cordial links with their successors, moved from city to village, and shifted modes. Whereas I used to promote my own

"Waaseta (Personal Connections)" by Whitney Azoy as appeared in *Bangor Daily News,* February 9–10, 2002, p. A9.

country (of which I remained proud, not least for our rule of law as cited by the dean), now I tried to learn what I could of another culture, that of backwoods northern Afghanistan where Persian is *lingua franca.*

Waaseta—the concept of personal connections—was everywhere. Your family core group was a given; what really mattered were your personal connections beyond home and hearth. You were defined by it: enabled by knowing some people, limited by not knowing others. "Name" or reputation—the currency of old-time, hinterland politics among both great *khans* and small peasants—was ultimately reckoned by whom you knew . . . and whom you could get to do favors for you. As waaseta moved from countryside to city, it quickly acquired all the trappings of what we call "corruption." Read "The Shah's Last Ride," by William Shawcross, which describes that phenomenon and Reza Pahlevi's consequent downfall in Iran. Afghanistan was going the same way, albeit less spectacularly because it has no oil.

As an American (and a former official to boot), I was first assumed by rural folk to have extraordinary urban connections: with Kabul's bureaucracy, with Washington's presidents and Cabinet members. Endlessly I explained that (a) I knew no one of importance; and that (b) America didn't work that way anyhow. I cited Nixon's fall from power. I quoted the Iranian dean. The illusion of my well-connectedness peaked early, gradually subsided, but never quite went away.

Regrettably, not even now. On the phone last week was a voice I last heard in 1977 northern Afghanistan. How "Hedayatullah," now a refugee in Germany, found me remains unclear but after half an hour of reminiscences he got to the point. "I have this project for the reconstruction of Afghanistan. You and I can do it together. I have the people. You can get the U.S. government money. You have the waaseta—the personal connections."

It's not a bad project, and I said so. I also said that I'll do what (little) I can, and I will. But then I reminded Hedayatullah of our conversations on waaseta a quarter century ago, of how I had no special connections, and of how America depends more on law and merit than on

pull. I even reminded him of the Iranian dean. About the rule of law. About checks and balances.

All refugees are necessarily news addicts. Why? Their survival depends on knowing what's what in an alien environment. No refugees (save perhaps the Vietnamese) are as long on enterprise and short on self-pity as the Afghans. I should have known that Hedayatullah would be up to speed.

"That Iranian dean is out of date," he said. "Isn't Enron all about connections? Nixon was president too soon. But the great Bush, thanks to God, is safe. Now it's all waaseta."

We were speaking in Persian, and I got lost in the *non-sequiturs.* "Slow down," I said, using the phrase (*"aastaa buru"*) from an Afghan wedding song which speaks to the need for care in creating connections. "What does Enron have to do with Nixon? And Nixon with Bush? And how come you like Bush so much."

"Nixon fell then, but he wouldn't now. Not even with Enron giving him money," said Hedayatullah. "We like Bush because his bombs delivered us from the Taliban, much as his father's chief, the great Reagan, gave us Stingers to defeat the Soviets. Who cares if Bush has been on Enron's payroll? No one can touch him."

"Whoa," I said in cowboy lingo defense of my Texas president. "Hold your horses. No one can touch Bush because he's never been paid by Enron. Not even to the value of one *afghani* [the Afghan currency, now trading at about 35,000 to the dollar]. Check your facts. Enron simply contributed to his election campaigns."

"Election campaigns? Not that we Afghans care, but how did Bush, may God protect him, ever come to have election campaigns?" asked my no-longer-backwoods friend. "How was that last election campaign decided? What about Florida? What about the Supreme Court?"

"What about them?" I countered with some asperity. While skeptical myself, I don't like it when non-Americans take pot shots at our domestic politics.

"It was all waaseta," he said. "All personal connections. Even America's that way now. And all I want from you is a little waaseta."

Please check the three questions in paragraph no. 1.

36

The Modern State
Nation-Builder or Nation-Killer?

Pierre L. van den Berghe

Pierre van den Berghe received his PhD from Harvard University in 1960. He has written extensively on ethnic and race relations, sociobiology, tourism, and genocide in sub-Saharan Africa and Latin America. He is a professor of sociology and an adjunct professor of anthropology at the University of Washington.

Torrents of scholarly and political ink have flowed about the modern "nation-state" (Almond and Coleman, 1960; Coleman, 1958; Coleman and Rosberg, 1964; Connor, 1990; Deutsch, 1966, 1969; Deutsch and Foltz, 1963; Emerson, 1960; Gellner, 1982; Hodgkin, 1956; Huntington, 1968; Masur, 1966; Seton-Watson, 1977; Smith, 1979, 1981; Snyder, 1976; Tilly, 1975; Tiryakian and Rogowski, 1985; Wallerstein, 1967; Whitaker, 1962). The strong pro-state bias of most of that literature has often been unrecognized because the authors' underlying statist premises have been implicitly shared by a broad political spectrum ranging from classical liberals to Marxists. My own approach is frankly anarchist. Simply stated, my theses are that the process euphemistically described as nation-building is, in fact, mostly nation-killing; that the vast majority of so-called "nation-states" are nothing of the sort; and that modern nationalism is a blueprint for ethnocide at best, genocide at worst.

CURRENT STATIST MYTHS

Let me first state, then demolish, the often unstated premises of the dominant statist tradition in the literature on nationalism:

1. States are inevitable. You need them to keep the peace.
2. Stable political regimes must rest on legitimacy. Violence is an insecure basis of statecraft.

3. Large states are better than small states because they are more economically viable. "Balkanization" and "tribalism" are bad. Nation-building is good.
4. Since states are supposed to be the political organ of the nation, it is best not to scrutinize too closely their claim to legitimacy. The distinction between state and nation is best obscured by indiscriminately referring to all states as "nation-states" (except for states one dislikes).

To which I respond:

1. States are obviously not inevitable. They have only existed for about 7,000 years of human history. We have done quite well as a species for millions of years without states. Why should we all of a sudden need them? It is true that states have been devastatingly *successful* in recent human history, because they constitute an effective way of organizing coercive violence. State-organized societies have generally won over stateless societies, and have grown rapidly through conquest. Once a state emerges in a region, it typically conquers its non-state neighbors, or forces them to develop states in self-defense. And, of course, big states gobble up small states, so that the general trend of history has been toward bigger and bigger states. The only inevitability in all this is the advantage to those who organize collective violence better. States, far from keeping the peace, wage external war on their neighbors, and parasitize their own citizens through intimidation. Let me offer, if not a definition of the state, at least an apt description of what many states do much of the time: States are killing machines run by the few to steal from the many. A state is really a big gang or mafia that extracts booty from its rivals and "protection money" from its own citizens through the use or the threat of violence. Conversely, gangs or mafias are embryonic states.

"The Modern State: Nation-Builder or Nation-Killer" by Pierre van den Berghe from *International Journal of Group Tensions,* Vol. 22, No. 3, 1992, pp. 191–207. Reprinted with kind permission from Springer Science and Business Media.

2. Legitimacy is at best an elusive concept. It rests on a state-invented ideology to justify the existence of the state and to disguise its parasitic, exploitative and tyrannical nature. The most that can be said about legitimacy is that, to the extent that the state ideology is believed by the people, the state can economize on the use of repressive violence. It is, however, unlikely that states can fool most people most of the time, and that state domination rests primarily on legitimacy. Even many of the self-proclaimed democracies (e.g. Ancient Athens, the United States, Israel, South Africa) are or were minority governments, or "*Herrenvolk* democracies" as I called them, with political rights restricted by age, gender, legal status, religion, race or ethnicity. These states ruled not by the consent of the governed, but by the consent of the governors. George Washington's or Thomas Jefferson's slaves did not sign the Declaration of Independence or vote on the constitution. State power rests in the last analysis on violence or the threat of violence. Murder and theft are at the root of statecraft. Claims of legitimacy are merely the self-serving rationalizations of those with an interest in hiding the coercive and parasitic nature of the state.

3. If one likes states, then it stands to reason that one should also like them big and powerful. Economic viability or "economies of scale" are invoked to keep large states from breaking up. That world mafia of state-controlling elites misnamed "United Nations," for example, always rallies to the support of existing states, no matter how obnoxious, when they are threatened with "Balkanization" or "tribalism." The argument linking size of state to economic viability is sheer nonsense. What is or was economically unviable about Genoa, Bruges or Luebeck, or, today, about Lichtenstein, Singapore, Abu Dhabi, or Monaco? Yet, this inane argument has been used both to deny entities as large and prosperous as Quebec a right to independence, and to prevent basket cases like Ethiopia and Pakistan-Bangladesh from breaking up. Surely, the size of states and economic prosperity are totally independent variables. There is simply no evidence of the superiority of big states over small ones, except as killing machines. This is the only sense in which, say, Iraq is superior to Kuwait, Germany to Belgium, the Soviet Union to Poland, the United States to Grenada, South Africa to Lesoto. Large states have the ability to conquer small states, but no other evident mark of superiority.

4. The obfuscation of the distinction between state and nation, both in the social science literature and in common parlance, is not simply an innocuous piece of intellectual sloppiness. It serves the interests of ruling elites. The most common sleight of hand is that most insidious of hyphenations, the "nation-state." To be sure, there *is* such an animal: Japan, Swaziland and Somalia, for example, are genuine nation-states. The overwhelming majority of their inhabitants speak the same language, share the same culture and history, look on one another as a single ethny. In common parlance, however, "nation-state" has come to mean *any* state: Nigeria, Zaire, India, Switzerland, Yugoslavia, Canada, Trinidad, you name it. That is, the term "nation" has been made redundant to "state."

In fact, some 73 per cent of the world's independent states are multinational (by the criterion of a nation-state as an entity where 95 per cent of the population speak the same language), and, conversely, 42 percent of ethnies or nations are split up between several states (e.g. Basques, Kurds, Koreans, Hungarians, Ewe, Bakongo and many others) (Neilsson, 1985). Until the advent of the "modern" state (using 1789 as a convenient birthdate for such an animal), it was totally unthreatening for states to recognize their multinational character. The Ottoman, Moghul, Czarist, Hapsburg, British, French, and other empires quite happily termed themselves multinational, or *Vielvölkerstaaten* in German parlance. Even the late but unmourned Soviet Union, that gold medalist in murdering its own citizens, had the saving grace of still recognizing its multinational character. Contemporary events clearly show how realistic that perception was.

THE NATIONALIST STATE: A FATAL MUTATION

The French Revolution, however, destroyed the candor of traditional empires. This brings me to the heart of my argument, namely that the modern state, inspired by the French Revolution and its ideology of nationalism and popular sovereignty, underwent a lethal mutation. In order to understand what makes modern states so ethnocidal and genocidal, let us first define what makes states modern. The modernity of states has three main ingredients, the first technological, the second ideological, and the third a corollary of the first two:

1. Modern states have an industrialized technology of destruction and mass terror.
2. Modern states legitimate their existence by claiming to represent popular sovereignty.
3. Modern states increasingly shift their lethal violence from external to internal use, and direct much of it toward ethnocide (efforts to stamp out cultural, linguistic or religious diversity) or genocide (murdering people on ethnic or racial grounds).

Let us expand on each of these points.

1. The first one is obvious. Modern state killing has become much more efficient. Not only have weapons become much better, but they can be mass-produced rela-

tively inexpensively by a vast industrial machine (or purchased from other states or private arms dealers). States, in short, can get more and more bang for their buck, and some weapons of mass destruction are quite cheap (automatic small arms, poison gas). The French Revolution coincided roughly with the Industrial Revolution, and already Napoleon's armies could blast their foes with thousands of cannons. But the real breakthrough in mass killing came half a century later with repeating firearms, especially the machine gun, and railways and steamships for rapid transport of troops, horses and artillery. The American Civil War, the Crimean War, and the Franco-Prussian War were among the first large-scale industrial wars, but the same technology also facilitated the last colonial expansion of Europe in Africa and Asia. The great superiority of white over black was that of the Gatling gun over the spear.

So long as the advanced killing technology was beyond the reach of large parts of the world, as was the case until World War II, it could be used quite effectively for conquest. Now, however, small guerrilla bands with AK47's, ground-to-air missiles and plastic explosives can stalemate major powers, and upstart dictators of small countries can blackmail them with threats of unacceptable damage (as Saddam Hussein tried to do in 1990 though he overplayed his hand somewhat). Since World War I, external wars between sizeable states with comparable armaments have become a negative sum game: everybody loses. The impact of the two World Wars on all European belligerents is a case in point. Only the United States emerged as a real victor, and then mostly by getting into the war late and at a distance. Its homeland was still beyond the reach of its enemies. The latest example of the increasing unwinnability of international war is the Iran-Iraq war which was a repeat on a small scale of World War I (trench warfare, human wave attacks, poison gas) with the same outcome: stalemated exhaustion. Modern states, in short, have become vast military-industrial complexes with enormous but increasingly unusable overkill. The Soviet Union is the first major state to have collapsed in good part under the unwieldy deadweight of its military and repressive machine. The hypertrophy of the army, the police and the Gulag have produced the sclerosis of the state. The state apparatus of external and internal terror drowned in the torrent of blood it produced. The parasitic state nearly killed its host society, and ultimately committed suicide.

2. The second characteristic of modern states, noted by most analysts of nationalism (e.g. Deutsch, 1966, 1969; Emerson, 1960; Huntington, 1968; Seton-Watson, 1977; Smith, 1979; Snyder, 1976), is that, in the aftermath of the French Revolution, a new ideological fashion spread. States increasingly claimed legitimacy through "popular sovereignty," to replace the divine right of kings, paternalism, or the simple but effective notion that might is right. Now governments claimed to incarnate the "will of the people," and started creating new supposedly representative institutions. But who is "the people" whose collective will is supposedly expressed? If it has a collective will, it presumably is a community, not a mere assemblage of individuals. Social classes or estates would not do because their interests are too clearly at variance. Besides, the revolution was fought against class interests and privileges. There was, however, another pre-existing collectivity, the nation, which was ideally suited to become the new legitimating myth of the state. The people was simply the nation.

Nationalism antedated, of course, the modern state but not until the 19th century did nationalism become *the* legitimating myth of the state. The new state could only be legitimate if it was the political arm of a nation, and, conversely, a nation now had a claim to statehood. If, in fact, most states had been nations or something close to it, and most nations had a state, the new ideology would have been a description of reality. However, even the birthplace and prototype of the modern state, Jacobin and Napoleonic France, did not come close to being a nation until a century or so later, as Eugene Weber (1979) has so well documented. The *grande nation* only became so by ruthlessly suppressing the languages and traditions of a dozen *petites nations* all around the periphery of Ile de France: the Flemings, Bretons, Alsacians, Corsicans, Catalans, Occitans, Basques, and others. The blueprint for nation-building was born: ethnocide (the cultural suppression of ethnic and linguistic diversity), or genocide (the physical extermination of ethnies). If the state is to become one nation, there is obviously no room for other nations.

Nation-building and nation-killing become complementary aspects of the same policy of fostering the ethnic, religious, linguistic, political and economic interests of those who control the state at the expense of all others. The state becomes identified with one ethnic group (not even necessarily a numerical majority, e.g. in South Africa the ruling Afrikaners are barely eight per cent of the population), what the Germans aptly call the *Staatsvolk*. Everyone else is subordinate.

It may be argued that domination of the state by one ethnic group is not a modern phenomenon. Was not, for instance, the Ottoman Empire a Turkish state? The answer is that, in many important ways, it was not. Non-Muslim minorities (especially Jews, Armenians and Greeks) not only had considerable autonomy and privileges under the millet system, but they were disproportionately represented in the upper echelons of government and business, as indeed were a number of foreign advisers and mercenaries. The Janissaries, the backbone of the army, were drawn from non-Muslim, non-Turkic groups. Christians and Jews had full freedom of worship. Everyone was free to speak his own language, and Greek, for instance, continued to be widely spoken in urban areas. Istanbul was a Babel of peoples and tongues. The ruling class of the Empire, in short, was largely indifferent as to what languages people spoke so long as they remained docile and paid their taxes.

The fatal mutation came during World War I when the Ottoman Empire disintegrated into would-be national states, half-a-dozen Arab ones under British and French tutelage (including Palestine and Lebanon, future hotbeds of endless nationalist conflicts). The rump of the Empire became the Turkish Republic under the militant nationalists known as the Young Turks. The outcome was the first great genocide of the 20th century, the murder of over a million Armenians (Hovannisian, 1986). Since then, the history of Turkey has been one of intolerance towards all non-Turkish minorities, even Muslim ones like the Kurds, whose very existence is denied. There are no Kurds, the Turkish government tells the rest of the world, only "mountain Turks." As for the Armenian genocide, it never happened if one is to believe the Turkish government; lots of people died during the war, including some Armenians, but that was just the unfortunate consequence of the inevitable turmoil of war according to official Turkish historiography. Turks too suffered. (One is reminded of Himmler's commiseration for his SS who had such a tough job running concentration camps.)

Traditional empires were generally tolerant of, or at least indifferent to, ethnic, linguistic or even religious diversity. For the most part, they even rejoiced in their subjects' diversity. Colonial India, Nigeria, or Congo were made-to-order for a policy of dividing and ruling. The more tribes, castes and religions, the merrier, as far as the ruling class was concerned. Even the French were much less than half-hearted in their supposed policy of assimilation in Asia or Africa. The French state was ruthlessly assimilationist within the *hexagone* (metropolitan France). In Senegal, Madagascar, Indochina or even Algeria, it never really believed that all those dark colonials were potential Frenchmen. Systematic suppression of ethnic diversity is the hallmark of modern nationalism. Colonial empires can live quite happily with a Babel of tongues and cultures.

3. As a corollary of the first and second characteristics of modern states, there has been a shift from external to internal violence. As weaponry became more and more destructive and equally distributed between states so that even third-rate powers could threaten massive destruction, external wars became less and less attractive and winnable. The Vietnams and Afghanistans of the world can reduce superpowers to bloody and costly stalemates and even defeats. Even the "victory" of the Gulf War is a Pyrrhic one: Kuwait was destroyed before it was saved. At the same time, the would-be nation-states are riddled with hostile, captive nations within their own borders which they seek to subdue in the name of nation-building.

The figures are eloquent. Harff and Gurr (1987), who compiled a necrology of mass state violence since 1945, document that, at a minimum, two thirds of all people killed by states have been internal victims of genocides or what they call "politicides." Estimates of internal bloodbaths yield totals of 6.8 to 16.3 million victims (megadeaths, for short) between 1945 and 1987, depending on whose figures one accepts. This compared to 3.34 megadeaths in international wars between 1945 and 1980. There were six internal megadeath events by their account, involving the USSR, the People's Republic of China, Indonesia, Pakistan-Bangladesh, Kampuchea, and Afghanistan. The one clearly international event in the same league was the Iran-Iraq War, not included in the Harff and Gurr statistics since these stop at 1980 for international conflicts. Harff and Gurr have a third category for "colonial and civil wars" which included such protracted conflicts as the Indochina War and the Nigerian Civil War, which made another 3.13 megadeaths. Many of these civil wars were scarcely distinguishable in nature from politicides and genocides, or at least included within them major massacres by governments of unarmed civilians within their own state boundaries.

Whichever way one classifies acts of state-sponsored murder, it is clear that, since World War II, something like three quarters of all fatalities were caused by states butchering their own citizens in genocides or politicides. Ten megadeaths for the period seems a reasonable middle estimate.

THE "NATION-STATE" A LEGITIMATION MYTH

My analysis will no doubt displease and offend many. First, state-controlling elites insist that their ethnocides and genocides are internal affairs, and that world order rests on governments giving each other *carte blanche* in butchering their own citizens. Such was obviously the dominant "gentlemen's agreement" at the United Nations (a sad misnomer for Squabbling States). In that sanctimonious forum of state-controlling elites, delegates have achieved near-unanimity on only one issue: to make sure that the Genocide Convention would remain, quite literally, a dead letter (Kuper, 1981, 1982, 1985). Second, most social scientists have done their best to befuddle the issue of nationalism for the benefit of state-controlling elites. It is to that scholarly conspiracy of befuddlement that I shall now turn. Political and other social scientists could easily have called the bluff of state-controlling elites calling themselves "nation-states," yet scholars seldom did because of their own statist bias.

How did social scientists cope with the embarrassing fact that most of the world's states are not nations, nor most nations, states (Neilsson, 1985)? The simplest ploy was the uncritical acceptance of the hyphenation "nation-state." The unexamined confusion characterizes at least 90 per cent of post–World War II authors on nationalism and the state. But there were more ingenious forms of befuddlement as well. One is the subjectivist, or "instrumentalist" view of ethnicity and nationalism, which denies the ethny or nation any external or objective reality, and holds that ethnicity or nationhood is whatever people, especially political elites, say it is. If Mobutu says Zaire is a nation, then by definition it is. This radical subjectivist view of nations as the figment of political imaginations in the service of political gains is, in fact, the dominant position in social science.

Another ploy was to redefine nationalism, or to distinguish different types of nationalism in different parts of the world or in different periods. The Africanist literature, especially in the 1960's, is a good example of these mental convolutions (Coleman and Rosberg, 1964; Hodgkin, 1956; Wallerstein, 1967; Young, 1965). Many analysts observed that "nationalism" in Africa was something different from what it was in Europe, yet they overwhelmingly accepted the misnomer. It is plainly grotesque to characterize as "nationalist" the civilian or military kleptocrats who have appropriated African states for private gain, and typically live on incomes 100 times their countries' average, and equally preposterous to call these countries "nation-states" when nine tenths of them are patchworks of ethnies thrown together by artificial colonial boundaries. What we have in nearly all of Africa are small Western-educated elites who inherited an alien, colonial system of government; perpetuated their minority rule through graft, corruption and violence; and appropriated all organs of state control for private exploitation and gain, through a complex network of nepotism and ethnic favoritism. This is about as "nationalist" as the Sicilian mafia, the Medellin drug cartel or the Moghul Empire.

Why then, did scholars persistently misuse these labels? The answer is suggested by the prevalent use of another set of terms dear to Africanists: tribe and tribalism. These terms, be it noted, are seldom used in political analysis, except in Africa and in aboriginal North America. In Africa, they have clearly derogatory connotations. Nationalism is good, modern and progressive; tribalism is bad, traditional and reactionary. African politicians are praised for seeking to maintain "national unity" against the divisive threat of the primitive, atavistic savagery of tribal hatreds. All this invidious vocabulary used to describe African politics and all the supposedly unique features of African conflicts are revealed as an ideological smokescreen when one realizes that what is called "tribalism" in Africa is in fact authentic nationalism, while the so-called "nationism" of African states and their ruling elites is nothing of the sort.

Such perverse misuse of terms was sustained by a multinational coalition of elites. Africanist scholars (mostly from Europe or North America) have been conditioned to look at Africa through a racist prism that made it seem eminently sensible to label groups "tribes" if their members were darkly pigmented, and "nations" if light in color. Thus, the Amhara, Yoruba or Zulu are tribes; the Finns, Danes or Croats are nations. African elites, on the other hand, were also happy with that terminology because it justified their murderous repression of dissident movements as progressive, and appeared to legitimate their claim to be ruling "nation-states." Colonial prejudices and neocolonial interests converged on the perpetuation of analytical obfuscation. The misuse of terms made it easy, for instance, to apply a double standard of judgment to the use of repressive violence in South Africa and the rest of the continent.

A state like South Africa, which never pretended to be a nation, can be safely condemned as reactionary for maintaining an archaic colonial system of racial segregation and ethnic domination, even though its level of murderous repression is moderate compared to the state-sponsored genocidal orgies perpetuated during recent decades in Burundi, Ethiopia, the Sudan, Liberia, Cambodia, Iran, Iraq, or Syria. Sure, the South African police operates death squads and murders political prisoners in detention (or, at least, did until recently), but it does not blanket Bantustans in mustard gas as, for instance, Saddam Hussein did with Kurds in 1988. Sure the South African government periodically bulldozes black urban settlements, but it never forced marched, executed and starved hundreds of thousands of people out of Soweto as the Khmer Rouge did in Phnom-Penh. South Africa has only known one major episode of state-encouraged genocide: the extermination campaigns against the San ("Bushmen") in the Cape from the late 17th through the mid-19th centuries. South Africa is a Herrenvolk democracy, an unwieldy hybrid of a parliamentary regime for the *Staatsvolk*, the Afrikaners, and a garden-variety settler-colonial regime for the black population. It would be a more murderous state if it claimed to be a nation-state.

THE ROUTINIZATION OF GENOCIDE

Notwithstanding, then, the scholarly tradition that would make the Nazi Holocaust a unique or at least exceptional event, the genocide against Jews in the Second World War was merely one of the largest and best documented genocides unleashed by modern nationalism. It was, in fact, only one of *two* genocides perpetuated by the Nazi regime, the other being that of the Rom ("Gypsies"), and one of hundreds of genocidal massacres by scores of states during the last two centuries. If one defines genocide as a deliberate state-sponsored or supported attempt to decimate large numbers of people on the basis of race or ethnicity, by direct execution, death camps, death marches, induced famines or other methods designed to kill, then the instances certainly run into the hundreds.

The majority of them are small-scale, but nonetheless highly successful events, involving the virtual extermination of small marginal groups that only a few anthropologists have ever heard of, and who therefore can be killed silently and away from the spotlight of unwanted publicity. This has been the fate of countless "aboriginal" groups in Australia, Southern Africa and America, and continues to this date in Amazonia. But even massive genocides involving hundreds of thousands or even millions of "civilized" victims in Europe have been recently "rediscovered," e.g., the deliberate decimation by starvation, exposure and unchecked epidemics of perhaps up to 800,000 German prisoners of war in U.S. and French camps in 1945, an atrocity almost certainly attributable to Dwight Eisenhower (Bacque, 1989) and the genocide by famine of between three and eight million Ukrainians by Stalin in 1932–33 (Commission on the Ukraine Famine, 1988; Conquest, 1986). Hitler, Stalin and Eisenhower all belong in the great fraternity of leaders of genocidal states. The terror and horror of mass genocidal killing are not aberrations of the modern state; they are in the very nature of it. We live in an era of routinized holocausts. If *the* Holocaust has a distinctive characteristic it is that it was conducted with Teutonic *Gründlichkeit*; otherwise, it was fairly routine.

SOME HINTS ON GENOCIDE PREVENTION

Is genocide inevitable in modern states? Obviously not; not all states are genocidal all the time. There are alternatives, and it is important not only to spell them out, but to understand their limits.

1. Small, weak states with citizen-armies or no armies at all tend to be less lethal than large, strong ones with mercenary armies. This is especially true of small states in the fear-shadow of big ones, like Luxembourg or Switzerland. However, small weak states that are effectively isolated from pressures by neighboring states, and even from news coverage, can conduct genocide with impunity, as shows, for instance, by Burundi.

It is also true that states can be so weak as to be unable to prevent orgies of communal violence that are largely privately sponsored. Sri Lanka is a good example,

but, even though most of the ethnic massacres were not state-sponsored, the state provoked Tamil nationalism by adopting ethnic quota policies systematically favoring the Sinhalese. Lebanon is another case in point, though one greatly complicated by Syrian, Palestinian and Israeli intervention.

2. True nation-states are, by definition, less likely to be internally genocidal, because of lack of targets. Thus, given an acceptance of nationalism as the basis of legitimation for states, the break-up of multinational empires into smaller, weaker, mono-ethnic states is desirable. Not only the rest of the world, but many groups within the former Soviet Union, for example, are breathing more peacefully since the empire began to break down. However, even genuine nation-states can find small minorities to scapegoat. Jews and Rom (Gypsies) together made up under one per cent of Nazi Germany's 1938 population, and, furthermore, most German Jews were so assimilated that, objectively, they were in no sense an alien nation. Still, the Final Solution was only implemented after German conquest incorporated millions of foreign Jews. The Holocaust was overwhelmingly an external, not an internal genocide. Of the two greatest state killers of this century, Nazi Germany and the Stalinist Soviet Union, the former, a nation-state, was externally genocidal, while the latter, a multinational empire, was internally so (to the tune of 30 to 60 million, according to the most credible estimates). The seeming German exception, in fact, confirms our second proposition.

3. Short of a break-up into independent nation-states, multinational states best approximate a Swiss model of a loose confederation of autonomous ethnic or even sub-ethnic groups, like the Swiss canton. Confederal solutions of local autonomy are especially attractive where ethnic groups are largely territorialized as in the case in countries like Belgium, Switzerland, Yugoslavia, the Soviet Union, Canada (between Anglo- and Franco-Canadians), India, and many others. The more territorially dispersed ethnic groups are, and the more multi-ethnic areas (especially *urban* areas) become, the thornier ethnic problems grow. The lesson is that states should not devolve power to local authorities, but discourage colonization settlements, e.g. of Russians in non-Russian parts of the Soviet Union, of Jews in the West Bank of Palestine, or of Javanese in Borneo and West Irian, to mention only three state-sponsored designs to extend the domination of the Staatsvolk to ethnically alien areas. Every colonization scheme contains the seeds of ethnic conflict and potential genocide.

4. What to do about the world's many ethnically scrambled areas where neat territorial partition along natural lines is not possible or would be too costly? Even then, partition may turn out not to be such a bad solution, as the relatively successful Cypriot example shows

(imposed though it was by Turkish arms). Over a third of the island's Greek and Turkish population had to move at great personal cost and suffering, but ethnic violence has ceased since partition and the creation of two ethnic micro-states. Palestinian partition might also have worked, had it not been undone by Israeli conquest in the 1967 war. However, let us admit that partition is often unrealistic and undesirable.

There are many types of ethnically and/or racially "scrambled" situations, each with its special kinds of problems: post-slavery situations such as in the Caribbean, Brazil and the United States; massive waves of immigration as in Canada, Argentina, Australia and the United States; temporary labor migration as in many African and European cities, "middleman" mercantile communities as the overseas Chinese and Indians in South East Asia, Eastern Africa and the Caribbean, and so on. The very diversity of such situations defies simple solutions, and state policies have varied enormously, with equally diverse consequences. At one extreme have been genocidal massacres (e.g. of Chinese in Indonesia); encouraged terrorism to foster mass flight (e.g. of Palestinians in Israel during wars); and state-managed expulsions (e.g. of Asians from Uganda under Idi Amin). At the other end of the spectrum, some states have institutionalized what Lijphart (1977) has called "consociationism." In countries like Belgium, Canada, Yugoslavia, and others, the state has an official policy not only of federalism based on multilingualism and recognition of ethnic distinctions, but also a system of ethnic proportional representation in the organs of government.

In between these extremes of intolerance and encouragement of ethnic diversity fall a wide range of state policies. Some states, notably France and most of Latin America (with the partial exception of Paraguay), have resolutely ignored cultural and linguistic diversity and pushed through the dominant language and culture through official monolingualism and propagation of the "national" culture of the ruling elite. State-encouraged assimilation to the dominant ethny is the essence of the much vaunted "nation-building" efforts of many governments and can itself range from passive ethnocide through "benign neglect" of minority cultures presumed to be on a "natural" road to extinction, all the way to the active genocide of prohibiting the use of languages, forcing people to change their names, banning cultural practices, and imposing ethnically based legal restrictions on property-holding, marriage, trading, employment and so on.

It is also frequently the case that the same country can simultaneously or sequentially practice several forms of repression ranging from genocide to "benign neglect." E.g. the United States has sequentially used the whole panoply of repression against American Indians: genocide, expulsions, land "relocations," land theft, linguistic and cultural suppression, kidnaping of children in government schools, encapsulation into internal colonies ("reservations"), the "benign neglect" of the "termination policy," and the parody of "national autonomy" based on continuously broken "treaty rights."

In a slightly different mode, some countries have practiced different forms and degrees of repression against different ethnic groups. For instance, Turkey has conducted genocide against Armenians, and repeated attempts at forceful ethnocide against Kurds, but has been relatively tolerant of Jews. The variations, in short, are legion (Horowitz, 1985; van den Berghe, 1981, 1990; Wirsing, 1981). Even supposedly benign policies such as "reverse discrimination" or "affirmative action" have frequently had adverse consequences for their supposed beneficiaries, and have turned out to be, in fact, policies of tokenism and internal colonialism (Glazer, 1975; van den Berghe, 1981).

TOWARD A DENATIONALIZED STATE

Assuming that one seeks tolerance of ethnic diversity and the maximum preservation of individual rights to conduct one's life through the linguistic and cultural medium of one's choice, a few prescriptions and caveats emerge from past experiences of many states. Ideally, the state should not be associated with any particular group, but should be the neutral, common property of all of its citizens. I am simply advocating an extension of the principle of secularization in the religious sphere to language and other cultural domains. Much as the state should tolerate all religions but be associated with none, the state should also be "denationalized."

This is a difficult prescription, especially in the linguistic sphere, because, while it is easy enough to transact government business without reference to religion, one must use some language to communicate. Almost inevitably, the language of the majority (or of the ruling elite) becomes dominant. The state, however, has no need to declare any language "national," and no mandate to push, protect or even encourage any language at the expense of others. Competing languages operate in a sort of marketplace of utility in which the state best not interfere, except perhaps in the field of education, where schooling at all levels should be made available in the languages of choice of individuals (or their parents), and in government services, which should also be available insofar as possible in the language of choice of those served.

This prescription implies a flexible, demand-based policy of pragmatic multilingualism in ethnically mixed areas, wherein the state would refrain from either declaring any languages official or allocating any definite language rights to officially recognized ethnic groups, but simply provide multilingual facilities to people *as individuals*. For instance, in the Sun Belt of the United States with large Hispanic minorities, any parent, whether Hispanic or Anglo, would have the practical option of sending his or her children to a Spanish-medium, English-medium, or bilingual school, of taking standardized tests in either language, and so on. This is quite distinct from conceding a special right to Hispanics to go to Spanish-medium schools, for such a policy of special rights to minority groups is inevitably resented, and frequently carries a stigma of inferiority for the minority group.

The state then should not only denationalize. It should also incorporate all of its citizens strictly as *individuals*, endowed with strictly equal rights, without any official recognition granted to any group affiliation. Ethnic or racial self-identification should be protected by the state as an individual option (provided it does not entail discrimination against others), but the state itself should pay no attention to the way people choose to identify themselves, much less base policies on such identifications. In fact, the state should not even ask ethnic or racial questions on its census, any more than it should ask religious questions. Ethnicity, in short, should be entirely in the private sphere, as is religion in secular states.

A corollary of the above is that states should also refrain from ethnically or racially based policies of granting special rights or preferences to groups it sees as in need of redress or remedial action. Reverse discrimination, quota systems, and "affirmative action" based on race or ethnicity, whatever their purported benevolence, almost inevitably backfire because they are widely resented by supposedly privileged groups, demean minority groups, result in tokenism, detract from broader class-based solutions to systemic inequalities, set minority groups against each other, benefit the already privileged within the disadvantaged groups, and generally exacerbate ethnic and racial conflicts and perpetuate prejudices. Redressive policies should be based on *class*, not race or ethnicity, and should follow social democratic principles, such as progressive taxation, need-based welfare programs, and the like, with qualifications strictly by individual socioeconomic criteria, not group affiliation.

The French and American Revolutions created the secular state, and that was probably their greatest advance over the preceding age of religious tyranny and conflict. When the state stopped taking sides and interfering in religious conflicts, the latter largely withered into the sphere of private competition. The same revolutions unfortunately created the monster of the nationalist state. Two hundred years of state-sponsored ethnocide and genocide are quite enough. If we must have states, which I am not prepared to concede, let them be small, weak, and hemmed in by broad supra-state economic agencies like the European Community. Above all, let them be not only secular but denationalized. Genuine nation-states are bad enough in their parochialism. Multinational states that masquerade as nations have such a lethal historical record that they can no longer be tolerated. At the very least, they should be exposed with favor toward none.

ACKNOWLEDGMENT

This article is a revision of a paper presented at the First International Congress on Prejudice, Discrimination and Conflict, held in Jerusalem on July 1–4, 1991.

REFERENCES

Almond, G. A., & Coleman, J. S., eds. (1960). *The Politics of the Developing Areas*. Princeton: Princeton University Press.

Bacque, J. (1989). *Other Losses*. Don Mills, Ont.: Stoddart.

Coleman, J. S. (1958). *Nigeria, Background to Nationalism*. Berkeley: University of California Press.

Coleman, J. S., & Rosberg, C., eds. (1964). *Political Parties and National Integration in Tropical Africa*. Berkeley: University of California Press.

Commission on the Ukraine Famine (1988). *Investigation of the Ukraine Famine, 1932–1933, Report to Congress*. Washington: United States Government Printing Office.

Connor, W. (1990). When Is a Nation? *Ethnic and Racial Studies 13*, 92–103.

Conquest, R. (1986). *The Harvest of Sorrow*. New York: Oxford University Press.

Deutsch, K. W. (1966). *Nationalism and Social Communication*. New York: MIT Press.

———. (1969). *Nationalsim and Its Alternatives*. New York: Knopf.

Deutsch, K. W., & Foltz, W. J., eds. (1963) *Nation Building*. New York: Atherton.

Emerson, R. (1960). *From Empire to Nation*. Cambridge, Mass.: Harvard University Press.

Gellner, E. (1982). *Nations and Nationalism*. Oxford: Basil Blackwell.

Glazer, N. (1975). *Affirmative Discrimination*. New York: Basic Books.

Harff, B., & Gurr, T. R. (1987). Genocides and Politicides Since 1945, *Internet on the Holocaust and Genocide*, December, Special Issue 13:1–5.

Hodgkin, T. (1956). *Nationalism in Colonial Africa*. London: Muller.

Horowitz, D. L. (1985). *Ethnic Groups in Conflict*. Berkeley: University of California Press.

Hovannisian, R., ed. (1986). *The Armenian Genocide in Perspective*. New Brunswick: Transaction Books.

Huntington, S. P. (1968). *Political Order in Changing Societies*. New Haven: Yale University Press.

Kuper, L. (1981). *Genocide*. New York: Penguin Books.

———. (1982). *International Action Against Genocide.* London: Minority Rights Group.

———. (1985). *The Prevention of Genocide.* New Haven: Yale University Press.

Lijphart, A. (1977). *Democracy in Plural Societies.* New Haven: Yale University Press.

Masur, G. (1966). *Nationalism in Latin America.* New York: Macmillan.

Nielsson, G. P. (1985). States and "Nation-Groups," A Global Taxonomy, in E. A. Tiryakian & R. Rogowski, eds., *New Nationalisms of the Developed West.* Boston: Allen and Unwin.

Seton-Watson, H. (1977). *Nations and States.* London: Methuen.

Smith, A. D. (1979). *Nationalism in the Twentieth Century.* Oxford: Martin Robertson.

———. (1981). *The Ethnic Revival.* Cambridge: Cambridge University Press.

Snyder, L. (1976). *The Varieties of Nationalism, A Comparative View.* Hinsdale, Ill.: Dryden Press.

Tilly, C., ed. (1976). *The Formation of National States in Western Europe.* Princeton: Princeton University Press.

Tiryakian, E. A., & Rogowski, R., eds. (1985). *New Nationalisms of the Developed West.* Boston: Allen and Unwin.

van den Berghe, P. L. (1981). *The Ethnic Phenomenon.* New York: Elsevier.

van den Berghe, P. L., ed. (1990). *State Violence and Ethnicity.* Niwot: University Press of Colorado.

Wallerstein, I. (1967). *Africa, The Politics of Unity.* New York: Random House.

Weber, E. (1979). *Peasants into Frenchmen, The Modernization of Rural France: 1870–1914.* London: Chatto and Windus.

Whitaker, A. P. (1962). *Nationalism in Latin America, Past and Present.* Gainesville: University of Florida Press.

Wirsing, R., ed. (1981). *Protection of Ethnic Minorities.* New York: Pergamon Press.

Young, C. (1965). *Politics in the Congo, Decolonization and Independence.* Princeton: Princeton University Press.

Deceptive Stereotypes about "Tribal Warfare"

Neil L. Whitehead and R. Brian Ferguson

Neil Whitehead is an Oxford D.Phil. He has specialized in historical anthropology, especially of lowland South America and the Caribbean. He teaches at the University of Wisconsin in Madison.

R. Brian Ferguson teaches in the Department of Sociology, Anthropology and Criminal Justice, Rutgers University, Newark. He has long been interested in warfare and has published extensively on the subject.

Who would have imagined the current nostalgia for the cold war? We lived with the threat of imminent nuclear destruction for decades, but at least the battle lines seemed clear. East versus West, Communism versus capitalism. Any brushfire war, anywhere in the world, could be forced into this mold. To be sure, this interpretation blinded us to many realities, but at least it was tidy.

That sense of order is missing today. The great polarity has evaporated, and we are left with proliferating local conflicts that seem to be getting more savage all the time. Groping for a framework to make sense of the carnage, pundits and politicians are tapping into old ideological currents about "tribal warfare." These explanations, however, are contradicted by much recent research. Rather than illuminating the wellsprings of violence, they only muddy the waters.

The human species is held to be inherently tribalistic. We are said to cleave to others like "us" and to react with unreasoned fear and hostility to "them." Humans form tribes, it is said, and the relations between tribes are hostile. Applied to recent outbreaks of violence around the world, the concept of tribalism suggests that a weakening of control by central governments allows an upsurge of primal antagonisms. The violence seems to erupt from the people themselves.

These views are based on mistaken, but deeply ingrained, ideas about the origin and nature of tribes.

"Tribe" itself is a loaded term. In the rhetoric of European expansionism during the heyday of colonialism, it was used as a disparaging label for indigenous peoples whose political organization did not exhibit the hierarchical, centralized authority of a state. In this pejorative sense, *tribal* was contrasted with *civilized.*

But tribe also refers to a genuine kind of polity, a group that anthropologists describe as being bounded and distinct from its neighbors to some degree, capable of a measure of coordinated political action, yet lacking a stratified central structure. Many indigenous peoples do not exhibit this cohesion, their highest sovereign units being families or more extended groups of kin.

But true tribes often were created in the areas that European colonialists governed, in response to a gradual process of colonial expansion during the past 500 years. For example, the Mohegans emerged out of Algonquian populations in New England to become a distinctive tribe by taking sides in 17th-century colonial wars.

Frequently, tribal peoples have engaged in brutal, horribly destructive wars, a direct inspiration for Hobbes's "war of all against all." The loudly trumpeted mission of Europe's colonialists was to put a stop to such carnage, to "pacify the savages."

The problem with this interpretation is that, in cases from all over the world, comparing the *earliest* reports of European contact with indigenous peoples to later reports shows that tribal warfare sometimes was absent when the Europeans first arrived, or at least was much less intensive than it was after they appeared. Perhaps more astonishing, the tribes that are so prominent in later accounts often were unrecognizable as tribes when the Europeans initially arrived.

"Deceptive Stereotypes about 'Tribal Warfare'" by Neil L. Whitehead and R. Brian Ferguson as appeared in *The Chronicle of Higher Education,* November 10, 1993. Reprinted by permission of the authors.

The central point in the volume that we recently edited, *War in the Tribal Zone* (School of American Research Press, 1992), is that both the transformation and intensification of war, as well as the formation of tribes, result from complex interactions in an area that we call "the tribal zone." The zone begins at the points where centralized authority makes contact with peoples it does not rule. In tribal zones, newly introduced plants, animals, diseases, and technologies often spread widely, long before the colonizers appear. These and other changes disrupt existing sociopolitical relationships, fostering new alliances and creating new kinds of conflicts.

Thus, life and war on the American Great Plains took on an entirely new cast when smallpox, horses, guns, and displaced peoples arrived from distant frontiers. The arrival of priests, traders, soldiers, and settlers in a tribal zone always complicated circumstances and often encouraged new kinds of wars (for example, as various tribes took different sides against rival colonial powers), along with new patterns of trade and political alliances. The new people who arrived had trouble dealing with the lack of boundaries and the independence of the native peoples that they encountered, so they encouraged the formation of politically unified groups—tribes. Even without such direct encouragement, the extreme conflict frequently generated by the arrival of colonialists promoted tribalization, as local people were compelled to band together just to survive.

To be sure, both warfare and tribes have existed for a very long time in human history. But the often horrifying tribal bloodshed that was, and continues to be, used to justify the expansion of European control in most cases was a reaction to a colonial presence. Thus, research done by one of us shows that the formation of a distinctive Carib people in northern South America, and the devastating warfare reported in the region, was a response to the initial bloody colonization by rival Spanish and Dutch powers from the 16th through the 18th centuries.

Research by the other author on the Yanomani of the remote borderlands of Brazil and Venezuela, who often are said to be one of the most violent peoples on earth, shows that their violence is tightly connected in timing, targets, and intensity to changes in the presence of Westerners stretching back for centuries.

How is this relevant to contemporary conflicts? We are in danger of allowing our misunderstanding of tribal conflict, a misunderstanding that is a product of our own cultural history, to prevent us from grasping the real causes of contemporary violence in various countries.

To speak of "ancient tribal hatreds," as many observers of conflicts in Somalia and in the former Yugoslavia have done, invokes an image of timeless, unchangeable political oppositions. In fact, tribal boundaries are highly changeable; they can arise, dissolve, or shift as a result of diverse circumstances. Labeling current conflicts as tribal also promotes the idea that violent conflict is a predictable outgrowth of cultural differences between groups. In fact, tribes often are from identical cultures, and cultural difference itself is a very poor predictor of violent conflict—just as cultural homogeneity is not necessarily a predictor of peace. Consider the fact that Somalia is one of the most culturally homogeneous states in all of sub-Saharan Africa.

To invoke tribal warfare in areas such as the former Yugoslavia is especially misleading. The essence of tribal political organization and of real tribal warfare is that it is based on extensive discussion and consensus among local leaders. In the Balkans, authoritarian leaders give the orders. If the fighting has become increasingly polarized along cultural lines, it is because self-aggrandizing heads of state have deliberately played on existing cultural differences. When soldiers who have been encouraged to think of themselves as defenders of one ethnic group are ordered to rape women of another, ethnic hatred will grow. It is clear that ancient animosities do exist in the culture of the region, but these seeds of violence only blossom when they are cultivated by politicians.

Another danger is that we may accept the stereotypical assumption that tribal warfare is irrational, perhaps even an expression of atavistic biological impulses. In contrast, close study of the decision making involved in genuine tribal warfare usually reveals canny strategizing about very tangible interests. Moreover, the main circumstances shaping tribal military decisions are rarely purely local, as is often claimed, but instead involve the connections between local groups and the outside world. Very frequently, the fighting is about who will benefit more or suffer less from ties to colonial power centers. Thus, from the 17th-century Mohawk Indians to the 20th-century Yanomani, wars have been fought to gain monopolistic control over the physical space around Western colonial outposts and missions.

These observations suggest how we should understand war in places such as Somalia. A variety of power bases exist, growing out of the local organization of subsistence and exchange, but also shaped by a long history of political interactions with foreign governments. The ruling groups in Somalia were supported by the superpowers during the cold war, then abandoned. United Nations forces now have become entangled in this political web, becoming identified with one side against another in a conflict where the sides themselves are defined largely by the nature of their relationship with outside powers. For example, in this complex political field, Ali Mahdi Mohammed has been the most prominent leader aligned with United Nations forces, and Mohammed Farah Aidid has been painted as the U.N.'s foe, even though earlier he had also cooperated with and benefited from the U.N. presence.

A broad-ranging debate over the newly elevated principle of "humanitarian intervention" is just beginning. The issue will be with us for years, if not in Somalia or Bosnia, then somewhere else. It is a confounding issue, and each case will be disquietingly unique. But our un-derstanding will always be clouded if we view local wars as eruptions of primitive tribal animosities. A better conception is that violence emerges and is structured by the intersection of local and external forces. Any act of humanitarian intervention will itself become a part of that interplay. If such interventions continue in Somalia or elsewhere, we must recognize and continually monitor their effects—and that means avoiding deceptive stereotypes about tribal wars.

– 38 –

Participant Observation on a Motorcycle

Andrew Cornish

Andrew Cornish is an anthropologist who has carried out fieldwork in Thailand.

A short while after arriving in the field in southern Thailand, I managed to acquire a motorcycle. While I did not actually possess a licence to ride it, some kind words to those in high places by patrons who had taken me under their wing had cleared the way for me to be turned loose on the roads of Thailand without hindrance unless, it was sharply stressed, I was foolish enough to get involved in an accident. At an early stage I had wondered whether I should mention that my licence at home had been repossessed by a couple of incredulous policemen who took a very dim view of creative driving, but I felt that to try and explain this in Thai would probably lead to misunderstandings, and might well have caused my hosts unnecessary anxiety.

Come St. David's Day, the inevitable accident occurred. I had been on an afternoon jaunt on my freshly cleaned motorcycle, merrily weaving through the traffic, and thinking how interesting it was that Thai motorists actually lived out the theory of loose structure in their driving. During this course of musing I decided to make a right-hand turn, and still being rather set in my Western ways, slowed down to do so. This was an ethnocentric mistake. As I began to turn, another motorcyclist, complete with an ice chest full of fish and a large basket of oranges on the pillion seat, decided that this was the ideal moment to overtake. I was much too slow, he was far too fast, and our subjective constructions of existence spectacularly collided with the limits of the material world.

What followed was actually quite pleasurable for the brief but slow-motion moments it lasted. A massive surge of metal, flesh, fish, and disintegrating oranges swept me

from behind, then passed overhead in a surrealistic collage as my body easily performed a series of gymnastic stunts that I had been totally unable to master at school. As always in life, the brief pleasure had to be repaid with an extended flood of unwelcome pain, relieved only by the happy realization that I, and the other motorist who had flown so gracefully above me, had narrowly but successfully avoided truncating our skulls on a Burmese ebony tree.

Anxious to reassure myself that nothing was broken, I got quickly to my feet, dusted myself off, and walked over to switch off my motorcycle engine, which by now was making a maniacal noise without its exhaust pipe. Then I walked back to the other rider, who was still lying rigidly on his back and wondering whether he should believe what was happening. I politely asked him if he was all right, but the hypothesis that in a crisis everyone reverts to speaking English clearly required some revision. Months of Thai lessons began to trickle back, but far too slowly, and in the meantime he had also stood up. It was only then that I realized the pair of us had been surrounded by a rather large crowd of onlookers.

Television in Thailand does not commence broadcasting until 4:30 p.m. so our little accident had a good audience, with local residents coming out of their houses and shops, and cars, motorcycles, and trucks stopping to take in the scene. The other rider began talking to some people near him, and a shopkeeper who knew me came and asked if I was all right. From that moment, I never had a chance to speak to the other rider again. We were slowly but surely separated, each of us in the centre of a group, the two groups gathering slightly apart from one another. I had a sudden and horrible realization that I was in the middle of one of those dispute settlement cases that I had intermittently dozed through as an undergraduate. With an abrupt and sickening shock, participant

"Participant Observation on a Motorcycle" by Andrew Cornish from *Anthropology Today*, December 1987, pp. 15–16. Reprinted by permission of Blackwell Publishers.

observation had become rather too much participation and too little cosy observation.

Some of the other rider's newly acquired entourage came over to ask the fringes of my group what exactly had happened. I pleaded my version to those standing close to me, and it was then relayed—and, I should add, suitably amended—back through the throng to be taken away and compared with the other rider's tale of woe. While this little contest was going on, a number of people from both groups were inspecting the rather forlorn wreckages of our motorcycles and debating over which one appeared to be more badly damaged. "Look at this!" someone cried, lifting a torn section of the seat and helpfully making the tear more ostentatious in the process. "But look at this!" came the reply, as someone else wrenched a limply hanging indicator light completely off its mounting. After a series of such exchanges, the two groups finally agreed that both motorcycles were in an equally derelict state, though I could not help feeling, peering from the little prison within my group of supporters, that those judging the damage to the machines had played a more than passive role in ensuring a parity of demolition.

Physical injuries were the next to be subjected to this adjudication process. I found my shirt being lifted up, and a chorus of oohs and aahs issuing from the crowd, as someone with jolly animation prodded and pinched the large areas of my back which were now bravely attempting to stay in place without the aid of skin. My startled eyes began looking in opposite directions at the same time, while somewhat less than human groans gargled out of my mouth. From similar sounds in the distance I deduced that the other poor rider was being subjected to a similar treatment. He frankly looked rather the worse for wear than I did, but whenever his group claimed this, my supporters would proceed to show just what excruciating pain I was suffering by prodding me in the back and indicating my randomly circumambulating eyes as if to say "see, we told you so."

On issues of damage, both mechanical and physical, we were adjudged by the two groups to be fairly evenly scored. Fault in relation to road rules had never been an issue. Then came a bit of a lull, as if something serious was about to happen. A senior person from the other group came over and spoke to me directly, asking if I wanted to call the police. A hush fell over everyone. I, of course, was totally terrified at the prospect—no licence, visions of deportation, and so far only one meagre book of field notes to my name. I put on my best weak pathetic smile and mumbled that I thought it was not really necessary unless the other chap insisted. A culturally appropriate move: Everyone looked happily relieved, and the other rider's spokesman said generously that it would only be a waste of time and cause unnecessary bother to bring the police out on an errand like this. It was to be a few months before I realized that, like many other motorcyclists, the other rider was also probably roaming the roads without a licence, and that in this part of the country calling the police was generally regarded as a last, and unsporting, resort.

The final agreement was that we should settle our own repairs—to both body and vehicle—and let the matter rest. A visible sigh of relief passed through the two groups that had gathered, and they slowly began to disperse. For the first time since the collision, I saw the other rider face to face, so I walked towards him to offer my apologies. I never managed to reach him. The dispersing groups froze in horror, then quickly regathered around me. "What is wrong now?" I was interrogated on all sides. Was I not happy with the result? I had clearly made a serious blunder, and it took a while to settle things down once more. A perceptive shopkeeper from nearby grabbed my arm and dragged me off to his shop for coffee, explaining to me that the matter had been settled and that further contact for any reason with the other rider or his group would only prolong an unpleasant situation that could now be forgotten by all involved.

So it was that later that evening I was able to start my second book of field notes with an entry on dispute settlement, though painful twinges up my back and throbbing between the ears made me wish I had relied on some other informant to provide the ethnographic details. I made a silent vow to myself to discontinue this idiosyncratic method of participant observation, and managed to some extent to keep the vow for the rest of my stay. Thereafter I successfully steered clear of motorcycle accidents, and instead got shot at, electrocuted, and innocently involved in scandal and otherwise abused. But all that, as they say, is another story.

RELIGION

*How Do We Make Sense of Peoples' Beliefs
and Ritual Practices?*

WHAT DOES IT MEAN to be religious? Is belief rational? Can we have faith in science? Why do we wear appropriate clothing on ritual occasions? What foods go with which meals? The greater part of our existence is devoted to making sense of the world rather than telling the truth about it. Indeed, French anthropologist Claude Lévi-Strauss argues that the distinctive characteristic of humans is precisely our capacity to make meanings in order to make sense of ourselves. In such projects, he argues, humanity has an *a priori* classification system that is ingrained before practical utilization of knowledge. The reason why we eat certain foods on certain occasions and dress appropriately for certain rituals or activities is based on this classification system. The analysis of this deeply embedded system is called **structural analysis.** The more basic this system of classification, the more difficult it is for us to reconcile activities involving mutually incompatible categories. For example, the distinction between human and animal is fundamental, and this would explain why bestiality is still viewed with horror in most societies.

Our day-to-day knowledge, then, is built upon and supported by a prior system of knowledge that is gratuitous (in opposition to the Western notion that systems of thought always have practical ends in view). This is why in our day-do-day life we operate on a mass of assumptions and partial understandings and accept the authority of our society as mediated through physicians, electricians, and lawyers. Actions are based on a mixture of faith and experience. If we fail to achieve our ends, then we might seek alternative explanations. Thus the failure of a lightbulb might eventually be attributed to "Chance," which would be the structural equivalent of "God" in another society.

One of the ways we accentuate difference between ourselves and others is by exaggerating others' propensity to have "weird" beliefs and practices in contrast to our own eminently rational and logical beliefs and actions. They are always held to be guided and influenced by "sorcery" and "superstition." Nowhere is this expressed more strongly than in the realm of **magic** and **religion.** Most of us have a strong faith in the "technological fix" for solving our problems. The problems of famine, starvation, and even AIDS, we believe, rhetoric notwithstanding, will be solved by science. Science will provide us with the technological means of neutralizing the problem, thereby freeing us from the necessity of changing our behavior.

Isak Niehaus shows why witchcraft has been a central theme for anthropology and discusses the major theories used to explain it. He then goes on to show why witchcraft beliefs persist in the "modern" West, existing alongside and competing with scientific worldviews.

By subjecting ship-launching ceremonies to a classic structural analysis, Silvia Rodgers explains that our beliefs frequently override technology. She describes how the religious beliefs (superstitions?) of sailors (including even senior officers), their symbolic classification of the ship, the extensive reincarnating power of a ship's name, and the relationship between women and ships all play an important role in how sailors believe and act. Furthermore, these are sailors with high educational qualifications and experience, who literally control earth-shattering means of destruction in the form of nuclear weaponry.

By connecting beliefs to actual practices, these articles demonstrate that anthropologists are as interested in beliefs as they are in the embodiment of belief through individual and collective practices. Indeed, one of anthropology's major contributions to understanding religion is through the study of ritual processes. Victor Turner, for example, is famous for his analysis of rites of passage and the experience of **liminality,** the experience of being "betwixt and between" social statuses that people feel as they move through a ritual. In her article, Irish anthropologist Sian Sullivan offers an analysis of a certain kind of ritual experience, comparing how Namibian Khoesaan and London "ravers" enter into trances through dancing. She raises the interesting observation, drawn from her own experience as a "raver" and professional dancer, that trying to understand such subjective experiences in terms of language or conscious thought misses the fact that people can have transformative and transpersonal experiences through bodily movement.

We end this chapter with a transformative event of another kind, the events of September 11, 2001, when jets crashed into the World Trade Center and the Pentagon. A number of prominent media outlets and politicians have framed this event as the actions of irrational terrorists bent on the destruction of Western civilization, justi-fying the mobilization of a new global "war on terror" and war in Iraq. Like many people, anthropologists were shocked at these events, but many have insisted that prejudicial attitudes against "fanatical Muslims" are neither necessarily accurate nor the productive basis for understanding what happened that day. In this section of "Anthropology and Public Debate," two prominent anthropologists and public intellectuals take differing positions on how to understand 9/11. Lionel Tiger, a sociobiologist, sees it as a manifestation of a basic problem all societies face: what to do with young males who exhibit chaotic energy. In this case, they were harnessed to the destructive political ideology of Osama Bin Laden. William Beeman argues that the root cause cannot be found unless we consider the troubled relationship between U.S. foreign policy and the rest of the world. The terrorists have done these things, not because they follow Osama Bin Laden, but because of their indignation against American foreign policy and their belief in the rightness of their cause.

·········· FOCUS QUESTIONS ··········

As you read these selections, consider these questions:

✦   Why do beliefs in the supernatural persist in Western cultures, even though many believe that "irrational" behaviors should be replaced by science and "rationality"? What social purpose do these beliefs have?

✦   How and why can different ways of knowing and believing coexist within a society?

✦   Is it really possible to understand someone else's beliefs? How?

✦   It has been said that "it is the unbeliever who believes that the believer believes." What do you think this means? Is it true? Why or why not?

✦   Can you think of other anthropological explanations for the events of 9/11?

39

Witchcraft in Anthropological Perspective

Isak Niehaus

Isak Niehaus received his PhD from the University of Witwatersrand and is a senior lecturer in the Department of Anthropology at the University of Pretoria in South Africa. He is the author of Witchcraft, Power and Politics: Exploring the Occult in the South African Lowveld.

Europeans and North Americans often regard the belief in witchcraft as unique to the witch persecutions of the Inquisition and Reformation. Whereas there was profound skepticism about witchcraft in early medieval Europe, this entire religious milieu changed with the Crusades and the Reformation. Witchcraft beliefs became enshrined in the theology of the church, and clergy assigned the administration of evil to Satan and witches. Since Satan was believed to be spiritual, he could only acquire physical bodies in which to do his work by entering people through possession. Otherwise Satan signed pacts with them to do as they were bid in return for mundane considerations (Parrinder 1963; Thomas 1971).

These changes precipitated the Inquisition, during which thousands of suspects were tried on charges of witchcraft, heresy, and devil worship by secular and ecclesiastical courts. As confessions were obtained voluntarily or wrung from the accused by torture, the belief in witchcraft attained greater credibility. A papal bull issued in 1484 by Pope Innocent VII identified witches as the prime enemy of the church. Three years later the book *Malleus Maleficarum* ("hammer of the witches") was published as a sort of handbook on the discovery, trial, torture, and execution of witches; it came to be used by Catholic and Protestant clergy throughout Europe. Passages were cited from the Scriptures—for example, "Thou shalt not suffer a witch to live," which is from Exodus. At least 300,000 witches were publicly executed at the stake.

Although the Reformation was partly a reaction against the Inquisition, Protestants did not halt witch persecutions. In fact, Geneva, Calvin's native city, became a center for witch-hunting. Clergy blamed Geneva's many disease epidemics on witches whom Satan allegedly incited to spread the plague. Large numbers of men and women were apprehended for making pacts with Satan and were accordingly tortured and burnt. These beliefs were also prevalent among Calvinists in Scotland and in New England; in 1692, two hundred suspected witches were arrested in Salem, Massachusetts. Of these, nineteen were hanged and one other was hounded to death (Boyer and Nissenbaum 1974). The reasons behind Calvinism's fear of witchcraft include the propagation of a dualistic worldview, a belief in the inevitability of sin, and the literal interpretation of biblical texts.

Actually, witchcraft beliefs are much more widely distributed in time and place. They are encountered throughout history on virtually all continents—in native North America, South America, Africa, Asia, and in the Pacific—and continue to be an important feature of contemporary times. Hunter-gatherers such as the Bushmen and Australian aboriginals are exceptional in that they do not believe in witchcraft. Due to its widespread distribution, witchcraft has become a staple topic of anthropological research.

DEFINING WITCHCRAFT

In his famous study of the Azande of Anglo-Egyptian Sudan, Evans-Pritchard (1937) distinguished between "witchcraft" and "sorcery" by their technique. He defined the former as an innate, inherited ability to cause people misfortune or to kill them. For Azande, witchcraft involves unconscious psychic powers, and it emanates from an oval black swelling, located near the liver. By contrast, Azande referred to sorcery as the performance of rituals, the uttering of spells, and the manipulation of organic substances such as herbs, with the conscious intent of causing harm.

Middleton and Winter (1963) find Evans-Pritchard's distinction appropriate for east Africa, and Stephen (1986) insists that it illuminates the situation in many Melanesian societies. However, Turner (1964) shows that the distinction between "witchcraft" and "sorcery" is not made in the largest part of Africa, nor in many other parts of the world. Following Turner and many contemporary authors, I use the terms *witch* and *witchcraft* more broadly to denote both types of persons and modes of action. (In this review I retain the word *sorcery* only where it is used by the authors in the original texts.)

In an overview of several ethnographic studies, Mayer points to the recurrence of identical details, common to witchcraft beliefs nearly everywhere.

1. Though human, witches incorporate nonhuman power. Witches are possessed by Satan, have pythons in their bellies, work with animals such as snakes, cats, baboons, and owls, which they own as familiars, or themselves change into the shape of animals.

2. Witches are nearly always adults, who are said to inherit their destructive power. They may bear physical stigmata like a red eye, a devil's mark, or a special witchcraft substance.

3. Witches tend to become socially important in times of crisis, when all sorts of misfortune—sickness, death, drought, or plague—are ascribed to them.

4. Witches harm their own kin and neighbors rather than strangers. For example, residents of the South African lowveld believe that no witch can cross a river.

5. Witchcraft is motivated by envy and malice, rather than by the pursuit of material gain.

6. Witches reverse usual expectations of behavior. For example, they may stand backward when they knock on doors, ride baboons facing the tail, and negate all Christian values during the witches' Sabbath. Witches work at night, commit incest, practice cannibalism, and go naked instead of clothed.

7. Witchcraft is nearly always immoral.

CLASSICAL ANTHROPOLOGICAL THEORIES OF WITCHCRAFT

Anthropologists have generally left open questions about the actual performance of witchcraft. While some people may perform (or at least attempt to perform) witchcraft, even the most optimistic fieldworker does not expect to see people flying around on brooms. Rather, the classical anthropological theories of witchcraft by Fortune, Kluckhohn, Evans-Pritchard, and Marwick seek to unearth the social and psychological realities underlying witchcraft beliefs and the cultural meanings they encode.

Fortune (1932) analyzed "sorcery" on the island of Dobu, Melanesia, as a conception of mystical power. Here small exogamous villages were the basic political and territorial units, and clusters of equal villages formed endogamous localities that united for purposes of warfare. Dobuans made allegations of sorcery against their allies in war, whom they married, rather than against outsiders with whom they waged war (p. 35). Fortune argues that these allegations expressed tensions, resulting from conflicting solidarities between the *susu* (a matrilineal group of brothers, sisters, and sisters' children) and the marital group (comprising the husband, wife, and children). Moreover, because of rules of alternate residence, each Dobuan village sheltered a heterogeneous collection of "men of different village alliances who distrust each other thoroughly" (p. 9). He suggests that in such a political system—with no rank or titular authority—Dobuans perceived prowess in sorcery as a component of leadership and power. They conducted life as a covert series of night battles in which individuals used sorcery to assert themselves at the expense of others. According to Fortune, Dobuans used sorcery "for collecting bad debts and enforcing economic obligation, in vendetta to avenge one's own sickness or one's kinsmen's death, to wipe out any serious insult" (p. 175).

Evans-Pritchard (1937) demonstrated how witchcraft formed an "ideational system" among the Azande of Anglo-Egyptian Sudan. From the point of view of the individual, in particular situations, he argued, the beliefs presented a logical explanation of unfortunate events. Evans-Pritchard insisted that witchcraft beliefs supplemented theories of natural causation. They did not exclude empirical knowledge of cause and effect but provided answers to the particularity of misfortunes. He cites the famous example of a granary that collapses, injuring those sitting beneath it. The Azande could explain this event in empirical terms: Termites had eaten the supports. According to this explanation, the fact that people sat beneath the granary when it collapsed was purely coincidental. However, the theory of witchcraft links these events. It explains why these particular people sat under the particular granary at the particular moment that it collapsed.

Kluckhohn (1944) elaborated a psychological theory of witchcraft. He insists that among the Navaho, witchcraft served as a channel for projecting emotions of guilt, desire, and aggression. By investing the witch with responsibility for misfortune, Navaho absolved themselves of blame. Their forbidden desires, such as incest, also found an outlet in fantasies of witchcraft. Moreover, under stressful conditions, witches were scapegoats for hostile impulses. The rigid rules of decorum among the Navaho allow little means for expression of hostility, except through accusations of witchcraft. Such accusations funnel pent-up negative emotions against individuals, without upsetting the wider society. Accusations of witchcraft also permit the direct expression of hostile feelings against people to whom one would otherwise be unable to express anger or enmity.

In his influential analysis of witchcraft beliefs and accusations among the Chewa of Northern Rhodesia (now Zambia), Marwick (1965) draws on sociological theories of conflict. He contends that witchcraft accusations reformulated problematic social relations that were not susceptible to judicial processes. Marwick found that 60 percent of sorcery accusations occurred within the matrilineage. As the matrilineage grew beyond the size that its resources could sustain, tensions over inheritance and succession became apparent. The leaders of different matrilineal segments then jockeyed for position and often attempted to discredit their rivals by accusing them of sorcery. In retrospective accounts, sorcery justified segmentation. It served as an idiom for initiating processes of fission and enabled the accusers to break off redundant relations and to discard unwanted obligations. Marwick (1965) notes that sorcery accusations were absent in the case of conjugal relations, because hostilities between spouses could easily be expressed and redressed by alternative means. The Chewa could attribute misfortune at home to the transgression of taboos, and the courts could easily dismantle conjugal relations by granting divorce.

Since the 1970s two different approaches have predominated in the study of witchcraft. On the one hand neo-Marxists demonstrated the instrumentality of witchcraft in political economic struggles. For example, Steadman sees the killing of witches by the Hewa of Papua New Guinea as an outcome of competition for resources between different roofing and flooring parties. By executing the members of other parties who threatened their interests, the witch killers generated fear and communicated their capacity to use violence to protect their interests. On the other hand, interpretive studies delineated the meanings of witchcraft beliefs within wider conceptual terms. In this tradition, Kelly (1976) shows that there is an analogical relation between witchcraft and sexual intercourse among the Etoro of New Guinea. He contends that the Etoro perceived both acts as transmitting life forces from one person to another. In witchcraft, the witch appropriates the victim's life forces to acquire added strength and vigor. Likewise, men suffer weakness

and eventually death through the depletion of their semen, in which their life forces are concentrated. Women are the agents of this depletion and men the beneficiaries.

THE MODERNITY OF WITCHCRAFT

Witchcraft beliefs and accusations are far from an archaic tradition that has disappeared with the growth of knowledge, modernization, and development. Recent studies show that modernization itself spawns new forms of witchcraft and that the occult has flourished precisely in the most modern sectors of society—such as sports, institutions of formal learning, politics, and new forms of entrepreneurship. There are deep anxieties throughout Africa and Melanesia about new forms of witchcraft that are reproducing on an increased scale. Indeed, the "modernity" of witchcraft has become a decidedly popular theme in anthropological studies since the 1990s (Comaroff and Comaroff 1993; Lattas 1993; Ciekawy and Geschiere 1998; Geschiere 1997). These studies subvert the certainties of the unilineal modernist scheme and highlight the inconsistencies and ambiguities of the modern.

Ciekawy and Geschiere contend that because witchcraft is so open-ended it becomes an obvious discourse for interpreting modern changes to linking local realities directly with global changes. "Witchcraft discourse forces an opening in the village and the closed family network: after all, it is the basic interests of the witch to betray his or her victims to outsiders" (Ciekawy and Geschiere 1998:5). They argue that it is through the opening of witchcraft that people or resources are withdrawn from the local community and disappear into the outer world. Hence, witchcraft is about "transgression and constantly redefining boundaries" (Ciekawy and Geschiere 1998:5). Not only do witchcraft discourses enable people to conceptualize the way in which the opening up of local communities has been accelerated by new technologies of transport and communication, but they also express people's concern about the selectivity of the opportunities and benefits that these processes provide.

Lattas (1993) shows how these processes are apparent in Papua New Guinea. He suggests that among the Kaliai of New Britain sorcery constitutes a kind of political language, containing a cultural critique of colonialism. He shows how powerful institutions such as the state and church are conceived of as fusing with the powers of indigenous sorcerers. Because the colonial state prevented reprisals against sorcerers the Kaliai perceived whites as somehow complicit in sorcery and as providing Melanesian sorcerers with a license to kill (p. 56). They argued that sorcerers supervised government cash crop projects, magistrates used the powers of sorcery to travel to different villages and to extract fines, and the Catholic Church destroyed its opponents by magic. Moreover, the Kaliai believed that sorcerers incorporate European symbols, offices, and commodities. People were said to learn and swap sorcery skills on the plantations and to purchase sorcery substances such as a very powerful herbicide on the marketplace. In this way "a violent space of death" "grows alongside, and is coextensive with commodity production" (p. 59). Moreover, dreams reveal Europeans as inhabiting Melanesian sorcery shrines.

Focusing on the Cameroon, Geschiere (1997) contends that witchcraft plays a vital role in modern politics and that rumors of witchcraft have overrun all political spaces, from village communities to the highest affairs of the nation-state. Colonial chiefs, educated elites, and modern politicians alike are purported to command occult forces called *djambe*. These forces even explain the superior rhetorical prowess of notables in the chiefly councils. *Djambe*—a small being that lives in a person's belly—transcends the opposition between good and evil. It is possessed by all and is the principle behind all success. *Djambe* can be used both constructively and destructively. At night a witch's *djambe* flies out to attack its victims. There were definite parallels between the lack of transparency and capriciousness of President Ahidjo's autocratic one-party system and the occult world of witchcraft, where actors and their acts are hidden from view. President Biya's multiparty democracy brought about political debate in all villages, but also greater insecurity, which made villagers resort to supernatural protection. Like conspiracy theories, witchcraft renders political processes and events comprehensible.

New forms of wealth, too, have found expression in witchcraft discourses. Sons of the villagers, who occupy important positions in the bureaucracy, act as brokers between clients in their home villages and the repressive state. In this context witchcraft constitutes a "popular mode of political action" against reticent urbanites who fail to further the interests of villagers. Rumors in Cameroon also denounce the nouveaux riches as a new brand of witches who transform their victims into zombies in order to get rich through exploiting their labor. Local witches are now supposed to work together with the mafia, organizing a worldwide zombie traffic in which Mt. Kupe—of old the place where zombies were taken—has become no more than a "relay station."

Geschiere (1997) shows that the state is experimenting with new ways of containing witchcraft. Since the 1970s regional courts in Cameroon's East Province have sentenced witches to terms of imprisonment for up to ten years, purely on the basis of testimony provided by certified *nkong* (diviners). Those convicted are poorer persons, deemed to present an anti-modern threat to progress. He sees this initiative as a logical outcome of the state's "hegemonic project," which aims to secure dominance over all domains of society, including the occult. (Also see Fisiy 1998.)

WITCHCRAFT IN THE WEST

Witchcraft does not belong merely to former Third World countries and to the early beginnings of the modern European and North American world. As Cardozo (1972) and Steadman (1985) point out, the parallels between witchcraft and U.S. Senator Joseph McCarthy's dreams about Red agents is indeed a close one. Moreover, Jean and John Comaroff point to a cluster of images in the popular culture of North America that address the contradictions of advanced capitalist societies: the "Fatal Attraction" of the corporate harridan who would destroy the home, husband, and family—and will not die; the dangerous market woman of Wall Street who will consume all before her, including the honest "Working Girl"; and the callous babyminder whose "Hand . . . Rocks the Cradle" and aborts social reproduction (Comaroff and Comaroff 1993:xxviii).

Witchcraft beliefs assume an even more concrete form in many Mediterranean societies, where it is believed that the envy of certain persons can bring harm to their objects through envy and an "evil eye." Envy and the evil eye are invoked to explain recurrent, persistent, and vague illnesses that doctors cannot cure, rather than obvious physical injuries or illness (Delamont 1995). The aggressors either cast the evil eye deliberately or do so unintentionally. Stewart (1991) reports that shepherds in Naxos, Greece, saw the evil eye as a "projectile of envy" that can strike a person, animal, or even valuable possessions such as television sets or motor bikes (p. 232). Victims were diagnosed by dropping oil into water—if it coagulated, an evil eye had been at work. Once a diagnosis had been made, Naxiotes removed the evil eye by saying a prayer invoking the Trinity and by dropping a cross into a glass of water and then sprinkling the bubbles of water from the cross onto themselves. In the Portuguese town of Vila Branca, amulets were fixed around the garments of babies, the sign of the cross was painted onto the houses of both the bride and groom before a wedding, and curers could lift the evil eye from its victims (Lawrence 1982).

When Favret-Saada did fieldwork in Brocage, an area in the northwest of France, between 1968 and 1971, she found that peasants did not want to discuss witchcraft with her. To talk about witchcraft with intellectuals from Paris would label them as backward and could endanger them because witches do not like their victims talking about witchcraft. To do so would render them liable to insanity. Jean Barbin—an impotent alcoholic whose cows had brucellosis—was convinced that a malevolent neighbor had bewitched him. Barbin fixed on Favret-Saada as an unwitcher, whose task it was to take the witchcraft and send it back onto the witch. If that works, only the witch suffers. But if the unwitcher is not strong enough, the witchcraft can leave the original victim and attack him or her instead. As long as Favret-Saada did not believe in the existence of witchcraft, she could act (or pretend to act) as an unwitcher. However, she eventually began to believe that witchcraft was a better explanation of Barbin's impotence than anything orthodox psychiatry could offer and found herself believing that the witchcraft had indeed been diverted from Jean Barbin to her. She began to experience a series of inexplicable accidents.

Favret-Saada (1980, 1989) argues that witchcraft beliefs and the ways Brocage families tried to divert witchcraft from themselves "worked" better as therapy and as a resolution for family problems than psychiatry did. In these ways the tensions generated inside families were diffused onto unspecified neighbours by the unwitcher.

More recently, La Fontaine (1992, 1997) suggests that, from an anthropological perspective, allegations about the sexual assault of children in rituals described as witchcraft or satanic worship in contemporary England can be seen as a modern day witch-hunt. The sexual assault of children exemplifies a major form of evil that is destructive of all order, and its perpetrators place themselves outside normal society or even humanity as a whole. Characteristically, the figure of the witch personifies such inhuman evil.

British child protection workers, therapists, and Christian fundamentalists made the allegations that, in secret gatherings, robed or masked people sexually abuse children in rituals that also include bestiality, forced abortions, animal and human sacrifices, and even acts of cannibalism. The founder of a British charity expressed the view that 4,000 children had been sacrificed in Great Britain alone.

Confessions of participation in witchcraft rituals and the rather incoherent accounts of survivors clothe the idea of witchcraft and devil worship with a unique air of realism. The fact that various forms of occultism do exist also supports modern allegations of satanism. The lack of corroborating evidence from police investigations and from the courts lends credence to thoughts about an international conspiracy and protection by important members of society.

La Fontaine argues that tensions arise from the perception that the fundamental assumption of parental altruism that underpins the concept of the family is being destroyed. In England the victims of child abuse come from unstable families in areas of long-term deprivation. They are marked by high unemployment, residence in run-down urban estates, histories of broken marital relations and police arrests, and considerable child neglect. Many children had suffered from delayed development or from emotional problems.

CONCLUSIONS

Witchcraft cannot simply be dismissed as a frill, on the edge of fantasy. Witchcraft relates to perennial problems of human existence such as misfortune, suffering, death, morality, desire, and inequalities in wealth and power. These problems of existence rank among the most compelling forces that motivate people to action. As Geschiere (1997) shows, the power of witchcraft beliefs derives precisely from their open-endedness and from their capacity to incorporate such multiple and diverse meanings. The indeterminancy of discourses allows for the constant integration of new themes and permits alternative interpretations that make witchcraft hard to refute. It is for these reasons that witchcraft exists in so many different times and places and that it deserves to be taken seriously by anthropologists.

REFERENCES

Boyer P., and S. Nissenbaum. 1974. *Salem Possessed: The Social Origins of Witchcraft.* Cambridge, Mass.: Harvard University Press.

Cardozo, A. Rebecca. 1972. A modern American witch-craze. In *Witchcraft and Sorcery,* edited by Max Marwick. Harmondsworth: Penguin.

Ciekawy, Diane, and Peter Geschiere. 1998. Containing witchcraft: Conflicting scenarios in postcolonial Africa. *African Studies Review* 41 (3):1–14.

Comaroff, Jean, and John Comaroff. 1993. Introduction. In *Modernity and Its Malcontents: Ritual and Power in Postcolonial Africa,* edited by Jean Comaroff and John Comaroff. Chicago: University of Chicago Press.

Delamont, Sara. 1995. *Appetites and Identities: An Introduction to the Social Anthropology of Western Europe.* London: Routledge.

Evans-Pritchard, E. E. 1937. *Witchcraft, Oracles and Magic Amongst the Azande of Anglo-Egyptian Sudan.* Oxford: Oxford University Press.

Favret-Saada, J. 1980. *Deadly Words: Witchcraft in Brocage.* Cambridge: Cambridge University Press.

———. 1989. Unwitching as therapy. *American Ethnologist* 16 (1):40–56.

Fisiy, Cyprian F. 1998. Containing occult practices: Witchcraft trials in Cameroon. *African Studies Review* 41 (3): 143–164.

Fortune, Reo F. 1932. *Sorcerers of Dobu: The Social Anthropology of the Dobu Islands of the Western Pacific.* London: Routledge.

Geschiere, Peter. 1997. *The Modernity of Witchcraft: Politics of the Occult in Postcolonial Africa.* Charlottesville: University of Virginia Press.

Kelly, Raymond. 1976. Witchcraft and sexual relations: An exploration in the social and semantic implications of the structure of belief. In *Man and Woman in the New Guinea Highlands,* edited by P. Brown and G. Buchbinder. Washington, DC: AAA Special Publications No. 8, 36–53.

Kluckhohn, Clyde. 1944. *Navaho Witchcraft.* Boston: Beacon Press.

La Fontaine, Jean. 1992. Concepts of evil, witchcraft and the sexual abuse of children in modern England. *Etnofoor* 5 (1/2): 6–20.

———. 1997. *Speak of the Devil: Tales of Satanic Abuse in Contemporary England.* Cambridge: Cambridge University Press.

Lattas, Andrew. 1993. Sorcery and colonialism: Illness, dreams and death as political languages in West New Britain. *Man* (n.s.) 28 (2): 51–77.

Lawrence, D. L. 1982. Reconstructing the menstrual taboo. *Anthropological Quarterly* 55 (2): 94–98.

Marwick, Max. 1965. *Sorcery and Its Social Setting: A Study of the Northern Rhodesian Cewa.* Manchester: Manchester University Press.

Middleton, John, and E. Winter, eds. 1963. *Witchcraft and Sorcery in East Africa.* London: Routledge and Kegan Paul.

Parrinder, Geoffrey. 1963. *Witchcraft: European and African.* London: Faber and Faber.

Stephen, Michele. 1986. Introduction. In *Sorcerer and Witch in Melanesia,* edited by Michele Stephen. Carlton, Victoria: Melbourne University Press, 1–14.

Stewart, Charles. 1991. *Demons and the Devil.* Princeton, N.J.: Princeton University Press.

Thomas, Keith. 1971. *Religion and the Decline of Magic.* New York: Charles Scribner's Sons.

Turner, Victor. 1964. Witchcraft and sorcery: Taxonomy versus dynamics. *Africa* 34 (4): 314–325.

40

Feminine Power at Sea

Silvia Rodgers

Silvia Rodgers was awarded her doctorate in anthropology at Oxford University for her research on "the symbolism of ship launching in the Royal Navy."

The ceremony that accompanies the launch of a Royal Navy ship is classified as a state occasion, performed more frequently than other state occasions and to an audience of thousands. But until now it has never been the subject of research, either historical or anthropological.

If the ceremony of launching looks at first sight like the transition rite that accompanies the ship as she passes from land to water, it soon becomes clear that the critical transition is from the status of an inanimate being to that of an animate and social being. From being a numbered thing at her launch, the ship receives her name and all that comes with the name. This includes everything that gives her an individual and social identity, her luck, her life essence and her femininity.

My research into the ceremony sheds light not only on the nature and development of the ceremony itself but also on the religious beliefs of sailors, on the symbolic classification of a ship by sailors, on the extensive and reincarnating power of the ship's name, and on the relationship between women and ships and mariners. It is the last aspect on which I want to concentrate here.

Most of us know that sailors refer to a ship by the feminine pronoun. But the extent of the metaphor of the ship as a living, feminine and anthropomorphic being is not, I think, appreciated. Furthermore, it is this metaphor that shows up the quintessential and extraordinary nature of the launching ceremony. I say "extraordinary" because this ceremony is unique in our society and any of its auxiliary societies in that it symbolically brings to life an artefact. It looks more like a case of animism than of personification. Its status in the Royal Navy as a state occasion makes all this even more remarkable, particularly as it is accompanied by a service of the established Church.

There are of course other new things that are inaugurated by secular or sacred means. But in none of these instances does the artefact acquire the properties of a living thing, let alone a feminine person. There is the proclivity to personify virtues and institutions in the feminine, but these are not conceptualized as living and human beings. Personal articles are given human attributes, with a name and even a gender. But this is not a social rule, nor a rule of grammar, as in the case of the personified ship. Nor is life, name and gender instilled through the public enactment of a prescribed ceremony.

Members of the Royal Navy, and indeed the merchant navies, talk about a ship as having a life, a soul, a spirit, a personality and a character of her own. These notions are not necessarily differentiated, and the terms are used interchangeably. Whether the word "soul," "life" or "spirit" is used depends on the informant. What is constant is the gender of the ship. In the English language, which allows gender only to human beings and animals of determinate sex, it is the rule to refer to a ship as "she" or "her." While reflecting the strength of the metaphor, the rules of grammar also indicate its limit. The linguistic boundary lies in the region of the relative pronoun. According to Fowler it is correct to say: "The ship that lost her rudder" and the "*Arethusa* that lost her rudder" or "*Arethusa* who lost her rudder." Sailors frequently drop the "the" in front of the name of a ship. They explain that if I went to see a friend I would not say "I am going to see the Sally" but "I am going to see Sally" and that this applies to a ship.

The image of the ship as a fictive woman is established in diaries and chronicles, is legally encoded in naval and legal documents, and celebrated in poetry and prose. It survives masculine names, figureheads and the labels East-Indiamen and men-of-war. In the current Royal Navy, as I have indicated, the metaphor is as strong as ever. But what kind of woman is she? A ship is represented as possessing the attributes of more than one category of woman. All are stereotypes that are idealized by sailors. Two images predominate: the all-powerful mother who nurtures and offers womblike protection; and the enchantress of whom a man can never be certain. Other images intrude, but all inspire romantic and consuming love, awe and constant devotion. When Conrad (1960) writes of "the mysteries of her (the ship's) feminine nature" and how the love of a man for his ship "is nearly as great as that of man for a woman, and often as blind" he expresses the sentiments of modern sailors.

"Feminine Power at Sea" by Silvia Rodgers from *Royal Anthropological Institute News,* Vol. 64, October 1984, p. 204. Reprinted by permission of Blackwell Publishers.

Conrad not only depicts vividly the ship as a woman, but brings out the whole environment of being at sea. My informants frequently explain to me, with some emotion and with interesting detail, the reality at sea. It is disorienting, frightening as well as awe-inspiring. This environmental context is crucial when we look for reasons for the feminine nature of the ship. In an environment which is not the natural habitat of human beings, a man may feel himself to be especially vulnerable if as a species he is incompletely represented. That vulnerability could well account for the partnership of an all-male crew with a feminine ship. It is significant that the male and secular principle is complemented not by a secular and natural woman, but by her metaphysical and metaphorical manifestation. Needham (1980) has gathered enough ethnographic evidence from diverse and land-based societies to suggest that the complementary opposition men:women-temporal:mystical is widespread if not archetypal. It is easy to understand that the oceanic environment exacerbates the need for mystical protection that emanates from women. In addition, in circumstances where uncertainty and the likelihood of sudden death is increased, the symbol of rebirth in the form of the mother would be particularly welcome. Nor should we omit to look at the metaphor from the point of view of the archetypal figure of the mother and the mother goddess which according to Neumann is deep within the human psyche. Neumann (1974) also explains how the ship has served as the symbol of the mother, of rebirth, and salvation for many cultures over many periods; and not only for people that go to sea.

It comes as a surprise to find that unlike the life essence of the ship, the universality of the ship as a symbolic woman is undermined by some ethnographic data. Nevertheless it is very widespread and historical, and cross-cultural material helps to underline the supernatural power of women in the oceanic domain. Hornell (1946) finds that from the Mediterranean to the Pacific Ocean, and from Ancient Greece to the 20th century, "ships are generally considered to be feminine." He believes the feminine principle is often introduced when the ship is dedicated to her tutelary goddess at the launch. He describes such cases from the coast near Madras. Hornell points out that sometimes there is an identifiable icon of the deity. Malinowski (1932) relates how the Trobriand canoes are closely associated with the Flying Witches, whose Power is on occasion concentrated in the carvings at the prow.

In western societies, from the coasts of Preclassical Mediterranean to Catholic Europe, patron saints of mariners are usually feminine. Figureheads, now no longer extant on British ships, were particularly efficacious if the image was a woman, especially if she was bare-breasted (Kemp 1976). There is some ground for concluding that this icon symbolized the mother who suckled the infant god, and that this made her a powerful intercessor especially against the devil. However one hardly needs this evidence to recognize the existence of a special relationship between women, ships and mariners in British fleets.

First and foremost is the irrefutable feminine nature of the ship. Then there is the launch at which the two most important personages are both feminine: the ship and her sponsor. It is the role of the sponsor, a woman of high rank by ascription, to exercise her mystical powers to imbue the ship with luck and life by naming her in strict adherence to the ritual detail: the bottle must move, the ship begin to move, the name (the generator of the luck and life) be pronounced—all at the same moment. Anything else augurs bad luck for the ship. Unfortunately, a ship at her launch is hypersensitive towards her sponsor and may react with self-destructive wilfulness to any lapse by the sponsor in her manner of dress or rendition of the formula. There are many accounts of instances when a ship has refused to move or moved too soon, making it impossible for the bottle to break at the right moment. When a ship behaves in this way she puts her own luck at risk, but it is always the sponsor who is blamed. The sponsor's power to bless has inadvertently turned into the power to curse.

There are several ethnographic examples where positive power coexists with negative power in one and the same person: a coexistence that had been spotted earlier by Jacob Grimm (in Briffault 1927). But negative power, where ships of the Royal Navy are concerned, usually emanates from ordinary women. Strict taboos attempt to restrict this harmful influence. A woman on board a ship at night is regarded with particular misgiving. She is bound to bring bad luck, and sophisticated technology is no proof against this. On the contrary, it may itself be a target. This is nicely demonstrated by the true story of the Rolls-Royce engine of a destroyer that blew up when a woman computer programmer had spent the night on board. It was perfectly true that the manufacturers had omitted to drill a critical hole, and the engine could have blown up at any time. But why, the officers wondered, had it blown up on the one night that a woman was on board? (The reasoning is Azande, the granary is waterborne.) The taboos excluding women from critical areas extend to the part of the dockyard where ships are under construction. We know that equivalent taboos are described in a host of ethnographies. They also operate on oil rigs and down coal mines in Britain, and are very stringent in fishing communities here and across the world.

With modern technology no match for the vicissitudes of luck, it is not surprising to find that the ceremony of the launch is as indispensable as ever, and part of the regulations of the Royal Navy. Nor is it surprising that it is still believed that if the bottle fails to break at exactly the right time, the fate of the ship is in doubt.

At the launch of a destroyer in 1975, a distinguished naval officer was alarmed when he thought that the sponsor had failed to break the bottle across the bow. "After all," he told me, "I might be in command of her one day." The role of the sponsor has if anything increased. Advanced technology has made it possible for her to be seen to control not only the mystical but also the technical part of the launching. From 1876, engravings in the *Illustrated London News* portray Royal sponsors setting the ship in motion and releasing the bottle with just a touch of the finger. It may have been coincidental that this overall control mechanism was installed at the same time as the Christian service was added to the ceremony.

But the very existence of a Christian service presents a puzzle. The critical part of the launching ceremony is concerned with imbuing the ship, an artefact, with luck and the soul and personality of a feminine entity—hardly in accord with Christian doctrine. Although this naming ritual has always been called a "christening," the term is misleading: the subject of the ritual is not a human being but an artefact; the liquid is not water but wine; the celebrant is neither ordained nor male. The duties of the sponsor (or godmother as she is sometimes referred to) are in any case not consistent with that of a Christian godmother, apart from the secular obligations that start after the launch.

The puzzle comes no nearer to solution when one looks at the varying attitudes of ministers of the Church to this ceremony. Some clergymen in the 19th century voiced strong disapproval of the naming ritual and of its being called a baptism. Today, incumbents of parishes local to the shipyards are happy to conduct the service at a launch. The only aspect that continues to baffle them is that no higher ranking ministers are ever invited to officiate, not even when the Queen Mother is the sponsor. Although the service was inaugurated by the Archbishop of Canterbury in 1875, since then it has been the rule for the local incumbent to conduct it. But if the ceremony of the launch seems to bother the main body of the Church, for naval chaplains the problem is even more complicated. Among the duties of the Chaplain of the Fleet is the keeping up to date of the launching service, and approving the minister chosen to conduct it. Yet, as a senior naval chaplain was at pains to point out to me, according to the Naval Chaplaincy no naval chaplain should himself ever take part in a launching. Incidentally, this same chaplain shares, and with conviction, the view of sailors that the ship is a living and feminine entity, though he does deny the ship her soul, that hallmark of a Christian being.

To understand the religious beliefs of sailors one has to look beyond the tenets of Christianity. The power of a ship's name, the naming ceremony, the metaphor of the ship as a fictive woman, the taboos relating to women: all are part of the beliefs of sailors which they themselves call "superstitious." It is well known in our own society that sailors are superstitious. What is not appreciated is that when sailors describe themselves as being superstitious, and they do so frequently, it has none of the usual pejorative connotations. They explain it as a natural consequence of life at sea, which makes them see things in a different way. An acceptable part of their syncretic religion, it comes near to the sense that adhered to *superstitio* in early Classical Rome: a valued and useful quality (Benveniste 1973).

Historical investigation shows that this so-called superstition has always existed in British navies, though specific manifestations may have changed. A ceremony to mark the launch of a new ship seems to have been imperative for centuries. But it has undergone such transformations that it is unrecognizable from, for example, the one performed in Pepys's time. The ship has always been feminine, but the relationship between women and ships had shifted over time. That the power of women has remained confined to the supernatural plane will come as no surprise.

With so much emotion invested in a ship, one may well ask why the demise unlike the launch, of a Royal Navy ship, is marked only by routine, and not by ritual. The answer must surely lie in the name through which the life, luck and personality survive the body of any one ship. The choice of names is vast, but the same names recur time and again: the present *Ark Royal* is the fifth ship of that name; the first belonged to Elizabeth I. If a name is outstandingly lucky and illustrious, it is reincarnated more frequently than others. The name as the keeper of life, as integrator into society and its history, has ethnographic parallels. Mauss draws on North American Indian material to show that the name of a person is part of the stock of the tribe, and that it reincarnates the original ancestor (. . . , 1979). When Gronbeck describes the power or the names in *The Culture of the Teutons* (1931) he could be writing about names of Royal Navy ships. But unlike the societies studied by Mauss and others, the Fleet, or the society of Royal Navy ships, consists entirely of feminine personages.

REFERENCES

Benveniste, Emil. 1973. *Indo-European Language and Society.* London: Faber.

Briffault, Robert. 1927. *The Mothers: A Study in the Origins of Sentiments and Institutions.* 3 vols. New York.

Conrad, Joseph. 1960. *The Mirror of the Sea.* London: Dent.

Gronbeck, V. 1931. *The Culture of the Teutons.* London: Oxford University Press.

Hornell, James. 1946. *Water Transport.* Cambridge, England: Cambridge University Press.

Kemp, Peter. 1976. *The Oxford Companion of Ships and the Sea.* London: Oxford University Press.

Malinowski, Bronislaw. 1932. *Argonauts of the Western Pacific.* London: Routledge.

Mauss, M. 1979. (1950). *Sociology and Psychology,* trans. by B. Brewster. London: Routledge.

Needham, Rodney. 1980. *Reconnaissances.* Toronto: Toronto University Press.

Neumann, E. 1974. *The Great Mother,* trans. by R. Manheim. Princeton, NJ: Princeton University Press.

41

On Dance and Difference

Bodies, Movement and Experience in Khoesaan Trance-Dancing—Perceptions of "a Raver"

Sian Sullivan

Sian Sullivan is a Research Fellow at the Center for the Study of Globalization and Regionalization at Warwick University. Her research explores discourses and practices that contest the normalized subjectives of modernity in contemporary resistance to neoliberal globalization. She is co-editor of Political Ecology: Science, Myth, and Power *(2000, Edward Arnold) and has published in ecology and anthropology journals as well as in a range of edited volumes. Sian also dances.*

If there is one feature of indigenous life which has been the subject of the cinematographer, be they commercial, professional, academic or tourist, it has been dancing. (Gordon 2000, p. 1)

As the quotation above says, the dances of "the primitive Other" have fascinated observers from the time of European contact to today. In particular, the perceived abandonment exhibited by "the dancing native"—epitomised by ecstatic states of trance through dancing—has been a key maker of cultural and ethnic difference itself. As Widlok (1999:234) describes for Khoe-speaking Nambian Haiǀǀom, for example, "[a] close examination of the Haiǀǀom medicine [trance] dance is promising with regard to questions of cultural variability and diversity because it is . . . an important ethnic marker. . . ." Contemporary tourism, and its tendency to show a sacralized and noble Other, have further reinforced dance as an indication of authentic and traditional ethnic identity, offsetting both what Durkheim identified as the anomie of modern life *and* reiterating the civilised and advanced state of the observer (Garland and Gordon 1999; Gordon 2000). As Rony (1996:65 in Gordon 2000:1) argues, indigenous peoples are identified with the body in a way that affirms the conventional dualisms of the modern world:

between mind, culture and civilisation on the one hand, and the body, nature and wildness on the other. It is not difficult to locate where the various observers of ritualised dances fall in relation to this conceptual divide, and where, by default, the indigenous participants of communal dances are situated.

In this essay, I suggest that these distinctions and separations tell us more about what distinguishes an Occidental culture of observers than about the particular defining traits of those being observed. My arguments are based on observations of Khoesaan[1] dances—in filmed material, through ethnographic fieldwork with Khoe-speaking Damara people in northwest Namibia, and via secondary sources—and on my participation and ethnographic work in largely urban-based dance events or "raves," i.e. those that focus on the *experience* of trance-like states through dance movement. I emphasise the term experience because it seems to me that a commitment to the *experiential* aspects of participant observation in an anthropology of the body and of dance often is missing from analyses of ritual and performative events based on body movement and varied subjective states. In this regard the language through which I understand and interpret the significance of dance movement is that of movement itself—drawing on my own experience and training in a range of dance movement practices (see Thomas 1995). These include long-term training in classical ballet; preliminary training and practice in dance movement therapy, "authentic movement" and the "5 Rhythms" movement system formulated by Gabriellle

"On Dance and Difference: Bodies, Movement and Experience in Khoesan Trance-Dancing—Perceptions of 'a Raver'" by Sian Sullivan from *Africa e Mediterraneo Cultura e Societa*, December 2001, Vol. 37, pp. 15–22.

Roth; performance work in contemporary dance with London-based Gravitas Dance Company; and, in particular, my participation as "a raver" in the dance-based events characterising a more-or-less "underground" dance "sub-culture" in London.[2]

I explore here some commonalities that I believe exist between the trance-dance practices of Khoesaan peoples located in southern Africa and those of dancers in the rave events that have emerged in industrialized and technocratic society. These suggest to me a universal ability to attain trance-like states through dance movement.[3] Given the global dominance of what Laughlin (1992) describes as the "monophasic" culture of "the west" (i.e. a culture that values the perceptual mode associated with waking, rational consciousness above all else), an ability to experience a range of perceptual processes, coupled with the cultural valuing of these experiences, has significant psychological, socio-cultural and political implications (Lumpkin 2000).[4] By extension, I argue that resistance to such experiences (because of their supposed "deviant" nature), reveals more about the characteristics and psychological "ill-health" of a conventional Occidental patriarchal and capitalist culture than about anything else (Deleuze and Guattari 1988 (1980)).

I focus on three aspects of trance-dance experiences and events. First, I describe some components of the individual experience of a trance-like state, especially the attainment of such a body-mind state through unchoreographed repetitive dance movement. Second, I explore some social and cultural phenomena associated with spontaneous and improvised dance movements, including the interplay between ritual and theatre, and of spectator and performer. I draw particularly on the explanatory relevance of the Polish theatre director Jerzi Grotowski's concept of "paratheatre" (Kumeiga 1985). In brief, this refers to a striving towards open-ended performative spaces where conventional divisions between artist and audience are broken down, and the spontaneous rather than rehearsed unfolding of dramatic creativity is encouraged. Finally, I draw some parallels between the cultures of Khoesaan "groups" and "ravers," reading dance events and other practices both as multifaceted assertions of autonomy, autarky and affective affluence. Social theorists such as Lefebvre (1971) and de Certeau (1984) are especially useful for helping us understand individual and group participation in dance events as powerful political acts that involve the appropriation of bodyspaces, mindspaces and physical spaces from an otherwise all-encompassing situation in which the body and its spaces are built on conceptual dualities (e.g. mind-body, nature-culture, male-female, etc.), economic affluence and control (Foucoult 1961, 1973, 1975; Deleuze and Guattari 1988). Throughout, I am interested in issues related to the authenticity and legitimacy of the experience of trance-dance: asserting, for example, that the transrational (Lumpkin 2000), transpersonal and transformative *experiences* articulated as part of the practice of dancing for many ravers, as well as the subculture of rave itself, are no less authentic or culturally situated than contemporary trance-dancing rituals performed by indigenous peoples such as Khoesaan.

DANCE LIKE NOBODY'S WATCHING

"When I'm dancing . . . it feels like my stomach is in my heart, like a burst of energy, like a glow. You feel like expressing yourself. You can dance however you want. . . . people can express themselves and let themselves out and have no fear." (rave dancer quoted in Malyon 1998, p. 188)

The songs of the trance dance, . . . are said to possess *n|om*, a special kind of energy or spirtual power. *N|om* is invisible, dwelling in the *n|om* songs and in the bodies of the trancers, . . . There it lies latent *until it is activated by the singing and the dancing.* (Biesele 1993, p. 74)

Although using different words, oral testimony accounts of the mind-body experiences described by individual dancers are remarkably similar: whether these are by Khoesaan participants of an age-old tradition of social trance-dances, or ravers participating in the various underground dance events held every weekend in the industrialised world in formal venues, warehouses, squatted buildings and country fields. Particular similarities are the experience of a powerful energy rising through the body upwards from the base of the spine as movement and rhythmic music begins to "take over" the dancer (e.g. Katz 1982); the experience of a "loss-of-ego-self" and a sense of what the psychologist Abraham Maslow (1973) framed as "transpersonal" (or beyond-the-self) experiences, connecting the self with both other people and with the dance-space or environment (Fox 1990); and the accessing of "other worlds" or alternative "mindspaces" through movement and setting. These are *empirical* phenomena in that they generate knowledge based on *experience* and the validity of sense-data (The Concise Oxford English Dictionary 1982:315). They also are verifiable, in the sense that similar individual experiences can be, and are, reproduced at different dance events.[5]

In terms of the form and content of dance movement involved in such events, again, there are numerous parallels. In both contexts, and as Malbon (1999:86) describes, ". . . dancing is a conceptual language with intrinsic and extrinsic meanings, premised upon physical movement, and with interrelated rules and notions of technique and competency guiding performances." This implies an importance of *form* in guiding the types of dance movements that are acceptable. Dancing thus is a nonverbal expressive and communicative *language* that can both cement and extend bonds between individuals. Given an oft-quoted statistic that verbal communication comprises only around 7% of all communication, dancing in and of itself thus can be said to have a cohesive and socially "healing" effect (e.g. as described by dramatherapist and anthropologist Sue Jennings as a primary outcome of social trance dances among Senoi Temiar of Malaysia (1995:2).[6] At the same time, there is the possibility for individual dancers to experience, express and extend their individuality through movements that are unique and idiosyncratic. The setting of communal dances encourages individual spontaneity of movement: i.e. comprising an up-welling of the body-based intelligence of the dancer that allows ". . . internal, inner dimensions, rhythms, [and] patterns" to ". . . open through the body into space" (Dymoke 1999:19). Such a retreat into inward repetitive energies of the mind-body can propel the dancer into a meditative state: a "quieting of . . . inner dialogue" and an integrative experience of "reality" that is ". . . unsullied by the categorizing imperatives of language" (Moxley n.d.). As Roth (1989) describes, stillness and associative clarity can be found in the extremes of spontaneous and both rhythmic and chaotic movement.

Among Khoesaan peoples, an ability and inclination to trance-dance is highly valued. As Biesele (1993:75) describes for Juǀ'hoan, ". . . trancers go through a fearful discipline . . . in learning to trance," and trances are considered to require ". . . the courage a man needs to 'die and then come alive again'." The act of trance-dancing thus is one of bravery in which dancers experience a "mini-death" through temporarily relinquishing the power of the rational mind over the body, as well as undertaking possibly fearful metaphysical journeys to a powerful "other world." That this is a common and cross-cultural trajectory of traditional trance-dance rituals is illustrated by Jennings" (1995:xxviii) descriptions of the risky business of forgetting the self, articulated as crucial to the communal trance-dances of the Senoi Temiar of Malaysia.

In the West, spontaneity and creativity of dance movement, entwined with the opening up of patterns of movement and internal experiences of the body, has become the basis for a range of dance movement and body-based psychotherapies. In these, and based on the premises ". . . that mind and body are inseparable," and "that what is experienced in the mind is also experienced in the body" (Levy 1995:1), knowledge of "the self" is accessed bodily, with verbal articulation signifying integration into an always shifting conscious or ego self (e.g. Rowan 1988;

Whitfield 1988; Boadella 1988). Significantly again, such integration may involve the loss or death of previously held constructions of the self, in order that a more healthy psycho-somatic self may emerge. The movement therapist Mary Starks Whitehouse in Frantz (1999:23), for example, asserts that "[a]n authentic movement is in and of the Self at the moment it is done. . . . When I see someone moving authentically, it is so real that it is undiluted by any pretense or any appearance or images. . . . *to get to this authenticity a sacrifice* [i.e. of the ego-self] *is involved*" (emphasis added). As such, and as articulated by ravers, trance-dance experiences in the context of raves can be personally transformative and, I would suggest, may qualify fully for a description as courageous, in the same way as applied to Khoesaan and other "traditional" trance-dancers.

As observed elsewhere (e.g. Malbon 1999), these experiences conform well to Victor Turner's notions of *liminality* and *antistructure*. These describe significant aspects of culturally important rites of passage, in which a subject ". . . becomes ambiguous, neither here nor there, betwixt and between all fixed points of classification; he [*sic*] passes through a symbolic domain that has few or none of the attributes of his past or coming state" (Turner 1974:232). Gordon and Sholto Douglas (2000:239) utilise these concepts to explain the positions of Bushmen in relation to a broader and dominant political economy to suggest that, like the liminal subject, Bushmen ". . . are *in* but not *of* the world. They are different but alike, *despised yet held in awe*. They have both animal and human qualities and possess both secular and mystical power." Similarly, ravers pursuing trance-dance and alternative mind-body experiences can be seen to travel a rite of passage sanctioned and legitimised by a rave subculture (cf. Malbon 1999), *and* to place themselves in an ambiguous state *vis à vis* the mind-body and other activities legitimised by modern society. In both contexts the liminal subject, as individual and group, is vilified as peripheral to the norms of conventional society, and also perhaps viewed with an element of awe in their ability to maintain a certain degree of autonomy and autarky.

Tellingly for all marginal groups, and as Gordon and Sholto Douglas (2000:239) remind us, ". . . those seen as outside or anti the structure of the state are always persecuted; and such persecution requires discourses which dehumanize them." Thus while the heroism and ego-strength that accompanies an ability to trance is appreciated and valorised by participants, it comes as no surprise that an Occidental culture of dance-*observers* views such practices with a range of responses from bemusement to disgust. As Bourguignon (1973:342) states, "The nineteenth-century view of progress, not only from simple to complex but from a primitive mentality to a civilized one, is associated with an evaluation of the ecstatic as savage and childlike." Just as the colonial and typically male cinematographer would not permit himself to abandon his rational control by allowing his body to become "entrained" with the dance movements of the "the observed native" (Gordon 2000), so a "phallogocentric" (Irigaray 1977) establishment of the modern world distances itself from a rave subculture built on alternative experiences of the "mind-body-spirit" nexus, and seems set to put in place increasingly punitive measures to disallow the possibilities for different ways of being-in-the-world (Heidegger 1962). Organisers and participants of rave dance events (frequently free or low-fee parties) thus have been vilified by the media and the state, and subjected to systematic harassment by the authorities with the support in the UK of the Criminal Justice and Public Order Act of 1994 (Bender 1998; Malyon 1998). Further, a whole gamut of legislation imposes controls over a citizen's freedom of choice and responsibility regarding mind-body experiences. As discussed below, it is perhaps tribute to the growing *power* of an emerging culture that has alternative mind-body experiences and ways-of-*being*-in-the-world at its core that formal society is and has been so virulent in its suppression of such experiences and their political correlates.

RESURRECTING THE FESTIVAL: FROM RITUAL TO PARATHEATRE

As Jennings (1994:8) points out, conventional analyses of ritual, drama and theatrical performance have posited a number of polarised relationships: primarily between ritual and drama on the one hand, and theatre on the other (e.g. Schechner 1988). In these terms, the enacting of "traditional ritual," and the immediacy associated with drama (i.e., "as a creative action based on improvisation" Jennings 1995:8)), are considered distinct from the "high art" of theatrical performances. Moreover, an evolutionary relationship frequently is considered to exist such that theatre emerged from ritual. Within these schemata, the trance-dances of Khoesaan peoples would be considered as rituals, with the cultural functions of facilitating healing events and promoting social cohesion. Raves on the other hand, might also qualify in some respects as comprising both elements of ritual and drama: it is perhaps unlikely that they would be considered as theatre or art.

These categories, however, are of limited heuristic value in exploring the properly theatrical and creative dimensions of trance-dance events in both contexts. As Lefebvre (1971:36) points out, they also leave as unproblematic the alienation from everyday life that art in the West, including theatre, perhaps embodies, having become "an increasingly specialized activity . . . , an ornament adorning everyday life but failing to transform it."

I would suggest that communal events with music-driven spontaneous movement and the possibilities of transformative trance-dance experiences at their core shatter the boundaries between these categories. Thus, "traditional" rituals involving dancing usually also involve a range of other creative and skilled activities (singing, musicianship, costuming, etc.) and involve complex interrelationships between elements of performance, improvisation and spectatorship. Similarly, raves comprise spaces where creative behaviour is not limited to an élite of artists. Instead, and as clearly articulated in the interview transcript below, all participants potentially are themselves artists as in "art-producers": in costuming; in dance; in contributions to the visual art shaping dance spaces; in playful and imaginative conversation and interactions with others, including dance improvisation. Given this appropriation of creativity by everyday culture, such events are suggestive of the potentially revolutionary "resurrection of the Festival" called for by Lefebvre (1971:36).

This spontaneity of creativity, coupled with a breakdown of the distinctions between audience and spectator, and between art specialist and the 'ordinary person,' has been a dream of Western theatre directors in the latter part of the 20th century. Perhaps the most famous proponent of these potentialities is Jerzi Grotowski, whose Theatre of Sources was an attempt to plumb the direct primeval experience and the creativity of ordinary people (Grotowski 1969 *in* Jennings 1994:10). In the latter part of his career, Grotowski endeavoured to create situations where "paratheatre" might occur: "a genuine encounter between individuals who . . . as they lose their fear and distrust of each other move towards a more fundamental encounter in which they themselves are the active and creative participants in their own drama of rituals and ceremonials" (Roose-Evans 1984:154 *in* Jennings 1994:10). Might not rave constitute an embodiment of the paratheatrical process that Grotowski was seeking? The following interview transcript, from Dot, a rave participant who herself has a background in the performing arts, would suggest this to be the case:

> "Sometimes, at the end of a rave, when the lights come up, the music fades out, and everyone begins to clap and cheer, I have the sensation that it's not just the DJ and the organisers that we're applauding—it's also ourselves. It's as though there's an unspoken acknowledgement that we are *all* responsible for the success of a night. *Our* performances, the characters we've played, the selves we've created and the spectacles we've participated in as observers, work together with the music played, the lighting and the décor. At the end of it we

deserve applause too, because we've been part and parcel of the creation of an experience—both as creative performers and as spectators." (Interview with Dot, 23 November 2000)

IF I CAN'T DANCE, IT AIN'T MY REVOLUTION

> The failure of modern society lies in our alienation—a sense of powerlessness in trying to influence the world in which we live; of meaninglessness in our search for guides to conduct and belief; of isolation from others; of estrangement from one's self. For modern society to have meaning, to convey a sense of coherence, it must find some purpose beyond consumption. Lefebvre argues that it ought to be the production of autonomous, thinking, feeling individuals able to experience their own desires and develop their own style. (Wander 1984:ix)

> The judges of normality are present everywhere. We are in the society of the teacher-judge, the doctor-judge, the educator-judge, the "social-worker"-judge; it is on them that the universal reign of the normative is based; and each individual, wherever he [sic] may find himself, subjects to it his body, his behaviour, his achievements. (Foucault 1975:304)

From the 19th century to recent decades, assertions of Khoesaan 'Bushman' identity by scholars and observers have served to prevent them from participating as full citizens in wider discourses of modernity. They have been explained as coming prior to humans on the evolutionary scale, due to various assertions of their difference, manifest as primitiveness. It was considered, for example, that "[t]he inclination of the moment is decisive to him" (Ratzel 1897:267), such that they display no "drive to create something beyond everyday needs, to secure or permanently to improve systematically the conditions of existence, even the most primitive ones like the procurement of food," and thereby "lack entirely the precondition of any cultural development" (Schultze 1914:290). Such assertions reappear in different guises throughout this century, usually justifying further exclusion of Bushmen from opportunities to participate economically and politically as citizens at least equal to "blacks" as classified under the South African administration's schemata of colour.

Again, there are parallels between these perceptions of "Bushmen" and descriptions of those choosing variously autarkic existences in the industrialised West. As well as rave-participants, we might think, for example, of New-Agers, travellers, communitarians of various descriptions, anti-capitalist protesters, and a growing DIY-culture with many shapes and forms (McKay 1998). In other words, those people portrayed variously as a rag-bag bunch living on the margins of formal society deemed incapable of participating in wider (capitalist) society (particularly when it comes to investing in the future); seen as revelling in immediate-returns, pleasure-seeking and irrational behaviours such as trance-dancing and other mind-body altering practices; and generally considered a threat to the norms and ideals of what Lefebvre (1971) terms a bureaucratic society of controlled consumption (Floyd 2001).

But an adherence to such practices and internally reinforcing behaviours instead might be interpreted as assertions of autonomy and autarky *vis à vis* a colonising and dominant cultural mainstream. Among Khoesaan peoples, for example, and paraphrasing Gordon and Sholto Douglas (2000:234–5), the strength of Bushman ideological autonomy needs to be viewed against the need of the colonial project to colonise the minds of indigenous peoples through the internalisation of the norms, categories and values of the industrial capitalist world: one that is a properly Cartesian world of rational individuals. Similarly, rave-participants and groups attempting degrees of self-sufficient and communal existences in the West might be viewed as comprising individuals making various choices towards lifeworlds comprising "affective affluence" (Van der Sluys 2000),[7] while perhaps remaining in relative financial poverty (McKay 1998). Against this backdrop both rave and a current resurgence of Bushman trance-dances (e.g. Shostak 1990 (1981):219; Widlok 1999) might be interpreted more broadly as acts of defiance and resistance in relation to the multiple constraints effected by the political economy and culture of modernity.

In this reading the mind-body experiences articulated by trance-dancers in both rave and Khoesaan contexts become possibilities for transcending the mundanity of everyday life (Lefebvre 1971; de Certeau 1984). They echo Foucault's validation and pursuit of "limit experiences": the practice of extending oneself *beyond* socially defined dictates of the person (Miller 1994). Given the apparently anarchic aspect of spontaneous and improvised dance movement (Dymoke 1999:20), and combined with the possibilities of transformative experiences offered by spontaneous movement and trance-dancing, particularly in communal settings, the acts of dancing can be articulated as powerful individual and group expressions of political will and autonomy. Each dance act thus becomes a multifaceted political act of appropriation: of one's own mind-body space; of physical spaces in which communal dances are located; and of a shared identity marginal to that sanctioned by modernity.

CONCLUDING COMMENTS

> The modus operandi of nomad thought is affirmation. . . . (Massumi 1988:xiii)

In this chapter I have drawn on a range of theoretical, ethnographic and experiential perspectives to explore possible concordances between the trance-dance practices of Khoesaan indigenes and participants of an emergent rave culture in the industrialised and bureaucratised West. By way of a conclusion, I wish to affirm the importance of a serious scholarly engagement with the social, cultural, political and historical significance of subjective practices that embrace so-called alternative mind-body experiences. This is particularly important if one concedes that the emancipatory potential of poststructural and postmodern thinking has to a large extent been hijacked by an emphasis on a representational and linguistic analytics. These seem to suggest that experience exists only in the retelling, and that language and importantly the text thereby are the sole areas worthy of academic analysis and reflection (e.g. Cupitt 1998). As potently articulated several decades ago in a critique of patriarchal society by Mary Starks Whitehouse, "Words have become his primary means of communication and realization . . . movement is non-verbal and yet it communicates. . . . just as the body changes in the course of working with the psyche, so the psyche changes in the course of working with the body. We would do well to remember that the two are not separate entities but mysteriously a totality" (1999 (1958):41–2).

Living also is embodied and experience is felt. "Literacy" in these domains offers great possibilities for critical analysis and for wise interpretation. By embracing the dynamic and plural potentialities made possible by a poststructural attack on modernity's ontological certainties (e.g. Deleuze and Guattari 1988 (1980); Irigaray 2002), we might also accept that subjective reflection and dynamic awareness confers possibilities for *agency* and choice, both within, and with the ability to affect and transform, broader structures (Giddens 1985). The states of consciousness embodied in trance-dance practices, and the suggestions here of experiential resources between these practices in broadly different cultural contexts, suggest to me that here is a domain of activity where identity and ideas of difference are explicitly malleable, being subject to individual intentionality and possible transformation. This may pose a threat to some and liberation to others. But following Lefebvre, it also may be a significant means of thinking and experiencing beyond the phallogocentric cultural confines defining what is legitimate in terms of the constructed bodies and experiences of modernity; thereby actualising the creative potential both latent and present in everyday life.

NOTES

1. The term "Khoesaan" refers to those southern African peoples who are part of a "click" language-cluster comprised of Khoekhoegowab (spoken by Nama, Damara and Hai l lom) and a variety of Saan (or "Bushman") languages (Haacke et al. 1997). Although I draw here on trance-dance practices among Khoesaan peoples, I believe that many of the same arguments could be made for other peoples for whom trance-dance events are important parts of social and ceremonial life. For example, see Jennings' (1995) ethnography of social and individual significances of trance-dance and dramatic events among the Senoi Temiar of Malaysia

2. By "underground" I mean a dance culture that involves actions and norms framed as "deviant" and/or illegal by formal society; predominantly the use of psychoactive substances ("drugs") and the "squatting" or appropriation of disused urban and other spaces. For more information on these various dance practices see Chodorow 1991; Pallaro 1999; Roth 1989 (1998) and 1997; Collin and Godfrey 1997; Saunders 1997; Malbon 1999; Silcott 1999.

3. By "universal ability" I mean that the *potential* to access trance-like states through body movement is something akin to Merleau-Ponty's (1961) concept of cross-cultural bodily constants (see Couzens Hoy 1999, p. 6). As the rest of the chapter should make clear, however, and following Foucault (e.g. 1977 (1975)) I also consider that possibilities for accessing these types of experiences are deeply influenced by the situatedness of body, self and subjectivity in socio-political and cultural contexts.

4. As psychological anthropologist Erika Bourguignon (1973:11) states on observing "[t]he presence of institutionalised forms of altered states of consciousness in 90% of . . . sample societies" it would seem that this is ". . . a psychological capacity available to all societies."

5. The experience of dancing at "raves" frequently is accomplished by consumption of psychoactive drugs, predominantly MDMA (3, 4-methylenedioxymethamphetamine) or "ecstasy." Indeed, it is the *interaction* of imbibed chemicals *with* new genres of popular music (from the original 1980s House, Garage and Techno to the more recent sounds of Psychedelic Trance, Hardcore and Gabba) that usually is credited with responsibility for the subcultural phenomena that comprise "rave" (Collin and Godfrey 1997; Robb 1999). This significance of psychoactive substances makes the experiential aspects of rave events easy to discredit by an establishment that is profoundly fearful of, and anti-"recreational-drugs" (unless, of course, these are alcohol or tobacco). It might also be used to suggest that the movement experiences of ravers somehow are less legitimate than those participating in "traditional" trance-dance practices and rituals. This is not the place to enter into a discussion about the legitimacy or otherwise of mind-body experiences facilitated or enhanced by consumption of psychoactive substances (although see Saunders, Saunders and Pauli 2000). What I would suggest, however, is first, that such consumption does not necessarily detract from the subjective significance of trance-dance experiences for an individual; and second, to point out that the supposedly more authentic ritualised trance practices of "the native Other" are themselves

frequently accompanied and enhanced by consumption of various substances—from tobacco amongst Khoesaan, to the profoundly psychoactive ayahuasca consumed by indigenous peoples of the Amazon.

6. As an aside, this significance of nonverbal communication makes me wonder at the current lack of body-awareness and movement training available for anthropologists and other social scientists. It seems to me that the success or otherwise of ethnographic and participant observation research practices rests crucially on a sensitivity to bodily aspects of communication and to nuanced "readings" of these.

7. Following Markovi (1974) in Wander (1984:xvii–xviii) affective affluence might be described as affirming some or all of the following aspects of being: a range of sensory experiences and imaginative possibilities; capacities for communication and creative activity, and abilities to harmonize interests with other individuals, choose between alternative possibilities, and develop a critical consciousness of the self.

REFERENCES CITED

Atkinson, A. 1991. *Principles of political ecology.* London: Belhaven Press.

Bender, B. 1998. *Stonehenge: Making space.* Oxford: Berg.

Biesele, M. 1993. *Women like meat: The folklore and foraging ideology of the Kalahari Ju\|'hoan.* Bloomington and Indianapolis: Witswatersrand University Press and Indiana University Press.

Boadella, D. 1988. Biosynthesis. In Rowan and Dryden (Eds.), *Innovative therapy in Britain.* Milton Keynes: Open University Press.

Bourguignon, E. 1973. *Religion, altered-states-of-consciousness, and social change.* Columbus, OH: Ohio State University Press.

Chodorow, J. 1991. *Dance therapy and depth psychology: The moving imagination.* London: Routledge.

Collin, M. & Godfrey, J. 1997. *Altered state: The story of ecstasy culture and acid house.* London: Serpent's Tail.

The Concise Oxford Dictionary (7th ed.). 1982. Oxford: Oxford University Press.

Couzens Hoy, D. 1999. Critical resistance: Foucault and Bourdieu. In Weiss and Fern Haber (Eds.), *Perspectives on embodiment: The intersections of nature and culture.* London: Routledge.

Cupitt, D. 1998. *Mysticism after modernity.* Oxford: Blackwell.

de Certeau, M. 1984. *The practice of everyday life.* Translated by S. Rendall. London: University of California Press.

Deleuze, G. & Guattari, F. 1988 (1980). *A thousand plateaus: Capitalism and schizophrenia.* London: The Athlone Press.

Dymoke, K. 1999, October 30. Improvisation, a territory of the body, a body based theory or anti-theory? The internal landscape. In Briginshaw (Ed.), *Exploding perceptions. Performing theory: theorising performance.* Proceedings of a conference organised by the Society for Dance Research in collaboration with University College, Chichester.

Floyd, P.B. 2001, July 1. Is dancing terrorism? http://www.urban75/Action/news137.html, visited 29 October 2001.

Foucault, M. 1990 (1961). *Madness and civilization: A history of insanity in the age of reason.* London: Routledge.

Foucault, M. 1990 (1973). *The birth of the clinic: An archaeology of medical perception.* London: Routledge.

Foucault, M. 1977 (1975). *Discipline and punish: The birth of the prison.* Translated by A. Sheridan. London: Penguin.

Fox, W. 1990. *Towards a transpersonal ecology: Developing new foundations for environmentalism.* London: Shambhala.

Frantz, G. 1999. An approach to the center: An interview with Mary Whitehouse. In Pallaro (Ed.), *Athentic movement: Essays by Mary Starks Whitehouse, Janet Adler and Joan Chodorow.* London: Jessica Kingsley Publishers.

Garland, E. & Gordon, R. 1999. The authentic (in)authentic: Bushman anthro-tourism. *Visual Anthropolgy, 12,* 267–287.

Giddens, A. 1985. Time, space and regionalisation. In Gregory and Urry (Eds.), *Social relations and spatial structures.* Basingstoke: Macmillan.

Gordon, R.J. 2000, May. "Captured on film": The claptrap of "performance primitives." Paper presented at the Anthropological Association of Southern Africa conference on "The African Renaissance" held in Windhoek.

Gordon, R. & Sholto Douglas, P. 2000. *The Bushman myth: The making of a Namibian underclass* (2nd ed.). Oxford: Westview Press.

Heidegger, M. 1962. *Being and time.* Translated by J. Macquarrie and E. Robinson. Oxford: Blackwell.

Irigaray, L. 1977, May. Women's exile. Translated by C. Venn. *Ideology and Consciousness,* no. 1, pp. 62–76.

Irigaray, L. 2002. *The way of love.* Translated by H. Bostic and S. Pluhácek. London: Continuum.

Jennings, S. 1995. *Theatre, ritual and transformations: The Senoi Temiars.* London: Routledge.

Katz, R. 1992. *Boiling energy: Community healing among the Kalahari Kung.* Cambridge, MA: Harvard University Press.

Kumeiga, J. 1985. *The theatre of Grotowski.* London: Methuen.

Laughlin, C. 1992. Consciousness in biogenetic structural theory. *Anthropology of Consciousness, 6* (3), 17–22.

Lefebvre, H. 1984 (1971). *Everyday life in the modern world.* London: The Athlone Press.

Levy, F.J. 1995. Introduction. In Levy (Ed.), *Dance and other expressive art therapies.* London: Routledge.

Lumpkin, T. 2000, May. Perceptual diversity: Is polyphasic consciousness necessary for global survival? Paper presented at the Anthropological Association of Southern Africa conference on "The African Renaissance" held in Windhoek.

Malbon, B. 1999. *Clubbing: Dancing, ecstasy and vitality.* London: Routledge.

Malyon, T. 1998. Tossed in the fire and they never got burned: The Exodus Collective. In McKay (Ed.), *DiY culture: Party and protest in nineties Britain.* London: Verso.

Markovi, M. 1974. *From affluence to praxis.* Ann Arbor: University of Michigan Press.

Maslow, A. 1973. *The farther reaches of human nature.* Harmondsworth: Penguin.

Massumi, 1988 (1980). Translator's foreword: Pleasures of philosophy. In Deleuze and Guattari, *A thousand plateaus: Capitalism and schizophrenia.* London: The Athlone Press.

McKay, G. (Ed.) 1998. *DiY culture: Party and protest in nineties Britain.* London: Verso.

Merleau-Ponty, M. 1961. *Phenomenology of perception.* London: Routledge & Kegan Paul.

Miller, J. 1994. *The passion of Michael Foucault.* London: Flamingo.

Moxley, W. 2000, November 20. The center of the universe. http://www.psychedelic-library.org/univch3.htm.

Pallaro, P. 1999. *Authentic movement: Essays by Mary Starks Whitehouse, Janet Adler and Joan Chodorow.* London: Jessica Kingsley Publishers.

Ratzel, F. *The history of mankind*, Vol. 2. London: Macmillan.

Robb, J. 1999. *The nineties: What the f**k was that all about?* London: Ebury Press.

Rony, F. 1996. *The third eye.* Durham: Duke University Press.

Roose-Evans, J. 1984. *Experimental theatre from Stanislavski to Peter Brooks.* London: Routledge & Kegan Paul.

Roth, G. 1989 (1998). *Maps to ecstacy: A healing journey for the untamed spirit.* London: Thorsons.

Roth, G. 1997. *Sweat your prayers: Movement as spiritual practice.* Dublin: Newleaf.

Rowan, J. 1988. Primal integration therapy. In Rowan and Dryden (Eds.), *Innovative therapy in Britain.* Milton Keynes: Open University Press.

Saunders, N. 1997. *Ecstasy reconsidered.* London: Nicholas Saunders.

Saunders, N., Saunders, A. & Pauli, M. 2000. *In search of the ultimate high: Spiritual experience through psychoactives.* London: Routledge.

Schechner, R. 1988. *Performance theory.* London: Routledge.

Schultze, L. 1914. *Sudwestafrika Meyer, Hans Das Deutsche Kolonialreich,* Vol. 2, pt. 2. Leipzig: Verlag des Bibliographischen Instituts.

Shostak, M. 1990 (1981). *Nisa: The life and words of a !Kung woman.* London: Earthscan.

Silcott, M. 1999. *Rave America: New school dancescapes.* Toronto: ECW Press.

Starks Whitehouse, M. 1999 (1958). The tao of the body. In Pallaro (Ed.), *Authentic movement. Essays by Mary Starks Whitehouse, Janet Adler and Joan Chodorow.* London: Jessica Kingsley Publishers.

Sullivan, S. 2001. Difference, identity and access to official discourses: Hai I om, "Bushmen," and a recent Nambian ethnography. *Anthropos, 96,* 179–192.

Thomas, H. 1995. *Dance, modernity and culture: Explorations in the sociology of dance.* London: Routledge.

Turner, V. 1974. *Dramas, fields and metaphors.* Ithaca, NY: Cornell University Press.

Van der Sluys, C. 2000. *Gifts from the Immortal Ancestors: Cosmology and Ideology of Jahai Sharing.* In Schweitzer, Biesele, and Hitchcock (Eds.), *Hunters and gatherers in the modern world: Conflict, resistance and self-determination.* New York: Berghahn Books.

Wander, P. 1984. Introduction to the transaction edition. In Lefebvre, *Everyday life in the modern world.* London: The Athlone Press.

Whitfield, G. 1988. Bioenergetics. In Rowan and Dryden (Eds.), *Innovative therapy in Britain.* Milton Keynes: Open University Press.

Widlok, T. 1999. *Living on Mangetti: "Bushman" autonomy and Namibian independence.* Oxford: Oxford University Press.

– 42 –

UNDERSTANDING 9/11

What Motivated the 9/11 Hijackers?

Lionel Tiger is Charles Darwin Professor of Anthropology at Rutgers University. Canadian by birth, he received his PhD from the London School of Economics and is well known for his work trying to bridge the gap between natural and social sciences. He is author of a recent controversial book The Decline of Males, *in which he argues that women are surpassing men in economic, social, and reproductive status, and that the cause of this is not political or moral, but biological.*

William O. Beeman is professor of anthropology and theatre, speech and dance, as well as director of Middle East Studies at Brown University. His research focuses on language styles and sociocultural patterns in Iran, cross-cultural comparison of performative genres, and peasant societies. He is a regular columnist for Pacific News Service.

. . . .

Osama Bin Laden's Man Trouble *Why His Young Men in Groups Are So Scary*

Lionel Tiger

An outstanding characteristic of the miserable band of insane worshippers responsible for the savage events of Sept. 11 is that they're all male. Virtually all the fist-shakers we see in news clips of anti-American demonstrations in Pakistan and elsewhere are men, too, usually relatively young ones. What does this have to do with Sept. 11, Osama Bin Laden, the Taliban, and the future?

One of the most difficult tasks for any social system is figuring out what to do with its young males. These are invariably the most lurchy, impressionable, energetic, socially exigent, and politically inept members of any group. They cause trouble for their elders and ruthlessly hassle each other. (See the Sharks and Jets of *West Side Story* and

the Bloods and the Crips of the West Coast story.) They pose chronic danger to public order when they drive, drink, and drug.

Various communities cause their young men to endure a startling and often gory array of harassing rituals and trials in order to become acceptable adults. In his autobiography, Nelson Mandela says that only after his circumcision at the age of 15 did he feel ready to assume the chieftaincy he inherited. I have been a so-called expert witness in lawsuits on behalf of young men physically abused by fraternity brothers during hazing and initiations: One was turned into a quadriplegic. Often, only when they have made their bones in some grim initiatory expedition are young men able to contemplate the next steps of courtship and marriage.

The terrorism of Bin Laden harnesses the chaos of young men, uniting the energies of political ardor and sex

"Osama bin Laden's Man Trouble" by Lionel Tiger from *Slate*, October 7, 2004. Reprinted by permission of United Feature Syndicate, Inc.

in a turbulent fuel. The structure of al-Qaida—an all-male enterprise, of course—appears to involve small groups of relatively young men who maintain strong bonds with each other—bonds whose intensity is dramatized and heightened by the secrecy demanded by their missions and the danger of their projects. Like such highly trained and prestigious warriors as the Army's Rangers or the Navy's SEALS, they are screened before they are allowed to earn their stripes in a program of militaristic training in isolated and demanding environments. Selection to the group is prestigious. It confers unquestionable, if radical, Islamic credentials and associates them with the tides of history sketched for them in their training. For many, nothing in the rest of their often sorry existences can compare with the authoritative drama of what they hope to do and with the sense of purpose flowing from their commitment to the leaders they accept.

Their comfort in an all-male world begins with the high sex segregation of many of the Muslim communities from which the terrorists draw. While there are great variations among Islamic communities, the sharp tendency is toward sexually segregated societies. Contact between the sexes is tightly restricted by draconian moral codes. Not only are women's faces veiled, so is their behavior. This means that men and women have relatively little to do with people of the opposite sex. Therefore, they develop a great deal of reliance on those of their own. Most men in most societies marry, or try to. This is more difficult than usual in polygamous societies in which powerful men may have as many as four wives, leaving three potential husbands without a date for Saturday night—or any night. For example, Osama Bin Laden is thought to have several cave-mates, as many as four, including his most recent bride, a teeny-bopper who's presumably an earnest theological theorist. There are also substantially more men than women in Afghanistan, which augments the deprivations of polygamy. So, some of his troops have no choice but to accustom themselves to relatively monastic lives. The sexuality and reproductive potential of such young men is not an unimportant matter politically. The United Arab Emirates, not normally considered forerunners of the progressive movement, have taken an inventive action that reflects how difficult it is for men and women to mate in a traditional manner. To marry a local woman, men in that nation must provide gifts, feasts, and ritual performances that may cost as much as $40,000—an impossible accumulation for all but a few. Many would choose a foreign wife instead, which is unattractive to the government. So now when a man marries a local woman, the government supplies a grant sufficient for his ceremonial obligations. Bin Laden and his ilk provide no such marriage benefit. (In a grim reversal, they offer bonuses to the kin of those who commit suicide.) So, his young men have to rely for emotional and social succor on their fellow-marchers to the triumph of grandly effective death. It is in the crucible of all-male intensity that the bonds of terrorist commitment and self-denial are formed. As they move from Hamburg to Cleveland to Lima to Havana to Jersey City, they are enveloped in tacit camaraderie with their associates who've endured the same training, the same deprivation, the same expectation of enjoying death and heaven in the same shiver. They share the sweet-sour prospect of striking a fiery suicidal blow for the self-evident purity of a religion of love. They are not lonely psychopaths but demented special forces wearing anonymity like a uniform. They share and catalyze swirling energies and religious absolutism, forces immensely useful to those operators such as Bin Laden who are able to turn young men's need for a cool place in the hot sun outward, to other societies, to attack infidels at large.

It's all something grand to do. So much better than the few jobs available, the threadbare economies, the ramshackle societies run either by altogether corrupt cynics, autocratic monarchies feeding princes foie gras, or theocracies that mistake reading ancient books for action.

Will the situation change? There are countless young men in poor "states of concern" whose only plausible luxury may lie in the symbolic realm of moral and theological triumph. They are likely—at best—to have to scrape out a minimally tolerable existence that pales beside the images of sensual and material peril—America! America!—their leaders seek to hide from them but cannot. "The Great Satan" strictly translated is "the great tempter." A select few, perhaps the most angry or lonely, perhaps the most pious or theoretical, will decide not to try to become part of America or its way of life but to destroy it. To do this they can enroll in stirring academies such as Bin Laden's. The danger of belonging to them enhances their excitement and feeds their sense of worthwhile enterprise. Their comrades provide them an emotional haven and a clear focus for the turbulent energies at the intersection of youth and despair. Their basic weapons are intensity and insane commitment, not the usual visible armament of warriors. American and other forces will have to find, confront, and destroy something new. They may well succeed in rooting out at least the more overt groups. But the much larger and longer-term problem for us and the world at large— that there are millions upon millions of these young men, not just Bin Laden's thousands—will finally have to be faced by the currently feckless leaders of the grim societies that have produced and nurtured such wild theological pathologies.

Article URL: http://slate.msn.com/id/116236/

Understanding Osama bin Laden

William O. Beeman

The United States risks a severe miscalculation in dealing with the destruction of the World Trade Center and the attack on the Pentagon on Tuesday. This event is not an isolated instance of violence. This is not an "act or war." It is one symptom of a cancer that threatens to metastasize. The root cause is not terrorist activity, as has been widely stated. It is the relationship between the United States and the Islamic world. Until this central cancerous problem is treated, Americans will never be free from fear.

Merely locating and hunting down a single "guilty party" in this case will not stop future violence: Such an action will not destroy the organization of terrorist cells already established throughout the world. Of greater importance, it will do nothing to alleviate the residual enmity against America. The perpetrators of the original attack on the World Trade Center in 1993 were caught and convicted. This did not stop the attack on Tuesday. The chief suspect is the Saudi Arabian Osama bin Laden, or his surrogates. He has been mischaracterized as an anti-American terrorist. He should rather be thought of as someone who would do anything to protect Islam.

Bin Laden began his career fighting the Soviet occupation of Afghanistan in 1979, when he was 22 years old. He has not only resisted the Soviets, but also the Serbians in Yugoslavia. His anger was directed against the United States primarily because of the U.S. presence in the Gulf region, more particularly in Saudi Arabia itself—the site of the most sacred Islamic religious sites. According to bin Laden, during the Gulf War America co-opted the rulers of Saudi Arabia to establish a military presence in order to kill Muslims in Iraq. In a religious decree issued in 1998, he gave religious legitimacy to attacks on Americans in order to stop the United States from "occupying the lands of Islam in the holiest of places." His decree also extends to Jerusalem, home of the sacred Muslim site the al-Aqsa Mosque.

Bin Laden will not cease his opposition until the United States leaves the region. Paradoxically, his strategy for convincing the United States to do so seems drawn from the American foreign policy playbook. When the United States disapproves of the behavior of another nation, it "turns up the heat" on that nation through embargoes, economic sanctions or withdrawal of diplomatic representation. In the case of Iraq following the Gulf War, America employed military action, resulting in the loss of civilian life. The State Department has theorized that if the people of a rogue nation experience enough suffering, they will overthrow their rulers, or compel them to adopt more sensible behavior. The terrorist actions in New York and Washington are a clear and ironic implementation of this strategy against the United States.

Bin Laden takes no credit for actions emanating from his training camps in Afghanistan. A true ideologue, he believes that his mission is sacred, and he wants only to see clear results. For this reason, the structure of his organization is essentially tribal, or cellular, in modern political terms. His followers are as fervent and intense in their belief as he is. They carry out their actions because they believe in the rightness of their cause, not because of bin Laden's orders or approval. Groups are trained in Afghanistan, and then establish their own centers in places as far-flung as Canada, Africa and Europe. Each cell is technologically sophisticated, and may have a different set of motivations for attacking the United States.

Palestinian members of his group see Americans as supporters of Israel in the current conflict between the two nations. In the Palestinian view, Ariel Sharon's ascendancy to leadership of Israel has triggered a new era, with U.S. government officials failing to pressure the Israeli government to end violence against Palestinians. Palestinian cell members will not cease their opposition until the United States changes its relationship with the Israeli state.

Above all, Americans need to remember that the rest of the world has an absolute right to self-determination that is as defensible as our own. A despicable act of terror such as that committed in New York and Washington is a measure of the revulsion that others feel at U.S. actions that seemingly limit those rights. If we perpetrate a cycle of hate and revenge, this conflict will escalate into a war that our great-grandchildren will be fighting.

"Understanding Osama bin Laden" by William Beeman from Alternet.net, September 17, 2004. Reprinted with permission from www.alternet.org.

XII

CHANGE

What Does It Mean to Modernize?

CULTURES CHANGE ALL THE TIME, but the most dramatic instances are to be found in the confrontation between small-scale and large-scale societies. By 1900, hardly any autonomous tribal people were left on the globe because most had been conquered and subjugated by powerful forces of Western technology and ideology. This takeover changed political relationships profoundly. It was not Western culture per se that confronted these people, but a worldwide economic system that made use of this inexpensive labor administered usually by some form of colonialism. It was in this **economic exploitation** that these people were transformed.

The results of this transformation were hardly uniform. Industrialization or colonialism did not shape new household or other cultural forms; rather, any new forms were the product of how so-called tribal people *interpreted* their colonial experiences and acted on the basis of these interpretations. Some cultures are clearly more amenable to culture change than others, and explanations of culture change have been sought in a variety of interlocking factors including relative deprivation, exploitation and economic inequality, and congruence of cultural elements. Frequently culture change is manifested in terms that are the antithesis of the colonial situation. Thus, for example, if the colonized are treated hierarchically, the culture change movement might stress **egalitarianism.** This is known, in terms formulated by the anthropologist Victor Turner, as a form of antistructure or liminality.

Perhaps the most dramatic forms of these movements are those known as **cargo cults** or **millenarian movements**—typically religion-based movements that promote social change. They are also movements to make sense of what is a bewildering and frustrating experience for many of the colonial underdogs. Much interesting work has been done on this subject, and some anthropologists have even gone so far as to apply these models to their own society. The rise of Christianity, for example, shows many similarities with Melanesian cargo cults. Both are very much the products of an oppressive colonial system, and both led to the formulation of an alternative lifestyle and ideology. The major difference is, of course, that Christianity went on to become a successful movement, whereas most of these movements are rather short-lived.

What one makes of these movements depends on whose point of view is taken. The Mau Mau, for example, was a movement in Kenya that the colonial authorities saw as a terroristic movement that used "sick" rituals like the slaughter of goats and people to intimidate the local populace. Later analyses, however, showed it to be not a fanatical cult but a highly effective anticolonial movement. Outsiders' preoccupation with the esoteric and their inability to communicate because of language barriers have often resulted in outsiders projecting their own fantasies onto such movements—a situation abetted by the need of such movements to maintain some secrecy.

After gaining independence, many Southern Hemisphere countries were given massive foreign aid to help in their development. Much of this aid is believed to be misplaced. When financial aid was originally provided to these countries, anthropologists were rarely consulted, for a number of reasons: They were believed to favor "traditional culture" and thus were against change; moreover, they took too long to do their studies since they insisted on fieldwork. But after some particularly dismal failures of foreign aid, anthropologists are increasingly being called upon to provide the local perspective, because they are believed to be well qualified to serve as bridge personnel who understand both the world of the local people and that of the planners. They are supposed to help identify the unanticipated consequences of large development projects and can have important benefits.

Anthropologists are by no means unanimous as to what their role should be in these social engineering projects. Their attitudes range from seeing them as simply another form of recolonization, to disillusionment, to damage control—accepting that such projects are inevitable. James Brain's and James Ferguson's papers point to the truth of Pogo's adage that "We have met the Enemy and he is us." Brain's concern is more with the anthropology of the development expert, while Ferguson asks a more basic question: What does development do? Of course, aid not only is provided to promote development, but often is also a response to war, famine, or other disasters, raising key intellectual, political, and methodological questions that Alex de Waal examines in his article.

It is important to recognize that anthropological voices that are critical of development exist alongside and draw their authority from the voices of an increasingly loud chorus of people who themselves have been the "victims of progress" and development projects. Some indigenous groups, like the Zapatistas of Mexico, are united in their refusal of outsider-dominated development, reflected in their motto "Ya Basta!" (Enough Already!). Frédérique Apffel-Marglin's article explores how one particular social movement in the Andes presents itself as a counterdevelopment initiative that is actively working to regenerate a space for Andean worldviews and social practices, in direct opposition to Western ideas of development.

FOCUS QUESTIONS

As you read these selections, consider these questions:

✦ What are some of the forces that motivate cultural change? What happens to "tradition" in the context of cultural change?

✦ Anthropologists both work in and criticize development. What is development? Why are some anthropologists critical of development? What are some of the ethical dilemmas for an anthropologist working in the aid industry?

✦ How are some indigenous people in the Andes responding to development and cultural change?

43

The Ugly American Revisited

James L. Brain

James Brain first experienced Africa, where he has done fieldwork, as a welfare officer for the British Colonial Service. He went on to study anthropology at Syracuse University, which granted him a PhD in 1968. He is now an emeritus professor of anthropology at the State University of New York College at New Paltz, and his research specialties include social organization, social change, sex roles, and Swahili.

In 1958 the publication of the novel *The Ugly American* by William J. Lederer and Eugene Burdick caused a great furor. In that year alone there were twenty printings. Its emotional and political impact were instrumental in the founding of the Peace Corps and perhaps the establishment of the National Defense Education Act. A sense of shame and dismay was aroused among most liberal-minded educated Americans by the idea that our State Department representatives abroad could be so naive and gullible, so isolated in a cocoon of air-conditioned American technological culture, so lacking in any knowledge of alien cultures and languages, that they would do more harm than good to American real interests. Many of us felt guilty and even outraged that the ignorance and ethnocentrism of our aid administrators were getting us hated in the world.

Many people never read the novel and assumed from its title that it was about the ugliness of the American image abroad; indeed, it became common to say "He's a real ugly American." In one sense this idea correctly identified the message of the book; in another, it is ironic that one of the book's few heroes was the person referred to: a small ugly modest man who understood the real needs of the people and wanted to initiate schemes such as the construction of simple water pumps using a bicycle as the power unit. The snag that the little man discovered was that such schemes were of no interest whatever to anyone in the State Department. The reasons can be simply stated and they are just as strong today: (1) They are not spectacular even though they might revolutionize people's lives; (2) they would only cost a few thousand dollars; nothing that costs less than several millions is even considered; (3) no American institution—companies, contractors, universities—would make a big profit.

I recently saw the book in a flea market, bought it and re-read it. It was horribly resonant to me as I recently worked for US AID on a two-year contract in Tanzania. I resigned after one year filled with dismay. Nothing has changed: we are still making the very same mistakes, spending huge sums of our tax money, and getting ourselves cordially hated for it.

Tanzania has been the recipient of perhaps more non-military aid than any other country in Africa, taking it from all kinds of sources, both east and west. Like every Third World country, its economy has suffered severely from the massive rise in oil prices and from the low prices for the kind of crops on which it depended in the past for its foreign exchange—coffee, cotton, sisal, tobacco. At the same time it is very shocking for someone like myself who went there first some 32 years ago to see the depths of poverty, inefficiency, and squalor to which it has been reduced. The reasons are many and complex. Chief among them are undoubtedly: (1) the nationalization of the wholesale and retail sector of the economy: shops have virtually nothing in them most of the time; bare requirements of sugar, flour, rice, cooking oil, etc. arrive at irregular intervals—sometimes weeks or months apart—and are sold out immediately (the majority of the people live by subsistence agriculture so although they can no longer get any luxury goods (sugar, margarine, luxuries!) they don't starve, otherwise the country would collapse in a month); (2) the nationalization of the highly effective producer cooperative movement started under the British in the nineteen fifties: the government is now the sole buying agent and pays poor prices, pays late, or even in IOUs; (3) the omnipresent party which really runs the country and which together with the huge bureaucracy constitutes an exploitative regime that makes the former colonial period look benign indeed; (4) the policy of compulsory "villagization" carried through in the seventies which has left a legacy of bitterness, cynicism, and passive resistance among the peasants.

Leaving this all aside—hard but just possible if we really want to help the people—what sort of things are being done in the way of international aid? There seems to be a correlation between the size of the country and the effectiveness of its aid program: the smaller the better; the larger, the poorer—with us, of course, the largest. For instance, Norway trains forestry experts—essential for a country with no other fuel resources as yet tapped. Denmark trains veterinarians—crucial for a country that has millions of cattle, sheep and goats, yet where meat and dairy products are almost unobtainable. Even the Republic of Ireland has a useful little scheme running a carpet factory to make carpets from the sisal it is hard to sell (the man running it was a gem: he had started a darts club at the local bar and was totally one of the boys). If you visit the German aid organization you will find it very modest, yet it is doing an excellent job and is very popular. The Dutch have a good scheme constructing small village wells and pumps. There is no Dutch aid office; it is part of the embassy.

Contrast this with the United States. The AID office occupies two air-conditioned floors of a large office block and is considerably larger than the embassies of most countries. The U.S. Embassy is some three miles away in a mini-fortress (originally made for the Israelis until they had to leave the country) inconveniently located for everyone except perhaps the ambassador. Outside the AID office is a large sign which includes the logo of two clasped hands. It used to have one black hand and one white—the latter representing the United States—until someone finally realized that all Americans are not white and all aid recipients are not black. The hands are now both the same neutral color. (Incidentally, a few blocks away is the USIS office which has everything captioned in English for a population of whom perhaps ten percent know English. Why? "We are only interested in the educated elite," I was told by the officer in charge. As far back as 1965 I was protesting to the ambassador that American projects had notice boards describing them to the public only in English, and even volunteered to translate them into Swahili, which is known to the entire population, unlike most African countries where there is a multiplicity of languages. When the Chinese were giving aid to Tanzania a few years ago all their projects had large signs in Chinese, English and Swahili. In that same year, I now recall, a highly intelligent young woman whom I

had trained in Swahili and who came out as an officer in the information service, was hurriedly removed to another country after pressure from the State Department community who were outraged that she should be friendly with one of the most important Tanzanian ministers. She was white.)

Inside the AID office one is met by a massive photograph of the incumbent president, the floors are carpeted, a pretty receptionist and glamorous secretaries all add to the impression of a huge organization. The impression is only too correct. Two busy floors of highly salaried officers are dreaming up six-million-dollar schemes. Nothing less is ever considered—as someone once said: "The paper work alone costs that much."

The process goes something like this. Someone has an idea for a project. Since it is going to be very expensive a lot of work has to go into preparing it. The preparation of a contract can take a long time and the final resultant document has all the size of a family bible. All kinds of congressional conditions have to be met—many of them concerned with certifying that the country to whom the aid will be given is not hostile to the U.S. It is very easy to evade these conditions, but the amount of paper required is almost incredible. Doubtless some of the schemes proposed and which have been carried out in the past have been of value to Tanzania; many have not. Why, one might ask, does a country like Tanzania accept such schemes? The answer, as one might expect, is that there is something in them for a lot of people. Usually every scheme will mean some free vehicles, some new buildings, salaries for some staff positions, and perhaps most importantly, some scholarships for Africans to go to the U.S. for advanced degrees. Why do we get involved? The answer is much the same: there is something in it for a lot of people.

When a scheme has been processed through Washington and agreed to by the country concerned, it is put out for tender—perhaps the most bizarre system of any aid system. The bidders are usually land-grant universities. They claim to make no profit out of such a deal; on the other hand, many of their faculty members get free trips out as consultants, salaries for faculty and staff members at the home university are met, other faculty members can be shipped off for a few years at the government's expense (who will then become "experts"), and the university will get the students who have been awarded scholarships. One might question the value of involving agricultural institutions in this country committed to an "agribusiness" approach in the agriculture of countries at a largely subsistence level; or the sense of sending students to such institutions where they will learn almost nothing of any practical value to them at home. Moreover, one often wonders what on earth anyone from, say, Colorado or Utah has to contribute as a consultant on a three-week visit.

The persons recruited to go out for two or three years (like myself) are called "contract staff." They are the second-class citizens of the AID hierarchy. The real mandarins are the career officers of the State Department—and I hasten to add that many of them are decent, hardworking people, but caught in a system that is absurd. As I said, their job is to dream up new schemes—never less than six million dollars, remember—and, of course, to be "project officers" to keep a vague eye on the hatched chicks that actually make it through the astounding jungle of regulations in Washington. To do this they received—in 1981—a minimum salary of $50,000 plus a substantial post allowance, commissary privileges (including duty-free liquor), travel allowances for home leave annually for themselves and their families, a large house surrounded by a chain-link fence and guards. In effect they live at a level far above what most would expect in jobs in this country, far, far above the level of any of the previous colonial service officers. They are totally out of contact with the ordinary people. None that I met spoke more than a few words of any local language. Their social contacts are confined to the upper elite of the government and the diplomatic corps. Many of them are able to retire in their forties on a pension. As I said before, many of them are good, kind people, but they are trapped into a crazy, expensive, wasteful and largely useless system that gets us no credit and a lot of hatred.

Not only are most of the career officers totally out of contact with the people of the countries in which they are working; they are also astonishingly ignorant of the cultures of those countries. Peace Corps Volunteers usually get a good training in the language, history, political development and culture of the country. They are only there for two years. Career officers of the State Department are often in a country for many years but know nothing of it beyond the capital and the game parks.

To someone like myself who was involved in the Peace Corps from its first inception, the ironies of contrast are constant. Whereas Peace Corps Volunteers really know a lot about the country where they are going and have to have some proficiency in the language, AID personnel have no preparation other than a pamphlet about the cost of living and what to take. There is no language requirement on them even though they may stay in a country for several years. Peace Corps Volunteers live not too differently from the local people, travel by local transportation, have to speak the language. They have done a great deal to change the image of rich Americans. Even contract AID officers (and this included me) are supplied with a large house, a refrigerator and large freezer, have to purchase a car, and have salaries considerably larger than they would get in the U.S.—enormous by local standards. Perhaps it is necessary to get qualified people; volunteers are just starting their careers; most AID contract officers are taking an unpaid leave of absence. There is usually some antagonism between the Peace Corps and the AID organization—the former feeling sometimes a little holier than thou and the latter feeling guilty about the stark contrast between themselves and the local people.

What kind of schemes am I talking about? Let us take a couple: first, the one with which I was connected. I have to backtrack a little to explain my connection. I worked in extension work in Tanzania and Uganda from 1951–63. In 1971, as an anthropologist, I returned for the summer to do research on belief systems. The dean of the agricultural college, who had known me for many years, instantly coopted me to give a series of lectures to the students on extension work because nowhere in their technically-oriented syllabus did they learn how to put over what they had learnt. It seemed to me to be a very useful idea and so in 1980 I applied for and was to be given a Fulbright fellowship to do this for a whole year. At this juncture I was approached by AID and asked wouldn't I like to do the same thing for two years at a high salary ($36,000 as compared to the $16,000 of the Fulbright)? Greed won out and I turned down the Fulbright: a decision I deeply regret. To my astonishment I found that the college had gone from the sublime to the ridiculous, with the establishment of an entire academic department devoted to agricultural education and extension. My idea is that students need perhaps two courses: an introduction to cultural anthropology to help them to understand how communities function, and a course on how to teach a practical subject. They certainly do not need courses on the philosophical and psychological foundations of education. Part of the scheme was to supply three faculty members, part to send Tanzanians to the States to do doctorates, part to build a large training center for courses, workshops, conferences and the like. Admirable, one might think, but there are dozens of idle buildings around where one could do any of these things without spending a large sum of money.

As I was about to leave, a new project was shaping up in which a big western state university would send out about twenty researchers with Ph.D.s to carry out research on the latest buzz-word—farming systems. Obviously, such a scheme will be very costly—each officer in the field costs $100,000 a year for a start—and I constantly voiced two major criticisms. First, most of the information required is already well known if someone were to do a little reading of the archives. Second, it would be quite possible for a trained anthropologist with a good knowledge of Swahili to obtain all that is needed in a few weeks at most; in many cases a few days would be enough. To bring in American farming experts with no background in East Africa, with no knowledge of the language or culture, unfamiliar with the history, is like throwing American taxpayers' money down the drain. But, of course, the university concerned will make a lot of money, all kinds of lucrative contracts will result, instant experts will be created—and then they will be able to be called in to advise on similar problems elsewhere.

In Africa in general and Tanzania in particular one major cultural matter of supreme importance has so far escaped the experts' notice, just as it escaped the notice of the colonial regimes of the past: that the farmers of Africa are usually the women. At the very least the women work on the farms as much as the men—they also fetch the water, cut and fetch the firewood, pound corn in a mortar, do the cooking, take care of the children. The only politician in all Africa to realize this fact is the often maligned Hastings Banda of Malawi, one of the only countries in Africa to be self-supporting in food. How? Dr. Banda invites the women from a particular area to the capital, gives them a big dance with lots of beer and food and a present, and then exhorts them to go back home and do everything the extension officers tell them.

The impression that I constantly got was that most AID people mentally perceived a "farmer" to be a tall white man, wearing blue jeans, boots and a Stetson staring out over his wide acres. Ronald Reagan receiving the Queen of England at his ranch would be a good model. The idea that a farmer might be a woman was not something that had really sunk in. Given the sharply divided sex roles of African society, a man cannot deal with women; on the other hand, a well-educated woman—African or American—can be accepted by both men and women. Plainly, we should send women experts and train more African women.

What should we do then? We might take a lesson from the smaller countries and think small. Abolish the wasteful AID offices and their career persons whose task it is to produce these expensive and largely useless schemes. One or two officers attached to the embassy should be entirely sufficient to act as liaison with the government and the contract workers. Get involved in small-scale schemes which don't need large buildings and vehicles. The kind of training that extension workers might get in India, Egypt, Israel, or even China would be of far more use than anything they could get in this country. Must we always make a profit? Would it be too much to pay for people to go elsewhere, to admit that we don't have all the agricultural answers, especially for small-scale peasant agriculture that is likely to remain the mode for the foreseeable future? If the millions poured into the present schemes were channelled into research in intermediate technology it would be much more useful. Simple hand grinding machines and small-scale wells and pumps could make life less burdensome for the real producers of food—the women.

An even more radical idea was propounded in 1966 by Charles Hynam when he wrote an article with the intimidating title of "The Disfunctionality of Unrequited Giving." He pointed out that long ago in anthropology it was noticed that the principle of reciprocity is one of the most basic in human social organization. If you continually give things to someone which he cannot return he will feel a sense of obligation to you which in time will inevitably turn to dislike, hatred even. The application of this to the international aid scene is obvious. The more aid we give the more we shall be hated. His solution is one of supreme simplicity. Instead of all the bilateral aid agreements, everyone should channel funds to the World Bank which would then set up local branches all over the Third World like savings and loan associations. One of the major hindrances to development is often lack of initial capital on a small scale. By having a local bank it would be possible for individuals, or even cooperatives or whole villages, to obtain loans to finance projects which would be repaid with reasonable rates of interest. No one would be obligated to anyone and a lot of development would result. The beauty of the idea is that it does not prescribe a capitalist mode of development or a socialist one but could assist both individuals or groups.

It is sad enough that we should be wasting such astronomical sums on crazy weapons. Should we not make sure that the money we do spend to help Third World countries does in fact help them?

44

The Anti-Politics Machine

"Development" and Bureaucratic Power in Lesotho

James Ferguson (with Larry Lohmann)

James Ferguson is a political and economic anthropologist who specializes in southern Africa. He teaches at the University of California, Irvine. Larry Lohmann writes on themes development, ecology, and tropical forestry.

In the past two decades, Lesotho—a small landlocked nation of about 1.8 million people surrounded by South Africa, with a current Gross National Product (GNP) of US$816 million—has received "development" assistance from 26 different countries, ranging from Australia, Cyprus and Ireland to Switzerland and Taiwan. Seventy-two international agencies and non- and quasi-governmental organizations, including CARE, Ford Foundation, the African Development Bank, the European Economic Community, the Overseas Development Institute, the International Labour Organization and the United Nations Development Programme, have also been actively involved in promoting a range of "development" programmes. In 1979, the country received some $64 million in "official" development "assistance"—about $49 for every man, woman and child in the country. Expatriate consultants and "experts" swarm in the capital city of Maseru, churning out plans, programmes and, most of all, paper, at an astonishing rate.

As in most other countries, the history of "development" projects in Lesotho is one of "almost unremitting failure to achieve their objectives."[1] Nor does the country appear to be of especially great economic or strategic importance. What, then, is this massive and persistent internationalist intervention all about?

CONSTRUCTING A "DEVELOPER'S" LESOTHO

To "move the money" they have been charged with spending, "development" agencies prefer to opt for stan-dardized "development" packages. It thus suits the agencies to portray developing countries in terms that make them suitable targets for such packages. It is not surprising, therefore, that the "country profiles" on which the agencies base their interventions frequently bear little or no relation to economic and social realities.

In 1975, for example, the World Bank issued a report on Lesotho that was subsequently used to justify a series of major Bank loans to the country. One passage in the report—describing conditions in Lesotho at the time of its independence from Britain in 1966—encapsulates an image of Lesotho that fits well with the institutional needs of "development" agencies:

> Virtually untouched by modern economic development . . . Lesotho was, and still is, basically, a traditional subsistence peasant society. But rapid population growth resulting in extreme pressure on the land, deteriorating soil and declining agricultural yields led to a situation in which the country was no longer able to produce enough food for its people. Many able-bodied men were forced from the land in search of means to support their families, but the only employment opportunities [were] in neighbouring South Africa. At present, an estimated 60 per cent of the male labour force is away as migrant workers in South Africa . . . At independence, there was no economic infrastructure to speak of. Industries were virtually non-existent.[2]

THE INVENTION OF "ISOLATION"

To a scholar of Lesotho, these assertions appear not only incorrect but outlandish. For one thing, the country has not been a "subsistence" society since at least the mid-1800s, having entered the twentieth century as a producer of "wheat, mealies, Kaffir corn [sic], wool, mohair, horses

"The Anti-Politics Machine: 'Development' and Bureaucratic Power in Lesotho" by James Ferguson with Larry Lohmann from *The Ecologist*, Vol. 24, No. 5, September/October 1994. Reprinted with permission.

and cattle" for the South African market.[3] Nor were the local Basotho people isolated from the market. When they have had surpluses of crops or livestock, the people have always known how to go about selling them in local or regional markets. According to *The Oxford History of South Africa*:

> In 1837 the Sotho of Basutoland . . . had grain stored for four to eight years: in 1844 white farmers "flocked" to them to buy grain. During 1872 (after the loss of their most fertile land west of the Caledon) the Sotho exported 100,000 *muids* [185-lb bags] of grain . . . and in 1877 when the demand for grain on the diamond fields had fallen, "large quantities" were held by producers and shop-keepers in Basutoland.[4]

Livestock auctions, meanwhile, have been held throughout the country since at least the 1950s, and animals from central Lesotho have been sold by the Basotho as far afield as South Africa for as long as anyone can remember. Far from being "untouched" by modern "development" at the time of independence, colonial rule had established a modern administration, airports, roads, schools, hospitals and markets for Western commodities.

The decline in agricultural surpluses, moreover, is neither recent nor, as the Bank suggests, due to "isolation" from the cash economy. More significant is the loss by the Basotho of most of their best agricultural land to encroaching Dutch settlers during a series of wars between 1840 and 1869. Nor is migration a recent response of a pristine and static "traditional" economy to "population pressure." As H. Ashton, the most eminent Western ethnographer of the Basuto, noted in 1952, "labour migration is . . . nearly as old as the Basuto's contact with Europeans"[5]—indeed, throughout the colonial period to the present, Lesotho has served as a labour reservoir exporting wage workers to South African mines, farms and industry.

Large-scale labour migration, moreover, preceded the decline in agriculture by many years and may even have contributed to it. Even in years of very good crop production, from the 1870s on intermittently into the 1920s, workers left the country by the thousand for work. In the early stages, it seems, migration was not related to a need to make up for poor food production but to buy guns, clothing, cattle and other goods, and, from 1869, to pay taxes.

LESOTHO REALITY

In fact, far from being the "traditional subsistence peasant society" described by the Bank, Lesotho comprises today what one writer describes as "a rural proletariat which scratches about on the land."[6]

Whilst the World Bank claims that "agriculture provides a livelihood for 85 per cent of the people,"[7] the reality is that something in the order of 70 per cent of average rural household income is derived from wage labour in South Africa, while only six per cent comes from domestic crop production.[8] Similar myth-making pervades a joint FAO/World Bank report from 1975, which solemnly states that "about 70 per cent of [Lesotho's] GNP comes from the sale of pastoral products, mainly wool and mohair." A more conventional figure would be two or three per cent.[9]

Also false is the "development" literature's picture of Lesotho as a self-contained geographical entity whose relation with South Africa (its "rich neighbour") is one of accidental geographic juxtaposition rather than structural economic integration or political subordination, and whose poverty can be explained largely by the dearth of natural resources within its boundaries, together with the incompleteness with which they have been "developed." If the country is resource-poor, this is because most of the good Sotho land was taken by South Africa. Saying, as USAID does in a 1978 report, that "poverty in Lesotho is primarily resource-related" is like saying that the South Bronx of New York City is poor because of its lack of natural resources and the fact that it contains more people than its land base can support.

REARRANGING REALITY

A representation which acknowledged the extent of Lesotho's long-standing involvement in the "modern" capitalist economy of southern Africa, however, would not provide a convincing justification for the "development" agencies to "introduce" roads, markets and credit. It would provide no grounds for believing that such "innovations" could bring about the "transformation" to a "developed," "modern" economy which would enable Lesotho's agricultural production to catch up with its burgeoning population and cut labour migration. Indeed, such a representation would tend to suggest that such measures for "opening up" the country and exposing it to the "cash economy" would have little impact, since Lesotho has not been isolated from the world economy for a very long time.

Acknowledging that Lesotho is a labour reserve for South African mining and industry rather than portraying it as an autonomous "national economy," moreover, would be to stress the importance of something which is inaccessible to a "development" planner in Lesotho. The

World Bank mission to Lesotho is in no position to formulate programmes for changing or controlling the South African mining industry, and it has no disposition to involve itself in political challenges to the South African system of labour control. It is in an excellent position, however, to devise agricultural improvement projects, extension, credit and technical inputs, for the agriculture of Lesotho lies neatly within its jurisdiction, waiting to be "developed." For this reason, agricultural concerns tend to move centre stage and Lesotho is portrayed as a nation of "farmers," not wage labourers. At the same time, issues such as structural unemployment, influx control, low wages, political subjugation by South Africa, parasitic bureaucratic elites, and so on, simply disappear.

TAKING POLITICS OUT OF "DEVELOPMENT"

One striking feature of the "development" discourse on Lesotho is the way in which the "development" agencies present the country's economy and society as lying within the control of a neutral, unitary and effective national government, and thus almost perfectly responsive to the blueprints of planners. The state is seen as an impartial instrument for implementing plans and the government as a machine for providing social services and engineering growth.

"Development" is, moreover, seen as something that only comes about through government action; and lack of "development," by definition, is the result of government neglect. Thus, in the World Bank's view, whether Lesotho's GNP goes up or down is a simple function of the current five-year "development" plan being well-implemented or badly-implemented: it has nothing to do with whether or not the mineworkers who work in South Africa get a raise in any particular year. Agricultural production, similarly, is held to be low because of the "absence of agricultural development schemes" and, thus, local ignorance that "worthwhile things could be achieved on their land." In this way, an extraordinarily important place is reserved for policy and "development" planning.[10]

Excluded from the Bank's analysis are the political character of the state and its class basis, the uses of official positions and state power by the bureaucratic elite and other individuals, cliques and factions, and the advantages to them of bureaucratic "inefficiency" and corruption. The state represents "the people," and mention of the undemocratic nature of the ruling government or of political opposition is studiously avoided. The state is taken to have no interests except "development": where "bureaucracy" is seen as a problem, it is not a political matter, but the unfortunate result of poor organization or lack of training.

Political parties almost never appear in the discourse of the Bank and other "development" institutions, and the explicitly political role played by "development" institutions such as Village Development Committees (VDCs), which often serve as channels for the ruling Basotho National Party (BNP), is ignored or concealed. "The people" tend to appear as an undifferentiated mass, a collection of "individual farmers" and "decision makers," a concept which reduces political and structural causes of poverty to the level of individual "values," "attitudes" and "motivation." In this perspective, structural change is simply a matter of "educating" people, or even just convincing them to change their minds. When a project is sent out to "develop the farmers" and finds that "the farmers" are not much interested in farming, and, in fact, do not even consider themselves to be "farmers," it is thus easy for it to arrive at the conclusion that "the people" are mistaken, that they really are farmers and that they need only to be convinced that this is so for it to be so.

In fact, neither state bureaucracies nor the "development" projects associated with them are impartial, apolitical machines which exist only to provide social services and promote economic growth. In the case of the Canadian- and World Bank–supported Thaba-Tseka Development Project, an agricultural programme in Lesotho's central mountains, Sesotho-language documents distributed to villagers were found to have slogans of the ruling Basotho National Party (BNP) added at the end, although these did not appear in any of the English language versions. Public village meetings conducted by project staff were peppered with political speeches, and often included addresses by a high-ranking police officer on the "security threat" posed by the opposition Basutoland Congress Party. Any money remaining after project costs had been repaid went to the BNP's Village Development Committees—leading one villager to note caustically, "It seems that politics is nowadays nicknamed 'development.'"

Tellingly, when I interviewed the Canadian Coordinator of the Thaba-Tseka Project in 1983, he expressed what appeared to be a genuine ignorance of the political role played by VDCs. The project hired labour through the committees, he stated, because the government had told them to. "We can't afford to get involved with politics," he said. "If they say 'hire through the Committees,' I do it."

It seems likely that such apparent political naivete is not a ruse, but simply a low-level manifestation of the refusal to face local politics which, for institutional reasons, characterizes the entire "development" apparatus.

INEVITABLE FAILURE

Because the picture of Lesotho constructed by the Bank and other "development" agencies bears so little resemblance to reality, it is hardly surprising that most "development" projects have "failed" even on their own terms. Thus after years of accusing local people of being "defeatist" or "not serious" about agriculture, and even implying that wage increases at South African mines were "a threat" to the determination of farmers to become "serious," Thaba-Tseka project experts had to concede that local people were right that little besides maize for local consumption was going to come out of their tiny mountain fields, and that greater investment in agriculture was not going to pay handsome rewards.[11]

Casting themselves in the role of politically-neutral artisans using "development" projects as tools to grab hold of and transform a portion of the country according to a pre-determined plan, "development" officials assumed that the projects were givens and all they had to do was "implement" them.

In the case of the Thaba-Tseka project, for example, planners assumed that it would be a relatively simple matter to devolve much of the decision-making to a newly constituted Thaba-Tseka district, in order to increase efficiency, enable the project to be in closer touch with the needs of "the people" and avoid its becoming entangled in government bureaucracy. But what the planners assumed would be a simple technical reform led—predictably—to a whole range of actors using the reforms for their own ends.

The project's Health Division, for example, was partly appropriated as a political resource for the ruling National Party. Power struggles broke out over the use of project vehicles. Government ministries refused to vote funds to the project and persisted in maintaining their own control over their field staff and making unilateral decisions on actions in the district. An attempt to hire a Mosotho to replace the project's expatriate Canadian director was rejected, since as long as the programme's image remained "Canadian," there could be no danger of bringing about a real "decentralization" of power away from Maseru, Lesotho's capital.

Instead of being a tool used by artisans to resculpt society, in short, the project was itself worked on: it became like a bread crumb thrown into an ant's nest. Plans for decentralization were thus abandoned in 1982. Yet Thaba-Tseka's planners continued to insist that the project's failure resulted somehow from the government's failure to understand the plan, or from the right organizational chart not having been found. Needing to construe their role as "apolitical," they continued to see government as a machine for delivering services, not as a political fact or a means by which certain classes and interests attempted to control the behaviour and choices of others.

A DIFFERENT KIND OF PROPERTY

Another example of "failure" stemming from the "development" discourse's false construction of Lesotho is that of livestock "development."

"Development" planners have long seen Lesotho's grasslands as one of the few potentially exploitable natural resources the country possesses,[12] and the country's herds of domestic grazing animals as an inertia-ridden "traditional" sector ripe for transformation by the dynamic "modern" cash economy. What is required, according to planners, is to develop "appropriate marketing outlets," control grassland use to optimize commercial productivity through destocking and grazing associations, introduce improved breeds, and convince "farmers to market their non-productive stock."[13]

Far from being the result of "traditional" inertia, however, the Basotho's reluctance to treat livestock commercially is deeply embedded in, and partly maintained by, a modern, capitalist labour reserve economy. In Lesotho's highly monetized economy, an item such as a transistor radio or a bar of soap may be subject to the same market mechanisms of pricing, supply and demand as it is anywhere else. Cattle, goats and sheep, however, are subject to very different sorts of rules. Although cash can always be converted into livestock through purchase, there is a reluctance to convert grazing animals to cash through sale, except when there is an emergency need for food, clothes, or school fees.

This practice is rooted in, and reinforced by, a social system in which young working men are away in South Africa supporting their families for ten or eleven months of the year. (Mines hire only men, and it is very difficult for women from Lesotho to find work in South Africa.) If a man comes home from the mines with cash in his pocket, his wife may present him with a demand to buy her a new dress, furniture for the house or new blankets for the children. If, on the other hand, he comes home with an ox purchased with his wages, it is more difficult to make such demands.

One reason that men like to own large numbers of livestock is that they boost their prestige and personal networks in the community, partly since they can be farmed out to friends and relatives to help with their field work. They thus serve as a "placeholder" for the man in the household and the community, symbolically asserting his structural presence and prestigious social position, even in the face of his physical absence. After he has returned to the household because of injury, age or being laid off from the South African mines to "scratch about on the land," livestock begin to be sold in response to absolute shortages of minimum basic necessities. Grazing animals thus constitute a sort of special "retirement fund" for men which is effective precisely because, although it lies within the household, it cannot be accessed in the way cash can.

Hence a whole mystique has grown up glorifying cattle ownership—a mystique which, although largely contested by women, is constantly fought for by most men. Such conflict is not a sign of disintegration or crisis; it is part of the process of recreating a "tradition" which is never simply a residue of the past. If the cultural rules governing livestock in Lesotho persist, it is because they are made to persist; continuity as much as change has to be created and fought for.

Investment in livestock is thus not an alternative to migrant labour but a consequence of it. If livestock sellers surveyed by "development" experts report no source of income other than agriculture, this does not mean that they are "serious stock farmers" as opposed to "migrant labourers"; they may simply be "retired."

However useful and necessary they may be, moreover, livestock in Lesotho is less an "industry" or a "sector" than a type (however special) of consumer good bought with wages earned in South Africa when times are good and sold off only when times are bad. The sale of an animal is not "off-take" of a surplus, but part of a process which culminates in the destruction of the herd. A drop in livestock exports from Lesotho is thus not, as the "development" discourse would have it, a sign of a depressed "industry," but of a rise in incomes. For instance, when wages were increased in South African mines in the 1970s, Basotho miners seized the opportunity to invest in cattle in unprecedented numbers, leading to a surge in import figures from 4,067 in 1973 to 57,787 in 1978. Over the same period, meanwhile, cattle export figures dropped from 12,894 to 574. A boom in exports, on the other hand, would be the mark of a disaster.

Not surprisingly, attempts to "modernize" Lesotho's "livestock sector" have met with resistance. Within one year of the Thaba-Tseka project attempting to fence off 15 square kilometres of rangeland for the exclusive use of "progressive," "commercially minded" farmers, for example, the fence had been cut or knocked down in many places, the gates stolen, and the area was being freely grazed by all. The office of the association manager had been burned down, and the Canadian officer in charge of the programme was said to be fearing for his life.

This resistance was rooted in more than a general suspicion of the government and the "development" project. To join the official "grazing association" permitted to use the fenced-in land, stock owners were required to sell off many poor animals to buy improved ones, ending up with perhaps half as many. Such sales and restrictions in herd size were not appealing for most Basotho men. Joining the association not only meant accepting selection, culling and marketing of herds. It also meant acquiescing in the enclosure of both common grazing land and (insofar as any Mosotho's livestock are also a social, shared domain of wealth) animals. It thus signified a betrayal of fellow stock-owners who remained outside the organization, an act considered anti-social. Prospective association members also probably feared that their animals—which represent wealth in a visible, exposed, and highly vulnerable form—might be stolen or vandalized in retaliation.

THE SIDE EFFECTS OF "FAILURE"

Despite such disasters, it may be that what is most important about a "development" project is not so much what it fails to do but what it achieves through its "side effects." Rather than repeatedly asking the politically naive question "Can aid programmes ever be made really to help poor people?" perhaps we should investigate the more searching question, "What do aid programmes do *besides* fail to help poor people?"

Leftist political economists have often argued that the "real" purpose of "development" projects is to aid capitalist penetration into Third World countries. In Lesotho, however, such projects do not characteristically succeed in introducing new relations of production (capitalist or otherwise), nor do they bring about modernization or significant economic transformations. Nor are they set up in such a way that they ever could. For this reason, it seems a mistake to interpret them *simply* as "part of the historical expansion of capitalism" or as elements in a global strategy for controlling or capitalizing peasant production.

Capitalist interests, moreover, can only operate through a set of social and cultural structures so complex that the outcome may be only a baroque and unrecognizable transformation of the original intention. Although it is relevant to know, for instance, that the World Bank has an interest in boosting production and export of cash crops for the external market, and that industrialized states without historic links to an area may sponsor "development" projects as a way of breaking into otherwise inaccessible markets, it remains impossible simply to read off actual events from these known interests as if the one were a simple effect of the other. Merely knowing that the Canadian government has an interest in promoting rural "development" because it helps Canadian corporations to find export markets for farm machinery, for example, leaves many of the empirical details of the Canadian role in Thaba-Tseka absolutely mysterious.

Another look at the Thaba-Tseka project, however, reveals that, although the project "failed" both at poverty alleviation and at extending the influence of international capital, it did have a powerful and far-reaching impact on its region. While the project did not transform livestock-keeping, it did build a road to link Thaba-Tseka more strongly with the capital. While it did not bring about "decentralization" or "popular participation," it was instrumental in establishing a new district administration and giving the government a much stronger presence in the area than it had ever had before.

As a direct result of the construction of the project centre and the decision to make that centre the capital of a new district, there appeared a new post office, a police station, a prison and an immigration control office; there were health officials and nutrition officers and a new "food for work" administration run by the Ministry of Rural Development and the Ministry of Interior, which functioned politically to regulate the power of chiefs. The new district centre also provided a good base for the "Para-Military Unit," Lesotho's army, and near the project's end in 1983, substantial numbers of armed troops began to be garrisoned at Thaba-Tseka.

In this perspective, the "development" apparatus in Lesotho is not a machine for eliminating poverty that is incidentally involved with the state bureaucracy. Rather, it is a machine for reinforcing and expanding the exercise of bureaucratic state power, which incidentally takes "poverty" as its point of entry and justification—launching an intervention that may have no effect on the poverty but does have other concrete effects.

This does not mean that "the state," conceived as a unitary entity, "has" more power to extract surplus, implement programmes, or order around "the masses" more efficiently—indeed, the reverse may be true. It is, rather, that more power relations are referred through state channels and bureaucratic circuits—most immediately, that more people must stand in line and await rubber stamps to get what they want. "It is the same story over again," said one "development" worker. "When the Americans and the Danes and the Canadians leave, the villagers will continue their marginal farming practices and wait for the mine wages, knowing only that now the taxman lives down the valley rather than in Maseru."[14]

At the same time, a "development" project can effectively squash political challenges to the system not only through enhancing administrative power, but also by casting political questions of land, resources, jobs or wages as technical "problems" responsive to the technical "development" intervention. If the effects of a "development" project end up forming any kind of strategically coherent or intelligible whole, it is as a kind of "anti-politics" machine, which, on the model of the "anti-gravity" machine of science fiction stories, seems to suspend "politics" from even the most sensitive political operations at the flick of a switch.

Such a result may be no part of the planners' intentions. It is not necessarily the consequence of any kind of conspiracy to aid capitalist exploitation by incorporating new territories into the world system or working against radical social change, or bribing national elites, or mystifying the real international relationships. The result can be accomplished, as it were, behind the backs of the most sincere participants. It may just happen to be the way things work out. On this view, the planning apparatus is neither mere ornament nor the master key to understanding what happens. Rather than being the blueprint for a machine, it is a *part* of the machine.

WHAT IS TO BE DONE? BY WHOM?

If, then, "development" cannot be the answer to poverty and powerlessness in Lesotho, what is? What is to be done, if it is not "development"?

Any question of the form "What is to be done?" demands first of all an answer to the question "By whom?" The "development" discourse, and a great deal of policy science, tends to answer this question in a utopian way by saying "Given an all-powerful and benevolent policy-making apparatus, what should it do to advance the interests of its poor citizens?"

This question is worse than meaningless. In practice, it acts to disguise what are, in fact, highly partial and interested interventions as universal, disinterested and inherently benevolent. If the question "What is to be done?" has any sense, it is as a real-world tactic, not a utopian ethics.

The question is often put in the form "What should *they* do?" with the "they" being not very helpfully specified as "Lesotho" or "the Basotho." When "developers" speak of such a collectivity what they mean is usually the government. But the government of Lesotho is not identical with the people who live in Lesotho, nor is it in any of the established senses "representative" of that collectivity. As in most countries, the government is a relatively small clique with narrow interests. There is little point in asking what such entrenched and often extractive elites should do in order to empower the poor. Their own structural position makes it clear that they would be the last ones to undertake such a project.

Perhaps the "they" in "What should they do?" means "the people." But again, the people are not an undifferentiated mass. There is not one question—What is to be done?—but hundreds: What should the mineworkers do? What should the abandoned old women do? and so on. It seems presumptuous to offer prescriptions here. Toiling miners and abandoned old women know the tactics proper to their situations far better than any expert does. If there is advice to be given about what "they" should do, it will not be dictating general political strategy or giving a general answer to the question "what is to be done?" (which can only be determined by those doing the resisting) but answering specific, localized, tactical questions.

WHAT SHOULD WE DO?

If the question is, on the other hand, "What should *we* do?" it has to be specified, which "we"? If "we" means "development" agencies or governments of the West, the implied subject of the question falsely implies a collective project for bringing about the empowerment of the poor. Whatever good or ill may be accomplished by these agencies, nothing about their general mode of operation would justify a belief in such a collective "we" defined by a political programme of empowerment.

For some Westerners, there is, however, a more productive way of posing the question "What should we do?" That is, "What should we intellectuals working in or concerned about the Third World do?" To the extent that there are common political values and a real "we" group, this becomes a real question. The answer, however, is more difficult.

Should those with specialized knowledge provide advice to "development" agencies who seem hungry for it and ready to act on it? As I have tried to show, these agencies seek only the kind of advice they can take. One "developer" asked my advice on what his country could do "to help these people." When I suggested that his government might contemplate sanctions against apartheid, he replied, with predictable irritation, "No, no! I mean development!" The only advice accepted is about how to "do development" better. There is a ready ear for criticisms of "bad development projects," only so long as these are followed up with calls for "good development projects." Yet the agencies who plan and implement such projects—agencies like the World Bank, USAID, and the government of Lesotho—are not really the sort of social actors that are very likely to advance the empowerment of the poor.

Such an obvious conclusion makes many uncomfortable. It seems to them to imply hopelessness; as if to suggest that the answer to the question "What is to be done?" is: "Nothing." Yet this conclusion does not follow. The state is not the only game in town, and the choice is not between "getting one's hands dirty by participating in or trying to reform development projects" and "living in an ivory tower." Change comes when, as Michel Foucault says, "critique has been played out in the real, not when reformers have realized their ideas."[15]

For Westerners, one of the most important forms of engagement is simply the political participation in one's own society that is appropriate to any citizen. This is, perhaps, particularly true for citizens of a country like the US, where one of the most important jobs for "experts" is combating imperialist policies.

This article is a summary of some of the main arguments of *The Anti-Politics Machine: "Development," Depoliticization and Bureaucratic Power in Lesotho* by James Ferguson, published by the University of Minnesota Press, 1994.

NOTES

1. Murray, C., *Families Divided: The Impact of Migrant Labour in Lesotho.* New York: Cambridge University Press, 1981, p. 19.

2. World Bank, *Lesotho: A Development Challenge.* Washington, DC: World Bank, 1975, p. 1.

3. "Basutoland," *Encyclopedia Britannica,* 1910.

4. Wilson, M., & L. Thompson (Eds.), *The Oxford History of South Africa* (vol. 1). New York: Oxford University Press, 1969.

5. Ashton, H., *The Basuto: A Social Study of Traditional and Modern Lesotho* (2d ed.). New York: Oxford University Press, 1967, p. 162.

6. Murray, C., op. cit. 1.

7. FAO/World Bank, *Draft Report of the Lesotho First Phase Mountain Area Development Project Preparation Mission* vols. I and II). Rome: FAO, 1975, Annex 1, p. 7.

8. Van der Wiel, A. C. A., *Migratory Wage Labour: Its Role in the Economy of Lesotho.* Mazenod: Mazenod Book Centre, 1977.

9. FAO/World Bank, op. cit. 7, Annex 1, p. 7.

10. World Bank, op. cit. 2, p. 9.

11. See "Appraisal of Project Progress During the Pilot Phase and Review of Plans to Expand Agricultural Programs in Phase II of Project Operations." Ottawa: CIDA, 1978, p. 39.

12. See, for example, FAO/World Bank, op. cit. 7, Annex 1, pp. 10–12. For a related South African history of government intervention into "traditional" livestock keeping, see W. Beinart & C. Bundy, "State Intervention and Rural Resistance: The Transkel, 1900–1965." In *Peasants in Africa,* ed. by M. Klein. Beverly Hills, CA: Sage, 1981.

13. CIDA, op. cit. 11.

14. Quoted in Murphy, B., "Smothered in Kindness." *New Internationalist,* No. 82, 1979, p. 13.

15. Foucault, M., "Questions of Method: An Interview." *Ideology and Consciousness,* Vol. 8, 1981, p. 13.

45

Counter-Development in the Andes

Frédérique Apffel-Marglin

Frédérique Apffel-Marglin received her PhD from Brandeis University in 1980. Her initial research was on Indian classical dance, but now she focuses mainly on development and social movements in the Andes. In the late 1980s, she was a research advisor at the World Institute for Development Economics Research in Helsinki. As a result of this work, she has coedited several books that critique development and its forms of knowledge, including (among others) The Spirit of Regeneration: Andean Culture Confronting Western Notions of Development *and* Decolonizing Knowledge: From Development to Dialogue. *She is a professor of anthropology at Smith College.*

Colonized peoples have three choices in response to colonization, according to Yvonne Dion-Buffalo and John Mohawk in a recent article: to become "good subjects," accepting the premises of the modern West without much question; to become "bad subjects," always revolting within the parameters of the colonizing world; or to become "non-subjects," acting and thinking in ways far removed from those of the modern West.[1] Dion-Buffalo and Mohawk advocate the latter not only for Native Americans but for all colonized peoples, which includes not only indigenous peoples everywhere but most of the so-called Third World. Formal colonization may have ended but the global market with its attendant intellectual and cultural colonization spread via the imperial road of development makes colonization a contemporary reality.

Dion-Buffalo and Mohawk's notion of "non-subjecthood" seems to have captured the historical moment, for one finds something very similar to it articulated by a group of indigenous writers in the Peruvian Andes. The group, called PRATEC (Proyecto Andino de Tecnologias Campesinas), was formed in 1987. Its core members are academics and government bureaucrats who left their positions to form a nongovernmental organization devoted to researching and writing about traditional Andean technologies, knowledge and world-view. PRATEC has been teaching a course aimed at would-be rural developers—

mostly agronomists—in which it presents the Andean world-view and also assesses modern Western knowledge from a native Andean point of view, and its voice has since become well known throughout the Andes.

PRATEC's conception of "non-subjecthood" emerges from its perception of what it calls "officialdom." Officialdom from the point of view of the people native to the Andes is a colonizing entity: it not only covers all governmental organizations and opposition political parties and movements but includes also the knowledge system pervading schools and universities, the judiciary system and the Church. Officialdom's perception of native peoples and cultures is to exalt them when safely dead and in the past—make them emblems of "national" identity enshrined in museums and history books—folklorize ancient ceremonies for the tourist industry where lucrative; and where it is not, relegate native contemporary practices to the marginalized status of "backwardness," anachronism and even illegality.

PRATEC's presentation of Andean world-views is always contrasted to modern Western knowledge which it sees as undergirding all branches of officialdom. The modern Western knowledge system is assessed not from an unsituated "objective" perspective but from an indigenous Andean point of view. PRATEC emphasizes the situatedness of its Andean point of view, and rejects claims to universality and absolute truth. PRATEC sees the Andean cosmovision as emerging from the very soil and air of the Andes, inseparable from its landscape and its history. Indeed, the very process of assessing modern Western knowledge from an Andean point of view has the powerful effect of revealing the historico-cultural particu-

"Counter-Development in the Andes" by Frédérique Apffel-Marglin from *The Ecologist*, Vol. 27, No. 26, November/December 1997, pp. 221–224. This article first appeared in The Ecologist, www. theecologist.org. Reprinted with permission from the publisher.

larity of modern Western knowledge, by which PRATEC refers to the globalization of what originated in Western Europe and which continues to be imported and channelled to the rural areas through all manner of development endeavours. To look at this hegemonic knowledge system from such a light robs it immediately of its claims to universality, and places it within the context of a particular cosmology rooted in Western European culture and history.

PRATEC's radical critique and rejection of the cosmology of the modern West consists of a rejection of basic assumptions about nature, about the nature of humans, of knowledge, etc. It rejects evolutionary paradigms which lead to a utopian pursuit of "development." It rejects the rather hollow notion of "preserving the best from tradition with the best of modernity." Neither is its stance that of a knee-jerk rejection of all that is foreign to the Andes, but rather PRATEC's position is a dialogical one.

A dialogical stance is inherently a pluralist stance, one that rejects a linear evolutionist vision of the future and entertains the possibility that industrial or post-industrial civilization and the global market are not the inevitable futures for everyone. A dialogical stance is not an oppositional or an essentialist stance either, rejecting whatever comes from a foreign source. The late Eduardo Grillo Fernandez, who was a core member of PRATEC, liked to compare the Spanish conquista with the advent of frost, hail or pests in the peasants' fields:

"Just as when frost or hail falls in the fields of our peasant communities it is because some of us have disturbed the harmony of the world with our incorrect conduct, similarly the apparition (arrival) of the Spanish invaders is due to a disturbance in the harmony of our own world. To free ourselves from colonization we have to recuperate our own internal harmony. It will then be impossible to colonize us, just as in a healthy and strong person, in whom life flows fully, illness cannot penetrate. It is not a question of acting directly against the invader because while we remain perturbed another can always come and invade us."[2]

PRATEC's writings are not primarily aimed at the international academic community; nor are they designed to increase the store of universal knowledge about peoples and their cultures in the manner of social sciences. They are meant rather to re-identify another world in which to live for those who dwell in the Andes today but have been convinced of the inevitability of modernity, post-modernity or any of its other hybrid variants.

PRATEC's writings point to the fact that the Andean peasants have been in existence for over 10,000 years and possess the dynamism and the resources to regenerate themselves creatively without breaking with their history. The issue is an important one for PRATEC. They argue that with the collapse of the formal economy in Peru, the spectacular failure of most development projects, the rapidly deteriorating environment and the chaotic political situation in the country, the only vibrant, non-destructive and dynamic sector of the country is the Andean peasantry. Today the peoples native to the Andes have fully recovered from their demographic collapse after the conquest, and constitute an actual majority of the Peruvian population. With the collapse of the hacienda system in 1968 and the failure of subsequent governmental co-operative schemes, indigenous modes of relating to the land are spontaneously expanding throughout the Andes.

Non-subjecthood, what PRATEC calls "cultural affirmation," should not be confused with a political movement. PRATEC is emphatic on this point: Julio Valladolid Rivera went to great lengths to explain to me that PRATEC was not a movement or a political organization at all (the word *movimiento* is in South America inextricably linked with political movements). As Eduardo Grillo has pointed out:

"... it is not a matter of forming another political party, because such formalism would undermine the decentralized creative capacity necessary for the task of decolonization. Nor is it a matter of using violent means to deactivate the apparatus of colonization. We consider that what is adequate is to affirm ourselves each time more in our own Andean culture, dispensing with having recourse to the colonial authorities, leaving them thus without function and obsolete . . . we believe rather that violence justifies the presence and the action of the police, the army, the magistrates and the rest of officialdom. First of all, to decolonize ourselves is to affirm our Andean culture and to reject the imperialist pretension of homogenizing peoples. Consequently, to decolonize ourselves is to break with the global enterprise of development."[3]

Cultural affirmation corresponds to the third path of "non-subjecthood." It can be understood as a cultural politics that "support(s) alternative (non-Western) discourses of reality that legitimate entirely unfamiliar stories and versions about how the world works."[4] Cultural affirmation or non-subjecthood are stances that question the evolutionary inevitability of something called "progress" or "modernization" while at the same time recognizing the continued relevance and vitality of ways of life that existed long before the advent of the Europeans.

Just as the Andean landscape is one of the world's most ecologically diverse, it also harbours a great diversity of human ways of life. In its work, PRATEC has attempted to articulate the sources from which all this diversity keeps emerging. Thus, rather than giving us snapshots of reality in the manner of empiricist social sciences, their efforts are aimed towards capturing something like a world-view, what they call an Andean cosmovision. It is a point of view that goes behind or beyond the happenings of everyday life with their inevitable rough spots and difficulties as well as small triumphs. It is an approach less intent on giving knowledge about a world and more akin to an invitation to enter that world.

A phrase which perhaps more than any other captures the heart of the Andean ways of life is *"criar y dejarse criar"* (to nurture and let oneself be nurtured). Since the translation does not do justice to the original, let me quote some examples. In the Andes it is common to hear the breeders of alpacas say: "Just as we nurture (or raise) the alpacas, the alpacas nurture (or raise) us."[5] In a first fruits ritual in the region of Puno in the southern altiplano, the wives of the ritual leaders mix the first fruits or seeds at the time of the harvest with those preserved from the ritual of the previous year. The ritual leader, becoming the voice of the old seeds and fruits, addresses the new fruits and seeds as follows: "As we have nurtured these people, now it is your turn to also nurture them."[6]

What is clear from these two examples is that nurturing is not the sole prerogative of humans, but also that of nature and of all that inhabits the world. This mutual nurturing between humans and the rest of the world happens through dialogue, conversation and reciprocity. As one Bolivian peasant explains:

> "We have great faith in what nature transmits to us. These indicators are neither the result of the science of humans, nor the invention of people with great experience. Rather, it is the voice of nature itself which announces to us the manner in which we must plant our crops."[7]

Thus the position and brilliance of stars, for example, speak to the peasant about aspects of the weather; the frequency, intensity, odour and colour of the winds speak to the farmer about the coming weather; when and how a particular wild plant flowers tells the farmer that this fallow land is now ready to be cultivated again. These are only a few examples; there are thousands of such signs that speak to the Andean farmer. The peasants learn the language of the world and respond to it, thus engaging in a constant conversation. It is out of these dialogues and conversations that life generates and regenerates itself. Nature speaks to the peasants just as the peasants speak to nature and to their deities (*huacas*). Given the great diversity of ecological niches, of micro-climates, given the great changeability of the weather as well as the diversity of human communities, no two conversations are the same. Out of these conversations emerges an immense diversity.

Indeed, the Andes have been identified by the great Soviet plant geneticist Vavilov as one of the eight centres of origin of cultivated plants. The enormous variety of cultivated plant species continues to astonish plant geneticists today. The peasants grow and know some 1,500 varieties of quinoa, 330 of *kaniwa,* 228 of tarwi, 3,500 of potatoes, 610 of oca (another tuber) and so forth.[8]

This mode of conversing with all the inhabitants of the world—be they rock, tree, animal or human—is one which we should be careful not to assimilate with current prevalent notions. To assume when a peasant tells you that she is conversing with the soil or the wind that she is speaking metaphorically is to assume that Andean peasants are the intellectual heirs to the Reformation and the Scientific Revolution, in which nature does not speak directly, but can be interrogated in the laboratory through experiments, in which to "hear nature speak" one has to be specially trained and taught to construct mechanical devices for proper interrogation. As Robert Boyle, the first experimentalist and inventor of the air-pump in the seventeenth century explained, the experimenters must be "priests of nature,"[9] having received lengthy intellectual training as one would need in order to become a priest. This is very different from the idea of conversation, for which the signs which comprise nature's language—known as *lomasas* in Aymara—cannot be reduced to mere "representations" or "symbols" as they were after the Reformation.[10] Rather, Andean peasants do not experience themselves as being apart from the rest of the inhabitants of the world. Just as we humans speak, so do the other inhabitants of the world. To hear these other inhabitants speak, no special training is required, just attention and practice. No special training and certification is required, rather it is open to all those willing to listen and hear. Openness, attentiveness, receptivity and respect are the attitudes that foster conversation. The senses are not apprehended as limiting or distorting. With the beginning of experimental science, the senses were seen as "infirmities," as obstacles to correct understanding. These "infirmities" were to be remedied and enhanced by the use of experimental devices and instruments. Such denial of the senses in the pursuit of knowledge can only arise in a world-view that has already separated humans from the natural world. In the Andes, rivers, mountains, lakes and rocks have eyes and ears: everything is sentient.

Some mountains, streams and lakes, as well as some animals and plants are *huacas* (deities). In Quechua, the human community is called the *runa;* the rest of the natural world is called the *sallga.* The three are interconnected and together form a living whole called the *pacha.* The three realms meet at the site of the *chacra,* the field where the peasants raise their crops but also any site where the human community, the natural community and the community of deities converse and reciprocate in order to regenerate life.[11]

> "What happens between the Andean communities of humans, deities and nature is reciprocal dialogue, a relationship which does not assume any distancing and objectification between those dialoguing, but rather an attitude of tenderness and understanding towards the life of the other. Such dialogue does not lead one to a *knowledge about the other,* but rather to emphasize and attune oneself with its mode of being, and, in company with that other, to generate and regenerate life. It is a dialogue . . . that leads [not to knowledge but] to wisdom"[12] (Rengifo Vasquez).

Many of the graduates of PRATEC's course have returned to their *ayllus* (communities in the broadest possible sense) of origin as did Marcela and Magdalena Machaca, two sisters from a peasant community near the central Andean city of Ayacucho. There they work to counteract the influence of the state educational system which devalues the peasants' ways of doing and living. They work to recuperate practices and knowledge which many among the younger generations have abandoned. Marcela and Magdalena had made it to the university in Ayacucho from their villages, seeking there to "better themselves." Magdalena told me that when they arrived at the university in the school of agronomy:

> "All knowledge in the university is against the life of our mother culture. My professors did not speak of that culture. As a result my sister and I were very disillusioned. All the knowledge we had acquired in our work in the field was not reflected in the university curriculum. We became confused."[13]

Many other graduates of PRATEC's course have instead returned to their university or government posts, in the hope of initiating profound transformations. I met with twelve instructors of the faculty of agronomy of the University of Cajamarca during my visit there. All twelve were graduates of PRATEC's course. Isidro Rimarachin Cabrera explained to me that, out of a faculty of sixty, their group is in the minority. They have organized themselves and struggled for the representation of Andean culture and agricultural knowledge in the university curriculum. The struggle was not easy but as of 1993 what had been an informal course of Andean agriculture has become an accredited part of the curriculum. Isidro explained that up to then agronomy textbooks taught about such things as spring, summer and fall wheat, all of which are European and do not correspond to local crops or seasons. Since the majority of the student body (as well

as the faculty) is of peasant origin, this learning alienates them from their own experience and knowledge. Isidro and his friends have created an alternative curriculum, where Andean culture and knowledge is taught.

Teoladio Anguro, another member of Isidro's group of twelve, explained:

> "We spent a whole year living in the villages, learning the rhythms of life of the farmers. We observed that the peasants practise *ayni;* the families help each other and pool labour and other things. We did not observe from the outside, which is what is usually done in rural development schemes. Rather we worked with families, we integrated ourselves in the community. We observed that farmers also had house gardens next to their *chacras.* We noticed that they had two gardens: one laid out according to the instruction of the visiting agronomist and another according to the farmer's ways. When the agronomist visited he was shown the agronomist's garden. We have ignored the agronomist's garden and have worked in and studied the farmer's garden. We no longer take seeds from the farmer for improvement in the university's experimental station. The farmers themselves propagate their seeds and those of their relatives. We have compared the productivity of the two kinds of seeds and have found them to be equivalent."

The experience of this group was summed up for me by Juan Seminario:

> "We ourselves who are agronomists were profoundly surprised to discover the immense wealth of seed varieties that the farmers grow. A veil has been covering our eyes; we have been told that the region is a degraded zone and that everything has been lost. That is not so; we do not need seeds from the outside. We have the vitality to grow our own. We are not poor; we are not eroded. Some seeds and knowledge have been lost but others have been raised."

From Puno in the south to Tarapoto in the north-east of the Peruvian Andes, through Ayacucho, Cajamarca and Moche, I met with dozens of graduates of PRATEC's course. What struck me was the tremendous transformative power of that course. All the students I met had come to PRATEC's course out of a deep malaise with what they had learned or taught at schools and in the universities, as well as with their experience with rural development schemes. They have all in their various ways dedicated themselves to learning from the peasants, seeking out particularly the elders of the community in order to salvage some of the knowledge which is being eroded by the activity of the state and international agencies.

Meeting so many of PRATEC's graduates I had the opportunity to see for myself that Eduardo Grillo's vision of a decentralized and dispersed society is in fact a reality. None of the groups formed by these graduates of PRATEC's course is dependent on PRATEC or in any way organizationally or financially related to PRATEC. There is no party line to be followed. PRATEC plants seeds in people and communities and most of them seem to have flourished in their own soils and in their own manner. Everywhere in the Andes, even in Lima, sprouts of non-subjecthood have emerged and are flourishing, quietly and unobtrusively regenerating an ancient but always new world.

REFERENCES

1. Dion Buffalo, Y., & Mohawk, J., "Thoughts from an autochthonous centre: postmodernism and cultural studies," *Cultural Survival Quarterly,* Winter 1994, pp. 33–35.

2. Grillo Fernandez, E., "El Paisaje en las Culturas Andina y Occidental Moderna" in *¿Desarrollo o Descolonizacion en los Andes?* PRATEC, Lima, 1993, p. 24.

3. Ibid., p. 306.

4. Dion-Buffalo, Y., & Mohawk, J., op. cit., p. 35.

5. Rengifo Vasquez, G., "Educacion en Occidente Moderno y en la Cultura Andina" in *¿Desarrollo o Descolonizacion en los Andes?* PRATEC, Lima, 1993, p. 167.

6. Valladolid Rivera, J., "Las Plantas en la Cultura Andina en Occidente Moderno" in *¿Desarrollo o Descolonizacion en los Andes?* PRATEC, Lima, 1993, p. 86.

7. Rengifo Vasquez, G., op. cit., p. 168.

8. Valladolid Rivera, J., op. cit., p. 88. "Agricultura Campesina Andina: Crianza de la Diversidad de la Vida en la Chacra" in *Crianza Andina de la Chacra,* PRATEC, Lima, 1994, p. 342.

9. Shapin, S., & Shaffer, S., *Leviathan and the Air-Pump: Hobbes, Boyle and the Experimental Life,* Princeton University Press, 1985, p. 319.

10. Uberoi, J. Singh, *Science and Culture,* Oxford University Press, Delhi, 1978: Pena Cabrera, A., "Notas caracteristicas de la tecnologia occidental" in *Filosofia de la Tecnica,* UNI, Peru, 1986.

11. Valladolid Rivera, J., 1993, op. cit., p. 79: Rengifo Vasquez, G., op. cit., p. 173.

12. Rengifo Vasquez, G., op. cit., p. 168.

13. Note: Julio Valladolid used to have a chair at the school of agronomy at the university in Ayacucho before he joined PRATEC.

– 46 –

In the Disaster Zone
Anthropologists and the Ambiguity of Aid

Alex de Waal

Since taking his doctorate at Oxford, Alex de Waal has been involved with numerous NGOs (nongovernmental organizations) concerned with human rights, disaster relief, and development in Africa. He is the author of a definitive study on the Sudanese famine and co-director of the organization African Rights.

A decade ago, a researcher investigating the languages of northern Uganda came upon an anthropological first: the subjects of an ethnographic monograph asked him for advice in taking legal action against the author of a book. The Ik, made notorious as the cultureless villains of Colin Turnbull's *The Mountain People* (1972), wanted to sue for libel.

Turnbull's description of life and death among the Ik is a harrowing account of how, under the stresses of chronic famine, a people apparently abandoned all their social norms in favor of totally selfish and wantonly aggressive behavior—some of it directed against their unhappy ethnographer. Turnbull described it as a society mutilated beyond recognition. The only approach to ritual he noted consisted of throwing cow dung against a tree. Turnbull concluded that the Ik "were driven to survive against seemingly invincible odds, and they succeeded, at the cost of their humanity." He recommended that the community should be dispersed.

According to the information gathered by the linguist Bernd Heine and published in the journal *Africa* in 1985, the Ik would have had a strong legal case against Turnbull; at the very least, they could probably have obtained a court injunction banning further sales of the book. Judging by the critical reaction to *The Mountain People,* most professional social anthropologists would have testified in favor of the Ik, though perhaps admitting to

an apprehensive tremor as to what other litigation the case might unleash.

Called to account in the furor that followed publication of *The Mountain People,* Turnbull responded in a letter in the journal *Cultural Anthropology* that "there was no culture to kill." In the 1970s, he might have escaped with such a comment; his critics had few comparative ethnographies of disaster with which to compare his book. There is no doubt that today *The Mountain People* would be rejected as unpublishable, though it remains on the reading lists for many undergraduate courses in anthropology. With the benefit of a decade's worth of research on the subject, anthropologists know increasingly well how people react under such stresses, and it is not as Turnbull describes. Like the media images of Beirut and Mogadishu, such descriptions tell us more about the disturbed psyche of their author than the social realities of disaster.

The Ik homeland lies a few hundred miles south of the Upper Nile Valley where British social anthropology came of age. Since the classic texts of the 1940s and '50s were written, the peoples of the region have undergone a succession of calamities with few parallels in the modern world. Only now is the discipline catching up with what has happened to some of its most important subjects.

The Nuer of the southern Sudan, for example, became celebrated as a result of Edward Evans-Pritchard's series of monographs, based on field-work done in the 1930s. Nuer pastoralists became the archetypal stateless society. In the seamless anthropological present of Evans-Pritchard's writings, stories of cosmic turmoil were located in a mythical past, even though the Nuer had at that time only just emerged from decades of hunger,

"In the Disaster Zone: Anthropologists and the Ambiguity of Aid" by Alex de Waal from *Times Literary Supplement,* 16 July, 1993. Reprinted with permission.

bloodshed and resistance to Arab and European colonialism. Indeed, it was the very recalcitrance of the Nuer in the face of the first attempt at colonial administration that was the spur to Evans-Pritchard's investigation. His fieldwork was conducted on the anthropological front line.

In retrospect, periods of peace in southern Sudan appear as intervals in a cycle in which upheaval and violence alternate with relative tranquility. The region returned to war in 1963, soon after independence. This has wreaked havoc on southern Sudanese societies, but it kept the anthropologists away. War itself was not seen as a suitable subject for investigation. Peace came in 1972, but such are the slow rhythms of academe, anthropologists only began to return to the area at the end of the decade—just in time for the second civil war which broke out ten years ago. To today's ethnographers of Sudan, there can be nothing mythical about stories of global chaos: the apocalypse is now.

One such ethnographer, Sharon Hutchinson, revisited the Nuer in the 1970s, forty years after Evans-Pritchard. Nuer society, she found, was still overwhelmingly pastoral and largely acephalous, but important elements had been transformed by ready access to firearms. Among the Nuer, guns have now become part of bridewealth payments; communal ownership of them demarcates social groups; people adorn themselves with images of firearms and use cartridges as jewelry. Killing with rifles has a wholly different set of connotations to killing with spears; it involves less skill and effort, and is depersonalized; it is difficult or impossible to trace the trajectory of a bullet from rifle to victim.

During the current civil war, the Nuer have suffered famine, displacement and massacre at the hands of the government army and rival southern factions. Some of this is in reprisal for the carnage inflicted by the Nuer militia on their enemies—as major protagonists in the war, Nuer fighters have earned a fearsome reputation. So the Nuer survive, though their numbers may be depleted.

The convulsions of north-east Africa present greater perils for smaller and less well-armed peoples like the Mursi of the Ethiopia-Sudan borderlands. The Mursi are a small pastoral society, numbering perhaps 6,000, who have found themselves victims of both guns and a lack of rain. In 1971–73 there was severe drought and famine among the Mursi. Many died—most from disease and hunger, some violently and a few from suicide by starvation. The anthropologist David Turton witnessed the famine. In a paper for the specialist journal *Disasters* that he now edits, Turton wrote that the Mursi "came through this experience with their social and economic institutions intact and an undiminished sense of their cultural identity."

More recently, the Mursi were again victims, this time of a massacre. They had the misfortune to be neighbors to a people whose very name indicates the centrality of modern automatic weapons to their life. Formerly known as Nyam-Etom ("Elephant-Eaters"), this group now calls itself Nyang-Atom ("Carriers of New Guns"). The Nyangatom were given Kalashnikovs by the Sudan government in order to fight against southern rebels; the Mursi had only a few aging rifles. In February 1987, between 600 and 800 Mursi were killed in a surprise Nyangatom attack: a devastating demographic loss, but, equally importantly, a profound break in the pattern of inter-communal relations in the region. The Mursi were compelled to evacuate the southern part of their territory. At considerable risk of suffering another massacre, they began to plan what they themselves called a "return match" to even the score. Fortunately for the Mursi, the Nyangatom fell foul of the Kenyan government when they murdered two policemen in a cattle raid: the Kenyans fought the second leg of this encounter with helicopters and armored cars, and the Nyangatom withdrew with 200 fighting men dead.

David Turton found himself in an increasingly common position for members of the discipline: defending the integrity of a people threatened with the demise of their way of life, even the extinction of their society. This is a new and more brutal version of the familiar phenomenon of ethnographers trying to protect their subjects from the onslaught of commercial interests embodied in development-oriented nation states. This time, however, international organizations are commonly seen as the savior rather than the threat. Western relief operations are regarded as necessary, but also recognized to be late, inefficient, and culturally insensitive. Social anthropologists are finding a new niche: advocating more and improved aid to "their" peoples, and simultaneously making international aid programs more effective and appropriate.

Nobody can oppose increased and better lifesaving assistance. But putting anthropology in the front line of the relief encounter has its hazards. Aid agencies waver between being representatives of the Humanitarian International and the vanguard of a new philanthropic imperialism. The Pharanonic projects of the 1960s and '70s—the dams and resettlement schemes that are now so reviled—were the result of similar benevolent developmentalism. In future decades, surveying the economic and social ravages brought to the African continent by an over-supply of food aid, we may condemn today's advocates of emergency humanitarianism as equally misguided.

This is the dilemma of disaster sociology: do social scientists have enough faith in the fundamentals of their discipline to hold to them when lives are in the balance?

Common sense tells us that academic principles should be abandoned when giving food rations that might save children from death—but good sociology regularly debunks common sense.

It is one step from recognizing that peoples can survive disasters with their social fabric intact to arguing that they do in fact survive them better without external intervention of any kind. Certainly, Turton ascribed the Mursi's resilience in the face of the 1970s famine in part to the fact that the international community did not come to their aid. A few sacks of food were left by the Ethiopian Relief and Rehabilitation Commission at the border of Mursi territory, and the Mursi allocated the food as they saw fit. Doubtless a feeding program devised by nutritionists could have saved more lives, but the Mursi, even if they had had that option, would probably have preferred benign neglect.

The closer one comes to a people suffering famine, the less effective international interventions appear. Almost every detailed investigation of a famine has concluded that it is a moot question whether food aid did more good than harm. Those who recommend simple, externally provided solutions do so only from a distance. The antidote to such simplistic thinking is detailed field-study. But conducting field-work in a famine raises a range of practical and ethical difficulties. What is "participant observation" in a famine? Observing starvation is one thing, participating in it is something entirely different. Perhaps a social anthropologist might want to endure hunger in order to gain a better understanding of the trauma of famine. Raymond Firth had no option but to do this on his second stay in Tikopia in 1952–53, when a combination of drought and hurricane devastated the crops and caused famine. Few modern anthropologists are exposed in this way, however, and none have actually gone so far as to deliberately get life-threateningly undernourished as part of their field-work.

Investigating wars is still more problematic. Participating in a war for research purposes would certainly raise eyebrows at the ethics committee of the Economic and Social Research Council. It would also be hazardous: the Geneva Conventions, even were they respected, do not draw a distinction between sociological investigators and spies. Glynn Flood, a young anthropologist studying the Ethiopian Afar pastoralists, was murdered in 1975, almost certainly by the Ethiopian security forces, who were planning a military campaign against the people he was studying.

Wars are also different from famines in that "survival strategies" like gathering wild food—now something of a *cause célèbre* in the literature on famine—are often simply impossible. People who try them may be shot or blown up. Certainly there are traditional rules of warfare in many societies, and established mechanisms for protection of civilians. In Somalia, for example, religious communities have provided sanctuary for civilians of the "wrong" clan caught up in the fighting, and some clans have negotiated neutrality in the conflicts. Where there is a history of reciprocal raiding between neighboring peoples, if there is an approximate balance of armaments, a negotiated truce is likely.

However—particularly since the advent of automatic firearms, with their capacity for industrialized carnage, and pocket-sized antipersonnel landmines, which cannot distinguish fighter from villager—such solutions are precarious at best. There is no traditional method of clearing minefields, save stepping on the mines.

Modern warfare shows both the value and the limits of anthropological method. A social anthropologist may be well placed to understand a conflict, but that does not automatically lead to identifying solutions. It is fashionable to advocate the use of international forces to intervene in civil conflicts and "save" the suffering civilians. Some Somali social scientists advocated this last year. In turn, the US military tried to enlist anthropological expertise in formulating its post-invasion policies. Here is another dilemma: should an anthropologist collaborate with an occupying military force?

In an ironic manner, front-line anthropology is returning the discipline to its early role as an intelligence system for the administration of native peoples. The avowedly humanitarian motives for the operations made the ambiguities scarcely less comfortable. With relief organizations providing one of the few growth areas in employment opportunities for anthropology graduates, this situation is unlikely to change.

Much of the current anthropological corpus already consists of "grey literature," chiefly consultants' reports for aid agencies. Typically, an agency wants a social and economic assessment of an area where its relief operations are running into unexpected difficulties. These reports are researched and written under severe time constraints, for an audience of even more time-pressed managers of relief programs, and with specific administrative or logistical goals in mind. Perhaps from a visceral loyalty to the discipline, the authors of these reports often include far more sociological detail than their institutional readers will ever appreciate. Sometimes typed in the field, usually Xeroxed and with only a dozen copies extant, such documents are rarely archived in academic libraries. None the less, grey literature is probably the richest sociological source material for many parts of Africa today.

At its best, anthropology in the service of the relief agencies can snatch specific remedies for individual communities. The protection and resettlement of Sudanese Uduk refugees in Ethiopia by the United Nations High Commission for Refugees, at the behest of their long-time ethnographer Wendy James, is an excellent example of this. At its worst, such activities can provide a liberal gloss for a new humanitarian imperialism. Having called for the US Marines to invade Somalia, the American relief agency CARE has been actively recruiting social scientists to make its programs more user-friendly. Should the United Nations forces in Somalia become a party to the conflicts, anthropological analyses will undoubtedly feature in their counter-insurgency manuals.

With a few notable exceptions, exemplified by Conrad Reining's *The Zande Scheme*, anthropologists have been reluctant to subject the "aid" industry to the same critical scrutiny as the supposed beneficiaries of its largesse. Enough trained anthropologists have participated in its machinations for there to be a formidable reserve of material; anecdotes suggest that many have observed their colleagues with a critical sociological eye as well. This second front for disaster sociology may prove vital for the health of the discipline. By making the monsters of concern more accountable, it might even assist the well-being of the disaster-stricken, aid-recipient peoples of Africa and elsewhere.

OLD ISSUES, NEW CONTEXTS

What Does the Future Hold for Anthropology?

THE PHILOSOPHER KIERKEGAARD once wrote that there are two ways—one way is to suffer and the other is to be a professor of another's suffering. In this sense we are all potential professors. Anthropologists, drawn largely from the affluent middle class, have made a career out of studying "others" who are typically less privileged, and they especially have an obligation to profess.

The fact is that the "others" have suffered in the past, are suffering now, and will continue to suffer in the future. Sometimes the suffering is so unpleasant that we do not want to hear about it. This is one reason why genocide is a topic hardly ever discussed. Yet its implications for understanding the banality of evil are awesome. The horrors of present-day genocides (Rwanda's Tutsis being a well-known recent example) do not stay at the forefront of reporting and concern for long, and **AIDS** runs the risk of becoming similarly "invisibilised," even though it continues to spread in all parts of the world. Some of the most dramatic reports of its recent spread come from Asia, a continent where there were once few reported cases.

It is important to address these issues. Before World War II, anthropologist Everett C. Hughes had studied a small German village that was so close to one of the concentration camps that the villagers could literally see the smoke from the smokestacks. After the war, Hughes returned to the village, and he discovered that the villagers had hardly been touched by their proximity to the death camps. He wrote a classic essay entitled "Good People and Dirty Work" on how people could symbolically tune out such disturbing aspects of their lives. In our increasingly interdependent global "village" we cannot afford such luxuries. Part of the problem is not that we do not want to see, but that we do not know *how* to see.

For example, the gap between rich and poor and between white people and people of color has increased substantially. In 1960 the wealth of the richest 20 percent was some 30 times greater than that of the poorest 20 per-

cent. By 1989 the gap had increased to 60 times, and by the end of the twentieth century it was estimated to be over 150 times greater. At the beginning of the twenty-first century, it is estimated that the rich (predominantly white) countries, which have only about one-quarter of the world's population, consume more than 70 percent of the world's energy, 75 percent of its metals, 85 percent of its wood, and 60 percent of its food.

Even among countries receiving aid from industrialized countries, there are major discrepancies: The richest 40 percent of Southern Hemisphere countries, for example, receive more than twice as much aid as do the poorest 40 percent. This proves the adage that development aid is like champagne: In success you deserve it, and in failure you need it. And, like the South African government that was accused of providing the more affluent Zulus of Chief Buthelezi with weaponry, countries that spent heavily on arms—more than 4 percent of their gross national product—received twice as much aid as did more moderate military spenders.

In an era when selfishness and egoism have been elevated to a virtue, it is important to take global interdependency not as a source of potential shame but as a source of moral responsibility. The political philosopher Robert Goodin (1985) has developed a comprehensive theory of responsibility based on the concept of vulnerability. More people are vulnerable to us—individually or collectively—than we have made commitments to in any sense, but we have the same sort of strong responsibilities toward all those who are vulnerable to our actions and choices. While we should try to protect the vulnerable, we should also strive to reduce their vulnerability. This approach fits particularly well with anthropology precisely because the people we "traditionally" study are especially vulnerable.

But inequality and vulnerability have important nuances. In his article, Steven Rubenstein explores the complexities of the relationship between the global core and periphery. The encounter between Ecuadorian Shuar migrant workers and *tsantsa*, or Shuar shrunken heads, in a New York City museum demonstrates the peripheral status of the Shuar in relation to North America. But it is not a simple question of the heads' physical location that shows this inequality, and these Shuar migrants seem little concerned about repatriating what was taken from them. What demonstrates the inequality is the lack of cultural and historical context around the shrunken heads in the museum: While Americans see these heads as examples of a "savage Other," Shuar see them as indications of their past involvement in world systems. The broader theoretical point here is that globalization is not a simple story of homogenization or Westernization, but of complex processes of encounter in which people of different cultures are increasingly sharing spaces, but not necessarily the same interpretations of their worlds.

There are many ways we can protect and aid the vulnerable on this globe. One collective form of protective action is that of **anthropological advocacy groups** like Cultural Survival, but there is also the possibility of individual, personal action. One anthropologist who is involved in personal advocacy is Faye Ginsburg, who writes here of the contribution that anthropologists can make toward significant public debates of our time (in this case, the abortion debate). As Ginsburg points out, the ethnographic approach helps us understand the cultural basis of each argument, thereby forcing us to move beyond easy stereotypes about our political enemies, in order to rescue the common questions that often get lost in polarized political discourse. Ultimately, this encourages us to contribute to the reframing of public debates based on what anthropologists can offer best: comparative perspectives based on sound ethnographic research.

What do anthropologists have to say about that other great public debate of our times, the "war on ter-

ror?" A lot, it turns out. In this final chapter we offer two positions on the discipline's relationship with military and intelligence activities related to the war in our "Anthropology and Public Debate" section. Murray Wax and Felix Moos take the position that Western civilization is under attack, and just as in past wars against tyranny, anthropologists have the moral and political obligation to ally themselves with the open and democratic societies of the West against despotic regimes and terrorist campaigns. Elsewhere, Moos has expressed this as a need to develop spies with sophisticated linguistic and cultural training (McCutcheon 2003). David Price, on the other hand, reaffirms a fundamental ethical precept of our discipline: We anthropologists have a duty to serve the populations we study. He argues that instead of serving the cause of warfare against minority populations, anthropologists should be revealing the oversimplified pictures of "the enemy" offered by politicians and the media.

We finish this chapter—and the book—with a look at the phenomenon that is changing the way many of us in North America communicate and gain information about the world—the Internet—although many of us might not be aware of just how it mediates our lives. Ellen Ullman, who is not an anthropologist but a technology consultant and writer, offers some interesting "anthropological" insights. She argues that discussion and advertising around the Internet and high technology represent public space and interaction as dirty and burdensome. In its place, a new "Net ideal" is being promoted—that each person is entitled to get exactly what he or she wants—something that is, at its base, antidemocratic and antisocial. In this new technologically mediated order, Ullman believes, there is no need for messy debate, government, tolerance of difference. This represents an undesirable retreat from political life and raises important questions we should all be concerned with about the future of cultural conversations in our society.

FOCUS QUESTIONS

As you read these selections, consider these questions:

✦   Do you think that anthropology has practical value? What services do you think anthropologists can provide to help resolve social problems?

✦   What do you think is the future of cultural diversity? Do you think that the future of the world is one of cultural homogenization? Why or why not?

✦   What cultural impact do you think new technologies like the Internet are having on our society? On political activism?

REFERENCES

Goodin, Robert. 1985. *Protecting the Vulnerable: A Reanalysis of Our Social Responsibilities.* Chicago: University of Chicago Press.

McCutcheon, Chuck. 2003. "Expanding the ROTC Concept to Train a Better Spy." Newhouse News Service (accessed on 10/17/04 at http://www.newhousenews.com/archive/mccutcheon081503.html).

47

Shuar Migrants and Shrunken Heads Face to Face in a New York Museum

Steven L. Rubenstein

Steven Rubenstein is associate professor in the Department of Sociology and Anthropology at Ohio University. He received his PhD from Columbia University in 1995. His research focuses on economic anthropology, colonialism, history, and tourism in the Amazon. He is author of the book Alejandro Tsakimp: A Shuar Healer in the Margins of History.

When I was in the Ecuadorian Amazon in the summer of 1998, the President of the Schuar Federation—a political organization of about 50,000 indigenous people—showed me twelve *tsantsa,* or shrunken heads, that had recently been de-accessioned from the National Museum of the American Indian. Leaders of the Federation hoped that I could help them develop a plan to build a Schuar museum, in which these heads would be placed along with other items. Thus, when I went to New York in 2003 to visit some Schuar friends, I thought it would be interesting to see what they thought of the shrunken heads on display at the American Museum of Natural History.

Movements of Schuar shrunken heads and Schuar workers are perfect examples of what Arjun Appadurai (1996:33,41) has called an ethnoscope—geography of "moving groups and individuals"—through which culture becomes deterritorialized and globalized. Here I respond to Appadurai's call to study the role of the imagination in the formation of global cultures. However, I take issue with his rejection of models of global culture that rely on a distinction between core and periphery (ibid:31–3). Appadurai argues that global capitalism is too disorganized (that is, lacking a clear and stable center), and that the relationship (and disjunctions) between the economy, culture, and politics is too complex for it to make sense according to the simple binary between core and periphery. However, as I observe it, people everywhere—whether they be in New York or in Ecuador—maintain their own core-periphery distinction. It is not just that some people identify with the core (or the First World, or civilization) while others identify with the periphery (or the Third World, or savagery), but as I argue here, people who identify themselves in these different ways also imagine the relationship between core and periphery somewhat differently.

GLOBALIZATION AND CULTURE

A fundamental issue in anthropology is at stake in the core-periphery distinction: how do we talk about non-Western peoples like the Shuar? At the time of contact (and conquest), Europeans were struck by differences, but they also looked for similarities. In the first few centuries following the conquest of the Americas, Europeans debated whether American Indians were living in a state of nature. (If they were living in a state of nature then there was a radical difference between "us," the "civilized," and "they," the "savage." In the nineteenth century most anthropologists came to accept that Indians were similar to us, at least in so far as they too have culture. But some, such as Lewis Henry Morgan, also wondered whether they could go further in their thinking and conceive of an actual connection between them and Westerners. The language of evolution provided a way to express a connection while recognizing (and explaining) differences. In this discourse Indian cultures represented an earlier stage of cultural evolution. (This way of thinking is echoed today in the way people contrast "modern" cultures with "traditional" or "primitive" cultures.) In the twentieth century—especially after World War I—anthropologists largely abandoned this evolutionary model and its implication that Westerners were more advanced than the people they had been conquering and colonizing.

Today most people recognize that Indians are not only "cultured," but that their cultures are often quite complex. Although many people still think of them as somehow "more natural" or "closer to nature," anthropologists work rather hard to avoid such language and the implied evolutionary opposition.

For most of the twentieth century, anthropologists were content to study non-Western cultures simply as "different" cultures, and tried to understand them in their own terms. Cultural theorists like Arjun Appadurai are not content to talk only of cultural difference; they have returned to the question of what might connect seemingly different cultures. Most anthropologists had long ago rejected the language of evolution, not just because of ideological doubts about notions of progress, but also because most nineteenth-century evolutionary models were speculative. However, we now have a great many fine historical studies, supplemented by archaeological studies, that help us reconstruct actual changes over the past several hundred years. These studies not only help us understand changes in any particular culture; they show how changes in one culture can lead to (and be influenced by) changes in another. Clearly, cultures need to be understood in terms of larger, even global, contexts.

Anthropologists have long been interested in cultural logics and social structures, so the question now is whether this global context, this world of interacting cultures, itself has a logic, a structure. The terms "core" and "periphery" provide one influential way of talking about a global structure. These terms come from the sociologist Immanuel Wallerstein, who characterized the global market in terms of an unequal division of labour in which low- (or non-) wage-earning workers in "peripheral" countries exchanged goods with high-wage-earning people in "core" countries (Wallerstein 1974:351). The profound insight is that two parts of the world can appear to be radically different (in terms of material wealth, social structure, and values) *precisely because* they have been in a relationship, each influencing each other.

World systems theorists such as Wallerstein were primarily interested in the relationship between different countries (for example Spain and Mexico or England and India). Anthropologists wondered if they could look at relationships between different—even vastly different—cultures in the same way. In his, ironically titled, *Europe and the People without History*, the anthropologist Eric Wolf argued that this core-periphery distinction provides a historical explanation for differences between so-called traditional (or primitive) societies and so-called modern societies, and would thus provide a productive basis for studying local cultures in global terms (Wolf 1982:22–3).

Appadurai (1996:32–43), however, suggests that this distinction functions as a surrogate for the opposition between civilized and savage. He argues that in a world where people and their values (both material and symbolic) circulate so widely and freely, such binary categorizations are anachronistic attempts to impose a false order. Although I share Appadurai's conviction that anthropologists must critique, deconstruct or transcend this opposition, I believe that we must take the distinction between core and periphery seriously—precisely because it helps explain why North Americans and other Westerners have imagined global cultures in terms of a divide between civilized and savage, and also because it helps us understand how and why indigenous people like the Schuar imagine global culture quite differently. This difference has its origin in the nineteenth century, when this ethnoscope first began to emerge.

DISCOURSES OF THE COLLECTOR

In the late nineteenth century Shuar culture was territorialized in the global imagination of Europeans and Euro-Americans through the circulation of shrunken heads. There is evidence that the Shuar and neighbouring groups, collectively called "Jívaro," shrunk the heads of enemies killed in warfare in the 1500s, prior to contact, but there is little evidence that Westerners were interested in this practice until the 1860s. When Euro-Ecuadorians began to settle the region in the 1880s they occasionally traded manufactured goods, like shotguns and machetes, with Shuar, in return for game, salt and shrunken heads. Settlers would sell these heads to dealers in the highlands, who often sold them on to Europeans and North Americans. At the same time the Shuar began to use Western-manufactured shotguns and steel lance-heads in warfare. As Jane Bennet Ross has remarked, the concurrent increase in intergroup warfare and guns-for-heads trade suggests that the Shuar began producing shrunken heads for export (Bennett Ross 1984:89–90; see also Steel 1999:754–9).

It is striking how Euro-Americans despite maintaining their moral and cultural differentiation from the Shuar, actually colluded with the Shuar in trafficking shrunken heads. This paradox is most evident in the story of F. W. Up de Graff and a few other North Americans panning for gold in the upper Amazon in 1899. One day they encountered a large group of Jívaro, who offered them protection from a neighboring group; the prospectors, however, suspected that these Indians were themselves a threat. At first they answered that they could take care of themselves, but then they explained that they themselves were a war-party and invited the Jívaro to join them in attacking a nearby community (Up de Graff 1923:252–3). Although Up de Graff claims that neither he nor his companions fired a shot during the ensuing raid, he does admit to lending his machete to one of the Jívaro, to aid in cutting the head off of a wounded, but still living, woman (1923:274).

Up de Graff admits that readers might misunderstand his motives. He emphasizes that the Jívaro methods of warfare are cowardly and distasteful to the *"true white man who is brought up to a code of fair play"* (1923:270). His heart, he insists, was not really in the butchery; all he really wanted was gold. But this precious metal was not the only thing he wanted to collect. After the slaughter the North Americans chose to stay with their Indian companions, in part, as Up de Graff explains, because "we were anxious to trade the Jívaros out of their trophies" (1923:285). Thus, the mercantile values of the core were crucial to his imagining of the distinction between civilized and savage: the Jívaro value the heads as trophies of warfare, but for Euro-Americans they are just another precious commodity found in the Amazon.

THE PUBLIC CLOSET: DONATING THAT WHICH CANNOT BE DISCARDED

Travelogues like Up de Graff's celebrate the act of collecting discursively. The end results of such acts are celebrated materially in such institutions as the American Museum of Natural History and the National Museum of Natural History. These museums did not acquire most of their shrunken heads through the efforts of adventurous curators or sponsored expeditions.[1] Most were donated by individuals who had come to possess, but did not want, these objects. Robert Carniero, curator of the Hall of South American Indians at the American Museum of Natural History, told me of a widow who had never liked her husband's shrunken head. While he was alive, she insisted that it be kept hidden in a closet; upon his death, she was finally able to get rid of it. On another occasion a young man discovered a head in a warehouse full of his late father's belongings. Informed that the warehouse was to be destroyed, he donated it to the museum. Significantly, none of these people could do what explorers and ethnographers report the Shuar as having done after the shrunken head feast, or after the death of the warrior: throw them away or bury them.[2] Even when unwanted they had to be hoarded and stored in a closet or warehouse. Where even that became unnecessary or impractical then they had to go to a museum—the public's (and public) closet.[3]

The American Museum of Natural History and the Smithsonian Institution, however, are examples of what Mieke Bal called "metamuseums"—large and ambitious museums that display not only their collections, but also older forms of display. In other words, they put themselves, and the very idea of "museums," on display (Bal 1992:260; see also Ames 1986). But they do so in a peculiar way, one that typically highlights the objects of collection while effacing the act of collecting so vividly described in travelogue. Though trophies of colonial expansion acquired by Euro-Ecuadorians in the Upper Amazon, shrunken heads are presented as trophies of Shuar warfare—so museums can present themselves not as collectors of shrunken human heads, but as collectors of tokens of "Shuar culture" (see also Torgovnick 1990 and Feest 1993). These tokens are in turn recontextualized as part of the much larger collection—one that makes sense only to the viewer who has access to the collection as a whole. As Susan Stewart has suggested, such collections privilege the position of the core as the centre of consumption on a global scale (Stewart 1993:162; see also Mitchell 1989).[4] Objects that were originally commodities become something else when they are collected and put on display—used but never used up, they are not so much objects of consumption as fetishes of consumption (Stewart 1993:164).

Although collectors and museum-goers see their distance, and difference, from the Shuar in shrunken heads, ethnographers have suggested that through shrunken heads the Shuar have subordinated difference and distance to social relationships—that is, to terms of affinity rather than alterity. Despite Up de Graff's claims that *tsantsa* were trophies of war, to this day the Shuar are adamant that they are not. Virtually all ethnographers agree that the value of the *tsantsa* lay in its serving as a container for the *muisak*, the avenging spirit of the victim. Some accounts suggest that, through the various rituals of the *tsantsa* feast, the wife of the slayer would have virtual sex with the *muisak*. This act accomplished a "gradual transformation of an unknown foe first into an affine, and at a later stage into a foetus to be born of a woman in the captors' group" (Taylor 1993:671; see Descola 1996a:276). Other accounts suggest that it was the slayer who would dream of, and perform, sexual intercourse with the *muisak*, in order to turn it into his servant (Karsten 1935: 367–8). Either way, these rituals express a belief that Carlos Fausto has argued is typical of Amazonia: "the overall reproduction of society is symbolically dependent on relations with the outside and otherness" (Fausto 2000:934).

When Euro-Americans began to offer manufactured instruments of production in return for shrunken heads they transformed this process—for the overall reproduction of Shuar society increasingly came to depend materially on relations with outsiders. In the early years of colonization most Shuar were encouraged by the state to raise cattle and sell lumber, but now Shuar have little to sell to Euro-Americans besides their labour. Leaders of the Federation (see Rubenstein 2001 for a history of the formation of the Federation) are salaried by the state, through agreements with ministries such as health and education, but virtually all Shuar—like their Ecuadorian neighbours—believe they can make more money working in the United States. Though present day Shuar no longer subscribe to the efficacy of *tsantsa* rituals, memories of these rituals nevertheless continue to play an important symbolic role in reproducing Shuar identity. The existence of actual *tsantsa* in North American museums force the Shuar to imagine the global ethnoscope of which they are a part.

FINDING ONE'S HEAD

Federation leaders are elected by Shuar, but are financed by the state and foreign NGOs; they represent the Shuar to outsiders, and outsiders to the Shuar. Thus, when the Smithsonian Institution organized the 1991 Festival of American Folklife, they invited Federation officials to consult with curators of the National Museum of the American Indian who were selecting objects for exhibition. At the request of these leaders, the museum returned twelve *tsantsa* to the Shuar Federation on 6 October 1995. For well over a century, it was only from the point of view of Euro-Americans (especially given the way *tsantsa* were displayed in museums) that the heads represented "the Shuar"; it was in part because of this metonymic function that the National Museum of the American Indian repatriated the heads to the Shuar Federation—they recognized the Federation as the legitimate representative of the Shuar (and, at the time, Achuar) people.[5] The return of the heads accomplished more than a recognition of the legitimacy of the Shuar Federation; the Federation claims to represent the Shuar nation and in this sense it could be construed as the restoration of a new political body (see Winans 1994 for a similar case in East Africa).

My Shuar friends in New York, however, expressed no interest in the repatriation of the heads at the American Museum of Natural History. Overwhelmed by the size of the museum, they immediately grasped its function to represent the power of the core. This power was communicated to them most immediately, although ambiguously, as we climbed the steps to the main entrance and they saw people lining up to present themselves to guards. They panicked, because they had no identification with them and spoke only Spanish—they were afraid of being detained. I explained that in fact the authorities of the museum were afraid of a terrorist attack, and that the guards were merely checking people's bags. As we silently submitted to the cursory search I realized how a

form of power I took for granted appeared to my friends as unpredictable and was easily misunderstood.

The museum also confirmed their sense that New York is at the centre of the world, while their awareness of their inability to read signs in English reminded them of their own peripheral status. At the same time, they experienced their position as consumers of the collection as liberating and exciting. When I later asked them what their favorite parts of the museum had been they did not mention the *tsantsa*, but rather what was exotica for them: the stuffed animals from Africa, gemstones and asteroids. They also emphasized that they saw only a small portion of the collections, and saw in their visit an opportunity to belong to a much bigger world than that they had previously imagined.

For similar reasons, they were content for the heads to remain in the museum: they still see *tsantsa* as a way to experience others in terms of relationships, rather than absolute difference. They assumed that just as they were interested in learning more about North American culture, the presence of the heads in the museum expressed North American interest in Shuar culture; moreover, they felt that the heads represent a Shuar presence in the centre of the world. Yet they commented on the fact that the heads were presented out of context—not just cultural, but also historical context. It is, I believe, this lack of historical context rather than the actual physical location of the heads that signals the peripheral status of the Shuar. To the Shuar this lack of context was tantamount to a lack of a sort of recognition, for they internalize the heads in terms of a complex sort of otherness. They do not see the heads as representing who they are (because they themselves do not shrink heads); the heads represent who they are *not*. In the nineteenth century what was important was that the heads were not Shuar, but were rather taken from the neighbouring Achuar (with whom they sometimes traded). Today this difference is no longer important; what matters is that the heads were not taken and shrunk by them, but by their ancestors. Either way, this "not" is never an absolute negativity. In the past it expressed not only distance but also proximity; today it expresses not only distance but also possession. They identify the heads with *their* ancestors. Thus the heads now serve as markers of their own past—in short, the heads are the most material and visible means they have for identifying themselves as a people with history.

The distance between the Shuar and their past—between these migrant workers in New York and their head-shrinking grandfathers or great-grandfathers—constitutes a largely unknown territory. Until recently the Shuar lacked a written history; even today the written history available to them is superficial and simplistic, and largely takes the form of textbooks for children. More-over, since such textbooks have mostly been written by missionaries or government bureaucrats, they reflect the ideological interests of the Church or the State.

Some books written by missionaries who have adopted an ethnographic voice, or even by Western ethnographers and translated into Spanish, do attempt to provide an "authentic" portrait of the Shuar. Yet Shuar are often confused or even alienated by these books, which describe, in the present tense, a way of life that is foreign to them. Of course they understand that these books were written many decades ago, and are meant to represent the past—but the stories these books tell do not even correlate with the stories their parents or grandparents used to tell. I do not think this means that classic ethnographies of the Shuar are wrong or mistaken. It might simply be that the story a Shuar would tell an anthropologist and the story a Shuar would tell his grandchild would be different: both stories equally partial, both stories equally true—but in different ways.

But I do know that the books the Shuar read about their own culture represent a dated, and in some ways, dubious project. For example, when Michael Harner wrote his classic ethnography *Jívaro: People of the Sacred Waterfalls* he worked within the twentieth-century paradigm of describing a culture in its own terms. Harner was delighted when, in the 1978 Spanish translation of his book, Aíjiu Juank wrote a preface explaining how the ethnography had value for Shuar, as it would "help us to rediscover our dignity and to regain the equilibrium that we need for an authentic development, based on our own values" (quoted in Harner 1984:xv). Harner did not know that Aíjiu Juank was actually Alfredo Germani, an Italian born Catholic missionary—which raises the question of whether this ethnography was being used to promote Shuar values or missionary values. This is a practical and a political question for many Shuar, who have concluded that missionary attempts to isolate Shuar from Ecuadorian society (in the course of what Germani calls "authentic development"), far from protecting them, only made Shuar dependent on missionaries for access to the larger world.

Today, Federation officials no longer depend on missionaries, and travel not only to Quito (the capital of Ecuador) but also to Europe and the United States (in order to participate in international conferences). Other Shuar, like my friends, travel to Los Angeles or New York in search of jobs. When they come upon *tsantsa* in a New York museum they not only encounter a physical piece of their past, but also evidence that their grandparents and great-grandparents also participated in a world system. The Shuar claim this territory as their own not in the sense that it is exclusively theirs—like their grandparents,

whether in Ecuador or New York they share space with others—but in the sense that an understanding of others might explain who they are and how they came to be. They are not sure what such an explanation might actually be, and as we stood by the display they shared some of the stories their fathers or grandfathers had told them. Ultimately, I believe, their curiosity about this moving past, this ethnoscope, is closely bound up with their own claim to territory.

IMAGINING HISTORY

As we spent over an hour lingering by the heads, and watching people pass by without so much as glancing at them, they began to suspect that their own imagining of this ethnoscope was different from that of others. I had hoped for (or rather, tried to contrive) encounters between my friends and other visitors, but I had forgotten how strong the invisible walls between people are when so many crowd together in one place. Of the dozens of people who passed the shrunken heads, only a few paused to look at them. One of my friends, who knows a few words of English, introduced himself, and I explained who we were. "They are beautiful, yes?" my friend asked. The others visitors looked startled, but said "yes." My friend spoke in Spanish and I translated: "He says that his grandparents made these, although Shuar no longer hunt heads." The other visitor said, "Yes, we know." We stood together for a few more moments, without saying anything, and the other visitor walked away.

My Shuar friends found the apparent passivity of visitors striking. They saw me as a local guide, translating and explaining different exhibits for them, and thought that the South American Hall should provide visitors with Indian guides who, they felt, would not only provide better explanations of Amazonian past: their very presence would reveal the Amazonian present—and the evident contrast between the present and past would demonstrate that Indians like the Shuar are peoples with history. They were sure this would be of profound interest to most visitors.

Others have argued that historical knowledge is partial and culturally mediated. I suggest here that people from the core and from the periphery mediate it in radically different ways—that is, we have very different attitudes towards our amnesias. In this the Shuar are strikingly different form other museum goers, who see "natural history," a history of the ontological other, and have forgotten the sociological history, the history of the political-economy by which these objects came to reside in one building in New York. Thus, whenever I ask my students who have seen shrunken heads what they thought, they ask me, "How did Shuar make them?" But when we returned to the apartment of one of my Shuar friends and, over dinner, I asked them what they thought of the museum exhibit, they all wanted to know, "How did our *tsantsa* end up in New York?" We all forget parts of our past, but some of us want to remember more than others.

NOTES

1. Most shrunken heads (though not the ones on actual display) are fakes, testimony to the earlier craze of Euro-Americans to acquire as many shrunken heads as possible.

2. For a similar clash between non-capitalist and capitalist values, involving the Zuni and the Smithsonian Institution, see Merrill et al., 1993: 546.

3. Similarly, many of the artefacts owned by museums were originally collected by wealthy private citizens. Those who still wanted to see and show off their stuff, but who had run out of room in their own homes or no longer wanted to pay for the insurance, could donate their private collections to a museum.

4. As Mieke Bal has observed, decontextualization in art collections has a more specific, but comparable, end. Namely, the claim of a universal aesthetic (Bal 1992: 559) and, by implication, the claim of an objective position from which one can recognize this aesthetic.

5. What occurred was not technically repatriation, as the National Museum of the American Indian had no legal obligation to give the heads to the Shuar Federation. They were given out of a sense of ethical obligation.

REFERENCES

Ames, Michael M. 1986.*Museums, the public and anthropology: A study in the anthropology of anthropology.* Vancouver: Ranchi Anthropology Series 9.

Appadurai, Arjun 1996. *Modernity at large: Cultural dimensions of globalization.* Minneapolis: University of Minnesota Press.

Bal, Mieke 1992. Telling, showing, showing off. *Critical Inquiry* 18(3): 556-594.

Bennett Ross, Jane 1984. Effects of contact on revenge hostilities among the Achuara Jívaro. In Ferguson, R.B. (ed.) *Warfare, culture, and environment* pp 83–124. Orlando: Academic Press.

Descola, P. 1996a. *The spears of twilight,* trans. Janet Lloyd. New York: The New Press.

Fausto, C. 2000. Of enemies and pets: Warfare and shamanism in Amazonia. *American Ethnologist* 26(4): 933–56.

Feest, C.F. 1993. Comments on "The return of the *Ahayu:da.*" *Current Anthropology* 34(5): 83–124.

Harner, M. 1984. *Jívaro: People of the sacred waterfalls.* Berkeley: University of California Press.

Karsten, R. 1935. *The headhunters of Western Amazonas. The life and culture of the Jíbaro Indians of eastern Equador and Peru.* Helsinki: Societas Scientiarum Fennica, Commentationes Humanarum Littararum VII(I).

Merrill, W.L., Ladd, E.J. and Ferguson, T.J. 1993. "The return of the *Ahayu:da.*" *Current Anthropology* 34(5), pp 83–124.

Mitchell, T. 1989. The world as exhibition. *Comparative Studies in Society and History* 31(1): 217–236.

Morgan, L.H. 1978. [1877] *Ancient Society* New York: Holt and Company.

Rubenstein, S. 2001. Colonialism, the Shuar Federation, and the Ecuadorian state. *Environment and Planning D: Society and Space* 19(3): 263–93.

Steel, D. 1999. Trade goods and Jívaro warfare: The Shuar 1850–1957, and the Achuar, 1940–1978. *Ethnohistory* 46(4): 745–76.

Stewart, S. 1993. *On longing: Narratives of the miniature, the gigantic, the souvenir, the collection.* Durham: Duke University Press.

Taylor, A.-C. 1993. Remembering to forget: Identity, mourning and memory among the Jívaro. *Man* 28(4): 653–678.

Torgovnick, M. 1990. *Gone primitive.* Chicago: The University of Chicago Press.

Up de Graff, F.W. 1923. *Head hunters of the Amazon: Seven years of exploration and adventure.* Garden City: Garden City Publishing Company, Inc.

Wallerstein, I. 1974. *The modern world system.* New York: Academic Press.

Winans, E.V. 1994. The head of the king: Museums and the path to resistance. *Comparative Studies in Society and History* 36(2): 221–241.

Wolf, E. 1982. *Europe and the people without history.* Berkeley: The University of California Press.

48

The Anthropology of Abortion Activism

Faye Ginsburg

Faye Ginsburg received a PhD in 1986 from City University of New York. Her research is on ethnographic film, indigenous media, gender and reproduction, and social movements in the United States. She has coedited several books, including Uncertain Terms: Negotiating Gender in American Culture *and* Conceiving the New World Order: The Global Politics of Reproduction. *She has also written* Contested Lives: The Abortion Debate in an American Community. *She is a professor of anthropology and director of the Program in Culture and Media at New York University.*

Like many people who are drawn to anthropology, I wanted to conduct research that would debunk common stereotypes about "natives." Unlike my colleagues who departed for distant shores to earn their Ph.D.'s in the early 1980s, I was drawn to the abortion issue in the United States. Why does it excite such profound emotions and political virulence in our society? What motivates activists? What kind of political activity occurs beyond the rhetoric and polarizing demonstrations organized by the leaders of both sides? Perhaps most important, I wanted to see whether activists in both camps could find any new, more-creative ways to deal with each other and the controversy surrounding abortion.

I felt that the abortion debate needed the kind of research that anthropologists and other qualitative social scientists undertake: studies that try to understand people as part of a community, getting to know them over time and in context, so that we can see the world from their point of view and comprehend why certain issues become more pressing than others in their lives.

Unfortunately, except for a few sociological works, such as James Davison Hunter's *The Culture Wars* and Kristin Luker's *The Politics of Motherhood,* as well as the historian Rickie Solinger's *The Abortionist,* most scholarly and popular writing on abortion seems to rely on stereotypes.

Journalists generally have focused on the most-violent aspects of the conflict—the headline-grabbing protests at clinics by Operation Rescue and the murders

of two doctors and three clinic workers by activists invoking what they considered to be the "Christian" principle of "justifiable homicide." And surveys and statistical research have relied on multiple-choice questions about variables assumed to influence attitudes on abortion, such as religion, income, or education.

Much of this research is enormously valuable. For example, the stability of public opinion on the issue for more than two decades—with half to two thirds of the public favoring abortion in some circumstances—is a stunning bit of data that has frustrated many an activist trying to push legislative change.

Yet such work does not provide a rounded, complex sense of who the activists are, the diversity of opinion and philosophical divisions within each side of the debate, or where new political possibilities for a solution to the conflict might emerge.

Scholarship can help place current "news" in the historical context of the ebb and flow of social movements. For example, the extreme violence that has characterized anti-abortion activism in the 1990s is a relatively new phenomenon. Through the mid-1980s, most activists on both sides of the issue were moderates—people who felt strongly but were fundamentally committed to public civility, such as non-confrontational protests and attempts to enact legislation.

Moderates still make up the majority of activists, but their presence is much harder to detect as radicals engage in deliberately provocative acts. Yet, despite all the clamor among activists and the shifting positions of politicians, the legality of abortion, established by the Supreme Court's 1973 decision in *Roe v. Wade,* has remained largely unchanged. And the confrontational and violent tactics of

"The Anthropology of Abortion Activism" by Faye Ginsburg as appeared in *The Chronicle of Higher Education,* January 26, 1996, p. A48. Reprinted by permission of the author.

anti-abortion extremists have turned off some potential supporters and aggravated philosophical differences among pro-lifers. Some more-moderate opponents of abortion have begun focusing on activities such as educational programs on fetal development and centers that try to help women with prenatal and obstetric care.

Academic work that looks beyond the front-page stories can help to illuminate new political possibilities that offer a brave counterpoint to the atmosphere of increasing violence. In a number of small cities, activists have grown tired of the polarized battles and are trying to find alternative ways to accomplish their agendas at the grassroots level. At a time when our country and the rest of the world seem dominated by the politics of hate, it seems especially important to locate and study how people are finding more-constructive ways to accomplish their political and social ends.

I was fortunate to encounter some of this activity while doing field research on grassroots abortion activists during the 1980s. My work focused on the small, prairie city of Fargo, N.D., where the opening of the Fargo Women's Health Organization in 1981—the first, and still the only, clinic in the state to offer abortion services—has provoked continuing local controversy. In Fargo, I witnessed some remarkable political creativity among activists on both sides, especially those involved in a group called Pro-Dialogue. For a brief time, those activists dared to step out of their stereotyped positions; they tried to imagine a way to work on their different agendas that was driven not by hate and violence, but by a desire to use the political process to improve the conditions faced by pregnant women.

Pro-Dialogue was formed during a meeting of the North Dakota Democratic Women's Caucus in March 1984, in preparation for that year's state Democratic convention. A pro-choice plank on abortion was proposed for the state party's platform, and, after much debate, was defeated. A woman who found she had friends arguing on both sides of the issue suggested a compromise position based on areas of agreement. The result read: "The North Dakota Democratic party believes public policy on abortion should provide some positive alternatives which would stress effective sex education, continued research on safer means of contraception, improved adoption services, support for parents of exceptional children, and economic programs which make it possible for parents to both raise children with love and pursue a productive work life."

Pro-Dialogue expired after only a few years, when Fargo—like many small American cities—was subject to prolonged anti-abortion protests by extremists from outside the community. Compared with the recent years of violence, Pro-Dialogue represented only a fragile moment in the abortion conflict.

But fragility is not the same as insignificance. In the past five years, the germ of the idea that emerged in Fargo a decade ago has begun to blossom independently; groups have formed around the country, made up of pro-choice and pro-life activists determined to find alternatives to divisive rhetoric and violence. Like strong families, these groups are finding ways to tolerate differences among their members and work toward common goals, such as helping women with difficult pregnancies. They have created an organization called the Common Ground Network for Life and Choice, whose members are trying to work together on issues such as teen-age pregnancy, ways to provide adequate resources for impoverished mothers and children, and guidelines for protests at abortion clinics.

When I first heard about Common Ground, I thought that it must have been founded by people who were interested in the abortion issue but had not put themselves on the front lines. In fact, exactly the opposite was true. Groups have emerged in places where the abortion battle has been the most prolonged and divisive—Buffalo, Milwaukee, Boston, St. Louis, and even Pensacola, Fla., the site of several abortion-clinic bombings in the 1980s and the murders of two doctors and one clinic worker in the 1990s. Indeed, one of the first local Common Ground groups to form was begun by the principal adversaries in the 1989 Supreme Court case, *Webster v. Reproductive Health Services*, a decision that allowed states to impose restrictions on abortion services, such as banning the use of public funds for counseling or for providing abortions.

Following that ruling, B. J. Isaacson Jones, the woman who directed the largest abortion clinic in St. Louis, and Andrew Puzder, the leading anti-abortion lawyer in Missouri, decided to find areas in which the two sides could work together. The efforts of the group they founded have resulted in legislation in Missouri providing assistance to drug-addicted pregnant women. Last year, the group issued a position paper on "Adoption as Common Ground."

Creative political imagination can flower in many different ways, inspiring people to protest peacefully, to dehumanize their opponents, or to commit murder in God's name. Public and even scholarly understanding of why people are driven to particular forms of activism is as rare as deep knowledge of the "exotic" people whom anthropologists and other social scientists traditionally have studied. Ethnographic research on a divisive issue such as abortion can give much-needed visibility to people who are trying to create new, positive action on social and political issues.

Perhaps if more attention had been paid to groups such as Fargo's Pro-Dialogue in the mid-1980s, we might have had a Common Ground network much earlier, which might have helped to prevent the murders of the past few years. Much as Margaret Mead studied other cultures, in part, to help Americans rethink their own cultural habits, contemporary anthropologists and other social scientists can, by the cases they choose to study and write about, help to redefine the way we think about cultural conflict and its resolution.

Social movements are built on trust and dialogue as well as on disagreement, but cooperative actions rarely attract as much media coverage as violent forms of protest do. Yet in an era of profound cynicism, when distrust of anyone unlike ourselves seems to dominate politics, it is crucial for academics to focus more research on people whose actions contradict our stereotypes. Such analyses can help expand and reframe the public discourse on controversial issues and, in the abortion debate, remind us of the key concern that seems to have been lost: how we can make our society more supportive of women in their childbearing years, and help people have and raise children under the best possible circumstances.

– 49 –

ANTHROPOLOGY AND THE WAR ON TERROR

What Is Anthropology's Role in the "War on Terror"?

Murray Wax is professor emeritus of sociology at Washington University and past president of the Society for Applied Anthropology. He received his PhD in sociology (and anthropology) from the University of Chicago in 1959, and his research focused mainly on education and society.

Felix Moos is professor of anthropology at the University of Kansas, Lawrence. He received his PhD from the University of Washington in 1963, and researches ethnology and applied anthropology, culture change and development, comparative value systems, and conflict in east, south, and southeast Asia and the Pacific.

David Price is associate professor of anthropology at St. Martin's College in Washington State. He received his PhD from the University of Florida in 1993, based on research on the evolution of irrigation in Egypt's Fayoum Oasis. In recent years, he has been writing a historical account of the influences of the cold war on anthropology, and has become a prominent public commentator on anthropological involvement in spying and warfare.

Commentary *Anthropology: Vital or Irrelevant*

Murray Wax and Felix Moos

Together with the "moral sciences"[1] generally, anthropology is among the remarkable achievements of civilization (viewed globally, cross-culturally, cumulatively). American anthropologists tend to think of their discipline as having emerged a century ago with the efforts of Franz Boas, and British to think of its emergence with Edward B. Taylor, but anthropology has a much deeper and richer genealogy, and thus a prolonged development associated with the evolution of human culture throughout the millennia.

As noted by ethnohistorians, local regions became ecumenes[2] (*oikoumene*), where scholarship, insight, and creativity flourished, and where then emerged critically engaged observers such as Heroditus, Ibn Khaldun, Snorri Sturlson, Montaigne, Goethe, and Locke. Their writings were transmitted, translated, and preserved, becoming the subject of argument, critique, and stimulation to later generations across the globe.

The pursuit of the moral sciences requires liberties and freedoms—of speech, writing, inquiry, argumentation, and conscience, and it was the presence of these freedoms—minimally for a limited few—that distinguished the ecumenes where innovative scholarship flourished. These freedoms also required a basis of social stability, grounded

Reproduced by permission of the Society for Applied Anthropology from Wax, Murray and Moos, Felix, "Anthropology: Vital or Irrelevant," SFAA 2004, *Human Organization*, Vol. 63, No. 2, pp. 246–247.

usually in "a concert of powers" or in a well-established imperial regime (as in 5th century Athens, Hellenistic Egypt, imperial Rome, and the Arab Renaissance). Because these freedoms can and will be used to challenge conformity and authority, their exercise can be fraught, and so threatened continually with limitations. These threats derive not only from external authority but from internal conformity, ethical corruption, and disciplinary self-censorship (the case of Socrates remains exemplary).

Because the moral sciences are a cumulative product of civilization as a whole, and because anthropology has emerged as a key discipline among these sciences, its practitioners have hoped to be able to situate themselves above the rivalries of local empires, communities, and nation states. Indeed, following the example of Boas—who championed cultural relativism above all else—many American anthropologists have considered themselves as if they were members of a secularized, pacific, and international (if not quite monastic) religious order, with no allegiances other than to the welfare of the communities and peoples they study. Unhappily, this detached and beneficent self-regard has proven to be an illusionary and fallacious conceit, as it disregards the fundamentals of institutional and financial support, political stability, and the potentials of military protection, deriving from their privileged positions within the United States and Western academe.[3] As a historical generality, religious orders (and monastic institutions) have not been able to function where a despotic regime was fearful of their role as an independent source of truth, or where a population had been subjugated by a hostile ideological system.

North American anthropologists may delude themselves with the belief that if they could only dissociate themselves from military and intelligence agencies, and avow that they were different from their fellow Americans, that then their bona fides would be globally accepted. However, such dissociation is irrelevant to the cynics whose views of knowledge and truth do not allow for freedoms of speech and inquiry, and who are ideologically opposed to the moral sciences which establish ethical parameters. As a recent conspicuous example, and one where American anthropologists remained largely disengaged, note how the Chinese Communist regime destroyed the Buddhist monasteries of Tibet, despite clear evidence of their pacifism and political detachment.

A half-century ago the necessity of protecting the democratic republics from barbarous despotism was clearly realized by the majority of anthropologists, including such influentials as Alfred Kroeber, Margaret Mead, Ruth Benedict, and E. E. Evans-Pritchard, when confronting the frightful destructiveness of the Nazi and Japanese fascistic regimes. Unhappily, an influential group of anthropologists (and intellectuals) were pathetically slow in disenchanting themselves of the despotisms masking themselves with ideological versions of Marxism. Nevertheless, there was a Gerald Hickey who worked selflessly and courageously among the mountain peoples of Vietnam. In a series of reasoned and ethnographically grounded communications, Hickey (1970, 2002) urged upon the military and the U.S. politicians the necessity of reasonable compromises. One should note that there were other involved anthropologists who put at risk their lives, reputations, and livelihoods. Had they been supported by fellow anthropologists, or at least been recognized for their ethical commitment, rather than disparaged, their words might have carried far more weight.

Again, today, not just the United States, but worldwide, civilization is under increasing attack. A loose alliance of terrorists has assaulted not only clear military targets but edifices and symbols from Buddhist statuary and Olympic athletes to the twin towers of the World Trade Center and tourist enclaves in Bali and the Philippines. In this process they have murdered thousands of noncombatant bystanders, including children. They have also held captive or murdered persons serving benevolent and independent welfare agencies in nongovernmental organizations, including the staff of local universities, as well as holding captive and torturing journalists and noncombatant observers. The weapons of choice have been the car bomb, the land mine, hijacked aircraft used as missiles, and the suicide bomber. In the background is a systematic campaign of ideological hatred, disseminated in schools and the mass media, and scorning the liberties and freedoms upon which anthropology is grounded, and on which depend its very existence.

In response, we again witness the disposition of intellectuals to ally themselves with the critics of the relatively open and democratic societies of Europe and North American, In the name of peace and justice they formulate rationales for despotic regimes and terrorist campaigns, just as so many once managed to defend the conduct of Lenin, Stalin, Mao, Ho Chi Minh, Pol-Pot, Kim Il Sung, and their ilk. In justification of primarily anti-Western protest movements, it is not difficult to find grievances, inequities, injustices. While these may justify organized protest, they do not justify evil, especially when manifested in massive slaughter; nor does ethical concern about such injustices justify disciplinary suicide or feigned ethical neutrality. What is strikingly paradoxical is for persons to advocate that the United States intervene military in situations of civil conflict, like Bosnia, Kosovo, and Rwanda, but who then dissociate themselves and their students from working with military or other pertinent agencies. Asymmetric warfare is a novel form of war and one that has received scant attention in the U.S. academe. Yet it has evolved as *the major challenge of our day*, demanding responses beyond pious platitudes. In this conflict, anthropologists have vital cross-cultural knowledge to offer and yet they have also much to learn. Privilege carries weighty responsibilities.

NOTES

1. The term "moral sciences" emerged in the Scottish Enlightenment and was employed by J. S. Mill. In historical context and for the subject of this essay, it is far more appropriate than "behavioral sciences."

2. Ecumene was introduced into anthropology by Kroeber (1952) and subsequently employed by Breckenridge and Appadurai (1988), Hewes (1961), and Wax (1993), as well as in the papers in the volume edited by Canfield (1991).

3. Max Weber (1921:78, emphasis in original) was clear-eyed: "If no social institutions existed which knew the use of force, then the concept of 'state' would be eliminated. . . . A state is a human community that (successfully) claims the monopoly of physical force within a given territory."

REFERENCES CITED

Breckenridge, Carol A., and Arjun Appadurai. 1988. Editor's Comments. Public Culture: Bulletin of the Project for Transcultural Cultural Studies 1(1):3.

Canfield, Robert L., ed. 1991. Turko-Persia in Historical Perspective. Cambridge: Cambridge University Press.

Hewes, Gordon W. 1961. The Ecumene as a Civilizational Multiplier System. Kroeber Anthropological Society Papers 25:73–110.

Hickey, Gerald C. 1970. Accommodation and Coalition in South Vietnam. P-4213. Santa Monica, Calif.: Rand Corporation.

———. 2002. Window on a War: An Anthropologist in the Vietnam Conflict. Lubbock: Texas Tech University Press.

Kroeber, Alfred L. 1952. The Ancient Oikoumenê as a Historic Culture Aggregate. *In* The Nature of Culture. Pp. 379–395. Chicago: University of Chicago Press.

Wax, Murray L. 1993. How Culture Misdirects Multiculturalism. Anthropology and Education Quarterly 24:99–115.

Weber, Max. 1921. Politics as a Vocation. *In* From Max Weber. H. H. Gerth and C. Wright Mills, trans. and eds. Pp. 77–128. New York: Oxford University Press.

Past Wars, Present Dangers, Future Anthropologies

David Price

Like many other anthropologists who contributed their professional skills to the waging of the Second World War, in 1943 Gregory Bateson enlisted in the Office of Strategic Services (OSS), the organizational predecessor to the CIA.[1] At the OSS Bateson wrote intelligence reports, undertook clandestine "black propaganda" radio campaigns, and even took part in manoeuvres with an OSS forward intelligence unit in the Burmese Arakan Mountains. Bateson applied his principles of *schismogenesis* to foster disorder among enemy minority populations, and some of this work prefigured the sort of psy-war, culture-cracking approach to conquest that was later employed by CIA operatives like Edward Landsdale in Vietnam and the Philippines. One intelligence report released by the CIA finds Bateson recommending that the Americans learn from Russian successes in conquering ethnic minorities, other reports show him analyzing ways the British could strengthen their colonial control of India in the post-war period.

"Past Wars, Present Dangers, Future Anthropologies" by David Price from *Anthropology Today*, 18(1): 3–5. Reprinted by permission of Blackwell Publishers.

These were very useful, albeit troubling, applications of anthropological skills in the service of war.

In the post-war years Bateson came to view this work with regret and disdain—not because of any failures, but because of the successes in which native peoples were ill treated, manipulated and disempowered. Some anthropologists had no regrets regarding their war activities, while others shared Bateson's sentiments in the post-war period, and the later wars of the 20th century found anthropologists supporting and opposing wars with a diversity of opinion and approach befitting the diversity of our field. Nevertheless, there remains a general hesitancy to take stock of the extent and meaning of past anthropological interactions with warfare.

The current crisis brings to the surface many of the buried issues faced by Bateson and hundreds of other anthropologists in past wars. Chief among these is the threat this "war on global terrorism" poses to the prospects of peace and sovereignty for indigenous peoples, ethnic minorities and separatist groups around the world. But the situation also raises numerous ethical issues that must be confronted by anthropologists and their colleagues—especially those concerning the integrity of the discipline of anthropology, as pressures to harness anthropological knowledge of other societies for military purposes and other objectives re-emerge.

PRESENT DANGERS

It is imperative that anthropologists critically evaluate and speak out about the dangers the war on terrorism will present to native and minority populations around the world if the governments managing them and their lands are given a new international legitimacy to repress them as "terrorists." The United Nations' support for new anti-terrorist policies is helping to establish new forms of cooperation among member nations, yet these arrangements proceed with explicit agreement that terrorism shall remain strategically undefined. International human rights groups and even the German Foreign Ministry have raised concerns that these policies will usher in renewed state terrorism against minority populations. But for the most part these objections have been suppressed in the interest of the Western world's new unity of purpose.

There are signs that US Secretary of State Powell-the-coalition-builder is purchasing the cooperation and approval of world leaders by adopting policies whereby the Unites States will not protest or intervene when these states suppress or attack their own ethnic minority populations. As the United States signals President Putin that it can learn to see Russia's bloody war in Chechnya as part of the global war on terrorism, this signal is welcomed by other world leaders hoping for a free hand to deal with domestic indigenous troubles.

Anthropologists know that most of the world's nation states are in internal conflict with one or more domestic groups contesting power relations; and these conflicts are frequently marked by violence and counter-violence. The idiom of power dictates that the violence of the state is legitimized as peace-keeping, while that of the dispossessed becomes terrorism. It is this hypocrisy that prevents the formation of a coherent behavioural definition of terrorism—and without such a definition the war on terrorism must be viewed with informed skepticism.

Anthropologists also know that colonial powers and nation states have long designated a wide range of cultural practices as terrorist threats. Historically, activities categorized as "terrorism" have not been limited to acts of violence. The historical range of non-violent practices defined as terrorism includes certain forms of speech, teaching native languages and a wide range of religious or cultural ceremonies. North American examples of this include outlawed cultural and religious practices associated with resistance or non-assimilation such as the Ghost Dance, potlatch, peyote rituals and lodge ceremonies. As terrorism

remains undefined we are left to wonder if world leaders will be freely allowed to oppress their own minority populations for engaging in similar nonviolent acts of rebellion.

There is a present danger of the wholesale categorization of people who resist domination as "terrorists"—thereby sidestepping all the issues that an in-depth cultural and historical analysis would raise. Whether it is the Basques in Spain, the Irish Catholics in Northern Ireland, the Tamils in Sri-Lanka, Zapatistas in Mexico, Chechens in Russia, post-colonial wars of Africa smouldering along ethnic lines, or the struggles of other excluded groups, there are contentious battles for power that will rapidly become even more lopsided if the currently ill-defined anti-terrorism campaign continues.

In the last few months the American Congress has given the CIA and NSA new authority to conduct global surveillance operations with minimal levels of supervision. Of particular concern to the international anthropological community is the passage of the "Patriot Act" and revisions to the Foreign Surveillance Intelligence Act that potentially impact all of us as well as those we study in the field. Relying on technologies already at work with the NSA's ECHELON program, all global telephonic and electronic communications are now increasingly subject to monitoring and scrutiny. These conditions mandate that anthropologists take extra precautions to protect their field data, and that communications from the field be made with high-quality encryption software such as PGP. As a discipline we can no longer afford the illusion that our field communications and research are not subject to inspection—and, if pertinent, use—by international military and intelligence agencies. The NSA and CIA have been taken off their leash and the world is now their unrestricted territory.

Many anthropologists bristled at the war rhetoric of Prime Minister Blair and President Bush as they cavalierly characterized the current military campaign as a fight between the civilized West and uncivilized Afghanistan. These representations are designed to limit public understanding, and to pre-empt the obvious comparisons between the violent acts against civilian populations committed by the terrorists and those perpetrated by the military. The complexities of Pashtun-, Hazara-, Aimaks-, Turkmen-, Baloch-, Uzbek-, and Tajik-contested Afghanistan are thus easily swept from view as the intricacies of Afghansitan are reduced to the inevitable chaos of uncivilized people. There is no need to examine the CIA's role in creating and maintaining instability in Afghanistan. Here in the US, narratives that accompany televised images of Fourth World poverty thus reinforce an implicit tenet which defines market consumerism as the peak of a hierarchical chain of evolutionary development.

Anthropologists have much to offer to the public and policy makers during this crisis. If the war continues, and grows, we should be concerned about the increasing probability of anthropologists serving less-public bodies within the world of military and intelligence community.

PAST WARS, PAST ANTHROPOLOGIES

Gregory Bateson's work and experience with the OSS was not an historical anomaly—and given a war on terrorism's inevitable focus on minority populations it is clear that the methods and skills used by Bateson and other wartime anthropologists will once again be in demand. Past wars have found anthropologists using their professional skills as analysts, spies, linguists, peace activists, interrogators, geographers, detention camp managers, cryptographers, military guides, propagandists, advocates for the humane treatment of prisoners, culture brokers and in dozens of other military capacities. If this turns out to be the new forty-year war promised by Bush, we will no doubt see many of these roles reprised by new generations of anthropologists.

Regardless of the immediate course of events—be it peace or war—we need to evaluate the impact and meaning of anthropological contributions to past wars, and to consider carefully the ethical and long-term impacts of these actions, if for no other reason than that some future war will find our profession drawn into conflicts in ways similar to our ill-considered past. Our history raises issues that must be discussed openly by anthropologists, but our past need not be our future. The various positions regarding the application of anthropology to warfare held by different factions of our profession need to be made known to the peoples we study so that they can take whatever actions are needed to protect their own best interests.

The ethical issues embroiled in the commingling of anthropology and warfare are both simple and complex. Simple, in that anthropologists' primary ethical duty must be to protect and serve those studied; and complex because when the drums of nationalism call, anthropologists at times find themselves conflicted (or compromised) between their duties to country, and to the culture which hosted them and their research. In past wars some anthropologists have not seen conflicts in these positions and have served their country without hesitation, while others resolved these conflicts by rationalizing war service as being in the best interests of the culture they found themselves fighting; some anthropologists have seen their duty as being to assist oppressed minorities and native peoples in time of war; still others have viewed the use of anthropology for warfare as ethically problematic. Some anthropologists held this last position during both World Wars. Boas' views concerning the propriety of mixing an-

thropology and espionage in the First World War are well known, and during World War Two Laura Thompson worried that wartime anthropologists were simply becoming "technicians for hire to the highest bidder."[2] Prior to joining the OSS Gregory Bateson wondered to what use anthropology would be put in the war, asking, "now that we have techniques, are we in cold blood, going to treat people as things?"[1]

The ethical guidelines of various national and international anthropological associations offer little consistent guidance on these matters. Some associations, such as the Association of Social Anthropologists of the UK and Commonwealth (ASA), do explicitly prohibit the use of anthropological research as a cover for espionage, while others (such as the American Anthropological Association) have intentionally removed such prohibitions from their ethical codes. But even the ASA's guidelines are less explicit concerning the propriety of anthropologists using information gathered in fieldwork to assist military or intelligence agencies at some later date. This issue has importance in "peace" time too, given the increased reliance on programmes such as the National Security Education Program in the United States (with its mandated payback clause) to fund graduate study. It is an issue of ongoing concern to all of anthropology.

It is unlikely that anthropologists in any one nation, much less throughout the world, will be of one mind regarding the ethics of anthropological applications in warfare. This is to be expected. What is important is that actions taken by anthropologists in the present situation be directed towards protecting the interests and safety of those groups likely to be victimized by this war on terrorism.

ANTHROPOLOGICAL ADVOCACY

Anthropologists as citizens and members of professional associations must monitor and speak out against the direct and indirect threats that the current war poses to various peoples around the world. In the past, calls for advocacy or action in opposition to wars and military actions on the part of various professional anthropological associations have provoked responses from some members that such organizations are not political bodies and it is therefore improper for them to get involved in political matters. But as David Aberle observed over three decades ago, in times of war there is no such thing as an apolitical course of action for anthropological professional associations, only inaction, which is in fact political action supporting prevailing military policies.[3]

Anthropological associations and research institutions have *always* been involved in political causes—it is just that these causes have seldom been considered as such unless they go against the grain of overriding political economic structures. Advocating around issues of gender, ethnic or racial equality or for basic human rights is common practice for professional anthropological organizations, and advocating for the groups who stand to be victimized by the new war on "terrorism" should be no different—though the consequences for such a stance will make some hesitate to engage in such advocacy.

We need to choose carefully the ways that we will use anthropology in this current war, for it seems likely that it will be used one way or another. We can help to reveal the complexity behind an oversimplified picture and to de-exoticize those who are being marginalized as uncivilized or reactionary. Thirty-five years ago anthropologists John Donahue, Marshall Sahlins and Eric Wolf helped invent the teach-in, creating a still-vibrant model of public education that bypasses the filters and constraints of traditional media outlets—and today this basic model has been adapted for an internet-ready world. Anthropologists can enrich public discussions of terrorism by "studying-up," and examining state terrorism, though as Jeffrey Sluka observes, thus far "among the well over 10,000 anthropologists worldwide, only a few dozen have chosen to study state terror."[4]

As anthropologists we have a duty to serve the populations we study by shifting political and media driven frames of analysis and advocating for the safety and independence of peoples around the world. This is not a conflict that anthropology can afford to sit out and watch from the sidelines, and we can learn from the regrets of Bateson and others who came to lament the application of anthropology to the cause of warfare against minority populations.

NOTES

1. Price, David 1998. Gregory Bateson and the OSS. *Human Organization* 57(4):379–384. As will be discussed in a forthcoming article in AT, hundreds of anthropologists—including Ruth Benedict, Carleton Coon, Felix Keesing, Clyde Kluckhohn, Margaret Mead, George P. Murdock and S.F. Nadel—contributed to the Second World War effort.

2. Thompson, Laura 1944. Some perspectives on applied anthropology. *Applied Anthropology* 3:12–16.

3. Aberle, David 1967. *Fellows Newsletter of the American Anthropological Association:* 7.

4. Sluka, Jeffrey 2000. *Death squad: The anthropology of state terror.* Philadelphia: University of Pennsylvania Press: 11.

The Museum of Me

Ellen Ullman

*Ellen Ullman is a computer programmer and freelance writer whose articles
on technology, gender, and culture have appeared in major media like the*
New York Times, Harper's, *and* Salon.

Years ago, before the Internet as we know it had come
into existence—I think it was around Christmas, in
1990—I was at a friend's house, where her nine-year-old
son and his friend were playing the video game that was
the state of the art at the time, Sonic the Hedgehog. They
jumped around in front of the TV and gave off the sort of
rude noises boys tend to make when they're shooting at
things in a video game, and after about half an hour they
stopped and tried to talk about what they'd just been
doing. The dialogue went something like this:

"I wiped out at that part with the ladders."

"Ladders? What ladders?"

"You know, after the rooms."

"Oh, you mean the stairs?"

"No, I think they were ladders. I remember, because
I died there twice."

"I never killed you around any ladders. I killed you
where you jump down off this wall."

"Wall? You mean by the gates of the city?"

"Are there gates around the city? I always called it
the castle."

The boys muddled along for several more minutes,
making themselves more confused as they went. Finally
they gave up trying to talk about their time with Sonic the
Hedgehog. They just looked at each other and shrugged.

I didn't think about the two boys and Sonic again
until I watched my clients try out the World Wide Web.
By then it was 1995, the Internet as we know it was beginning to exist, but the two women who worked for my
client, whom I'd just helped get online, had never before
connected to the Internet or surfed the Web. They took to

it instantly, each disappearing into nearly an hour of obsessive clicking, after which they tried to talk about it:

"It was great! I clicked that thing and went to this
place. I don't remember its name."

"Yeah. It was a link. I clicked here and went there."

"Oh, I'm not sure it was a link. The thing I clicked
was a picture of the library."

"Was it the library? I thought it was a picture of City
Hall."

"Oh, no. I'm sure it was the library."

"No, City Hall. I'm sure because of the dome."

"Dome? Was there a dome?"

Right then I remembered Sonic and the two boys; my
clients, like the two boys, had experienced something
pleasurable and engaging, and they very much wanted
to talk about it—talking being one of the primary ways
human beings augment their pleasure. But what had happened to them, each in her own electronic world, resisted
description. Like the boys, the two women fell into verbal confusion. How could they speak coherently about a
world full of little wordless pictograms, about trails that
led off in all directions, of idle visits to virtual places
closen on a whim-click?

Following hyperlinks on the Web is like the synaptic
drift of dreams, a loosening of intention, the mind associ-
ating freely, an experience that can be compelling or baffling or unsettling, or all of those things at once. And like
dreams, the experience of the Web is intensely private,
charged with immanent meaning for the person inside
the experience, but often confusing or irrelevant to someone else.

At the time, I had my reservations about the Web, but
not so much about the private, dreamlike state it offered.
Web surfing seemed to me not so much antisocial as aso-
cial, an adventure like a video game or pinball, entertaining, sometimes interesting, sometimes a trivial waste of

time; but in a social sense it seemed harmless, since only the person engaged in the activity was affected.

Something changed, however, not in me but in the Internet and the Web and in the world, and the change was written out in person-high letters on a billboard on the corner of Howard and New Montgomery Streets in San Francisco. It was the fall of 1998. I was walking toward Market Street one afternoon when I saw it, a background of brilliant sky blue, with writing on it in airy white letters, which said: *now the world really does revolve around you.* The letters were lower-case, soft-edged, spaced irregularly, as if they'd been skywritten over a hot August beach and were already drifting off into the air. The message they left behind was a child's secret wish, the ultimate baby-world narcissism we are all supposed to abandon when we grow up: the world really does revolve around me.

What was this billboard advertising? Perfume? A resort? There was nothing else on it but the airy, white letters, and I had to walk right up to it to see a URL written at the bottom; it was the name of a company that makes semiconductor equipment, machinery used by companies like Intel and AMD to manufacture integrated circuits. Oh, chips, I thought. Computers. Of course. What other subject produces such hyperbole? Who else but someone in the computer industry could make such a shameless appeal to individualism?

The billboard loomed over the corner for the next couple of weeks. Every time I passed it, its message irritated me more. It bothered me the way the "My Computer" icon bothers me on the Windows desktop, baby names like "My Yahoo" and "My Snap"; my, my, my; two-year-old talk; infantilizing and condescending.

But there was something more disturbing about this billboard, and I tried to figure why, since it simply was doing what every other piece of advertising does: whispering in your ear that there is no one like you in the entire world, and what we are offering is for you, special you, and you alone. What came to me was this: Toyota, for example, sells the idea of a special, individual buyer ("It's not for everyone, just for you"), but chip makers, through the medium of the Internet and the World Wide Web, are creating the actual infrastructure of an individualized marketplace.

What had happened between 1995, when I could still think of the Internet as a private dream, and the appearance of that billboard in 1998 was the near-complete commercialization of the Web. And that commercialization had proceeded in a very particular and single-minded way: by attempting to isolate the individual within a sea of economic activity. Through a process known as "disin-termediation," producers have worked to remove the expert intermediaries, agents, brokers, middlemen, who until now have influenced our interactions with the commercial world. What bothered me about the billboard, then, was that its message was not merely hype but the reflection of a process that was already under way: an attempt to convince the individual that a change currently being visited upon him or her is a good thing, the purest form of self, the equivalent of freedom. The world really does revolve around you.

In Silicon Valley, in Redmond, Washington, the home of Microsoft, and in the smaller silicon alleys of San Francisco and New York, "disintermediation" is a word so common that people shrug when you try to talk to them about it. Oh, disintermediation, that old thing. Everyone already knows about that. It has become accepted wisdom, a process considered inevitable, irrefutable, good.

I've long believed that the ideas embedded in technology have a way of percolating up and outward into the nontechnical world at large, and that technology is made by people with intentions and, as such, is not neutral. In the case of disintermediation, an explicit and purposeful change is being visited upon the structure of the global marketplace. And in a world so dominated by markets, I don't think I go too far in saying that this will affect the very structure of reality, for the Net is no longer simply a zone of personal freedoms; a pleasant diversion from what we used to call "real life"; it has become an actual marketplace that is changing the nature of real life itself.

Removal of the intermediary. All those who stand in the middle of a transaction, whether financial or intellectual: out! Brokers and agents and middlemen of every description: good-bye! Travel agents, real-estate agents, insurance agents, stockbrokers, mortgage brokers, consolidators, and jobbers, all the scrappy percentniks who troll the bywaters of capitalist exchange—who needs you? All those hard-striving immigrants climbing their way into the lower middle class through the penny-ante deals of capitalism, the transfer points too small for the big guys to worry about—find yourself some other way to make a living. Small retailers and store clerks, salespeople of every kind—a hindrance, idiots, not to be trusted. Even the professional handlers of intellectual goods, anyone who sifts through information, books, paintings, knowledge, selecting and summing up: librarians, book reviewers, curators, disc jockeys, teachers, editors, analysts—why trust anyone but yourself to make judgments about what is more or less interesting, valuable, authentic, or worthy of your attention? No one, no professional interloper, is supposed to come between you and your desires, which, according to this idea, are nuanced, difficult to communicate, irreducible, unique.

The Web did not cause disintermediation, but it is what we call an "enabling technology": a technical breakthrough that takes a difficult task and makes it suddenly doable, easy; it opens the door to change, which then comes in an unconsidered, breathless rush.

We are living through an amazing experiment: an attempt to construct a capitalism without salespeople, to take a system founded upon the need to sell ever greater numbers of goods to ever growing numbers of people, and to do this without the aid of professional distribution channels—without buildings, sidewalks, shops, luncheonettes, street vendors, buses, trams, taxis, other women in the fitting room to tell you how you look in something and to help you make up your mind, without street people panhandling, Santas ringing bells at Christmas, shop women with their perfect makeup and elegant clothes, fashionable men and women strolling by to show you the latest look—in short, an attempt to do away with the city in all its messy stimulation, to abandon the agora for home and hearth, where it is safe and everything can be controlled.

The first task in this newly structured capitalism is to convince consumers that the services formerly performed by myriad intermediaries are useless or worse, that those commissioned brokers and agents are incompetent, out for themselves, dishonest. And the next task is to glorify the notion of self-service. Where companies once vied for your business by telling you about their courteous people and how well they would serve you—"Avis, We Try Harder"—their job now is to make you believe that only you can take care of yourself. The lure of personal service that was dangled before the middle classes, momentarily making us all feel almost as lucky as the rich, is being withdrawn. In the Internet age, under the pressure of globalized capitalism and its slimmed-down profit margins, only the very wealthy will be served by actual human beings. The rest of us must make do with Web pages, and feel happy about it.

One evening while I was watching television, I looked up to see a commercial that seemed to me to be the most explicit statement of the ideas implicit in the disintermediated universe. I gaped at it, because usually such ideas are kept implicit, hidden behind symbols. But this commercial was like the sky-blue billboard: a shameless and naked expression of the Web world, a glorification of the self, at home, alone.

It begins with a drone, a footstep in a puddle, then a ragged band pulling a dead car through the mud—road warriors with bandanas around their foreheads carrying braziers. Now we see rafts of survivors floating before the ruins of a city, the sky dark, red-tinged, as if fires were burning all around us, just over the horizon. Next we are outside the dead city's library, where stone lions, now coated in gold and come to life, rear up in despair. Inside the library, red-coated Fascist guards encircle the readers at the table. A young girl turns a page, loudly, and the guards say, "Shush!" in time to their march-step. We see the title of the book the girl is reading: *Paradise Lost*. The bank, too, is a scene of ruin. A long line snakes outside it in a dreary rain. Inside, the teller is a man with a white, spectral face, who gazes upon the black spider that is slowly crawling up his window. A young woman's face ages right before us, and in response, in ridicule, the bank guard laughs. The camera now takes us up over the roofs of this post-apocalyptic city. Lightning crashes in the dark, red-tinged sky. On a telephone pole, where the insulators should be, are skulls.

Cut to a cartoon of emerald-green grass, hills, a Victorian house with a white picket fence and no neighbors. A butterfly flaps above it. What a relief this house is after the dreary, dangerous, ruined city. The door to this charming house opens, and we go in to see a chair before a computer screen. Yes, we want to go sit in that chair, in that room with candy-orange walls. On the computer screen, running by in teasing succession, are pleasant virtual reflections of the world outside: written text, a bank check, a telephone pole, which now signifies our connection to the world. The camera pans back to show a window, a curtain swinging in the breeze, and our sense of calm is complete. We hear the Intel-Inside jingle, which sounds almost like chimes. Cut to the legend: Packard Bell. Wouldn't you rather be at home?

In sixty seconds, this commercial communicates a worldview that reflects the ultimate suburbanization of existence: a retreat from the friction of the social space to the supposed idyll of private ease. It is a view that depends on the idea that desire is not social, not stimulated by what others want, but generated internally, and that the satisfaction of desires is not dependent upon other persons, organizations, structures, or governments. It is a profoundly libertarian vision, and it is the message that underlies all the mythologizing about the Web: the idea that the civic space is dead, useless, dangerous. The only place of pleasure and satisfaction is your home. You, home, family; and beyond that, the world. From the intensely private to the global, with little in between but an Intel processor and a search engine.

In this sense, the ideal of the Internet represents the very opposite of democracy, which is a method for resolving differences in a relatively orderly manner through the mediation of unavoidable civil associations. Yet there can be no notion of resolving differences in a world where each person is entitled to get exactly what he or she wants. Here all needs and desires are equally valid and equally powerful. I'll get mine and you'll get yours; there is no need for compromise and discussion. I don't have to tolerate you, and you don't have to tolerate me. No need for messy debate and the whole rigmarole of government with all its creaky, bothersome structures. There's no need for any of this, because now that we have the World Wide Web the problem of the pursuit of happiness has been solved! We'll each click for our individual joys, and our only dispute may come if something doesn't get delivered on time. Wouldn't you really rather be at home?

But who can afford to stay at home? Only the very wealthy or a certain class of knowledge worker can stay home and click. On the other side of this ideal of work-anywhere freedom (if indeed it is freedom never to be away from work) is the reality that somebody had to make the thing you ordered with a click. Somebody had to put it in a box, do the paperwork, carry it to you. The reality is a world divided not only between the haves and have-nots but between the ones who get to stay home and everyone else, the ones who deliver the goods to them.

The Net ideal represents a retreat not only from political life but also from culture—from that tumultuous conversation in which we try to talk to one another about our shared experiences. As members of a culture, we see the same movie, read the same book, hear the same string quartet. Although it is difficult for us to agree on what we might have seen, read, or heard, it is out of that difficult conversation that real culture arises. Whether or not we come to an agreement or understanding, even if some decide that understanding and meaning are impossible, we are still sitting around the same campfire.

But the Web as it has evolved is based on the idea that we do not even want a shared experience. The director of San Francisco's Museum of Modern Art once told an audience that we no longer need a building to house works of art; we don't need to get dressed, go downtown, walk from room to room among crowds of other people. Now that we have the Web, we can look at anything we want whenever we want, and we no longer need him or his curators. "You don't have to walk through *my* idea of what's interesting to look at," he said to a questioner in the audience named Bill. "On the Web," said the director, "you can create the museum of Bill."

And so, by implication, there can be the museums of George and Mary and Helene. What then will this group have to say to one another about art? Let's say the museum of Bill is featuring early Dutch masters, the museum of Mary is playing video art, and the museum of Helene is displaying French tapestries. In this privatized world, what sort of "cultural" conversation can there be? What can one of us possibly say to another about our experience except, "Today I visited the museum of me, and I liked it."

Glossary

a priori   In logic, working from the general to the particular; deductive reasoning.

age-grade   A category determined by age; each person goes through many categories of age during life.

age-sets   A group of persons initiated into an age-grade at the same time and who move together through successive age-grades thereafter.

agrarian society   Society in which food is produced by farming the land.

AIDS   Acquired immunodeficiency syndrome; a fatal disease resulting from infection with HIV, which is transmitted sexually, through contaminated blood products, and from a mother to child during pregnancy and/or through breast milk. Now pandemic.

anthropological advocacy group   Group formed to advance the rights of indigenous peoples.

anthropological perspective   The practice of viewing customs and institutions in their holistic and evolutionary context.

anthropology   The study of humankind, in all times and places.

balanced reciprocity   An exchange of goods in which those that are given and those that are received are of equal value.

cargo cults   A type of revitalization movement common in parts of the Pacific; adherents believe the ancestors will arrive in a ship loaded with white peoples' cargo and will drive whites out.

civilization   A type of society marked by the presence of urban settlements, social inequality, and a state type of political organization.

clan   A noncorporate group in which each member claims descent from a common ancestor without necessarily knowing the genealogical links to that ancestor.

colonialism   The unilateral assertion of political jurisdiction over a people and their territory by some other people.

common-interest group   A group formed for a specific purpose with membership based on an act of joining, rather than age, kinship, marriage, or territory.

communication   The transmittal of information from one individual to another, whether it be a hunger cry from an infant, words of a language, or flirtatious behavior.

cross-cultural   A comparative perspective based on the conviction that analyses of cultural problems and processes should not be limited to one culture or cultural type.

cultural anthropology   The branch of anthropology concerned with human behavior (as opposed to physical, also known as biological, anthropology).

cultural arrogance   The ethnocentric notion that one's own culture is superior to another.

cultural pluralism   Interaction socially and politically within the same society of people with different ways of living and thinking.

cultural relativism   The necessity to suspend judgment in order to understand a custom in its cultural context; essential for understanding other peoples' practices.

culture   The values and standards of a people that enable them to make sense of the world and to shape every aspect of their behavior.

dependence training   A way of raising children that promotes compliance in performance of assigned tasks and dependence on the domestic group, rather than personal independence.

development economist   An economist who studies or works with people whose lives are in the midst of cultural change.

dispute management   How a society handles disagreements such as ownership of land, marital rights, or dowry.

economic exploitation   Exploitation of one population's labor and resources by another population for the latter's benefit, at the expense of the former.

economics   The study of the production, distribution, and consumption of goods and commodities.

egalitarian ethos   The expectation that all should share equally in valued resources and have an equal say in making important decisions.

egalitarian redistribution   The redistribution of resources so that all members of the society share equally.

egalitarianism   A social system in which as many valued positions exist as there are persons capable of filling them.

enculturation   The process by which a people's culture is transmitted from one generation to the next.

ethnicity   Nonbiological expressions of group membership, an ethnic group being people who share foods, clothing, language, and so on.

ethnocentrism   The belief held by all people that one's own culture is superior in every way to all others.

ethnographies   Studies of particular cultures based on first-hand observation.

ethnology   The study of cultures from a comparative or historical point of view.

ethnoscience   The subdiscipline of anthropology concerned with explicating the characteristics of knowledge systems, including classifactory and taxonomic systems. A central goal is to reveal the emic (insider's) and etic (outsider's) logics that organize peoples' thinking.

exchange   The reciprocal giving of things, whether it be camels for wives, bananas for meat, money for manufactured goods, or whatever.

extended family   A kin group joined through marriage or blood relationships that does not necessarily share the same residence.

family   A residential kin group minimally composed of a woman, her dependent children, and at least one adult male joined through marriage or blood relationship.

fieldwork   The study of a society, or some segment thereof, carried out in that society itself.

foraging   The finding of food in nature, as opposed to food production through farming or herding.

gender   Culturally specific symbolic articulation of biological differences between men and women. Provides metaphors for ordering men and women in relation to each other and the social system as a whole.

generalized reciprocity   Exchange in which the value of the gift is not calculated nor is the time of repayment specified.

genocide   The extermination of one people by another, either as a deliberate act or as the accidental outcome of activities carried out by one people with little regard for their impact on others.

globalization   The development of global interdependency; the process by which the world's peoples become increasingly interdependent.

hierarchy   An organizational structure in which high-ranking elements subsume lower-ranking ones.

historical linguistics   The study of linguistic change and the relationships between different languages.

holistic perspective   A perspective by which anthropologists view things in the broadest possible context, in order to understand their interconnections and interdependence.

hunter-gatherer   One who lives on foods either hunted or gathered in the wild; preferred term now is *food-forager*, which incorporates hunting, gathering, fishing, and scavenging.

incest   Sexual relations between individuals normally declared "off-limits," usually between parents and children or siblings of opposite sex; in some cultures, however, other relationships may be considered incestuous.

independence training   A way of raising children that promotes independence, self-reliance, and personal achievement.

kindred   The maternal and paternal relatives of a particular individual to whom he or she can appeal for assistance and who gather together on important occasions in the life of the individual.

kinesics   "Body language"; system of postures, facial expressions, and body motions that convey messages.

kinship   A system of relationships and/or organizing principles by which people with common ancestry classify group members and allocate rights and responsibilities.

language   Communication by means of sounds that are put together in meaningful ways according to a set of rules.

language ideology   The interest in how language organizes peoples' lives, institutions, and their interrelations. It focuses on how language contributes to the construction and legitimation of power, the production of relations of sameness and difference, and the creation of cultural stereotypes about speakers and social groups.

law   Social norms, the neglect or infraction of which is regularly met by the threatened or actual application of physical force on the part of an individual or group possessing the socially recognized authority to do so.

liminality   Being at the point of change from one status to another.

lineage   A corporate group, membership in which is based on demonstrable descent from a common ancestor.

linguist   One who studies languages, their structure, and use.

linguistic anthropology   A branch of cultural anthropology that studies the linguistic behavior of humans.

magic   The idea that there are ritual formulas that if followed precisely, manipulate supernatural powers for desired ends.

market exchange   The buying and selling of goods and services with prices set by forces of supply and demand. In non-Western societies, usually occurs in a marketplace.

marriage   A transaction and resulting contract by which a woman and a man establish continuing rights of sexual access to one another and in which the woman involved is eligible to bear children.

matrilineal descent   Ancestry traced to a common ancestor exclusively through women.

matrilineal society   A society in which matrilineal descent is an important organizing principle.

millenarian movement   In a colonial or multicultural society, a revitalization movement that attempts to resurrect a group, with its own subcultural ideology, that has long suffered in an inferior social position.

multiculturalism   The doctrine that accepts the validity of groups within a larger society operating according to their own distinctive standards and values.

nation   A people who share a common language, culture, territorial base, political organization, history, and (often) religion.

natural selection   An evolutionary process by which individuals with characters best suited to a particular environment survive and reproduce with greater frequency than do those without them.

negative reciprocity   Contrasts with balanced reciprocity in that one party to the exchange tries to get the better of it.

nuclear family   Consists of husband, wife, and dependent children, living together in a single household.

Oedipus complex   In psychoanalysis, the term for the child unconsciously being attracted to the parent of the opposite sex while being hostile to the same-sex parent.

organizational principle   A principle, such as descent from a common ancestor, by which individuals are organized into groups within a society.

paralanguage   The extralinguistic noises such as grunts, cries, or laughter that accompany language.

patrilineal descent   Ancestry traced to a common ancestor exclusively through men.

patrilineal society   A society in which patrilineal descent is an important organizing principle.

physical anthropologist   An anthropologist who studies humans as biological organisms.

political organization   The means by which decisions are made, conflicts resolved, and order maintained within a society.

polygamy   A form of marriage in which one may have multiple spouses, that is, one man with two or more wives (polygyny) or one woman with two or more husbands (polyandry).

prehistorian   One who studies ancient societies for which there are no written records.

psychoanalytic theory   The theory of personality developed in the late nineteenth century by Sigmund Freud.

psychological anthropology   The branch of cultural anthropology that studies the interface between culture and the individual.

race   A repressive framework that divides people into groups ranked by arbitrary qualities of biological superiority or cultural worth.

racism   The ideology that evaluates people according to racial identity and provides a justification for discrimination.

redistributive exchange   The collection of goods by some central agent, be it a "big man" or the state, for subsequent redistribution.

religion   Rituals, with explanatory myths, that mobilize supernatural powers for the purpose of achieving or preventing transformations of certain events.

ritual   A repetitive action or set of behaviors that communicate symbolic meanings.

sex   Anatomical, biological, and physical characteristics of male and female bodies.

sexuality   Erotic desires, sexual practices, sexual orientation, or sexual identity.

social anthropologist   An anthropologist who studies the social life of human beings.

social class   In a nonegalitarian society, a class of individuals who enjoy equal or nearly equal prestige according to the system of evaluation.

social control   The control exerted on individuals by the institutions of their society.

social elite   In a nonegalitarian society, those who occupy important positions of power and have preferred access to valued resources.

social group   Any socially recognized group within a society.

society   A people who share a common territory and who share common cultural traditions.

sociolinguistics   The study of how language is used in particular social settings.

state   A centralized political system having the power to coerce.

stratification   The division of society into two or more groups of people (social classes) who do not share equally in the basic resources that support life, influence, and prestige.

stratified redistribution   A system of redistribution in which the redistributor withholds his or her own labor, retains the largest share, and ends up with more material wealth.

structural analysis   Analysis of the underlying structure of a myth or activity.

structural linguistics   The scientific study of the structure of a language.

subaltern   Subordinate.

subculture   The standards and values of a group of people within a larger society.

subsistence   Means of support of way of life.

symbolic indicator   Activities and positions indicative of one's position in a class-structured society.

Index